Protectors of Privilege

Protectors of Privilege

Red Squads and Police Repression in Urban America

FRANK DONNER

University of California Press

BERKELEY   LOS ANGELES   OXFORD

University of California Press
Berkeley and Los Angeles, California

University of California Press, Ltd.
Oxford, England

Library of Congress Cataloging-in-Publication Data

Donner, Frank J.
    Protectors of privilege : red squads and police repression in urban
America / Frank Donner.
        p.   cm.
    Includes bibliographical references.
    ISBN 0-520-05951-4 (alk. paper)
    1. Police—United States—Complaints against. 2. Political crimes
and offenses—United States. 3. Police patrol—United States—
Surveillance operations. I. Title.
HV8138.D66   1990
363.2'32—dc20   89-20290
                                                            CIP

Printed in the United States of America
1 2 3 4 5 6 7 8 9

To
Carey McWilliams,
editor, The Nation,
1955–1975,
who lived out his father's precept
to be "honorable in all things."

Contents

Acknowledgments

This book on urban police practices is the product of my work as director of the American Civil Liberties Project on Political Surveillance and complements my earlier volume on the same subject at the federal level, *The Age of Surveillance: The Aims and Methods of America's Political Intelligence System.* For its support and access to its resources I am deeply indebted to the ACLU, its director of development, Noel Salinger, and affiliates in cities across the country as well as to participants in the American Friends Service Committee's Program on Government Surveillance and Citizens' Rights.

This book could not have been written without the research contributions and devotion of Dana Frank and Priscilla Murolo, whose learning and commitment smoothed the tangled paths to the police response to urban unrest in the American past. I am also greatly indebted to Professor Paul Avrich, whose generous assistance and encouragement in the area of his specialty, American anarchism, taught me the true meaning of the phrase "a gentleman and a scholar."

Many journalists, scholars, activists, and lawyers helped me document police activities in various cities. I am deeply indebted to, among others, Michael Balter, Paul Bass, Haywood Burns, Douglas Cassel, Jai Chandrasekar, Paul Chevigny, Jeff Cohen, George Corsetti, Spencer Coxe, David Glenn, Gregory Goldin, Earnest Goodman, Herbert G. Gutman, Richard Gutman, Brownlee Hayden, Andrew Houlding, James Jacobs, Eugene Jiminez, David Kairys, Rob Koulish, Bruce Kramer, Ken Lawrence, Gary Marx, Mary Metzger, Aryeh Neier, Sheila O'Donnell, Marshall Perlin, Mark Rosenbaum, Harrison Salisbury, John H. F. Shattuck, Franklin Siegel, Daniel Stern, Flint Taylor, Linda Valentino, Nathan Weiss, and John Williams.

I owe much to Naomi Schneider, my editor at the University of California Press, whose initiative and devotion brought the book to life and to Professor Robert Goldstein, editorial adviser, who creatively restructured the text. For his endless hours of labor on the bibliography and footnote references, I owe much to Ben Chitty. Deborah Rossitto, a model of patience and devotion, has provided invaluable assistance through her typing and secretarial skills.

Acronyms and Abbreviations

AAPL	Afro-American Patrolmen's League [Chicago]
ACLU	American Civil Liberties Union
ACMHR	Alabama Christian Movement for Human Rights
AER	Alliance to End Repression [Chicago]
AFL	American Federation of Labor
AFSC	American Friends Service Committee
AIM	American Indian Movement
ANP	American Nazi Party
APL	American Protective League
APP	Afrikan People's Party
BAF	Better America Federation [Los Angeles]
BBIA	Black Brotherhood Improvement Association
BGA	Better Government Association [Chicago]
BLF	Black Liberation Front
BOSS	Bureau of Special Services [New York]
BPP	Black Panther Party
BUF	Black United Front [Baltimore]
CADRE	Chicago Area Draft Resisters
CAPA	Coalition against Police Abuse [Los Angeles]
CASA	Center for Autonomous Social Action [Los Angeles]
CCPR	Citizens' Commission on Police Repression [Los Angeles]
CCS	Criminal Conspiracy Section [LAPD]
CD	Civil Defense Squad [Philadelphia]

CDF	Campaign for Democratic Freedoms
CDS	Citizens for a Democratic Society
CII	Criminal Investigation and Identification [LAPD unit]
CIO	Congress of Industrial Organizations
CISPES	Committee in Solidarity with the People of El Salvador
CIVIC	Citizens' Independent Investigating Committee [Los Angeles]
CLS	Community Legal Services [Philadelphia]
COGS	Coalition on Government Spying [Seattle]
COINTELPRO	Counter-Intelligence Program [FBI]
CPC	Chicago Peace Council
CPD	Chicago Police Department
COPPAR	Coalition of Organizations for Police Accountability and Responsibility
CORE	Congress of Racial Equality
CRIC	Citizens' Research and Investigation Committee [Los Angeles]
CRLA	California Rural Legal Assistance Program
CRS	Community Renewal Society [Chicago]
CWP	Communist Workers' Party
DIU	Domestic Intelligence Unit [Memphis]
DSOC	Democratic Socialist Organizing Committee [Los Angeles]
ECTC	Emergency Committee on the Transportation Crisis
FOP	Fraternal Order of Policemen
GBI	Georgia Bureau of Investigation
HISC	House Internal Security Committee
HUAC	House Un-American Activities Committee
IOCI	Interstate Organized Crime Index
IPS	Institute for Policy Studies
ISD	Inspectional Service Division [Baltimore]
IWW	Industrial Workers of the World ["Wobblies"]
LADO	Latin American Defense Organization [Chicago]
LAPD	Los Angeles Police Department
LEAA	Law Enforcement Assistance Administration
LEIU	Law Enforcement Intelligence Unit

M&M	Merchants and Manufacturers Association [Los Angeles]
MCHR	Medical Committee for Human Rights
Mobe	National Mobilization Committee to End the War in Vietnam
MOVE	Philadelphia group [not an acronym]
MPD	Metropolitan Police Department [Washington, D.C.]
MSP	Michigan State Police
NAACP	National Association for the Advancement of Colored People
NAARPR	National Alliance against Racist and Political Repression
NCLC	National Caucus of Labor Committees
New Mobe	New Mobilization Committee to End the War in Vietnam
NSA	National Student Association
NSRP	National States' Rights Party
NYPD	New York Police Department
OEO	Office of Economic Opportunity
PCPJ	People's Coalition for Peace and Justice
PDID	Public Disorder Intelligence Division [Los Angeles]
PEJ	Philadelphians for Equal Justice
PLP	Progressive Labor Party
PUSH	People United to Save Humanity
RAM	Revolutionary Action Movement
RCP	Revolutionary Communist Party
ROCIC	Regional Organized Crime Information Center [Memphis]
SACC	Spanish Action Committee of Chicago
SCLC	Southern Christian Leadership Conference
SDS	Students for a Democratic Society
SIB	Special Investigation Bureau [Detroit]
SISS	Senate Judiciary Committee Subcommittee on Internal Security
SMC	Student Mobilization Committee [Philadelphia]
SNCC	Student Nonviolent Coordinating Committee

SWAT	Special Weapons and Tactical Squad
TPF	Tactical Patrol Force [New York]
UAW	United Automobile Workers
UFW	United Farm Workers of America
V and R	Veterans and Reservists against the War
VFW	Veterans of Foreign Wars
VMC	Vietnam Moratorium Committee
VVAW	Vietnam Veterans against the War
WAPAC	Washington Area Peace Action Committee
WPC	Washington Peace Council
WSP	Women's Strike for Peace
YAF	Young Americans for Freedom
YPA	Young Progressives of America
YSA	Young Socialist Alliance

Introduction

A strong case has been made for the thesis that in the course of the past hundred years urban police have served as the protective arm of the economic and political interests of the capitalist system. What is especially compelling is that specialized police units have openly performed such functions. Over time these units—sometimes referred to here as "red squads"—have vastly proliferated in American cities; at their peak in the sixties, they numbered in the hundreds and according to a 1963 report (see pp. 81–82) were served by a "nearly 300,000 man effort . . . pursuing subversion." These cadres have, beginning in the Gilded Age, predominantly engaged in political repression, which, in the context of policing, may be defined as police behavior motivated or influenced in whole or in part by hostility to protest, dissent, and related activities perceived as a threat to the status quo.

The damaging impact of this police mission on the protected freedoms was facilitated by the fact that the police charged with such responsibilities were typically engaged in line functions bringing them into direct contact with targeted dissenters and operated in a context of broad discretion (discussed below). These units developed an aggressive confrontational style in fulfilling their repressive mission.

The thrust and coverage of these police units have varied considerably over the past century from city to city and reflected such variables as power structure, political culture, ethnic considerations, the role of the press, and industrial development. Over the years, however, especially in the areas of target selection and operations, certain patterns have emerged that explain the process by which police repression was institutionalized throughout urban America. The repressive mission focused first on the classic outdoor protest modes prominent in the nineteenth century, such as demonstrations, mass meetings, rallies, picket lines, pa-

1

rades, and, in the 1960s, vigils. The tactics that have historically been associated with the police response to outdoor gatherings include dragnet and pretext arrests, use of force or the threat of force to disperse gatherings, indiscriminate clubbings, physical dispersal and banishment of targets, and mounted charges, along with vigilante offensives conducted with police support.

With the maturation of dissent agendas, organizational growth, and the politicization of protest, police intervention intensified. Indoor meetings and activities were also targeted, as were not only individuals ("agitators") but organizations as well. This expansion of coverage led to covert intervention through informer infiltration, a development strongly influenced by the operational style of private detective agencies. Another consequence of the police attack on organizations was the raid, typically conducted at times and in a confrontational manner intended to maximize intimidation.

In the early years of the history of police repression, police authority for intervention was "peacekeeping," a blanket excuse for a virtually unbounded range of activities, and the enforcement of such common law offenses as "unlawful assemblage," "incitement to violence," and "riotous conduct." In the Progressive Era a host of state statutes and local ordinances were added, creating a broad "law enforcement" excuse for restraining the exercise of rights that were then beginning to be recognized as involving constitutionally protected freedoms. An effective device for curbing dissent and protest was the denial by police authorities—directly or vicariously—of the permits required first for outdoor gatherings and then for indoor ones as well. And where indoor gatherings were not subject to permit requirements, they were controlled in a variety of ways: the discriminatory enforcement of fire, health, and building ordinances; intimidation of meeting hall owners or lessees; a requirement that hall owners or managers submit in advance the names of sponsoring organizations and speakers; and rulings that only English be spoken at meetings. When all else failed, police details flooded the entrances to meeting halls and turned away would-be attendees. Nor can we omit an intimidating practice used to monitor both indoor and outdoor gatherings: the assignment of note-takers, usually familiar with the language of the speaker, in uniform or plainclothes and sometimes accompanied by a guard, to record what was said.

Harsh police intervention spanned almost half a century, but was for the most part curbed by the 1930s as a result of a number of circumstances, most notably constitutional requirements. (However, such intervention was partially revived in dealing with the unrest of the sixties.)

In the thirties the traditional interventionist practices were subordinated to "intelligence." In its traditional configuration, intelligence consists of (1) physical surveillance of a "subject," usually conducted in secret and frequently termed "information gathering" or "data collection," benign usages characteristic of this system of repression; (2) a body of techniques that, in addition to informer infiltration, ranged from observation and mail opening to wiretapping and photography; (3) the compilation and dissemination of files and dossiers about individuals and organizational "subjects"; (4) the assessment of file data; and (5) the aggressive use of such data to do injury to the subject. Whether the monitoring of subjects was open or clandestine, passive or aggressive, intelligence by itself became a force that demoralized and intimidated many targets and their supporters—and was intended to do so.

From the very beginning, neither external nor internal standards of target selection and operations were imposed on police units—even though the targets were typically engaged in political expression—an area where precision in formulating restraints is constitutionally imperative. The head of the Chicago intelligence unit, Lieutenant Joseph Healy, summed up the matter when he testified at a 1969 Chicago conspiracy trial (see pp. 118–22) that his squad targeted for surveillance "any organization that could create problems for the city or the country." As will be seen, the Chicago unit and its big-city counterparts elsewhere not only engaged in a wide variety of passive operational practices, but in "dirty tricks" and harassment, such as forcing the eviction or firing of particular subjects.

The police units that emerged in their modern form in the thirties and thereafter—earlier in larger cities such as New York, Chicago, and Los Angeles—have undergone revealing transitions in missions, targets, and operations. Originally operating under a "peacekeeping" (later "crowd control") banner, they monitored behavior, especially the alleged potential for violence in conflict situations. Their mission was explicitly broadened in the Progressive Era to cover prevention of violence generally, and later, in the modern era, to include the protection of an assertedly endangered national security. A parallel development saw a shift from passive monitoring, giving rise first to harassment and confrontation short of arrest, then to on-the-spot arrests for allegedly deviant conduct or speech. Clandestine surveillance designed to gather information and to flaunt a "presence" in particular discrete situations evolved into "intelligence" work focused on ongoing involvement with targets, not as an investigative means to a decision-making end, its blueprinted purpose, but as a (punitive) end in itself. This distortion was glaringly revealed by the failure of the urban units to serve a predictive-preventive role as recommended by national commissions investigating the ghetto riots of the late sixties; instead of probing for social causes, they insisted that evil plotters ("subversives"—the successors to the "agitators" of an earlier day) were the source of ghetto unrest. In the same way, ideology almost wholly replaced behavior as a police concern; the original focus on individuals such as strikers and their leaders and supporters gave way to a reflexive blaming of social unrest on political conspiracies. By the forties the congressional antisubversive committees developed techniques of expanding the boundaries of subversion* to include a broad spectrum of peaceful dissent, which in turn served as a proscriptive model for political oppression by government agencies on all levels, including by urban police units. This model reflected our national obsession with conspiracy and with scapegoating evil forces in our earthly paradise—insightfully explored by scholars such as David Brion Davis and Richard Hofstadter. The transition from behavior to ideology, from suppression of violence to curbing peaceful dissent, was thus completed: the new, enormously expanded police mission was legitimated by our countersubversive political culture, which in turn was enriched by police contributions to its fear-based assumptions. Moreover, engaged as they were in the pursuit of a common enemy, police units scattered throughout urban America formed a national network and also replaced their historic class allies and protectors in the private sector with state and federal support. In addition, this embrace of openly political concerns escaped the adverse fate of some police abuses in part because of its lofty aim—how could one challenge police programs designed to preserve our very existence as a nation?—and its secrecy.

The institutionalization of radical-hunting in the United States can best be understood as the culmination of historical stimuli beginning with the Haymarket bombing in 1886 and its aftermath. This was followed by another traumatic spur: the Russian Revolution and domestic post–World War I unrest. To these must be joined the police response to the protests spawned by the Great Depression of 1929; the beginnings of the Cold War and consequent recruitment of local police units as part-

---

* The expansive formula was developed and refined by the congressional committees: first, by the application of notions of vicarious, imputed, and derived guilt; second, by a process of cross-fertilization that proscribes an organization through the individuals associated with it and the individuals through their relationship to the organization; third, by increasing the number of condemned organizations through their links to one another; fourth, by treating subversion as permanent, irreversible, and even hereditary, with the result that a dossier, no matter how old, never loses its importance nor a subject his "interest."

ners of the FBI in spy-hunting; and, finally, the disturbances in the wake of the assorted protests of the sixties. Of these influences, Haymarket is the most notable, in the areas both of overt police behavior and covert surveillance. A survey published by the International Association of Chiefs of Police assesses the role of Haymarket in this way:

> The Haymarket bomb was responsible for the first major red scare in American history, and led to the immediate popular condemnation of Socialism, Communism and Anarchism by the national press and opinion leaders. In addition, the bomb resulted in the establishment of the first sustained American police intelligence operation aimed at leftist groups. Two years after the Haymarket riot the Chicago police declared that they had learned an invaluable lesson in 1886, that "the revolutionary movement must be carefully observed and crushed if it showed signs of growth."[1]

At the time of their greatest impact in the early sixties, these units had become, in some quarters, a welcome balm to the fear and dependence spawned by the youth revolt, riots, campus disturbances, and an ever more aggressive antiwar movement. The debate among scholars in the sixties on whether police authoritarianism and brutality are rooted in psychological or occupational influences was never resolved.[2] What is clear is that police antiradical units became the dominant voice of the countersubversive tradition (with a new, added note—racism) and, as in the past, attracted passionate ideologues, venerated by the far right, who served as "culture bearers" (in Karl Mannheim's phrase) of the countersubversive tradition, members of the "Gallery of the Obsessed" as they are called here.

At root the embrace of the protection of national security as a prime mission reflected the thrust of almost a century of police repression: to define protest in such a way as to warrant the most freewheeling target selection and the most punitive modus operandi. In a society programmed for fear, this mission served as a protective barrier against challenge and a sure-fire path for ambitious police officials, the "Big Men" who, in an earlier day, had instead sought the patronage of the elites whose interests they guarded.

But popular fear and dependence, autonomy and elitism, professionalism and secrecy gave leaky shelter when, beginning in the late sixties, hard rain began to fall on the red squads and, indeed, on the police generally. It could no longer be concealed that the red-hunting units and their leaders had invented or exaggerated the subversive threat posed by their targets in order to deflect criticism and to fabricate an acceptable justification for violating the constitutionally protected rights of peaceful dissenters. And it was too late for a revival of the timeworn political rescue efforts of grateful powerholders. Coalitions of civic groups, lawsuits, legislative probes, urban power shifts, the outcries of victimized minorities, and a new generation of adventurous journalists, supported by a media turnabout, all contributed to the restoration of police behavior to reform agendas despite the die-hard rescue efforts of congressional committees and their constituencies.

1 Haymarket

Prelude and Aftermath

The Nineteenth Century: Jittery Urban Elites

The headlong growth of business and manufacturing during the Gilded Age resulted in vast increases in the number and populations, especially in the East and Midwest, of cities dominated by capitalists through political machines and a support network including the press, churches, and, most important for our purposes, the police structures. By the end of the century, the police force in large cities had become the spearhead of the movement to control unrest and protest. This movement was powerfully fueled by a spirit of Babbitry: nothing must be permitted to impede the steady expansion of a profit-yielding economy; growth was its own justification. Boosterism and glorification of wealth accumulation were at root seen as justified by God's grace bestowed on a divinely chosen people and nation. The secular version of the notion of chosenness also nourished a Manichean perception of opposition and dissent, an appetite for scapegoats along with a sense of the contingency and fragility of the American dream. Finally, almost from the very beginning, fear—the anxiety that our earthly paradise might be invaded and corrupted by the forces of darkness, evil conspirators allied with foreign principals—had assumed social proportions and served as a powerful influence in the growth of police repression.

The prevailing climate of fear of a proletarian uprising after the Paris Commune in 1871 made a countersubversive response to unrest grist for nineteenth-century journalistic mills.[1] Disturbances, rooted in social and economic discontent, were feverishly exaggerated and attributed to foreign subversive inspiration. The press exploited the fear of violent dislocations of the status quo and in the process ratified this fear and shaped the rhetoric and images associated in the popular culture with protest.

7

As has been observed by urban historians in the post–Civil War era, the growing cities were viewed as seething centers of unrest, poised on the cusp of riot and rebellion and rooted in the fear of the "dangerous classes"—the tides of toughs, vagabonds, gang members, "plug uglies," and assorted scalawags that swept the cities. These images and fears were intensified by mounting class conflict. As an English observer noted, wealthy Americans seemed "pervaded by an uneasy feeling that they were living over a mine of social and industrial discontent with which the power of the government, under American institutions, was wholly inadequate to deal, and that some day this mine would explode and blow society into the air."*[2]

These anxieties, constantly refueled by a febrile press, as well as by ministers' sermons based on a biblically rooted apocalypticism, contributed to the strengthening of stereotypes that reflexively identified industrial conflict with violence by its worker participants and screened out evidence to the contrary.† This fear syndrome attributed to the immigrant worker a central role in labor disturbances and stamped him with a "brand of unworth."

Not in handouts or leaflets distributed in dark alleys, but in the most respectable publications, editorial writers depicted immigrant workers

* The mine metaphor and similar images—the fuse and the dynamite bomb, the spark and the tinder box—expressed the fears of the establishment generated by the ease with which bombs could be made with newly invented dynamite. Other versions of a feared eruption also proliferated. According to Wilbur P. Miller, by the 1860s, "the image of a volcano under the city became a cliche" (*Cops and Bobbies* [Chicago: University of Chicago Press, 1977], p. 141). Writing in 1859, Samuel B. Halliday warned, "We are sleeping under a volcano, from which already there are irruptions [which] . . . are comparatively mild premonitions of the more terrible irruptions that are certain by and by to belch forth with an all-consuming power" (*Lost and Found; or, Life among the Poor* [New York: Blakeman & Mason, 1859], p. 332). The impact of the Paris Commune greatly impressed Charles Loring Brace, who wrote in 1872, "Let the law lift its hand from them for a season or let the civilizing influences of American life fail to reach them, and, if the opportunity offered, we should see an explosion from this class which might leave the city in ashes and blood" (*The Dangerous Classes of New York and Twenty Years Work among Them* [New York: Wynkoop & Hallenbeck, 1872], p. 29). See also Robert Wiebe, *The Search for Order, 1877–1920* (New York: Hill & Wang, 1967), pp. 77–79, and Murray Edelman, "Myths, Metaphors and Political Conformity," *Journal for the Study of Interpersonal Processes*, August 1967, which deals with the importance of metaphors in shaping political values and perceptions in order to promote conformity.
† Anxieties that a "final conflict" was nearing are reflected not only in the works of social critics and reformers but also in popular literature. For example, Ignatius Donnelly's populist classic *Caesar's Column: A Story of the Twentieth Century* (1890; reprint, Cambridge, Mass.: Harvard University Press, Belknap Press, 1960) portrayed a terrifying class war.

and protesters as depraved, delinquent, and degraded (wild-eyed, bad-smelling, deadbeats, immoral, loud-mouthed cowards, loafers, wife-beaters, drunkards), as criminals (thieves, assassins, bloodthirsty, looters), as bestial (jackals, hyenas, wolves, venomous reptiles, harpies), and as loathsome (vermin, offal, rats, dung, scum). These felicities were augmented by more general epithets such as "fiends," "riff-raff," "rag-tag and bobtail cutthroats," "rubbish," "outscourings," or "dregs" of Europe.* Apart from this *Schimpflexikon*, these workers were widely perceived as adherents of foreign revolutionary movements, easily inflamed to reckless acts by falsely attributing to this haven of democracy the oppression of the despotic regimes they had fled. It is not too much to say that immigrant workers were considered a caste without civic identity and unqualified to share our precious "heritage of freedom." Why should these dastardly ingrates, who did not even speak our language, be allowed to enjoy the "blessings of liberty"? Such status deprivation embittered workers as a class, including even the native-born, who were tarred with the same brush.

It requires no profound psychological insight to recognize that a complex reality was displaced by a scenario in which a crazed, marauding rabble, drawn from the "dangerous classes," was repulsed and contained by the forceful intervention of the authorities. In the course of time, urban elites looked to the police for order and property protection; they

---

* These characterizations were common in the newspapers of the time. For samples, see John Higham, *Strangers in the Land: Patterns of American Nativism* (1955; reprint, New York: Atheneum, 1963), pp. 53–54, and Herbert Gutman, *Work, Culture and Society in Industrializing America* (New York: Vintage Books, 1977), pp. 71–72. The latter includes a particularly gruesome contribution by the *Chicago Times* to the effect that Slavic Chicagoans were descended from "the Scythians," "eaters of raw animal food, fond of drinking the blood of their enemies whom they slew in battle, and [men] who preserved as trophies the scalps and skins of enemies whom they overthrew." Through epithets of bestiality and loathesomeness, the immigrant worker was dehumanized: the characterizations—because they were so widely, indeed, almost reflexively used—effectively replaced what they were supposed only to suggest, and this dehumanization process must have been particularly true of nineteenth-century nativists prone to view the unwelcome Other with the gut horror that echoes in the biblical cry "Unclean!" It is significant that at the time of the 1919 red scare, a similar vocabulary was used to express hate and loathing for the reds (see Murray B. Levin, *Political Hysteria in America* [New York: Basic Books, 1971], ch. 4, "Vermin, Feces and Secrets: Anxiety and Appeals to the Irrational," pp. 141–76). During the fifties, too, far-right nativists used comparable dehumanizing terms to describe their enemies (see, for example, Leo Lowenthal and Norbert Guterman, *Prophets of Deceit: A Study of the Techniques of the American Agitator* [1949; reprint, New York: Harper & Brothers, 1966], pp. 58–60). In the sixties these denigrations were transformed into "animals" and "creeps."

became, in Max Weber's phrase, "the representative of God on earth."[3] But in the immediate post–Civil War period, the official police forces, for a variety of reasons (ethnic and class loyalties, small numbers, lack of training), were not trusted to provide this protection. In this setting, the Pinkerton Detective Agency became a vital resource.

Founded in the Civil War era for military espionage purposes, the Pinkerton Agency's exploits, symbolized by the logo of a watchful eye and the motto "The Eye That Never Sleeps," captured the popular imagination.[4] The agency scored an early triumph and attracted fascinated attention as a result of its 1868 Mollie Maguire investigation.[5] The fascination with the Mollie Maguire case focused on the role of a detective infiltrator, a familiar-enough weapon in the modern police armory, but rare in nonmilitary contexts in the post–Civil War period.*

The fear of the unwashed, alien-branded lower classes only increased as a result of the depression of 1873–78 and the wave of unemployment demonstrations that resulted. In New York City, for example, police refused to authorize a demonstration planned for January 13, 1874, at Tompkins Square, and then brutally attacked an estimated 7,000 people who gathered there to protest the permit denial. While almost all of the violence at the "Tompkins Square Riot" was the result of indiscriminate

---

* When retained in the case, Allan Pinkerton's initial move was to send investigators to track down those of the area's Irish Catholics who belonged to a fraternal order, the Ancient Order of Hiberians (AOH), of which the Mollies were an unruly, runaway lodge. Pinkerton then recruited a young Irish Catholic agent, James McParland, to infiltrate the Mollies. Over time, McParland became a folk hero of sorts. With a masked cover identity, that of a criminal on the lam, he made his way to the Pennsylvania anthracite region, the home of his targets, and proceeded to penetrate the outer circle of the AOH. While McParland worked his way toward the hard core, pressure was put on the periphery—the Catholic Church and the AOH—to disavow the Mollies. This campaign, coupled with more ruthless and aggressive tactics by Pinkerton operatives deputized as Coal and Iron Police, isolated the inner conspiratorial circle. Demoralization, fear, and defections completed the process. McParland ultimately became the Mollies' nemesis and the principal witness against them in mass trials for murder in 1876. Under cross-examination, McParland justified conduct condemned as that of an agent provocateur on two grounds: (1) he had acted as he did to preserve his cover, and (2) in any event, he had tolerated and even counseled criminal acts only because he was assigned not to forestall crimes but to secure a conviction. In 1877 the Pennsylvania Supreme Court upheld this plea and ruled that "a detective who joins a criminal organization for the purpose of exposing it and bringing criminals to punishment, and honestly carries out that design is not an accessory before the fact, although he may have encouraged and counselled those who were about to commit crime, if in so doing he intended that they should be discovered and punished, and his testimony therefore is not to be treated as that of an infamous person" (*Campbell v. Commonwealth*, 84 Pa. 187, 193).

clubbing by mounted police, the press responded with the usual denunciations of a "rabble of blackguards mostly foreigners" and "a parcel of vagabonds of the worst stamp." The *New York Herald* blamed the disturbances on "noisy conspirators" linked to the Paris Commune who were financed by the "booty of the plundered churches of Paris."

In the aftermath of Tompkins Square, New York City police undertook a new mission of assigning special detectives to spy on labor and socialist meetings, while the New York police board accused the radicals of conspiring to set fire to churches and to store arms and ammunition in preparation for a bloody showdown.

The Great Upheaval of 1877: Tentacles of the Paris Commune? More than any single stimulus, the chain of railroad strikes that rocked the country in 1877 created a sense among powerholders of beleaguerment and promoted the search for a response strong enough to contain and repress future threats to the established order. The unease generated by the 1877 disturbances was nourished by an earlier series of railroad strikes and a fear, fueled by the press, that the pent-up miseries of the 1873 depression would erupt into a catastrophic disturbance rivaling the Paris Commune.[6]

The 1877 "Great Upheaval," as it has come to be called, is noteworthy for its broad social impact: the recognition by businessmen that they could no longer boast that this country was free of the class conflict and attendant unrest that rocked nineteenth-century Europe, and, in wider sectors, the sense that the rowdy strikers and their supporters were despoilers of the dream of a new world untainted by the evils of the old. This setting provided a receptive response to press charges that the strikers were agents of communism and assured a market for the wares of private guard and detective agencies such as the Pinkertons.

Police and military everywhere responded forcefully to the 1877 disturbances. In New York, socialist sympathy meetings for the strikes were disrupted, picket lines dispersed, strikers beaten, and strike breakers protected. The police commissioner boasted in 1884 that although the city had "a larger Communistic population than elsewhere in the country," bloody confrontations were prevented because the radicals respected the police determination to enforce the law impartially.[7]

In Chicago, where the police unambiguously served as the arm of the dominant manufacturing and commercial interests, police roamed the city dispersing meetings of strikers and their supporters, brutally raided a peaceful meeting of the Workingman's Party, a magnet for socialistically inclined German immigrants, and opened fire on a hall where frightened demonstrators had fled, wounding dozens and killing at least one person in what a judge later termed a "criminal riot" by the police. Although altogether thirty people were killed and about two hundred wounded as a result of police and military action in suppressing the 1877 disorders in Chicago, few tears were shed in respectable circles over their actions. Thus, the *Tribune* declared the police were entitled to "all praise" for their actions, while the world owed "extermination rather than a livelihood" to the "dead-beats, vagrants, drunkards, thieves, guttersnipes, Communists and vicious loafers who came to the front and demanded it in the recent riots."[8]

The primary result of the 1877 upheaval was to promote the erection of armories, the reinforcement of state militias, and a general strengthening of police forces to fulfill a new mission: the monitoring and control of working-class unrest and threats to the public order.[9] It marked the quickening of a process by which industrialism transformed the police from neutral peacekeepers to aggressive partisans. And the combined assault of police, military, and "Citizens' Associations"* sparked awareness in labor and socialist circles of the need for a defense preparedness and led to the launching by German immigrants of armed units (*Lehr und Wehr*) to repel future attacks. Finally, the indiscriminate assault by the pro-employer forces, not only on violence-prone radicals, but on the organizing activities of trade unions in the skilled crafts with modest goals quite removed from the demands of the radicals deepened and expanded the class consciousness of working people. The resulting polarization laid the foundations for the Haymarket tragedy of 1886.

Haymarket and Its Legacy

On May 3, 1886, the workers at Chicago's McCormick Harvester works who were striking for an eight-hour day held a mass meeting in support of their demands.[10] The police, under the command of Captain John Bonfield, fired into the crowd, killing at least four strikers. The next night a meeting was held in Haymarket Square, where some two thousand persons gathered to hear denunciations of the murders. Toward the close of the demonstration, when the crowd had thinned out to about two hundred, a police detail of one hundred eighty under the command of Captains Bonfield and William Ward entered the area. Shortly after Captain Ward issued a dispersal order to the stragglers, a bomb

* This benign usage was adopted in the post–Civil War era by employers and their supporters in conflicts with workers and other protest forces. These associations became the core of later vigilante activities and, through their control of the mainstream press, a powerful propaganda instrument.

was thrown by an unknown (and never identified) individual, resulting in the deaths of seven policemen and injury of seventy others. In the subsequent tide of fear and hysteria that engulfed the city, Captain Michael J. Schaack, a fiery foe of trade unionists and anarchists, who were prominently involved in the protest, led a witch-hunt and round-up, not only of radicals and anarchists, but of individuals identified with the mainstream labor movement who were opposed to anarchism.

On May 27, 1886, eight men were indicted as accessories to the murder of a policeman by pistol shots and, in a catch-all charge, general conspiracy to murder.[11] Subsequently, after brief deliberations, the jury found all of them guilty and the judge sentenced seven to execution while the eighth (Oscar Wiebe) received a fifteen-year sentence. After the U.S. Supreme Court refused to intervene, pleas for executive clemency (strenuously opposed by prominent merchants and manufacturers) led Governor Richard J. Oglesby to commute to life imprisonment the sentences of Samuel Fielden and Michael Schwab. A third defendant, Louis Lingg, killed himself by exploding a detonating cap in his mouth, and the remaining four, Albert R. Parsons, Adolph Fisher, George Engel, and August Spies, were hanged on November 11, 1887. On June 26, 1893, Governor John P. Altgelt pardoned Fielden, Wiebe, and Schwab.

Our purpose here is not to recount the oft-told tale of Haymarket, but to focus on the conduct of the police principals. During the two decades after the 1871 fire, the Chicago police were, according to Herbert Asbury, "probably the most inefficient organization of its kind in the United States . . . poorly paid and riddled with graft . . . and unable to handle with any degree of intelligence the railroad and streetcar strikes of 1877 and 1885 . . . and the other labor troubles and radical outbreaks that kept Chicago in almost constant turmoil."[12] It was not that the force loafed: in one year alone (1879) the police made 28,480 arrests on charges of disorderly conduct, primarily in connection with labor disturbances and riots.[13]

The reliance by the Chicago business community on repressive police tactics to deal with labor unrest was unconcealed. Indeed, the Chicago police were as much the minions of the business community as hired Pinkertons. The leadership role of Captain (then Inspector) Bonfield in both the May 3 and May 4 episodes was no accident. He had impressed the business community with his "shoot to kill" orders in an 1885 streetcar strike, and his readiness to order clubbings had led his victims to dub him "Black Jack." As a result of the indiscriminate clubbings he instigated on the morning of July 2, 1885, during the course of the streetcar strike, one man was beaten senseless, another died, and others never fully recovered from the injuries inflicted by the police.[14]

In February 1886 Bonfield posted a security guard of three hundred policemen around the McCormick Works to implement a lockout of some 1,482 workers, and on March 1 the police began escorting strike-breakers into the plant. On March 2, without warning, Bonfield's men clubbed a number of locked-out workers peacefully gathered outside the plant. In the ensuing confrontation, the police shot at the workers, killing at least four of them while they were in flight.

Bonfield's role in the Haymarket affair is illuminated by the fact that when he was informed at the station house by Mayor Carter Harrison at about 10:00 o'clock that the meeting was about over and that it had been peaceful,* he nevertheless stayed on until the mayor left, and then led his men to the tragic encounter in the square.[15]

We must now turn to Captain Michael J. Schaack, who dominated the stage after the bombing. In the wake of the bombing, he was assigned to assist the state prosecutor, develop his case, and bring to justice others who were implicated. Schaack may well be called the founding father of modern police antiradical theory and practice: his operational methods, ideological assumptions, exploitation of mass fear, and use of publicity together form a legacy that became the foundation of a police specialty in subsequent years.

Subsequent to the bombing, Schaack's men (they were frequently referred to as his "boys")[+] commenced a terror campaign during which well over two hundred sixty individuals were rounded up. They raided and ransacked homes, made illegal arrests, dragged people out of their beds, subjected dragnet victims to intimidation and torture, and bribed several into becoming prosecution witnesses.[16] The justification offered for these tactics was a claimed vast revolutionary conspiracy targeting the city and, ultimately, the nation.

The Chicago Citizens' Association and its allies raised funds used by Schaack to bribe witnesses and pay off informers. In addition, it apparently hired Pinkerton agents to assist the police,[‡] raised over $30,000 to

---

* He hardly needed to be told the news: all during the evening he had plain-clothesmen or informers (it is not clear which) shuttling between his post and the meeting to alert him to developments.
† The singular, "Schaack's man," was used for a close associate, an agent or alter ego.
‡ One of the hired Pinkerton agents subsequently wrote: "The false reports written about anarchists as told me by the writers themselves would make a decent man's blood boil" (C. A. Siringo, *Two Evil-Isms, Pinkertonism and Anarchism* [Chicago: C. A. Siringo, 1915], p. 3). One agent infiltrated an anarchist

succor the families of the dead and wounded policemen,* donated land to the federal government to be used "for military purposes," that is, as a redoubt for rapid troop deployment without delay when needed to curb disturbances in the city, and subsequently, in 1899, collected funds to build an armory for the same purpose.[17]

As the city writhed in fear, kept at a high pitch by a frenzied press, Schaack took center stage as a detective-hero, casting himself in the role of master detective, a figure that in the nineteenth century gripped the popular imagination, whose daring and skill would unlock mysteries and bring him acclaim as the man who had not only solved "the crime of the century" but rescued the city and nation from destruction. How could his vision be marred by such piddling details as apprehending the actual bomber? Instead, he bragged unceasingly of his cleverness and courage in rooting out secret conspiracies, confident that no one in the fear-ridden city would dare challenge his boastful disclosures, however absurd or incredible.

This self-styled master detective left no stone unturned to keep himself in the public eye. Not only did he falsely announce the discovery of bombs, but he actually sought to set up anarchist cells on his own. Three years after the bombing, on May 10, 1889, Police Chief Frederick Ebersold told the *Chicago Times* in an interview:

> Captain Schaack wanted to keep things stirring. He wanted bombs to be found here, there, all around, everywhere. I thought people would lie down to sleep better if they were not afraid their homes would be blown to pieces any minute. But this man, Schaack . . . wanted none of that policy. . . . After we got the anarchist societies broken up, Schaack wanted to send out people to organize new societies right away. . . . He wanted to keep the thing boiling, keep himself prominent before the public.[18]

---

group prior to Haymarket and surfaced as a witness at the trial (Lum, p. 87). As Henry David points out (*The History of the Haymarket Affair* [New York: Farrar & Rinehart, 1936], p. 222), it is unclear whether the agents hired after the bombing were employed by the Citizens' Association or by one of its prominent members, Melville E. Stone, editor of the *Chicago Daily News*.

* At the trial's closing, Judge Joseph E. Gary told the jurors that they "deserve some recognition . . . because of the meager compensation you have received" (Lum, p. 189). Subsequently it was proposed that they be rewarded by a fund raised by grateful citizens. However, it is unclear whether in fact such a fund was actually raised.

Ebersold's charges were probably prompted by Schaack's attack on him in his book *Anarchy and Anarchists,* published in February 1889, sixteen months after the Haymarket executions.[19] This volume was prepared to advance Schaack's career as a master anarchist hunter and to exploit his national reputation as the hero of Haymarket, and it was circulated by the Pinkerton Agency to induce employers to engage its services. The exaggerations and inventions in the book—admitted by Schaack himself later to be (at least) one-third lies[20]—also reflect the narrative strategies of nineteenth-century police thrillers, and they are clearly intended both to sow and to exploit mass fear. The book is a handsome volume of 697 quarto pages, with 191 illustrations (a great many bomb-related), and its title page blazes with three subtitles: *A History of the Red Terror and the Social Revolution in America and Europe; Communism, Socialism and Nihilism, in Doctrine and in Deed;* and *The Chicago Haymarket Conspiracy, The Detection and Trial of the Conspirators.*

Anarchy and Anarchists is embroidered with tales of creepy encounters with strangers, meetings with mysterious women veiled in black, heroic penetrations of clandestine meeting places, anonymous missives, and so on. At the outset, the author startles us with the assurance (p. 74) that "Socialism in the United States may be regarded as synonymous with Anarchy." Well-meaning, naive strikers were duped by the "Socialists-Anarchists" in 1886 "to strike a blow which would terrorize the community and inaugurate the rule of the Commune." Moreover, the bloody streetcar confrontations in the summer of 1885 had not been due to Inspector Bonfield's detail at all, but resulted from "prearranged plans" of "the Anarchists and Socialists of Chicago [who] did everything to create a bloody conflict between the police and the strikers."

Dipping into Social Darwinist wisdom, Schaack treats his readers to an extended paean to the glories of free enterprise and the perils of a socialist, equalitarian society, which not only offers no incentive to great achievements in art, literature, or invention, but places everyone on an equal footing, "the profligate with the provident and the drunken wretch with the industrious" (p. 84).

Arrayed against kindly and generous employers are the "Huns and Vandals of modern civilization," the socialists and anarchists who demand ten hours' pay for eight hours' work in the hope that employer resistance will lead workers who secretly profess socialism "to the point of violence" (p. 103). All of the conflicts preceding Haymarket were planned preliminary stages in a vast takeover conspiracy, culminating in what Schaack repeatedly refers to as the "Monday Night Conspiracy," to be ignited by the Haymarket demonstration on the following day. This plot, a product of Schaack's febrile imagination, was assertedly proposed by Engel and endorsed by Fisher and contemplated that bombs be thrown into police stations; riflemen of the *Lehr und Wehr* would post themselves outside, and whoever came out of the station would be shot down. They then would come into the heart of the city, where the fight would commence in earnest. When all the conspirators finally reached the center of the city, they would set fire to the most prominent buildings, attack the jail, open the doors, and free the inmates to join them. And why did it not take place? The reason "is not explicable upon any other hypothesis than that the courage of the trusted leaders failed them at the critical moment."

Schaack had control of a slush fund provided by the Chicago Citizens' Association for such purposes as bribing witnesses and purchasing the services of informers—called "privates" or "secret service men." In an illuminating passage, Schaack describes how his network operated:

> I did not depend wholly upon police effort, but at once employed a number of outside men, choosing especially those who were familiar with the Anarchists and their haunts. The funds for this purpose were supplied to me by public spirited citizens who wished the law vindicated and order preserved in Chicago. I received reports from the men thus employed from the beginning of the case up to November 20, 1887. . . . At each Anarchist meeting I had at least one man present to note the proceedings and to learn what plots they were maturing. (pp. 49–50)

Like so many authoritarian radical-hunters, Schaack was revolted by activist women:

> In many of the smaller meetings . . . a lot of crazy women were usually present, and whenever a crazy proposition to kill someone or blow up the city with dynamite [was made], these "squaws" proved the most bloodthirsty . . . they would show themselves much more eager to carry it out than the men and it always seemed a pleasure to the Anarchists to have them present. They were always invited to the "war dances" . . . and they fairly went wild whenever bloodthirsty sentiments were uttered. . . . At one meeting on North Halsted Street [were] the most hideous-looking females that could be found. . . . Some of them were

pock marked, others freckled faced and red haired and
others again held their snuff boxes in their hand while
the congress was in session. One female appeared at one
of these meetings with her husband's boots on and there
was another about six feet tall. She was a beauty! She
was raw boned, had a turned up nose and looked as
though she might have carried a red flag in Paris during
the reign of the Commune. (pp. 207–8)

The "slut" image of radical women was augmented by stereotypical
denunciations of their slovenly housekeeping and callousness to the
needs of their children. On the other hand there were some—but only a
few—decent women, good housekeepers and good mothers, who deplored the political involvement of their spouses.

Schaack then regales the reader with a stream of pulp-style spy
stories:

One of his "privates" is accused of being a spy; the plant
then charges his accuser, a bona fide anarchist, with being a Pinkerton agent and asks the assemblage whether
he should kill his accuser; he is told to take him out
somewhere and kill him. The accuser, overcome by the
countercharge, "ran for his life." But the plant, fearing
exposure, successfully urges adjournment explaining that
his accuser, being a police spy, would return with police
reinforcements. (pp. 208–9)

Between May 7, 1886, and November 1877, Schaack was a very busy
man—supervising surveillance programs, coaching witnesses, planting
informers, having holes bored in walls and floors at which eavesdroppers
were positioned, and fending off attempts to do him in or spy on him
(p. 215).

Schaack's prime post-Haymarket objective was to stoke the fires of
fear and panic, which the trial and executions might quench. Vigilance
cannot be relaxed; the danger is greater than ever. In addition to the
75,000 men, women, and children who are socialists, we must remember
the 7,300 dangerous anarchists! (Wholly invented figures, as his book's
appendices show.) He cannot warn us often enough that we must be
prepared for a fight to the death:

All over the world the apostles of disorder, rapine and
Anarchy are today pressing forward their work of ruin,
and preaching their gospel of disasters to all the nations
with more fiery energy and a better organized propa-

ganda than was ever known before. People who imagine
that the energy of the revolutionists has slackened, or
that the determination to wreck all the existing systems
has grown less bitter, are deceiving themselves. The conspiracy against society is as determined as it ever was,
and among every nation the spirit of revolt is being gal-
vanized into a newer and more dangerous life. (p. 687)

Schaack comes through as the quintessential political sleuth, the fore-
runner of a long line of zealots who, with the support of the business
community, used their countersubversive specialty to achieve self-
promotion, power, fame, and profit. Like the police red-hunters who
walked in his tracks, he thirsted, in Shakespeare's words, for "the big
wars / That make ambition virtue" (*Othello* 3.3.349–50).

Schaack and his detail blazed a trail in another area—corruption and
greed. While such failings were endemic in the nineteenth-century police world, they were particularly notable in areas where the urban elites
of the Gilded Age felt threatened by the unrest of the lower classes and
were hence ready to pay whatever was needed—tolerating graft or direct
payoffs—to ensure police aggression in restraining troublemakers.*

All three of the police officials identified with Haymarket would have
strongly endorsed Iago's advice to Roderigo: "Put money in thy purse"
(*Othello* 1.3.345). In September 1885 the *Daily News* uncovered a series
of scandals revealing that Bonfield, jointly with another official (Captain
Ward), was running an extortion and bribery ring involving payoffs
from gambling houses and prostitutes. According to a *Chicago Times*
exposé on January 5, 1889, both Bonfield and Schaack were receiving
immunity bribes from local taverns and prostitutes. The story also revealed that a great deal of stolen merchandise had been traced to policemen under Schaack's command, including the gold cuff links of

---

* Schaack made much of the fact that the anarchists' victims were not a lot of
nobodies, but valiant guardians of the public order. Indeed, the fact that the
victims were such noble fellows in itself proved that the defendants were fiends.
An ironic commentary on this attempt to glorify the murdered policemen
emerges from the fate of Thomas F. Birmingham, the policeman who served as a
model for the statue memorializing the victims of the Haymarket bomb. In 1890
and 1899 he was charged with collaborating with criminals and selling stolen
merchandise for his own gain. Subsequently, according to Emma Goldman's account, he became a petty thief and a skid-row drunk, and died in the county
hospital. See William J. Adelman, *Haymarket Revisited: A Tour Guide of Labor
History Sites and Ethnic Neighborhoods Connected with the Haymarket Affair*
(Chicago: Illinois Labor History Society, 1976), p. 39. The Birmingham statue
became a repeated target of assaults in the sixties by young radicals, who forced
its removal.

Haymarket defendant Louis Lingg. In reprisal, Schaack, repeating a tactic used against the radical press in 1886, promptly ordered the shutdown of the *Times*, then owned by Carter Harrison, a liberal former mayor of Chicago. But even more startling was the discovery that Schaack was the bagman of a $475,000 fund collected by Chicago businessmen for a continuing war on subversion. In the course of a prosecution of the wife of one of Schaack's boys, Jacob Lowenstein, she released documents establishing that her husband and Schaack had stolen and fenced a considerable amount of property, including possessions of the Haymarket defendants as well as property seized in the course of the subsequent terror campaign. Later, in 1889, after an investigation, the recurring scandals led to dismissal of a group of officers. Schaack managed, after an interval under a cloud in the wake of the corruption exposé, to retain leadership of the East Chicago Avenue station because of his supportive German ethnic constituency. In 1898 he died in peace.

Haymarket was exploited in a crusade to broadly tar peaceful labor activities with the brush of violence. As in the aftermath of the Great Upheaval, conspiracy concepts were extended by statute to peaceful labor activities and enlarged police forces in industrial cities were encouraged to apply vaguely worded common law restraints ("trespass," "disorderly conduct") and newly enacted ordinances to justify disruption of peaceful labor activities.[21] Thus, Haymarket created a climate in which Schaack-style abuses, both in targeting and operations, were not only overlooked, but encouraged in major industrial centers. The stereotypes applied to immigrant laborers and radicals (see pp. 8–9) were spiced with new epithets branding them violence-prone fiends armed with bombs and dynamite. The Haymarket tragedy also marked the emergence of a new form of policing: anarchists were indiscriminately surveilled not only as a means of crime suppression, but for ideological reasons alone. This targeting concentration embraced identifiable individuals (leaders, activists) as well as the organizations with which they were identified. The emergence of professional "anarchist chasers" led to the organization in large American cities of "bomb" and "anarchist" squads and resort to infiltration by informers as a surveillance technique. This style of ideological warfare against anarchism broke ground for subsequent similar police initiatives against socialism and communism and marked the beginning, in Richard Drinnon's phrase, "of the rationalization of conformity."[22]

Thomas Byrnes: Protector of Plutocrats. In New York the post-Haymarket syndrome of increased police surveillance was typified by the emergence of Inspector Thomas Byrnes, who paralleled Schaack's role both as an outstanding anarchist chaser and as a manipulator who used the fears of the business community and the general corruption of the time to line his purse. Finley Peter Dunne later recalled:

> The celebrated Inspector Byrnes whose fortune was made by scaring millionaires into the belief that there was about to be an uprising of anarchists and assembling an army of cops to surround a few hundred garment workers in Union Square who had gathered to hear a squeaky little tailor rant in Yiddish against the tyranny of Capital.[23]

Dunne did not overstate Byrnes's success in milking his wealthy patrons by his alertness in protecting their interests. After apprehending a blackmailer of Jay Gould, he became Gould's intimate and explained his fortune of $350,000—an enormous sum in those days, especially for one on a salary of $2,000 a year—as the reward of sound investment advice.[24] As in Chicago, a sense of beleaguerment after Haymarket intensified the felt dependency of the business community on Byrnes's protective resources and loosened its purse strings. Byrnes was quick to cash in on such fears: during his years as chief of detectives and inspector, he dispatched details to block anarchist meetings and assigned plainclothes note-takers to monitor them.

In August 1893 an anarchist scare was triggered by hysterical press accounts and police reports of an occurrence, promptly labeled a "riot," involving a wrecked East Side hall. Anarchists were held responsible for the disturbance—although there was no proof of their involvement—because Emma Goldman had delivered a passionate speech in an adjacent hall to an audience of the unemployed.[25] Word spread that a true riot inspired by anarchists was about to erupt as meetings were held to protest police misconduct. All police leaves were canceled, meetings were infiltrated, and the city prepared for the worst. Police hustled known anarchists out of their meeting rooms and headquarters and broke up peaceful meetings, which then moved to new sites, only to be broken up again.[26]

Emma Goldman fell afoul of Byrnes's anarchist hunt when she was arrested in Philadelphia on August 31 on a violence-incitement charge arising from a speech she had made on August 21, 1893, in New York's Union Square to develop support for a public works program to alleviate the needs of the victims of the economic depression. Byrnes's vigorously repressive response to the August scare, culminating in the Goldman arrest, won him acclaim as a fearless anarchist chaser, a "man of the hour."[27]

Ferocious in dealing with labor unrest and radicals, Byrnes was tender in his toleration of grafters and boodlers under his command, not only among the rank and file but higher up as well. After one of his captains laid bare the systematized profit sharing between the police and the owners of brothels and gambling dens, the curtain came down on Byrnes's career and he was forced to resign—to the regret of his wealthy patrons. Fittingly enough, in 1898 he launched a detective agency head-quartered on Wall Street.[28] But Byrnes's tradition lived on: by the turn of the century, political dissidents and strikers in New York were routinely surveilled and sometimes harassed.

The Progressive Era: The Police Assault on Freedom of Association

The Mythicizing of Worker Violence. As a result of the influence of power elites on opinion formation, violence in the post-Haymarket era and well into this century was, in our industrializing society, associated with organizing efforts, strikes, and related collective labor activities. Over time, the labor-violence equation became a social myth—that is, a (distorted) version of reality requiring no proof of its validity.[29]

The shaping of the violence myth in the Progressive Era is not difficult to trace. The dimming memory of the Haymarket bombing was revived by such events as Alexander Berkman's attempt on the life of the industrialist Henry Frick (1892), President McKinley's assassination in 1901, assassinations and attempted assassinations of European royalty between 1880 and 1900, the arrival of émigrés from the abortive Russian revolution of 1905, the murder-bombing of Idaho's governor, Frank Steunenberg, in 1905 (the defendants were acquitted in a law court but not in the court of public opinion),[30] the anarchist scare of 1908, and the *Los Angeles Times* bombing in 1911. Within a short time, the violence stigma became more unqualified, the selective perception of reality more pronounced, and the yellow press more inflammatory in dealing with this issue. The nineteenth-century fear syndrome reemerged, although in the form of a latent, more restrained angst.[31] Thus, the openly denounced "rabble" and "scum" of the earlier period became, in President Theodore Roosevelt's characterization, "undesirable citizens"—a *de haut en bas* put-down that drew angry responses.*

* Roosevelt was referring to the defendants in the Steunenberg bombing case; it is believed by some that this slur helped persuade the jury to return an acquittal verdict.

The image of worker violence that came to dominate popular perceptions of industrial conflict was powerfully reinforced by the deployment through employers' instigation of state militias and federal troops in such conflicts. The fact that the soldiery was called out in itself served as proof that workers and their allies had once again disturbed the public order and in a manner beyond the control of local authorities. Further, such call-outs brought resentment among the respectable citizenry against workers for blemishing the fair name of their city.[32]

Perhaps the most important stimulus in the development of the violence myth was the "agitator," cast as the prime instigator of violence. The agitator became the scapegoat for unrest; it was his rabble-rousing talents alone that sparked a crowd into a riotous mob.* That this troublemaker alone had manipulated an otherwise contented work force was demonstrated by the fact that he was an "outside agitator" (or alternatively a "professional agitator"). And this identification was plausible since eloquent anarchists and Wobblies were sometimes recruited

---

* The fear of crowds ("contentious gatherings" in Charles Tilly's formulation) and the scapegoating of the agitator were linked to the thesis, inherited from the past and rationalized in the Progressive Era by Gustave Le Bon, that crowd behavior was inherently disorderly and that the anonymity afforded by mass meetings encouraged the participants to shed rational restraints and to give expression to hidden violent proclivities without fear of detection. This view was challenged by liberals and reformers of the time, who used the Hyde Park safety-valve model to support the contention that the frustration and resentments of the lower classes could be defused by setting apart public areas for unrestrained speech and assembly (see pp. 28–30, 54–55, 61). Le Bon's thesis of the potentially "unrestrained frenzy" of crowd behavior has been largely rejected in the writings of later historians, who observe that historically crowds have behaved rationally and with only limited force to achieve their objectives. See Gustave Le Bon, *The Crowd: A Study of the Popular Mind* (London: T. F. Unwin, 1910); George Rudé, *The Crowd in History: A Study of Popular Disturbances in France and England, 1730–1848* (New York: John Wiley & Sons, 1964); Charles Tilly, *The Vendée* (Cambridge, Mass.: Harvard University Press, 1964); E. P. Thompson, "The Moral Economy of the Crowd in the Eighteenth Century," *Past and Present*, February 1971; Charles Tilly, "Repertoires of Contention in America and Britain, 1750–1830," in *The Dynamics of Social Movements*, ed. Mayer N. Zald and John D. McCarthy (Cambridge, Mass.: Winthrop Publishers, 1979), pp. 127–55. On the other hand, the thesis that grievances and frustrations could be defused by a public airing is supported neither by psychological studies nor by the historical record in this country, Ireland, and England. See, for example, Helen M. Lynd, *England in the Eighteen-Eighties* (New York: Oxford University Press, 1945), p. 282. Finally, it is worth recalling that after the cresting of outdoor protest modes in the thirties, public spaces used for such purposes were taken over by eccentrics, cultists, disputatious atheists, soul savers, and similar types and became a source of popular humor. More recently these sites have become a marketplace for drug traffickers in some cities.

from outside to charge up crowds—literally to agitate them—in conflict situations.

Violence! Violence! Who'll Buy My Violence?

The violence thesis was invoked to justify intervention in industrial conflicts by police, the courts, and private agencies such as the Pinkerton Agency, and, in the Progressive Era, the Burns Agency and others. The Pinkerton Agency and its progeny performed two separate functions: they supplied employers with strikebreakers and guards in industrial conflicts and pioneered in the field of labor espionage. As early as the mid eighties, Pinkerton agents had become a standard employer response to labor unrest. Both guard and spy functions were quickly enfolded in the police and criminal justice system, a circumstance that virtually eliminated the fear of punishment for otherwise indictable offenses. In 1885 the Pinkerton Agency was hired for strike duty at Chicago's Mc-Cormick Harvester works. Its agents shot and killed several bystanders when hooted by a crowd of strikers. The indicted killers were never tried. Governor Altgelt's subsequent pardon message observed, "The prosecuting officers apparently took no interest in the case, and allowed it to be continued a number of times, until the witnesses were worn out, and in the end the murderers went free."[33]

After the Haymarket bombing, the agency was hired to work with the police and volunteers to track down anarchists and to penetrate their meetings. Pinkerton men not only participated jointly with the police in raids, but also infiltrated the anarchists' ranks and reported their doings to the police and (in some cases) to the media. The guard work of the private agencies and their strikebreaking activities made them welcome police allies, with potential "turf" clashes only in cities and towns where workers' political strength had helped influence the outcome of elections. Indeed, the strikebreakers and thugs deployed by the private agencies were frequently sworn in as police deputies, given badges and clothed with police powers (which they often exceeded or ignored altogether).

An outstanding example of the role of private detectives in developing national support for the violence thesis is the 1910 bombing of the *Los Angeles Times* building, which was traced to the brothers James B. and John J. McNamara, associated with the Iron Workers' Union in Indianapolis (John was reelected its secretary-treasurer during his trial). William J. Burns, the McNamara brothers' nemesis, was retained in the case by local authorities and worked closely with the police in Los Angeles as well as other cities (Indianapolis, Chicago) not only to hunt down his prey but, through trickery, to deliver them for trial. The *Los Angeles Times* bombing and its aftermath produced an impact remarkably reminiscent of Haymarket, including a wave of restrictive ordinances and police repression similar to that spawned by Haymarket.

Given their stake in labor violence, it was almost inevitable that the Pinkertons and their rivals would promote and provoke it. A fear-mongering violence pitch was used first to obtain employer clients, and continued violence—spontaneous or provoked—was needed to maintain the arrangement. In short, violence protection became a commodity for which a demand had to be stimulated. But this was not too difficult given the background of the cadres recruited for industrial detective and guard work. According to Robert Hunter, writing in 1914:

> There are unquestionably numerous agencies in this country where one may employ thugs, thieves, incendiaries, dynamiters, perjurers, jury fixers, manufacturers of evidence, strike breakers and murderers. A regularly established commerce exists, which enables a rich man without great difficulty or peril to hire abandoned criminals who, for certain crises, will undertake to execute any crime. If one can afford it, one may have always at hand a body of highwaymen or a small private army.[34]

The Commission on Industrial Relations noted in its 1915 report that in many strikes not only was "one of the greatest functions of the State, that of policing, virtually turned over to the employers or arrogantly assumed by them, but criminals employed by detective agencies [were] clothed, by the process of deputization, with arbitrary power and relieved of criminal liability for their acts."[35]

The Attack on Freedom of Assembly and Association

In addition to exploiting the fear of a bloody class confrontation and discrediting organizing activities by workers, the claim of actual or threatened violence served as an all-purpose police weapon in dealing with protest activities of all kinds. During the Gilded Age, both before and after the Haymarket tragedy, gatherings were not infrequently disrupted or forbidden by police on violence-prevention grounds.

The confrontational onslaughts by police against the rights of expression and association continued during the Progressive Era, but with a range of added justifications based on ordinances, triggered in part by the *Los Angeles Times* bombing and paralleling the already-discussed post-Haymarket measures, dealing with disorderly conduct, traffic obstruction, unlawful assemblage, littering, vagabondage, failure to obtain a license, and other misdeeds. The availability of such an arsenal for use against protest and dissent inevitably invited police repression. For dissenters and radicals in the Progressive Era, the baton-wielding police officer—on horseback, he was a "Cossack"—symbolized the injustices of the larger society.

The most common site of political expression and protest was the street corner. In every large city, activists—either solicited for their oratorical gifts or volunteers—regularly addressed passers-by until a crowd formed. All aspects of soapboxing became the concern of radical groups: what were the most desirable corners, how long did it take for a crowd to gather at a particular location, could hecklers be expected, what was the best time to begin and end, and, perhaps most important, what about police interference, a circumstance that varied considerably, depending as it did on the exercise of police discretion.[36]

The size and spirit of larger outdoor gatherings—"monster" meetings and rallies, "indignation" meetings,* marches, parades, and demonstrations—varied with the importance of the issues, the organizing efforts of the sponsors, size of constituency, site, and, again, the extent of police interference. Large outdoor gatherings were typically intended to develop group identification ("us" against "them"), to inspire confidence in those who considered themselves powerless so as to strengthen their commitment, and to convey defiance and solidarity, sharpened by the

---

* The "monster" meeting—sometimes described as a "monster mass meeting"—was the characterization by an Englishman of the meetings organized by Daniel O'Connell, leader in the 1840s of the Irish movement for repeal of union with England, to demonstrate the extent of support for Irish independence and to assure his gigantic audiences (more than half a million in some cases) that Repeal would triumph and bring better living standards. The meetings were scornfully called "monster," a term used at the time to describe an immense balloon. However, like "agitator," it was embraced here and shorn of its original connotations. See William J. O. Daunt, *Eighty-Five Years of Irish History, 1800–1885* (London: Ward & Downey, 1886), 2: 73–84; William O'Connor Morris, *Ireland, 1798–1898* (London: A. D. Innes, 1898), pp. 131–32. "Indignation" meetings were gatherings that expressed a (prompt) response to some injustice or abuse. The Haymarket meeting to protest the previous day's attack on the McCormick strikers would appear to be a classic "indignation" meeting—although this term was apparently not used to describe it. For descriptions of other meetings so designated, see, for example, Kenneth Stampp, *Era of Reconstruction: America after the Civil War, 1865–1877* (New York: Vintage Books, 1965), p. 205, and C. Vann Woodward, *Tom Watson, Agrarian Rebel* (London: Oxford University Press, 1955), p. 177.

participants' readiness to risk anticipated police abuse and hostile action. In short, the participants sought to make a political statement through what has been aptly called "body rhetoric." As John Berger has written,

> A mass demonstration can be interpreted as the symbolic capturing of a capital. . . . The demonstrators interrupt the regular life of the streets. They march through the open spaces they fill. They cut off these areas and, not yet having the power to occupy them permanently, they transform them into a temporary stage on which they dramatise the power they still lack.[37]

The enormous proliferation of outdoor protest activities in the pre– World War I years gave the police new public order responsibilities, both on the scene and in the witness box. The waning nineteenth-century image of rampaging, out-of-control animals, whipped into a fury by agitators, still influenced the police response to mass gatherings, and it accounts for the indiscriminate resort to batons when participants lagged in complying with demands to "break it up" or "move on," and for mass arrests on such grounds as "disorderly conduct" and "unlawful assembly." But whatever the police efforts were at "crowd control," their priority was the agitator-speaker, who, however innocuous his utterances, was not infrequently arrested for "inciting to riot," especially if he were widely known, had a reputation for radicalism, and was an outsider.

The effectiveness of outdoor agitation and discussion was limited in many respects. To begin with, police conducted surveillance, and when they were not using the "hickory," they still managed to dampen enthusiasm and attendance by their sheer presence.* Other limiting cir-

---

* The use of the police on peacekeeping pretexts to monitor public meetings for evidence of illegal utterances was a sore point among American dissenters and radicals. Police spying of this nineteenth-century kind became a public issue as a result of a disturbance (frequently referred to as a "riot") at Mitchelstown, County Cork, Ireland, on September 9, 1887. In the course of a public meeting, an official note-taker—a stock identifiable figure on the platform at Irish protest meetings—tried, after the meeting had begun, to force his way through the densely packed crowd of 8,000 to record the speeches. After several police attempts to move the note-taker into position, the police fired on the crowd from their barracks, killing two or three (the accounts differ) and seriously wounding others. No attempt was made to punish the responsible policemen. As with other aspects of the movement for Irish independence, the news of Mitchelstown became known here first among the large body of supporters of the struggle for Irish independence and then more widely. Indeed, the affair was referred to by Michael Schwab in his address to the Haymarket jury. Accounts of the Mitchelstown confrontation may be found (in sharply varying versions) in Sir James

cumstances included weather, noise,* hecklers, logistics, street bullies, and, most important, the lack of opportunity for follow-up educational and organizational activities. Indoor meetings were thus an imperative mode of harnessing the anger and support of members of the audience for more organized forms of politics and protest.

Indoor meetings were initially not as intensively surveilled or monitored as outdoor gatherings. But increase in membership and consolidation of constituencies led to greater use of enclosed meeting sites, more organized protest styles, and diversified issue agendas. This heightened activity also resulted in more intensive surveillance by plainclothes officers and detectives—the outdoor protests were typically policed by uniformed officers—and a more furtive style. Detectives and undercover police officers in plainclothes invaded meeting halls for the claimed purpose of obtaining evidence of violation of laws against incitement to riot or criminal syndicalism. Here, the note-taking detective or police stenographer (the latter sometimes accompanied by a plainclothes protector) replaced the uniformed police officer as an instrument of intimidation. In most cities, police permits were required for outdoor meetings and, in some cases, even for indoor meetings; in others the sponsoring organization was required to identify itself and submit in advance a list of the names of speakers. Indoor meetings were controlled in a variety of other ways, such as fire, health, and building ordinances, intimidations of the owner or lessee, and flooding entrances with police officers.

But the arrest of speakers both before the meeting (on "suspicion") and afterward on pretexts was a preferred form of restraint. An instructive example of the extent of this abuse: from 1908 until 1911 the anarchist leader Emma Goldman was arrested on improvised grounds such as "incitement to riot" an estimated one hundred times in the course of delivering some three hundred lectures.[38]

The grave and systematic character of the invasions of freedom of assembly and of political expression by local authorities during the Progressive Era is reflected in the 1914 convention of the American Sociological Association, which was devoted entirely to this subject. Edward

---

O'Connor, *History of Ireland, 1798–1924* (London: Edward Arnold, 1925), 2:128; T. P. O'Connor, *The Parnell Movement: Being a History of the Irish Question from the Death of O'Connell to the Present Time* (New York: Cassell, 1891), pp. 319–23; and Liberal Unionist Association, *The Speaker's Handbook on the Irish Question* (London: Cassell, 1889), pp. 158–61.

* This was partially overcome by the sound amplifier, which came into use in the late twenties.

A. Ross, a prominent sociologist who was then head of the association, told his colleagues:

> During the last dozen years, the tales of the suppression of free assemblage, free speech and free press by local authorities or by the State operating under martial law have become so numerous as to have become an old story. These rights . . . are attacked at the instigation of an economically and socially powerful class, itself enjoying the full advantages of free communication but bent on denying them to the class it holds within its power. . . . The constitutional rights of free communication have been denied to socially insignificant persons . . . usually in order to spare certain employers the risk of a successful strike or the snaffle collective bargaining imposes upon their arbitrary will.[39]

Most of the abuses aired at the sociologists' convention were not finally curbed until the Supreme Court's decision in *Hague v. C.I.O.* a quarter of a century later. However, beginning in 1908, a grass-roots campaign against the suppression of rights ("free speech fights") was conducted by the IWW (Industrial Workers of the World, or "Wobblies"), resulting in forcing a retreat by the authorities in a number of cities from repressive clampdowns on public meetings.

For example, in San Diego in 1912, Wobblies won the right to speak on the streets, but only after hundreds of them were arrested and beaten by the police and then turned over to vigilantes, who beat them some more before running them out of town. Two Wobblies died from their treatment at the hands of the San Diego police. Where free speech was directly involved in strike activities, however, the authorities generally did not back down. Thus, during an IWW-led peaceful strike in the Paterson, New Jersey, silk industry in 1913, the authorities indiscriminately arrested over 2,300 strikers, disrupted peaceful picket lines, rallies, and demonstrations, closed down all of the city's meeting halls, and succeeded in crushing the walkout. Paterson Police Captain Andrew McBride explained the police rationale: the authorities, he maintained, were duty-bound "to prevent trouble rather than wait until it is too late."[40] The crushing of the Paterson strike made it clear to libertarians that the basic rights of workers to speech and assembly were held hostage by employer-controlled police, a realization nourished by similar misconduct in strikes in Lowell, Massachusetts, Passaic, Akron, and other cities.[41] Constitutional protection had to be extended to peaceful labor activities such as meetings, organizing, picketing, demonstrating, and striking. Moreover, given the frequently formless, leaderless state of protest movements, such protection—to preserve its purpose—had to extend to the "outsider."

The Development of Urban Red Squads. While some large cities like Chicago and New York had already developed progenitors of the modern "red squad" before the turn of the century, it was only after 1900 that these units developed widely and took on increasing functions to meet the demand to surveil and repress radicals amidst the climate of increasing labor strife, the rise of militant groups like the Socialist Party and the IWW and the yearly floods of hundreds of thousands of suspect aliens entering American cities from abroad. Although each city's red squad frequently had its own operational style, all were typified by close ties with the local business community, which frequently fostered blatant corruption. While often starting out with a focus on anarchists, the red squads expanded vaguely defined missions, which led them to encompass increasingly wide rings of suspects in their surveillance nets.

NEW YORK. In New York, anarchists were a major target of police surveillance, and the assassination of President McKinley in 1901 spurred an offensive to drive them from the city. When this initiative failed, the city resorted to flooding anarchist meetings with police and the occasional arbitrary denial of permits.[42] In 1906 an "Anarchist Squad" was formally constituted, focusing on harassing and arresting anarchists on pretexts, intimidating hall owners, and blocking the distribution of the anarchist journal *Mother Earth.* Aside from the timeworn peacekeeping justifications for these interventions, the police relied on the New York State Criminal Anarchy Act, passed after the McKinley assassination, as a justification for surveillance.

This period was also marked by continuing intervention on the side of employers in labor disputes—not only through harassment of strikers and picketers, but in the arrest and station-house beating of strike leaders.[43] For the New York police, all forms of labor protest were the work of anarchists, socialists, or communists. Furthermore, in the shirtwaist makers' strike in the winter of 1909–10, the police arrested 723 women strikers—of whom 19 were sentenced to the workhouse, while others were released on exorbitant bail (an average of $2,500 each).

In April 1914 Arthur Woods took over as police commissioner with promises of changes in police response both to labor disputes and political dissent. At this time it became settled policy that public meetings outdoors required no license and were to be protected from hostile interference by hecklers and members of rival groups. However, clandestine pressure on hall owners continued, as well as resistance by precinct cops to headquarters' policies—a resistance implemented by routine charges of incitement and blockage of traffic. But the price for the free-speech concession was high: large meetings, especially those with far left sponsorship, were routinely saturated with detectives, many of whom were also deployed for undercover work. In short, the relaxation of open restraints on freedom of assembly resulted in the actual extension of covert, more discreet police antiradical tactics—an irony that, as we have seen (see pp. 27–29), widely characterized efforts in the Progressive Era to reform police behavior.

Thus, on August 1, 1914, Commissioner Woods created a new unit, the Bomb Squad, commanded by Inspector Thomas J. Tunney, who was to report directly to him. By the end of 1914, the unit boasted an undercover detail, some of whom were assigned to infiltrate anarchist circles and charged with flushing out those responsible for two bombings in October in St. Patrick's Cathedral.[44] A would-be infiltrator was exposed, but a replacement, one Amadeo Polignani, was chosen and provided with an assumed name and cover. Polignani played a prominent role in the case in which two anarchists, Frank Abarno and Carmine Carbone, were charged with attempting to bomb St. Patrick's Cathedral. The defendants charged a police frame-up—specifically, that Detective Polignani had masterminded the bomb attempt. Accounts of his role differ sharply, but Polignani did admit that he had purchased most of the bomb's components and rented the premises where they were assembled. What also emerged from the trial evidence was that the bomb was actually a "fizzler," no more dangerous than a firecracker, used merely as a prop in a scenario staged to entrap the defendants. But the jury was not persuaded, and the defendants were given six- to twelve-year prison terms.[45]

During this year it became clear that infiltration by Bomb Squad detectives had become a common practice. Polignani's counterpart was Detective George Gilbert, who successfully infiltrated the Wobblies and kept Inspector Tunney informed of all Wobbly activities in New York and northern New Jersey. In 1916 it was revealed that since 1895 the police had tapped 350 phones, including those of labor unions and churches.[46]

CHICAGO. The origin of the modern Chicago red squad is interwoven with the career of Haymarket veteran Herman Schuettler, a protégé of Schaack's who inherited the mantle of his disgraced sponsor as the country's premier anarchist chaser. Although regarded by many as a model officer, Schuettler was clearly carried away by his anarchist mania and was especially relentless in his vendetta against Emma Goldman.

Schuettler intimidated Chicago hall owners to deny her rentals and to cancel previous rental agreements. In the wake of the attempted assassination of Police Chief George M. Shippy and his son in March 1908, Schuettler charged that the assailant (killed by Shippy) was the agent of an anarchist conspiracy. (The anarchists denied that he was an adherent of their movement). Schuettler's reputation shone with renewed luster as he indiscriminately arrested suspected participants in the plot.[47]

In 1916 Schuettler (then assistant police commissioner), apparently in need of some sensational plot to spice the effectiveness of anarchism as a fear stimulus, announced the discovery of an anarchist conspiracy to kill priests and bomb churches, city halls, and police headquarters all over the country. In short order arrests were made in Chicago and New York; the Chicago office of the anarchist publication *Alarm* was raided, while invented stories sprouted in various newspapers. This panic was generated by the mysterious illness of a number of guests at a banquet in Chicago honoring Archbishop George William Mundelein. Schuettler concluded from the disappearance of Jean Crones, a chef, that he had laced the soup with arsenic and that Crones was an anarchist who was assigned to activate the conspiracy. While Crones was clearly the culprit and the soup undeniably poisoned, no evidence of his whereabouts, his claimed anarchist connections, or the existence of a conspiracy was ever produced. Schuettler's dreams of a glorious new Haymarket came to naught.[48] He died two years later.

Schuettler's career as an anarchist hunter overlapped that of Make Mills (as he came to be called), a Russian émigré who became a legend in the red-hunting world and was the leading figure in the Crones investigation.[49] He became a sergeant in 1907 and a lieutenant in 1925, heading first the Bomb Squad and later its clone the Industrial Squad. Mills was proud of his operational triumphs, particularly of the clandestine variety: infiltrators were planted in a broad spectrum of left groups. In the years immediately preceding World War I, one of Mills's agents, Detective McDonough, successfully infiltrated the IWW: he became a highly trained and effective street-corner orator ("soap-box artists" as they were called by the Wobblies) and an eloquent fund collector and literature salesman. He first aroused suspicion when he advised a group of strikers to plant a bomb in their boss's car.

PHILADELPHIA. In the nineteenth century Philadelphia police had gained no glory from their brutal responses to riots and mob actions. In the early twentieth century, although radicals and strikers were not perceived as threats to the city machine's power, they still fell victim to police abuse—especially in periods of antiradical hysteria. However, even at their height, such abuses did not match the police performance in other large cities. This difference was not a reflection of greater police discipline, but is more clearly attributable to the passive style of protest movements in Philadelphia, the influence of the Quaker tradition of toleration, and the effective assimilation of immigrant city-dwellers.

At the turn of the century a small number of anarchists entered the city attempting to organize the unemployed. In 1902 Mayor Samuel Ashbridge, a paladin of the Republican machine, boasted of the city's success on this front: "The suppression of seditious utterances has been brought about by the vigorous action on the part of the Police Bureau. This city is freer from the objectionable class of people than any other large city in the country."[50] In 1908 Sergeant Theodore Fenn and three other patrolmen received commendations for heroic action in suppressing a "riot" of the unemployed and arresting its ringleaders.[51] Fenn's commendation resulted from a confrontation when mounted police charged a march toward City Hall of anarchist demonstrators (the "Broad Street riot").

The campaign against the anarchists continued in October 1909, when the director of public safety first denied Emma Goldman the right to lecture, and then reneged, but only on condition that she submit her lecture notes for police perusal. When she refused, the police forcibly prevented her, as well as the audience, from entering the hall.[52]

LOS ANGELES. The Los Angeles red squad was above all characterized by an undiluted nativism and a blatant patron-client relationship with local business interests, which was openly proclaimed and implemented against the local labor movement over the years, with only minimal concessions to changes in the political climate, accountability requirements, reform movements, recurring corruption scandals, and adverse court decisions.

The extraordinary bias, power, lawlessness, and resistance to reform movements of the Los Angeles Police Department (LAPD) and its red squad are a tribute to a unique support structure in the private sector.[53] Virtually from its early beginnings, the red squad served as the operational arm of the anti-union crusade of the Merchants and Manufacturers Association (M&M), a confederation of over 80 percent of Los Angeles's business firms, whose stated purpose was to "break the back of organized labor" and make the city "a model open shop town" in order to ensure its members a supply of cheap labor and to attract new industries. Employers who attempted to deal with unions were subject to an assortment of pressures, including the denial of credit. In return for services rendered, the M&M actively promoted the squad's funding and growth.

Another red squad support group, the Commercial Federation, was also active in the early part of the century to further the campaign of the "better element" against radicals and unions. It was succeeded by the Better America Federation (BAF), an organization with the same constituency as its predecessor, but more broadly involved in all aspects of repression—data collection, surveillance, propaganda, anti-union activism, lobbying, the promotion of censorship, and collaboration with state and city agencies in keeping Southern California free from radical taint. (Harry Haldeman, the grandfather of President Richard Nixon's aide H. R. Haldeman, a prominent Watergate principal, was the BAF's founding father.) The BAF and its organizational offspring—over the years it gave birth to no fewer than nine groups, functioning under a variety of aliases—adopted as their first priority the promotion of the Southern California version of civic virtue: the identification of business and property interests with Americanism, morality, and religion. Initially financed by public utilities, the BAF furthered its ideological crusade through pamphlets, a speakers' bureau, and congressional testimony. It shared the M&M's antilabor concerns and developed a standard smear response (Bolshevistic!) to trade unionism, liberal political movements, regulatory commissions, and even measures such as the initiative, referendum, and recall. A tenacious champion of the red squad, the BAF supported the unit's budgetary requests and fed it file material from its own voluminous dossier collection. One of its early triumphs was the passage in 1908 of an ordinance barring all organizations except religious groups from holding street meetings. This ordinance became an early victim of the Wobblies' free-speech fight when, after a six-month struggle by the IWW along with two socialist allies, the measure was repealed.

Support of the red squad by the M&M and BAF was furthered by such institutions as the right-wing evangelical churches and the public schools. But it was the *Los Angeles Times* that courted and developed an approving constituency for the unit's antilabor and ideological mission and its lawless tactics as well. Beginning in the 1890s, the *Times* took command of the area's countersubversive network.

Indeed, the Los Angeles story begins at the turn of the century with the efforts of the Los Angeles Typographical Union to organize the printers employed by Colonel Harrison Gray Otis's *Los Angeles Times*. The union's struggle against the *Times* triggered a citywide movement by the entire business establishment to resist unionization. No one, Otis was sure, would decline an opportunity to join a posse "armed with pick handles that would drive the lawless union laborites, closed shop, murderous vermin into the sea."[54]

The struggle with Otis and his constituency had been an unequal one from the beginning; it climaxed in the dynamiting of the *Times* building in 1910, which claimed twenty lives and was followed by the discovery of unexploded bombs at the homes of Otis and the secretary of the M&M. The *Los Angeles Times* bombing was one of those disturbances that have historically served to inspire fear of subversion, heighten dependency on the police, and legitimize antiradical aggression by intelligence forces. In the wake of the McNamara trial, the police force was increased to 500 men, the city's budding reform movement was wrecked, and its supporting Protestant (social gospel) component severely set back. The police also were provided with an arsenal of laws to legitimate their vigilante practices. In 1910, as a result of pressure by the M&M and its president, Felix J. Zeehandelaar, a close friend of Otis's, a second harsh ordinance was passed directed against public assemblages and picketing. This measure became a highly effective weapon in combating strike and organizing efforts. In a replay of 1908, the police attacked and dispersed an indignation meeting in December 1913 with drawn revolvers and clubs, killing one demonstrator and clubbing many others. The better to cope with future protests, a "strong-arm" squad was formed to rid the city of troublemakers such as the IWW. These and related local measures, along with the 1919 Criminal Syndicalism Act, institutionalized the use of pretexts to screen what was essentially a form of guerrilla warfare.

The World War I Influence: Transition to Ideology. Beginning with the post–World War I era, the police role in labor disputes was absorbed by a more comprehensive mission: the ideological war on radicalism. Although this antiradical function had already become part of police agendas in America's largest cities, it is clear that World War I pollinated the modern police surveillance and intelligence-gathering functions in the ideological realm. An early venture into this twilight zone took the form of collaboration with the American Protective League (APL). Wartime fears of espionage, sabotage, and disloyalty spawned the APL, a huge vigilante-style civilian network that at its peak boasted over 350,000 members in an estimated 1,600 urban units. Organized into police-style hierarchies, the APL adopted a cloak-and-dagger modus operandi complete with oaths of secrecy, code numbers, and a confidential manual. Its mission was primarily to check on the loyalty of individuals, report rumors harmful to the national security, round up draft dodgers and deserters, and collaborate with federal agencies in the surveillance of enemy aliens. Prominent citizens headed the group nationally and locally, but the operational work was performed by superpatriotic volunteers and in many cities—Detroit, Chicago, Tulsa, Minneapolis, San Francisco, and Milwaukee, to name a few—by moonlighting policemen.[55] In addition, APL members were deputized by local police and given the power to arrest, resulting in operational collaboration in rounding up deserters and draft evaders with police units in cities such as Minneapolis, Detroit, New York, and Philadelphia. Although the APL's mission was supposed to be confined to the matters indicated above, it gave prominence to a sweeping offensive against political and labor radicals, a concern stemming from the leadership role of members of the business community.

As in the earlier police–private detective partnership, league members engaged in such undercover surveillance activities as wiretapping, planting undercover agents, impersonation, subterfuge, and infiltration. In Chicago, Cleveland, and other cities, combined police and APL forces monitored speakers at socialist and Wobbly rallies and conducted raids on their closed-door meetings.[56]

Although local APL units were directed by the Justice Department to turn over files to area U.S. attorneys, it is clear that in large cities (New York, Chicago, and Los Angeles, for example), APL files were instead added to local police antiradical file collections.[57]

During the war and its aftermath, ideology supplemented behavior as a police concern; the police became guardians not only of public order but of the safety of the Republic itself. Ironically, the police resumed a function of social restraint that had dominated their operations in the nineteenth century, but the target this time was radicalism or subversion rather than "the dangerous classes." Radical-hunting by urban police was also spurred by collaboration with federal forces, first in the storming in 1917 of the IWW headquarters in eleven cities and the subsequent arrests of hundreds of union leaders, and then as an important operational resource in the 1919 red raids and round-up arrests. Bomb explosions in June 1919 that shattered buildings in eight cities and caused a number of fatalities were perhaps the most important single spur to the involvement of urban police in monitoring radicals.[58]

The postwar repressive climate spawned a third wave of restraints on freedom of association (paralleling the reaction to 1877 and to Haymarket): some cities not only required permits for meetings in private halls, but also advance police approval of speakers and programs, requirements that served as a justification for compiling lists of potential sponsoring organizations and speakers subject to challenge. Police regularly dissolved and disrupted assemblages for alleged failure to obtain a license or claimed departure from the time or site for which the permit had been granted. Included in these strictures were laws and regulations banning the exhibition of red flags or requiring a display of the American flag, which also gave police a pretext for monitoring radical gatherings. A typical solution to the constitutional protection of the distribution of literature was provided by littering ordinances authorizing arrests and fines for dropping paper on the street by either the distributor or the recipient.

But the police, especially in industrial towns controlled by business interests, continued the practice of the prewar era of arresting without charges, interrogating their victims, and after a time releasing them with a warning to get out of town; in some cases the police accompanied the radical miscreant to the town line. Another typical police response to a planned speech by a radical was to arrest the speaker without grounds and detain him until after his scheduled appearance.[59]

The Labor Beat: Countersubversion to the Rescue. The post–World War I growth of the labor movement and the resolve of industrialists to halt or reverse labor gains won in the war produced serious clashes, in which urban police played a harshly repressive role. Two outstanding examples were the Seattle general strike of February 1919 and the steel strike of the fall of 1919. On February 6, 1919, Seattle was gripped by the first major general strike in American history.[60] Seattle Mayor Ole Hanson and the chief of police viewed the strike, which focused on wages and hours, as a "revolutionary conspiracy." Preparations were made for a bloody confrontation. Police and 1,000 special deputies were armed and instructed to shoot on sight anyone causing disorder, and City Hall was converted into an armed fortress guarded by an army of soldiers, volunteers, and hundreds of county, state, and federal police. Despite expectations of bloodshed, unusual order prevailed before the strike collapsed, although police nonetheless made numerous arrests and raided the offices of newspapers and the Socialist Party. Raids on radical meeting halls continued in Seattle for months after the strike ended.

The 1919 steel strike of 350,000 workers convulsed the industry and drew a response unmatched in its ferocity.[61] Company police, sheriff's deputies, the Pennsylvania constabulary, private detectives, strikebreakers, federal agents, and local police joined forces to crush the strike.

While much attention has been focused on the more violent components of this army, the role of the police in cities and towns in monitoring the strike and enforcing local ordinances and regulations limiting the right of assembly is equally notable. Strikers were routinely arrested on violence-prevention grounds despite the fact that the areas in which meetings were banned by ordinance provided no record of strike-related violence. And in the few places where meetings were not banned, no violence occurred. Similarly in strike-bound areas of Ohio and West Virginia where meetings were permitted, no violence occurred.[62]

The widespread suppression of basic rights had a substantial impact on the strike's effectiveness, the morale of the strikers, and the ability to maintain solidarity. Police authorities worked closely with a network of company agents and detectives supplied by private agencies both to protect strikebreakers and as infiltrators: information obtained by spies (much of it wildly inaccurate) was channeled to police chiefs, who in turn reported to federal authorities.[63] This resulted in federal raids and deportation efforts.*

The record indicates that police clubbed arrested strikers and detained them for long periods of time without legal justification; some arrested strikers and supporters were turned over to mill management. It is equally clear that the police turned a blind eye to the physical violence and provocations committed against strikers, especially by the employees of private agencies.[64]

The reign of terror—no other words will do—against the strikers and their leaders was the work of the "Steel Trust," whose propaganda claimed that if the strike succeeded it would lead to a general strike that would be the curtain raiser for revolution. These appeals were fueled both locally and nationally by a servile press, whose accounts were frequently grounded in the invented tales of hired undercover agents.[65] In the attack on the steel strikers and their supporters, a vastly expanded range of innocent targets were attacked because of their asso-

---

* The modus operandi employed to undermine the strike is well described by a federal official who testified before the Senate. The in-house undercover operatives on the company payroll reported to the private detectives working for the agencies hired by management. "The detectives in turn report to the chief of police of the city. Generally, the chiefs of police in these small cities around Pittsburgh were placed there by the corporations. . . . The corporation orders an organization raided by the police department, the members are taken into custody, thrown into the police station and the department of justice notified. . . . They usually let all but a few go" (Interchurch World Movement of North America, Commission of Inquiry, *Report on the Steel Strike of 1919* [New York: Harcourt, Brace, 1921], p. 225).

ciations, however flimsy, with ideologically condemned individuals and causes. This technique of protecting the status quo by invented linkages to communism became a standard weapon in the police war on subversion.[66]

The official disruption of the strikers' collective activities on the pretext of violence-prevention and the hysterical and almost paranoid fear of a Bolshevik revolutionary takeover combined to defeat the strike. The popularly held image of the strikers and their revolutionary motivation was fortified by such conflicts as the 1919 Seattle general strike, the Boston police strike, and a train of walkouts in textile mills, railways, extractive industries, clothing factories, and public employment. It is clear that the fears and anxieties that surfaced in 1919 became the building blocks of a countersubversive myth system exploited by conservatives to discredit change movements of all kinds.

The Red Squads in the Postwar Period. The hysterical antiradicalism of World War I and the postwar red scare fostered the further growth and development of urban police red squads and provided them with the momentum that carried them through the 1920s until the next major burst of radical activity in response to the Great Depression. As in the prewar period, urban red squads generally maintained close and often corrupt relationships with local business interests, and their lack of clear direction or definition provided them with virtual carte blanche to engage in uncontrolled surveillance of radicals, labor unions, and anyone else who struck their fancy.

Beginning in the twenties, police monitoring of labor disputes became a routine function whether or not violence was reported. In the larger cities, strikes became a highly prized assignment for money-hungry bluecoats. In the guise of disbursements for overtime and meals, employers paid off police details assigned to patrol their strike-bound plants. And they were particularly generous when the police managed to engineer the arrests of organizers and leaders. Their gratitude also embraced the command structure, especially the officer in charge, who sometimes received a lump sum in advance to be divided among his subordinates, from which he deducted a share. At the conclusion of a labor dispute, employers sometimes distributed rewards measured by the value of the service rendered. In cities such as Chicago and New York, unions also contributed to the take by bribing patrolmen not to molest picketers.

In areas of protest outside of industrial conflict, police activity largely flagged during the twenties. In large cities police routinely tolerated dissident gatherings, although strict controls persisted.

NEW YORK. The New York red squad, known as the Bomb Squad, found plenty of work in the 1917–19 period cooperating with federal agencies and the Republican-controlled legislature. Legislative enthusiasm for red-hunting led in 1919 to the authorization of a joint committee to investigate "enemies of the government." Chaired by State Senator Clayton R. Lusk, the committee solicited testimony on the sources and character of the revolutionary movement in the state, especially its Soviet connections and its influence on education. Locally, Mayor John Hylan's 1919 red scare ban on the display of red flags was interpreted by the police as new justification for surveilling meetings, including those in public halls. Even though the war was over, Hylan ordered the police to exercise "extreme vigilance" in observing leftist demonstrations, rallies, and marches, to report the time and place of such gatherings promptly, and suppress those threatening disorder or promoting "hostility to the United States."[67] Pressure from superpatriots triggered a series of police raids, illegal searches and seizures, groundless arrests, disruption of meetings protesting police repression, and confiscation of radical literature that made 1919 the most repressive year in the bomb squad's history. First came a raid in March on the headquarters of the Union of Russian Workers. The brainchild of Sergeant James F. Gegan, it was ostensibly designed to obtain evidence to support deportation proceedings and was conducted jointly with federal agents led by William J. Flynn, then an area chief of the Federal Bureau of Investigation. Patrol wagons were stuffed with some 162 arrested aliens; all but 4 were subsequently released. During the summer of 1919, the Bomb Squad collaborated in a series of raids undertaken by the Lusk Committee in cooperation with the state police and American Protective League (APL) volunteers.[68] The most spectacular of these occurred on June 22, 1919. In a triple offensive considered the most aggressive in the city's history, state and city police armed with warrants obtained by the Lusk Committee raided the socialist-oriented Rand School, next the headquarters of the left-wing sector of the Socialist Party, and then the headquarters of the Wobblies, seizing several truckloads of literature and organizational records. These records netted a large number of radicals, who were arrested and held for trial under the Criminal Anarchy Act. But the greatest haul resulted from a committee raid on November 8, 1919, the day after the Bomb Squad raided the Union of Russian Workers in collaboration with the Justice Department. A huge detachment of seven hundred (including police in uniform and plainclothes and red squad operatives) descended on seventy-three branches of the newly formed Communist Party and the premises of fifty radical publications, confiscating tons of documents and making almost a thousand arrests, though only twelve convictions, and a few deportations, were finally obtained.[69]

The red scare persisted in New York into the early twenties—long after it had subsided in the rest of the country. But the years from 1922 to 1929 were quiet ones except for occasional police interference with protest meetings near proscribed sites (embassies, City Hall, Wall Street, and the like) or dealing with banned issues (birth control) or to quell disorders caused by clashes between rival leftist groups. However, indiscriminate arrests continued on grounds such as "disorderly conduct," as did attempted pressure on hall owners and disruption of marches, either to the site of a planned gathering or thereafter to present grievances, on the ground that they were "parades" requiring permits.

PHILADELPHIA. The red scare in Philadelphia resulted in the formal organization of a bomb squad in 1919 to investigate radical demonstrations and labor activities, as, it was alleged, a "necessary precaution" against the "mounting tides of Bolshevism in America." The squad was given a free hand, including the administration of a highly restrictive permit system. As in New York City, it closely cooperated with the U.S. Department of Justice and with police from other cities.[70] Indeed, as in many other cities, a major influence on the creation of the squad was the need for an operating arm for the repressive federal campaign against radicals. In 1921 Mayor J. Hampton Moore's police superintendent, William Mills, formed a "gas squad" consisting of police officers and World War I veterans with experience in handling explosives, to be trained in the use of tear gas against protesting groups.[71]

The post–World War I era, with its labor unrest, saw the emergence of labor relations in Philadelphia as a police specialty, linked to antiradical investigations by the thesis that strikes and related disturbances were subversively inspired.[72] Active police suppression of labor activities, however peaceful, became commonplace. On March 21, 1921, it was announced that the police would not interfere with any legitimate meeting of strikers to discuss their own affairs "so long as the meeting is orderly and not of radical character, but all meetings of a radical character will be prohibited or broken up."[73] Since the police assumed that radicals were working hand in glove with unions, such a statement gave them carte blanche to continue to suppress all union activity.

The antiradical unit was particularly active in the late twenties and through the depression years, when the squad was headed by Lieutenant Jacob Gombrow. The police modus operandi was quite simple: they refused permits for indoor meetings as a way of intimidating hall owners;

if the owners nevertheless did not retreat, the meetings were usually, if not always, held without police interference despite the permit refusal.[74]

DETROIT. As in other cities, the Detroit police forged ties to private employers during the World War I era via their cooperation with the APL and participated in the federally sponsored round-up of the Wobblies in September 1917 and in the raids on the Union of Russian Workers and mass arrests of its members in the fall of 1919.[75] The Detroit APL was actively funded by business and right-wing elites, whose fear of labor radicalism was fueled in the post-1910 period by an influx of workers, often foreign-born, into the large automobile plants where the labor force was concentrated. Detroit early became a bastion of the open-shop movement, with the result that IWW organizing efforts and demonstrations became police priority targets based on the assumption, shared by the city's industrialists, that unionism was per se the offspring of radicalism and to be prevented and neutralized at all costs.

LOS ANGELES. In Los Angeles, business and conservative groups continued to fund and support the red squad in the postwar era. Perhaps the most important contribution of the Better America Federation to official repression was the 1919 Criminal Syndicalism Act, which, it boasted, became law because of its lobbying efforts. To ensure the act's effective enforcement, the BAF financed a stable of professional informer-witnesses, who were used in virtually all of the prosecutions under the act. An investigation disclosed that in the postwar era, the BAF was subsidized by secret contributions from California's public utilities.[76]

The post–World War I red squad also enjoyed the operational assistance of the American Legion, whose "law and order committee," spearheaded by a military component, took steps in October 1919, after consultation with Mayor Meredith P. Snyder, the chief of police, the district attorney, and the sheriff, to develop a modus operandi that included arrangements for deputizing legionnaires. Immediately thereafter a meeting of the IWW was invaded by a gang of twenty-five legionnaire vigilantes; four persons subsequently required hospitalization and five were arrested on charges of "inciting a riot."

At the beginning of 1920 the IWW had all but faded from the Los Angeles scene. Yet in April 1921, in response to pressure from the BAF, the red squad was expanded and assigned to combat radicalism generally and, in particular, to deal with the surviving remnants of the IWW. The Wobblies' offices and meeting hall were subjected to raids, and supporters were indiscriminately arrested on pretexts and beaten. This reign of terror climaxed in a mass assault with clubs and axes that resulted in many serious injuries to men, women, and children. Wobbly leaders were kidnapped, driven to a deserted area, beaten unconscious, and left for dead. Although many of the raiders were identified by their victims, no charges were ever filed against the culprits.[77]

The 1923 strike of longshoremen in San Pedro, Los Angeles's port city, set the pattern for subsequent red squad intervention in the labor disputes of the twenties and thirties. The strike was, in a sense, a test of whether the area labor movement had recovered from the 1910 McNamara disaster. The M&M and the police sought to crush the strike in a pincer movement; the employer group mobilized scores of gun-toting professional strikebreakers, while the police arrested both peaceful strikers and their supporters.

In June of the following year, a vigilante band armed with clubs, blackjacks, and guns descended on the IWW hall, demolished the furniture, clubbed men, women, and children, scalded several children by dipping them in a coffee cauldron, and abducted a number of men to the desert, where they were tarred and feathered. Both the 1923 and 1924 episodes were furthered by the collaboration of the Los Angeles police.[78]

In its attacks on political leftists, the red squad of the 1920s (called for a period the "Radical Bureau") developed a "Cossack" style, which became its trademark: destructive raids on pretexts; censorship of meetings on public sites (in 1925 the police chief announced, "I will not allow any man to deny the existence of God down there in the plaza"); and arrests of scheduled speakers on invented charges of "suspicion of violation of the Criminal Syndicalism Act," followed by detentions, harassments, assaults, and false arrests of those protesting police interference with a scheduled meeting or demonstration.

In labor disputes the police routinely disrupted union meetings, assaulted strikers and arrested them on pretexts, and guarded nonstrikers and even deputized them as "special police," while denying protection to union pickets against armed thugs hired by employers. What unified the operations in both areas was a special brand of lawlessness unrelieved by a perception of legal risk or fear of internal discipline—a vivid reflection of the red squad's role as an instrument of the Los Angeles establishment.

2 　 The Growth of the Red Squads from the Thirties to the Sixties

Congressional Committees, the FBI, and the Red Squads

After the relative passivity of labor and radical groups in the early and mid twenties, the unrest of the Great Depression spurred a torrent of protest and organizational activity in the late twenties—demonstrations, rallies, mass meetings, neighborhood gatherings outdoors in summer and indoors in winter—rivaling, if not exceeding, the pre–World War I activity.[1] This revival of radicalism was in turn met by a new repressive police response. This shift to a more repressive police role was catalyzed by the House Special Committee to Investigate Communist Activities in the United States (the Fish Committee).

Following the earlier lead of the New York Lusk Committee (see p. 40), the Fish Committee held hearings in 1930 on the red menace and how to deal with it.[2] The committee had a triple purpose: to make a case for the renewal of a federal countersubversive authority (cut off by Attorney General Harlan F. Stone in 1924), to encourage the institutionalization on a local level of surveillance of radicals by publicizing and encouraging police activities in this area, and, finally, to accomplish these goals by renewing in our political culture the fears and anxieties in which countersubversive structures are rooted. All three of these objectives were promoted by a long line of witnesses from various cities: a succession of police officials, private detectives, consultants, army intelligence personnel, superpatriots, and legionnaires.

In their hyperbolic assumptions, strained inferences, and overheated conclusions, the Fish Committee proceedings largely echo their Lusk Committee precursors. But what is strikingly new is the extent of disclosures of surveillance both of organizations and of individuals. It would appear that while the earlier resort to indiscriminate arrests on trumped-up charges continued, it was supplemented or replaced in part by surveillance and dossier compilation. Moreover, police in industrial areas continued to resort to groundless detention of those deemed to be agitators and troublemakers.[3]

The challenge of Depression-related demonstrations led to an expansion of red squads and an increasingly selective focus of the police labor mission on left-wing leaders and organizations, especially in areas of sharp conflict such as shipping and agriculture. Aggressive police response was also fueled by growing protest against the criminal justice system: police brutality and claimed miscarriages of justice and frame-ups such as the Mooney-Billings, Sacco-Vanzetti, Gastonia, and Harlan County miners' cases. These and related issues were aired in angry gatherings from coast to coast and quickly transformed into symbols of disaffection. During this period, too, the felt hostility and hate of the police for radicals and dissenters generated similar sentiments among the targets. Quickly, hostility to the police became permanently enfolded in the politics of protest.

By the mid thirties, communism had become an all-purpose justification for red squad operations not only in the large cities but in smaller cities and towns as well, and the range of targets spread from labor to a spectrum of radical activities of all kinds. Much of the surveillance and confrontational police activity of the thirties culminated in raids designed to seize literature for possible use in criminal syndicalism prosecutions. One important area of police concentration was education and alleged efforts by subversives to poison the minds of students. A student anti-war strike in 1934 touched off police clashes on campuses throughout the nation,[4] and a number of state legislatures voted for investigations of college radical activities on campuses in their states. These ad hoc probes used the urban police as an operational resource. In addition, beginning in the late thirties, state intelligence units were clothed with jurisdiction over such radical activities and mandated to work with their urban police counterparts.[5]

In 1938 the Fish Committee's successor, the House Special Committee on Un-American Activities, known as the Dies Committee, launched a marathon countersubversive investigation that created a favorable climate for red squads, featured red squad operatives as witnesses, and poured out a cascade of printed hearings, reports, and indices that became vital police tools for countersubversive targeting.

The fear of spies and saboteurs in the period leading to World War II resulted in an activation of federal countersubversive forces—most no-

WED

tably the FBI—in intelligence-gathering programs. On September 6, 1939, President Roosevelt signed a document requesting local police officers and other law-enforcement cadres "promptly to turn over to the nearest representative of the Federal Bureau of Investigation any information obtained by them relating to espionage, counter-espionage, sabotage, subversive activities and violations of the neutrality laws."[6]

Subsequently it was made clear that federal agencies were to assume primary responsibility in the area, while local police units were to channel information dealing with security threats to the FBI and the military. The red squads were thus given an intelligence-gathering role and treated as a filter for the processing of privately disseminated data—a precaution designed to prevent the self-help, mob violence, and vigilantism associated with the World War I era. In a replay of the thirties, a number of states empowered special intelligence units to investigate reports of subversive activities and maintain liaison with the FBI and local red squads. In addition, cities such as Boston and Milwaukee established red squads for the first time.[7] While the FBI took center stage in war-related intelligence gathering, local police units played a highly important operational role in the program—especially in the use of electronic eavesdropping and wiretapping in situations where the bureau was reluctant to take constitutional risks.[8]

Beginning in World War II and continuing in the Cold War years that followed, subversion-hunting was glamorized by the mystique of intelligence: the humdrum routines of keeping track of radicals and giving them a hard time acquired a derring-do, cloak-and-dagger luster. As in the case of World War I, the close of World War II sent a stream of veterans into local and federal agencies seeking to build careers based on intelligence skills acquired in the armed services. In a significant Cold War development, the growth of red squads was accompanied by institutional separation from traditional categories of policing and crime detection. Red-hunting was not only a professional calling with a national provenance ("political intelligence"), but an elitist one, with duties ranging from weeding out questionable applicants for speaking permits on the basis of file data, traveling the luncheon circuits, and exchanging information with and answering inquiries from other cities to selecting wiretap targets, running informers, and developing press outlets.

This institutional consolidation was matched by new functional responsibilities. In states such as Maryland, Illinois, and New Hampshire, as in the thirties, ad hoc investigating commissions and attorneys general used local police units to ferret out subversives. Cities also delegated to red squads the implementation of ordinances requiring employee loyalty oaths and security clearances and the registration of communists.[9] Beginning in the forties, J. Edgar Hoover sought to establish the primacy of his FBI in the countersubversive realm and to encourage bypassing the red squads. Citizens with information about subversion and subversive individuals, he insisted, should deal only with the bureau, which alone possessed the expertise and professionalism needed to evaluate such data and to weigh its importance in the light of the FBI's nationwide anticommunist operation.[10] This bid enabled the FBI to dominate the headlines as nation-savior, but it also made it possible for financially strapped police units to tap FBI funds to pay informers. Ultimately, however, the FBI had to depend for input to the radical community on the red squads, with their day-to-day experience, investigative resources already in place, and file collections.

It was, in any event, too late for the FBI to overtake and subordinate the flourishing red squads in the late forties and fifties. These units were adrenalized by the anticommunist crusade of the Catholic church led by Cardinal Francis J. Spellman. Many Catholics in large urban police units came to regard anticommunist policing as a highly congenial calling by reason both of their religious beliefs and the sense that it offered a means of identifying with the larger society.[11] Indeed, Irish patrolmen in more conventional police work eagerly sought red squad appointments.

But in the fifties, the red squads were all dressed up with nowhere to go. Despite the favorable political climate and the consequent reduced perception of risk, the red squads languished during the fifties—a circumstance due primarily to the overkill and intimidation of dissenting movements and causes. It was the unrest of the sixties that revitalized these units and brought them to new levels of growth and prominence.

The New York Red Squad, 1930–1960

It is plain from testimony before the Fish Committee by John A. Lyons, chief of the New York Radical Bureau (formerly the Bomb Squad), and his operatives[12] that the undercover network of the New York red squad was huge, that it was responsible for the compilation of dossiers on Communist Party leaders, members, and supporters both in New York City and elsewhere, and that it cooperated with federal agencies to pinpoint illegal immigrants among strikers and exchanged files with police in other cities. The already-vibrant bureau was reinvigorated in 1929 by the appointment of a new police commissioner, Grover A. Whalen, who intensified police harassment of demonstrators just as the onset of the Depression spurred increasing protest activity. Whalen's enthusiastic antiradical binges reflected financial and political support from New York business and financial interests (he had formerly managed the John Wanamaker Department Store and was politically sponsored by a major investment banker).[13]

These interests clearly got their money's worth: the Radical Bureau engaged in mass arrests of dissenters and hundreds of skirmishes with demonstrators and strikers and regularly posted observers, usually identifiable, at both indoor and outdoor protest meetings. Police brutality against protesters culminated in a frenzied attack on participants and leaders in a demonstration of over 50,000 protesting unemployment on March 6, 1930. The Union Square gathering elicited more official lawlessness than similar meetings held that day under Communist Party auspices in large cities throughout the country. A confrontation resulted when, at the end of the demonstration, monitored by scores of police, Commissioner Whalen, who was observing the meeting from a booth, denied the request of a delegation of participants to march to City Hall—about a mile away from Union Square—to present their demands to the mayor. When the crowd was told of the commissioner's refusal, people responded by starting for City Hall anyway. The police, presumably on Whalen's authority, went wild, blindly clubbing everyone in sight, including those who remained behind in the square, and pursuing others and beating them without mercy. Scores of casualties resulted.

In an interview with the *New York Times*, Whalen's hunger for publicity overcame his professional discretion. On March 9 the *Times* reported:

> "I thought I would crack my sides laughing at some of the undercover men who figured in the Union Square demonstration last Thursday," said Commissioner Whalen. "They went there as Reds, singing the International and other revolutionary songs of the Communists. They carried placards and banners demanding the overthrow of the government and made as much noise as the genuine Reds."[14]

The pattern of surveillance, arbitrary police interference in peaceful meetings, hostility in dealing with strikers, and overreaction to defiance and provocation by leftist targets continued after Whalen's departure in 1930 and into the early thirties.[15] It was not until the three-term reform mayoralty of Fiorello H. La Guardia (1934–45) that police abuse receded in two areas: the disruption of outdoor meetings (which in any event had declined from their former popularity as a mode of protest) and labor disputes.[16] But undercover surveillance of far-left targets continued.

Although the Radical Bureau underwent many changes during the thirty years following the Whalen era, partly to convey reassurances to the public that the crude repressiveness of its early days was forever gone, among the constants of its mission were a continuing crusade against radicalism, a movement away from law enforcement to intelligence, and a shift from result-oriented investigations to continued surveillance and data collection. Like its counterpart in other large cities, the New York red squad was adrenalized by President Roosevelt's spy-watching order of September 1939. Even during World War II, when it turned its attention to Bundists and other native fascists, the red squad continued to assign large numbers of operatives to long-term penetration of the Communist Party and other left groups.

By the mid fifties, the New York red squad, now known as the Bureau of Special Services (BOSS), seemed to be at the end of its glory days, as the Cold War red scare and the Communist Party both appeared to be fading away. As Anthony Bouza, a historian of BOSS, observes:

> The fifties were a quiescent time, even though former undercover agents were testifying before government committees and exposing communists well into the sixties. There was little real activity in New York of a threatening nature and [the] Bureau of Special Services settled into a kind of rut of inactivity and disuse. The increasing interest and involvement of the Federal Bureau of Investigation in the espionage area and in the communist field served to restrict the operations of the Bureau of Special Services.[17]

The unrest of the 1960s thus provided a frustrated BOSS with an opportunity to climb out of its "rut" and to develop the highly ramified infiltration program (discussed on pp. 172ff), that had been activated by radical activities in the wake of the Great Depression.

The Chicago Red Squad, 1930–1960

Chicago Police Lieutenant Make Mills* openly boasted before the Fish Committee in July 1930[18] that the men of his radical squad (as Chicago's

---

* The name was supplied by the immigration authorities when he entered this country from Eastern Europe. Because they were unable to spell or pronounce his true name, they suggested, "Make it Mills." An immigration officer made it "Make Mills."

red squad was then known) systematically kept track of and dispersed demonstrations and public meetings whenever advance permission had not been obtained. Obtaining permits was not a routine matter: Mills frequently arbitrarily denied permits or delayed their issuance so as to set demonstrators up for mass arrests. (Demonstrations at a number of Chicago relief stations organized by Unemployed Councils were not infrequently met with such tactics as the driving of police cars into assembled crowds, demands for reductions in the size of the assemblages, limitations on the time allowed speakers, brutal police clubbings, and, in a few instances, fatal shootings of unarmed demonstrators.)[19]

Mills told the Fish Committee that thirteen demonstrations in the first six months of 1930 had produced 313 arrests and a huge album of arrest photos, a radical rogues' gallery that the witness made available to the committee. In addition, Lieutenant Mills's radical squad had over a six-month period monitored some 132 meetings ("there are sometimes 3 or 4 meetings a night").

Mills made another committee appearance in 1940, when he was summoned by the Dies Committee.[20] He staggered the committee chairman when he casually announced that he had a file of index cards, not only of 5,000 local communists, but of "75,000 names all over the United States." His treasury of names also specified the occupation, nationality, age, and leadership role of each individual indexed. Members of the squad monitored meetings of "fronts," of which, he said, there were about one hundred. Mills declared his records would show that all major strikes and labor troubles were the work of the reds. They had infiltrated the University of Chicago ("All of these Communists used sex" to "bring men into the party") and had greatly prospered with the organization of the CIO, which "was invented and inoculated from Russia."

Mills's special concentration was labor—its activities, unions, and leaders. His Industrial Squad simply carried on a long tradition of violent police intervention on behalf of employers in organizing and strike activities.[21] Under Mills, the labor unrest fueled by the Depression resulted in systematizing the formerly sporadic practice of employer payoffs to police. This form of institutionalized bribery was well described by Gordon Baxter, a Chicago attorney:

> There was a police detail in Chicago known as the Industrial Squad, in charge of a Lieutenant Mike [*sic*] Mills. When a strike occurred, Mills would arrange to arrest the leaders. They'd beat them up, put them in jail, make it pretty clear to them to get the hell out of town. Mills got tips, $1,000, or if it was a serious thing, $5,000. He

made a hell of a lot of dough to get the agitators, as they were called.[22]

Mills's industrial squad played an important role in collaborating with employers in strikebreaking, not only by assaulting picketers and protecting scabs, but in supplying dossiers (usually for a fee) to the right-wing press (the Hearst *Chicago American* and the *Chicago Tribune*) discrediting striking unions and their leaders. Well into the strife-torn forties, the labor detail served as a defense corps for AFL unions embraced in "sweetheart" contracts with employers to repel CIO organizing efforts, as well as combating rank-and-file revolts against repressive AFL union leadership.

Given the history of the police response to labor unrest in Chicago, the bloody confrontation on Memorial Day, 1937, at the South Chicago Republic Steel plant between demonstrators and police should come as no great surprise.[23] As a result of police gunfire, ten participants were killed, some thirty others suffered bullet wounds, and an estimated sixty more (including women and children) suffered injuries (mainly clubbings) of varying degrees of severity. Thirty-five policemen received minor injuries.

Police allegiance to Republic Steel was made clear: the police set up their headquarters in the plant, ate in the company cafeteria, unloaded company supplies, and used ammunition furnished by the company. Most important, despite the pronouncements of the mayor's office and the ruling of the corporation counsel that peaceful picketing should not be disturbed, five police officers made their own highly restrictive decisions about the site of picketing and about the permissible numbers of pickets.

The mushrooming of racketeering, the emergence of Chicago as a center of organized crime and the abuses (venality was the worst) of the labor-relations detail produced a clamor for a more effective and professional intelligence unit and led in the early fifties to the reorganization of the Chicago red squad. But changes in structure had no effect on function and file accumulation. Thus, in a 1963 speech to a national conference of police intelligence officers, Lieutenant Frank J. Heimoski boasted of the Chicago red squad's priceless files, as well as of the service it had performed in repelling the threat of subversion. But the task, Heimoski said, was endless:

> Before anyone gets the impression that our services have been mainly in behalf of agencies outside of our municipal jurisdiction, I would like to emphasize that subversive activity has been a constant problem in our City and

continues so to the present day. Issues dealing with labor, wages, working hours, strikes, peace, housing, education, social welfare, race, religion, disarmament and anti-militarization still provide fertile grounds for agitation. Our job is to detect these elements and their contemplated activity and alert proper authorities. Presently, subversive elements have made every effort to inject themselves into the racial situation now prevailing—despite efforts on the part of legitimate organizations to bar them. Our presence during their activity has been a deterrent to more aggressive action on many occasions. Our existence as a Police Department Unit has proved a thorn in the side of the subversives and many attempts have been made by them and their sympathizers to eliminate us as a police function.[24]

The Philadelphia Red Squad, 1930–1960

The behavior of the Philadelphia police in the late twenties and early thirties was typically marked by a barely leashed aggression: demonstrations were conducted after parleys with the police, who, even when permission was granted, monitored the scene and took photographs. But sometimes even this tolerance was denied: when leftists marched to City Hall on February 14, 1930, for a demonstration, members of the radical squad (whose existence had been first publicly disclosed shortly before by Police Superintendent William Mills in response to reactionary warnings of an imminent radical catastrophe in Philadelphia) blocked their procession and attacked the crowd with nightsticks. Twelve demonstrators were hospitalized and seventeen were arrested for "parading without a permit," "resisting arrest," and "attacking police." With the advent of a new administration in 1932, a new police policy was announced barring plazas adjacent to City Hall for meetings and rallies. On May 1, 1932, bloody riots erupted when police broke up a march to the forbidden sites "with a brutality," according to the American Civil Liberties Union, "that broke all records in the city." More than a score were arrested on a variety of charges. But in the fall of that year a court rebuked the police and all cases but one were dismissed, thus vindicating the demonstrators and opening up the disputed sites for meetings, rallies, and demonstrations.[25]

But freedom of expression was no bed of roses in the thirties and forties. According to official records from 1929 to 1937, the police surveilled more than 6,000 meetings of alleged radicals.[26] One of the more notable instances of police repression took place on April 2, 1940, when agents of the House Un-American Activities Committee (the Dies Committee) together with Lieutenant Albert Granitz and thirty Philadelphia police officers raided the Communist Party headquarters and the local branch of the International Workers' Order, confiscating two truckloads of documents and literature. On May 4, 1940, Federal Judge George A. Welch ruled the raid illegal, violative of the First Amendment's protection against unreasonable search and seizure.[27]

By the end of the forties, the Philadelphia antiradical unit had more or less embraced the cloak-and-dagger style of other big-city red squads: indiscriminate targeting, surveillance, secrecy, informers, wiretaps, and file-keeping. The unit was renamed the intelligence squad and its official mission was stated to be "to investigate subversive activities and to cooperate closely with the Federal Bureau of Investigation and other agencies in such matters." The new squad kept a low profile during the fifties and rarely stirred public criticism—a consequence of the defeat of the Republican machine and the election of reform mayors closely identified with the city's libertarian tradition.

The Detroit Red Squad, 1930–1960

In 1930 the Fish Committee came to Detroit in its ongoing campaign to stir up harsher police responses to radicalism.[28] A key disclosure at the hearings emerged from the testimony of Jacob Spolansky, the country's leading red-hunter specializing in the labor movement. The chief witness at the hearing, Spolansky explained that he had come to the Detroit area in 1927 at the request of the National Metal Trades Association (of which the automobile manufacturers were members) and the Employers' Association of Detroit. Flourishing copies of documents obtained from police files, he left no doubt about his close ties to the city's police.[29] A police detective, Albert Shapiro, explained to the panel that the creation, in January 1930, of a special operation "to work on the Bolshevik and Communistic activities in the city of Detroit" owed much to Spolansky's "great help." And it would appear from the testimony of the director of General Motors' Industrial Relations Department that the input of information about radicals in company plants came entirely from Spolansky and the New York City police department.[30]

From the evidence of these hearings, it would appear that in 1930 Detroit was not as active on the radical-labor front as such manufacturing sites as Flint, Pontiac, and Dearborn—all wholly dominated by automobile manufacturers—where mass arrests, raids, and collaboration with plant espionage personnel were routine.[31]

The committee's session was a huge success: it helped consolidate police ties with the area's right-wing and superpatriotic constituencies, especially in the local American Legion post, which claimed "one thousand Bolshevik bouncers."[32] In the wake of the committee's hearings, the Special Investigation Bureau, a new police unit, was formed, with an assortment of responsibilities including the monitoring of radical activities. The SIB was blueprinted by Mayor Frank L. Murphy and reflected the mayor's view that police abuses could be curbed only through professionalism and sound training.[33]

For Mayor Murphy, libertarian values were not merely pieties recycled from the Progressive Era. Insisting that the issuance of outdoor speaking permits be given priority, he strove to win approval for a permanent designated site for public meetings and overrode the police commissioner's fear of traffic congestion. Ultimately forced by the police and their allies on the city council to abandon his plan for an established site, the mayor nevertheless exerted himself to ensure that the protests of the unemployed were given a forum free of police interference.

The test of the police commitment to Murphy's goals came with a bloody confrontation on March 7, 1932, involving demonstrators, Ford Motor Company guards, and the Dearborn police, resulting in the killing of four demonstrators—subsequently called the "Dearborn massacre." The Detroit police, while not principals, played a role in the tragedy: they participated in the arrest of some of the marchers and later that day raided Communist Party headquarters to flush out the organizers of the march. When the ACLU's Roger Baldwin protested the action, Murphy revealingly replied, "There will be no lawless policy on the part of the police that I can control."

Murphy thus focused on a problem that had uniformly frustrated and defeated police-reform efforts from the very beginning: the inability of political leaders and administrators to impose effective restraints on police behavior based on inbred values and assumptions. Murphy's breach with the communists over police misconduct intensified toward the close of his term, and he became deeply embittered as a result of the savage response (tear gas, mounted charges, indiscriminate clubbings) to a June 6, 1932, hunger march organized by the Auto Workers Union (the predecessor of the United Automobile Workers) and, later, in February and March 1933, over police shootings, clubbings, mass arrests, abuse of prisoners, and a raid. Moreover, the SIB was permitted to plant police spies in a broad working-class sector.[34]

Conflicting assessments of blame in these and lesser clashes resulted in an agreement between Murphy and the ACLU authorizing the monitoring of certain gatherings. Some civil libertarians insisted that, allowing for occasional lapses largely due to lack of control, Murphy deserved high marks for restraining the police under trying circumstances, but for the communists and their followers, as well as others, police misconduct led to disillusionment, not only with Murphy, but with the ACLU as well.[35] In the end, the mayor's commitment to the protection of constitutional freedoms was overcome by the backward tug of countersubversion, the power of the city's bankers and industrialists, and the crisis atmosphere in which the commitment was tested. As elsewhere, the concessions to moderation in the use of overtly repressive tactics turned out to be largely cosmetic and, in any event, simply provided a justification for institutionalizing surveillance and file-keeping.

The mayor's frustration and sense of powerlessness contributed to his midterm resignation in May 1933 to accept the post of governor-general of the Philippines. But the SIB did not really grow into its style until after Murphy's departure, when Heinrich Pickert took over (in 1933) as police commissioner. Prominently identified with Detroit's upwardly mobile German ethnic community, Pickert reorganized the red squad and provided it with an aggressively antiradical investigative agenda; at the same time, under his direction, the SIB became a scourge of picket lines of all kinds.

Pickert brought gleaming credentials to his post. A past commander of the Order of the Purple Heart, he was also prominent in the councils of the American Legion, which in the thirties were the keystone of an elaborate structure of private groups—including private detective agencies and in-house corporate security structures—that monitored labor and left-wing political activities in the area.[36] In addition, Pickert enjoyed a special relationship with the Ford Service Department chief, Harry Bennett, who in those years collaborated with a network of patrioteers, labor spies, fundamentalist preachers (Gerald L. K. Smith, Frank Norris)* and Father Charles E. Coughlin's following (the Workers' Council for Social Justice) to combat unionism and create a climate hostile to radical initiatives.

---

* Norris was a power-conscious fundamentalist with a 10,000-member congregation in Detroit whose monthly newspaper, *The Fundamentalist* (with a claimed circulation of 6,376,500), targeted radicals, organized labor, and Jews. Appearing on the same platform as Pickert, Norris praised him and his department for their support and offers of assistance. He told the audience that he especially respected Pickert for the enemies he had made. See Lorraine Majka, "Organizational Linkages, Networks and Social Change in Detroit" (Ph.D. diss., Wayne State University, 1981), p. 160.

While a number of overlapping groups had served as red squad constituencies and collaborators, in some cases, these groups developed intelligence operational and data-exchange liaisons with the red squad on their own. I cannot leave unmentioned one other "friend" that provided "a little help"—the Ku Klux Klan and its successor, the Black Legion.[37]

In Detroit, the Black Legion acquired a powerful following, which included numerous supporters and sympathizers among the Detroit police, as well as among the officials of suburban communities. Like other Detroit-area right-wing groups, it placed strong emphasis on anticommunist intelligence activities. When the Black Legion was charged with responsibility for the murder of blacks, strikers, and people accused of communist ties, its Detroit police following (of an estimated one hundred members) was forced to reduce its profile. More than fifty Black Legion members were convicted of an assortment of crimes such as arson, kidnapping, flogging, and plotting to kill various individuals. The Black Legion was also tied to a number of bombings of radical meeting places and bookstores. Through its police members, the vigilante group transmitted lists of suspected communists to the service departments of area automobile manufacturers. Pickert barely escaped disgrace when the Black Legion–police connection came to light. Evidence emerged indicating that he had been a concealed Black Legion member, a charge confirmed by the fact that, according to an investigator, he "frantically promoted all those police officers who could compromise him."[38]

But for many years the Detroit red squad's closest "friends" were the federal countersubversive committees. Beginning with the Fish Committee, these panels served to legitimate the unit and consolidate its nativist constituency, a development furthered by an enthusiastic red-hunting press. In return, the red squad provided the committee with membership lists, photographs, literature, and other sources for "exposé" hearings. The first of these collaborative efforts took place in 1938 in a series of hearings held in Detroit and Washington that focused primarily on subversion in the Detroit area.[39]

Both the Washington, D.C., and Detroit sessions featured two red squad agents, Sergeants Harry Mikuliak and Leo Maciosek (called by their targets "Mick" and "Mack"), who had been attached to the operation since its inception. "Mick" and "Mack," and the Detroit police superintendent and his counterparts in other Michigan cities, as well as a member of the state police, tried to provide support for the committee's thesis that the 1937 sitdown strike had been part of a communist takeover offensive.

The 1938 hearings, for all their lengthy disclosures of names and activities, did not produce the expected impact and were widely criticized by labor and civic groups. The sense—nourished by the Black Legion disclosures, indiscriminate raids, unauthorized searches (such as the illegal seizure from a private apartment of documents relating to the medical examinations of Spanish Civil War recruits), as well as pretext arrests, provocative confrontations, and pervasive racism—that the police were out of control in their war against radicals was confirmed by an ACLU survey in 1939 rating the department's civil rights and liberties performance "very poor" and concluding that "perhaps the most flagrant violation of the civil rights of Detroiters occur at the hands of the Special Squad organized by Commissioner Pickert, commonly called the Red Squad."[40]

As in so many other police departments, repression was the handmaiden of corruption: in 1939 a grand jury investigation led to disclosure of an extensive bribery and payoff system, which resulted in the indictment of the mayor, county prosecutor, police superintendent, and eight officers. The protests and corruption disclosures combined to force change. The department was reorganized and the red squad—after a decade of abuse—was abolished.

However, only a few months after the disbanding of the squad, it was revived by the outbreak of World War II in Europe, and its functions extrapolated (as in the case of Cleveland, Buffalo, and other cities) from President Roosevelt's September 1939 order (see pp. 45–46, 49). In June 1940 the red squad emerged with a new mission: the monitoring, through intelligence techniques, of sabotage and espionage. This assignment gilded the unit with a "national security" justification and initiated a period of intensive collaboration with the FBI.

The major concentration of this reincarnation of the red squad turned out in the postwar period to be identifying and rooting out claimed "subversive elements" in the local unions and work forces in area plants, on the assumption that all labor unrest was subversively inspired to help the enemy. Such developments as the organization in 1947 of a state-level Un-American Activities Committee and the passage, without opposition, of a statute requiring the registration of "agents of foreign countries" (promptly declared unconstitutional), reflected a resurfacing of the Michigan nativist-patriotic tradition and the creation of a climate favorable to new countersubversive forays.[41]

Supplementing these developments was the establishment in 1947 of the Detroit Loyalty Commission by a charter amendment vote. This extraordinary measure, prominently supported by UAW mayoral candidate George Edwards, authorized the political investigation of city employees suspected of disloyalty. Like the red squad, the commission assembled data on communist activities during major strikes, which it transmitted to the mayor. The commission also developed a liaison with the FBI— not very difficult since the long-term chief of the commission was a former FBI agent.

In 1950 the Detroit red squad acquired a much more important "friend" than the commission, which over the years gave the local unit more than a "little help." This ally was the state countersubversive unit (the security squad as it came to be called), which was unanimously authorized by both houses of the Michigan legislature in 1950 as part of a revision of the Michigan Criminal Syndicalism Act. This unit formalized state police operations that had been conducted for many years. According to its first annual report, its prime mission was "to discourage the employment of subversive individuals." The city and state units shared investigative information and files, conducted joint operations, and consulted in such matters as target selection. The city unit during this period also strengthened its role as an operational resource of federal agencies such as the FBI and the Immigration and Naturalization Service. Although necessarily transient, the red squad's involvement with HUAC investigations in preparation for its 1952 and 1954 hearings was uniquely close.

By the early fifties, red-hunting became entrenched on both city and state levels despite the city's strong libertarian constituency among union members, leftists, professionals, and segments of the ethnic population. The reasons for the power of the antisubversive forces are not difficult to identify. To begin with, the city had since the twenties been subject to a strong white nativist influence rooted in urban migration from the South; this influence was most aggressively projected in the role of the American Legion. The automobile manufacturers, concerned about radical infiltration of the work force, also had a stake in repelling leftist influence on the city's political processes and labor unions, especially the UAW. The UAW, despite its professed programmatic hostility to political repression on a national level, became a silent partner in the antisubversive offensive in its own backyard, another "friend" of the red squad, reflected in such developments as its barely concealed support of the 1952 HUAC hearings, its sponsorship (through Edwards) of the Loyalty Commission, and its apparent failure to develop an opposition, even among legislative representatives from union constituencies, either to the ill-fated 1947 foreign-agent registration measure or to the 1950 stat-

ute creating a state police antisubversive unit (both passed without opposition). Ironically, officials of the international and local union
members became surveillance targets in the late sixties.

During the fifties, the countersubversive activities of the red squad
were focused on two priorities: the harassment of left-wing unionists
and the tracking of radical groups such as communists, socialists, and
"fronts"—an increasingly ecumenical targeting made possible by the absence of meaningful restraints (guidelines, ordinances) and freedom
from effective internal supervision and control. But the already-noted
decline in the fifties of investigative opportunities resulted, by the end of
the decade, in the decline of the red squad to a staff of six members.
What probably provided the unit with its chief raison d'être was its
availability as an investigative resource primarily for the FBI, but also
for other intelligence operations: the state antiradical unit, other area red
squads, and file-maintenance programs.

The Los Angeles Red Squad, 1930–1960

The two dominant police intelligence figures in Los Angeles in the
late 1920s and 1930s were Police Chief James E. Davis and the head of
the Intelligence Bureau (as the Los Angeles red squad was then known),
Captain William Francis ("Red") Hynes, who was made its commanding
officer in 1927 after serving as a labor spy for private employers and
then as a police infiltrator-provocateur after joining the police in 1922.[42]
More than any other single individual, Hynes was influential in shaping
the agenda of the modern red squad and in exploiting the career opportunities of its chief. In October 1930 he appeared before the Fish Committee and presented testimony and exhibits dealing with the red menace
in encyclopedic scope—over 1,500 pages, complete with photographs,
dossiers, and documents.[43] This mammoth tour d'horizon became part of
the file capital of red squads throughout the country and brought him
national acclaim as a top expert in the field and bids from other cities for
guidance in setting up their own units.

As in the case of his counterparts, Hynes's career reflected a close
linkage of repression and corruption. In a classic version of the Bargain
made familiar by Chicago's Captain Schaack and Philadelphia's Frank
Rizzo, as well as by a number of others, he was permitted by the city's
ruling powers to pillage at will in return for protecting their interests.
His ties to the area's open-shop forces were unconcealed. Indeed, for a
period of time his office was situated in the Chamber of Commerce
building in order to expedite a prompt, coordinated response to labor

disputes. When a major dispute arose, the employer involved would communicate with Hynes, who assigned a detail to the strike. Picket lines were assaulted with nightsticks followed by tear-gas projectiles and guns, frequently supplied or paid for by strike-bound employers or those confronted with organizational picketing. In large-scale disputes, the union involved was infiltrated by spies and provocateurs—frequently professionals hired by employers and operationally supervised by Hynes. M&M also supplied strikebreakers, who were placed under Hynes's command. In return for his services, Hynes was paid in cash out of secret employer slush funds. Members of his detail were also rewarded with cash payments, usually disguised as compensation for expenses—recorded in grossly padded bills for meals, accommodation, and overtime. Hynes did not permit jurisdictional barriers to impede his mission and frequently worked for employers outside the city limits. For example, he orchestrated a 1934 campaign by Imperial Valley growers that was marked by the bombing of the union's headquarters, vigilante night raids, and the brutalization of strikers and their families. In the course of this terror, hundreds of strikers were gassed, clubbed, and held incommunicado for weeks on end.[44]

The red squad's response on the ideological front was equally savage. Not as a casual or optional matter, but as official routine, the unit broke up every demonstration of organized communists and similar groups, raided communist halls every two weeks, confiscated literature, broke up Depression-related protest gatherings, and flexed its muscles on all occasions.[45]

By the mid thirties the Hynes-led Intelligence Bureau had, according to a 1938 description submitted by Hynes, acquired jurisdiction over a number of broadly defined areas in addition to vague "confidential" investigative duties. Of these specified responsibilities, the most important were the investigation, surveillance, arrest, and prosecution "of illegal activities in connection with ultra-radical organizations and individuals" and "all forms of sedition and treasonable activities"; preparation of intelligence reports and dossiers; the study of radical literature; the enforcement of federal, state, and local laws ranging from the federal Sedition Act to ordinances dealing with handbill distribution, unlawful assembly, and incitement to riot. A parallel labor-dispute assignment area broadly covered surveillance of strike disturbances, picketing, sabotage, and indeed all forms of labor activity considered threatening to "legitimate business," including the formulation in cooperation with employer groups of "plans of action in dealing with projected strikes . . . and radical and racial disturbances." The unit's leadership was explicitly authorized to develop "close contacts with the various civic, patriotic, business, educational and fraternal organizations and clubs" in order to provide them with file material on subversive activities, to represent the department in speaking engagements before such groups, and to supply the press "with the news, information and data as is deemed advisable."[46] The mission to cooperate with private groups and to feed the press was distilled from Hynes's prior pattern of operations and became part of standard red squad operating procedure in cities throughout the country: all the larger cities in Southern California, for example, maintained political intelligence units, which over the years became notorious for their excesses.

Two initiatives of the Hynes unit typify its modus operandi. On October 30, 1931, a red squad detail broke up a mass meeting at Philharmonic Auditorium called to support the movement to free Tom Mooney and the Harlan County, Kentucky, miners. As thousands surged around the entrance demanding entry, the police responded with verbal abuse, gas bombs, and clubbings. A spontaneous outdoor protest demonstration was similarly disrupted—this time with the aid of uniformed marines and sailors. Seven demonstrators (five of them women) were arrested, first on charges of "suspicion of criminal syndicalism," later reduced to disturbing the peace and battery, and finally to disturbing the peace and distribution of handbills.[47] On the night of January 3, 1932, Hynes and his minions crushed a licensed demonstration of the unemployed by wading into the ranks of unarmed men and women with clubs, slingshots, and brass knuckles, beating many of them indiscriminately to the ground.[48]

In 1934 four lawsuits filed by the ACLU succeeded in enjoining Hynes and his squad from interfering with peaceful meetings. In addition, the plaintiffs prevailed in two civil actions for damages against Hynes and some of his squad members. The deterrent effect was reflected in the success of Mayor Frank Shaw's edict reopening the plaza (the traditional free-speech site) and school buildings to meetings and demonstrations by leftists.[49]

The red squad and its supporters invariably responded to complaints of misconduct with charges that the critics were red-tainted and their complaints politically motivated. To the claim that even communists were protected by the Constitution, Hynes indignantly retorted: "They haven't any rights. I'm going to keep right after them." Socialists fared no better; Police Commissioner Willard Thorpe denounced them as "outrageous, deplorable, appalling, Un-American and uncivilized."[50]

During most of the period Hynes headed the Los Angeles red squad, the police chief was James E. Davis whose tenure (1926–29, 1933–38) was interrupted during reforms following a vice-squad scandal. Davis was the first in a line of ultraconservative Los Angeles police chiefs, big men who uniquely embodied and symbolized the rightist political culture of their time and place. When he was first appointed chief in 1926, he quickly succumbed to the courtship of the business community and became its spokesman in defense of the American Way of Life, hostility to unionism, expert in the machinations of the Menace, and preacher of morality. Davis himself was not merely indifferent to graft; he defended it, shared in the spoils, and dismissed criticism as red-inspired. Indeed, Davis's use of police power uniquely reflected the dialectic of the Bargain: the pursuit and harassment of dissent in exchange for the toleration of corruption.[51]

Davis not only sanctioned the shenanigans of the Hynes unit but, to please his anti-union mentors, encouraged it to engage in ever more blatant strikebreaking operations. During the administration of Mayor John Porter, the red squad was periodically called in to develop material for use as leverage against the mayor's critics, disillusioned by City Hall's abuses. In the mid thirties, Mayor Frank Shaw's administration was, in turn, overtaken by rapidly spreading graft and corruption, which once again inspired a reform movement. At the mayor's request, Davis organized a "secret service" unit to monitor and blackmail his rivals and reformer critics. For Davis this assignment was quite congenial. From the start he viewed his department as a client of the power structure, and there was an even greater stake in serving the mayor's political needs than in doing the bidding of the business community. If the mayor lost an electoral race and was replaced, the power-hungry Davis knew, his own future would be jeopardized. Had he not been demoted after the Porter victory in 1929? Mainstream political surveillance thus joined red-hunting as a priority concern. In three years the secret service unit spent almost a quarter of a million dollars in monitoring threats to the Shaw administration. The files of the unit reflected the indiscriminate targeting of political figures, writers, ministers, journalists, and prominent citizens. The custodian of the files and chief of the unit was Captain Earl Kynette, one of the most disreputable figures to emerge from the milieu of LAPD corruption.[52] After he was implicated in a vice-squad scandal (for shaking down prostitutes), Kynette was recruited by Davis to lead his secret service unit.

The downfall of the red squad was precipitated by a scandal that erupted in 1938 in the course of a campaign by an aroused reform constituency against the police corruption of the Shaw administration. The investigator for the reform group, the Citizens' Independent Investigating Committee (CIVIC), was critically injured when a bomb was placed in his car. Although the LAPD denied complicity, an investigation by the district attorney's office established that the bombing had been engineered by Captain Kynette. Kynette and an accomplice were subsequently convicted and jailed. At the close of the trial the city council voted to reject Shaw's request for $90,000 to fund his spy squad.[53]

The rise to power of Davis and Hynes illustrates the career opportunities offered by union-busting and radical-hunting in the twenties and thirties. These specialties became a path to advancement and political office throughout the public sector. In Southern California a powerful alliance of businessmen, boosters, superpatriots, and right-wing evangelicals, transplanted from middle America, made this specialty a particularly attractive path to power, not only in the police world but in the political realm. In turn, state legislative committees investigating subversion reinforced the Los Angeles unit by providing a punitive publicity outlet for the exposure of its targets. The local squad freely placed its operational resources at the disposal of the state panel and routinely referred useful right-wing sources in the private sector to the state committees for sponsorship and funding. This collaboration was particularly useful in discrediting reformers and libertarian critics who attacked both the Los Angeles and state units.

Countersubversive investigations by California state legislative committees spanned a period of thirty years (1940–71), a record unequaled in any other state. The chairman of the first legislative committee to launch an investigation of subversive activities was Samuel W. Yorty, a state assemblyman from Los Angeles County and subsequently mayor of Los Angeles. The Yorty Committee had functioned for only a year (1940) when Yorty resigned to run unsuccessfully for nomination to a seat in the U.S. Senate. He was succeeded by another Los Angeles County assemblyman, Jack Tenney, whose committee, the Fact Finding Committee on Un-American Activities, functioned continuously for eight years (1941–49).

In 1947 legislative opposition to the committee was stiffened by its characterization of two assemblymen as subversive. The committee, it was subsequently learned, kept files on many legislators, particularly those who voted against its appropriation requests. In 1949 pressures from libertarian and religious groups forced the termination of the panel under Tenney's leadership.[54]

A replacement for the Tenney Committee under Senator Hugh Burns was launched as a reform gesture; it would eschew the bad old Tenney pattern of widely publicized smear hearings and issue objective reports based on verified documentation—it would, in short, serve as a model for "the right way to fight Communism." But it soon became apparent that the more things changed procedurally, the more they remained the same (or got worse) substantively. Like its predecessor, the Burns panel maintained ties with an established network of organizations—patriotic, veteran, agribusiness, and right-wing—that supplied it with (frequently questionable) information and served as a conduit to privately sponsored informers.[55]

The Burns Committee operation was headed by the legendary Richard E. Combs. For virtually the entire twenty-one years of the committee's functioning, Combs was its chief investigator, counsel, and "senior analyst." A prominent member of a national community of red-hunters (the Gallery of the Obsessed), Combs was venerated in political intelligence and countersubversive circles generally as a tough expert on subversion. From his mountain retreat at Three Rivers, California, he orchestrated a network of informers (volunteers, paid for by outsiders or hired by the committee), apprentice sources, investigators, and contacts cloaked in secrecy and intelligence hugger-mugger (drops, code names, safe houses). As in the case of the Tenney Committee, whose antics had cooled business support, the Burns panel folded in 1971 (a year after Combs's retirement) without strong objection by business forces. In March 1971 the coup de grace was delivered when, in a replay of the Tenney Committee's demise, James Mills, state senate president pro tem, discovered that the committee's 20,000 file cards included dossiers on a score of legislators, including himself.[56]

3　The Surge of the Sixties

New Targets, Tactics, and Technology

Center Stage for the Red Squads

As the sixties erupted in a seemingly endless series of demonstrations, rallies, marches, mass meetings, vigils, and riots focused on ending the Vietnam War, equality for minorities, and New Left and campus
agendas, defenders of the status quo inevitably responded that the whole
dissident spectrum was part of a vast plot. Subversive agitators were,
they insisted, at the root of all the unrest of the sixties. Police antiradical
cadres thus became a vitally important source for such charges. But how
to ideologize in this way a movement of such scale and diversity, especially given the moribund state of the old (communist) left? The entire
intelligence apparatus—both federal and local—was faced with the need
to identify and control new actors on a new political stage—no easy
matter in view of the anarchic protest milieu, characterized by highly
mobile and anonymous young people who tended to be hostile to formal
organization and leadership. The social remoteness of the new radicals
concentrated in tribal, self-contained groups made it all the more difficult to identify them. An additional difficulty was presented by ghetto unrest and riots, which seemed, in most cases, spontaneous and
unplanned.

The most ambitious and significant campaign to discredit the role of
youth in the burning causes of the sixties was mounted by J. Edgar
Hoover. In testimony, press releases, special articles, and reports, the FBI
chief sounded repeated warning cries against the red menace on the campus during the sixties. In 1963 he vainly called for a ban on communist
speakers at colleges on the grounds that their propaganda was too insid-
ious for the unwary student. His increasingly fierce charges, patrioti-
cally cited by sympathetic members of the security establishment,

65

reached a climax in his annual report for 1965: "The unvarnished truth is that the Communist conspiracy is seizing this insurrectionary climate to captivate the thinking of rebellious-minded youth and coax them into the Communist movement itself or at least agitate them into serving the Communist cause."[1]

But Hoover could not make his stern warnings credible. For example, he "documented" his charges of subversion among the demonstrators involved in the University of California free-speech movement with a claim that of the almost one thousand demonstrators, some thirty-eight had "subversive backgrounds" of an unparticularized character. (And not even all of the thirty-eight were asserted to be students; some were identified as "connected with the University of California in some manner.")[2]

Furthermore, federal structures, typified by the FBI, were based on anachronistic targeting criteria dominated by an old left composed of "communists," "fellow travelers," and "fronts." Intelligence files were choked with millions of dossiers of aging and dead radicals. This gap gave urban police surveillance functions a unique importance. The core of the red squad operation was identification—of anyone and everyone involved in protest activities. The names and associations of activists—a sixties coinage reflecting the rejection of hierarchical organizational structures—were recorded and filed. Lists and dossiers of subjects were coded, stored, indexed, and disseminated to other intelligence agencies (federal, state, and urban). Police countersubversive agencies multiplied greatly as "intelligence" became a standard branch of urban police practice even in cities where it had theretofore played a relatively minor role. Young college graduates were offered career opportunities in intelligence, and intelligence-related instruction was provided both for urban and campus security police. The launching of such units and the strengthening of existing ones became a top priority, strongly recommended by federal and state countersubversive committees and (for entirely different reasons) by commissions appointed to study the causes of, and prescribe cures for, ghetto and campus disorders. As these units increased in number and size, they assumed a variety of names—anti-subversive squad, intelligence unit, civil disobedience unit, public disturbance intelligence division.[3]

The lure of professionalization, the mastery of operational techniques, the accumulation of files, and the growth of a brotherhood of specialists—insiders who shared secret information about subversives and their activities—all led to the perception of radical-hunting as an elite calling, charged with the awesome responsibility of protecting government and society from grave threats. Such influences were reflected in structural changes: the traditional police responsibility for public order, which served to legitimate a "prevention" rationale for surveillance, was subordinated to "intelligence," a professional specialty.[4] The political intelligence mission was in some cases assimilated to existing criminal intelligence units, launched in the fifties to meet the challenge of organized crime. This seemed, for some, a natural union: crime and subversion could both be classified as forms of deviance requiring monitoring. But the countersubversive cadres in some cities insisted that professionalism required a divorce from criminal intelligence operations. In either case, the specialists in political intelligence were viewed as highly skilled professionals and were assigned to conduct departmental educational projects and briefings as well as external activities such as speeches, conferences, lectures, and testimony before legislative committees. Indeed, in the sixties, in cities such as Chicago, Philadelphia, and San Francisco, more police personnel were on political intelligence assignments than were engaged in fighting organized crime. Similarly, the police in small and medium-sized cities, plagued by organized crime, proudly boasted that they were hot on the heels of radicals.[5]

The selection of targets for surveillance initially presented problems. The established urban units were at first confined to already-acquired assets: internal files and records, police texts, congressional committee reports and right-wing newsletters. (The newer units had to begin from scratch.) But these were rapidly supplemented by fresh listings of organizations and of individuals seen and photographed in protest activities. In addition, the drug culture provided an important source of names, a circumstance that created not only a reason for surveillance but a pretext for raids.[6]

Perhaps most important was the heavy surveillance of blacks. Such surveillance, not only in large cities but even in smaller ones and towns, was considered self-justifying, much like the surveillance of aliens in the twenties. The campus also became a theater of intensive surveillance operations by both public and campus agents.

The glamor of this police milieu was burnished by a wide assortment of technological assets, accumulated primarily in response to urban race riots and the activities of the New Left.[7] Since the prime emphasis of the urban units was identification, it is not surprising that photography became an operational concentration. Police in communities throughout the country systematically photographed the entire range of outdoor protest activities from parades to the presentation of petitions to congressmen. Technological sophistication brought the following changes in surveillance photography: it (1) expanded the coverage area; (2) lengthened the possible distance between the subject and the police camera; (3) made feasible 24-hour surveillance; (4) concealed the identity of the cameraman, and even the fact that the picture was being taken at all; and (5) made possible instantaneous review and identification. A sophisticated still camera used in police surveillance combines high-powered binoculars, a camera, and a telecamera. This device enabled the surveillants to stand more than half a mile away and take clear identification pictures of an area as large as a football field. Another camera, the Cyclops, which features an electro-optical device that converts light into electricity, permitted surveillance at night.* To speed the use of this new surveillance technology, the Law Enforcement Assistance Administration (LEAA), an offspring of the 1968 Omnibus Crime and Safe Streets Act, allocated funds to state and local police units for the purchase of such surveillance gear as 24-hour infrared closed-circuit television cameras, which were attached to telephone poles on city streets to monitor radical activities.[8]

Indeed, it was television and videotape that truly revolutionized police photographic surveillance. The application of low-light-level television (LLLTV) to cable systems permitted videotaping at night. The use of television cameras from helicopters for crowd viewing also spread. In Washington, D.C., for example, the police department used television cameras to surveil demonstrations. A television camera could be installed in any of the department's three helicopters and monitored at the Police Operations Center, where, in addition, two-way radio communication was maintained with the helicopters, squad cars, and patrolmen. The videotape recordings were retained in police files as evidence. In addition, the surveillance capability included portable television cameras. According to a police official, these looked "just like a commercial T.V. camera" and could be carried by a plainclothes officer for close-in surveillance of crowds.[9]

Street surveillance by closed-circuit television cameras also became commonplace. These systems operated in cities such as San Francisco, Mount Vernon, Hoboken, and New York City. They typically consisted of stationary low-light-level television cameras positioned on the tops of buildings or on high poles. All of the cameras were usually encased in what is known as "environmental housing." Protected from rain by windshield wipers, they were capable of functioning in temperatures

---

* Similarly, sensors and other electronic gadgetry developed for the military in Indochina were adapted for domestic intelligence and tested on an experimental basis in a number of cities.

from -20°F to 140°F, and some could be remotely controlled to tilt, pan, zoom, and rotate 355 degrees. Such equipment permitted the police to obtain close-ups of faces half a mile away, even in darkness.*

Like other aspects of the intelligence process, photography became an end in itself, a means of intimidating the subject. To achieve this objective, subjects were sometimes photographed from as close as three feet. A team tactic was typically employed: a policeman or detective pointed to a particular target for a cameraman to photograph. Some police officers extolled the deterrent effect of open photography and even resorted to pretending to snap pictures long after they had run out of film.† To convey and conceal photographic equipment, panel trucks were sometimes used, occasionally camouflaged to resemble vehicles conveying television gear. Not infrequently, surveillance photographers acquired spurious press credentials, and bona fide cameramen were induced to share their photographs with the police.

Photographs of individuals not already known to the police were submitted to informers and undercover agents for identification. Sometimes tentative identifications were verified by automobile license numbers systematically recorded by police at meetings and rallies and outside the homes of "known militants." The identified individuals then became the subjects of files and indices, which were passed on, as the commander of the New Orleans Police Department's intelligence division explained, to "every conceivable authority that might have an interest in causing prosecution or further investigation of these persons."[10]

In spite of judicial and constitutional restraints, wiretapping and electronic bugging were also common, both in connection with local investigations and on behalf of the FBI.[11] But a perhaps more noteworthy operational practice was the planting of informers drawn from police ranks. In the early years of this century, police garnered information from informers planted by private agencies, employers' associations, and patriotic groups. By the thirties, big-city police had begun to recruit

---

* With the aid of LEAA funds, a Cleveland educational and cultural community known as University Circle served as a test area for a highly sophisticated surveillance system. Everyone walking the streets within a two-square-mile area could be viewed by at least one of two television cameras installed on the tops of two high buildings. The image taken by the cameras was transmitted to police headquarters by laser beam, capable of transmitting over a million television signals simultaneously and so powerful that a police photographer could count the number of stones in the wall of a church half a mile away. *Cleveland Plain Dealer*, July 28, 1972.

† When asked to comment on this practice, a police cameraman told the author: "Sometimes I go out on an assignment with an empty camera. Just taking the pictures cools the agitators."

their own informers from the private sector and acted as the spy's "handlers," "contacts," or "controls," only rarely themselves resorting to impersonation, dissembling loyalties, and the fabrication of cover identities. It was one thing to hire an agent as an independent contractor to do the dirty work of spying, but quite another for a public servant to do it himself. But in the sixties, police, not only in Chicago and New York but in many smaller cities—San Diego, Houston, Oakland, New Orleans, and Columbus to name a few—went underground, and the "undercover agent" became commonplace.*

The red squads did not engage in surveillance in a vacuum. Intelligence theory and practice virtually mandate the storage of accumulated data in files, dossiers, and indices. With the exception of major cities, arrest records had previously served as the only means of preserving a target's past delinquencies, and police agencies in the thirties were not infrequently asked for such records by chiefs in more remote areas in order to gauge a suspect's subversive background. But the development and maintenance of a file system of "suspects"—individual and organizational—became indispensable in the sixties. The file entries were concerned not so much with prior arrests—although the file cards usually called for arrest records along with aliases, color of eyes, height, and similar police blotter–style information—as with the subject's political biography. The file collections became precious police assets; they gave a cachet of reliability and accuracy to the entries, treated the subjects as deviants, and contributed to the mystique of professionalism. Sheer accumulation of entries—signature on a peace petition, presence at a demonstration protesting welfare cuts, receipt of left-wing literature, a speech at a panel on police brutality, each innocuous in itself—leads the intelligence mind to the conclusion that the subject is subversive. Quantity is transformed into quality; the end result is greater than the sum of its parts.

Intelligence files became a highly important resource in the development of support for antiradical operations and an effective weapon in discrediting critics. The large urban units frequently funneled file material both to their supporters within the police hierarchy and to journalists.† Files, in short, became a form of "documentation," really a

---

* In some cases an undercover assignment was made part of a police training program, but in others where special qualifications—ethnicity, race, language skills, age, education—were needed to conform to the nature of the target, a larger pool of police officers or cadets was used.
† At the 1963 libel trial brought by John Henry Faulk, it was revealed that one of the defendants, Vincent Hartnett, had operated a highly profitable "smear and

kind of aggression, deepening and reinforcing the chilling effect produced by surveillance. The mere existence of a file inspired fear in the subject and confirmed the intelligence thesis that dissent is a form of original sin—permanent, incurable, and contagious. A file made the individual a "subject" with a record he could not change, tied forever to political views and associations that he might long since have abandoned.

Political intelligence functionaries were proud of their file collections and glowed as new entries boosted the total. They kept count of the number of requests for file data from other agencies—urban and federal. A trade-off system gave them favorable press coverage in exchange for requested file data about an individual or organization. File access became a means of blackmailing political opponents and critics. But a problem troubled the police functionaries: how was all this accumulated dirt about these radicals and their carryings-on to be used? It would appear that they possessed valuable assets that were, however, non-negotiable. Received intelligence wisdom required secrecy in operation and discretion in revealing its fruits. (But if the public only knew what a tremendous job the police were doing in keeping these agitators at bay!) And even if other difficulties were overcome, there remained budget problems. There was no provision in urban budgets for the sort of publicity about file contents for which the police functionaries yearned.

The combined need to do injury to the subjects and to reap rewards for their achievements led to a sort of partnership with congressional countersubversive committees. This connection served two additional purposes: it helped legitimize the questionable authority of local police units to engage in virtually unrestrained targeting and gave the committees new targets to expose, a fresh source of material to revive the languishing countersubversive tradition and, perhaps most important, a means of ideologizing the unrest of the sixties, of documenting the thesis—especially cherished by southern legislatures—that riots in the black ghettos, agitation against discrimination, and campus disturbances were all inspired by communists and their allies.

---

clear" service, in which he exposed individuals in the entertainment world and used the threat of exposure to extract investigative fees from sponsors. When Hartnett was asked on the witness stand to reveal the source of his extensive information about individuals, he testified that he had called Lieutenant Thomas F. Crane of the New York City red squad some seventy times for information or verification about the political backgrounds of certain entertainers and writers, and that on thirty occasions he received information from the unit's files. John Henry Faulk, *Fear on Trial* (New York: Simon & Schuster, 1964), p. 326.

The Police–Congressional Committee Alliance

The weightiest treatment of the thesis that subversion was at the root of the unrest of the sixties was developed in a 25-part, three-year investigation begun in 1967 of "Riots, Civil and Criminal Disorders" by the Permanent Subcommittee on Investigations of the Senate Committee on Government Operations, headed by Arkansas Senator John L. McClellan (the McClellan Committee). In addition to witnesses from other law-enforcement sectors, the committee, in the course of its marathon investigation, elicited detailed testimony from sixteen police officers from cities throughout the country. After hearing the witnesses from only four cities, Senator McClellan proclaimed that "militant agitators . . . were deliberately inciting to riot . . . Communists are at work through every channel that is available to them to sow the seeds of discord and exploit any dissent they can find among our people."[12]

The police witnesses set the tone for the hearing by their proudly submitted lists of names, identifications of leaders and members of target groups, wiretap logs, photographs, informers' reports, dossiers, minutes of meetings, flyers, and pamphlets, as well as literature and publications distributed by local groups under surveillance obtained through "confidential sources" (informers) or raids. The Fish Committee and later the House Un-American Activities Committee (Dies Committee) had provided an outlet for bulging local surveillance files, but there was no precedent for the sixties outpouring of urban police intelligence files into the investigative records of congressional committees—not only of the McClellan panel but, as will be shown presently, of the standing antisubversive committees of House and Senate.

In all of these committee hearings where local police witnesses testified, one can sense through the cold print of their testimony the self-preening on their cloak-and-dagger triumphs: the informers they had successfully run, the albums of photographs and mug shots, the literature surreptitiously acquired, the stolen diaries, maps, and financial records, followed by portentous conclusions about the conspiratorial root of it all.[13] As with earlier police performances before congressional committees, the McClellan Committee members complimented the praise-hungry police witnesses and sought to encourage the greater use of intelligence-related tactics.*

* Early in the McClellan hearings, Senator Mundt asked a witness from the Houston Police Department: "Is it entirely impossible for a law enforcement agency such as yours to put some plainclothes people, some undercover people, into these groups. . . . Don't you think there is some way to develop a counter-

At the same time as the McClellan Committee hearings, the House Internal Security Committee (HISC) held hearings (*Subversive Influences on Riots, Looting and Burning*)[14] that again documented the thesis that the disturbances of the sixties were caused by subversives, and that greater intelligence efforts by the police were required to isolate and neutralize the radical troublemakers. The star witness at the hearings was Captain Charles Kinney, the Newark Police Department's intelligence chief, who told the committee:

> In Newark, certain individuals conspired, and are conspiring to replace the leadership of the Newark Police Department. Other individuals conspired and are conspiring, to turn out of office the present city administration before its lawful term expires.*
>
> Still other individuals conspired, and are conspiring, as part of the movement to replace this system of government under which we live in the United States of America, using any means to do so, including the use of force and violence.
>
> To these conspirators, the insurrection that occurred in 1967 was a means to an end which they welcomed and exploited to serve their plot.
>
> To these conspirators, the accomplishment of any or all of the aforementioned goals was paramount.[15]

HISC was particularly smitten by photographs supplied, for the most part, by local red squads. In five HISC hearings between 1968 and 1972, a total of 378 photographs were published in appendices.[16] These include mug shots (in some cases of individuals who were never tried or who were acquitted after trial, and, in some cases, of juveniles), pictures taken by police during demonstrations, passport pictures, and photos obtained from the press, from television cameramen doubling as police photographers, and from student newspapers. All the countersubversive

---

offensive?" The witness agreed that greater deployment of "undercover people" was required, but he complained that his own force, "like most police departments throughout the Nation," was undermanned and underpaid. Senate Committee on Government Operations, Permanent Subcommittee on Investigations [McClellan Committee], Hearings, 1967–69: pt. 1, pp. 171–72.

* Captain Kinney had made an earlier television charge that the 1967 Newark riots were instigated by the Newark Community Union Project, whose director, Tom Hayden, Kinney claimed, "traveled with both black and white people from Newark to Bratislava, Czechoslovakia, for a meeting behind the Iron Curtain where they received instructions."

committee hearings, but especially HISC's, are also freighted with a fantastic variety of police-file documents, likewise reprinted in appendices.*

But despite HISC's praise for their accomplishments, local law-enforcement officers came under increasing attack for their operational tactics and because they divulged the results of surveillance for publication by the committee. As a result, local police officers became increasingly reluctant to testify in public.†

Perhaps the strongest and most enduring ties with the urban countersubversive police were forged by the Senate Judiciary Committee Subcommittee on Internal Security (SISS). The collaborative arrangement between the police and SISS is documented in twelve volumes of hearings full of testimony by local intelligence officers as well as by surfaced police informers.[17] In a series of hearings, SISS took testimony by an assortment of informants that American campuses were crawling with reds who fraudulently exploited student grievances, infiltrated their organizations, and generally employed "amoral means to pervert and ex-

---

* These include private letters, maps, photocopied checks, transcripts of interviews, membership lists, press releases, publication lists, invitations to conferences, lists of participants at meetings, delegates to conferences, newsletters, minutes of meetings, rent receipts, film transcripts, constitutions of target organizations, articles of incorporation of peace groups, university rules and regulations, organizational registration and application forms, career recruitment posters, student newspaper articles, bank signature cards, agendas for demonstrations, petitions to Congress, Department of Defense directives, newspaper articles, and financial data of all kinds.

† For example, in 1971 Herbert Romerstein, a staff witness, was asked to identify his sources. He replied: "No, sir, I cannot. At the request of the law enforcement agencies we were requested not to make their identities known. The reason for this is that while these law enforcement agencies have been engaging in the proper and the correct carrying out of their duties they have received a certain amount of criticism for their activities.

"Now the activities in particular are the surveillance of the actions of groups such as Progressive Labor and the placing of undercover informants in such groups. We have seen the police departments, the Federal Bureau of Investigation, and the Department of Defense criticized for their activities in observing groups that are planning and directing acts of violence on our country. The cooperative law enforcement agencies have therefore requested we not make their names public at this time."

MR. PERRY: "Did any of the law enforcement agencies indicate a willingness to appear and testify?"

MR. ROMERSTEIN: "No, sir. They said they would not wish to appear and testify at this time" (House Internal Security Committee [HISC] Hearings, 1971: *America's Maoists*, p. 405).

In explaining the negative police response, their HISC proxies frequently resorted to a stock bit of intelligence jargon: the fear of "compromising" a "sensitive" investigation.

ploit the idealism of youth." In 1965, SISS released a "special study" on *The Anti–Viet Nam Agitation and the Teach-In Movement*, charging that the teach-ins were "extremist influenced."

In a 1967 set of hearings, SISS elicited additional testimony about leftism among youth. The subcommittee's investigative assaults on student radicalism were marked by the unprecedented testimony of representatives of local police bodies, engaged since the early sixties in a campaign to equate student charges of police brutality with subversion. They blamed urban riots on subversives and darkly hinted to the subcommittee that radical youth must be curbed in the interests of sound law enforcement.

The ability of SISS to attract witnesses from the intelligence world may have been a dividend of its investment in liaison with, and coordinating efforts in, the intelligence community. In May 1970, SISS's chief investigator, Alfonse Tarabochia, told the Fifteenth Annual Conference of the Law Enforcement Intelligence Unit (LEIU), a national network of urban police intelligence units,[18] that his colleagues on the SISS research staff maintained "an almost daily liaison with various Federal, State and local law enforcement agencies throughout the country."

In a hearing in 1970, SISS's chief counsel, J. G. Sourwine, described the subcommittee's mission in these words:

> We seek information with respect to the persons who head . . . subversive organizations and are active in them and who participate in them, the persons who support them; about the interconnections, the channels of authority, and the sources of funds.
>
> We are asking police departments from all across the country to sift their records and bring these facts here for the committee . . . by gathering all of the available information from leading police departments throughout the country, the committee hopes to be able eventually to present a picture. We are charting the organizations in each area, the persons in each area who are connected . . . and we hope when we finish we will have a picture which will show just what this country is up against.[19]

The SISS hearings teem with identifications, photographs, and documents. No effort is made to conceal the fact that the committee's purpose was to publicize the contents of police intelligence files. In the wake of the SISS hearings, at least three lawsuits for damages were filed against intelligence officers.*

The criticism of police agencies that had cooperated with the committee and fear of further lawsuits brought to a close the airing of police intelligence files. But the partnership continued in another form: the police files were made available to committee staff members, who used them as a source for "staff studies," a popular format in the seventies. In addition, the police operational style, with its great stress on identification of individuals, accumulation of photographs, and print minutiae was adopted by HISC, which began to assign staff members to operational tasks.

The Short Life of Intelligence as a Shield against Riots

The congressional committees in effect recruited the police units as allies in their ideological attack on the movements of the sixties. Support and encouragement for local police riot-prevention programs also came from less biased quarters. A series of urban riots confronted a frustrated nation with the need for predictive intelligence: Why did we have to wait until violence actually erupted? Was it not possible to forestall outbreaks of violence by careful monitoring of the social sectors most likely to "blow"? After all, was not evaluation the end purpose of collecting information, so that decision makers and, where appropriate, law-enforcement officers could take preventive measures?

The countersubversive committees had implicitly rejected such a role for the police. As we have seen, they concentrated instead on the agitator-subversion thesis, which in effect denied the relevance of social and economic factors as the cause of unrest. But when criticism of both

---

* *Cannon v. Davis,* a suit against a Los Angeles police official, is discussed below. In a second case, *Napoleon Holmes v. Church,* the plaintiffs sued the city of New Rochelle, its police chief, and intelligence officers who had testified in the SISS hearing. A third suit, *Yaffe v. Powers,* charged that the chief of police of Fall River, Mass., and an intelligence officer had taken surveillance photographs of the two plaintiffs at a peace memorial service, released them to the press, and posted them on a bulletin board in police headquarters. In addition, the police wrote a surveillance report included in dossiers it maintained on the plaintiffs. As in the New Rochelle case, the surveillance activities of the defendants became known to the plaintiffs when their SISS testimony was released to the press. In the seventies SISS sought to repay and assist the besieged red squads in two extensive hearings: *Assaults on Law Enforcement Officers* (parts 1–5, 1970) and *The Nationwide Drive against Law Enforcement Intelligence Operations* (parts 1–2, 1975).

the committees and their police allies mounted, the committees discovered a new agitator-type scapegoat, terrorists, and belatedly defended the intelligence role of the police as our most valuable defense against the threat of terrorism, frequently called "urban guerrilla warfare." So it was that in a 1975 SISS hearing Francis J. McNamara, a bulwark of the countersubversive establishment, testified: "Just as the C.I.A. is our first line of defense against terrorism on the international front, the police departments are our first line of defense domestically, and if they have no intelligence or inadequate intelligence, then the American people basically have no security against terrorism."[20]

The endorsement of political intelligence as a form of therapy against the threat of riots came at a time when authorities were becoming increasingly aware of the need for criminal intelligence in fighting organized crime. So it was that the 1965 report of the President's Commission on Law Enforcement and Administration of Justice, *The Challenge of Crime in a Free Society*, recommended that the formation of intelligence units to fight organized crime receive high priority on police-reform agendas. Following the ghetto rebellions in Detroit and Newark in 1967, the National Advisory Commission on Civil Disorders (Kerner Commission) observed that the police had been totally unprepared for the outbreaks. Both the on-the-spot police response to serious disturbances and the long-term planning needed to be improved. The commission concluded that: "An intelligence unit staffed with full-time personnel should be established to gather, evaluate, analyze and disseminate information on potential as well as actual civil disorders. . . . It should use undercover police personnel and informants."[21]

Reinforcing the cries for improved intelligence, the sixties saw the birth of a nationwide youth antiwar movement, of which the campus was the core component. Police in cities and towns that were sites of college campuses extended existing surveillance operations and developed new ones focused primarily on college radicals; typically such operations were coordinated with campus police duties.

The police intelligence surge was quickened by the establishment of the Law Enforcement Assistance Administration (LEAA), a source of grants to local police units in accordance with a statutory mandate to give special consideration to grant requests for "programs and projects dealing with the prevention, detection and control of organized crime and of riots and other violent civil disorders." This entire movement for intelligence solutions to unrest, with its promise of grant goodies, produced an extraordinary proliferation of new police units and an equally extraordinary expansion of established ones.

This climate further promoted the institutionalization of political intelligence. In city after city, guidelines and regulations were adopted, courses of instruction inaugurated, and operational specialties—such as wiretapping, photography, and lock-picking—taught through lectures and briefings by equipment suppliers. The urban authorities generously provided budgets for additional staff and equipment. (Who could deny a request for funds to protect an imperiled citizenry?) But it is hard to point to any contribution that the police intelligence units made to improve the response to urban unrest in the sixties. Instead, there was an enormous expansion of surveillance targeting of the traditional counter-subversive variety: the black ghettos were monitored with special intensity. The Kerner Commission and other such panels recommended that in addition to undercover agents and informers, the police "should also draw on community leaders, agencies and organizations in the ghetto." What the Kerner Commission pleaded for were community-relations resources that would be a source of information, mediation, and predictive intelligence.

On the assumption that racially motivated riots and lesser circumstances could be anticipated and defused by police personnel assigned to participate in community and neighborhood affairs, units with such benign missions—typically called "human relations" or "community relations" squads—were activated. In a few cities, such units did perform a useful function. But police officials typically resisted these recommendations, complaining that policemen were not "sociologists"; in other cases, such units were viewed as offshoots of the communist campaign against the police ("commie relations squads" they were jeeringly called). They most commonly served as a cover for efforts to penetrate the ghetto and conduct intensive surveillance and, at the same time, to make plausible the pretext that surveillance was really designed to protect its targets.[22]

The blood-and-bones countersubversive formula was, in effect, tailored to ignore the causes of the unrest and to substitute the subversive plot-agitator explanation, which became more entrenched than ever before. Instead of meeting a desperate social need, the police charged ahead under the tattered banner of "national security." One example should suffice: despite a total absence of proof and evidence to the contrary, the New Jersey State Benevolent Association released a report in 1968 that the riots in Newark and three other North Jersey cities were the work of a "criminal conspiracy." An "armed rebellion" orchestrated by "Communist conspirators" had used "criminal elements" to implement their plot. The report took sharp issue with the conclusions of the Kerner

Commission and a state commission, which not only rejected the conspiracy thesis, but charged that police forces had resorted to brutal tactics in putting down the riots.[23]

The Law Enforcement Intelligence Unit: The Countersubversive Imperative

The American obsession with radicalism and conspiracy has historically been exploited as a diversion from grave, immediate problems facing the nation. We need only be reminded of the manner in which the 1871 Paris Commune was domesticated and scapegoated for the turbulence of the 1870s; anarchism for the movement for an eight-hour day; labor violence for employer resistance in the Progressive Era to organization by workers; the substitution in 1919 by the Senate Overman Committee of "Bolshevik propaganda" for its original mandate to investigate German brewing and liquor interests; the focus on communists rather than Nazis in the political investigations of the World War II era. In our recent past, we need only recall the attempts to link drug abuse with the radicalism of the sixties; terrorism with peaceful dissent; urban riots and ghetto unrest generally with subversive conspiracies and "guerrilla warfare."[24]

Nothing so sharply illustrates the manner in which radicalism overshadowed crime on police intelligence agendas as the history of the Law Enforcement Intelligence Unit (LEIU). Organized in 1956 by Captain James Hamilton, then commander of the Los Angeles Police Department's criminal intelligence unit, the LEIU owed its formation to the recognition, already referred to, of intelligence as a tool in the fight against organized crime.[25] A second spur was the resentment of local police functionaries over the fact that the FBI, while denying police access to its file resources, routinely used the fruits of police investigations to burnish its image, without ever giving credit to police contributions.*

---

* The LEIU was not a public agency. Its records were not published, but were distributed in typescript or mimeographed copies to its membership. The FBI monitored the LEIU over the years; the comments and reports of the bureau on the LEIU released under the Freedom of Information Act and used as a source in this section are understandably acerbic for the reasons suggested in the text and, additionally, because the bureau suffered a kind of institutional paranoia about police agencies it could not control. Carmen Dekle ("Deke") DeLoche, J. Edgar Hoover's hit man in this area, made several shrewd observations in a 1962 memo about the emergence of the LEIU and its shift to an intelligence focus: that police enjoyed using trendy intelligence terminology and that LEIU gatherings were perks providing free travel, "social enjoyment," and "relaxation" for members and their wives.

This network of some 230 local law-enforcement agencies avowed that its purpose was "to promote the gathering, recording and investigating and exchange of confidential information not available through regular police channels, concerning organized crime." Based in four regions spanning the United States and Canada, it limited its membership to state and urban law-enforcement agencies with functioning intelligence units. Although its constitution suggests that the LEIU was conceived as an investigating body, its core function was to serve as a clearinghouse for file data ("intelligence") supplied by its members. A manual system of "face cards," constantly augmented by new entries, identified the subject in police-blotter style, serviced the requests and needs for information of member agencies, and was organized into various categories (gambling, loan-sharking, narcotics, etc.) including a catch-all designation, "others of interest to law enforcement." In 1971 the LEIU received an LEAA grant to assist it in "interfacing some of its files with the computerized Interstate Organized Crime Index (IOCI)." A second grant in 1974 implemented a more sophisticated project automating the storage and dissemination of LEIU file-card data. (Altogether both LEAA grants totaled almost $2 million.) This system, which became operational in 1978, gave LEIU member agencies a WATS line and a computerized search system linked to a data center located in California. This headquarters of the LEIU's IOCI system was staffed by employees of the organized crime and criminal intelligence branch of the California Department of Justice.*

Despite the fact that LEIU member units were public bodies, that a state agency operated the system with state employees, that LEIU face cards and publications were printed at state expense, that LEAA grants were the lifeblood of the LEIU, and that urban treasuries financed trips by members to annual conferences and zone sessions, the LEIU insisted that it was a private organization with tax-exempt status. Indeed, it was so registered in the California Registry of Charitable Trusts. As a Michigan legislative report noted, the LEIU required "all member agencies to maintain files on government property and to perform LEIU tasks while on the government payroll." Indeed, as the report concluded, "It appears that the LEIU would not exist were it not for taxpayer support. Yet the LEIU and its members have resisted all taxpayer attempts to in any way control their operation."[26] Plainly the LEIU persisted in the pretense

* The IOCI was required by the LEAA to store "only public records information." It is also likely because of LEAA restrictions that the processing of computerized political intelligence–related data was limited. Such information was, however, processed, as I shall show, through the LEIU manual system.

that it was a private group in order to avoid accountability and the forced disclosure of its files—through investigations, lawsuits, or requests under local and state "sunshine" laws.* The pretense of being a private group and file-secrecy protocol were specifically decreed by fear of embarrassment in the event of disclosure through file entries of the extent of the LEIU's focus on political subjects unrelated to organized crime.

The evidence of the LEIU's deviation from its basic mission to combat organized crime is overwhelming, although here too, LEIU leaders persisted in denying that the group had ever dallied in the groves of political intelligence. It is difficult to fix a starting date for this departure, but the reasons for it are fairly clear. Member units, both local and state, had engaged in identification, confrontation, monitoring, and the storage and dissemination of data in the area of dissident political activity well before the LEIU was organized. In many cases this mission was, as I have already noted, institutionally assimilated to organized crime intelligence on the grounds that in both cases the police were dealing with a breeding ground for deviant behavior—what could be more lawless than plotting a revolutionary overthrow of the government?

The protest movements of the sixties had sharpened the police perception of this linkage between the two areas. In 1962 an LEIU Northwestern Zone meeting scheduled as a major subject of discussion "police intelligence units' role in securing information concerning protest groups, demonstrations and mob violence."[27] The November 1963 LEIU Eastern Zone Regional Conference featured a panel discussion on "Investigation of Subversives—An Intelligence Task" moderated by Captain Hamilton and joined by three panelists from the New York and Chicago police departments and the Texas Department of Public Safety. The report on the discussion states:

> The panelists left no doubt in the minds of the Conferees
> that the investigation of subversives and subversive ac-
> tivity is a definite interest of the Police Intelligence Unit.
> Through logic and common reasoning, the responsibility

---

* A strong indication of the LEIU's secrecy commitment surfaced in 1978 when, in the course of an investigation of police intelligence operations in Seattle, the head of the Seattle Police Department's intelligence unit, V. L. Bartley, turned over his LEIU cards to the zone chairman in California with a letter stating: "It would not surprise me if the Mayor seized our files at any time. . . . I'm forwarding our LEIU files to you since I can no longer assure their security. Please retain the cards until the situation has improved or until we are forced to resign from LEIU membership." Bartley was subsequently removed from his post and a judge ordered the cards returned.

> of being informed locally as to the intents of certain dissident groups is properly a local police function. Certainly the nearly 300,000 man effort of local police pursuing subversion coupled with the 6,000 to 7,000 man federal investigators [sic] so concerned is an important group to contend with these individuals and organizations that reject our system of government.[28]

Moreover, the panelists reported, under no circumstances should an investigator be charged with simultaneous probes of criminal and subversive subjects: "The field of subversion is too technical and too expansive to permit an investigator to have a dual familiarity with other criminal investigations." This report was preceded by an address by one of the panelists, Lieutenant Frank J. Heimoski of the Chicago political intelligence unit (whom we have already met), on "Investigation of Subversives—An Intelligence Task?" The speaker emphatically concluded that indeed it was, since it would identify agitators around such issues as

> labor, wages, working hours, strikes, peace, housing, education, social welfare, race, religion, disarmament, and anti-militarization. . . . Our existence as a Police Department Unit has proved a thorn in the side of the subversives and many attempts have been made by them and their sympathizers to eliminate us as a police function.[29]

A 1965 conference in Las Vegas heard the LEIU's national chairman, Thomas F. Fitzpatrick, warn against the threatening character of campus free-speech demonstrations and other "subversive movements." Another speaker, a representative of the Immigration and Naturalization Service, offered the conferees access to the agency's huge file (33 million subjects), which, while not useful as evidence in a criminal prosecution, "can give the police officer many new leads on investigation of foreign born persons involved in subversive activities."[30]

A workshop on civil disobedience and the showing of a film by Chairman Fitzpatrick—captioned "A Peaceful Demonstration in San Francisco . . . Participated in by the W. E. B. DuBois Club and Members of the Communist Party"—were major features of the 1966 LEIU national conference in Detroit. In the same year, the Northwestern Zone conference scheduled as a topic of discussion the "Criminal Conspiracy of the Communist Movement." Was it not apparent, the panelists concluded, that communism was simply a branch of organized crime? Congressional committees also illuminated the LEIU's shift to political concerns. In

1967 Captain John Sorace of the Nashville police intelligence unit told the McClellan Committee that his monitoring of dissidents was aided by LEIU contacts.[31]

At the 1968 combined Eastern and Central Zone meeting, a guest speaker was SISS staffer Alfonse Tarabochia, who addressed the gathering on "Castro's Influence on Student Uprisings."[32] In 1969 the Moloch of countersubversion had almost swallowed whole the LEIU's organized crime concerns. At the Palm Springs national conference that year, the main topic was "Revolution 1969" with the guidance of guest speakers such as Attorney General John M. Mitchell, whose address blended organized crime and subversion. Then California Governor Ronald Reagan enlightened the audience on campus disruptions, followed by a McClellan Committee investigator's discourse on "International Influences on Current Disorders" and Sergeant Robert Thoms of the Los Angeles Police Department on his specialty, "Dissident and Militant Funding." The centerpiece of the session was a "briefing"—a favorite intelligence usage—conducted by a panel of seven police officers, on—in the language of an FBI report—"names of local militant organizations, top leadership, identifying traveling members, financial support, and sources of other support and influence."[33] What a magical journey the LEIU had made from organized crime to political intelligence!* Scottsdale, Arizona—matching earlier host resort cities such as Bar Harbor, Las Vegas, and Palm Springs—was the site of the LEIU's 1970 annual conference on the theme "The Organized Destruction of America," featuring as the keynote speaker Senator Barry Goldwater on the topic "Revolution in the Streets."

During these years, the LEIU continued to deny that it was involved in the traditional forms of data exchange on political subjects. Presumably, the group felt that its mission was too important and its commitment to secrecy too sacred to permit disclosure. But these denials were refuted by the release in 1978 of FBI files dealing with the agendas of the LEIU's national and regional meetings (discussed above), state investigations by the Michigan and California legislatures, and the publication of LEIU face cards obtained by the plaintiffs' attorney in a lawsuit, who estimated that about 10 percent of the three to four hundred cards he examined in Chicago could be classified as political.[34]

The eight dossiers, complete with photos and printed headings to be filled in such as "D.O.B." (date of birth), "Description," "Physical Odd-

---

* Other subversion-related topics included "National Militant Problems," "Tactical Intelligence during Riots," and "Coordinating Intelligence Information."

ities," "Hangouts," "Modus Operandi," "Summary of Arrests," and "Associates," reflected close surveillance of political activists.* Dated from January 1971 through June 1974, these cards highlight the political activities of the subjects. For example: (1) a black militant nationalist without an arrest record dossiered because he is the head of a group called the Republic of New Africa; (2) a Marxist professor at a university in the Northwest characterized as a "political activist . . . present at many demonstrations"; (3) a subject labeled as a "recognized leader in peace movements. . . . He organizes meetings and arranges financing"; (4) a well-known civil rights leader characterized as a "long-time Communist Party member . . . who has assisted in organizing many radical groups and publications in Southern U.S."; (5) a West Coast subject described as a "member of the Black Panther Party . . . believed to be associated with the TRIAD Development Group (Real Estate)";† (6) the "miscellaneous information" entry on this subject's card reveals that he "has been associated with the New Left Movement in the New Orleans area since the late 70s [sic]" and had been involved in various antiwar demonstrations; (7) and (8) two leaders of the American Indian Movement (AIM) identified as burglars and robbers based on charges arising from the Wounded Knee occupation, without stating that neither was convicted on these charges.

We come finally to the operational role of the LEIU. It is indisputable that the network provided operational instruction in workshops on such subjects as surveillance and wiretapping. In the area of informer operations, an example came to light of the LEIU's recycling of blown informers, a capacity for which the countersubversive intelligence world has frequently expressed a need. According to the statement of Douglas Durham to congressional investigators, prior to his recruitment as an FBI informer, he had begun his career as an informer in the service of the intelligence unit of the Des Moines, Iowa, police. When he was exposed and his identity revealed, he was, as a result of an arrangement with the LEIU, detailed to work undercover on political surveillance as-

---

* The eight cards indicated that they were submitted for dissemination to other LEIU members by police departments in Louisville, New Orleans, Pasadena, Redlands (Calif.), Seattle, and South Dakota. Additional cards listing political affiliations or activities—not made public due to privacy concerns and copying costs—were obtained by the Chicago police through the LEIU from police in Denver, Fort Worth, Miami, and San Francisco.

† This is quite inaccurate. The subject insisted that he had never heard of such a group, and no trace of it could be found in area telephone books or other records. In addition, the card failed to note that he had left the Black Panther Party before the card was circulated.

signments for police intelligence units in Lincoln, Nebraska, and Cedar Rapids, Iowa.[35]

Widespread concern over the possibility that the LEIU might become the core of a national political police network finally forced suppression of its political proclivities. However, given the tug of radical-hunting, the power of the savior syndrome that grips police, and the outlet it provides for ambitious officers eager to transcend humdrum routine duties, fears of a revival are hardly groundless.

Making It Big: The CIA Connection

Although the FBI's Washington headquarters harbored an ongoing hostility toward the LEIU's intelligence programs and aspirations, local police cadres and special agents in charge (SACs) routinely cooperated in assorted liaison arrangements, operational assistance, and data exchange. The FBI's police academy, for which local officers were recruited, was a major instrument of influence; and while the director had his enemies in the police world—such as Los Angeles Police Chief William H. Parker— he also had pets, police officers who catered to his ego needs. A key FBI tactic in maintaining ties with the police community and at the same time preventing challenges to the bureau's primacy was to cultivate and cooperate with factions in police structures favorable to its hegemonic claims. The riots of the sixties and the need for a cooperative approach to tactical problems also brought local and federal agencies closer together.

In addition, local radical-hunters worked closely in the Johnson-Nixon years with the Internal Revenue Service and a number of White House intelligence-gathering programs, such as the Interdepartmental Intelligence Unit, White House "plumbers," and Interagency Committee on Intelligence, as well as with the Internal Security Division of the Justice Department, the Treasury Department's Alcohol, Tobacco and Firearms Division, and the Army. In 1968 the Army launched a "Civil Disturbance Orientation Course" at its Military Police School at Fort Gordon, Georgia, which prepared weekly instructions on riot control for local, regional, and state police officers.[36] (This was one of the several LEAA-funded programs to provide "a basic vocabulary and a unified, commonsense . . . planning for all types of forces likely to be involved in restoring law and order in a civil disturbance situation, and to delineate the respective roles of municipal, state, and federal agencies during such a situation."[37] All these liaison arrangements ratified local programs and police countersubversive values and assumptions, ideologized the causes of unrest, and cast the stereotypical radical agitator as a triggerman. But it was the Central Intelligence Agency that most directly shepherded the locals into the shadowy glens of "pure intelligence," spookery focused on domestic "security," unadulterated by such mundane concerns as the prevention of disorder or the containment of riots.[38]

Despite the CIA's charter, which bars the agency from exercising "police, subpoena or law enforcement powers or internal security functions," the tug of domestic countersubversion prevailed. Beginning in the sixties and until the mid seventies, the CIA conducted police training courses for close to seven weeks in such subjects as surreptitious entry, photo surveillance, and audio surveillance. The first of these consisted of instruction on "surreptitious entry planning." This ten-day course was designed to instruct the students in the theory and practice of "clandestine entry." The prospectus states: "The student will fabricate a set of lock-picking tools, and will learn how to employ them against a variety of luggage, lever, wafer and pin-tumbler locks." In addition, the students were required to "participate in practical work exercises" and, at the conclusion of the course, in a "field exercise."

The audio surveillance course explored the use of microphones, line amplifiers, transmitters, recorders, and telephone taps. But it would not do to leave the tenderfoot in the dark about the steps needed to cover up the planting of, say, a microphone. So the audio surveillance course concluded with a day's instruction on "plastering and wall restoration."

The CIA's Training Branch insisted on a practical demonstration ("hands on participation") of what the trainee had learned through the entire range of courses. For this purpose the prospectus called for a sort of graduation exercise: "The students had to survey, case and penetrate three Safesites [structures used by the CIA for instructional purposes] using surreptitious entry, photography and audio surveillance." In addition, the agency offered what might be called a graduate course, ten days in duration, in key surveillance areas.

Also prominent in the operational intelligence curriculum was training in the use of explosives. According to released CIA documents, the agency conducted five seminars for police officials dealing with explosives, including one gathering that featured "a demonstration of explosive and incendiary devices fabricated from common household articles."

But training and instruction were not the only CIA contributions to police intelligence sectors. It provided ("loaned") an extraordinary assortment of material, equipment, and gadgetry, including explosives, recorders, receivers, transmitters, explosive-detection kits, safes for storage of sensitive material, photographic equipment, lighting equipment, microphones, radio-equipped cars, forged identification cards, and polygraphs.

But we are not through yet: the agency donated the use of its safe houses and photography labs to police personnel. Participants in training sessions were provided with food, drink, and entertainment and offered recreational options such as golf, fishing, and hunting. Nor were the lowly beat-pounders entirely neglected: the CIA safehouse in Miami was offered to a patrol officer and the car rental charge ($800) of another was paid by the agency. (We can only note in passing its lavish courtship of police dignitaries: sumptuous entertainment, gifts, free use of cars at vacation spots, travel by limousine, and so forth.)

The beneficiaries of the CIA's largesse, from instructional courses to Roman-style feasts, included, according to one source, "at least forty-four state, local and county police departments." The files indicate that the following departments enjoyed active training or equipment relationships with the agency: Washington, D.C.; Fairfax County, Fairfax City, Arlington County, Alexandria, Falls Church (all in Virginia), and the Virginia State Police; Montgomery County, Prince George's County, and Baltimore (all in Maryland); New York City; Chicago; Philadelphia; Los Angeles; San Francisco; Boston; Miami and the Dade County Public Safety Department (both in Florida); and Lewes (Delaware). Various forms of CIA involvement with the following law-enforcement agencies are documented in CIA files: in California, the city police departments of Long Beach, San Clemente, San Diego, Oceanside, National City, Imperial Beach, Coronado, Chula Vista, Escondido, Costa Mesa, Fullerton, Santa Ana, Buena Park, and Newport Beach and the sheriffs' and district attorneys' offices of San Diego and Orange County; Minneapolis and suburban police departments; the Minnesota Bureau of Criminal Apprehension; the Pennsylvania Division of the International Association for Identification; and the Ohio Identification Officers' Association.

Why did the CIA conduct an operation in seeming disregard of its charter? Certainly, the most plausible answer is that the agency hoped to fill the vacuum created by the FBI's largely negative relationship with the local police and, not to be ignored, by the bureau's reluctance to take the risk of involvement in legally questionable and intrusive surveillance programs. A revealing clue to the CIA's purpose in courting the police is supplied by a memorandum by Howard Osborn, director of the CIA's Office of Security, which states in part: "Some aspects of Agency support to police operations have served to greatly enhance our working relationship and to secure, in return, police commitment to activities and operations which might otherwise have the departments' negative response." In short, these manifold liaison initiatives were conducted as a means of coopting police resources to promote the agency's domestic surveillance activities. Such activities included implementation not only of domestic programs such as the 1967 Operation Chaos—a CIA program of domestic surveillance—but targeting critics and enemies such as *Ramparts*, a magazine that in March 1967 published an exposé of CIA campus involvements, and Bernard Fensterwald, whose Committee to Investigate Assassinations had raised the charge of the CIA's possible complicity in John F. Kennedy's assassination.

As far as the record shows, the police came through nobly to meet the CIA's needs. Thus, the agency obtained "eighteen to twenty" police identification cards from the Washington police to infiltrate Capitol-area antiwar demonstrations. In return for the loan of radio cars and drivers and related favors during antiwar demonstrations between 1968 and 1971, the Washington, D.C., Metropolitan Police Department supplied the agency with intelligence reports on antiwar activists. Police were also used by the agency to investigate its own employees and, more seriously, to protect its "assets" (such as informers) from arrest and prosecution for criminal conduct.

The severance of the CIA's alliance with the police was brought about by vigorous congressional investigation and the exposure of an assortment of pretexts and denials. But, as in the case of the LEIU, a renewal of social tensions and dissenting movements may restore this partnership. Nor would the restraints of the 1947 charter legislation offer assurance to the contrary. In 1981 a presidential executive order (E.O. 12333) authorized the CIA for the first time to conduct "administrative and technical support activities within and outside the United States." The dangers posed by a renewed liaison between the CIA and the police are made clear by a section of the order that broadly authorizes all intelligence agencies to "cooperate with appropriate law enforcement agencies for the purpose of protecting the employees, information, property and facilities of any agency within the intelligence community." Beyond all this, the executive order authorizes intelligence agencies to "participate in law enforcement activities" in this country for the purpose, among others, of combating or preventing "clandestine intelligence activities by foreign powers, or international terrorist activities." This vague provision, as has been argued, would not only sanction the kind of partnership relationship described in these pages, but actually legitimate its expansion.[39]

Now that we have completed the dark journey from the pre-Haymarket era to the early seventies of this century, when red squad activities subsided, we must retrace our course—but along different paths. We need to explore in greater detail the recent history of police intelligence in large cities where dissent and protest flourished: the diverse political settings from which repression emerged; the similarities and differences in police target selection and operations (the "signatures" of these units); the relationships of the red squads to the power structure; red-hunting as a path to political power and as an aid to the achievement of the career goals of ambitious red-hunters ("Big Men") who walked in the footsteps of Captain Schaack; and the role of the press in these matters. Fittingly enough, we first visit Chicago—the source of the Haymarket legacy.

4 Chicago

The National Capital of Police Repression

Until its dissolution in September 1975, the political surveillance operation* of the Chicago Police Department was the outstanding example of its kind in the United States—whether measured in terms of size, number, and range of targets or operational scope and diversity. The police department's wide-open, no-holds-barred style of surveillance had been evolving over three-quarters of a century and historically was the product of a number of political and social influences. Chicago has been a center of three major American radical movements: anarchism, syndicalism (the IWW), and communism. In the middle and late sixties, the city was a theater of considerable antiwar activity and ghetto unrest. In addition, it was the headquarters of the Students for a Democratic Society (SDS) and the site of the 1968 Democratic Convention, which stimulated new surges of repressive police activity in response to organized protests. The power of the unit and its freedom from accountability were nourished by a superpatriotic "Americanist" tradition, a socially conservative constituency rooted in compact ethnic neighborhoods, a boss-ridden political structure, a right-wing press, racism both within the police department and in the city as a whole, and a corrupt police department. Indiscriminate targeting and autonomy were further assured by the power needs of the Daley administration and its political machine, which used the department's countersubversive resources as a weapon against critics. The mission of the red squad, the "subversive section" as it was called in the sixties, was murky: to identify and possibly prosecute "individuals, groups and organizations who advocate the

---

* Its last official title was Security Section of the Intelligence Division of the Bureau of Inspectional Services. I shall frequently refer to it simply as "the red squad."

disruption of the democratic process and government through the use of violence and criminal activity."

In 1970 the authorized strength of the entire intelligence operation was 382, with 49 assigned to the subversive unit; however, the latter figure is highly deceptive since "all personnel within the Intelligence Division are available for specialized assignments and functions in the event of any major occurrence." Indeed, if the occurrence were sufficiently "major," not only patrolmen from other departmental divisions but personnel from other law-enforcement agencies (state and county) were pressed into service.* According to reliable reports, prior to the 1968 Chicago Democratic Party National Convention, the subversive squad complement swelled to more than 500, and an equally large number were recruited for the 1969 SDS convention. In a press interview in June 1969, Illinois State Police Superintendent James T. McGuire reported that more police personnel were on antisubversive assignment than were fighting organized crime. In the Chicago area alone, he said, an army of more than 1,000 men from federal, state, and local agencies were working on undercover assignment. McGuire estimated that over $2 million would be spent in that year alone for intelligence work.[1]

In 1971 the subversive section was renamed the Subversive Activities Unit and charged with a new mission, even broader than its former one: "through covert and overt activity" to gather intelligence on all "organizations and individuals which present a threat to the security of the

---

* Nor was the pursuit of Chicago's dissidents confined to officially assigned or coopted personnel. For example, Wendell O'Neal, a black trust analyst employed by a Chicago bank, discovered a confidential memo dated February 28, 1968, in the documents dealing with the burglary of his apartment: "Mr. Wendell O'Neal is a black extremist and associated with various militant organizations. His home is decorated with Black Militant sayings and pictures of Stokey [*sic*] Carmichael and other Negro Militants. A check at the Intelligence Section (pax 241) shows that he has an extensive file #964-G-Item 30-31-1 (Subversive)." It was signed by Lieutenant Leo T. Crotty, D.D.A. #1 Burglary.

O'Neal was puzzled: what was there in his record that had so disturbed Lieutenant Crotty? He had an All-American boy background, including a progression through all the ranks of scoutdom to the heights of Explorer Scout. His Air Force service record was distinguished, capped by a Good Conduct Medal with cluster. To be sure he had joined the NAACP while stationed in Alaska. But what made him a "subversive" with an "extensive file" was the fact that for a few months he had been a member of a group that had tried to organize tenants in slum buildings and had encouraged a partially successful rent strike. Like other black intellectuals in quest of their heritage, O'Neal had decorated his walls with a zebra skin and spear; hung a portrait of Malcolm X (not "Stokey" Carmichael) in his living room; acquired a few dashikis and some African statuettes. See "The Agony of Wendell O'Neal," *Chicago Journalism Review*, April 1969.

country, state or city" and to investigate and identify the financial supporters, leaders, and members of "organizations or groups" (without limitation of any kind). In addition, the record establishes that the unit was formally concerned not merely with conduct or programs presenting an actual threat to security but with a "potential for disruption." Where surveillance was not warranted for such reasons, a nonpolitical reason was made available: crowd or traffic control. This broad mandate was renewed in 1973.[2]

Nor was the reorganized unit confined to passive data collection. A special dirty tricks program launched in 1974—unique among political police units in this country—blueprinted the "neutralization" of organizational and individual targets by causing them "to cease or change in direction." A principal tactic of this operation was the dissemination of file material for the purpose of doing damage to targets held in disfavor.[3]

Targets and Files

The Chicago Police Department boasted in 1960 that its security unit had accumulated information on some 117,000 "local individuals," 141,000 out-of-town subjects, and 14,000 organizations. In the fall of 1974 the department, through its attorneys, admitted the destruction of Intelligence Division files on some 105,000 individuals and 1,300 organizations. This step was taken after the police learned through an informer that a local group, the Alliance to End Repression (AER), was planning to sue the police for unlawful spying.* In addition, the destruction included files revealing the identities of some 220 informers.[4]

Documents that survived the purge establish that the sweep of organizational and individual surveillance was enormous: approximately 1,000 conventional files dealing with organizations (some 300 opened between 1961 and 1965) and eighteen volumes of confidential files deemed too "sensitive" for routine filing. In addition, "case files" were maintained on groups or individuals who were the subjects of a particularly active, ongoing investigation. Finally, personal files were maintained on some 500 individuals of special intelligence interest. Supplementing the organizational files (documents and reports totaling some 400,000 pages) was an index system summarizing the individual

---

* An informer's report concluded: "Note: it seems this time they are finally ready to proceed with the lawsuit. It would only seem reasonable that any steps that can be taken to prepare for the possible problems ahead should be taken as soon as possible. It may be too late if postponed." Released file document, September 1973.

references contained in the files and designed as a data-retrieval resource.*[5]

The Targeting of Civic Groups and Prominent Citizens

Preparations for monitoring the Democratic Convention of August 1968 (discussed below) triggered an expansion of the red squad, with increased diversity of targets and operational techniques. Prior to the late sixties, the organizational and individual targets of the red squad were typically confined to ideological (the Communist Party, the Socialist Workers' Party, and affiliated organizations), minority, and antiwar groups. The standard evaluative procedure was to link, by ever-lengthening chains of inference, the subjects, organizational and individual, with communism. Despite the fact that this rationale of imputed subversion embraced such improbable targets as the ACLU, NAACP, Rev. Jesse Jackson's People United to Save Humanity (Operation PUSH), the National Lawyers' Guild, and similar groups, the squad's excesses stirred little critical response. A vivid illustration of this classic technique of imputed subversion comes from the file of black alderman A. A. ("Sammy") Rayner. Long under red squad surveillance, his politics were analyzed by the unit in this way:

> Rayner now believes that the black people will arise and a revolution will ensue. He also believes that if the black people do not get their "just due" there will definitely be trouble. Rayner now believes the words of Stokely Carmichael; however many of the statements made by Rayner indicate several things—they may not be his own thoughts, or he may have been instructed to relate them in this manner by persons unknown at this writing; nevertheless he has shifted his position in relation to militancy.

Beginning in the postconvention years—a time of mounting criticism of the Daley machine and the police department—the range of surveil-

---

* A subject's index data consisted of a "face card" with salient identifying data followed by cards with additional entries summarizing activities or affiliations, along with references to the number and page of the organizational file from which the data had been extracted. These cards were essentially inchoate files: multiple index-card entries and the prominence of a subject were in themselves sufficient grounds for the opening of an individual name file. The files and indices were based on informers' reports as well as compilations of documents and reports by officers engaged in overt surveillance.

lance targets, already enormous, was expanded to include scores of civic and citizens' groups, such as Businessmen for the Public Interest, the Lawyers' Committee for Civil Rights under Law, League of Women Voters, American Jewish Congress, World Council of Churches, Kenwood-Oakland Community Organization, Parent-Teacher Association, Save the Children Federation, Community Renewal Society (CRS), and university campuses and churches.[6] Police Superintendent James Rochford defended the surveillance as a legitimate attempt to "keep the peace and protect the public from violence and disorder." The approved targets, he insisted, were either revolutionary, terrorist, or marked by a history of violence and disruption. But the released files establish that this was a pretext for an extraordinary offensive against participants in the mainstream political process—in effect, an enemies' list.*

The files on the CRS are illustrative.[7] An affiliate of the United Church of Christ, the organization was involved in a range of inner-city problems such as slum rehabilitation and assisting neighborhood groups, as well as training ministers and community organizers for such work. Although its methods were entirely peaceful, its objectives laudable, and its directors drawn from among the most prominent civic leaders, it was accused in the intelligence reports of aiming to "secure a political and-or social revolution in the United States" by advocating social changes "detrimental to democratic principles." The report's conclusion makes its political thrust all too clear: "It is known and documented in this report that many of the individuals associated directly or indirectly with the Community Renewal Society have views and goals diametrically opposed to those of the administration of this city." These and similar findings were based on an investigation conducted from October 1969 to February 1970 that produced almost 1,000 pages of reports. In the course of this huge investigation, some 31 police agents were deployed, who reported on 1,669 individuals and organizations, including 235 clergymen and 161 churches.

The investigative techniques were as ludicrous as the report's conclusions; for example, three intelligence officers were assigned to spy on the CRS's annual dinner meeting on December 31, 1969. The leaders and supporters of the group, Chicago-area bankers and businessmen, were intensively investigated, including details of their private lives. The personal life of the CRS executive director, Rev. Donald Benedict, was the subject of a ten-day intensive surveillance by two intelligence

---

* Additional file subjects of this same kind were later recorded (see p. 97 and footnote).

agents. Their report for a sample day records his goings and comings; car and license number; mode of dress ("blue suit, with a white shirt and tie"); when he parked his car and where; when and where he dropped his wife off at her place of employment; the color of his wife's dress; and so on.

In the case of the CRS, as with other priority targets, the Intelligence Division did not neglect more aggressive tactics. A major offensive consisted of fueling two IRS attempts to impose tax sanctions on the group.

Equally revealing is the range of individuals who were surveilled either as primary targets or because of their alleged links with proscribed civic groups. Any individual who attended more than one meeting of an organization was listed as a member. Among those surveilled were Arthur Woods, chairman of Sears, Roebuck and Company; newspaper columnist Mike Royko; Rev. Theodore Hesburg, president of Notre Dame University; Republican State's Attorney Bernard M. Carey; Hampton case prosecutor Barnabas Sears; Dan Walker, author of the controversial Walker Report, critical of the police role in convention-week violence, and later governor; Albert Jenner, a prominent Republican attorney; U.S. Senator Charles Percy; seven sitting or former city aldermen; fifteen members of the Illinois General Assembly (of whom seven were black); John Hoellen, Richard Daley's Republican adversary in the 1975 mayoralty race; Gaylord Freeman, chairman of the First National Bank; Gayle Sayers, former star running back of the Chicago Bears; Rev. Jesse M. Jackson; Terrence Bruner, executive director of the Better Government Association (BGA); Lutrell Palmer, black radio commentator; Kermit Coleman, an ACLU attorney; and Ralph Metcalfe, a black congressman.[8]

These individual files, too, teem with inaccuracies, absurdities, personal gossip, and biased characterizations. One well-known businessman associated with the CRS was accused of having been, when he was nine years old, a leader of a Communist Party branch in a distant city he had never visited! A 49-year-old businessman, head of a paint and home-care chain of stores, is identified as a 20-year-old member of a revolutionary group. It is plain that here, as in the case of the organizational surveillance, the dominant concern was the monitoring and harassment of opponents of the Daley administration and its policies.

The purpose of blackmailing enemies is close to the surface. For example, an insider confided to the columnist Mike Royko that several detectives were assigned to surveil Dan Walker after the issuance of his report. "They wanted to see if they could get something on him that was dirty . . . something out of his personal life that would be used to discredit him. . . . There wasn't a move he made that they didn't know about."[9]

Mayor Richard J. Daley alternately denied (under oath) knowing about red squad surveillance programs, insisting that they had ended, and justifying them as protective, violence-prevention measures. But his denials were contradicted by Police Superintendent James Rochford, who insisted that the mayor had consulted the intelligence reports.[10] Besides, the record shows that Daley's office regularly received, on printed transmittal forms, weekly intelligence summaries prepared by the squad's analytical section, which were also forwarded to high departmental officers.[11] Moreover, the file of George Clements, a Roman Catholic priest, civil rights activist, and chaplain for the Black Panthers, revealed that on May 24, 1968, the mayor's office requested and received intelligence material about him.[12]

The mayor's denial of complicity in the red squad espionage is rendered wholly incredible by disclosures that during the sixties his office was served by a Watergate-style "plumber," John J. Clarke.[13] A long-time city employee, Clarke was on paper a paid consultant to the police department, a cover that gave him unlimited opportunity to roam the radical scene as the mayor's "eyes and ears." In the mid sixties, he developed a unique surveillance operation after he was recruited by the chief judge of the criminal court, Joseph A. Power, a friend and former law partner of the mayor's, who reviewed Clarke's reports and transmitted them to Daley. Among the targets of Clarke's intelligence operation were the Southern Christian Leadership Conference, Students for a Democratic Society, Black Panther Party, and a number of other student and peace groups. In addition to these local targets, Clarke in 1968 conducted a surveillance of the Southern Christian Leadership Conference at its Resurrection City camp in Washington, D.C. In the same year he went to Oakland, California, to spy on a Black Panther Party conference there.

Clarke admitted that his agents infiltrated a group in New York City, sabotaged its plans to organize demonstrations at the 1968 Democratic National Convention in Chicago, and collaborated with police groups in other cities for the same purpose. In addition, he planted spies in the Chicago office of the National Mobilization Committee to End the War in Vietnam (Mobe) who engaged both in the transmittal of information and in dirty tricks designed to discourage attendance and to disrupt meetings. He also directed a network of Chicago agents in an infiltration of the November 15, 1969, Washington Peace March.[14]

An important occupational hazard of the spy master is his inability to resist the temptation to appropriate for his own use funds in his control for the payment of informers. Because such funds are rarely processed through conventional accounting procedures (the informer might be exposed), spy masters not infrequently pocket them. Despite his cover, Clarke was sentenced in federal court to three years in prison in January 1974 after switching his plea to guilty on charges of obstructing justice and filing false income tax returns. Shortly before his conviction, it was revealed that Clarke, in the hope that he could hold off prosecution, offered five police lieutenants in charge of vice-control units bribes to track down information through prostitutes, narcotics addicts, and gamblers that could be used to blackmail U.S. Attorney (now governor) James R. Thompson and his aides.[15]

The Pursuit of the Alliance to End Repression

The Chicago unit was particularly alert to organizations and movements aimed at police abuses. Thus, the eighteen-month infiltration of the Chicago chapter of the National Lawyers' Guild by security squad agent James Kostro (Operation Church) was inspired by rumors that the organization was preparing a lawsuit charging members of the department with brutality. The operation terminated when it became certain that the suit would not be brought.

Another early target of surveillance and open harassment was the Afro-American Patrolmen's League (AAPL), an association of black patrolmen critical of the police. Thick files on the AAPL and its leader, Renault Robinson, established that the group, devoted to combating discrimination both internally and in law enforcement, was the target of a pattern of reprisals that bespeaks a profound racism. Moreover, the evidence is clear that the Daley administration was actively involved in a program to destroy the AAPL and its leadership.[16]

But the most detailed and illuminating account of police reprisal against a critic is documented by its files on the Alliance to End Repression (AER). In May 1971 the AER, a coalition of fifty-one Chicago religious, civic, and community groups with shared concerns about civic issues, especially in the criminal justice field,[17] organized a Surveillance Task Force with a view to exploring the possibility of a lawsuit challenging the constitutionality of the red squad's surveillance-related operation. The squad promptly responded by launching "Operation Watchdog," a project intended both to monitor the task force's activities and, more aggressively, to "neutralize" the project. Two undercover police officers, Geno Addams (confidential informant "C.I. 3549") and David Cushing (confidential informant "C.I. 3538") were assigned to infiltrate the Surveillance Task Force and report their findings immediately.[18]

The informers' reports on the activities of the AER (not confined to the Surveillance Task Force) were summarized in two detailed analytic reports by Cushing. These documents are marked by the already-noted hyperbole characteristic of the unit's evaluative endeavors. The first, submitted at the end of December 1971, is fifty-seven single-spaced pages long (exclusive of seven appendices) and concludes on wildly strained grounds that the AER is a subversive organization.* At the end of the following year, a second analytic summary ("Watchdog"—Phase II) found its way into the files; in this Cushing ventilated his fears that the dangers posed by the AER might well be underestimated.†

The core reasons for the AER's surveillance are not concealed in the Cushing documents:

The AER was "actively involved" in forcing the trial of former State's Attorney Edward V. Hanrahan for the 1969 Black Panther raid and in defeating Hanrahan in the 1972 election.

The group's "greatest strength" was that its leaders "do their homework, know what they are about and have enough law behind them to prove their point."

In addition, "they can and do continually develop issues where they are 'right' and the [police department] powers that be are 'wrong.' People gradually become aware that the Alliance is really fighting for the people."

As it became clear in 1973 that progress was being made in the preparation of a legal challenge, the police agents were ordered "to obtain any and all information regarding the lawsuit against the Red Squad." About a year after the special investigation had begun, a paid civilian confidential informant, Adele Noren ("C.I. 5633"), successfully infiltrated the AER and (along with Cushing) became a member of its steer-

---

* The extraordinarily detailed raw materials reviewed by Cushing include a speech made by the author at an annual dinner at the Chicago Theological Seminary on May 8, 1971, co-sponsored by the AER and the Chicago Committee to Defend the Bill of Rights.
† In recommending "Watchdog"—Phase III, to commence on January 1, 1973, Cushing noted that while the AER could not on the evidence be designated a communist front, it was nevertheless "actively campaigning to disrupt some of our established institutions, particularly our law enforcement agencies."

ing committee.* As part of her work, Noren volunteered to assist the plaintiffs' attorney in the preparation of the suit by interviewing potential plaintiffs concerning their evidence. In carrying out that assignment, she obtained and turned over to the defendants a copy of the interview questionnaire developed by the plaintiffs' attorney. Moreover, she delivered to her control officers the answers received from these questionnaires and turned over copies of the texts of her confidential interviews with five potential plaintiffs, containing the detailed accounts of their allegations and supporting evidence.†

In addition to the questionnaires, the infiltrators gathered intelligence concerning the evidence that was to be used in the lawsuit, the legal strategy, preparations, and litigation schedule.

This clandestine spying by the police department defendants in the lawsuit continued even after the litigation commenced in November 1974 and despite a ban on police spying early in 1975. Adele Noren did not terminate her undercover surveillance of the plaintiffs' legal preparations until the spring of 1975, when she was exposed. Similarly, while the deputy police superintendent for inspectional services, one of the defendants, told undercover police officer David Cushing to withdraw from the AER, he left only after attending a March 11, 1975, alliance meeting, during which the informer Geno Addams was exposed, and after a public exposé on March 20, 1975, by the AER (discussed below) of police officers spying on civic groups.

The information gathered by the security section was used in a variety of attempts to undermine the AER lawsuit, including the destruction of quantities of documents, already described.‡ Similarly, information

---

* Noren attained this post as a representative of the United Methodist Board of Social Concerns, Northern Illinois Conference. The fact that the conference was opposed to political spying made it an ideal cover. Cushing served on the AER steering committee as a delegate of the Southwest Community Organization for Peaceful Equality.

† Red squad files reflect knowledge that the alliance intended "to use this information in a federal suit." Noren's control officers had previously reported that they would "obtain and report information regarding questions members of the Alliance Surveillance Task Force are asking various groups to be used in a later lawsuit against the Security Section."

‡ The judge presiding over the AER lawsuit ruled: "While the destruction of documents here in issue occurred *before* the suit was filed in November, 1974, plaintiffs have convincingly demonstrated that defendants obtained reports that plaintiffs were about to file suit from paid informants who infiltrated plaintiff Alliance to End Repression. . . . Defendants have nowhere stated that document destruction here in issue was in the ordinary course of business nor have they

obtained by Noren from an attorney's letter to his clients setting forth the deadline for adding new parties to the planned suit was relied upon by defendants in support of their responses to the plaintiffs' legal moves.

Not surprisingly, the AER and its co-plaintiffs sought from Judge Alfred Y. Kirkland, the federal district court judge trying their lawsuit, an injunction restraining the red squad from persisting in the surveillance of their legal preparations or using the fruits of prior surveillance. The lawyers for the red squad did not deny the allegations that the AER legal team had been infiltrated, but indignantly resisted the granting of the requested relief, asserting, "We are entitled to present a defense and we intend to present a defense with whatever material we have available to us." The court granted the injunction and on March 1, 1971, a federal court of appeals in Chicago unanimously turned down the police department's appeal. The U.S. Supreme Court subsequently rejected a request by the department for review of the adverse rulings.[19]

In an extraordinary perversion of the judicial process, the department attempted to use pretrial discovery interrogation to compel the individual plaintiffs in the AER lawsuit to answer questions relating to their organizational affiliations, contributions, and political views. In denying this request, Judge Kirkland ruled that the only purpose of seeking such information would be "the completion of files defendants allegedly maintained on these individuals . . . to employ discovery in this suit to further [defendants'] alleged intelligence gathering activities."*

Another tactic in the department's pretrial offensive was a "dirty tricks" campaign. Anonymous letters to AER supporters charged that the group was a Communist Party front; that it had falsely accused innocent people of informing for the red squad; that its general counsel and leading officers were CIA agents; and that the group itself was a CIA offspring, created to discredit the police as a means of controlling their operations. Similar bogus letters called on leftist organizations to demonstrate against the AER. This poison-pen program implemented a red squad project "to negate or nullify sympathetic and political influence, financial and organizational support and the operational activities" of the group.[20] Because of its damaging thrust, the police department

---

shown any written authorization for that destruction." *AER v. Chicago*, 561 F Supp. 537, 542–43 (N.D. Ill.) 1982, memorandum opinion and order on sanctions, November 10, 1976, p. 3.

* The court registered its reluctance "in a suit alleging invasions of privacy to allow defendants to discover the very information they allegedly have been seeking by overt and covert means" ("Rule Court Not Cop-Spy Tool," *Chicago Daily News*, April 1, 1976).

went to great lengths to frustrate a court order requiring the disclosure to the AER of file material relating to its campaign against the organization.[21] More direct was the squad's offensive against John Hill, the AER's executive director, which included open surveillance of his marriage ceremony. Twice before and twice after the lawsuit was brought, the windows of his car were broken, while other cars parked on the same street were untouched.[22]

The effectiveness of the AER in publicizing the documentary material unearthed in its lawsuit, particularly in disclosing on March 20, 1975, the squad's infiltration of civic groups and identifying the infiltrators, resulted in a media storm, which prompted other public-interest groups whose surveillance was uncovered by the AER to file similar actions.

In an effort to contain the mounting criticism of the red squad, Chicago Police Superintendent Rochford, along with a deputy and informers Noren and Cushing and their control officer, Eugene Dorneker, testified before the Senate Internal Security Subcommittee on July 11, 1975, charging that the AER was a "Communist front organization"* plotting the subversion of the squad's valiant efforts to protect the city from violence.[23] The strained charges and inferences, not to speak of factual misstatements both in the hearing testimony and the subcommittee's final report, were coldly received in Chicago. When the hearing transcript and the SISS press release were released on January 13, 1976, both the *Chicago Sun-Times* and the *Chicago Daily News* editorially attacked the testimony as a "smear campaign" and a "rubbish pile." Senator Charles Percy of Illinois noted that "the guilt by association and 'Communist front' allusions contained in the release accompanying the document hearken back to the smear tactics of the 1950's. . . . The dangerous subversive threat to our way of life is not from the Alliance to End Repression, but widespread illegal police surveillance."[†24]

---

* The testimony was given in secret and then made public in January 1976 along with an approving press release by the subcommittee. An equally approving final committee report ("The Erosion of Law Enforcement Intelligence and Its Impact on Public Security") was issued in 1978.

† This was not Percy's first clash with red squad witnesses. In June 1969 two of the squad's commanding officers, Lieutenant William L. Olsen and Sergeant Joseph P. Grubisic, testified in Senate hearings on "Riots, Civil and Criminal Disorders" (Senate Committee on Government Operations, Permanent Subcommittee on Investigations [McClellan Committee] Hearings, 1969: pt. 20, pp. 4434–98). The Illinois senator rebuked Grubisic (at pp. 4478–80) for his charges of subversion either wholly unsupported or based on "guilt by association of the worst type." See "Percy Raps Tactics of Police 'Red Squad,' " *Chicago Daily News*, July 1, 1969.

Rochford's successor, Police Superintendent James O'Grady, had another go at the AER in September 1978 when he testified before the House Intelligence Committee. Although the AER's lawsuit focused entirely on political surveillance, unrelated to law enforcement, the superintendent charged that the lawsuit had rendered the Chicago Police Department "virtually helpless to protect the city from terrorist activity" and "completely frustrated any legitimate intelligence activity."[25] In fact, at the time the charges were made, the CPD's generously funded intelligence division was operating eight intelligence squads, including one specializing in terrorism. The AER lawsuit had resulted in only two curbs on political spying: the restraint already mentioned on surveillance of the plaintiffs' legal team and another forbidding the destruction of evidence.

The police department had good reason to frustrate the lawsuit by stigmatizing the AER. In the course of the litigation, the association's lawyer, Richard Gutman, had received, pursuant to a court order, a payroll list of Intelligence Division personnel. Under the caption "Assignment Unknown," he discovered the name "Howard Pointer," an already identified and self-admitted infiltrator of Rev. Jesse Jackson's PUSH between 1970 and 1974. Ingenious detective work led Gutman to the conclusion that at least three other police officers similarly listed were being transferred out of the informers' ranks in the aftermath of the filing of the AER lawsuit. Two so identified were Marcus Salone, who, beginning in 1972, had served two terms as president of a local community group, the Organization for a Better Austin, and Melvin Barna, the leader for three years of a chapter of a civic group called the Citizens' Action Program, which was apparently targeted because it opposed a cross-town expressway favored by Daley. Similarly, the identity of the AER's Geno Addams as a police officer was confirmed by a documentary analysis, as was that of an infiltrator in the Metropolitan Area Housing Alliance.[26]

The last barrier to the identification of the informers was overcome in March 1976, when the court, in a sweeping ruling in the AER case, ordered that the names of informers that had been deleted in the 21,000 pages of files turned over to the plaintiffs, be restored. While recognizing the need to protect the identities of informers, the judge ruled that such protection ("informer's privilege" in legal usage) did not extend to the surveillance of noncriminal conduct. This landmark ruling rejected the claim, usually made in such cases, that identification would expose the spy to violent reprisals. The court noted that since a gag order prevented the disclosure of the contents of the released files, this contention "lacked credibility."[27]

The Cook County Grand Jury Report

On March 20, 1975, the very day the AER aired its charges in the press, State's Attorney Bernard M. Carey subpoenaed six undercover red squad operatives to appear the following week before a Cook County Grand Jury convened to determine whether the police had violated the law.

On November 10, 1975, the grand jury issued a report, "Improper Police Intelligence Activities," strongly condemning the red squad: "The evidence has clearly shown that the Security Section of the Intelligence Division assaulted the fundamental freedoms of speech, association, press and religion, as well as the constitutional right to privacy."[28] It explained that the cover-up of evidence had deprived the grand jury of sufficient grounds to indict the responsible higher-ups and left only the minor operatives who were carrying out departmental orders. The higher police officials who were most culpable "were insulated from prosecution by level upon level of police officers who invoked their privilege [against self-incrimination] under the Fifth Amendment." The report deplored the efforts of supervisory police officers and the city administration to thwart the investigation by hiring top criminal lawyers at the taxpayers' expense to represent all the police witnesses, by coordinating collective stonewalling, and by the destruction of physical evidence and records.* For example, potentially incriminating records of illegal electronic surveillance prior to 1973 were assertedly destroyed in 1973. But the panel heard considerable testimony from several police witnesses that they were aware that electronic surveillance was used to gather intelligence information.† In addition to illegal electronic surveil-

---

* The department's systematic evasion and resistance of the panel's search for information was indeed ironic; as the grand jury observed, "a primary duty of the Chicago Police Department is to produce evidence for the Cook County Grand Jury."
† In response to grand jury questions about electronic surveillance, illegal entries, and burglaries, former Police Superintendent James B. Conlisk replied that he knew of such practices, knowledge "an uncharitable person could consider improper or even illegal." This response was part of an obstructive pattern that marked Conlisk's grand jury testimony ("Testifies He Knew about Cops Bugs," *Chicago Daily News*, June 3, 1975). Conlisk sought to protect himself and others against a possible future indictment by disseminating, in defiance of a gag order, detailed memoranda to potential witnesses and law-enforcement figures, a virtual transcript of his grand jury testimony, an action State's Attorney Carey called "arrogant and outrageous" ("Open Probe of Conlisk Disclosures," *Chicago Daily News*, June 4, 1975; "Conlisk Bares Spy Probe Replies," *Chicago Sun-Times*, June 4, 1975). Carey denounced as particularly reprehensible a letter accompanying Conlisk's memoranda to the U.S. Army's chief of intelligence that

lance, police officers admittedly engaged in burglaries, thefts, incitements to violence, destruction of mailing lists, and other criminal acts because "they believed it their duty."

The grand jury rejected the justification by police witnesses that surveillance was necessary because of the violent nature of the groups monitored, pointing out that both the record of activities by members of the groups and informants' reports refuted this justification. The grand jury concluded that the dominant motivation for the surveillance was almost uniformly the opposition of the targets to Mayor Daley and the policies of his administration. In the same way, as the grand jury pointed out, "groups which received the most intensive scrutiny had also been openly critical of some policies of the Chicago Police Department."

Police witnesses had also attempted to justify the surveillance of community groups on violence-prevention grounds by pointing to the October 1969 SDS disturbance in Chicago (the "Days of Rage," discussed below). But the report notes that undercover police agents had successfully infiltrated the Weatherman group that had organized the "Days of Rage" and had reported their plans to create a disturbance far in advance of the event. When asked by the grand jury why they did not proceed in advance to prevent the disturbance, the police witnesses replied that "the acts of violence must actually occur before any charges can be brought." But this, as the grand jury observed, "is absurd and totally wrong." In Illinois, as elsewhere, the crime of conspiracy is consummated when an act in furtherance of the agreement is committed. It was ironic, the grand jury observed, that "peaceful groups were spied upon and disrupted for apparently political reasons while a violent group was permitted to carry out their intended plan of violence."* The report con-

---

falsely stated: "I have been instructed by representatives of the present state's attorney to perform duties of a special investigator for the grand jury to seek out records of burglaries, illegal entries and illegal eavesdropping by members of the Chicago Police Department" ("Act against Conlisk in Spy Jury Contempt," *Chicago Tribune*, June 12, 1975).

* The irony was even more piercing. The unit had not intervened with conspiracy charges primarily because it would have involved the exposure of its informers and, in addition, forfeited the opportunity to settle accounts remaining after the convention-week disturbances of the previous year, which had generated widespread criticism of police misconduct. Equally ironic is the contrast between the earlier grand jury's report and the Cook County Grand Jury Report, which returned indictments in December 1969 arising out of the October confrontations between the police and the SDS. After returning a total of sixty-four indictments against the SDS militants and none against the police, the Cook County Grand Jury issued a report on December 19, 1969, urging that the "Communistic" connections of the SDS be widely publicized and denouncing the leniency of

cluded that the police department had nothing to show for its infiltrations and the criminal acts of its agents "except a substantial waste of money and time and a serious intrusion into the constitutional rights of the people of Cook County." Many were surprised at its failure to return an indictment against particular culprits in view of its characterizations, the underlying patterns of illegality that had dominated the unit's operations over the years, and the formal programs of aggression and dirty tricks that the unit had implemented.

Overt and Confrontational Tactics

During the sixties the Chicago police used their powers in highly repressive ways, frequently marked by violence and threats of violence, to disrupt and punish, outside the forms of law, gatherings of all kinds that were perceived as threatening not only to political orthodoxy but to police personal values as well. If by a highly strained reading, the record on this score was ambiguous in the early sixties, it was made overwhelmingly clear by the "police riot" (no other words will do) when an out-of-control force clashed with radical demonstrators at the 1968 Democratic Convention.[29] The history of this mode of police repression in American cities demonstrates that such confrontationist tactics typically are augmented or replaced by surveillance ("intelligence").

Intelligence operations are traditionally divided into overt and covert categories. The former practices were widely used in American cities both because they are a natural extension of conventional peacekeeping and traffic and crowd control procedures and because they are less costly than covert practices such as infiltration and wiretapping. In Chicago both modes were used extensively. We begin with the pretext raid, typically triggered by informers' tips, and designed to serve both confrontational and intelligence ends. An outstanding example of this practice

---

lower courts in handling charges against student radicals. It commended the red squad for its "splendid work," expressed appreciation for its dedication and bravery, and urged other communities "to resort to this effective manner of obtaining information relative to the subject." It also took care more broadly to commend the police, still smarting from the charges of convention-week misconduct. "In contrast to the many other things said about them, the Chicago Police Department conducted themselves in a most exemplary and restrained manner"—praise that wholly ignored, among other things, the brutal mass raid, largely warrantless, on an Evanston church on October 11, 1969 (discussed below). The text of the grand jury report is reprinted in the *Chicago Sun-Times*, December 20, 1969. See also "Havoc in Chicago Called S.D.S. Aim," *New York Times*, December 20, 1969.

was the raid of December 4, 1969, that resulted in the fatal shooting of Fred Hampton and Mark Clark, Panther leaders.* An earlier (April 8, 1967) red squad raid on a fund-raising party for a liberal cause sponsored by a University of Chicago professor, which resulted in an assortment of criminal charges, was ultimately exposed as a prearranged frame-up based on the pretext that minors had been illegally sold alcohol. All the convictions in the case were invalidated in 1970 by the Illinois supreme court.[30] Another technique, an updating of earlier practices, was the thwarting and sabotaging of peace demonstrations—a program in which the red squad played a prominent role.

While raids yielded the maximum punitive return (physical confrontation, arrests, destruction, thefts, and court appearances), they could only be used in limited situations and required warrants. The routine overt practice was the physical monitoring of both indoor and outdoor meetings: identification of individuals through observation; taking down license plate numbers or tailing arriving and departing participants in meetings, rallies, or demonstrations; and, most important, tape recording and photography. While the claimed purpose of such surveillance was peacekeeping and violence-prevention, its basic aim was to sabotage and thwart gatherings. This goal was typically served by denying or frustrating attempts to obtain a license. For example, an attempt by a coalition of Chicago-area groups to organize a peace demonstration on April 27, 1968, was first met by a dilatory and obstructive response at City Hall.† An investigating commission's report condemning the police role in instigating violence and disorder at the April parade and demonstration noted that, "A line of plainclothes officers (including Red Squad detectives) for no apparent reason . . . marched eight abreast at the parade head."[31]

At large gatherings, red squad plainclothesmen usually supplemented uniformed policemen posted to keep order and regulate traffic. But by

* The raid was ordered by State's Attorney Edward Hanrahan, but was executed by Chicago policemen assigned to his office.
† The attempt to obtain legal redress was itself considered suspect. A memo in the police files from Captain Lyons to Deputy Superintendent Mulchrone reads in part: "Reliable information has been received by the intelligence division that the American Civil Liberties Union is planning to file a brief in Federal District Court on Friday, April 19, 1968 seeking an order to allow the April 27th Parade Committee to use the Grant Park Bandstand Shell and the Civic Center Plaza for their activities on April 27, 1968.

"Further information indicates that Clark Kissinger, leader of the April 27, 1968 Parade Committee, will attempt to attract wide publicity to this city's refusal to allow anti-war groups to assemble and parade on the 27th of April."

This form of "intelligence" recurs quite frequently in the files.

the early seventies, efforts at disguise—turtlenecks, sneakers, (well-pressed) jeans, and peace pendants (purchased for $2.95 each at Sears, Roebuck)—themselves proclaimed the identity of the wearer. When the crowd was smaller than anticipated, as was usually the case, the red squad surveillers stood out in ludicrous profusion. For example, at a modest peace rally in October 1970, with no more than two hundred participants, some thirty-four readily identifiable agents were observed monitoring the crowd.

But the squad's big gun was the camera, theoretically employed for identification and file purposes, but in reality—like physical surveillance—a highly efficient instrument of intimidation. Thus, the investigating commission already referred to concluded that the red squad's pervasive photographic activities at the April 1968 demonstration effectively intimidated the participants. Demonstrators who tried to photograph the police, particularly when they were assaulting others, were beaten with special savagery. In addition, cameras were smashed and films were forcibly confiscated and exposed.*

The red squad played a similarly repressive role in an overall city strategy of intimidating participation in a Hiroshima Day demonstration on August 10, 1968.[32] On the day before the scheduled demonstration, the intelligence unit's Captain Thomas J. Lyons transmitted to Deputy Superintendent John Mulchrone a five-page report about the demonstration, which included "a series of photographs, which will be distributed to the Commander of the First Police District, of individuals, who, given the opportunity will undoubtedly attempt to embarrass the city officials and the Chicago Police Department by agitating or inciting others to perpetrate unlawful acts."

To avoid the embarrassment of the April melee, in which photographers identifiable as intelligence officers had dominated the scene, the Intelligence Division was inspired to experiment with the deception that its surveillance photographers were television camera crews. But such deception (I shall return to it later) could only be used at important, newsworthy meetings, press conferences, parades, and rallies and, in any event, was repeatedly exposed by vigilant participants. The department

---

* The importance of photography as a weapon in the unit's intelligence arsenal was amusingly demonstrated during the Chicago conspiracy trial arising out of demonstrations in connection with the 1968 Democratic Convention. By court order, photographers were excluded from the federal court house during the trial in order to safeguard the integrity of the judicial process. But this prohibition unwittingly closed a valuable surveillance channel, and the order was hastily amended to permit intelligence photographers to ply their trade.

then fell back on the insistence that there was nothing illegal in photographing individuals in public for intelligence purposes.

Photographs taken by sophisticated cameras at varying distances from a site were used to pinpoint targets for subsequent illegal searches, verbal abuse, electronic eavesdropping, and press publication to discredit the subject.* But the still camera, focused for close-up shots, remained the chosen instrument for crowd photography. To be sure, cameras slung around necks almost immediately led to the conclusion that police agents were on the scene. But it was precisely this intimidating consequence that was sought. Here as elsewhere intelligence-related discretion was sacrificed to punitive need.

The confrontationist dynamics of crowd surveillance, Chicago-style, are readily distilled from interviews, court records, and press accounts. When the meeting gets under way, the detail fans out through the crowd, usually in teams, taking pictures and recording the speeches. If there is an automobile procession, a number of the squad members, including photographers, will crowd into cars and join it. Sometimes they are challenged: "Aren't you from the red squad? Isn't that why you're taking those pictures? What are you going to do with all those pictures?" Occasionally bona fide participants will join the picture game and photograph the photographers. (This was considered a subversive tactic.) The cop cameraman pretends to be nonchalant: either he stares straight ahead, elaborately ignoring this tit for tat, or he tries to conceal his face, especially if he is taking a picture; or, if he is not, he furtively eyes his opposite number in confusion: "What's that beatnik doing taking my picture? I'm supposed to be taking his." As the police continue

---

* Of many examples of such photographic harassment, one will have to suffice. In 1970 John Kearney, a Chicago civic figure, then executive administrator of Friendship House, directed a summer camp called "Childerly," located in Wheeling, Illinois, and rented the camp to various groups for use in weekend conferences, retreats, and the like. In August 1970 he rented the camp for that weekend to an ad hoc coalition of groups including the Chicago Peace Council, the American Friends Service Committee, and others for the purpose of a conference to study nonviolent ways to end war, racism, and repression. A red squad team set up photographic equipment opposite the camp and photographed all those present at the conference. They also interrogated both the caretaker and the cook connected with the camp about the participants in the conference and its purpose. The agents were accompanied by a *Chicago Tribune* reporter, Ronald Koziol, who wrote a story published September 1, 1970, which stated that "radicals" and "Communists" had used the property for a "secret revolutionary planning session." Despite its patent falsity, this disclosure caused Childerly's board of directors to relieve the administrator of his post, an action that ultimately resulted in the loss of his position as executive administrator of Friendship House.

monitoring the event, the resentment of the targets mounts. They become bolder and sometimes ask their stalkers to leave. The professional cool of the agent evaporates; verbal abuse ("Get movin', you fuckin' creeps!") gives way to arrests and physical harassment.

Police Informers: The Chicago Pattern

Like most red squads in large cities, the Chicago unit made extensive use of undercover agents, both police and civilian. Police informers were drawn from two sources: the first, cadets or other candidates for jobs as police officers who had not been publicly exposed and (an added qualification) whose manner did not proclaim a line policeman's background; the second, veteran policemen who were attracted to the work by reason of ideology and, equally important, occupational benefits. The undercover agent was obviously not required to wear a uniform; in contrast to the cadet recruits, he could influence the choice of targets and was not required to give more than a rough accounting of how he had spent his time or otherwise report on the manner in which he had performed his mission.* Nor did the work require a financial sacrifice: as we shall see, he rapidly converted his targets into sources of income, to replace those he had developed in regular police work. The classic Chicago spy pattern (before it was upgraded in preparation for the 1968 Democratic Convention) is illustrated by the tale of an infiltration network that flourished in 1966 and 1967.[33]

In January 1967 Morton Frankin, a Chicago detective attached to the organized crime section of the Intelligence Division, was forced to end his assignment as an infiltrator of Chicago's gambling rackets when his identity became known to his targets. An experienced sleuth of fifteen years' service on the force, six of them in intelligence, he was reassigned to the security section. But his cover was blown when a peace activist recognized him in the witness chair in December 1967 testifying in a racketeering case. Adopting the name "Martin Frankel," he had a brief, but extraordinary, career as an infiltrator. Frankin, as I shall call him, was instructed at the time of his undercover assignment to infiltrate certain organizations. As he later told it on the witness stand:

> It was left up to me as to which ones I would get into,
> and I was able to infiltrate the Chicago Peace Council

* Newly assigned undercover operatives, especially rookies, were provided with a "Training Bulletin" ("Limited Distribution") designed primarily to prevent exposure—precautions that were frequently ineffective.

and the Latin American Defense Organization [LADO], the Socialist Workers' Party, a more or less senior member of CADRE, Chicago Area Draft Resisters . . . and I had contact with numerous other organizations.[34]

Frankin made his first undercover sortie in the spring of 1967, when he appeared at a meeting called by a loosely organized group with no formal membership requirements, the West Side Organization, to mobilize ghetto support for a planned peace march. When those in attendance were requested to introduce themselves, Frankin said that he was Martin Frankel, a merchant seaman interested in working for peace. He attended several meetings of peace groups in the spring and summer of 1967. These groups welcomed a broadly representative attendance and regarded Frankin with his firsthand experience as a merchant seaman on vessels conveying ammunition to Vietnam (that was his cover story) as a valuable addition to the group.

During Frankin's eleven-month stint with the "radical element," as he put it, he moved from loose ad hoc groups to more cohesive ones. Infiltration targets are selected by two tests: (1) will the problem of security be manageable or are the risks of exposure too great? (2) will entry into the group offer an opportunity to extend the range of surveillance to more promising targets? Frankin's progression shows how he successfully preserved his security in the primary target and then moved into other organizations, seven in all. He chose as his base LADO, a community organization formed after a ghetto riot in 1967 to improve conditions in the ghetto. Frankin decided, ironically enough, that his most authentic cover and passport to other groups was as a specialist in police brutality. His simulated passion about police misconduct and sympathetic response to grievances of ghetto dwellers on this subject led to his attendance, as a LADO representative, at a meeting of the Citizens for a Democratic Society (CDS), held on August 18, 1967, at the Hyde Park Cooperative for the purpose of discussing this issue. At the end of his denunciation of the police, Frankin launched into a peroration to soften up the audience for the fund-raising speech to follow: "If we don't unite now against the police we'll get more of the same. We sailors know how to take care of the cops and the blacks are learning. You just have to beat the shit out of them. You have to meet violence with violence."[35]

Frankin's farewell appearance before his exposure was at a meeting to plan a demonstration, sponsored by CADRE, to be held early in December in opposition to the draft. He unsuccessfully pressed for the adoption of a proposal that as a condition for participation in the demonstration, each adult should be required to sign a statement committing himself to "aiding and abetting" draft resistance, a step that would have constituted a criminal act.

The chairman and moderator of the August 18, 1967, meeting was one John Valkenburg. Indeed, it was Valkenburg who had recommended that Frankin be invited to speak at the meeting as a LADO representative. Like Frankin, Valkenburg was a police agent.[36] Originally a uniformed patrolman, he aspired to a red squad assignment because as he put it, "the subversive activities squad was a very elite unit," as reflected, for example, in the fact that its members worked without uniforms. Perhaps a more compelling inducement was his superpatriotic passion, which embraced as heroes George Wallace, General Douglas MacArthur, and Richard Daley ("He's the greatest mayor in the world. When he's gone the city will probably collapse.") and condemned with a visceral loathing all varieties of political liberalism. Unwilling to wait until his application for a transfer was acted on and eager to demonstrate his qualifications, he began a one-man vigilante countersubversive operation while still a patrolman.[37]

After an initial apprenticeship, Valkenburg infiltrated the CDS, where he was warmly welcomed and promptly elevated to the post of moderator of its meetings and forums. This achievement required no great deception: like almost all of the infiltrated organizations, CDS was informal in structure and without a roster of officers. Its meetings, held in a church, the Hyde Park Co-op, or members' homes, were all open to the public. Valkenburg's prominence in the CDS gave him access to the SDS, of which CDS was an adult version; he attended a national SDS convention and participated in other SDS activities, requiring trips to Indiana, Wisconsin, and Michigan, where he stayed with the SDS leader Tom Hayden. In addition, he surveilled a constellation of Chicago dissident groups, including the Fellowship of Reconciliation, CADRE (of which he became chairman and treasurer and which he claims to have destroyed through disruption and thefts), and the ACLU. The range of his individual targets was extraordinarily ecumenical: he even reported on presidential candidates Eugene McCarthy, George McGovern, and Lester Maddox.

In a sworn deposition in May 1979 in connection with the AER lawsuit, Valkenburg admitted that on at least one occasion he tried to provoke members of the CDS to attack police with guns;* on another he

* Asked by the AER attorney Richard Gutman whether he had advocated attacks on the police, Valkenburg replied: "Well, I advocated the getting on top of

recommended that a demonstration be held during rush hour to paralyze downtown traffic; and on a third participated in a break-in to steal furniture. Also notable is Valkenburg's testimony describing how, assertedly on his own, without authorization by his superiors, he wiretapped the telephones of two professors by blackmailing a telephone company supervisor ("He was a white person, and he had had a black prostitute in the truck with him").*

Even after Valkenburg's spy role became known, he, along with two fellow spies, Michael Randy and Alfred Vallejo, infiltrated the Conference for a New Politics held in Chicago's Palmer House over the Labor Day 1967 weekend.[†] He contributed to the disruption of the conference by charges that Dr. Martin Luther King, Jr., was a communist puppet and that black delegates were being manipulated by the civil rights leader. With the aid of Randy, he stole five hundred tickets to the conference and pocketed the proceeds from their sale. In addition, all three police officers stole electric typewriters (worth an estimated $1,500), which they kept, and Randy made off with two microphones, which he subsequently sold. In his deposition, Valkenburg claimed that the purpose of stealing documents was to discourage membership through fear of exposure and thus to dry up contributions. Similarly, he defended such capers as the pocketing of contributions, the embezzlement of trea-

---

the buildings along Madison St. and shooting at the police officers" (Valkenburg deposition, p. 136; quoted in "Red Squad 'X' Urged: Fight Cops," *Chicago Sun-Times*, May 11, 1979).

* Valkenburg's deposition (see n. 36), pp. 15–20. This noisome explanation of how maverick wiretap operations were accomplished was apparently widespread. Still, it strains credibility: how often could a compromised telephone linesman or supervisor turn up? It may well be that this blackmail claim was devised in advance as a cover to protect both the telephone company and the red squad. In any case, this explanation, whether true or false, has an authentic only-in-Chicago flavor.

[†] Valkenburg claimed that he felt free to function as a spy-disrupter after he was identified as a police agent because the leaders of the victimized groups "were afraid of me . . . they were embarrassed to think that they had been observed with me and close to me and I was eating in their homes and . . . living with them." This explanation appears to have been wholly invented. The leaders who knew of Valkenburg's spy role decided not to make it public on the-devil-you-know grounds: their organizations had nothing to hide, and it was not difficult to protect themselves against his greed for money. Expulsion and publicity would only demoralize members of the group and make it vulnerable to a replacement and unsettling suspicions as to his identity. There was an added double-agent inducement—they traded their silence and a cash sweetener for information about the red squad's undercover activities (Valkenburg deposition, p. 128; "Police Spy Revealed as Double Agent," *Chicago Daily News*, June 6, 1975; interviews with author).

suries, the stealing of stamps and unused expense money, and related forms of self-enrichment as proper aggressive intelligence practices designed to weaken the victimized groups.

Valkenburg served as a control and mentor of Michael Randy, who was assigned as an infiltrator from June 1967 until December 1968. Randy was a familiar enough undercover type—the Jimmy Higgins who makes himself indispensable by hanging around and doing the unpleasant work shunned by others. Among other chores, he laid floors for the Chicago Peace Council and the Fellowship of Reconciliation, became a volunteer office worker for the Conference for a New Politics, and did clerical work for other peace groups and manned their phones—coverage made possible because the offices of all of the target peace groups adjoined one another in a building on West Madison Street. He attended peace meetings with the diligence of a patrolman covering a beat, became (along with his wife) a faithful member of the Communist Party, and hosted meetings in which he and his fellow spies played a dominant role.[38]

When the clouds of suspicion darkened, Randy fell back on an ingenious gambit to avert his exposure. Valkenburg was already burned, so why not arrange to strengthen his cover by denouncing his fellow spy? But the plan fell through and the suspicions intensified. By the beginning of October, Randy was played out. He began to explore the possibility of targets other than the peace movement and seized upon the CDS, where Valkenburg had done so well. But here, too, his efforts failed.

The intensive surveillance of the groups singled out by the subversive squad for infiltration is hard to justify, even in police terms. The Chicago Peace Council, the most heavily infiltrated of all the organizations that claimed the attention of the subversive unit, was an open organization. No attempt was ever made to restrict either its membership or to conceal its program. When the three infiltrators were exposed at the end of 1967, Karl Meyer, the CPC's director, observed: "At our meetings they invariably took the most militant positions, trying to provoke the movement from its non-violent force to the wildest kind of ventures. They had strewn around leftist and Marxist literature in the hope presumably that they could entrap 'subversives.' " Meyer added that the three had participated in the planning of almost every CPC demonstration during the preceding nine months "and were about our most active members." What made the wholesale infiltration totally incomprehensible, Meyer added, was that "our meetings are open and we call the police whenever we are planning a demonstration and tell them where and when it will be held and how many will participate."[39]

The Keystone Kops flavor of the infiltration is distilled in the case of a fourth agent, assigned to penetrate LADO. Obed Lopez, its executive director, announced early in December 1967 that a man who had joined the group under the name of Alfredo Perales was really Alfred Vallejo, a police agent. The police had tried twice to infiltrate LADO in 1966 but the would-be spies were promptly discovered.* In July 1966 in the wake of ghetto riots the previous month, Vallejo became a familiar figure around the LADO office. He tried to bring Spanish-language copies of the *Spartacist*, a far-out Marxist periodical, into the office. "I told him," Lopez later said, "that we didn't have any use for that stuff." In the same vein, Vallejo tried to involve a friend who was active in the Progressive Labor Party in LADO's activities, but he was rebuffed by Lopez, who pointed out that the organization would be handicapped by an association with the far left. In the fall of 1967 a member of another organization told Lopez that he recognized Vallejo as a policeman. A check of his license plate revealed his true name, and a credit check led to the discovery that he had listed his employer as the Chicago Police Department.

The LADO infiltration was a prelude to a more rewarding intelligence gambit. On the night of September 9, 1967, in response to a hint from higher-ups that "it would be nice to disrupt" LADO, Valkenburg and Randy burglarized LADO's offices at 1306 North Western Avenue. There was no need to break in; Vallejo had given them a key. They made off with correspondence, address files, and a list of the names of some three hundred LADO members and supporters—materials pinpointed by Vallejo. Assertedly to make the raid look like a genuine burglary, they also stole two typewriters, a portable and a decrepit Underwood. Two weeks later, after they had been offered a reward of two hundred dollars by their superior, Sergeant Joseph Grubisic, the two police thieves performed a replay of their earlier burglary, this time in the combined offices of the Fellowship of Reconciliation, Women for Peace, and the Chicago Peace Council at 1608 West Madison Street. This time the keys were supplied by Randy, since this was his turf. All three organizations were stripped of their files and correspondence and, again assertedly to make it look like a conventional robbery, mimeograph machines, typewriters, office equipment, supplies, stamps, and money were also stolen. In both cases, Valkenburg spray-painted slogans on the walls and elsewhere designed to promote racial conflict and to suggest that the burglaries were the work of black nationalists or revolutionary whites.

---

* One of the exposed spies, Tom Braham, was an Anglo who spoke Spanish fluently, having gone to school in Venezuela. We shall meet him again.

The two robberies placed the revolutionary desk at police headquarters in a bind: it was one thing to justify violation of the rights of free association and privacy, but quite another to steal property. The police thieves were therefore ordered to return the stolen office equipment, but not the files.* The undercover men sold some of the stolen equipment and delivered the rest of it (a mimeograph machine and two typewriters) at a pick-up spot. Valkenburg called one of the robbery victims and in a crudely mimed black accent (in order to further the "black power" burglary deception) told her where she could retrieve the remaining loot.

Valkenburg delivered the file booty from the two break-ins to his superiors at the red squad's secret Navy Pier office, from which it was transported to headquarters for integration into the unit's file collection. Although the testimony disclosed that high departmental officials (including two police superintendents and a deputy) knew about the burglaries, neither they nor Valkenburg and his accomplices were ever indicted or disciplined. Valkenburg was transferred out of the unit to protect him from publicity and subsequently (in 1975) was encouraged by Police Superintendent Rochford to plead the Fifth Amendment when the burglaries were investigated by the Cook County Grand Jury.

We must not leave Valkenburg and Randy without commenting on the reports filed in the aftermath of the thefts.[40] None of the victimized groups bought the crude, scapegoating provocations planted by the thieves. On September 19, 1967, the head of the Fellowship of Reconciliation and the Chicago Peace Council advised the police by telephone of the robbery, listing the items stolen from the office, including mail, business files, clippings, cash, checkbooks, uncashed checks in the amount of approximately five hundred dollars, seven typewriters, and other equipment. The caller stated that the attempt to blame the Black Power movement was transparently false and suggested that right-wing Minutemen were responsible. The report solemnly records the fact that two officers were dispatched immediately after the break-in, but they "did not succeed in catching the burglars."

All four of the police agents discussed above were veterans transferred from other police units. Indeed, it can be argued that their backgrounds as policemen had led both to their venality and their carelessness in developing a plausible cover. Now consider the case of infiltrator Tom West, who typifies the cadet recruit. While still a student at a junior college, West was given an informer assignment to an

---

* Randy justified the theft of the files as a deterrent to contributions: "People may slow down sending money in for fear that who knows where their name may appear" (*AER v. Chicago*, Randy deposition, pp. 50–51).

old left target, the Young Socialist Alliance, the youth branch of a Trotskyist group, the Socialist Workers' Party. West functioned as an infiltrator in the YSA from December 1967 until he surfaced in December 1969, subsequently testifying (in April 1970) at a congressional committee hearing. Straight in appearance and conventional in manner, he nevertheless survived in his undercover role, primarily because his target put no great strain on his feeble powers of deception. Indeed, YSA members prized the very qualities in him that should have aroused suspicion. As one of his victims put it to me, "West fitted into our group. We thought he was sort of backwards [sic] politically. But we felt it was our job to educate him." West functioned for the most part as an "organization man" and rarely crossed political lines to expose himself to outsiders, who might have found him oddly cast in the role of revolutionary.*

Tooling Up for the Convention

Documents in the files of the intelligence division establish that the city's officialdom seriously believed informers' reports and newspaper accounts that an army of demonstrators planned to invade the city and take over the August 1968 Democratic Convention.† The threats, rang-

---

* To members of the New Left, West exuded "bad vibes," and they were cautious even in casual contacts with him. One young woman active in movement work described in an interview why she suspected West but did nothing about it: "Well, Westy used to wear like these white sweat socks and these funny pants and these funny shoes and shit you know. He was always available whenever you wanted a car to go around like to stick up posters, you know . . . on buildings and stuff and me and this girl went and he had this bright, shiny new car like he was always available anytime you wanted to do anything, you know. 'I'll go with you, I'll help you.' Like we were organizing like crazy, we slept like five hours a night and we went out with him one night and he had this bright, shiny new car outside and I said well, where did you get, is that your car? Immediately I was suspicious. . . . I said, wow, this is a far out car, where did you get this car. . . . And he said oh it's my brother's, I had this old jalopy, it's this year and it's this make and it broke down tonight and I really wanted to go with you all so I asked my brother if I could borrow his car. . . .

"And then he turns on the tape deck, not the radio, the tape deck, which has all these like Glen Miller weirdness you know. Okay, it's his brother's car and he's turning on the tape deck because he wants to listen to this shit and then he starts humming along with it like he knows all the words to all these songs. At which point it was pretty clear what was happening. . . . I just hipped other people in the collective to him, that was all."

† The movement literature boasted that some 100,000 to 200,000 demonstrators would invade the city. But according to the best estimates, no more than 5,000 demonstrators came from out of town.

ing from burning the city down by flooding the sewers with gasoline to dumping LSD in the water supply, were all accepted at face value. Although such threats were disseminated (mainly by Yippies) as a form of "theater," the Daley administration was ready to swallow any absurdity that would justify crushing the demonstrators. And the police department, unwilling or unable to tell whether they were being put on, prepared for the convention demonstrations as though for Armageddon.[41]

The regular intelligence unit was beefed up by coopting officers, detectives, and investigators from the entire force. Investigators on the staff of the state attorney's office were borrowed for the impending showdown with the forces of evil. Liaison was established with federal agencies; arrangements were even made for employees of the Social Security Board of Chicago to suspend their regular duties prior to the convention and to patrol the city in teams assigned to cars on the lookout for troublemakers. All of the arrangements were supervised by a convention planning committee that included representatives of a number of police branches (such as intelligence, patrol, detectives, task force) as well as of state and federal agencies. According to the minutes of the committee, every precautionary detail, from the availability of sufficient numbers of vans for mass arrests and the activation of "canine units" to the selection of the ten major hospitals in the city for the treatment of "injured police personnel," was provided for. The local surveillance network was extended by a nationwide chain of cooperating intelligence units.*[42]

The planned surveillance modes were highly varied, including, separately and in combination, crowd surveillance by perimeter plainclothesmen, electronic eavesdropping, round-the-clock physical surveillance of individuals by "tails," tips from street informants, exchange of information with other units, literature and document analysis, and civilian and police infiltrators. The department also developed a variety of spookish practices, such as disguises, dummy business fronts, and similar deceptions. Line policemen were assigned as delivery van drivers for phantom television repair services and pizza parlors. The entire covert program was orchestrated from the secret office of a dummy corporation, Mid-Continent Import and Export, located on the lakeshore Navy Pier. Media employees, newsmen, and photographers were solicited to cooperate with the subversive unit in exchange for information or to become moonlighters for pay.

---

* Surveillance and infiltration of the demonstrations were independently conducted by the FBI and Naval and Military Intelligence.

A *Chicago Tribune* news story on September 7, 1968, presented revealing evidence of the scope of the undercover operation.[43] According to the *Tribune*, a spy disguised in hippie regalia had penetrated the top councils of the demonstrators and worked in their office, where he managed to discourage prospective visitors from coming to Chicago. Those activists who did come, he assigned to apartments rented by the police and presumably bugged. Information also came from undercover agents in New York and California. In addition, constant police checks were made "at every toll booth on highways between Chicago and New York."

The infiltration of the ranks of the demonstrators was a high priority of the convention intelligence program. The 1969 trial of movement leaders for conspiracy to incite riots (the Chicago 7) illuminates the new role of police informers in the late sixties and early seventies. The three star witnesses for the prosecution—Irwin Bock, William Frapolly, and Robert Pierson—were part of the new specially trained informer network organized in preparation for the convention. Of these three, perhaps the most effective was Irwin Bock, who was planted in the Veterans for Peace in the fall of 1967.[44] Bock used as a cover the claim that he had been sickened by what he had witnessed on active duty in Southeast Asia; in fact, his background was far more prosaic: he had been stationed in the United States for his whole nine-year Navy stint as an instructor of marine fliers in survival techniques in the event they were shot down. During his entire two years as a police informer, he continued to use a prior American Airlines job as a cover, which his fictitious employer helped maintain. For example, whenever he was called at the airline, the caller was told, "Mr. Bock is not in at the moment. Do you care to leave a message?"

Bock rapidly rose from the ranks of the veterans' group to membership on its executive committee and then, because he seemed to have so much free time, to the post of delegate to the Chicago Peace Council, that protective haven for a train of Chicago informers. In July 1969 the council made him one of its delegates to the New Mobilization Committee to End the War in Vietnam ("New Mobe"), and he was promptly coopted to its planning group, the steering committee, a post that brought him into contact with the country's most committed and well known opponents of the Vietnam War.

For all his usefulness, Bock inspired suspicion, an elusive feeling that he was not authentic, based in part on his habitual prying. According to Sholem Leibowitz, one of the officers of the Veterans for Peace, there were many other reasons for suspecting Bock. For one thing, most of the members had a defined politics, were studious types, were largely unmarried, and, if married, childless. Here was "a career Navy man," not "the typical bookish type of person," and "far more conventional than any of us."

Suspicion was also fueled by the fact that Bock would never offer his home for a meeting or attend social gatherings in other members' homes, and by his habit of prying about for membership lists. In any event, these suspicions never outweighed Bock's undeniable usefulness. While he made no contributions to discussions, he "would volunteer for those God-awful jobs . . . stuffing envelopes . . . doing all the legwork . . . errands . . . picking up newspaper bundles . . . had a car . . . and was generally quite co-operative." His methodical manner and efficiency also disarmed suspicion, not to speak of his readiness to sit grimly for hour after boring hour through long meetings. Utterly without humor ("even when he smiled, he looked glum"), he came through in the end as the long-hoped-for convert from middle America. No fuss or feathers, just a solid fellow.

What really tipped the beam in this seesaw alternation between acceptance and suspicion was Bock's extraordinary ability to leave his job and to travel.

In the spring of 1968, Bock's infiltration began to pay dividends as he moved up to the Chicago Peace Council. Here, too, he was strongly suspected—especially by the late Sidney Lens, author and peace activist, whose wife, Shirley, was the council's vice president. The Lenses got to know Bock quite well and "almost from the beginning" thought there was something fishy about him. As Lens put it: "He never had his wife around, didn't bring his family anywhere . . . didn't seem to have any roots in any kind of a political movement in the past and he was never active in anything in the past."

Came a day in the summer of 1969 when Lens asked Bock point-blank whether during the marshals' sessions the previous summer or at any other preconvention gathering he had heard any discussion of violence or seen any preparations for any criminal activity. "Bock said, 'No, very definitely, nothing of that kind.' So I said, 'Are you willing to give us an affidavit to that effect?' " Bock agreed; but before he visited the defendants' lawyer, Leonard Weinglass, to execute the affidavit, he consulted his control officer. Bock not only absolved the defendants of criminal conduct, he explained to Weinglass how his own experience in the jungles of Southeast Asia had brought him to a realization of the horrors of the Vietnam War and even offered to supply corroboration from other marshals of his exculpatory statement. (On the witness stand he was not asked whom he had in mind—other informers or bona fide marshals.)

Bock is about as close as one can get to the model spy: an effective cover, a placid temperament, neither carried away nor tempted into provocation, but still capable of projecting an image of concern and involvement despite his ideological bias and hostility toward the target and conscientious enough to take advantage of opportunities to obtain information beyond the formal limits of his assignment. At the conspiracy trial, most of his testimony elaborated on what he had heard by eavesdropping, including plans for fire-bombings, "wall-to-wall sit-ins," window-breaking in the Chicago Loop, and smashing street lights. But when Attorney Weinglass asked him whether he had ever seen any of the defendants engage in these or similar acts, he admitted that he had not.

If Bock is a textbook example of the passive "straight" spy, William Frapolly and Robert Pierson represent the "freak" types. When Frapolly entered Northeastern Illinois State College (NISC) in 1966 as a psychology major, he was also serving as a part-time police cadet.[45] In February 1968 a red squad officer, Kenneth Carcerano, asked him to attend a NISC Peace Council meeting, and thereafter, under instruction from various squad officers, he altered his appearance, grew a goatee, mustache, sideburns, and long hair, traded his conventional clothing for a hippie-style costume, and, guided by his police controls, attended on a regular basis, first, meetings of SDS and the Student Mobilization Committee, and then, in the summer of 1968, the Chicago Peace Council and the New Mobe. He became a campus leader of the SDS and, in the summer of 1968, was named a marshal for the convention demonstration—along with Irwin Bock and Dwayne Oklepek, an informer who worked for Jack Mabley, a columnist for Chicago Today. In the spring of 1969 he led an SDS sit-in and participated in a Weatherman action that culminated in throwing the college president off the stage, conduct that led to his expulsion.* In a hearing before an appeals committee, he defended himself on the grounds that as a revolutionary, he felt that by such tactics alone could injustice be eliminated. The appeals committee received this plea quite coldly; they not only upheld the suspension punishment but extended it for an additional semester.

After his suspension, Frapolly concentrated on ingratiating himself with the national leadership of the Weatherman faction and actively recruited for it on the campus, in particular for participants in the

---

* The rest of the participants were outsiders.

Weatherman-sponsored "Days of Rage" in the fall of 1969. As a witness at the trial, he conceded that during convention week he had proposed schemes for sabotage of police cars and public facilities.

Like Bock, Frapolly never entirely escaped the suspicion that he was a spy. When he was taxed with his background as a police cadet, he admitted it, but insisted that his "mother made him go but he dropped out." Because NISC is a college with a "straight," largely working-class student body, Frapolly's long hair, goatee, and hippie garb authenticated him. The handful of more adventuresome students at the college belonging to SDS looked to him for guidance and as a link to the national leadership in Chicago. The top SDS leaders in turn assumed that he was the only one on the NISC campus who was really committed to the SDS. He was a beneficiary of the special indulgence extended to the convert, the individual reborn into a faith or cause but still a partial captive of his rejected past. To his victims, male and female, Frapolly's exotic behavior demonstrated his sincerity in trying to overcome his "bourgeois past" and to escape the clutches of a domineering mother who had forced him into the hateful choice of police work. One had to understand and "work with" Frapolly. Then, too, it did no harm that he owned a car: "People were really hard up for cars in the collective so we would like to borrow his car."

Even when there were reasons to suspect him, they were never brought to the surface. Frapolly presents us with yet another instance of the manner in which the most revealing clues to the spy's true identity (here, his police background and his nervousness) are dialectically transformed by his trusting targets into evidence of his authenticity.

Robert Pierson, the last of the three, is a good example of the "freak" informer whose cover is his machismo.[46] More experienced and more self-assured than Frapolly, he was a veteran policeman, having worked in some branch of law enforcement since 1954. He was the son of a retired police lieutenant and the nephew of the police commander, Howard L. Pierson, in charge of the police district where the convention was to be held. Pierson's background, besides the Chicago Police Department, included investigations for the state's attorney's office (a job he held immediately before his undercover assignment), liaison work in counterintelligence, attendance at the Army counterintelligence school at Fort Holabird, Maryland, and a three-year stint as chief of security for a hotel.

When Pierson received his assignment, he was also given a cover apartment on the North Side and an identity as a burly "biker" named Bob ("Big Man") Lavin. Through the intercession of "Sunny," an Amazonian, pistol-packing member of a motorcycle gang, Pierson became the bodyguard of the Yippie leader Jerry Rubin. Shortly before Pierson appeared on the scene, the police warned Rubin that they had learned from intelligence reports that he would be assaulted by a motorcycle gang. This made him highly receptive to the offer of Pierson's services, especially when his friends learned of the warning and insisted that he get a bodyguard.

Pierson's undercover service is probably the shortest on record. After meeting Rubin on August 25, he became his bodyguard on August 26, but his identity was discovered on August 28 in a chance meeting with a member of the Blackstone Rangers, a South Side street gang, who recognized him. He scored his greatest coup when Rubin entrusted him with his personal diary and told him to hold onto it at all costs. Pierson later excused himself to go to a washroom in the park. Instead, he later claimed, he "picked a fight" with a policeman and got himself arrested. While in detention, he turned over the diary to the police. After his release through an attorney obtained by Rubin, he (falsely) told Rubin that he had destroyed the diary when he was arrested rather than to permit it to fall into police hands. On August 31, only three days after Pierson was exposed, the *Chicago Tribune* printed a lurid leaked account of his exploits, including how, in order to gain Rubin's confidence, he threw rocks and bottles and hurled epithets at the police.[47]

Pierson's trial testimony focused primarily on Rubin's shouts of "Kill the pigs." On one occasion, he said, Rubin pointed at the picture of a policeman with a nightstick and exclaimed, "Look at that fat pig. We should isolate one or two pigs and kill them." Pierson not only construed these statements as actual threats of and incitements to physical violence, but relied on them as the principal basis for a complaint against Rubin that resulted in state charges.* At a press conference, Rubin categorically denied ever urging demonstrators to kill policemen and charged that Pierson himself was "the wildest man in the park, all the time talking about attacking pigs, a real agent-provocateur" who had been specifically assigned to frame him on trumped-up charges.

---

* On the night of August 28, the police arrested Rubin and charged him with state law violations: solicitation to commit mob action, disorderly conduct, and resisting arrest. This disorderly conduct charge arose out of the release of a pig in the Chicago Civic Center. The other charges were based on the overheated reports of Pierson and interpretations of entries in Rubin's stolen diary. While the charges against Rubin were still pending, on October 31, 1968, Pierson repeated them in a public hearing of the House Internal Security Committee (vol. 1, p. 2381). Rubin ultimately pleaded guilty to reduced charges and spent sixty-six days in an Illinois jail.

The Civilian Informer Does His Thing

Political police in American cities not infrequently develop an identifiable "MO" (modus operandi), an operational signature that distinguishes them. The Chicago MO is heavy reliance on civilian informers. The extraordinary saturation of the Chicago scene with civilian spies was documented when, in March 1976, a sweeping order by Judge Kirkland forced the CPD to turn over to the plaintiffs in the AER lawsuit some forty thousand pages of documentary records, previously withheld, of police surveillance of noncriminal activities. Rejecting the CPD's pleas of the danger of the exposure of its informer sources, the court ruled that the traditional "informer's privilege" protecting the identities of informers and undercover agents did not extend to the surveillance of targets, individual and organizational, not accused of criminal conduct.[48] The documents released identified some ten police spies and six civilian informers. However, as I have already noted, a list that named an estimated six hundred civilian spies was destroyed before the court ordered its release, and many were identified from internal clues gleaned from the spy reports released under court order, while others were exposed earlier.[49] In addition, an estimated two hundred and fifty civilian spies supplied information only sporadically—they were designated as "OIS" (occasional information source).

It was not uncommon for three or four infiltrators to monitor a single organization, or for police and civilian spies to target the same group and monitor one another.* Like their police counterparts, civilian spies were assigned a "confidential informant" (CI) code number and a control officer, to whom they reported either orally or in writing. Some were paid a fixed monthly stipend or a fee for each meeting reported, while others volunteered their services gratis and were reimbursed for their expenses. The motivations of the civilian recruits varied. They came from three overlapping constituencies. The first were driven by a passionate anticommunism, folkish† or ideological, and not infrequently became spies to implement their hostility to a particular neighborhood or dissident group. Others volunteered because, as police groupies, they relished the role of insiders, privileged participants in a world they ad-

---

* Sometimes rival spies got in each other's hair. Valkenburg, for example, charged that he was being surveilled by an FBI spy and took steps to have him removed.

† A gray-haired informer who identified herself only as "Granny" told reporters, "I am a police spy and I am proud of it. I do police work because, as far as I am concerned, God and country come first" ("Granny Tells Why She Spies," *Chicago Daily News*, June 10, 1978).

mired. A third spy source consisted of aspirants to a coveted job in the department—for which, it was hoped, undercover work would improve their prospects.

Family ties sometimes created a recruiting opportunity, as in the case of Morton Frankin, whom we have already met. Frankin's cousin, Richard Markin, was a graduate student in the social sciences at the University of Chicago. Markin selected as a subject for his Ph.D. thesis a study of "The Value Orientation and Role of the Medical Committee for Human Rights." The MCHR, a group of health professionals at odds with the conservative views of the medical establishment, was considered subversive by the red squad. With his thesis research as a cover, Markin became an MCHR member and used it as a springboard to enter the Chicago Peace Council and its constituent organizations simply by volunteering as MCHR's delegate to the CPC. In short, he followed precisely the same procedure as his cousin, who used LADO as his passport into the CPC.

Markin also infiltrated the Center for Radical Education, a project headed by activists Staughton Lynd and Rennard Davis, which had a high intelligence priority because it provided access to black circles.* If Frankin paved the way for Markin's penetration of certain liberal or radical organizations, Markin returned the favor on a number of occasions. It was Markin who introduced Frankin to Professor Marlene Dixon, a University of Chicago radical social scientist who had been Markin's faculty advisor. Under Markin's tutelage, Frankin developed a new cover: an interest in "socialist theory." (On one occasion he and Markin attended a communist meeting at the home of informer Michael Randy, ostensibly for the purpose of studying Marxism. Of the seven participants, four were red squad agents.) To polish up his Marxism even more brightly, Frankin joined his cousin as a student in Professor Dixon's one-night-a-week class, held in the summer and fall of 1967 as a part of a Free School project at the University of Chicago.

When Frankin was exposed in December 1967, the MCHR concluded that Markin had duped them and declined to continue cooperation with Markin's research, a step that led to his loss of standing as a candidate for a Ph.D. In addition, members of the Social Science Department felt

* The flow of intelligence from the Chicago black ghetto in 1966 and 1967 was extremely thin, a lack the police hoped to remedy by planting white agents in groups that might possibly yield an opportunity to penetrate the ghetto. It was not that the police lacked black patrolmen who might be groomed for undercover work; they simply did not trust the black men on the force. And street informers were an even more unreliable lot.

that his record was unsatisfactory and that his conduct had violated the ethics of social science research.

In December 1968 Markin sought readmission to the graduate program, claiming that Ms. Dixon had discriminated against him because of his political beliefs. Two red squad members called on university officials to vouch for Markin's innocence. While his case was under consideration, the university authorities announced that Dixon's contract would not be renewed. At about the same time, Markin was readmitted to the doctoral program—not, the authorities insisted, because of his charge against Dixon, but because unpromising academic qualifications were considered insufficient grounds for rejecting a doctoral candidate already admitted to the program.

The red squad did not end its pressure with a visit to the university authorities. On the morning of January 31, 1969, alongside a story of the commencement of a student protest sit-in against Professor Dixon's termination, an article entitled "Controversial Prof Taught Revolution Policeman Recalls" appeared in the *Chicago Tribune* under the byline of Ronald Koziol, summarizing "detailed information on Mrs. Dixon's activities . . . contained in previously confidential files of the Chicago Police Department compiled by Mort Frankin." The agent had not only submitted reports but had made tapes of the class lectures and discussions.

Extracting from his "confidential" source what he presumably considered the quintessence of incendiary Bolshevism, Koziol cited such items as:

> Mrs. Dixon denounced the local city government and cited the good in the Chinese and other Communist systems of handling public administration.
>
> Mrs. Dixon said that city officials respect only one thing, the threat of black power groups to burn down the city.
>
> According to Frankin, Mrs. Dixon would give her class lists of Marxist books to read and would end the evening by telling her students to "read and think radical thoughts until the next class."

It is hard to quarrel with the conclusion of the *Chicago Journalism Review*:

> Whatever the reason for the decision to dismiss Ms. Dixon and readmit Markin, it is clear that police spying on the campus has clouded the issues, distorting the

teacher-student relationship, the ethics of social science research and ordinary human decency. If the practice were common enough, free inquiry and serious social thought at universities would suffer.[50]

Another civilian informer worthy of note was David Emerson Gumaer, who served as a red squad undercover agent from October 11, 1965, until September 1967 using the alias David LeMarc. A militant right-winger, he was recruited for undercover work by the red squad's Sergeant Joseph Grubisic, who had met him at a John Birch Society meeting. Impressed by Gumaer's James Bond–like schemes for foiling the Reds through "counterintelligence," Grubisic enlisted him as a spy at the regular rate and became his control officer. While C.I. 162, as he is designated in the files, spied on the Chicago Peace Council and the CDS, his primary assignment was the Chicago-area W. E. B. DuBois Club, a communist youth group. As he intensified his involvement with the encouragement of Grubisic, his reports became more detailed: even the license numbers of cars parked in front of the target's headquarters were included. In his reports on the music played at the group's convention, he wrote, "I believe many young impressionable children are sucked into this atheistic vacuum by communistic folk-rock music and brainwashed into accepting the Party line without being aware of it." "A rough drawing of the office layout of SUBJECT organization [the DuBois Club]" is attached to the June 14, 1966, report of C.I. 162. On July 29 that year, the office was burglarized: membership and mailing lists were stolen, which subsequently emerged in the red squad file on the group.

But Gumaer was eager for madder music and stronger wine. As a volunteer social worker for the Fall 1967 Conference for a New Politics (infiltrated as we have seen by Randy and Valkenburg), he stole substantial quantities of material for the red squad. In addition, he looted office files for his own purposes, selling a list of names to a right-wing purchaser and transmitting correspondence dealing with the Mississippi Freedom Democratic Party to the Senate Internal Security Subcommittee. Grubisic thought he had an exclusive right to his services and fired him because his protégé shared his information with others on the far right. But C.I. 162's experience served him well: he became the John Birch Society's intelligence expert, a contributing editor of *Review of the News*, a Birchite weekly, and a lecturer on intelligence in the right-wing world.[51]

Civilian spies were even recruited by the Chicago red squad for service beyond its legal jurisdiction. Dissident groups in Evanston, Illinois, were monitored in the mid sixties by a red squad informer whose targets included the Democratic Party of Evanston, the Fellowship of Reconciliation, local chapters of national civil liberties groups, the Baha'i religious sect, and peace and civic groups. Her reports included summaries of meetings, lectures, and services; identification of attendees; the license plate numbers of cars parked near homes where meetings were held; and dossiers on activists. The author of these reports, who used the pseudonym "Joan Evans," was an emotionally troubled high school dropout whose red squad service began at the age of sixteen.[52]

As far as the record indicates, the most productive and industrious of the red squad's civilian spies was Sheli Lulkin, exposed in the fall of 1977 in the course of the AER litigation. Lulkin, code designation C.I. 436, infiltrated some eighty-eight organizations in the course of her ten-year career as a spy.[53] A leader in the Chicago Teachers' Union, she served on its executive board, as head of its publicity committee, and as a trustee of its pension fund.

According to associates and targets in the union and antiwar movement, Lulkin was regarded as "articulate," "energetic," and "efficient" and quickly moved into leadership positions in nearly every organization she joined, including the Radical Teachers against the War, Teachers for a Radical Change in Education, Teachers for a Free Society, Women's Strike for Peace, and Vietnam Veterans against the War (VVAW).* She became a close personal friend and almost constant companion of Sylvia Kushner, the Chicago Peace Council's executive director. Elected to the national coordinating committee of an antiwar group, the People's Coalition for Peace and Justice, she helped organize peace demonstrations at the 1972 presidential conventions in Miami.

As the peace movement flagged in the early seventies, Lulkin began to back feminist causes. She was named co-chairperson of the Women's Rights Committee of the American Federation of Teachers and the AFT's delegate to the Chicago Coalition of Labor Union Women (CLUW), and in 1975 she attended the International Women's Year Conference in Mexico City as an AFT delegate.

Lulkin's specialty as an infiltrator was supplying the police with the mailing lists of her targets. Her greatest coup occurred early in her ca-

---

* The ecumenical range of Lulkin's targets even included a meeting on April 20, 1968, of the Midwest Jewish Council in memory of the victims of the Warsaw ghetto massacre. She characterized the council as "pinkish" because "it has always been anti-Israel and anti-Zionist" and does "not recognize the use of the Hebrew language." The principal speaker, Lulkin reported, was Congressman Abner Mikva, who "urged support and understanding for the fight for 'black rights' "; she also identified an attendant who "applauded loudly for the resolution to end the war in Viet Nam" (File 443, May 6, 1969).

reer as a spy. In 1968 Pierre DeVise, her professor in an urban studies course at De Paul University, selected her as a research assistant and recording secretary of the Sparling Commission investigating police abuses, of which he was the executive director. The police file contains accounts of the meetings of the commission as well as reports of private conversations between the executive director and others in his classroom or at the commission's office. It also contains copies of each successive draft of the commission's final report.[54]

Lulkin's reports stressed criticism of the police as well as dissension within the ranks of the commission and served as the primary source for an eight-volume, thousand-page secret document prepared by the police on the work of the commission. Lulkin also spied on DeVise, adding to a police dossier that went back to 1955.* DeVise noted after reading Lulkin's reports about him: "She must have had a very powerful microphone in her purse; she picked up verbatim conversations."

In 1978 Lulkin was honored at a Washington dinner sponsored by the Council against Communist Aggression.[55] At the affair, she announced she was taking a leave of absence from the Chicago school system to obtain a Ph.D. in "Terrorism and Propaganda." "We haven't told the American people the truth about terrorist organizations operating in the United States under the guise of citizens exercising their First Amendment rights." She added that lawsuits such as the one that exposed her cover "have stripped the American people of the protection that they had."†

Patrick Maurice Dailey: His Dreams and Games

Wish-fulfilling dreams or daytime fantasies are staples of human behavior. They help ward off frustration, sustain hope, and mask failure. The literary hack dreams of writing the great American novel, the dauber of turning out a priceless masterpiece, the sandlot's hitless wonder of batting a homerun with the bases loaded and converting defeat

---

* In the police dossier, DeVise was described as "anti-police," having "expressed radical anti-police statements in the past and [been] critical of Mayor Daley in his classroom."

† In September 1985 Lulkin lost her bid for a seat on a Chicago area community panel because of objections to her past role as a spy. A board member who supported her candidacy also admitted that he had served as a "student informant" for the Chicago intelligence unit ("Former 'Spy' Causes Stir at ECC," *Sunday Star* [a Chicago North Side community newspaper], September 15, 1985; "Former Red Squad Spy Loses ECC Board Bid," ibid., September 22, 1985).

into victory in a World Series game. Where the daily reality mocks expectation of reward or anonymity and dull routine thwart a longing for recognition, compensatory fantasies are almost inevitable—not only in individuals but in groups occupationally unified by a shared sense of boredom, loss, and failure.

Because their exalted "mission" to protect internal security contrasts so sharply with the dreary reality of their duties, intelligence personnel in the late sixties, almost as an occupational necessity, fantasized, Walter Mitty–style, about uncovering a subversive plot: in the nick of time they nip it in the bud and seize the plotters (already defined in the police mind by images of bestiality and terror) along with their weapons and explosives.[56] They then testify in a dramatic trial, resulting in long prison sentences, and earn the undying gratitude of the nation, not to speak of promotions, publicity, and awards. The happy ending of an arrest makes the dream complete, but even short of that, the fantasy of radical terror is consoling in itself because it vindicates the premise of threatened revolutionary violence that is, after all, the primary justification for the huge expenditure, the files, the days, months, and years of boring surveillance, the bursting albums of police photographs, the informer networks, and the minatory propaganda. The boy who cries wolf must somehow produce the animal if he is not to forfeit his credibility— and lose a promotion.

Chicago policeman Patrick Maurice Dailey may possibly have been bemused by such dreams of glory when, on street patrol during convention week, he found a notebook in Lincoln Park belonging to a member of a religious collective called Heavenly Blue Lodge (an alternate name for the group in the files is Heavenly Blue Light), which consisted of two couples who lived together. After making appropriate changes in his appearance* and taking another name, he used his notebook find as a cover for ingratiating himself into their group. Eager to set up an arrest, he talked to the four about blowing up department stores in Chicago's Loop, but received no encouraging response. Dailey not only badgered them to produce a bomb recipe but, as he later admitted in court testimony, rented an apartment where the ingredients were stored and combined.[57] The record of the court trial of the four defendants includes these curious revelations excerpted from Dailey's undercover reports:

* In grand jury testimony on this subject taken on October 9, 1968, Dailey said that during this time he "had a growth of beard" and wore beads and "hippie clothing"—"white levis, no socks, moccasins."

> He said, "We will pick up the cotton and the empty bot-
> tles but I don't have any money." So I [Dailey] gave him
> ten dollars. . . .
>
> I [Dailey] picked up two pints of nitric acid and two
> pints of sulphuric acid and about forty or fifty bottle
> stoppers. . . . As they were walking out of the building
> they were arrested. The officers then placed me in cus-
> tody with them.

The arrest of the four alleged plotters and Dailey was carefully
staged. The Daley administration had come under sharp attack as a result of the convention week disorders, characterized by the Walker Report as a "police riot." Dailey's exploit was a made-to-order vindication
of the police and a clear demonstration to the nation that young radicals
were in fact bent on revolutionary violence as the city administration
had insisted all along.

To the red squad and its leaders, the plot and the subsequent arrests
were the dream fulfilled. But the trial judge could not suppress or ignore
Dailey's prominent part in the plot. He sentenced the four to five years'
probation, noting that the defendants were all twenty-two or younger
and that "a police undercover agent had purchased chemicals to be used
in making the bombs and that a police chemist testified the bomb was
neither flammable nor explosive."* On November 15, 1969, Police Superintendent James Conlisk announced that Dailey, in addition to a promotion, would receive the department's commendation award for his
"initiative, courage and dedication to duty."[58] (The operative word may
well have been "initiative.")

The affair served to hone Dailey's antisubversive zeal and set him in
pursuit of a less equivocal version of the dream. Dailey—or "Maurie"
as he was usually called by his radical targets—surfaced to become, for
Chicago's radical community, "Mr. Red Squad,"[59] a front-row occupant
of the Gallery of the Obsessed. By the fall of 1969, Maurie, in his new
open role, was possessed of a pure and shining version of the dream: to
rout the SDS Weatherman members and to expose and capture the so-
called "Weather Underground," a group of SDSers who were either in
flight from criminal charges or who had chosen to go underground as a
protective environment for their extremist politics. Maurie's dream fo-

---

* Attacking the judge for rejecting his recommendation for three-to-five-year
prison sentences, State's Attorney Edward V. Hanrahan told the press, "The
Judge seemed to be more concerned with the age and ineptness of the defendants
than for the safety of society" ("4 Get Probation in Plot to Bomb Department
Stores," *Chicago Sun-Times*, September 10, 1969).

cused on the pursuit and capture of two leading Weather people, Bernadine Dohrn and Mark Rudd. He made a study of both these fugitives
and boasted that he knew more about their habits, their appearance,
their way of walking, talking, and standing than any other person in the
world. He scornfully dismissed the FBI's efforts: "You could line up all
these FBI guys against the wall and have Mark Rudd walk by and they
wouldn't even know what he looked like." Pursuing the fugitives like
Victor Hugo's Javert, Maurie traveled to Washington, D.C., Buffalo,
New York City, and California. Maurie's intensity, his obsessive hunt for
his quarry, personal involvement, and obvious pleasure in his work
make him an almost larger-than-life model of the ambitious, up-front
political detective consumed by the hunt.

By the late sixties and early seventies, the red squad cadres in Chicago and elsewhere moved from passive hostility to aggressive confrontation, and Maurie became a symbol of this new mode. When he was
not tracking leads to the fugitive Weather people, he grimly harassed
other targets in a highly personal way. An initial move in this transition
was calling a participant in a meeting or demonstration or rally, presumably a stranger, by his first name—a way of telling a subject that the
police knew who he was. The subjects, especially veteran activists, responded in kind and identified the detective by name. In many cities this
first name exchange—the "game"—was not uncommon; in Chicago it
became an almost stylized dialogue, all the more frequently engaged in
because surfaced undercover agents were routinely assigned to overt surveillance and were recognized by their betrayed victims. A familiar form
of the "game" was to introduce the agent to the audience, as if observing a social amenity: "Ladies and gentlemen, I want you to meet
[whomever] from the red squad, sitting three rows from the back on the
right-hand side."

A wealth of material, some of it almost legendary, has accumulated
on Maurie's game.* Because red squad surveillance in Chicago was extraordinarily intensive, the subject was made much more aware of the
agent, and vice versa, than in any other city. In face-to-face confrontations, Maurie signaled his subjects that he knew all about them; and
they, in turn, tried to demonstrate a similar familiarity with his movements and background.

The personal encounters between subject and agent that gave rise to
various versions of the game were supplemented by more aggressive tac-

---

* The Yiddish word *shtick*, a prank or sly turn, is perhaps a better description of
Maurie's modus operandi.

tics, such as pretext raids. Red squad raids in which Dailey played a prominent role crested in the fall of 1969, when the unit launched a round-the-clock offensive against the SDS and especially the Weatherman group, in part to arrest law-breakers in hiding and in much greater part to harass movement members and supporters, generally on the pretext that they were harboring fugitives.

Here are two samples of the Dailey raid pattern. The first is by a young movement lawyer:

> There was a time when there were demonstrations that the Red Squad was interested in and arresting people for, and, for example, the opening day of the Chicago Eight conspiracy trial. There was a big demonstration in Chicago and only two people were busted at the scene and the Red Squad spent the next two weeks raiding every movement house in the city and rounding people up. . . .
>
> They would bust through the door. They would just . . . Maurie is real good at names and faces and so he . . . he would look around and see who's at the demonstration, not bust them there because maybe it would cause too much of a scene and then literally, you know, six in the morning, go through the door and clean up the house and take everybody out and bust who he wanted.

Now the recollections of a young woman former member of a Weatherman collective about the "scene" in the fall of 1969 and Maurie's role in it:

> They used to come around a lot. They used to watch us whenever . . . wherever we went, wherever they knew we went—they knew from our phones. They watched us at demonstrations. . . . And they came to our apartment a couple of times also. Well, there were several apartments and they came to each several times.
>
> And they came to the back door which had a big glass window in it and held a warrant—this was Maurie Dailey—held a warrant up to the back door, up to the window, and then busted through the glass and then busted the frame of the door and busted a lock on the door and busted in and pulled guns on us. And there were about . . . oh, there were a lot of them. There were about eight of them and they made us all, you know, put our hands up and stuff. . . .

> And then they would come back and after they'd got-
> ten good and drunk with no warrants. None of this was
> very legal but we weren't in any kind of a position to
> question their legality, you know. . . . So they would
> come without a warrant and . . . with guns drawn. And
> they would bust into an apartment and pull their guns
> on everyone.
> They came to one apartment and this girl was sleep-
> ing on the couch and they made her take her socks and
> shoes off and tickled her feet and said, "Police brutal-
> ity." And this one guy got an asthma attack and
> they . . . they took him and opened the window and
> hung him out of the window by his ankles. It was like a
> third floor apartment . . . until he stopped coughing and
> then pulled him back in. And . . . you see, the thing
> was, everything that they were doing was completely il-
> legal, you know.

Arrest on a trumped-up charge was a favorite game. The most common arrest pretexts were for using or possessing marijuana, traffic violations, and on the basis of claims that the subject was a criminal
fugitive. To be sure, agents in other cities used claimed law violations to
harass subjects. But in Chicago it was not only that the arrests were
selective and politically motivated; they were typically launched with
the agent's full knowledge that the asserted reason for the arrest was
fabricated. And the purpose was not to obtain a conviction (the charges
were almost invariably dismissed; sometimes the charging officer didn't
even appear in court) but simply to burden the suspect with the trouble
and inconvenience of making a court appearance.

Maurie and other red squad members played a special version of the
game with women subjects that consisted of sexual taunts, frequently
couched in vile language. These gibes formed a pattern: "propositions"
to engage in sexual relations, suggestions that the subject is insatiably
promiscuous ("Who did you fuck last night?") or, conversely, totally
lacking in sexuality. Maurie's sex-baiting proclivities are reflected in this
excerpt from an interview with one of his subjects (Courtney Esposito):

> The one I absolutely know the best is Maurie, the one
> that I've had the most personal contact with. In October
> [1969], there was a raid on a church in Evanston that we
> were all staying at and I was one of the people that they
> had a warrant for. . . . But they were like looking over
> everybody in the church after they had raided it and I

was sitting down on a chair with another woman and another man and Maurie was there just getting his kicks and fooling around. And he made all these sexual allusions and, you know, all the other cops sit around and laughed and giggled and thought it was cute. You know, he said, "Don't worry, you'll get bailed out because there are at least five men out there who are waiting to bail you out and raising money 'cause they all want to sleep with you tonight."

He has this thing about liberated women, that he hates them a lot. Like, I don't think he hates anyone more than he hates Bernadine [Dohrn]. But he can't decide whether they're men or they're women, you know, because he has no models in his whole life to compare them to. So he . . . he would switch that night between talking to me for about half an hour about my sexuality in all kinds of perverse ways and he would say things like that when I went to the bathroom I didn't have to take my pants down because I was his . . . I was going to the bathroom like a man. Then he would say that I could sit on a fireplug if I wanted to because all of my orifices were so enlarged from, you know, making it with all these men and stuff. I mean, he was obviously hung up about something, you know, and he couldn't decide what it was. He said to me and the other woman, he said, "You know, you two both smell, just like Bernadine" and he was hateful, you know. He hates Bernadine. He wants nothing more in the world than to be the person who is in charge of catching her.

The flamboyant cowboy style of surveillance used in the war against the SDS gave way in the seventies to nonviolent but nevertheless highly intimidating tactics. The game became a means of release, an outlet for the political sleuth's hostility. One of the targets put it this way: "Their general purpose remains harassment but they enjoy themselves very much. They have fun when they do it." Another subject: "They've never tried to do it in a subtle way, you know. When they follow you in your car, they're right behind you. They wave, you know."

The Postconvention Red Squad

Despite the widespread criticism of police misconduct during the 1968 Democratic Convention, by the end of the sixties the intelligence unit intensified its harassment and intimidation of public demonstrations and protest activities and, as already noted, expanded its surveillance coverage of all shades of dissidents. The unit's complement was increased* and, in order to maintain a low profile, many intelligence operatives were switched to other sections of the Bureau of Inspectional Services and undercover infiltrators were also rotated out into new assignments. With the increasing emergence of civic and neighborhood groups, the police surveillance network was extended to cover this new front.[60] Even marches of welfare recipients were swelled by red squad detectives and undercover agents.

At the June 1969 SDS conference, special security arrangements were made to bar potential spies as well as members of the commercial press.[61] The unit's detectives were forced to make their surveillance headquarters in a room on the third floor of a school building across the street.[62] Supplementary physical surveillance and photography were conducted by other agents scattered throughout the area. In answer to protests by civil libertarians against plainclothesmen who took hundreds of pictures of those entering, leaving, and passing the entrance to the Chicago Coliseum annex where the SDS convention took place, Frank Sullivan, public relations director of the Chicago Police Department, said: "This is America. People can take pictures without fear of harassment. Every American has the right to write down license plate numbers if he wants."[63]

In mid October, at 2:30 A.M., a party of seventy-five plainclothesmen (including twenty-six members of the red squad and twenty-five Evanston policemen) led by the red squad's Lieutenant William Olsen conducted a massive raid on the Covenant Methodist Church in Evanston, where approximately three hundred members of the SDS were being housed for a period of four days. Shortly before the raid, a Chicago Police Department undercover agent had been exposed in another church and had received a severe beating at the hands of several members of the SDS. The reprisal raid netted forty-four arrests: four on previously executed warrants and the remainder without warrants on various charges brought on the spot by three undercover agents.[64] In addition, a number of the raiders administered brutal beatings to some of the SDS

---

* Both the local antisubversive unit and State Attorney Hanrahan's undercover apparatus were enlarged. Hanrahan boasted that his contacts with informers in "street gangs and subversive and militant organizations" were better than ever (*FRED: The Socialist Press Service*, May 26, 1969).

members.* Most of the charges brought by the police were later dismissed, a common outcome of red squad charges.

The unit continued its heavy pressure on the Chicago peace movement and the SDS. The agents outnumberd the SDS supporters at a rally protesting ROTC in the fall of 1970. Even the friendly and protective *Tribune* raised a mildly disapproving eyebrow, noting that "there were almost as many, if not more police than demonstrators. Most of them were members of the Red Squad dressed in civilian clothes, but they were easily identified because they all seemed to dress alike. . . . the police weaved in and out of the crowd, snapping photos with their Instamatics, trying to pick up snatches of conversation on tape recorders, writing down names."[65]

The red squad's writ ran to all the Chicago campuses. While members of the squad sometimes posed as students or dropouts, long-term informers were recruited to infiltrate campus groups and to spy on professors as well. Nor were youthful high school activists immune from the squad's surveillance. According to reliable accounts, not only were protest activities monitored, but guidance counselors cooperated with intelligence detectives in supplying data on student activities and identifying activists.[†]

---

* The raid became known as the "vengeance raid" because of the brutality of the raiding party. According to an intelligence operative, "When one of the police officers went up to an individual who was sleeping and told him to stand up, if that individual did not stand up immediately, he was hit with a night-stick. There were several who, as a result of that raid, had to receive hospital care."

† Early in 1970 two members of the Intelligence Division encountered a high school student, Mort Schaffner, at a convention of young radicals. After a while, Schaffner recalled in an interview, they said, " 'By the way, Mort,'—I had never told them my name—'how are you doing in school?' And when they started asking questions like this, I started not answering, and they looked at each other and they looked at me, and then one of them said, 'Say, I hear you've been getting into some trouble, something to do with home room,' and then they mentioned something else. And again, I paid no attention, and they said, 'Mort, on Monday, you're going to be suspended for four days.' And then, after a while, they came down with the specific reason for why I was going to be suspended and what teachers had sent in referrals on me for behavior. There were two referrals, and two different teachers sent them, and they told me their names and what the referrals were about and again said that on Monday I'd be suspended for four days.

"Monday I was still at the convention, but I returned to school on Tuesday, and when I went to the hall office to sign in and get an admit for classes, I was called into the hall principal's office, and I was in fact suspended for four days for the reasons they had given, the referrals that they had said had been written by two teachers were in fact written by those two teachers, and for the reasons they had said."

In 1970 the Chicago Black Panthers became a high-priority red squad target when they stepped up earlier criticism of the police. Agents hounded the Panthers on a round-the-clock basis and detained them on invented charges. In the summer of that year, they regularly stationed themselves in unmarked cars around apartments occupied by Panthers, took photos at front and rear entrances, flashed searchlights in windows, and even ascended in helicopters for overhead surveillance.[66]

The repressive practices of the unit led to the growing involvement of lawyers on behalf of harassed clients, a development that inspired reprisals against the lawyers. When, in the fall of 1970, members of the Hull House legal aid clinic complained of photographic harassment by red squad operatives, the unit's chief, Thomas J. Lyons, replied that his men often photographed subjects without explicit instructions and offered the stock justification that anyone in a public place was a legitimate subject of photography. Similarly, lawyers for blacks, dissenters, and the poor were routinely monitored and their clients harassed. In one instance, an activist lawyer, Ronald J. Clark, was confronted on the street by two red squad members who informed him that he was under surveillance, offered him a cash bribe (which they displayed) for information about one of his clients, and warned that if he refused to cooperate the surveillance would continue. Subsequently, Dailey maintained surveillance outside his law office. During the same period (1968 and 1969), the parents of William Willet, who had retained Attorney Dennis Cunningham, were questioned by police agents about Cunningham and urged that their son drop Cunningham as his lawyer because he was a "known subversive."

Members of the Chicago People's Law Office (a group of lawyers specializing in political cases) and their clients discovered that they were under constant heavy surveillance; the evidence is quite clear that mail addressed to the People's Law Office was monitored and its phone tapped. Here is an account excerpted from an interview with a member of the group:

> My attention was drawn repeatedly to the presence of unmarked vehicles parked conspicuously in the vicinity of the law office. Whether the vehicles were different on the two occasions, the occupants were the same two men identified to me as members of the Chicago Police Department, dressed in plainclothes. On each occasion, the men lurked in the vicinity for at least fifteen minutes. During that period of time, the principal business consisted of gesticulating and smirking belligerently at all those passers-by who had business at the law office. And

> this goes on all the time and we're not the people who
> suffer the worst from it. Clients are the people who suf-
> fer from it, who visit us, and after they leave, they will
> be stopped. Their cars will be searched occasionally. And,
> you know, it happens to people who have business with
> other places in the city, particularly movement offices.[67]

Nor did the squad neglect the ideological front. In the seventies, two documents emerged in the course of the AER litigation that may well be called countersubversive classics. One, by David Cushing, the unit's resident theoretician, is an appendix to a report on the AER (see p. 98) that sets forth the thesis that the neutralization and conquest of the police is the prime goal of a communist conspiracy manifested in the sixties riots, baseless charges of police brutality, deception of youth and the clergy to protest claimed police misconduct, the movement for civilian review boards and community relations programs, and the persistence of the courts in undermining law enforcement—the frontline protection against the mounting threat of communism.

For even higher ideological flights, we must turn to the Intelligence Division's training bulletin summarizing a lecture series on "Classic Patterns of Subversion." The bulletin deals with forty-five "current Communist goals"—some already almost completely achieved and others "in progress." In the former category we find the "use of technical decisions to weaken basic American institutions" by reliance on claimed civil rights violations; fomented student riots to protest the "programs or organizations which are under Communist attack"; the elimination of obscenity laws, cultural standards of morality, and prayer in the schools. In the "in progress" listing we find discrediting and eventually dismantling the FBI; infiltrating and controlling labor unions; discrediting the family by encouraging promiscuity and divorce; portraying homosexuality as "normal, natural and healthy"; "eliminat[ing] all good sculpture from parks and buildings [and] substitut[ing] shapeless, awkward and meaningless forms" as part of a larger campaign "to promote ugliness"; and gaining control of positions in the media and thus infiltrating the press. But the Chicago police could hardly complain of press subversion.

The Red Squad and the Media

The squad's enormous file collection was highly useful as a means of discrediting particular targets. The files were selectively leaked to rightist allies: a neighborhood committee opposed to integration, a rightwing group campaigning against an investigation of the police, a principal seeking the ouster of a radical teacher. Similarly, the unit's files were extensively used to protect the Daley administration and to discredit the Walker Report's condemnation of police misconduct during convention week.

But the most important outlet for file material was the press: its disclosures could do the most damage over the widest area—especially since the material could be presented (as it usually was) as prizes wrested from confidential, secret sources by the extraordinary daring or influence of the reporter. This collaboration was used in the early sixties to discredit antidiscrimination activists. For example, in 1963 when the Chicago school system and its superintendent, Benjamin A. Willis, were under attack by the Congress of Racial Equality, the red squad released the dossiers of about a dozen CORE members to the *Chicago American* to document its claims that the anti-Willis movement was subversively inspired.

Both the *Chicago Tribune* and its offspring *Chicago Today* "cooperated" with the unit in a familiar trade-off by which reporters, in exchange for favorable press coverage, received information about targets or activities in disfavor with the red squad.[68] In some cases press people were even more cooperative: they supplied information or photographs to the intelligence unit and even took the witness stand to buttress a case against a subject by establishing his identity, his presence at a meeting, or the content of his utterances. Others worked as moonlighters for the police for a fixed stipend or sold their wares at piece rates. A prosecution witness in the Chicago conspiracy trial, Dwayne Oklepek, infiltrated preconvention protest circles on behalf of Jack Mabley, reporter for *Chicago Today.*[69]

The undisputed dean of red squad collaborators was the *Tribune's* Ronald Koziol. By the late sixties, Koziol became an integral part of the intelligence system, used not merely to create a favorable image of the red squad's operations, but to discredit its targets, including those critical of the police or in disfavor with the Daley administration.[70] When the police came under attack because of their convention-week brutality, the Daley administration's response included sharing of the intelligence unit's files with Koziol. In the same way, Koziol relied on the squad's files as the basis for his disclosure of an alleged SDS "secret plan" to disrupt the Nixon administration's inaugural.*

---

* Kolziol's story did not improve on the accuracy of the original report in the files. The so-called secret plan had been abandoned many months before the convention, and information to that effect had been circulated over the wire services.

Another link between the intelligence unit and the press was the practice by unit detectives of posing as reporters and photographers. Illustrative is an incident that occurred on March 5, 1971, at a black student rally. Joel Havemann, a journalist specializing in education, and Jack Dyking, a photographer for the Chicago Sun-Times, assigned to the affair, were told by students from whom they sought information that they had already talked to a Sun-Times reporter. Subsequently, Havemann observed the imposter with a two-way radio conferring with other plainclothesmen. The editorial director of the Sun-Times complained to the police, and after an investigation Deputy Police Superintendent James Rochford admitted that the suspect was John Philbin, a young Vietnam veteran assigned to the subversive unit. According to Rochford, Philbin had violated departmental regulations and had been admonished by his superior, Lieutenant Robert D. Osmondson, that "he was in no way to pose as any type of news correspondent." Despite these grave words, police impersonation of newsmen and especially television cameramen was fairly common, to the despair of bona fide news gatherers.[71] Philbin's lapse was not the impersonation but getting caught.

The most important function of the Chicago press was the implementation of the red squad's neutralization programs. As we have seen, the press was frequently used as an outlet for damaging file material against individual targets. But it played an indispensable role in the planned disruption of organizations. One example is illustrative—the destruction of a Puerto Rican community group, the Spanish Action Committee of Chicago (SACC), in collaboration with a Chicago Tribune reporter, Robert Wiedrich.[72] In 1966 a squad infiltrator, Tom Braham, promoted defections from the SACC by planting charges that the group was being taken over by subversives. Pursuant to the plan, the defectors were persuaded by Braham to set up a new organization. To launch the new group, Braham introduced them to his partner, James J. Zarnow (as his close friend James H. Baron, an expert in the field of public relations). Zarnow took over the organizational problems and the writing and dissemination of press releases announcing the resignations and the formation of a new group and attacking the SACC and its leader, Juan Diaz. To ensure the success of the plot, Wiedrich was recruited to interview the chief defectors.* A red squad agent, pretending that he did not know

* According to the files, Braham and Zarnow reported: "On 31 August 1966, the investigators assigned contacted Mr. Bob Weidrich [sic] of the Chicago Tribune who expressed great interest and offered to help by working with us and

Wiedrich, monitored the interviews and coached the defectors to give the right answers. The file further discloses that the squad supplied Wiedrich with ten questions they wanted him to be sure to ask. Wiedrich's highly prejudicial stories, which appeared in the September 3 and 4, 1966, issues of the *Chicago Tribune*, fully reflected the red squad's view of the SACC, including "background" material from the unit's files. The articles produced the desired result: in the words of one of the group's officers, "Juan Diaz resigned, and then everyone else ran away. It broke the organization into pieces. They broke everyone in pieces." In June 1980 the SACC joined the AER lawsuit and sought $400,000 in damages (see pp. 354–55).

It is not only that a section of the Chicago press became an indentured retainer to the city's political police. Critics of the unit and its practices turned up in its files as subversives—a self-justifying practice that dates back to the twenties. When the Chicago newsman Ron Dorfman was summoned in March 1970 to appear before the Illinois Crime Investigating Commission, ostensibly in connection with its probe of the SDS, "I was confronted with a five-page single-spaced summary of my political activities over the years, including such minutiae as my 1961 sponsorship of a leaflet attacking General Edwin Walker, when that fanatic spoke at McCormick Place."[73] When *Chicago Daily News* reporter Larry Green criticized the behavior of the Chicago police, the red squad struck back by physical attack.

The aggressive quality of the squad's response to media criticism is well illustrated by the case of a National Educational Television (NET) camera crew. In September 1971 four cameramen and Marc N. Weiss, a photo-journalist, came to Chicago to prepare a segment of a documentary television film on surveillance for NET's Channel 13. The camera crew and Weiss rented an apartment and became well known to the squad members, whom they filmed and interviewed on a number of surveillance assignments.[74] After a few weeks, the five film makers rented an apartment across the street from the People's Law Office, which was under constant heavy surveillance.

---

using the story to expose S.A.C.C. . . . Investigator T. Braham composed a series of ten questions to be used by Weidrich [sic] during the press interview. A copy was given to Ted Ramirez, a member of the American Spanish Speaking People's Association, who was chosen to be their spokesman. Later that evening, the above investigator, pretending to be unknown to the newspaper man, was present to guide Ramirez in order to get the fullest impact for the press and to give courage and confidence to Ramirez who fears physical reprisal from Juan Diaz."

Dailey, in his customary taunting style, made no attempt to hide what he was doing. He slowly drove by the crew's quarters night after night in a Chevrolet Biscayne (the model used by the squad). On Friday, October 1, when Dailey drove by, two crew members equipped with a camera and a radio microphone rushed out to film. Both cameramen were taken into custody despite the fact that they showed their press credentials and identified themselves as NET employees. As they were being escorted to the police car, Weiss arrived; his knapsack, containing a tape recorder, was searched on the street at gunpoint and despite his protests, he, too, was detained.

After prolonged detention, the two cameramen were booked. In the words of one of them:

> They brought us up to the desk, and they started filling out forms, and I [again] asked, "What's the charge?" And he looked at me, and he said, "Suspicion of burglary." And I just looked at him, and I didn't say anything. Then, after a pause of 30 seconds, I said, "Suspicion of what?" And he said, "We saw you walking out of an apartment carrying a camera. Therefore, we're charging you with burglarizing that apartment."

Soon afterward all three were released.* On arriving home, they discovered that in the two-hour period of detention on the charge of burglarizing their own apartment, the place had been thoroughly searched. The lawyer for the group, who had been alerted to the arrests,† tried to enter the apartment and was told, "This house is being secured for a burglary."

Whether as a result of the "burglary" investigation or in some other fashion, the red squad discovered the store that had supplied the camera crew's equipment. Officer Irwin Bock appeared at the store. In the words of an employee:

> He had left a card with just his name and telephone number with the instructions that if we should hear from the NET crew again, if they were going to come to Chicago to do some more filming, that we should call this number and they would not answer that it was the

---

* A fourth person, a friend of one of the cameramen who had been left behind to guard the house, was also arrested and released after two hours.
† The arrestees had been forbidden to make a telephone call, obviously to prevent interference with the search. But one of them managed "to smuggle a dime out to somebody who was standing in the hall, and he made a call for us."

police department but it is, and to tell when the crew is coming and what equipment they were going to get but not to let the crew know that the Chicago Police Department was checking up on them.

The Chicago police, through Frank Sullivan, its director of news affairs, denied that the red squad was involved in the affair at all. The police also professed not to have been told that the cameramen worked for NET. But this fact, and indeed, the whole episode, is recorded on tape (which the author has heard). Sullivan also insisted that "at no time did intelligence division investigators enter the apartment." What is corroborated by eyewitnesses and by the physical evidence of slips of paper accidentally left behind is that several police officers entered and took possession of the apartment and examined the papers and notebooks of the four occupants.* The responsibility of the police (including Dailey) for the illegal conduct was confirmed in May 1974 when a federal judge awarded $4,000 in damages to Weiss and his two fellow plaintiffs.[75]

The Intelligence Network: Public Sector

To an extent not duplicated in any other city, the Chicago subversive activities unit worked closely with other intelligence agencies, both state and federal. According to a CIA memo, it was "the official policy of the Chicago Police to accept any training of a possible beneficial nature from any agency." The liaison with the FBI was close and ongoing. Not only was there an exchange of intelligence data, but FBI personnel conducted briefings on the goals and tactics of the radicals in the Chicago area. Moreover, federal involvement—as the Cook County Grand Jury report concluded—is reflected in the fact that "as much as $779,000 in federal

---

* Apparently this encounter stirred the squad's curiosity. The camera crew that had worked on the television program, a small group of film makers known as the Pacific Street Film Collective, had made a film about the New York City red squad. Early in 1973 the film was shown at the Whitney Museum and among its viewers was none other than Sergeant Grubisic. Shortly after Grubisic's visit, the collective received a note from James J. Zarnow of Suite 802, 1121 South State Street, Chicago, Illinois 60605, reading in part: "A friend of mine who just returned from the East told me he viewed a film of four documentaries relative to "Red Squad" type investigations by the police and F.B.I. A group of friends and myself who are actively engaged in local civic affairs and betterment would like very much to be able to view these films if it is possible. Please let me know if they can be made available either through loan or rental." Suite 802, 1121 South State Street, is one of the offices assigned to the red squad at the Chicago police headquarters building, and Zarnow is the red squad's "Dr. James Baron," whom we have met as a member of the SACC neutralization team.

funds was given to the Chicago Police Department Intelligence Division between 1972 and 1974."[76]

Similarly, close liaison was maintained in the late sixties and early seventies with the U.S. Army Region I, 113th Military Intelligence Group, then headquartered in Evanston, Illinois. In an interview, John O'Brien, a former Army intelligence agent assigned to the Evanston unit, recalled that he personally maintained liaison with the squad on both operational and command levels. Not only were intelligence reports routinely exchanged,[77] but

> In some instances we were allowed to take part in the interrogation of individuals who had been arrested by the Chicago Police Department and one of the biggest activities in which we were involved was the exchange of photographs and an attempt to identify those individuals singled out in the photographs to be of interest.*

The relationship between the Army and the Chicago red squad was not merely passive. One example of operational cooperation was the policing of antiwar activities on the campus of Northwestern University in Evanston, where the Military Intelligence group was headquartered.† In preparation for the 1969 Evanston raid, the red squad requested the Army intelligence office in Evanston to make arrangements with the Evanston Police Department for a joint operation. The raiding party also included two Army intelligence officers, and among those arrested was an informer for Army intelligence.‡

---

* According to O'Brien, the *Chicago Tribune* reporter Ronald Koziol was also used by Army intelligence as an outlet for information that could not be officially released. On one occasion "privileged information was leaked to Koziol" and as a result "there was a considerable flap within military intelligence circles as to how this information found its way to the press. . . . Koziol was advised that in the future that he should clear publication of any information . . . before taking it upon himself to publish it. . . . However, Koziol was contacted on a regular basis by the special operations officer . . . and did receive privileged information concerning army intelligence matters." And see "The Press and the Spies," *Chicago Journalism Review*, April 1972.

† In addition to overt surveillance, the Chicago police, according to O'Brien, planted an informer on the campus: "Up to March of 1970—from June of 1969, when I arrived—this one particular undercover agent was operational at that time. I don't know when his period of operation began. The individual was a Chicago police cadet and he was quite active at the University of Illinois-Chicago circle campus and quite active in new left activities—the anti-war activities here at Northwestern University."

‡ As O'Brien explained, both intelligence units were anxious to include the undercover spies in the arrests for two reasons: to remove them to a safe place and also to strengthen their cover. Later that morning when the others were

Official documents released under the Freedom of Information Act (FOIA), the report of the Rockefeller Commission's probe of CIA domestic activities, and files obtained pursuant to pretrial discovery in the AER case establish that the Chicago intelligence unit also worked closely with the CIA.[78] In December 1967, the CIA sent two of its agents to Chicago to evaluate the squad's intelligence-gathering and file-maintenance procedures and to make recommendations for their improvement. The team participated briefly in red squad field operations and made recommendations for improved "filing, collation and the assessment of intelligence information." Released file material also establishes that the CIA obtained data collected by the Chicago Police Department concerning protest groups and activities, in addition to conducting its own surveillance program, all in violation of its charter.

Close ties were also maintained with the House Internal Security Committee (HISC) and its predecessor, the House Un-American Activities Committee (HUAC). Red squad agents were used instead of federal marshals to serve the committees' Chicago area subpoenas, a modest form of baksheesh. In addition, the two units exchanged intelligence data and conducted joint surveillance operations against the SDS and other targets.

The Intelligence Network: Private Sector

Of the many ways in which urban intelligence conceals and cosmeticizes its basic thrust and bias, probably the most important is the claim that its operations are rigidly even-handed and that it is concerned just as much with internal security threats from the right as from the left. However, in practice even a restrained, low-profile intelligence system typically focuses on the left as the main target, by reason of both its ingrained political assumptions and the cultural bias of its cadres. And when, as in the case of Chicago, police intelligence moves from passive surveillance to punitive activism, the logic of this process inevitably forces a progression from benign neglect of the right to open alliance with it.* In our time, the heightened infusion of politics with culture and morals—from long hair and race relations to abortion and capital

---

arraigned, the spies for both units were kept in the custody of the police. They were subsequently taken to a motel, where they were debriefed and instructed to return to the SDS contingent.
* The intelligence coverage of right-wing, extremist groups in most cities was confined (as in Chicago) to the compilation of press clippings.

punishment—has enormously tightened the bond between the police and the ultra-right.

At least since the post–World War I days of the Chicago-based American Vigilant Federation, Chicago's political police have maintained important ties with the city's ever-blooming far-right groups. Beginning in the mid sixties, a secret tie was gradually formed between various parts of the Chicago law-enforcement structure—especially the red squad—and a group known as the Legion of Justice.[79] The legion's history and background are closely linked to that of its principal spokesman, a prominent Chicago divorce and corporation lawyer, the late S. Thomas Sutton. Once a liberal and a charter member of the United World Federalists, Sutton in 1966 helped organize homeowner groups in opposition to the open-housing demands of Martin Luther King, Jr., and his supporters. In 1968 he ran for the Republican gubernatorial nomination with the support of his enthusiastic white suburban ethnic constituency. He lost badly, but his campaign organization, plus some conservative Young Americans for Freedom (YAF) college students, became the nucleus of the Legion of Justice, which he took credit for naming. The Chicago operation blossomed, and in a little over a year, the legion claimed five or six units, each with forty to sixty members, in the city, and four in the suburbs of equal size, as well as affiliates in Ohio, Indiana, and Wisconsin.

A pattern soon clearly emerged from the legion's Chicago activities: burglaries, bugging, harassment, threats, disruption of meetings, and similar tactics, much of it criminal in nature. Court records, the Cook County Grand Jury report, interviews with victims, and the disclosures of defectors establish that in 1969 and 1970 the legion, in collusion with the red squad, engaged in a series of terrorist-style raids against left-wing groups.* In some cases, the targets, especially of break-ins to obtain files, were suggested by Chicago police. ("In a way it was funny. The burglaries would be reported to the Chicago police. Then a few days later, we'd be giving the police copies of records we had taken in the burglaries.") The collaboration between the red squad and the police department explains why it was that the legion burglarized left-wing offices with impunity during the time when they were being heavily surveilled by the security section, that the unit's detectives failed to

---

* "Seizure of Tapes, Files Told," *Chicago Daily News*, April 8, 1975. Two former Legion of Justice members, Stephen Sedlacko and Thomas K. Stewart, testified under oath that the red squad's Sergeant Joseph Grubisic and two of his aides, James Nolan and James Fitzgibbons, acted as their accomplices in the legion's attacks.

come to the aid of victims of legion violence even when they witnessed it, and that no serious effort was made to monitor the legion despite its lawless conduct.

The legion also maintained liaison with the police in De Kalb and other northern Illinois cities. The Army's Evanston-based 113th Military Intelligence Group contributed financially to the support of the legion and supplied it with tear gas, mace, and electronic surveillance equipment. Both the red squad and the 113th MIG shared the fruits of its file raids.

The legion's Chicago operation apparently began in July 1969 with the burglary of the office of Newsreel, a film collective. Three Chicago police cars were parked outside the group's offices when the break-in took place. No arrests were made, although one of the victims chased the escaping burglars while the police looked on. The loot—films and documents—was turned over to Army Intelligence. This was followed by an incident in February 1970 when, in the presence of the police, legion members assaulted a participant in a Young Workers' Liberation League meeting in a Chicago hotel and then threatened the victim with arrest. In March a peace rally was disrupted and the invaders burned the hand of Norman Roth, one of the organizers. When regular squad cars were called to the scene, the red squad officers helped the legion members flee and later arrested Roth.

An elaborate campaign of legion-police harassment targeted the Young Socialist Alliance, a youth arm of the Socialist Workers' Party. On November 1, 1969, the YSA bookstore-office was raided by a group of eight legionnaires.[80] After macing one YSA member and clubbing another, the raiders made off with books, files, records, tapes, and a cash box. At a press conference shortly thereafter, Sutton proudly displayed the stolen material "liberated," as he put it, by the legion. Richard Hill, Chicago organizer for the SWP, identified the stolen material and demanded that the police who were present arrest Sutton and two legionnaires whom he identified as members of the raiding party. The police conversed with Sutton on an amiable first-name basis and refused to arrest him.* Two days after the conference, Hill swore out a warrant

---

* One of Sutton's more devoted supporters was the red squad detective James Fitzgibbons, who covered Sutton's November press conference for the Chicago police. When Sutton finally appeared in court to answer the stolen property charge, Fitzgibbons was at his side; they even approached the bench together. In response to a protest, Fitzgibbons explained that he was off duty and present only as "an interested citizen." He was permitted to remain. ("Legion of Justice: No Law Protects Traitors," *Chicago Journalism Review*, May 1970.) According to

against Sutton for "unauthorized possession of property," a charge later dismissed on the ground that the prosecution had failed to show that Sutton had intended to keep the property, a resolve that was made quite clear from the videotape of the conference, which the prosecution refused to subpoena.

On the same day as the press conference, November 13, a legion supporter, Greg Schultz, attempted to gain entry to the YSA-SWP office, but was barred when he was recognized. Although he left without incident, he claimed that he had been forcefully excluded, and two leftists who had barred his entry were arrested on November 30 on charges of "illegal restraint" as well as assault and battery. On December 6, 1969, two days after the raid on the Black Panthers that killed Fred Hampton, a detail of thirty police, some with guns drawn, entered the YSA-SWP headquarters after several "anonymous" tips that a shoot-out was in progress. When the police learned that the tips were bogus, they nevertheless proceeded with a detailed search of the office. In the meantime, phone messages were received at YSA-SWP offices all over the country, from a caller posing as Hill, to the effect that the Chicago "office has been tommy-gunned. People are lying on the floor bleeding and unconscious and pleading for help." These false calls were clearly part of a collusive arrangement between the police and the legion, the source of the calls, to provoke armed protective measures, thus justifying a raid in the style of the earlier attack on the Panthers.

The campaign against the group intensified with another raid in December by men wearing ski masks and armed with mace, bats, and tire irons on a student apartment at the Northern Illinois University campus at De Kalb. The occupants of the apartment, which was also a bookshop, were maced and beaten, one of them so severely that he was hospitalized. The legion's responsibility was undisputed.* But the De Kalb police ignored the legion and, instead, quizzed the victims about their politics, blamed the raid on black militants, confiscated books and literature, and tried to get the students evicted.

The passivity of the police in the face of the legion members' violence was extraordinary. Early in 1970, a legion assault force harassed a con-

---

the testimony of Stewart and Sedlacko, already referred to (see p. 146), Fitzgibbons supplied tear gas bombs for the legion's arsenal.

* A few months later a young legionnaire bragged at a *Pro America* forum, "We went to De Kalb and closed down a liberal bookstore by beating all hippies and niggers in there."

ference of the Young Workers' Liberation League at the Sherman House and assaulted one of the conferees. The police, who had themselves infiltrated the conference, not only refused to act against the assailants but threatened to arrest the victim. A short time later, a smoke bomb was hurled into an apartment with a legion card attached but the police refused even to investigate.

A major legion concentration in collusion with the intelligence unit was the defense lawyers' office in the case of the Chicago 7, the antiwar activists tried in 1969 and 1970 for conspiring to incite a riot at the 1968 Democratic Convention. The legion stole records from the defense office, planted a bug in the office of the American Friends Service Committee (Quakers),* which, for security purposes, was sometimes used for defense planning, and invaded a Catholic church in Cicero suspected by military intelligence officers of being a secret repository of legal defense files. (In the course of this break-in, an armed robbery was committed in which about $1,000 in cash and four watches were stolen.) Red squad members checked out in advance whether the church had a burglar alarm system and reported their findings to the legion's break-in team.

Both the Army and the red squad played a role in legion gas-bomb attacks that disrupted performances of Russian ballet and Chinese acrobatic troupes in 1970 and 1971. Army Intelligence agents furnished the grenades to the Chicago unit, which it in turn passed to the legion through an intermediary, a right-wing businessman.

The legion also engaged in spookish dirty tricks. Beginning in July 1972, an organization calling itself the "Chicago Land Committee to Expose Police Spies, Informants and Provocators [*sic*]" mailed to eighteen groups and the alternative press (all long-standing red squad targets) bogus charges that certain named area leftists were either CIA agents or collaborators with countersubversive agencies such as the House Internal Security Committee. "Our evidence," the recipients were assured, "in the nature of statements, tapes and photos will be delivered to the Alli-

---

* The record indicates that the offices of the Independent Voters of Illinois were also bugged by the legion, one of a number of targets "suggested" by red squad members who regularly met with legionnaires in a motorcycle shop owned by a right-winger, which served as a clearing house for red squad "suggestions" and the transmittal of files, films, and tape recordings obtained through bugs and raids. For wiretapping, the division used direct ("don't get caught") assignments to its cadres or, as in the case of Valkenburg, assertedly permitted them to blackmail linemen caught in "compromising situations" ("Seizures of Tapes, Files Told," *Chicago Daily News*, April 8, 1975, and "Link Phone Linemen to Cop Spying," *Chicago Daily News*, April 14, 1975).

ance to End Repression, the Peace Council [sic] and other groups at the proper time." From August to September communiqués were issued repeating the charges, promising proof, and alleging that proof had already been submitted to the AER. It became plain that the entire operation was a right-wing stunt.*

Private surveillance and filing and dossier operations, less flamboyant than the legion's but with access to red squad files, abounded in Chicago. Some of them originated with ad hoc committees formed in the sixties to resist racial integration. Along with the *Tribune* and *Chicago Today*, they served as conduits for the subversive unit's dossiers. The congressional committees were also channels for the release of smear data. For example, in August 1970, two leaders of a conservative community group, the Lincoln Park Conservation Association, took the witness stand in a specially rigged SISS meeting (arranged after a long correspondence) to denounce as subversive a neighborhood coalition of liberals and minority groups. Together they presented the fruit of this "research," gathered with admitted help from the red squad's files (see pp. 93–95). Their main target was the North Side Cooperative Ministry, an association of twenty-six area churches. They claimed that the ministry had sponsored a long list of alleged subversive and revolutionary organizations. Red squad files were used to support the claims of revolutionary disruptions and "outside agitation."[81] The ministry categorically denied the charges.

A more modest vigilante-style surveillance unit was Rollen S. Church's self-described "band of patriotic spies" on the campus of Northern Illinois University at De Kalb. Church (a former Green Beret) collected campus intelligence on students and professors he considered "leftists" or "radicals," as well as on drug sellers and users, which he then transmitted to law-enforcement authorities in the area. Church and his patriotic spies are squarely in the tradition of World War I delators

---

* The Chicago Land Committee's charges were broadcast by Sherman Skolnick, the operator of an exposé service, "Hotline News," specializing in dredging up weird secret conspiracies linked by creepy by-plots, "tie-ins," and "pass throughs." A master of Hofstadter's paranoid style, Skolnick enjoyed a fervent local constituency in the early seventies. See Ron Dorfman, "The Sky Is Falling," *Chicago Journalism Review*, November 1972; "Don't Read This Unless You're Paranoid," *Village Voice*, June 7, 1973; "Watergate Murders?" *Los Angeles Free Press*, April 27–May 7, 1973; "How Jet Carrying Mrs. Hunt Crashed," *Washington Post*, June 3–4, 1973; and Skolnick's "Hotline News" article "Chicago 7—Are They for Real?" an "exposé" charging that the convention-week disturbances were a CIA plot organized by its agents, Tom Hayden and Rennard Davis, published by Skolnick's "Citizens' Committee to Clean Up the Courts."

who remained in the spy business after the war and of former Army officers bitten by the intelligence bug. His organization, the Vietnam Veterans' Association, was chartered in April 1970 with Sutton's help and with avowedly counterintelligence aims. He recruited a secret corps of undercover agents, mostly NIU students, to gather information about groups and individuals considered "a detriment to society." The data collected by his network was collated in dossiers, including the subject's photograph, telephone number, details of personal background, a description, and even the serial number of his or her car—information initially drawn from red squad files. In return, the red squad was supplied with the fruits of the group's surveillance.

Indeed, all of the organizations that served as outlets for the red squad's files themselves became sources of information, both to supplement the files and to open new ones. In at least one case, reports and photographs by a spy for the International Telephone and Telegraph Company (ITT) dealing with the movement in opposition to the Chilean junta, turned up in the Chicago unit's intelligence files.[82] In March 1975, a month after the ITT documents were placed in the files, the court in the AER case ordered the impoundment of the red squad files in the wake of the already-described disclosures of widespread surveillance of civic groups.[83]

Official Vigilantism: Chicago-style

The record indisputably establishes that Chicago's red squad for at least a decade engaged in a campaign of guerrilla warfare against substantial sectors of the city's population. What unifies and explains the operation of the security section is an institutionalized aggression, unique in the annals of any American city.

Its operational techniques were flamboyantly illegal and in many instances criminal. What is to be said in justification of a unit in a law-enforcement structure whose members engaged in burglaries, thefts of property and money, blackmail, warrantless wiretaps, pretext raids, illegal arrests, provocations, and a train of related crimes? Sworn testimony proves that red squad leaders (especially Sergeant Joseph Grubisic) repeatedly urged attacks on leftist groups by Legion of Justice hit men, who were given an intelligence division number to call in the event they encountered difficulties, and that Grubisic usually answered the phone and handled their problems.

The record makes it plain that law enforcement was replaced by intimidation, physical confrontation, and punitive self-help. Consider the case of Robert Oxley.[84] In January 1975 a group of demonstrators against police brutality attacked the police in a melee that resulted in the hospitalization of eight officers, including a policewoman. In mid October assault indictments against the protesters (seven in all) were dropped after the judge was told that Robert Oxley, one of the defendants accused of attacking a police sergeant with a board in the incident that had triggered the melee, was in fact a paid undercover police agent. The prosecutor angrily denounced Oxley's "outrageous action." In requesting that the charges be dropped, he told the court that the defendants "may have been outraged by the actions of the agent provocateur."

It would be wrong to suppose that we are dealing with a small clique of rogue officers, a few rotten apples in an otherwise sound barrel. When the 1967–68 infiltration-burglary pattern became known to the higher-ups in the department, its response was to protect the culprits. Similarly, the superintendent of police orchestrated a "closed ranks" silence to frustrate the grand jury. And when the grand jury failed to return an indictment, Superintendent James Rochford actually hailed it as a vindication of the police.[85]

The grand jury did, however, transmit to Superintendent Rochford a list of thirteen officers who had acted "far beyond their authority," in the hope that disciplinary action would be taken as "a deterrent to others." Instead, they were shielded and even commended for their silence through Fifth Amendment pleas. Moreover, it was not merely the department that was complicit. As we have seen, the mayor's office not only knew about the unit's shenanigans, but used it and its own surveillance resources to hound dissidents for smear and blackmail purposes.

As we shall see, in the seventies when the hard rain of exposure began falling on the police departments of American cities, many countersubversive operations were cut back or eliminated altogether. But in Chicago, the pressure of litigation, widespread public criticism, and a hemorrhage of press revelations merely sent the department to Washington in the quest for allies in congressional countersubversive committees to help in its rehabilitation.[86] In some cities, campaigns by civic groups based on disclosures of indefensible practices led to the passage of local ordinances banning or curbing political spying. But legislative attempts to curb such police spying in Chicago by means of a state statute were twice defeated—once by the House after the March 1975 revelations of the infiltration of civic groups and again in 1977 by a Senate committee. Similarly, a proposed city ordinance against political surveillance was sunk without a trace.[87] In all three cases Daley's Democratic machine lined up solidly and strenuously lobbied against the proposals. But we are not through yet. In December 1980 a proposed settlement of the federal litigation against the FBI and the city in the federal court suits discussed above was judicially approved, but final settlement of the charges against the Chicago police was blocked despite the fact that it, too, had been accepted by the department (after two years of negotiations) and approved by the court. The proposed settlement agreement prohibiting unwarranted surveillance by Chicago police was rejected at the last minute by Mayor Jane M. Byrne, who not only defended the record of the surveillance unit, but insisted on retaining carte blanche surveillance power to investigate political and civic targets without the restraint of requiring "reasonable suspicion" of law-breaking as an investigative trigger. How, complained the city attorney, could the police become "reasonably suspicious" without a preliminary investigation to determine whether such suspicion were warranted?* As a result of this claim to a roving commission, the police department remained free for a time to resume business at the old stand until curbed by a court of last resort. But in March 1981 the mayor retreated, and the city subsequently consented to a restrictive settlement agreement, including a court injunction (see p. 353).

For many it seemed that the police department had played its last card, and that risk of drastic penalties alone would ensure public compliance with the restraints imposed by the court's decree. But Richard Gutman, lead counsel in the AER case, was not so sure. In an interview in early 1982 he said:

---

* On January 3, 1981, the Chicago Police Department, in a document filed in federal court, admitted that the red squad had kept files for surveillance-related purposes on seventy-seven civic, religious, antiwar, civil rights, and political organizations, ranging from the Chicago Parent-Teacher Association to an assortment of church groups, raising to at least eight hundred the total number of such files. (Some files, such as those labeled "Miscellaneous," "Anti-pollution," and "Anti-police," recorded more than one target entry.) Moreover, individual dossiers were recorded in thousands of files and on tens of thousands of index cards. At the same time, the department insisted that it had "not committed any politically-motivated spying or harassment, neither before nor since 1975," and that the Chicago red squad engaged in great part in "appropriate police activities" and was "responsible for combatting criminal activities." *AER v. Chicago,* defendant's pretrial statement, December 24, 1980, par. 7, p. 6; par. 21, p. 13; par. 43, p. 20. The inconsistencies between the two submissions, though hardly inscrutable, seem to have eluded the city's attorney. ("Police Spied on 800 Groups," *Chicago Sun-Times,* January 4, 1981; "Police Need Right to Spy, City Contends," ibid., January 6, 1981; "PTA, 76 Others Listed as Targets of 'Red Squad,' " *Chicago Daily News,* January 6, 1981; "Why Defend the Red Squad?" *Chicago Tribune,* January 2, 1981.)

History teaches that the intensity of political surveillance is not constant. It ebbs and flows. When the political establishment feels its power or policies threatened, political surveillance will resume. That resumption may be marked by a court-ordered revision of our injunction based upon "changed circumstances" or by a resurgence of political intelligence activity by a government entity other than the Chicago city government, such as the county sheriff's office. . . . But resume it will.

Subsequent developments would appear to confirm this view (see pp. 353–58).

5 The New York City Intelligence Unit

The Tarnished Badge of Professionalism

In contrast to the Chicago unit's wide-open, Dodge City style, its scorn for the law it was supposed to uphold, a claim to professionalism dominates the self-image of the New York City red squad (BOSS, as it has commonly been called, an acronym for its formal title, the Bureau of Special Services). In the sixties, its spokesmen toured the country as "proselytizers for the cult of intelligence" and promoted periodic seminars on intelligence practice for police representatives both here and abroad. Within the department, the squad's agents bore a distinction akin to that of Green Berets; the department's press releases touted them as "the finest of the finest," as "total professionals" whose achievements were "the greatest story ever untold."

The unit's high standing in the national intelligence community was in part functional: in its heyday it transmitted to outside agencies three times as much intelligence information as it used in its own operations in New York City. Its more experienced operatives traveled to distant points to observe New York City–based targets and to exchange information with agents of other urban agencies.

The uninterrupted growth of the New York City unit reflects the fact that the city of New York is the center of a rich diversity of political movements, the site of the headquarters of the Communist Party, of the largest black community in the United States (Harlem), and of the United Nations and its delegations. A heavy concentration of leftists, liberals, ultra-rightists, aliens, militant trade unionists, and black dissident groups has, over the years, fueled intensive surveillance of a broad range of targets. Finally, the unit enjoyed an extraordinary autonomy during the sixties and was more independent in its functioning than other major urban police intelligence units.

BOSS: Recruitment, Training Operations, and Files

BOSS's headquarters was, as in Chicago, for a long time housed in a separate building, far removed from other police structures in order to avoid the normal flow of press and public. BOSS Captain George G. Gallagher, who organized the infiltration of the Communist Party in the 1940s, operated out of a midtown office fronting as an advertising agency. From this location, he organized and ran two antisubversive undercover details, Special Squads Nos. 1 and 2. In the sixties and seventies, BOSS was headquartered in a five-story warehouse building in lower Manhattan, but it also made use of several operational offices that it maintained in various public buildings throughout the city. By then, BOSS was headed by a deputy inspector who reported directly to the first deputy commissioner, reflecting BOSS's importance as well as its insulation from the rest of the police department.

The working force of field personnel was made up of approximately one hundred detectives, about equally divided among three ranks. The detectives performed the daily labors of BOSS, such as monitoring meetings and demonstrations, processing photos, servicing electronic equipment, and guarding dignitaries. The police department maintained a computerized record of the skills and achievements of every member of the force, which was used by BOSS to preselect choice recruits. Some candidates were recruited to fill a special need—if for a particular assignment the unit required an agent who was Spanish-speaking, under twenty-five years of age, and raised in Puerto Rico with some medical training, the department computer would produce a list of candidates so qualified.

New BOSS agents generally came from the other elite units of the force, such as the Tactical Patrol Force (TPF), whose members were usually selected for their special skills and dedication. A plainclothes detective who had been cited for outstanding achievement was likely to find favor with BOSS recruiters. Once recruited, the rookie was required to study a special instructional booklet that outlined every aspect of BOSS's functions. After digesting this written material, the new member was paired with a more experienced agent who guided him through his first several months. During this early period the recruit attended classes on the theory and practice of intelligence work, consulting a BOSS library of published and unpublished intelligence literature—including a text, "American Communism," edited by Captain Gallagher. Thereafter the new operative engaged primarily in on-the-job training, sometimes with a partner.

But the refinements of recruitment and training were dispensed with in implementing the most critical BOSS activity, undercover surveillance. This was the field responsibility of a corps of untrained recruits (discussed below) whose number is unknown and varied widely at different times. These spies were not listed as BOSS operatives on any official roster or salary chart. Nor could they be identified in budgetary sources. They did not even appear on any official record as members of the police force, and their ranks were secretly augmented as the need arose. For example, during the period of the "long, hot summers" beginning in the mid sixties, BOSS organized a special undercover unit as an antiriot safeguard. This was reassembled every summer thereafter by one of the BOSS lieutenants, who recruited more than fifty men from the rest of the department to serve primarily as temporary spies in the ghetto.

Equally secret was the budget of this unit. Indeed, it was as carefully guarded as the budget of the CIA. But no one can dispute that BOSS was an expensive operation. According to a 1974 estimate, it spent well over a million dollars in salaries alone for its overt assigned employees.

During the sixties, the unit launched a yearly average of one thousand intensive political investigations of dissident groups and individuals and about six hundred lesser probes. A cascade of information about an extraordinary range of targets,* based primarily on the official organs of target groups, press clippings, interviews, voluntary submissions, and informers' reports was sifted and boiled down into two daily reports to be read by the four highest-ranking members of the department. The unit did not confine itself to the passive transmission of facts; it "evaluated" the facts to enhance its own importance and to increase dependence on its services.

---

* These included apolitical groups such as Mensa, as well as right-wing, liberal, left, and far-left groups. Among the targets were CORE, NAACP, ACLU, SDS, Yippies, Fifth Avenue Peace Parade Committee, and Lower East Side Mobilization for Peace Action (*Handschu et al. v. Special Services Division et al.*, examination of Michael Willis, November 6, 1974, pp. 53–54). Individual targeting was equally ecumenical: even the homes of Greenwich Village "Bohemians" were surveilled. See "Police Intelligence Unit Watches Radical Activity," *New York Times*, July 27, 1968; "Police Undercover Unit Kept Tabs on Minutemen," ibid., November 1, 1964; "Crackpots Here under the Eyes of BOSS," New York *Herald Tribune*, November 24, 1963; Nat Hentoff, "A Lengthening List," *Village Voice*, June 24, 1971; "City Has Its Own Special Police to Keep Dossiers on Dissidents," *New York Times*, August 8, 1969; Jack Newfield, "Garelik and the 'Terrorists': New York's Agnew?" *Village Voice*, September 10, 1970.

In addition, BOSS maintained a four-hour log book listing every upcoming event considered important—demonstrations, meetings, conferences, labor disputes, the arrivals and departures of dignitaries, and similar matters falling within the unit's jurisdiction. This calendar was made available to other intelligence agencies. For example, an Army military intelligence agent stationed in the New York area in 1967–68 testified before Senator Sam Ervin's committee investigating invasions of privacy that "we received daily from the Bureau of Special Investigations of the New York City Police Department an itemized list of events that were to take place around the city."[1]

Each assignment, whether long-term or transient, resulted in a report, written on a form tailored to the kind of surveillance involved. The form used by infiltrators called for detailed information on "Future Plans, Unlawful Activities, Trouble Makers, Leaflets, Weapons, Speakers, Statements." BOSS boasted that by the time a subject was twenty years old, it could readily assemble a dossier of over sixty items relating to his or her personal history: criminal record, family background, social and political affiliations, bank and credit records, passport stamps, medical records, and related matters.[2] By 1968 the BOSS master index had well over one million entries. In February 1973 a publicly announced purge of BOSS's records resulted in the deletion of 980,000 names of individuals from the intelligence index (reduced from 1,220,000 to 240,000) and a reduction of organizational listings to 25,000 from 125,000. In addition, file folders on individuals were reduced to 2,500 from 3,500, and on organizations to 200 from 1,500.*

BOSS files were also used to develop court testimony and cross-examination, in addition to being a resource for bar examiners in determining political qualifications for admission to the bar, a source of information for other intelligence units, a propaganda resource, and a means of blackmailing or neutralizing hostile officeholders. For example, in late 1969, the New York Times reported that an "informed police

---

* "Police Intelligence Records Here Are Purged of a Million Names," New York Times, February 7, 1973. It was widely charged that despite the claimed purge, the file material remained available to insiders. Ken Auletta, "Your Friendly Local Spies," Village Voice, March 10, 1975; Nat Hentoff, "Rest Easy, G. Gordon Liddy," ibid., August 8, 1974; Nat Hentoff, "Still on the Track of the Red Squad," ibid., June 9, 1975. See also "Lawyers Assail Police on Files," New York Times, February 20, 1973 (lawyers for the complainants in the Handschu case pointed out that the claimed purge and accompanying guidelines reflected an attempt to block the litigation, that self-correction could not replace legal restraints, and that, in any event, the number of files retained reflected a continuing commitment to political surveillance unrelated to law enforcement).

source" had revealed that BOSS had developed dossiers on Mayor John Lindsay and some of his aides. One aide began using a public phone booth for sensitive discussions, and the mayor issued a statement saying that he would make no statement.[3]

The files were also used to implement private right-wing programs. In the 1963 libel suit brought by John Henry Faulk, it was revealed that one of the defendants, Vincent Hartnett, had operated a highly profitable "smear and clear" service, in which he exposed individuals in the entertainment world and used the threat of exposure to extract investigative fees from sponsors. When Hartnett was asked on the witness stand to reveal the source of his extensive information about individuals, he testified that he had called BOSS Lieutenant Thomas F. Crain some seventy times for information about or verification of the political backgrounds of certain entertainers and writers, and that on thirty occasions he had received information from BOSS files.[4]

In 1949 a BOSS lieutenant, Watkin Parry, filed a routine report based upon his interrogation of two young sisters in Brooklyn. The two girls confessed to Parry that they were members of a communist youth organization, the Young Progressives of America (YPA). Their father attended the questioning at the precinct house and became so alarmed that he invited Parry to their home to confiscate any and all material relating to the YPA. Along with a series of pamphlets and the like, Parry walked off with the YPA membership records, which listed a 16-year-old Brooklyn youth, Peter Bell, as a member. Seventeen years later, when Bell was a 33-year-old longshoreman on the Brooklyn docks, he lost his job and was barred from the docks by the Waterfront Commission on the grounds that he had lied to the commission about ever having been a member of the group.

For many years applicants for city employment were confronted with reports and photos from BOSS files identifying them as members of a proscribed organization or participants in a march or rally. Public school teachers were similarly investigated by BOSS under New York's Feinberg Law and charged with subversion. In 1970 a bar applicant was questioned extensively about his membership in an antiwar organization. When pressed to identify the basis for such questions, the committee referred to a report from "Police Department, Special Services." BOSS files were also used to verify statements made by applicants for public employment, city, state, and federal, and disseminated quite freely.[5] Efforts to limit file access by private investigators were consistently frustrated by the bribery of detectives.[6]

The Mantle of Elitism: Skilled Professionals
Entrusted with an Awesome Mission

As we have seen, the special status BOSS claimed in the sixties did not emerge from an official definition of its mission but was simply improvised. Anthony Bouza's basic contention is that the BOSS unit played a uniquely important role in the urban police structure: "Assignment to the Bureau of Special Services is 'a consummation devoutly to be wished.' It constitutes, for a patrolman, entrance into the most prestigious unit of the department."[7]

Intelligence, Bouza repeatedly tells us, is a highly skilled craft, to be sharply differentiated from conventional police or detective work. But we are not told why BOSS investigations required greater skill or ability than, say, investigations into organized crime. In the end, Bouza's claims of an elite role for BOSS are reduced to the asserted importance of its mission as a political police force. In short, BOSS agents were the lions guarding the throne, and it was the interest they protected, the government itself, that made them so special. And just for this reason, Bouza insists, it is unsound police practice to permit intelligence units to become mired in the normal departmental chains of command: "An intelligence unit belongs directly under the highest authority in a police department."[8]

It is a staple of intelligence theory that the surveillance unit serves only as the "eyes and ears" of the department, that it is confined to the neutral process of gathering information and nothing more. But Bouza assures us that it must be more than this: "The successful intelligence operations will not only secure the information but analyze and evaluate it and furnish logical alternatives or plans for coping with the event, whatever its nature."[9] Moreover, the unique character and urgency of intelligence work require a special command leadership to guide the unit to the fulfillment of its vital mission without obstructive standards of operation and accountability:

> It is also worthy of note that the very unit being discussed has evolved into its present form, naturally and effectively, without concrete mandates and without an analysis or description of its shape or direction. The process of evolution has been gradual and orderly but without chronicle and, therefore, dependent upon the individual proclivities or talents of its commanding officer.[10]

We need only note that the aspects of the New York City unit's operation that Bouza commends promoted precisely those evils made increasingly familiar to us by the evolution of political intelligence structures: exaggeration of political dangers, made possible by a fuzzy mandate; indiscriminate target selection; absence of limiting operational standards; unrestricted power for the intelligence chief; merger of the power to collect information with the power to evaluate it; and failure to establish procedures for external review.

If BOSS's countersubversive mission served to gild it with an elite distinction, its claims of professionalism made it gleam with an extraordinary luster. The growth of technology of surveillance in the sixties (see pp. 67–69) made it possible to depict political intelligence practices as a prestigious specialty, a "career service" not only intellectually demanding but requiring the esoteric skills of specialists bound together in an "intelligence community." (A minor, but illuminating, indication of BOSS's infatuation with intelligence cloak-and-daggerism was its organization into specialized "desks"—"extremist," "black," "Hispanic," etc.) This process of professionalization of data collection led to an arrangement under which twelve New York policemen, in September 1972, received four days of training in data handling from the CIA at its Langley, Virginia, headquarters.*

---

* It is clear that they were part of a CIA-initiated program offered to many police units (see pp. 86–87). Indeed, the CIA's director, Richard Helms, subsequently testified before a Senate committee: "And since we have files of this kind and have been using them for years it just seemed like a friendly gesture to tell [them] how to do it best . . . this was something I volunteered to help on out of what was the goodness of my heart and in a very public-spirited way." This program was unquestionably violative of the CIA's 1947 mandate barring it from domestic police functions. For this reason, it was kept a secret both by the CIA and its police pupils. The consciousness of impropriety is reflected in a memo to the CIA from a New York City police official seeking guidance on "how to handle [a] requested interview" by the *New York Times* reporter David Burnham. He was instructed to tell Burnham that it was "not unusual as the NYCPD also sends officers to the FBI Academy and to other U.S. government agencies to obtain assistance and training whenever it would be helpful to them." On December 12, 1972, at about the time of the requested interview and five days before Burnham's story appeared, the following judicious assessment of Burnham by CIA bigwigs found its way into an agency memorandum: "He was characterized as a 'Ramsey Clark liberal,' who is reasonably reliable but a very thorough investigative reporter." Finally, whatever the department's outlays for transportation and lodging, the record shows that the trainees and their superiors were given a party and provided with hotel accommodation and transportation by the CIA. CIA file releases; "C.I.A. Discloses It Trained Police from 12 Agencies," *New York Times*, February 6, 1973; "Ex-Head of C.I.A. Backs Its Training of Domestic Police," ibid., February 8, 1973; "Why Did C.I.A. Train Police?" ibid., February 11, 1973; "C.I.A. Will Curb Training It Provides Police Forces," ibid., March 6, 1973; "CIA to Discontinue Assistance to Local Police," *Congressional Record*, March 5, 1973, p. H1352;

But neither its professed nation- and city-saving goals nor its aspirations to professionalism could conceal the harsh reality of BOSS's operational practices, a subject to which I now turn.

Overt Intelligence Gathering: Intimidation and Harassment

During the sixties, most large urban police units moved from such legitimate functions as crowd control and peacekeeping to the deployment of patrolmen and detectives who made their presence known at demonstrations and rallies, developed countersubversive data—especially identification—about participants and speakers, and assumed an adversarial role. In varying degrees, a passive function was converted into a pattern of hostility and harassment, usually haphazard and unplanned—a transformation that reflected a deeply rooted conflict of values.

The New York City unit developed a detail of political detectives, headed by Lieutenant John Finnegan, that was similar in some respects to a patrol force deployed in high-crime areas. Finnegan and his men, usually equipped with cameras, monitored the city's political scene, deliberately presenting a high profile to their left-wing targets. But unlike law-enforcement patrolmen, BOSS detectives surveilled specific events, selected from the log book, as part of a larger strategy of intimidation and the use of techniques of provocation.

Finnegan, the classic "up-front" radical-stalker,* well qualified for admission to the Gallery of the Obsessed, became a legend in leftist circles.[11] Everyone had a Finnegan story. As one activist recalled:

> Finnegan at first came on as a wraith-like James Bond
> type. In the old days, when we asked him who he was
> and why he was there, he just shrugged his shoulders or
> walked away or took our picture. Then I found out who
> he was. . . . After a while, we began to call Finnegan by

"Prohibiting CIA's Engaging in Domestic Law Enforcement," ibid., June 6, 1973, p. H4399.
* Finnegan is the New York version of Chicago's Maurie Dailey; their less flamboyant counterparts emerged in every large urban political police unit in the sixties. Finnegan's predecessor as Mr. Red Squad was Fritz Behr, a more affable type, dubbed "the friendliest spy in New York." Unlike Finnegan, he occasionally donned disguises in order to deceive his targets. "Right or Wrong, Policeman Does Duty," *New York World-Telegram*, July 14, 1965.

his name and would kid around with him. Then he got
in the habit, even before we talked to him, of coming up
to a group of guys and calling each of their names. That
would freak some of them out.

While a number of other BOSS photographers took pictures at every
rally, Finnegan was the only one who made a point of being highly visible as he snapped the subject's front view, then his or her profile. And
when demonstrators from New York traveled to Chicago in 1968 and to
Washington, D.C., in 1969, it was Finnegan they observed in the company of local police officials pointing out various activists.[12]

Finnegan actively sought to deter demonstrations in face-to-face encounters with would-be demonstrators, and did not hesitate to use telephone warnings to accomplish his mission. For example, when a
demonstration was being planned against a New York firm, Finnegan
called the principal organizer, warned against the plan, and predicted
grave consequences. (There was no demonstration.) One of the risks of
crossing Finnegan was physical assault. Long-haired radicals particularly
stirred his juices, and on more than one occasion he was known to corner one of them, produce a pair of brass knuckles, and administer an
effective beating.

When Finnegan moved through the crowd at a demonstration, identifiable BOSS agents performed support functions. The speakers were
tape-recorded and photographed (see discussion below) and a selection of
their political statements later entered in a file. Other agents were assigned to pick up conversations of the better-known demonstrators, and
still others copied the license plate numbers of cars parked in the area of
the demonstration. Videotapes and films were made from nearby buildings, a simple matter when the demonstration was held in downtown
Manhattan.

BOSS's overt surveillance deliberately exploited its openness to intimidate its targets. But it did not scorn deception and ruses in special
situations. For example, a BOSS agent might on occasion disguise his
appearance or wear a wig or falsify his identity in order to decoy a subject, or spread false rumors. A favorite gambit was to pose as a reporter.
At one time, BOSS issued press cards with coded serial identifications to
its agents accrediting them as reporters for small metropolitan or suburban newspapers.[13]

The use of overly repressive tactics against a target group is well illustrated by the BOSS drive against Veterans and Reservists against the
War (V and R), a small New York–based group of disillusioned Vietnam
returnees, formed in the spring of 1967. Its primary activity was the

organization of other Vietnam veterans in the antiwar marches of the period. V and R members began to notice that Lieutenant Finnegan never missed a demonstration or meeting. On one occasion when V and R members were picketing outside a movie house showing the film *The Green Berets,* Finnegan ostentatiously posted himself on the curb across the street while numerous plainclothesmen mingled with the picketers and periodically reported to him.

In April 1969 a peace march took place in which a large number of participants, including V and R members, were beaten by the police and arrested. In the next several weeks, at least six V and R members were visited at their homes, usually late at night, by Finnegan and one of his aides. Typically these people would refuse to answer any questions and were then warned by Finnegan to keep away from V and R or to "watch yourself" at the next demonstration. One member was told by the angry lieutenant that his next demonstration "might be your last." When the subject was not at home, Finnegan would attempt to interrogate members of his family about his involvement with V and R. If no one was home, there might be a note like the one that was slipped under one member's door: "May 28—Detectives Judge and Finnegan visited—will try again." These tactics were highly effective: activity and membership declined and the group was forced to disband.* The leaders could hardly comprehend exactly what had happened.

At the April 1969 peace march, BOSS agents assumed the guise of demonstrators and provoked an incident that was used as a pretext for beatings by the police (a tactic gleefully described by Police Commissioner Grover Whalen in connection with a 1930 gathering).[14] Such provocative acts served as a routine formula for breaking up an assemblage under the cover of "crowd control," on which BOSS relied as justification for infiltrating large mass rallies, demonstrations, marches, and meetings. Often the disguised police infiltrators first heckled and abused the uniformed police, only to later join them in beating up their fellow demonstrators. This was done so blatantly during the 1968 Columbia University disorders, and created such public opposition, that the police department issued a statement promising to curtail the use of plainclothes infiltrators at demonstrations.[15]

Overt intimidation was not confined to broad sweeps—demonstrations, rallies, and the like—and their organizational sponsors. It was also highly intensive. Individual activists and leaders were frequently

---

* Contributing to the group's demise were the provocative actions of a BOSS infiltrator, discussed below.

surveilled by BOSS agents and developed a first-name relationship with their tails. When a subject resisted, for example, by trying to shake his tail, a harassing reprisal might well result—an arrest, an assault, or a raid on a pretext (drug possession was a favorite). In October 1969, when two university teachers, Jonah Raskin and Robert Reilly, were arrested along with numerous others at an antiwar rally, two BOSS agents emerged out of the crowd to identify Raskin and Reilly to the arresting officers as political activists. When they arrived at the 17th Precinct House for booking, Raskin and Reilly were separated out from the group and severely beaten throughout the night. Pictures of their bruised and bandaged bodies were displayed in several local newspapers. The New York Civil Liberties Union successfully filed police brutality charges before the Police Civilian Complaint Review Board. But the board cited only the four officers who had actually participated in the beatings in upholding the charge—the two BOSS agents were not mentioned.[16]

BOSS responded with special zeal to its critics. In 1970 three young film makers, Steven Fischler, Joel Sucher, and Howard Blatt, who called themselves the Pacific Street Collective, were targeted, as they were in Chicago (see pp. 141–43), while making a film about urban police surveillance, centering on the activities of BOSS.[17] After they were observed filming BOSS headquarters, Lieutenant Finnegan and his partner visited the home of Blatt's parents under the pretext that Blatt had been seen near the scene of an accident. They reached Blatt through a phone call from his parents' home and induced him to submit to interrogation under the barely concealed threat that if he did not cooperate, his parents would be subjected to further harassment. Subsequently, a second member of the collective was arrested on a pretext and interrogated.

Photography, Electronic Surveillance, and Third-Party Sources

The BOSS agents not only used cameras and video equipment for open surveillance but also took pictures covertly. It was a common practice for detectives to acquire "working press" cards for the purpose of covert photography. All such films were then developed at BOSS headquarters and the subjects identified wherever possible.[18]

In 1969 the department installed an "electronic war room" designed to receive videographed pictures on one of three screens: one 13×10 feet and two others 10×7 feet. The demonstrations were covered by fixed television cameras placed at frequently used demonstration sites and by mobile cameras mounted on helicopters.

Electronic surveillance practices included the planting of electronic devices in informers' cars and on the persons of informers, which in some cases both recorded and transmitted conversations to the cars of detectives within a five-block range. Two types of wiretaps were employed: warrantless taps of informers' phones in order to record their conversations with suspects and taps installed on the phones of the suspects themselves. In the latter case, warrants were usually obtained, but on the basis of highly questionable justification. Consider the case of Shaun Dubonnet whose representations were used as the justification for no fewer than six wiretaps. On October 18, 1968, the police in Brooklyn arrested a young black man who gave the name Shaun Dubonnet on charges of grand larceny. While being booked at the precinct, Dubonnet insisted that he had to speak to some detectives concerning the Black Panther Party. A special unit of detectives had been formed in Brooklyn at that time to investigate several recent ambush shootings of police officers. The head of this unit, Lieutenant Angelo Galante, came to interview Dubonnet. In return for a hint of leniency on the larceny charges and a weekly $100 pay-off, Dubonnet gave Galante what he wanted concerning the Panthers.

Describing himself as the lieutenant-in-charge of the Brownsville section of the Black Panthers, Dubonnet stated that he had attended a planning meeting for a police ambush that had occurred on August 2, and that he had been the driver for that ambush, although he was uncertain as to the names of the other Panthers involved. Galante noted then that Dubonnet might be "acting as a double agent," but he nevertheless certified Dubonnet as a reliable informant to appear as a witness before a grand jury. Dubonnet testified, and the Kings County district attorney used his testimony to obtain a court order for separate wiretaps of six Panthers mentioned by Dubonnet. Every item of information supplied by Dubonnet, including his claimed membership in the Black Panther Party, was ultimately proven to be totally fabricated.

Dubonnet, a substitute for his more prosaic real name, William Fletcher, had an extraordinary history. From the ages of fourteen to twenty-nine, he had been a patient at fifteen different mental institutions. All of them diagnosed him as a "paranoid schizophrenic," and several noted that he was a "pathological liar." His lengthy and bizarre criminal record on both state and federal charges included two arrests for impersonating a doctor and a police officer. At the time Galante was using him, he was wanted by the Secret Service for allegedly threatening the life of President Johnson, by the Philadelphia police on an all-points warrant, and by a state mental institution from which he had escaped the year before. Ironically, Galante himself soon discovered from one of the Dubonnet-inspired wiretaps that Dubonnet was lying to the police.

To obtain a court order for a wiretap based entirely on information supplied by an informant, the police must swear to the court that they have determined in one of three ways that the informant is "reliable."* None of the three methods was employed to qualify Dubonnet; Galante had in fact suspected him from the start. Yet Galante and others continued, each time they requested the district attorney for a renewal of the warrants, to vouch, under oath, for Dubonnet's reliability. The police suppressed information impugning his credibility and subsequently denied that they knew of Dubonnet's mental and criminal background. Once they discovered the informer's identity, defense counsel in the Panther 13 case had no difficulty uncovering his history within a matter of days, even without access to the special sources available to the police. Dubonnet himself stated the obvious when later questioned by an incredulous district attorney at a hearing to suppress the wiretap tapes:

D.A.: Anybody who is gullible enough to believe you is stupid, is that right?

---

* Three tests of justifiable reliance have been prescribed by the courts. The first is that information given in the past by the particular informant has proved to be accurate information of criminal activity (*McCray v. Illinois*, 386 U.S. 300 [1967]). This did not occur in Dubonnet's case. The first meeting with Dubonnet occurred on October 18, 1968; the police had not on earlier occasions received accurate information from him and made no such claim. The courts have consistently required information on "several" prior occasions and insisted that on each such occasion the information prove to be accurate. E.g., *United States v. Perry*, 380 F. 2d 356 (2d Cir.) cert. denied, 389 U.S. 943 (1967).

The second test of reliability is the character of the informant himself. Thus, where the informant is not the garden-variety underworld tipster, but a distinguished citizen, his identity alone might establish his reliability, as in *United States v. Ventresca*, 380 U.S. 102 (1965). Dubonnet's background, almost needless to say, is not the kind the Supreme Court of the United States had in mind in the Ventresca case.

The third reliability qualification is an independent police investigation of the facts involved that verifies the information supplied (*Smith v. United States*, 358 E. 2d 833 [D.C. Cir. 1968]). To establish that the information is credible, moreover, the independent investigation must corroborate some of the *incriminating* facts supplied by the informant (*Spinelli v. United States*, 393 U.S. 410 [1960]; *People v. Galligos*, 62 Cal. 2d 176 [1964]; *Draper v. United States*, 358 U.S. 307, at 314 [Douglas, J., dissenting]; see *Wong Sun v. United States*, 371 U.S. 471 [1963]). The affidavit must allege that an independent investigation was conducted to corroborate the information (*Aguilar v. Texas*, 378 U.S. 108 [1964]). Without adequate corroboration, information derived from the "untested" informant is not sufficient to establish probable cause (*Wong Sun v. United States*, cited above). No such claim was made in the police affidavits.

DUBONNET: That's correct.[19]

The district attorney obtained repeated renewals of the six wiretap orders based upon expert "interpretation" of what the police had overheard on the previous wiretap.

A few of the police "interpretations" will suffice to demonstrate how seemingly solid legal protections can be dissolved. Once an SDS organizer phoned the Panthers to invite them to a demonstration outside the State Office Building in Harlem. The Panther on the phone turned down the invitation. This was put forward as proof that the Black Panther Party believed only in violence. An account by two Panthers of how much they had enjoyed the movie *The Battle of Algiers* was submitted as evidence that the Panthers were engaging in guerrilla training, a fact incidentally refuted by the daily reports of BOSS infiltrators. The police kept exaggerating the gravity of the conduct they were supposed to be monitoring until, near the end, they were asking the court for a renewed wiretap order to check blossoming conspiracies to commit "Murder, Arson, Bombing, Kidnapping, Coercion, and other violents [sic]." Of course nothing ever came of these alleged plots, but they served to justify the wiretaps through mid March 1969.*

Finally, we come to the BOSS practice of interrogating third parties for information about subjects, especially their political views, activities, and associates. Unit detectives systematically sought information from landlords, employers, maids, college deans, bartenders, taxi drivers, storekeepers, and others, the fruits of which were entered in dossiers.

---

*One of these wiretaps did reveal a flickering plot of sorts. The police overheard a conversation about a Panther, Roland Hayes, who had (without the customary aid of a BOSS agent) procured a hundred sticks of dynamite, which an investigation traced to a source in Vermont at Goddard College, which Hayes had once attended. Detective Richard Hodgson, sent to investigate, interviewed or checked with the local detectives of the Department of Public Safety; the local agent of the Treasury Department; two college deans and Hayes's former college advisor; the proprietor of Vermont Explosives, Inc.; the Minnesota State Police; the Vermont Motor Vehicle Bureau; the local postmaster; college security officers; and the owners of a local gas station. Hodgson finally puzzled out that Panther Hayes had in fact purchased one hundred sticks of dynamite on December 13, 1968, from a college student at Goddard. After Hodgson returned to New York, the police were astounded to learn from one of their wiretaps that the suspect, Roland Hayes, was an informer for the FBI, which had supplied the money for the trip. *New York v. Lumumba Abdul Shakur et al.*, No. 1848 ½-69, "Application for Amendment of Eavesdropping Warrant," supporting affidavits (February 21, 1969), and "Order Renewing Eavesdropping Warrant" (February 21, 1969); "Panther Lawyer Says Dynamite Was 'Gift' from Ally of F.B.I.," *New York Times*, March 11, 1971; "The Mystery Witness at the Black Panther Trial," *New York Post*, March 9, 1971.

The BOSS Informer Network

The MO—the distinctive operational style—of New York City political surveillance was heavy reliance on planted informers drawn from the ranks of the police force, as opposed to civilians, a practice considered a mark of the unit's professionalism. However, BOSS did not spurn civilian spies for limited purposes. Two examples are noteworthy. In the case of V and R (see pp. 163–64), BOSS, in addition to its overt aggressive intelligence program, recruited a civilian infiltrator. Shortly after V and R was formed, Richard Lyons, a bank employee, joined as a fellow veteran. In the fall of 1967, V and R made plans to participate in the October march on the Pentagon. This was one of the group's first major activities, and Lyons was on hand, repeatedly urging the use of tear gas and smoke grenades against the troops guarding the Pentagon. In the spring of 1968, V and R planned to participate in another antiwar demonstration. Lyons urged the group to call for a public burning by GIs of their weapons-authorization cards, a federal crime. At a September demonstration in New York, where a pig was to be offered to presidential candidate Hubert Humphrey, Lyons suggested that the arrival of the pig be used as a signal for a mass charge at the police lines. Lyons also brought with him to these latter planning meetings a realistic plastic replica of a submachine gun, which he proposed should be carried by all V and R members. In each of these cases, as well as on other occasions, Lyons's suggestions were flatly rejected by V and R in favor of lawful and nonviolent tactics. Despite his best efforts, Lyons failed to provoke acts that might justify arrests. He was exposed in late 1968,* but the veterans' realization that they had become a BOSS target intensified a demoralization that had already set in as a result of more overt BOSS tactics.

---

* Lyons was arrested, along with others, in the fall of 1968 and charged with two offenses: one was disorderly conduct and the other was maintaining a live animal (a pig) without a permit. When Lyons, along with other V and R members, came to court to plead to these charges, he confidently expected that his case would be dismissed. Shocked when the court did not immediately dismiss his case at the arraignment, he turned bitterly to Detective Finnegan and threatened him, "I'll get you for this." Lyons was drunk at the time, a fact that may account for the violence of his outburst. He had, for a long time prior to the arraignment, sat in with the other defendants in consulting counsel. Prior to one of these sessions, he blurted out to the group's lawyer, Eleanor Jackson Piel, "You know. I'm a police spy." Ms. Piel then brought to the attention of the assistant district attorney in charge of the case the fact that a police agent had participated in the sessions planning legal strategy. Shortly thereafter, the case against all the defendants was dismissed, on motion of the district attorney. Interviews by author with Richard (Robin) Palmer and Ms. Piel.

Lyons was a volunteer. BOSS also sought on its own to recruit promising candidates for spy work. Illustrative is an incident that occurred on
the eve of the 1966 National Student Association (NSA) convention. A
Saint John's University (New York) coed, Gloria Kuzmyak, was visited
by BOSS detectives. Kuzmyak, then an officer in the NSA, was planning to attend the convention, which was to be held at the University of
Illinois. The BOSS men asked her "to keep a check on demonstrations
that were going to take place." Her help in this instance would be confined to giving BOSS the names of all New York NSA students and
representatives "associated with the liberal caucus." Kuzmyak, who had
been campus head of the Young Conservatives, admitted that for a while
she was "swayed by the patriotic tunes the police were giving me," but
she ultimately declined.[20]

The typical BOSS police agent was deployed in three modes of undercover surveillance: short-term infiltration in response to a tip that a
crime was being planned; a more prolonged, but still limited, infiltration
ostensibly to discover and report back evidence that might ultimately
show a violation of law; and long-term penetration primarily in order, as
Bouza puts it, "to develop access to the more sensitive informational
area." The classic deep-penetration agent, less frequently employed today because of the scanty yield of information and the immobilization of
detectives for long periods of time, was extensively used in the forties
and fifties to monitor the Communist Party.*

Two of the best known of the BOSS infiltrators of the forties were
Stephanie Horvath and Mildred Blauvelt, both of whom were recruited
as infiltrators while still in police training and remained with BOSS after
they surfaced. After two or three months training, Blauvelt was assigned to penetrate the Communist Party as an undercover agent. She
succeeded in her assignment and was recruited as a communist under an
assumed name in April 1943, but was expelled as a spy in September of
that year. Ordered by her superiors to gain reentry, she joined a communist group in another part of the city in April 1944 under another
assumed name. She was again expelled as a spy in November 1951, and
as a reward for her nine years' undercover work, she was honored with a

---

* Data on infiltration practices of this kind, developed in the record of the
Handschu case, indicates that as of 1977 BOSS had deployed five deep-
penetration agents beginning prior to 1974 and continuing beyond 1977. In
addition, nine informers were planted in fourteen target groups for the following periods of time: one for approximately six months; three for approximately
one year; two for about two and a half years; and three were continuing as
of 1977.

police department citation "for exceptional merit," an award "given for an act of bravery, intelligently performed, involving the risk of life."[21] She was the first policewoman to be so honored, but not the only woman infiltrator.

Stephanie Horvath, a BOSS detective, was a police trainee at about the same time as Blauvelt and, like her, was first assigned to infiltrate the Communist Party and, in her words "to report on the members and their activities." She was a police spy from 1943 to 1947, when she was exposed. Thereafter she engaged in more overt forms of surveillance, such as attending public meetings and taking stenographic notes of what was said.[22]

In June 1940 Margaret Disco was, on joining the police force, assigned to Special Squad No. 1 (a BOSS unit), where she and twenty-seven other police officers were trained to infiltrate the Communist Party. Disco was a spy for fifteen years. She became a good communist and eventually attained high office in the Party. Like Blauvelt's, her services were gratefully acknowledged through a series of honors and awards, culminating in November 1963 in appointment to head the Police-women's Bureau.[23]

The principal function of such agents was the identification of communists and other radicals and the transmission of information about the group's activities for entry in the log book. Nor were they all women, though female infiltrators were preferred because they disarmed suspicion. Another infiltrator of the forties surfaced in the 1947 trial of Carl Marzani, a former State Department employee, for perjury in denying past membership in the Communist Party. The chief prosecution witness was a black agent, a long-term Communist Party plant named Archer Drew, alias Bill Easley. Drew was a highly enterprising operator: singlehandedly he created a black radical organization on the lower East Side and organized a program of panel discussions, to which he invited speakers (including Marzani). He then turned their names in.

Typical of the informers of the sixties with limited missions was Frank Ferrara. After he emerged from the police academy, he was assigned to undercover work at Columbia University, where he posed as a student for two months. Ferrara was responsible for the arrest of Weatherman Mark Rudd during the university riots in April 1968. A similar figure was Steve Weiner, a plant who, using the cover of a taxi driver, drove a group of radicals to the site of a bank they planned to bomb. The bombing conspiracy was hatched at several meetings in Weiner's apartment, which were secretly recorded, as were conversations in his taxi cab.[24]

The Black Target Infiltration Program
of the Sixties

BOSS's response to the black protest movements of the sixties pivoted on a campaign to saturate the targets with spies, either recruited during police training or, to a lesser extent, coopted for temporary assignment to undercover work. This offensive culminated in a series of court cases, the records of which make it possible to chronicle the recruitment and development of an agent for undercover infiltration of black groups. Our composite subject is a young black man with an irregular employment record who has filed an application for a job in the police department.

Shortly after he begins his training at the academy, he is approached by a BOSS lieutenant (then Milton Schwartz, who had an office at the academy) in charge of recruiting rookie agents. After completing an extensive background investigation of our subject, the recruiter offers him an assignment with BOSS. The new recruit accepts; he immediately leaves the police academy before completing the training course. His personnel file is removed from the academy, leaving no record of his identity. Following a brief orientation, dealing primarily with the filing of daily reports, he is provided with a new identity, complete with all the requisite documentation and a "cover" apartment. He is introduced to his BOSS control and then sent into the street on a trial basis.

He is now, almost overnight, an undercover agent. He phones or visits his control sometimes two or three times a day during this initial period as he immerses himself in the outer circles of black radicalism, attending as many meetings and rallies as possible until his face becomes familiar to others.

During these first weeks or months, the agent joins an open, moderate political organization. There he is directed to establish himself as a supermilitant and to align himself with the more radical members of the group. When the time is ripe, he is ordered to leave and to join a more radical organization. With his militant credentials, he is quickly accepted. The agent spends several more weeks or months establishing himself within the target group, moving closer to the leadership.

After the agent has secured himself within the inner circle, his reports become repetitive and tedious. The group turns out to be more militant in word than in deed—the only crimes being committed are ones of possession, either of marijuana or guns. His superiors show no interest in these crimes, which the agent himself is also committing. The agent's superiors then begin to question him as to why nothing more substantial is turning up. BOSS has already decided that the group is subversive.

Having themselves already smelled the smoke, the superiors begin to imply that the agent must be failing for some reason to find the fire. The agent realizes that BOSS wants "results" beyond what his reports reveal.

The threat of a lost opportunity makes the agent more eager. He has already learned how to blow up his reports for the purpose of impressing his control, and he is now prepared to carry the process one step further. The use of violent rhetoric is routine among many left-wing groups, white and black. It is especially common among black radicals ("Off the pigs!") because their frustration is so great and the compensatory need to demonstrate their militance (and manhood) so demanding. And they can safely compete with each other in purely rhetorical militance because they are locked into their hostile verbalization by their lack of resources (plans, weapons, explosives, etc.), a deficiency that raises the rhetorical ante to higher and higher levels, since the players know (and each knows that the others know) that the risks are quite academic because no action is possible. Even when a plan is adopted to execute some violent proposal, assignments are given, a dry run is arranged, a car is obtained, and so on—by an unspoken understanding, the whole scheme is allowed to die. Instead, a new round of rhetoric fills the air—new threats and proposals, images of a fantasy by which the powerless revenge themselves on their oppressors.

Our agent himself immediately joins in the game. The violent rhetoric sometimes triggers his own pent-up rage and resentment, and, in any event, he must play in order to preserve his cover. But whatever subjective need fuels such talk, and however plainly its context indicates a tacit understanding among all the players that it is not intended to be acted upon, to the control and to the officer at BOSS in charge of the black radical desk, it sounds like a criminal conspiracy that needs only broader sponsorship and an "overt act" to justify an indictment. So the agent is urged to persevere and to produce evidence of the necessary commitment.

He presses the others to move from talk to action. They are shaken by the militance of this newcomer and, not to be outdone, develop *the* definitive plan. The agent is pleased; he has gotten enough discussion out of them to file his best report in months: specific members of the target group, especially the leaders, discuss the possibility of blowing up such-and-such, but at this stage, confront the obvious drawbacks—no dynamite, no knowledge of ballistics, not even a car. The members of the group again try to dismiss the proposal on practical, not political, grounds: "We have the guts but we have no dynamite," or guns, or maps, or cars, or whatever. The agent then plays his trump: he suggests that maybe he can get the dynamite and so forth from a friend of his. Thereafter the agent produces the goods and pushes the group to take the next step. Now the scenario is no longer a transient fantasy of the powerless but, for the first time, a realistic possibility.

The group, excited by its newfound resources, begins to treat the proposal as something it now has the power to execute. Whenever they hit a snag, the agent himself does a reconnaissance of whatever is needed to keep the "plan" going. But even when difficulties are resolved by the agent's industry, the scheme remains crude and often laughably impractical and risky, typically, for example, lacking a rational escape scenario.

Although the group never does actually attempt to implement the proposal—and indeed never could—it nevertheless does ripen into something that might loosely be called a conspiracy: there is an agreement to do something illegal as well as an "overt act," usually innocuous in itself, which is all that the law requires as long as it is "in furtherance" of the conspiracy. What is pitifully absent is either the power or the will to execute it.

But what gives the "plot" a surface plausibility is that the boasts and rhetorical derring-do of the plotters have not blown away and been forgotten the next day, but have been recorded on tape as "evidence" of the conspiracy. The agent has had his own phone tapped while talking to members of the group; the car he supplied them was bugged, and on several occasions he wore a wireless transmitter taped to his chest by a BOSS electronics expert (then Lieutenant Joe Harry Williams). The targets are seized in midnight arrests and charged at a press conference with plotting enormous destruction and mayhem. The agent is promoted to detective third grade, a post that would normally have taken him, if he were lucky, about twelve to fifteen years to attain. The newpapers blaze with feature stories on the "hero cop" who risked his life to capture the defendants. The target group never recovers, and the defendants are forced to remain in jail for a long time awaiting trial without bail.

The Infiltrator in Court: Four Cases

The profile of the infiltration process presented in the previous section is a distillation of pertinent portions of the record of five New York conspiracy cases involving BOSS agents and black dissident groups. I shall examine the first four only briefly[25] but deal in more detail in the section that follows with the fifth, the case of the Panther 13,* certainly the most revealing of all the BOSS court cases.

The Statue of Liberty case, as it came to be known, coincided with the development of a "Black Power" movement among ghetto activists.[26] The infiltrator in this case was BOSS agent Raymond Wood, who used the undercover alias "Woodall." Wood was first directed to join CORE, an open, broad-based organization. There he quickly established himself as a strong militant, impatient with CORE's slow pace. He eventually became the CORE chairman of voter registration and housing. Three months after he joined the organization, in July 1964, Wood talked the chapter chairman, Herbert Callender, into making a "citizen's arrest" of Mayor Robert F. Wagner, Jr. Callender was concerned about Wagner's failure to integrate the construction industry. Wood suggested they arrest Wagner to dramatize CORE's grievance and convinced Callender that such an arrest was perfectly legal, stating that he had learned as much at law school. (Wood had never attended law school and the proposed arrest was illegal.) Wood, Callender, and one other activist were arrested attempting to arrest the mayor. Wood was dragged away by the police defiantly flashing the victory sign with his fingers on his way to the paddy wagon. His fine on conviction was paid by BOSS. Callender was convicted and sent to Bellevue for psychiatric examination.

Wood soon moved on to the Freedom Now Party, and then to the Revolutionary Action Movement (RAM). Three members of RAM splintered off to form the Black Liberation Front (BLF), to which Wood was instructed to gain entry. Inside the BLF, Wood reportedly proposed a number of extraordinary actions, including blowing up the sewer systems by pouring gasoline into it. As it turned out, it was perhaps his most bizarre proposal that was adopted, blowing up national symbols of freedom such as the Statue of Liberty. Although Wood later weakly denied that he had originated the specific idea of blowing up the statue, he did admit to arguing for the plan and persuading those uncommitted to adopt it.

Wood was certainly the outstanding figure in the plot. While the others were still weighing his seriousness, Wood made, on his own initiative, a "test run" to the statue carrying a suitcase to convince them that there was no security problem. Wood then obtained money and a bugged car from BOSS in order to drive to Canada to purchase dynamite together with Robert Collier, the acting leader of the BLF. They smoked marijuana from New York to Canada and back, but returned without

---

* Originally twenty-one were indicted in this case, but only thirteen were tried.

dynamite. Two weeks later, one of the contacts they had made in Canada delivered some dynamite to a vacant lot in the Riverdale section of the city and phoned Wood to describe its whereabouts. Wood promptly notified Collier to go with him to pick up the dynamite. Once at the lot, Wood handed the dynamite to Collier to carry to the car, cueing FBI agents and local police to close in immediately and arrest him with the evidence of guilt in his hands.

Wood was instantly trumpeted in the press as the "hero cop." Collier and two others, the entire "cell" except for Wood, were convicted of two conspiracies: to smuggle dynamite into the United States and to destroy the Statue of Liberty.

Only a few months after Wood had made his splash in the press, a second case was born with the assignment of another BOSS undercover agent, Edward Lee Howlette.[27] In July 1965 Howlette was assigned to the South Jamaica area of New York, where he attended numerous meetings and rallies, which he reported in great detail.

He was directed to move closer to the Black Brotherhood Improvement Association (BBIA), which was headed by Herman Ferguson, then one of the highest-ranking blacks in the New York City school system and a leader in the embryonic community school control struggle. The BBIA was a small group of six to ten black intellectuals and professionals organized by Ferguson. Howlette not only penetrated but in fact helped to form several offshoots of the BBIA. One such group was the Jamaica Gun Club, chartered by the National Rifle Association. Howlette served both as vice president and head of the youth division.

Arthur Harris, a young community worker and a member of the gun club, is credited with having made the crucial conspiratorial statement in the case. One day, after Harris read a condemnation of the Black Power movement by several moderate black leaders in a newspaper advertisement, he reportedly said: "Those guys have sold out their own people. They should be offed." Howlette seized on the statement and pushed it toward a conspiracy. He reintroduced the idea at several meetings and began to initiate action proposals. Howlette first learned the address of Roy Wilkins, head of the NAACP and one of the ad's signatories, and then purchased a map of his home area. He next went to some lengths to draft an assassination note composed, kidnap-style, of individual words cut out of newspapers and pasted together. The note read in part: "This man should be eliminated because of actions against the people." Howlette then took Harris, in his bugged BOSS car, on a drive past the Wilkins residence to plan the assassination and getaway route.

Although the plot never developed further, the entire BBIA was arrested just as it was about to disband. Ferguson and Harris were featured in the press as the principal figures in a "terrorist cell." Because Ferguson had become a well-known figure, closely identified with the escalating controversy over community control of the schools, the case received extensive press coverage. Ferguson and Harris were each sentenced to three and a half to seven years in prison.

These convictions quickened the flow of BOSS agents into the black ghettos, among whom were Patrolmen Wayne Carrington and Timothy Hubbard, graduates of the police academy in February 1967. BOSS accepted them as part of a special unit on "temporary assignment" in the black ghettos and sent them into the streets in March 1968.

Carrington and Hubbard knew what they were after and wasted little time. Hubbard later was forced to admit in court that he wanted to become a detective; he knew undercover work might be a stepping stone; his future assignments would depend on the success of his BOSS assignment; arrests would aid his promotion; and, finally, he "might have" discussed with Carrington the added benefits of a "big arrest." The narrative that follows is based primarily on the testimonial admissions of both agents.[28]

The case of the Harlem 5, the third in our series, began when Carrington and Hubbard attended a three-day conference at a Times Square hotel sponsored by the National Black Anti-War, Anti-Draft Union. Carrington began courting one of the conference's more militant workshop leaders, Preston Lay, who had made angry and bitter statements concerning the recent murder of Martin Luther King, Jr. As Carrington would have it, Lay accosted him, though he was a virtual stranger, and in their very first private conversation proposed that they steal guns and rifles from the Kingsbridge Armory, even though Lay did not even know where the armory was located. Several days after the conference, Carrington pulled up at Lay's home and drove him to the armory in order to plan their theft and getaway. Carrington recommended a friend, Hubbard, who would definitely go along with their plan.

Thereafter the three, Lay and the two agents, met and appointed Lay the leader of their newly formed cell. Next followed several weeks of abortive meetings, always convened at Carrington's initiative, in which Carrington and Hubbard urged Lay to get others to join their plot. They eventually recruited four others, who haphazardly met with them to discuss the Kingsbridge Armory job. At one meeting where Lay was not present, the two agents steered the talk to the question of the "action" to be taken with the guns once they were stolen. This turned into an animated discussion of the many ways to kill a cop, during which Carrington recommended stretching a wire across a stairwell, a stunt that had delighted him in the movie *Rio Bravo*. This conversation, and others, were, of course, tape-recorded. When Lay learned of the discussion, he vetoed any such "savage" action. On May 15 two of the others told Carrington they were thinking of backing out of the plan. On May 16 Carrington summoned all the parties to a meeting and insisted that they all bring whatever weapons they had so that they would be available in one place in the event of a decision to move on their plans. When some arrived at the meeting empty-handed, Carrington sent them out again. It took several hours of coming and going to assemble four guns and some "home-made bombs" (several large firecrackers tied together). But when they finally had enough for a credible press release, Carrington gave a signal on his wireless transmitter and the police moved in.

The headlines credited BOSS with another major coup: "5 Held in Harlem Plot to Kill Cops, Stir Riot."[29] It became popularly known as the "kill-a-cop-a-week" conspiracy, in the wording of the police press release, and supplied telling support for the police claim that they were the innocent targets of wild black extremists. Carrington and Hubbard got their promotions to detective and permanent assignment to BOSS. They had, after all, produced a major indictment with only two months' work.

The defendants were not put on trial until nearly three years later, when the atmosphere had changed markedly. The jury acquitted the five on all the conspiracy charges and voted to convict four only on charges of possession of weapons. Two of the defendants were sentenced to three years in jail and two others to five years on probation. Its haste and clumsiness suggested that BOSS was getting a bit overeager to produce an annual save-the-city conspiracy indictment.

In a fourth (1969) case, involving agent Wilbert Thomas, BOSS completely overplayed its hand. Thomas infiltrated the Black Panther Party in Brooklyn in March 1969.[30] Following the indictment of the Panther 21 in April 1969, it would have been impossible to lure any bona fide Panther not working for the police into a classic BOSS plot. Agent Thomas had to make do with only the materials at hand, however unpromising: the endless fascination with guns and how to get them, a subject some Panthers were still willing to discuss. Thomas got things started in early August by beginning to carry a (BOSS-issued) revolver. One of the Panthers, Alfred Cain, asked Thomas if he could get guns for the rest of them, the first of several discussions in which Thomas and several other Panthers debated the matter of obtaining guns and, of course, what they would do with them.

BOSS never seems to have decided what the actual plot in this case was. The original indictment, a supporting affidavit, and press releases alleged that three members of the Panther Party, plus Thomas, had concocted a scheme to kill a policeman "as a diversionary tactic" while they robbed a welfare hotel in Harlem, all for the purpose of getting money to "aid the Black Panther Party," particularly the Panther 21. The references to murdering the policeman were quickly dropped after the initial releases; the most the prosecution could produce at trial were several conversations outlining the robbery scheme—and the "overt acts" of Thomas.

At a meeting where the crime was supposedly hatched, Thomas offered to steal a car and to case the hotel. He obtained a car from BOSS, not only bugged but also hot-wired to suggest it had been stolen. Thomas then drove one of the Panthers with him to the hotel and made a map of the scene. On August 16, 1969, Thomas and the soon-to-be Panther 3 were driving along the West Side Highway when they were pulled over and arrested. The indictment charged that the four were en route to the robbery, but a judge later found this claim to be entirely devoid of factual support.

BOSS was now beginning to sound much like the boy who cried wolf, and the press was becoming skeptical. The first trial of the Panther 3 ended in a hung jury, locked ten to two in favor of acquittal. When the case came to trial the second time, the presiding judge dismissed almost half the charges and the jury acquitted the defendants on all the rest except several minor possession charges. Thus, not with a bang but a whimper, ended the fourth of a series of cases that, together with several others,* traced a pattern of infiltration and provocation in BOSS's dramatic resurgence of the sixties. Never before in the agency's history had its operations been so revealingly bared to the public. The testimony of the surfaced agents weaves a pattern of provocative response to radicalism that clearly shows that BOSS had turned away from passive long-

---

* The most prominent of the earlier cases involved charges of violations of state law against William Epton for allegedly inciting the 1964 Harlem–Bedford Stuyvesant riot. The principal witness against him was undercover agent Adolph Hart, who was instructed in 1963 to infiltrate the Harlem branch of the Progressive Labor Party, a splinter Marxist group. Recruited by BOSS as an undercover agent even before he received a badge and police academy training, Hart became a hard-working PLP convert, performing tasks at the Harlem office and writing articles for the PLP's official organ, as well as its monthly newspaper, and attending lectures, classes, and meetings. He served on the group's defense squad at police demonstrations and as Epton's personal bodyguard at rallies. After the riots broke out in Harlem on July 18, 1964, Hart attempted to draw Epton into a compromising conversation about writing and distributing a leaflet on the manufacture of Molotov cocktails, while using a concealed tape recorder. See Donner, "The Epton Anarchy Trial," *Nation*, November 15, 1965; "Six Summers Ago in Harlem," *Rights*, September 1970.

term intelligence collection to activist involvement in, and control of, the life of the target, a style made familiar by the intelligence systems of czarist Russia.

The decision to prosecute in these cases was unquestionably influenced by the fascistic vendetta of the police against black dissidents, fueled by their fearsome rhetoric, a glut of expendable black agents, and the hope of exploiting urban fears of black insurrection. The racist quality of the prosecutions was not lost on black policemen. The Guardians' Association, an organization consisting of nearly all the city's black policemen, issued a release in June 1971 denouncing BOSS's exploitation of black agents for the betrayal of black radicals and insisted there were other, less offensive methods of surveillance.[31]

The Panther 13

The year 1969 may some day be called the Year of the Panther. In that year, J. Edgar Hoover labeled the Black Panther Party "the greatest threat to the internal security of the country." In the same year, the San Francisco police tear-gassed their way into the national headquarters of the Black Panther Party and arrested 16 people. The Los Angeles police raided the local Panther office and arrested 11. The FBI in Chicago raided the Panther office and arrested 8. The Detroit police followed next and arrested 3. Then in Denver 10 Panthers were arrested in a raid. In Sacramento the police raided and found no one to arrest; they destroyed the office and food-storage facilities, in an action strongly condemned by the mayor. The Chicago police again raided the local Panther office, destroyed it, and dragged away 3 wounded Panthers. The San Diego police raided their local Panther office. A Los Angeles Panther, Walter Toure Pope, was shot and killed by police. For a third time in Chicago, the police raided the local Panthers, killing 2 members, Fred Hampton and Mark Clark, in an action widely denounced as a police murder. The Los Angeles police again raided the local Panther headquarters and fought a five-hour gun battle during which 3 Panthers and 3 policemen were wounded and 21 Panthers were arrested. By the end of 1969, across the country, it was estimated that 30 Panthers were facing capital punishment, 40 faced life in prison, about 55 faced terms of up to thirty years, and another 155 were in jail or being sought.

But New York was a clear exception. Assistant District Attorney Joseph Phillips attributed this to the infiltration work of BOSS, which had put the local police "in much greater control" than in other cities and "on top of the situation." The decimation of the Panther Party in New

York was accomplished without the almost obligatory raid and shoot-out. The lethal instrument was a mass trial—the longest, most expensive, and most publicized trial in the history of New York State.[32] It was a trial overflowing with melodrama: BOSS infiltrators, FBI agents, double agents, wiretaps, wireless transmitters, over $1 million in bail, interrogations and confessions, pistols, rifles, dynamite, bombs, reams of "guerrilla literature," feature-length movies, terrorist plots to kill police and bomb women and children, heroic agents who escaped with their lives by inches, and last-minute arrests that saved the city from wide-scale death and destruction.

The public was first introduced to this case with headlines splashed across the papers on April 2, 1969: "Smash Plot to Bomb Stores" (*New York Daily News*); "Indict 21 in Midtown Bomb Plot" (*New York Post*); "21 Accused of Plot to Terrorize City with Bombings" (*New York Times*). Twelve of the twenty-one indicted persons were rounded up in predawn arrests on the morning of April 2. The arrests were elaborately staged. A total of more than two hundred policemen were mobilized including, in a complete break with precedent, the entire BOSS leadership. Press photographers were given advance notice of the various locations where "arrest scenes" would occur, and along with their stories, each of the papers ran a number of photos.

The press conference announcing the hastily delivered grand jury indictments was dramatized by the rare appearance of District Attorney Frank Hogan himself. To cover the fact that not much in the way of explosives had been produced, he told the press: "We believe they have other material cached away," which the police were said to be then tracking down.

The actual charges listed in the Panther indictment, after being amended once, ran to thirty individual counts against each defendant and covered a period of eight months. The indictment—an array of charges of criminal possession, criminal attempts, and several overlapping conspiracies—can be reduced to two basic plots.

The first was the "January plot," an alleged conspiracy to dynamite several police stations and the Queens branch of the Board of Education, and also to gun down any police escaping from the dynamited precincts. This plot was said to have culminated on January 17, 1969. The second plot became known as the "Easter plot," an alleged conspiracy to blow up the 42d Police Precinct, the New Haven Railroad, five department stores (Macy's, Alexander's, Korvette's, Bloomingdale's, and Abercrombie and Fitch) and, finally, the Easter flowers at the Bronx Botanical Gardens. The New York Supreme Court immediately set bail of

$100,000 for each of the defendants, an act later described by a federal district judge as "a euphemism for the denial of bail." There were two star witnesses, one for each plot: the BOSS infiltrator Ralph White testified about the January plot and the agent Gene Roberts about the Easter plot.

Ralph White was driving a truck at Kennedy Airport when he was accepted for police training two years after he had filed his application. In mid April 1968, after two months at the police academy, he was approached by Lieutenant Schwartz and offered an undercover assignment. He was directed in June to make contact with the not-yet-organized Panthers, who were meeting at the New York SNCC office.

At least six BOSS agents infiltrated the Panther Party right from the start, but White quickly shot ahead of all of them, a tribute to his carefully developed militant image.[33] He boasted to his comrades of robberies, burglaries, and muggings he had committed, described how he threatened his landlord with a shotgun, pointing to small bullet holes in the wall of his apartment, and urged others not to pay their rent. He testified that on a number of occasions he had taught Panthers how to fire guns (he had been a sharpshooter in the Army), and once he conducted a class with one other Panther on how to construct a time bomb. He also admitted that he once had gone to Connecticut to survey a jail where several Panthers were locked up in order to plan for a possible break-out, and had told the heads of the Harlem section to include him in if they made any plans to ambush police. White had once threatened to kill fellow informer Shaun Dubonnet because Dubonnet had never produced guns that White had given him money to buy.

White's supermilitancy was matched by his masterful oratory, and he soon became an official Panther spokesman and representative. In August 1968 he acted as spokesman for the Panthers at a Bronx Community Action Center meeting, then became the paid director of the Elsmere Tenants Council and hired two leading Panthers, Lumumba Shakur (the alleged ringleader of the January plot) and Thomas Berry, to work under him. Panther meetings were regularly held at the Elsmere Council or at White's apartment, partly because he was a host who was generous with marijuana. He engaged in sexual relations with a number of Panther women and supporters, a practice that later led the Guardians' Association to denounce undercover agents who "use black women sexually" while serving as spies.[34]

By September 1968, when the Panther chapter in New York was only two months old, White became section leader of all the Panthers in the Bronx. His functions as a section leader were to organize, to give training in "TE" (technical equipment, primarily meaning weapons) and to gain community support. White also testified that the Panthers were obsessed with problems of security and constantly discussed suspected infiltrators. At the trial, several of the embarrassed defendants recalled that a secret unit had once been formed to guard against spies. The head of the unit was Ralph White. While most agents have had only one control to guide them, Ralph White had five: he reported not only to two direct supervisors but to three other BOSS detectives as well.

White was on the witness stand for several weeks, most of which was consumed in cross-examination by six different lawyers and one defendant, Afeni Shakur. The cross-examination covered two principal areas: the many discrepancies between White's testimony and his reports* and the stillborn fate of all the multifarious criminal plans White attributed to the defendants, a circumstance that, to a more objective observer, would have plainly indicated that they were little more than verbalized fantasies.

Ralph White is an exaggerated version of a type: the informer whose involvement with his targets is so intense and intimate that he comes to share their values and goals. His formal role of the "cool" police operative is submerged by great waves of personal sympathy and political commitment. Unable to suppress these drives, he becomes both hunter and hunted, a good spy and a good Panther. And in betraying others, he betrays himself. This ambivalence produces in the agent profound feelings of guilt and self-hate, which drive him to a compensatory militance within the group. And the need to block his guilt feelings when his betrayed brothers are faced with punishment makes him a treacherous and vindictive witness, prepared, in self-justification, to attribute the most heinous crimes to his victims. Indeed, his need to protect himself from the psychic consequences of his betrayal forces him to view the defendants, his former friends, as unmitigatedly evil. Thus, on the witness stand, White repeatedly insisted that they were capable of committing almost any criminal or immoral act. The almost schizoid quality

---

* White's reports frequently omitted key items mentioned in his direct testimony. He regularly attributed this to carelessness or to the fact that he had "too much to remember" each day. At least one report, for November 28, 1967, appears to have been altered to conform to his direct testimony. In referring to activity at the Elsmere Tenants Council, White wrote: "nothing worth reporting happened at ETC." But, as an afterthought, the very end of the report describes how White had discovered that same day on the desk of Lumumba Shakur, a defendant, evidence allegedly linking the Panthers to a recent bombing—hardly something White could have completely forgotten in his initial presentation. See " 'Afterthoughts' a Panther Trial Key," *New York Post*, February 18, 1971.

of White's relationships made it easy to deceive his BOSS superiors about his real commitment to the Panthers and the Panthers about his spy role.

With the passage of time, White appears to have developed a fuller realization of his role. In a rambling and sometimes incoherent interview with a TV film producer in November 1971, six months after the Panther verdict, White, back at the police academy to continue the training he had barely begun before going undercover,* was asked about the "human side" of being an agent. He began by mumbling almost inaudibly: "I'm the original outsider," then raised his voice and continued without stopping:

> You're always there. . . . Did you read Richard Wright's book *The Outsider?* It's this very good book . . . kind of going into what being outside means . . . you're like a . . . I might even write a book about this . . . about playing games and shit. . . . I mean I'm being honest, but I'm still aware of what I say. If you're an outsider you're more aware of people. You're listening to people behind what they're saying . . . listening to the tone. . . . They never know. . . . See, most people would say: "Oh, Yedwa [White's Panther alias], you're a good brother, you're a nice cat," or "You're a funny nigger." And you're acting the part of a revolutionary, funny nigger, so to speak, in a way. Yet still you're very much aware of you're making them, you're controlling them, you're making them say this, you're making them act the way you want them to. . . . At the same time, too, you're recording everything that they say in your head.

White then ended this erratic monologue and explained that by controlling the Panthers, he did not mean that he framed them. He also said, in response to a further question, that it was "part of the game" to get humanly involved with the people in the target group, and that "sometimes you slip."

When asked why he had become a cop, White said that his basic motivation was a desire to help people, but that he also considered "the twenty-nine year retirement, the fringe benefits. I also considered a certain amount of prestige and notoriety and being looked up to by peo-

---

* Even before completing his police academy training, White was rewarded for his service as a spy by a promotion to the rank of detective, with a substantial increase in salary, which, as already noted, normally takes twelve to fifteen years for those few who make it.

ple . . . and a certain amount of self-respect also for yourself . . . and, you know, advancement, career."

The interviewer then began to discuss his infiltration, but before a question had actually been posed, White interjected: "Getting in was a story unto itself. Once you're in there . . . you never know that you're in, but all of a sudden you realize that you're in . . . and then you're trapped."

White was then queried about his BOSS superiors' credentials:

QUESTION: Did you feel that you were really being controlled in a way by these white people in this organization? Did you feel that they were manipulating you, using you against your own people?

WHITE: I felt that, sure.

White paused silently for a while, then tried to express his pride in the Panther Party and his feeling of brotherhood with those who used to look up to him.

> The only thing that hurt was the people who were in the Party to help people. . . . You see the Black Panther as an Eldridge Cleaver or a Huey P. Newton. You don't see him as a cat who doesn't. . . . Okay, now, if I were in my Panther garb, I would be a model Panther. I'm tall, when I'm standing I'm big. . . . I try to look very sharp. And if you saw me in my Panther garb, I take it you would consider me more of a Panther than you might consider some guy who was just running down the street with kinky hair, beat-up clothes, holes in his pants, you know.

Lumumba Shakur was the most respected of all the Panther defendants, and White's pervasive ambiguity about his role as an agent was distilled in his love-hate feeling for Shakur. White first condemned Shakur and then described how Shakur had told him of the crimes he had committed. He insisted he knew what was "in the back of the guy's head" because Shakur had "exposed his insides" to White when they used to get stoned together. But then he added that when they did get stoned, White could see Shakur as a human being, "and I loved that human being." He said he would not want to hurt Shakur and that if it ever had been necessary to expose himself as a cop in order to prevent Shakur from performing a serious criminal act, like murder, he would have done so—a stunning and wishful repudiation of the role he in fact did play.

About his own leadership role within the Panther Party, White said that he had done "some good things, some great things" as a Panther. As the interview then began to wind down, White was asked if he would do it again. This question triggered a tormented twenty-minute monologue. He began by vowing that he would never do it again, but proudly affirmed the worth of his Panther activities: he "worked very hard within the Party, to try to do something." But he criticized the militant Panthers for overriding the more political brothers who wanted to concentrate on community work. He then recalled a saying he used to quote from Mao Tse-tung to the effect that you cannot run ahead of the people: the Panthers had done this and it was their major mistake. During this sequence, White had lapsed completely back into his Panther identity.

When asked if the Black Panther Party did not have considerable community support prior to the arrest, he became defensive.

> No, I don't think it had that support. Are you asking me honestly? You know, I hate to say that because people say: "You know, you're an Uncle Tom. You're a real Tom." Oh, am I a Tom? Fuck you, I'm a Tom, man. I'm a Tom? Man, I'm not going to go into a thing about how great I am, what I have done for the black community, what I'd do. I worked, believe me, I worked my ass off. And I'm a Tom? Wow! I'd get results.

Describing the promise of the Black Panther Party, he criticized it for becoming "opportunistic" and laid bare his aching resentment at having been used.

> And then, okay, of course you're fighting with your bosses. They're saying [inaudible]. And you're saying: "Hey, I just can't hack this shit." Cause you got the blues, man, sometimes, the bad blues, man. Some bad nights. I lost some weight, man. And you say to your bosses: "Well, you know I really can't see this because, you know, so-and-so, they're not all that fucking bad." "Well, you know, Ralph, they're not *your* people." "Well they *are* my people [White shouts and slams the table]. You don't understand, they *are* my people." "But, no they're not your *kind* of people."

White was interrupted by the interviewer, who exclaimed: "Your superiors are saying this?" White responded with sudden hostility to the interruption and raced on to get it all out:

Don't jump on that. They're not saying that as being cops. They're saying that as being white people. They're saying that as being misinformed people. They're saying that as being people who are trying to protect. They're saying: "They're not your *kind* of people." But I picked it up. And I can also pick up the other connotation of "kind" that they are saying. I know they had that: "They were black, were gonna get guns, they were gonna ice cops." They were like little kids [mimicking]: "You're going to hurt me." So right away they had to beat these people down, you know what I mean? I felt that too. And, okay . . . maybe . . . I felt them saying. . . . But I'm saying, I felt that they were saying this because they were trying to protect me or they were trying to protect the police department. . . . In my own way, I was trying to protect the Panther Party, their image, you know what I mean? That's the whole thing. It's . . . most unfortunate . . . that some of the people locked up were locked up. It's a terrible waste of mankind. There was so much energy in the damn thing. It was terrible that it had to turn out that way. I don't say . . . I don't regret one second being in the Party. I regret quite a bit that . . . people . . . I'm very glad that it took wings, you know what I mean. The whole movement took wings. And its motivation has sucked many people into a consciousness, a conscious level, you know, they say [White rises, raising a clenched fist over his head]: "Oh yeah. Wow. Power! Beautiful! Beautiful!"

We now turn to the "Easter plot" and its star witness, Gene Roberts.[35] When Malcolm X was assassinated on the podium at the Audubon Ballroom in February 1965, one of his bodyguards immediately gave mouth-to-mouth resuscitation to the dying black leader. The bodyguard huddled over Malcolm X was Gene Roberts, BOSS agent. During his five years underground, the longest of any of the surfaced ghetto agents, he had penetrated many militant black organizations but he had never contributed to the staging of a BOSS conspiracy trial until he surfaced in the Panther case to testify about a plot that was lurid, fantastic, implausible, and comic.

In contrast to the volatile and ebullient White, whose temperament trapped him into overidentification with his targets, Roberts is the very model of the cool, unobtrusive, low-keyed operative—straight out of a James Bond scenario. So unobtrusive was he that when his role became known before the trial began, some of the defendants were unable to recall what he looked like or who he was. Roberts belongs to an identifiable class of informers common to all radical strata—quiet men whose commitment is taken for granted in part because they serve as foils for wordy theorists, foot soldiers who gladly permit themselves to be overshadowed by more flamboyant types struggling for leadership. Such spies usually bring to ignorant, poor, and powerless people the gift of a practical skill, connections, savvy—a bridge to the real world, the ability to procure weapons and dynamite, raise money, rent and drive cars, make available a meeting place, or provide some other resource necessary to keep the project from foundering before a conspiracy charge can be brought. Roberts was a bodyguard and driver—steady, dependable, and obedient. As one of the defendants put it: "If you told Gene to drive in a particular direction, he would drive in that direction without asking questions until he ran out of gas."

Roberts became a follower of Panther William King, his boyhood friend for eighteen years. And who could have asked for a better shield from suspicion than King? A familiar type of *fantaisiste* in black radical circles, King loved to play soldier, practice "Third World" guerrilla tactics grotesquely unsuited to the urban scene, study the chemistry of explosives, and prepare grandiose plans, never permitting the harsh realities—manpower, money, equipment, risk of apprehension and punishment—to intrude into his dreams of glory or the stillborn plans of yesterday and the day before and the day before to spoil the scripts for a succession of new battle plans for today and tomorrow and the next day. King was a self-taught master of the new tactics of urban guerrilla warfare, which were totally divorced from the politics they were supposed to implement, a strategist for an army that was perpetually on maneuvers.

Roberts, the born follower, and White, the charismatic leader, were both planted in the Black Panther Party right from its start and remained there during the incubation of both plots—but White testified that he knew absolutely nothing about the Easter plot; Roberts testified that he was unapprised of the January plot. For six months Roberts reported nothing of consequence. Then, in February 1969, he began to report a series of meetings, drills, training sessions, and the like, which together generated the outlines of a plot set to go off "sometime before Easter."

Roberts, as of February 3, 1969, won assignment to the security section led by King, the alleged innermost Panther Party cell. The other members of the unit were inexperienced youngsters who found it hard

to execute King's comic opera battle plans with the disciplined seriousness he expected. Roberts changed all that; he brought to his new assignment an exemplary earnestness and unquestioning willingness to
follow orders that kept the whole enterprise from dissolving into a child-
ish game. Assigned to execute reconnaissance missions, or "recons," of
several department stores and sites along the New Haven Railroad,
Roberts solemnly reported that they were appropriate targets for the
Easter plot.

The rest of the plot evolved piecemeal from various discussions, during which the priorities of a "coordinated attack" were listed: first, several police precincts were to be bombed, then the six sites selected along
the New Haven Railroad, then the department stores, and, finally, the
Easter flower beds at the Bronx Botanical Gardens.

Roberts testified in detail about numerous meetings at which a great
deal of fiery rhetoric was heard. While these statements indicated that
the Black Panthers were outraged and sometimes seething with hate,
they were hardly probative of the charges.

One of Roberts's early reports dealt with Ralph White. In his account
of a meeting on November 23, 1968, Roberts reported that White had
made an angry speech proclaiming that the Panthers would achieve their
ends "by any means necessary" and described White as the most militant member there. (Roberts admitted on cross-examination that he was
thereafter told by his superiors not to report any more on White.) Roberts testified to many discussions about obtaining weapons, from handguns to homemade explosives. At one point, one of the defense
attorneys, Robert Bloom, led Roberts through a series of questions covering seven pages of trial minutes referring to a long list of planned
violent actions against people and property that Roberts had reported.
Roberts admitted that not one of them had ever been carried out.

Nowhere did this bizarre contest between word and deed emerge so
clearly as in the testimony about the Easter plot itself. Roberts testified
that when he and another Panther, Walter Johnson, did a "recon" of the
midtown department stores, they ended up trying on leather jackets at
Macy's and looking at toys to purchase for Roberts's child. Later on, at a
meeting of the Panther security section where Roberts was supposed to
give a report on one of his recons, it was completely overlooked and
admittedly never brought up again. This was the only "hard" evidence
the prosecution presented to demonstrate that the defendants had seriously intended to bomb the five stores. Roberts was even uncertain
whether the recon of the railroad sites had simply been a routine training maneuver, unrelated to the bombing plot.

In a lengthy cross-examination, he made the following admissions: Lumumba Shakur had never had any dynamite to his knowledge and never gave Roberts orders to do anything but community work; Roberts himself was never given orders to bomb anything; there was never any agreement he knew of to place explosives at any particular department store; no one had ever agreed to place any explosives at the railroad sites; he did not recall anyone being assigned to bomb anything.

Questioned as to the final days prior to the Panthers' arrest on April 2, four days before Easter, he testified that on March 29 he went to a security section meeting and only four of the alleged conspirators showed up. The next day there was a similar meeting and no one but Roberts appeared. On April 1, he testified, he had driven the three alleged leaders of the plot to Baltimore and back on a mission to buy a rifle. In all the four days prior to the date of the arrest, described by District Attorney Hogan as the target date of the plot, not one word about the plot was mentioned, not even among the three leaders on the long drive to Baltimore and back. And finally Roberts stated that as of the date of the arrest itself, no exact date had been agreed upon; no particular type of explosive had been decided upon; no particular store designated—let alone locations within the stores; and no particular persons had been selected or assigned for the job.

Roberts nevertheless insisted that a plot had been formed and that it was to be executed "sometime before Easter." But Roberts's own testimony makes it all too clear that the plot was little more than clouds of hot air, which BOSS chose to treat as a real conspiracy. The reports of a planned bombing of precinct headquarters buildings and the gunning down of the escaping survivors ratified police fears of a massacre by blacks that had been triggered by ambush police slayings in the summer of 1968. The indictments were simply the explosion—if one may use that word—of accumulating pressures and tensions within the department. The flimsy and absurd January plot was dusted off and pasted on to the equally flimsy Easter plot to project a bloodthirsty *Schrecklichkeit*, thwarted in the nick of time only by the vigilance of BOSS. And the linkage of the two plots was necessary in order to provide a framework for jailing the entire Panther leadership and thus, at one fell swoop, destroying the organization—without a messy raid or a bloody shoot-out.

Intelligence agencies characteristically exaggerate the intentions of their subjects. And, in the same spirit, they broaden the base of responsibility from the individual suspect to the organization. Unverified political stereotypes about target groups are thus substituted for real evidence of individual guilt. This tension between the assumptions of intelligence and the requirements of law is resolved by heavy reliance on theories of conspiracy, which at once make possible mass charges, embracing even nonparticipants; the substitution of organizational for individual guilt to provide the framework of the criminal "agreement"; and the replacement of proof of criminal acts by vague and deceptive evidence of an intent to act. Quite apart from the credibility of the informer testimony on which this formula typically relies, it sagged in this case at a number of other points—especially the complete collapse of the proof of the defendants' intentions, let alone their power to execute the complicated and destructive plots charged.

As a result, this overkill strategy boomeranged. Despite the pretrial fanfare, one could safely conclude at the close of the trial that never in our history have such heinous charges been supported by such ludicrously unpersuasive evidence.

And so apparently concluded the jury. When the case finally reached them, two years after the Panthers had been arrested, the jury was charged with evaluating testimony that made up a trial record of more than 13,000 pages. The trial itself had lasted weeks and weeks and cost, according to the prosecution, well over $2 million. Justice John M. Murtagh had "simplified" the indictment for the jurors, reducing the number of counts against the thirteen defendants on trial from thirty to twelve, leaving the jury to return 156 individual verdicts.

A bare ninety minutes later, the jury reappeared. As the clerk read off each of the 156 counts, the soft lilt of Jury Foreman James I. Fox's West Indian accent sang out: "Not Guilty."[36]

For the Panthers it was a Pyrrhic victory. By 1971 their organization had been all but destroyed; they had lost two years of their lives to jail and the courts and emerged in a climate of suspicion and fear that killed hopes of regrouping.

A Court Strikes a Blow at BOSS

The damage to BOSS's prestige inflicted by the Panther acquittal was extended four years later by a judicial denunciation. On July 28, 1975, New York State Supreme Court Justice Peter J. McQuillan dismissed an indictment on weapons and conspiracy charges then pending against a black activist, Robert Steele Collier, in a devastating 56-page opinion.[37] Collier had been convicted in the already-discussed Statue of Liberty case and was also a defendant in the Panther 13 trial. Five days after the jury's acquittal of Collier in the Panther case, a black agent, Detective

Oswald Alvarez, was assigned to infiltrate undercover New York City's lower East Side community and to monitor community activities. This broad mission focused on Collier. At the time of the assignment, BOSS had no clear and definite reason ("probable cause") to believe that a crime had been committed. For two years, Alvarez told the court, he had acted on a roving commission with no specific law-enforcement objective. His two targets were, first, the Young Lords, a Puerto Rican community group, and, later, Collier. A BOSS official admitted on the witness stand that "there was no particular crime under investigation." Nor was Collier a promising target. Over the two-year period when Alvarez spied on him, he had earned a reputation as an extraordinarily effective community organizer and civic-minded activist.*

It was not merely that there were no law-enforcement grounds for the undercover assignment but, the court pointed out, the investigation was continued in the face of guidelines promulgated by the police commissioner on February 8, 1973, requiring, as the judge put it, "[some] probability of certain crimes being committed before an infiltration like that conducted by Alvarez could be undertaken."† When pressed further for a justification in the form of criminal activity warranting Alvarez's

---

* Three pages of the court's opinion cited, as a "selected sample," character testimony establishing Collier's commitment to community welfare from sources such as the president of the New York City Health and Hospitals Corporation ("His persistent advocacy for quality health care in the municipal hospitals has been positive and effective"); Planning Associates of the United Presbyterian Church ("Bob is a very valuable member of our community of people who are not content to ignore poverty, hunger, disease, war and injustice"); the executive director of Governeur Hospital ("He has been active and concerned in community affairs in the Lower East Side"); the director of the Medical Care Research Unit, New York University School of Medicine ("I have come to have great confidence in his honesty, his integrity and his desire to protect the safety and well being of the students with whom he works"); the administrator of the Community Relations Department, New York City Health and Hospitals Corporation ("Mr. Collier has been elected to the National Executive Committee of the Medical Committee for Human Rights and has continued to carry out the commitments required by the position"); the executive director of the Bellevue Hospital Center ("Mr. Robert Collier has been a member of the Bellevue Hospital Community Board since September 1972. . . . He has proven to be an interested and responsible member of the [Bellevue Hospital Center] Board and a worthy advocate for improving patient services. He is respected by his fellow board members and has shown considerable leadership abilities"); and the coordinator of the Community Medicine Program, New York University Medical Center ("Bob has . . . committed himself to upgrading the quality of life and cohesiveness of the Lower East Side community").
† The guidelines could be disregarded or altered at will since they lacked sanctions. See Paul G. Chevigny, "Politics and Law in the Control of Local Surveillance," *Cornell Law Review*, April 1984, p. 749.

assignment, his superior lamely acknowledged, "I don't know what criteria was [sic] used to institute the investigation."

The roles played by Alvarez and Collier present an ironic contrast. Collier was heavily involved in a wide variety of civic activities: he was a prominent member of school and election boards, housing associations, health centers, hospitals, and youth groups. Nor did he neglect his detective pursuer. The following exchange tells its own story. An attorney asked Alvarez: "Mr. Collier tried to reform you, so to speak, by offering you jobs, by trying to get you involved in community activities or political activities during the time you were undercover; isn't that a fair statement?" Alvarez: "Yeah." When Alvarez made the mistake of telling Collier he was interested in photography, Collier tried to get Alvarez into a vocational training course in film making—he could make films about housing and health problems. But the pursuer would not be diverted from his pursuit. Alvarez was after bigger game: to get the goods on Collier.

In the course of his two-year assignment, Alvarez accompanied Collier in his rounds of neighborhood improvement activities and endured endless meetings of civic groups. He went along when Collier showed films about the dangers of drug use, organized the Tompkins Square Community Center, recruited youths to a program for learning occupational skills, and performed his duties as a member of the Bellevue Hospital Advisory Board (Collier was a committee chairman), as chairman of the Lower East Side Health Council, and as co-chairman of the Parents' Union for the local school board district.

Invasions of the privacy and personal effects of the target were commonplace. On a number of occasions, he searched Collier's apartment—closets, mattresses, and even a shopping bag of groceries that Collier's wife had brought home. During the two-year infiltration his reports included accounts of Collier's efforts to gain admission to college, the presence of "political" pictures, books, and leaflets in Collier's home and such minutiae as the fact that Collier and his wife "went to the movies," or that they were going to visit her family.

In accordance with instructions, Alvarez routinely made duplicate keys of constitutionally protected premises, such as the apartment of one of Collier's friends, a community workshop where Collier "was working with those kids and teaching them some of those carpentry skills," and the office of the Community Service Center where Collier was a salaried employee for most of the period of the surveillance. He ran the gamut of spy capers: surreptitiously lifting samples from typewriters in private homes; removing and examining papers from a "found" wallet; stealing an address book and copying its contents; opening a briefcase; and lifting, examining, and copying papers while a guest at private homes.

These spookish activities were followed by two applications for search warrants in June 1973. The first was denied and the second was granted. But Justice McQuillan concluded that the evidence in support of the validity of the second search warrant was "simply too conflicting, too weak and too incredible . . . to accept." Accordingly, the court granted the defendant's motions to suppress the evidence as well as to dismiss the indictment altogether. In his landmark opinion, the judge renewed the historic warnings against the dangers of political espionage: "Unwarranted police surveillance will destroy our capacity to tolerate—and even encourage—dissent and non-conformity; it promotes a climate of fear; it intimidates, demoralizes and frightens the community into silence. . . . A ubiquitous secret police and an obsequious society go hand in hand."

"There is a compelling need for legislation to govern covert police activity," the court urged. Subsequent to Justice McQuillan's decision, an ordinance designed to curb open-ended BOSS people-watching practices was rejected by the New York City Council after the police establishment protested that it would block vital law-enforcement investigations.[38] At least until the late seventies, BOSS persisted in political surveillance.[39] It was not until 1985, ten years after the decision in the Collier case, that, in a changed political climate, the settlement agreement in the *Handschu* case (see pp. 356–57) finally brought to an end BOSS's most objectionable practices.

BOSS: Spearhead of a Politicized Department

The pattern of BOSS offensives against the city's black activists traced here is noteworthy because, to a far greater extent than elsewhere on the urban scene, it reflects a conscious decision to use the legal process. Indeed, sources within the department have claimed in interviews that the prosecutions were part of a trade-off to appease elements in the police that threatened self-help and vigilantism unless punitive courtroom measures were taken against the ghetto militants. What cannot be disputed is that in the sixties, the department (and especially BOSS) was highly politicized, its racist cadres eager for a showdown with the leaders of the roiling movements of the time. The emergence of a police crusade for action against the ghetto leaders is rooted in a power struggle in the mid sixties; more specifically, in conflict over a proposal in the election platform of mayoral candidate John Lindsay for a civilian review board to entertain and adjudicate complaints by civilians of police abuses.[40]

Despite the fact that the proposal was in no way unusual—such civilian review boards became commonplace in American cities by the mid sixties—the New York City Police Benevolent Association (PBA) fought it in 1966 by launching a highly racist campaign featuring professionally drafted full-page newspaper advertisements and television warnings of impending disaster. The proposal was backed by a coalition, Federated Associations for Independent Review, led by the New York Civil Liberties Union. The outcome was startling: the police won by a decisive majority (67 to 33 percent). Victory in the face of support for a civilian review board by then Senators Robert F. Kennedy and Jacob Javits, as well as by Mayor Lindsay, strengthened the hand of racist police elements, consolidated a right-wing political movement within the department, gave it a dominant voice in the PBA, and cemented police ties with an urban racist constituency. The antiblack forces won a second round in 1968 in a dispute centered in New York's Oceanville-Brownsville district over decentralized boards of education. This time the liberal forces and the mayor were defeated by Albert Shanker's United Federation of Teachers. By 1968 the police and their support groups were in the saddle, while an inept and bumbling city administration lost power to curb mounting police excesses. In August of that year, John J. Cassese, head of the PBA, shocked many New Yorkers by directing the 29,000-member group to ignore orders by their superiors to exercise restraint in dealing with demonstrators and rioters.

The racist thrust of the new police activism became manifest in September 1968 when many off-duty policemen, subsequently revealed as members of a hard-line police faction, the Law Enforcement Group, [41] joined a mob in an attack on Black Panther Party members and white sympathizers in a Brooklyn courthouse where a hearing was being held in the case of three Panthers charged with assulting a policeman. [42]

The extent of the police rebellion against a neutral peacekeeping role was dramatized in May 1970 when the police stood idly by as bands of construction workers rampaged through lower Manhattan beating antiwar demonstrators. [43] These developments both reflected and contributed to the politicizing of the police—a process nurtured by the "law and order" themes of the Nixon and Wallace presidential campaigns, the escalation of antiwar protest, the Chicago convention confrontation between the police and demonstrators, and, more broadly, a growing fear of ghetto violence fueled by macho Panther rhetoric ("Off the pigs!") and armed confrontation, as well as by the riots of 1967. *[44]

* In the late sixties, the John Birch Society claimed five hundred policemen as members. In other cities, such as Chicago, the Ku Klux Klan gained a foothold.

The police-demonstrator polarization provided BOSS with a counter-subversive agenda that both broadened the scope of its targeting to include police critics and created a climate that justified operational abuses as a response to rampaging "creeps" and "animals" (in police usage) threatening not only public order but the safety and status of the police themselves. For large sectors of the police force—and especially for BOSS, with its strategic (security) and tactical (demonstration-monitoring) missions—it was a war for survival.

But the climate created by the liberal policies of Mayor Lindsay, Police Commissioner Patrick Murphy's gestures (well-intentioned but skimpy) to defuse criticism, the filing of the *Handschu* lawsuit (discussed on pp. 356–57), the 1971 jury verdict in the Panther 21 conspiracy case, and Justice McQuillan's scathing opinion in the *Collier* case (1975) combined to restrain the hard-line countersubversive forces, especially in the attack on black protest. In the mid eighties, the police were confronted with charges of brutality in the treatment of blacks, but not in a context of racial or political protest.[45]

In 1970 the New York City Police Department, yielding to pressure from pro-war patrolmen, amended its regulations to permit the display of the American flag on police uniforms, and the following year the PBA endorsed James L. Buckley, a conservative, for U.S. senator ("Unprofessional Conduct," *New York Times*, July 14, 1971).

6   Rizzo's Philadelphia

Police City

> I'm gonna make Attila the Hun look like a faggot after
> the election's over.
>
> —Mayor Frank L. Rizzo on how
> he would deal with his political
> enemies after his 1975 reelection
> campaign.

The Biggest of the Big Men

While practices associated with the term *police state* abound in the
United States (and all other "free world" countries), beginning in the
sixties, police state modes of governance emerged in ominous perspective
in urban America. Among such subsequently disclosed police state patterns, Philadelphia's is outstanding. Not merely in a rhetorical sense,
Philadelphia became a police city. Police functions were converted by
Frank L. Rizzo into a path to political power. In the process, the police
department became an instrument for implementing Rizzo's moralizing
and racist politics, a symbolic embodiment of the values of his constituency, an elite force that abused its powers with impunity, and a sort of
palace guard mobilized to strike at his political enemies. This power
drive was fueled by a highly efficient political surveillance system based
on distinctive techniques for dealing with dissenters. Philadelphia's vigorous peace movement and large black community (according to the
1980 census figures, 42 percent of the population was nonwhite) were
early targets of this surveillance apparatus and the proving ground for
tactics later used against a broad spectrum of groups.[1]

The star of the police city story, Frank L. Rizzo, the son of a police
sergeant with forty-five years' service, joined the force in 1943 and rose
from the ranks—to acting commissioner in 1966, commissioner in 1967,
and mayor in 1972. He cultivated a tough, fearless image, and even after
he had climbed the advancement ladder, strongly identified with the cop
on the beat. Rizzo is the archetypal authoritarian personality. Like others of his breed—J. Edgar Hoover is a familiar example—he developed a
virtuoso skill in the uses of power: an arbitrary style in the exercise of
authority, deference to higher-ups, a demand for gratitude and loyalty
from the beneficiaries of his favor, contempt for the open-minded civility

197

of the liberal, ethnocentricity and racism, savagery toward the vulnerable or powerless who crossed him, and an ability to wait patiently for others, "like a tiger in high grass" to use his own metaphor, and pounce when the time was ripe. The secondary traits of the authoritarian personality are evidenced in his visceral hatred, a sort of tribal horror, for those who violate the taboos of the culture (sexual, moral, racial), a fanatical fastidiousness (three white shirts a day, a glistening shoeshine, sharply creased trousers, a fleckless car), and an obsession with toughness and masculinity.[2]

The destructiveness of such types is frequently diverted or blunted by the perception of risks. But in Rizzo's case personal passion, provincialism, and a stunted grasp of social reality reduced such restraints to a minimum. Thus, even when he was a line police officer, the norms of professionalism fought a losing battle with his punitive needs and prejudices—reflected most clearly in ham-fisted physical brutality, about which he actually boasted.* In his rise to power as a professed champion of law and order, he consistently displayed a reckless scorn for legal restraints in harassing, detaining, raiding, and arresting targets. Such confrontations were not only personally gratifying but, even if ultimately rebuked by the courts, productive of politically useful headlines.

Rizzo became aware early on that playing the part of a Savonarola, the charismatic scourge of permissiveness and immorality, brought the headlines for which he hungered, as well as an adoring following—first in the Philadelphia white ethnic communities and then among a sizable law-and-order constituency whose anxieties, fears, and prejudices he echoed. In the fifties when he was on the rise, Rizzo became known as "The Cisco Kid" and "Rizzo the Raider" for his flamboyant raids on street gangs, illegal bars, private poker games, and gambling parlors. Later he turned his attention to raiding coffee houses, "head" shops, and similar havens of Philadelphia's mildly bohemian subculture and harassing the habitués.[3]

---

* One example: "Like two weeks ago he gathered a small audience of reporters in a corridor behind City Hall courtroom and told them with great glee the story of a man he had beaten up. He told how he chased the man, caught him, and finally threw him to the ground.

" 'Then I come down with the old number twelve,' Rizzo said, stamping his foot on the floor, 'and the guy ain't walking right today.' Then Rizzo did an imitation of a man who cannot walk right" ("The Techniques of Frank Rizzo," *Philadelphia Inquirer,* August 18, 1967). Further accounts of Rizzo's head-beating proclivities may be found in Craig Walter, "Rizzo," *Philadelphia Magazine,* July 1967; Bernard McCormick, "God Bless Frank Rizzo . . . or God Help Us," ibid.; August 1969; and especially Fred Hamilton, *Rizzo* (New York: Viking Press, 1973), ch. 3.

His vendetta with the Electric Factory Coffee House in the late sixties is lengendary. The Factory, a replica of hundreds of similar places in other cities, became a gathering place for hippies, bikers, students, and guitar-playing singers, not to speak of tourists and curious respectable townfolk. It did well and its owners were careful to comply with all applicable laws and regulations in order to avoid the harassment suffered by the Factory's predecessors. Not long after the place opened in February 1968, Rizzo dropped in and told one of the owners, "You won't be an owner for long. You brought these people to Philadelphia and you're going to pay for it. I'm gonna make a parking lot out of this place." As an appetizer, he brought the owners into court for curfew violations and then moved to accusations that the cafe festered with homosexuals, transvestites, and a multitude of other varieties of "sex perverts," to use one of his favorite epithets.

When raids grounded in these claims collapsed, he charged that the Factory was a headquarters for traffic in hard drugs; when this claim, too, was rejected by the courts, he induced the city solicitor to bring an action to close the place down as a "nuisance." While this legal proceeding was pending in the courts, Rizzo kept a detail of about twelve plainclothesmen stationed outside the premises in order to scare off patrons. An injunction putting the Factory out of business, issued by a compliant lower court judge, was reversed on appeal. But ultimately the harassment proved too much for the proprietors and they closed down.

Rizzo's crusade as police commissioner against permissiveness focused, in large part, on the schools. His most memorable foray in this sphere occurred in November 1967 when school officials were meeting with a delegation of high school students to discuss a demand for a black studies program. An estimated crowd of 3,500 peacefully demonstrated on the outside in support of the students' demands. But when Rizzo arrived on the scene, he put "riot plan number three" into action, ringing the area with squad cars and uniformed police wearing riding boots and leather jackets. Reportedly on a signal from Rizzo ("Get their black asses!"), the patrolmen began to beat demonstrators indiscriminately. Ministers, school board officials, spectators, and students were clubbed. According to the ACLU's Philadelphia director, Spencer Coxe, "I myself was there and saw children who were fleeing from the police lying on the ground each with three patrolmen beating them unmercifully with clubs."

Rizzo not only stood his ground, rejecting claims of police brutality, but renewed his attack on the school system the very next month. In December 1967 the Philadelphia school board set up a program involving students, principals, and social scientists to find ways to ease racial tensions exacerbated by the earlier provocations. Meetings and seminars were held in an isolated mansion, used as a secluded study center, in the Chestnut Hill section. Unknown to the sponsors of the program, the police spied on the meeting, copied a list of those who registered, identified others from license plate numbers, questioned the manager of the center about the program, and compiled reports and dossiers on many of the participants.[4] When Rizzo became mayor in 1972 he promptly arranged for the ouster of the school superintendent, Mark Shedd, a nationally known progressive educator, whom Rizzo regarded as a bête noire of permissiveness.

Rizzo instinctively knew that there was political gold in his blend of moralizing and law enforcement. But in order to extract it, he needed the help of the media, and not merely as a passive conduit of the "news," which he could produce at will: a raid followed by a press conference, reckless courtship of danger, endless outpourings of good quotes (sometimes regretted or repudiated the next day), an eye-catching photo. In Rizzo's favorite Horatio Alger scenario of the poor kid who "came up the hard way," the press was cast in the role of an enthusiastic collaborator in an arrangement by which a continuing supply of "news" was exchanged for an equal amount of personal publicity. No police officer in America ever wooed the press as ardently as Rizzo. During his tenure as police commissioner, he systematically cultivated the company of reporters, did them favors, and even obtained patronage sinecures to supplement their incomes. And newspaper executives were his special pets.*[5] By the late sixties, Rizzo's image-building efforts paid off. He became an urban folk hero, a Big Man who overshadowed even such predecessors as Captain Schaack and Grover Whalen, and a sure-fire candidate for the mayoralty.

The Civil Defense Squad: Friend or Foe?

The power of the forces that made the Philadelphia Police Department a repressive instrumentality in the sixties is symbolically reflected in the history of the Civil Defense (CD) Squad. This police unit was launched in

---

* Rizzo's media courtship, political conservatism, cocksureness, narcissism, and passionate self-righteousness in vilifying his critics are further links to J. Edgar Hoover. Indeed, Rizzo greatly admired the late FBI chief and after his death in 1972 courted the Nixon White House in the hope of being named his successor. Compare the profile of Hoover's authoritarian traits in Donner, *The Age of Surveillance: The Aims and Methods of America's Political Intelligence System* (New York: Knopf, 1980), pp. 120–23.

1964 by the then police commissioner, Howard Leary. A liberal—he was subsequently, in 1966, chosen by New York's Mayor Lindsay to head the New York City Police Department—Leary instituted what was considered at the time an innovative police program to deal with the newly emerging problem of proliferating public demonstrations. However, like so many of its counterparts in other cities and despite its benign purpose, the CD was transformed by the countersubversive imperative. Leary projected the concept of a new police specialist, "The Civil Disobedience Man," who, by virtue of his background, experience, and training, could keep order and at the same time protect demonstrators' constitutional rights. The CD man was to be selected for his congeniality, "long fuse," patience, and maturity—young enough to be able to relate to demonstrators but with sufficient experience to stay cool under pressure. Those who qualified were then to be schooled by professionals in sociology, human relations, and civil rights law.[6]

In contrast to uniformed patrolmen, the plainclothes CD men were instructed to "establish rapport" with demonstrators and their leaders. A vital part of the plan called for the CD's encouragement of telephone calls from leaders of protest groups informing the police of the time, site, and estimated number participating in a planned demonstration. This would enable the CD to furnish adequate protection without wasting men. In order to gain the confidence of the demonstrators and to protect their constitutional rights, CD members were instructed to make arrests only as a last resort after prior warnings had been ignored. At the conclusion of a demonstration, the entire squad was supposed to meet in a self-criticism session.

But this benign and well-intentioned program went awry almost from the start. In an article in November 1966 on "The CD Man" in a leading police journal (*Police Chief*), Philadelphia Police Inspector Harry G. Fox stressed the importance of the intelligence function of this new "specialist." The CD officer must use his personal relationship with demonstrators and their leaders both to "develop intelligence about their connections, background, personal life and ambitions" and to collect literature in order to determine which "organizations are infiltrated, influenced or directed by hard-core communists and their sympathetic followers." In June 1966, in testimony before the Senate Internal Security Committe, Fox had already (unconsciously) revealed that Leary's conciliation perspective had given way to garden-variety adversarial surveillance. He explained to the senators that "the CD officers know by sight the hard-core men and women who lead and inspire demonstrations . . . their associations, family ties, techniques and affiliations with organizations leaning toward Communism both on and off the Attorney General's list. They see them day in and day out recruiting, planning, carrying signs and verbally assaulting the principles of democracy." It was all too much for flesh to bear. It "frustrates and alarms [the police] to see the cancer of subversive thought spread into our youth with its contamination and certain death."[7]

Neither Fox's testimony nor his article ever explained how the CD officer was to become matey with the demonstrators, their leaders, picket captains, and spokesmen and thus generate the "rapport" that would encourage cooperation. Why should a responsible activist confide in a CD man the details of a contemplated demonstration and thus make it easier for the police to photograph and develop files about himself and his fellows, to infiltrate his group with spies, and to condemn it as "subversive"? The newly decreed chumminess between the demonstrator and the CD man was little more than a technique for persuading the hunted to hold still long enough for the hunter to train his sights on him.

As the sixties progressed, the CD, under the leadership of Lieutenant (later Inspector) George Fencl, gradually reverted from its benign conciliatory mission to the hostile "red squad" style it was supposed to replace. Meeting and demonstration sites bristled with CD men whose very numbers were intended to be oppressive. Some were armed with tape recorders and cameras, either actively photographing or pointing empty cameras at targets in order to intimidate them.

The squad's use of photography was described by CD Sergeant Kenneth Hyland in the Berrigan (Harrisburg) trial, at which he was a prosecution witness. He testified that on February 24, 1970, "we anticipated a demonstration by various peace groups to start at City Hall and end up at Independence Hall, in the form of a march. I was assigned to photograph this demonstration" (a concededly peaceful rally by some three hundred antiwar protesters). Despite the fact that no arrests were made, the photographs were retained in a file: "We keep a record in the file of all the demonstrations we cover." The sergeant admitted that, in addition to the participants collectively, individuals were photographed who "are engaged in activity that we figure should be photographed."

But by Hyland's account it would be wrong to conclude that those procedures had anything to do with surveillance:

> We are not a surveillance group. We provide the necessary police service to demonstrators, to the general public to insure a peaceful demonstration. We maintain communications with organization leaders and community leaders to try and stop demonstrations before they start by keeping track of their problems.

Q.   Stopping disorder, not demonstrations?

A.   Well, sometimes certain groups will have problems that we can solve before a demonstration would come about.

Q.   And this particular demonstration had a lot of policemen present, did it not?

A.   It did have a lot of policemen present.

Q.   But there was no occasion to use the policemen because the demonstration was completely peaceful?

A.   It was completely peaceful. That is correct.

Q.   There were no arrests and there was no difficulty of any kind.

A.   That is correct.[8]

The implausibility of Sergeant Hyland's disclaimer of CD surveillance and his insistence on its protective peacekeeping and violence-prevention mission is illuminated by the CD's full operational pattern. To begin with, at the time Hyland was testifying, the CD had targeted virtually every dissenting Philadelphia organization, some six hundred in all. And these included groups such as the American Civil Liberties Union, the Quakers, and Resistance.

In interviews and group conferences conducted by the author in 1971, representatives of monitored groups and individual targets reported various forms of overt surveillance, such as the tailing of members or leaders for periods ranging from three to twenty days, physical surveillance of the organization's office, and recording the license plate numbers of those in attendance. Here are three accounts:

Student Mobilization Committee

By far the most common practice, which is common to the point of routine, is open surveillance of the SMC [Student Mobilization Committee] office by members of the Civil Disobedience Squad. Their normal practice is to sit in their car and watch the people coming in and exiting. They often appear to be taking notes. Frequently, when they notice someone going in who they don't recognize, they will go up to him, and, pretending to be interested passersby, try to find out what is going on inside the office, and, if they can, who the person is and what he does for SMC.

CORE

Still another surveillance technique leveled at CORE is to watch the office from stores in the area. This was learned when one merchant refused to let them use his store and informed CORE of the attempt. He also said that this had been done from other stores on the block. A particularly obnoxious aspect of this incident was that the refusing store owner had charges of some sort pending at the time of the request to use his store and the police indicated that his cooperation would lead to favorable results in his case.

Resistance

At the old Resistance office,* we used to have, quite regularly, people coming in saying that there are people across the street taking pictures or a cop outside taking down names or license plates and this used to really upset some of the volunteers. It was also the national headquarters of Women's International League for Peace and Freedom and United World Federalists, and they used to get quite upset about this.

Official protestations of a benign protective purpose were further mocked by the CD's infiltration apparatus, operated both on its own and with supplementary assistance from other units.

Target groups were regularly infiltrated by police officers, civilian spies, and, a Philadelphia contribution to the art, "pin money" informers—usually wives of regular police officers recruited through the inducement of a modest family income supplement. Ghetto tipsters "hooked" on criminal charges were also used. The CD's use of informers suggests not only the bogus character of its peacekeeping conciliation cover but a root purpose to injure and neutralize the target. Thus it took pains to taunt the infiltrated groups with tidbits of inside information. As a Resistance leader observed in an interview:

One of the things the CD Squad, especially Fencl, liked to boast about was having inside men. And they liked to

* In the course of an interview, a Resistance leader recalled: "Resistance had an office at 20th and Walnut on the 4th floor of Women's International League's national headquarters and it was a really beautiful old building. We began to have a certain amount of increasing harassment. And then one night the whole building burned down. It was really tragic. The police came and the firemen came and so forth. And we came down and talked to a bunch of the firemen and they said, 'You know that it just had to be arson because where it was set in the stairwell so that the stairwell, four flights up, acted as a chimney and there was nothing else there.' There wasn't anything, not even a rug, that could have caught on fire."

drop things to you like, "So, you're having a meeting on such and such a date," or, "Your leaflet had a spelling error," or, "Our informer told us such and such." They say that all the time and they enjoy doing it—in fact, the last time we were arrested they tried to convince us that Tony [Avirgan, a Resistance leader] was an FBI informer. . . . I have begun to believe that they like to make their presence known and to tell us that they have infiltrated our group with spies because they know it freaks us out.

Since informers were used as a punitive resource and not merely as a channel of information, they were planted in great numbers, a practice intended to create an internal fear of betrayal. Spy saturation was also used to form a pool of expendable decoys; plants were instructed to invite or arrange for their exposure by other spies to strengthen the cover of the latter. The format of secrecy and gravity poorly concealed a rough-and-tumble vaudeville in which performers took the stage, did what they could to pummel their victims, and departed. Small wonder that little was done to protect the security of even the most valuable spies. Robert Thompson, for example, a hard-working CDer who ran the Resistance office ("the first one in in the morning and the last one to leave"),* was exposed when his betrayed comrades visited him in the hospital: he was in a ward reserved exclusively for patients from the police and fire departments.

The evidence is quite clear that as early as the summer of 1967, the CD had access to a supply of informers, sponsored and paid by the Federal Bureau of Investigation. More important, collaboration between the FBI and the Philadelphia police in destructive counterintelligence initiatives against the Philadelphia black activists was used as a model for the bureau's aggressive intelligence program (COINTELPRO) in this sector, begun in August 1967 and expanded in February of the next year.

---

* Thompson was, if anything, a bit too dedicated. On one occasion, a group of Resistance members, including Thompson, staged a protest against war-related toys in front of the Lit Brothers Department Store, using plastic machine guns as a "guerrilla theater" prop. The CD, notified by Thompson, patrolled in an unmarked squad car. Departing from the script, Thompson enthusiastically turned his simulated weapon on his fellow officers in the squad car and simulated a vicious machine-gun burst, "Rat-a-tat, rat-a-tat." While it was probably done to protect Thompson's cover, it left the other demonstrators gasping. And was it a similarly misplaced zeal that led Thompson to injure himself in a touch football game with his Resistance associates, requiring the hospitalization described in the text?

In exchange for assistance on the informer front, the police supplied the FBI with the fruits of its electronic surveillance, an area in which the bureau was reluctant to tread. Resistance members became convinced that the police were tapping both office and private phones. Resistance members announced demonstrations of a fictitious nature through telephone calls to suspected phones. If the police showed up at the place where the fake demonstration was scheduled at the correct time, suspicion that the phone was tapped was confirmed. "When this happened repeatedly, we became sure. Just one example of this occurred in June of 1970. A demonstration was planned at the South Philadelphia Draft Board. Since it involved the ritual of pouring blood, it was felt that large numbers would be a hindrance so no advance announcements were made at all. The CD Squad, alerted by an informer, showed up anyway before pourers arrived." In some instances, the police would learn from a tap or an informer that a demonstration or meeting was planned and would then send plainclothesmen from door to door in ghetto areas warning householders to shun the targeted meeting because trouble was expected.

If the CD had ever been a shield for the protection of dissent, it was quite clear that by 1966–67, the beginning of the Rizzo years, it had become a sword.* To be sure, Fencl and his CDers did make a few gestures and indulged in the rhetoric of conciliation. But when Rizzo took over, even these concessions faded. In the eyes of the new commissioner, Fencl was a Leary man and shared his conciliatory style—he had favored a civilian police review board and had banned clubbing or shooting in the 1964 Philadelphia riot. But Rizzo's priorities were quite different: determined to transform the department into a source of dependence and political power, he exploited its law-enforcement resources with the aid of the media to frighten the citizenry—even civic-minded liberals—into embracing without reservation his promise of "protection" against the threats of the sixties posed by radicals, black militants, student activists, and their constituencies (*pace* Captain Schaack). This "protection" mission, designed first to sow fear and then to offer a haven,

---

* The polarization of the CD into an aggressive red squad was a result of a number of circumstances, beginning with Fencl's ambivalent conception of its role. Prominent influences were the recruiting of police types for whom neutrality and conciliation made no sense, training sessions that placed heavy stress on the sinister role of the "outside agitator" (according to one instructor a reliable clue to the identification of such a troublemaker is the use of revolutionary terms like "vested interest"), and the fact that CD posts were considered cushy jobs (minimal supervision and no uniforms) and typically filled by candidates with political sponsors.

inevitably elevated the police force as a whole into an autonomous body, shielded from accountability to the public for corrupt practices and other abuses. *

When Rizzo took over from this "gutless bastard," as he called Leary, he promptly summoned Fencl and barked, "The party is over," Fencl. You're just another cop now." Rizzo's contempt for the blueprinted mission of the CD ("Pussycats!") left no room for "bleeding heart" formulations about conciliation.

Rizzo's racism and barely concealed rage at nonconformity transformed the peacekeeping function, in the name of "protection," into an instrument of aggression. And this transformation, enveloping the entire department, including the CD, was reflected in mounting reports from the mid sixties on beatings of demonstrators. In effect, the nightstick style, a "let-me-at-'em" passion that hungers for a victim, became a recurring police modus operandi at demonstrations and other public gatherings.[†]

Bombs and the Man

Even more than on the federal level, urban law enforcement is reactive, a response to already-committed crimes. But the CD and its support units insisted that the surveillance of political targets was a vital requirement of advance law-enforcement intervention to prevent planned violence. Based on information typically supplied by a street tipster or casual informant, or "discovered" through several weeks of intensive surveillance by the CD, police would raid a private residence, where they assertedly found explosives, guns, or inflammatory literature. A torrent of Rizzo-inspired publicity would then link the raided

---

* Moreover, it was fostered by Democratic Mayor James Tate, eager to consolidate a populist constituency and especially to win the support of Philadelphia's ethnics and turn the city away from the reform traditions of its predecessors (Mayors Clark and Dillworth) and the community service goals of their police commissioners (Brown, Gibbons, and Leary) to Rizzo's fear-mongering "protection" mission. The Tate-Rizzo banner soon made most Philadelphians forget that, despite its aberrations, especially in the labor-relations field, the Philadelphia Police Department was regarded as "probably the best in the country" (Russell E. Weigley, ed., *Philadelphia: A 300-Year History* [New York: Norton, 1982], p. 659).

† On July 2, 1969, four Philadelphia civic groups (Americans for Democratic Action, Community Legal Services, Philadelphians for Equal Justice, and the American Civil Liberties Union) issued a statement charging that, to protect the police from identification in the beating of demonstrators, "the state police have counseled local policemen to remove identity badges lest the officers could later be made defendants in civil actions."

premises and the seized matériel to a group of militants, which, it usually suggested, was part of a larger and more powerful movement. Front-page stories under banner headlines would quote Rizzo's blood-chilling description of the plot, miraculously aborted, and the closeness of the city's escape from destruction. Bail would be set at astronomical levels, but prosecution of the culprits usually faltered. After long delays (months and even years) the back pages of the newspapers whose front pages had originally blazed with reports of the sensational arrests would limply record that the prosecution had been dropped altogether or the defendants had pled guilty to lesser charges (usually possession of weapons) or other, unrelated charges.

The brazen quality of this raid formula, its disregard of legal restraints, flowed directly from Rizzo's police-can-do-no-wrong credo. He repeatedly insisted that the police were "human beings" after all and if they made "mistakes," their misconduct should be condoned in view of the (invariably exaggerated or misrepresented) behavior of their accusers. These exculpatory pleas were rarely, if ever, tested in the local courts because of Rizzo's influence in the district attorney's office. And, in criminal cases in which the victim of police misconduct was a defendant, lower court judges were reluctant to dispute the accused officer. As a result, systematic abuse of the rights of minorities and dissenters became institutionalized. Raids on Black Panther centers climaxed a long train of harassment: vendors of the Panther newspapers were regularly abused, frequently arrested, and detained for hours without charges; Panther posters supporting political candidates were removed; members' cars were stopped and searched; Panthers were cursed and denounced if they merely looked tough; their cars were indiscriminately ticketed. On one occasion the owner of an inoperative, junked car received a ticket for "speeding." Similar tactics were used against members and leaders of other dissident groups, though not as systematically. For example, cars bearing peace windshield or bumper stickers or with long-haired drivers or passengers were frequently stopped and their occupants harassed. (The use of traffic laws to harass black targets became a joint enterprise of the police and the FBI even prior to the formal launching of the FBI's "Black Nationalist" COINTELPRO offensive, which frequently made use of this tactic with the aid of local units in other cities.)

The first "bomb" raid took place August 12, 1966, when eighty heavily armed policemen, supported by hundreds of backup men, staged simultaneous raids on four premises in the ghetto area of North Philadelphia. Rizzo, who had just been named acting commissioner by then Mayor James Tate, announced that the police had received a tip from an informant that the four apartments were meeting places for the

Student Nonviolent Coordinating Committee (SNCC) and were being used as private "arsenals,"* stocked with "hoards of dynamite, guns and ammunition." Nine persons were arrested, some of them at the time of the raid, others when they gave themselves up later. Six were held on $50,000 bail.

The raids netted two-and-one-half sticks of dynamite, found in one apartment under a couch. At subsequent hearings it was established that the dynamite had been hidden there by one of the nine arrestees, Barry Dawson, a mentally unstable ghetto resident.[9] The incident was hardly worldshaking; there was no legal ban at the time on the storage of dynamite, which, in any event, lacked detonators. But with the help of the media, Acting Commissioner Rizzo played endless variations on the theme that militants were plotting to dynamite the city and that "a major incident had been averted by the raid."[10] Rizzo said he had received information that "the meeting places for the militant groups were being used as storehouses of arms, ammunition and dynamite," and he warned that "five sticks of dynamite could reduce Independence Hall to a heap of rubble." He was also careful to point out that the defendants all had "histories of connection with various civil rights organizations." At the time, SNCC had neither cadres nor headquarters, but the raids still were constantly referred to as "the SNCC raids," the defendants as "SNCC members," and the apartments as "SNCC headquarters." It is true that several of the defendants had been active in SNCC at one time or another, but no evidence was ever produced to show that SNCC as an organization was implicated in any way in unlawful activity connected with the dynamite. Rizzo's publicity was effective, however, for the episode was long remembered by Philadelphians as "the SNCC dynamite plot." In August 1967 the charges against three of the defendants were dropped; three more cases were dismissed the following April, and the last two (Dawson having pled guilty to possession of explosives and subsequently having been placed on probation) were dropped in May.[11] But SNCC ceased to exist in Philadelphia.

The RAM Plots

In the summer of 1967 Rizzo discovered the RAM (Revolutionary Action Movement) plots. On July 27 of that year, two months after Rizzo was named commissioner, the police raided a house in the ghetto and confiscated quantities of pamphlets, manuals, and other literature of

---

* Virtually every raid site was characterized as either a "fortress" or an "arsenal."

a group calling itself the "Black Guard," an alleged offshoot of the Philadelphia RAM, which had long been a prime CD target. The raid followed the arrest of six officers and members of the group and was timed with inspired precision: On the very next day, July 28, 1967, Mayor Tate proclaimed a "limited emergency" (discussed below) that banned public meetings of twelve or more. Later Tate made a television announcement that the police were searching for "several large caches of dynamite, rifles and other contraband" hidden by the arrested conspirators, a development that conveniently served as an answer to the widespread demands for an end to the "emergency."

The black militants were initially charged with disorderly conduct and breach of the peace and, later, on the basis of the seized documents, with a conspiracy to incite to riot and other seditious plots, including a weird superplot, described in this way by Lieutenant Fencl:

> Men were solicited to create a riot in the city of Philadelphia; to commit murder, to cause public chaos by destruction of private and public property, literally to destroy the city by violence. It was their intention that once riots started in the city that poison would be distributed through their agents throughout the city for the purpose of placing it in the food and drink that would be distributed gratuitously to policemen assigned to the riot area. [12]

In October the *Totentanz* took a wilder turn when more alleged RAM members were seized and charged with plotting to dynamite public buildings and assassinate public officials, including Rizzo. All of the incitement charges were quickly dropped and the other charges (of dynamiting and assassination) were also abandoned. In exchange the defendants pled guilty to breach of the peace and were placed on six months' probation on that charge. [13]

The police had still another go at RAM in November 1968, when a detail from the CD Squad descended on a house that Fencl said had been placed under surveillance for "a period of time" as the suspected headquarters of the Black Guard. In the basement the police found an assortment of weapons—two rifles, two shotguns, two pistols, more than three hundred rounds of ammunition, and several knives—as well as tape recorders, a mimeograph machine, and three cartons of Maoist literature. The police said they also found a bullet-ridden Philadelphia telephone directory, which indicated that the basement had been used for target practice. An alleged member of the group, Odell Rogers, was arrested and held on the usual high bail—$20,000. Again, the prosecution was dropped; and RAM itself disappeared from the scene. [14]

The SDS Bomb Conspiracy

By 1969 many American cities had already experienced the impact of SDS militance. On Philadelphia campuses, however, SDS had never been very strong, and Rizzo found himself behind the times. Rizzo's problem was admirably summed up by Bernard Segal, a Philadelphia attorney, in a 1969 interview: "Rizzo is a 1969 guy. He's very modern, like the guy who wants to be the first on his block to have a [late model] car. And it bothered him that other cities were having trouble with SDS but Philadelphia wasn't. So he decided to have trouble with the SDS."

The National Caucus of Labor Committees (NCLC) was a miniscule offshoot of the SDS, quite removed from and scornful of the mainstream of dissent, proud of its militance, but unable to attract substantial support. When the NCLC became involved in a campaign directed against the city's public school system, Rizzo moved against it.[15] In February 1969 eight members of the group were arrested by the CD (over the vigorous protests of the Philadelphia branch of the American Civil Liberties Union) for distributing leaflets in front of two Philadelphia high schools.* In the same month, six visitors to the city were arrested for taking pictures of a ceremony outside a high school. The police justified the arrests on the grounds "that they were suspicious people in an auto with New York tags taking photos."†

In March Rizzo charged that the NCLC organizers were subverting the high schools and plotting to blow them up. He "documented" his charge with *Your Manual*, a pamphlet on how to make bombs and Molotov cocktails, which he reproduced in quantity for the local media and

---

* The leaflets were captioned, "Help the Fight against the University City Science Center at Penn." The eight were taken to the Police Administration Building, interrogated, photographed, required to provide information for use on an "intelligence summary" (discussed later), detained for three hours, and then released.

† Young people in cars with out-of-state license plates with long-haired drivers or passengers were frequently stopped "on suspicion." For example, in 1970 the son of Governor Cahill of New Jersey was stopped because he was driving an out-of-state car with a peace sticker on the side, which was parked in a black neighborhood. Young Cahill was arrested and charged with a marijuana law violation. The same year, the daughter of a prominent Quaker drove into town with a long-haired passenger and out-of-state license plates. She was stopped as soon as she crossed the line into Philadelphia, and when she asked the reason for stopping her, the police replied, "We just want to check on your identity. We want to know who the people are who come to Philadelphia." This "outside agitation" concern may well have been a cover. The evidence is strong that such targets were pinpointed by the FBI pursuant to the collaborative arrangement described earlier.

circulated with a memorandum stating: "The Students for a Democratic Society is the moving force behind the circulation of this booklet in Philadelphia." In fact, the pamphlet was published in San Francisco and referred to the local San Francisco scene only and was obviously not intended for use outside of that city. It had been seized and destroyed by the police there, except for single copies distributed by the Veterans of Foreign Wars (VFW) to urban police chiefs; the real "moving force behind the circulation of this booklet in Philadelphia" was Rizzo himself. In a letter to the Philadelphia ACLU dated April 11, 1969, he justified his action by saying that he knew the pamphlet had been distributed at an NCLC meeting in Philadelphia as recommended reading and he believed that "it is in the interest of the people of this city for them to be aware of the actions advocated by groups within our society." Rizzo refused to disclose the source of his knowledge of SDS's use of the pamphlet.

The attempt to attribute this how-to-do-it manual to the NCLC was marked by a particularly offensive irony. Rizzo had in the past confined himself to targets whose style and rhetoric might create an expectation of violence. But the NCLC had fought factions in the student movement and the SDS that were committed to anarchist-terrorist methods: it favored coalition politics, mass pressure, and ameliorating legislative programs. In short, the political police of Philadelphia attributed a revolutionary bomb plot to a group that had come into being and defined itself by rejection of bomb plots as a political instrument.

When the initial harassment, bogus arrests, and smear press releases failed to stop the NCLC, Rizzo once again resorted to the familiar bombplot scenario. On the night of April 9, 1969, after two weeks of around-the-clock surveillance, ten members of the CD Squad led by Lieutenant Fencl entered the apartment of Steven Fraser and Richard Borgmann, young activist members of the NCLC. Armed with a search warrant (applied for on the basis of a "tip from an unnamed informant") the detail found a can of explosive powder, three casings for pipe bombs, six metal pipe caps, a container of plastic explosive known as C-4, and a length of dynamite fuse. The incriminating explosives were "discovered" in or underneath a refrigerator in a corner of the kitchen, a location that enabled the policemen to "find" the contraband without being seen simply by walling the corner off with their massed backs.

Rizzo held a press conference on the day after the raid and recited his now predictable lines: those arrested "could have caused great grief in the community and great damage. People like this should be not permitted to roam the streets." The commissioner displayed sixteen photographs of the messy apartment and two separate close-up pictures showing four paperback novels with titles like *My Body Is Waiting.* "Just look at the filthy conditions in those pictures," he said. "They're self-explanatory." Given such degeneracy, who needed further proof of guilt?

At the preliminary hearing on the case, a set of seized bomb parts mysteriously made an appearance in police photographs as an assembled bomb. But even stranger was the police failure to take fingerprints. The following colloquy between defense counsel and Lieutenant Fencl tells its own story:

Q. Did you or any of the other officers who handled these items pick up either with tongs, tweezers or with handkerchiefs in order to preserve whatever fingerprints there might be on those cans to help identify the individuals who had been handling or having possession of the particular item?

A. No, we did not.

Q. Why not?

A. We just did not do it.[16]

At a hearing Fencl asked for $25,000 bail for each of the defendants and asserted that the NCLC was part of an "East Coast Bomb Conspiracy" centered in Boston whose first priority was the demolition of national monuments in Boston and Philadelphia. He added that Fraser had been present at a Boston meeting of the "conspiracy" the preceding March. The court granted Fencl's bail request, but on appeal, when Fencl admitted that he really didn't know that such a gathering had ever taken place, let alone that either Fraser or Borgmann had attended, the bail was reduced to $10,000 each. All this happened in the summer of 1969. Almost four years later, in 1973, the case was dropped on the grounds that the prosecution was unwilling to reveal its informer's identity.*

The Panther Police Assassination Plot

Commissioner Rizzo had been singularly unsuccessful in making any of his bomb-plot charges stick, and by 1969 he was beginning to have the same trouble as the boy who cried wolf. He was helped out of his di-

---

* Not long after this the NCLC turned sharply rightward. Its leader, Lyn Marcus, revealed himself to be Lyndon LaRouche, an ex-Trotskyist, and renamed the NCLC the U.S. Labor Party. The organization specialized in political and economic intelligence and sought to supply information to federal, state, and local police on left-wing activities. LaRouche and his lieutenants were eventually convicted on criminal charges of fraud.

lemma by nationwide scare publicity concerning the Black Panther Party, and he immediately went to work on the Philadelphia Panthers.[17] In mid September a bugging device was discovered behind a wall in the Philadelphia Black Panther Party (BPP) headquarters in Philadelphia.[18] A week later, on September 23, a police party including CD men and FBI agents entered the home of the sister of a BPP leader, Richard (Reggie) Schell, allegedly looking for a bank robbery suspect. They never found the man they claimed to be looking for, but they did find an M-14 military rifle, which they claimed was stolen. Schell was subsequently charged with stealing the weapon, although he did not live in his sister's house. Later that evening, Fencl's men entered the BPP headquarters by smashing a back door to the office and removed an armful of records and correspondence. The police also looted the office of its daily activities log book, personnel files, photographs, and signed petitions gathered by the party in its campaign for community control of the police. In addition, office equipment was destroyed or removed. Fencl denied responsibility, but the break-in and theft of records had all the earmarks of a CD job.

In March 1970 Fencl's squad, together with federal agents, raided another "fortress" in North Philadelphia and arrested eleven persons on various charges, including burglary and violation of the Uniform Firearms Act. Fencl told the press that seven of the suspects were members of a group "possibly allied with the Philadelphia Black Panther Party" and that the other four were "believed to be members" of the Black Panther Party. Nothing came of this foray.[19]

The final confrontation came at 6:00 A.M. Monday, August 31, 1970, when three separate police teams of about forty-five heavily armed police stakeout men, each team accompanied by eight to ten detectives, under CD leadership, simultaneously raided Black Panther Party offices on Wallace Street in West Philadelphia, Columbia Avenue in North Philadelphia, and Queen Lane in Germantown. As in all of the major Philadelphia raids, Rizzo mobilized a corps of newsmen and photographers to record and photograph the action.

The raids climaxed a bloody August weekend in a city already tense and fearful over a Panther-sponsored "People's New Revolutionary Convention" scheduled for the following weekend (September 5–7) for the purpose of drafting a new left-wing constitution. On Saturday, August 29, a policeman, Frank VonColln, was killed and his partner injured in a bungled attempt to blow up a police guardhouse in Fairmount Park. Five suspects were later arrested. Rizzo described them as members of the "Black Unity Council" and "revolutionaries" who were participants in a national conspiracy to kill policemen. On Sunday night, in a wholly unrelated incident, two highway patrolmen were shot and wounded by an unidentified gunman.

As a result of the Monday dawn raid, fourteen persons were arrested and three policemen were wounded, none seriously, by shotgun pellets fired by the Panthers in one of the raids. The fourteen Panthers were charged with a variety of assaults, all of which grew out of the raid, but in no case with complicity in the weekend shootings. Only one charge, violation of the firearms code, was based on conduct that anteceded the issuance and service of the search warrant. Yet the raids on all three buildings were authorized for the declared purpose of obtaining evidence in aid of the police hunt for the fugitive killer of VonColln. None of the weapons yielded by the raids was linked by the police to the killing.

The justification for the raids was questionable on its face. A more convincing explanation for them is Rizzo's ferocious hatred of the Panthers, intensified by the VonColln killing. Perhaps the clearest evidence that it was vengeful fury and not law enforcement that inspired the raids is the manner in which they were conducted and Rizzo's response to those who criticized them. The early hour at which the searches were made, the fact that the raiders were specially chosen for their marksmanship and wore bullet-proof vests, and Rizzo's taunting of a number of Panthers as "yellow" because they dropped their guns in response to a police order rather than engage in battle all suggest that the raids were planned as a pretext to provoke a shoot-out.

The questionable motivation for the raids was underlined by an eyewitness account of the Wallace Street foray published in the *Philadelphia Bulletin* on August 31, 1970, which told how "the suspects were all ordered against the adjoining wall and the men were instructed to strip naked. Police searched their clothes and handcuffed them." A photograph on the front page of the *Daily News* for August 3, 1970, distributed by the Associated Press, displayed six Panthers with bare buttocks. The pictures showed police standing with shotguns near the naked men, indicating that the raiders had required their captives to strip naked.

Rizzo savagely brushed aside objections to this humiliating procedure. A policeman had been killed; this was no time to waste sympathy on the Panthers. "Imagine," he gloated, "the big, black Panthers with their pants down!"[20] But this single indignity had an enormous impact on the Philadelphia establishment. It stirred a revulsion that recalled the reaction to the bloody November 1967 police assault on the high school demonstrators.

The vengeful thrust of the raid was again confirmed by a Panther press release of September 1, later verified by newsmen, stating that the raiders had not merely removed the guns and ammunition specified in the search warrant,* they cleaned out all three search sites—furniture, bedding, clothing, file cabinets, party records, and even, in some instances, refrigerators and stoves. In a rampage of destruction, they demolished the cinder blocks with which the Panthers had replaced storefront windows and knocked out house windows and covered them over with sheet metal. They even ripped out pipes in some of the bathrooms. They also made off with typewriters, tape recorders, cameras, and a duplicating machine, as well as a sum of money—estimated by the police at \$1,067 and by the Panthers at between \$1,500 and \$1,700.[†]

After initially denying these claims, Rizzo was later forced to concede their validity when corroborative evidence emerged.[21] As for the Panthers, Rizzo made his views clear in a statement after the raids:

> We're dealing with a group of fanatics, yellow dogs that they are. We are prepared for any eventuality. We are dealing with psychotics and must be in a position to take them on. These imbeciles and yellow dogs . . . we'd be glad to meet them on their own terms. Just let them tell us when and where.[‡]

On Thursday, September 3, three days after the raid, Federal Judge John Fullam issued an injunction restraining the police from violating the rights of the Panthers and from interfering with the New Left Convention proceedings scheduled for the next weekend. The judge warned that: "A madman out of control shooting at policemen is not much more dangerous to the community than a policeman who loses control and goes shooting up people's houses and raiding them."

On September 4, 1970, all fourteen persons arrested in the Wallace Street raid were freed when the police failed to produce evidence in support of the charges against them.[22] In May 1973, two and a half years later, Common Pleas Judge Edward J. Bradley ruled that the 1970 entry

---

* Grenades were also mentioned in the search warrant, but none were ever found. Pistols and rifles were seized, none of which matched the murder weapons. The law is plain that only those items listed in the warrant can be seized unless there are other items on the premises that may be the fruits of a crime.
† Assistant District Attorney Sprague admitted the illegality of these seizures. "The items that were not contraband or connected with the shooting of Von-Colln or the shooting of the police should not have been taken."
‡ This statement is another revealing clue that Rizzo had hoped to provoke a shoot-out; he apparently realized that he had said more than was safe, and he subsequently claimed that he had been misunderstood ("Courtoom Drama Stars Rizzo, Weinrott and Young Lawyer," *Philadelphia Bulletin*, September 1, 1970; "Rizzo Orders Return of Panthers' Property," ibid., September 2, 1970).

and search of the Columbia Avenue house were illegal and granted a defense motion to suppress the evidence seized in the raid. But by that time, the Philadelphia Panthers had almost entirely faded away.

Repeated courtroom setbacks in eleven raid cases did not bother the commissioner as long as his image as a city savior remained untarnished. On the eve of his drive for the mayoralty, he discovered a plot that assertedly made him a target—an ingredient of personal danger that improved the savior recipe. On Monday, November 31, 1970, the headline "Executive Probe Bares Plot to Kill Rizzo" was splashed over the front page of the *Daily News*. Underneath the subhead "Viet Cong Agent Planned Swap for Angela Davis" were pictures of Rizzo and Davis. According to the story, the police were conducting a "massive investigation" of a plot to kidnap Rizzo and hold him hostage for the black revolutionary. An Oriental "self-professed Viet Cong agent" was the mastermind of the plot, which included, first, bombings of a district police station and then of police headquarters. The kidnapping was to be sandwiched between the two bombings and as an alternative to trading the commissioner for Davis, he was to be used "for target practice" in the group's basement headquarters.

According to its press release, the police department, to obtain evidence, "conducted at least eight raids, all cloaked in secrecy, in which literature, weapons, ammunition and explosives have been confiscated" and stored at police headquarters. The bombing, the police insisted, was scheduled for Christmas Day, 1970, which came and went without mishap. Thus ended the great Oriental bomb-cum-hostage-exchange assassination plot. No arrests were made. Nor were any details of the plot made public thereafter.

The Free Press *War*

The most powerful motivation for surveillance and harassment was criticism of police abuses. Illustrative is the case of the *Free Press*, a Philadelphia collective composed of young working people, who published a radical newspaper. William Biggin, a Temple graduate student, and his wife, Judith, a hospital lab technician, were prominent among the *Free Press* activists and helped organize it. The *Free Press* became a voice of Philadelphia's radical community and Rizzo's harshest critic.[23]

Surveillance cars followed Biggin and his associates to and from the printer and maintained an all-night watch when the paper was being prepared for press. The tabloid's reporters were surrounded at demonstrations by CD men, who prevented them from circulating, communicating with others, or even observing the demonstration. Editors of the paper were repeatedly arrested on pretexts and sometimes beaten.[24]

The police moved into surveillance quarters, in one case across the street from the Biggins and in another next door to one of their associates, Roger Taus, a political science instructor. They not only made their presence known but, without a search warrant, broke into the locked homes of both of them. On one of several occasions when the police broke into Taus's apartment, they pointed a gun at him, ordered him not to move, and then left. They twice broke into Biggin's locked car. They also gave the full treatment of stationary and moving surveillance to David and Leslie Gross, Biggin's friends and co-workers. On one occasion, three plainclothesmen entered their apartment with a search warrant authorizing them to seize drugs allegedly kept on the premises. They found no drugs and instead carried away two "subversive" books belonging to the *Free Press*.

In February 1970 the CD broke up an anti–Vietnam War demonstration by a coalition of new left groups in which a number of demonstrators from the *Free Press* contingent were singled out, ambushed, and clubbed by the police. Early in the morning of March 13, after a session in which Biggin and his associates worked with the Panthers on a community newspaper, Biggin's car was surrounded by six police squad cars, and the occupants were taken from the car at gunpoint and held while it was searched. Later that morning, Biggin and his wife attended a court hearing involving one of the February demonstrators. Hearing a commotion outside the building, he went to investigate; when he tried to reenter the building to notify the lawyer of a man being illegally searched by the police, he was thrown down a flight of stairs by highway patrolmen and charged with assaulting an officer. Because his wife started to scream when he was assaulted, she was arrested and falsely charged with drug possession, breach of the peace, and disorderly conduct. While Biggin was detained in jail, he was visited by one of Rizzo's favorite officers, Captain Alfonse Giordano, who warned, "If you don't get out of town soon, we'll get rid of you!" (On March 30 all charges against the Biggins were dismissed.)

Early in the morning of Monday, March 16, Biggin's car was again stopped, this time by five police cars; he and his passengers were removed while the police searched the car and then released. Later that same morning, a police surveillance vehicle warned him again, "You are now in this big and we are going to follow you."

In fact, from the moment he left the courtroom on March 13, Biggin's house and that of another couple in the area were placed under massive surveillance, sometimes by as many as six unmarked cars at each site. In addition, a number of members of the *Free Press* board of editors were followed day and night.

Rizzo's justification for the surveillance (at an estimated weekly cost of $4,000) was that "a highly reliable source" had informed the police that in early March 1970 at an apartment, subsequently placed under surveillance, a meeting had taken place that was attended "by known members of the SDS Weatherman faction," at which plans were made to plant bombs in police cars.[25]

The massive police surveillance tapered off when it failed to uncover any activity at all that could be turned into a plot, but the harassment continued. In May 1970 Biggin and his group participated along with many others in a rally protesting the U.S. invasion of Cambodia. The ensuing events are well described by his lawyer, William Eichbaum, Jr.:

> Lieutenant Fencl picks them up, puts them in a wagon—Bill and two other guys—brings them down to police headquarters, takes them upstairs to Major Crimes and leaves them there. So they've got them. They had done absolutely nothing and no charges were filed. . . . So I finally went to Deputy Commissioner Golden and said, "I want these guys out." . . .
>
> About twenty-five minutes later Rizzo comes in and says, "Well, counselor, we are going to let Mr. Biggin and his friends go," and he gives me a big lecture about how bad these guys are. . . . by now, they have them down in the basement in the detention cell. So they took them back up. Rizzo waits around and they put them in a little room again and the poor guys were scared to death. They didn't see me when they first got off the elevator, they just saw Rizzo. These three kids, Rizzo and myself go in there. And Rizzo goes into one of these real things. He started out with, "Well, Mr. Biggin, we are going to let you go. I want you to know that your lawyers did a really good job for you. . . . Mr. Biggin, we know what you are up to. We know what kind of person you are and we don't want your kind of people in this city. . . . The thing I hate the most is that you're not even an American citizen, you're a Canadian national. . . . We are going to get you and run you out of this town; but when we get you, I'm going to get a big piece. We are going to step all over you."

In the summer of 1970, Rizzo let it be known that his May threat to "get" Biggin was not idle talk. He began by feeding a team of *Bulletin* reporters material from CD files about Biggin and his associates. One of the reporters was Albert Gaudiosi, subsequently the manager of Rizzo's mayoralty campaign and thereafter a top functionary in his administration. In July the *Bulletin* ran the product of this collaboration, a sensational series called "The New Revolutionaries," which made no attempt to conceal its "law-enforcement" sources. The range of the ten-article series can be gleaned from the headlines:

"Head of Rebel Paper Is Central Figure in New Left Here"

"100 Here Called Hardcore Revolutionaries"

"Young Activists Scorn Old-Line Communism"

"Visitor Reports Talk of Bombs in Powelton"

"Powelton Man Denies Charges about Bombs"

"City Social Worker David Gross Doubles as *Free Press* Staffer"

"SDS Member Is Veteran of 101st Airborne Services"

"Petite New Leftist Studied for a Year in England"

"*Free Press*' No. 2 Man Assails Bicentennial"

For all of the police bias reflected in the series, there was only one specific charge of violence or law breaking, a "confession" by one Terry Caldwell, a drifter from the West Coast, who claimed that early in July 1970 he had been requested by Kenneth Moberg, a psychology instructor and a leader of a neighborhood group, to teach a class in techniques for detonating explosives and to mark on a map selected targets for destruction. Biggin was dragged into the plot by allegations that he, along with Moberg, was reported by an informant to be listed among Caldwell's "contacts," and in the language of the joint CD/FBI affidavit supporting their application for a raid warrant, they "are known to associate with militant action groups whose avowed purpose is the destruction by the use of explosive devices of representative targets of the present system of government establishments [sic]."[26]

The raid was fruitless. Caldwell even told the raiders, "I talk too much. I've learned a good lesson to keep my mouth shut. I didn't think they were going to blow anything up. They were all intellectuals." What the police failed to reveal, and apparently did not want Caldwell to reveal, is that he had given the statement implicating Moberg and his group under duress. After he left town he repudiated his initial "confession": "The police made it clear to me that if I signed the statement then they would not prefer charges against me for possession of the few grains of marijuana they claim to have discovered somewhere around the apartment building." Neither Moberg nor Caldwell was ever charged with violating the law in connection with this incident.[27]

But Rizzo's pressures were effective. The printer who was named in the newspaper series refused to print any more issues of the *Free Press*. A principal advertiser was first phoned by the police and warned to stop buying space in the *Free Press* and then monitored by police cars outside his establishment. Several other regular buyers of advertising space were likewise warned off. Two activists were fired, one from a city job and the other from a publishing house. Temple University terminated Biggin's scholarship and proceedings were initiated, allegedly at the insistence of Rizzo, to deport Biggin, a Canadian national.

At the end of August 1970, Rizzo made it clear that he was ready for the final Philadelphia-is-not-big-enough-for-both-of-us duel with Biggin. In a telecast he warned that "Bill Biggin and the *Free Press* are even more dangerous than the Panthers."[28] Biggin could hardly afford to ignore the emerging signs of a bang-up raid. The *Free Press* quickly sought legal protection, and in November its attorneys, David Kairys and Peter Gale, applied to federal court for protection against police harassment. At a trial the court upheld the allegations of systematic police harassment of Biggin and his group and issued an order barring police from further interference with the exercise of rights of association and expression. In December 1971 the plaintiffs were forced to file a petition seeking to have the police adjudged in contempt of the court's original order. And in the fall of 1972, after Rizzo had long since ascended to the mayoralty, the police department through its counsel signed a consent decree that in these words banished the spectre of another bomb-plot raid:

> The police will not enter the homes of the plaintiffs, nor limit their freedom of movement, without a warrant, unless such warrantless action is preceded by the existence of sufficient evidence that will support a warrantless entry or limitation of freedom in accordance with the provisions and application of the Fourth Amendment of the Constitution of the United States. The police will not harass plaintiffs or violate any of their rights guaranteed under the Constitution of the United States.[29]

Files and Dossiers: How to Spot a Subversive

As we have seen in the preceding two chapters, urban intelligence fetishizes files and dossiers both as a form of legitimation and as a punitive resource. A revealing profile of the CD's identification and filing system was unveiled to the American public in the NBC telecast "First

Tuesday" of June 2, 1970, in which Rizzo played the leading part, with Fencl in a supporting role.

The television screen showed a peaceful demonstration; watching along with us are Fencl and Rizzo, engaged in identifying the participants, who are also being photographed by police cameras on closed circuit television. Fencl enlightens Rizzo about the dramatis personae. Rizzo observes of one picketer, "That little girl over there, she's at all these demonstrations." Fencl replies, "Yeah, we got her name," and he then proceeds to identify by name six other demonstrators. After being jolted by the spectacle of police officials engaging in public surveillance of peaceful protestors and visibly preening themselves on their ability to identify their subjects—a boastful reassurance to the viewing audience that in Philadelphia nothing escapes the Argus-eyed police—we are further shocked by films of the files of dissenters, many with their names showing on the screen. Now Fencl takes over, his voice aglow with the pride of accomplishment:

> We have made a record of every demonstration that we've handled in the City of Philadelphia and reduced this to writing, first by report and then taking out the name of persons connected with the different movements. We have some 18,000 names and we've made what we call an alphabetical file. We know the name and so forth that we handle. This card shows such information as the name, address, picture, if possible, and a little rundown on the person . . . which group he pickets with and so forth. Also, on the back of the card, we show the different demonstrations, the date, time and location, and the groups that the person has picketed with. We have some six hundred different organizations that we've encountered in the Philadelphia area. We have such organizations as the Ku Klux Klan. . . . And all the way over to the other extreme, the left organizations such as the SDS . . . the Student Mobilization Committee, the Friends' Peace Committee, Quaker Action Groups and so forth.

Here, as in virtually all other areas of CD activity, no plausible justification was advanced by either Rizzo or Fencl for the unit's monitoring and filing practices. Whenever the CD's surveillance was challenged by those in attendance at a gathering, its members insisted, "We are only here to protect your rights." But this hardly required CD's ubiquitous note-taking, tape recording, and photography at such gatherings. Besides, the monitoring practices were not confined to the brief intervals in which disorder might erupt, and neither were the fruits of the surveillance destroyed when an evidentiary purpose was no longer served.

Many of the Philadelphia Police Department's eighteen thousand file cards were compiled from conventional sources: press clippings; license plates; photographs; informer reports; FBI files; school and university, employment, credit, medical, and related records; investigative interviews with landlords, friends, taxi drivers, parents, and so on. But the most fertile source of the collection was, until 1971, information extracted from those held at police precincts. In Philadelphia the police routinely filled out an "intelligence summary" from information required of all persons taken into custody while engaging in unpopular political activities. The completed forms included such information as organizations to which the subject belonged, his political affiliations, the people he associated with, his religion, and his education. The police filled out the intelligence summary not only on persons arrested on criminal charges but also on those merely taken into custody and subsequently released without any charges being lodged against them. These individuals were often held in police custody for substantial periods of time until they cooperated. Individuals who were placed under arrest and refused to sign the intelligence summary were then charged with resisting arrest.

This intelligence summary was conceived for the express purpose of developing dossiers. In the late sixties the dragnet arrest and detention became commonplace in Philadelphia; mass arrests (from three to thirty) were frequent and individual harassing ("investigatory") arrests routine—especially for Panthers, who were usually detained on a pretext for from half an hour to three hours and then released.

The following account by a member of a peace organization of how this procedure operated is representative:

> Well, then we were arrested at that time, they brought us into a room and began taking pictures of the people there. Then they sat everybody down and asked them a whole series of questions, including what organizations we belonged to, what religion we were, nationality and so on. And it became apparent right away that this wasn't part of the normal booking procedure, but was really an intelligence system. And a number of us refused to answer the questions and those of us who refused were charged with resisting arrest, which is really strange.

In 1970 the Philadelphia ACLU sued to restrain the intelligence summary procedure as unconstitutional. Five of the fourteen plaintiffs alleged in the complaint that they had been subjected to intelligence summary questioning and released without being charged with any offense.

Seven of the plaintiffs, including a Haverford College professor, William Davidon, had been interrogated to obtain information to fill out the summary and then charged with an offense; the other two plaintiffs were college students who averred that the use of the intelligence summary had deterred them from exercising their right of public advocacy of antiwar views. The complaint charged that political dissidents "are told that they will not be released until they cooperate . . . and they often are held in police custody for substantial periods of time for this purpose." In June 1971, as a result of the suit, the police department agreed to abandon the use of the intelligence summary.[30]

In the spring of 1969 members of Resistance, a well-dossiered target, made application to the Fairmount Park Commission for permission to hold a meeting at the John F. Kennedy Plaza. A permit was granted and then revoked on Rizzo's insistence. At a subsequent hearing Lieutenant Fencl testified that the group was not entitled to a permit because the CD files indicated that the applicants, all members of Resistance, were "known troublemakers." The group then filed a federal court suit that forced the granting of a permit.

The dossiers of both local and out-of-town left-wingers from the CD collection were regularly fed to Rizzo's Philadelphia press lackeys, and on most occasions the press was cooperative. Once, however, it refused to play its assigned role. In mid July 1967 Rizzo persuaded then Mayor James Tate that the city faced the threat of a riot and that a "proclamation of limited emergency" was required to hold the rebellious blacks in check. The mayor wasted no time; Rizzo had spoken, and for Tate, Rizzo's words were law. He promptly issued a proclamation prohibiting groups of twelve or more from gathering on the streets and in the open areas of the city, except for organized recreation. One hundred thousand yellow 8 × 14 posters reproducing the proclamation were distributed by the police throughout the city. Rizzo was delighted. "It gives us tremendous power; if people gather we can tell them to move on. If they refuse, we can arrest them without gathering a lot of evidence. Refusing to move on is the offense." It was the first time that such a measure had ever been invoked anywhere in the nation to maintain order, but Rizzo insisted the danger was real. He had accumulated "overwhelming evidence" that militants were plotting to foment racial disorder.

On July 30 twenty-two people who had demonstrated to test the constitutionality of the proclamation were arrested.* On Tuesday, August 8,
reporters were called in by various city officials, who had been coached
by Rizzo, and were told about "a great exclusive": no fewer than eight
of the twenty-two arrested demonstrators were "card-carrying communists." When reporters and their city desks were reluctant to use this
"exclusive" because no evidence had been produced or offered in support
of it, Rizzo personally called the reporters to his office and tried unsuccessfully to sell the story on the basis of undocumented reports.[31] The
test suit was dismissed because the "state of emergency" had expired.[†]

Enemies and Enemies' Lists

Although Philadelphia's city charter bars the commissioner of police
from political involvement, Rizzo almost from the start became deeply
involved in politics and freely used his new powers to further his political ambitions. When he became the city's chief cop, Rizzo formed
an alliance with the Philadelphia police establishment, represented by
Philadelphian John Harrington, national head of the Fraternal Order of
Policemen (FOP), a tireless lobbyist for police interests, which he

---

* Twenty-one were booked (and of course required to submit information for
the intelligence summary). The twenty-second was ACLU's Spencer Coxe, who
was discharged since he was present just as an "observer" and not considered
part of the group ("22 Arrested in Test of Ban on Gatherings," *Philadelphia
Bulletin*, July 31, 1968).
† After the litigation concluded, frustrated by the collapse of his campaign to
discredit the challenge to the proclamation as subversively inspired, Rizzo repeated his card-carrying charges in a speech on August 15 to a group of federal
officials. He also convoked an entourage of reporters in the hallway and fresh-
ened up the story with charges that he also had "reservations" about the political orthodoxy of some of the others arrested in the demonstration. And, in a
final stab at their apathetic response, he darkly observed that several "agitators"
who had been seen in two riot-torn cities (New York and Detroit) had traveled to
Philadelphia. In a press conference the next day, Mayor Tate was asked by reporters whether he supported Rizzo's charges about the subversive source of the
challenge to the proclamation. The question gave him a little trouble, but he
finally replied, "If Rizzo's against communism, I'm for Rizzo" ("Eight Card-
Carrying Reds in Group That Defied Tate Ban, Rizzo Says," *Philadelphia Inquirer*, August 16, 1967; "Tate Supports Rizzo's Charge against the Reds," ibid.,
August 17, 1967). There are two reasons why Rizzo did not reveal the sources
for his charges: (1) they were based on FBI files (Rizzo referred only to an
anonymous "government spokesman"), which reflected rather murkily that only
two of the eight were believed to be active communists, and (2) by 1967 the
Communist Party had long since abandoned the practice of issuing membership
cards, as Joe McGinniss acidly pointed out ("The Techniques of Frank Rizzo,"
Philadelphia Inquirer, August 18, 1967).

equated with law and order. Through their combined pressure they forced Mayor Tate to dissolve the Civilian Advisory Review Board set up by an earlier reform administration. They joined forces to make the department autonomous and to eliminate or weaken not only the institutional checks on the police but also efforts by private groups to make the police accountable to the citizenry. Among the organizations that entered the lists as litigants and pressure groups against the police were the Philadelphia branch of the American Civil Liberties Union, Philadelphians for Equal Justice (PEJ), the Coalition of Organizations for Police Accountability and Responsibility (COPPAR), Operation Alert (a "police-watching" project), and the Community Legal Services (CLS), an OEO-funded agency. In addition, a group of aggressive and imaginative young lawyers made their services available to the victims of police abuse.

In 1969 Rizzo and Harrington furiously attacked the United Fund, a citywide coalition of nonprofit groups, because it helped fund agencies that hired lawyers "to take us on" and thus demoralize the police. They not only effectively dried up police contributions to the United Fund but stampeded the business community and the fund's chairman to sue for peace. As the price of peace, the Legal Aid Society, the chief target of the attack, was forced to submit all complaints against the police to the commissioner and to instruct its lawyers to offer "no voluntary statement of alternative procedures available." Rizzo was further placated by making him the fund's vice-chairman.

But in 1970, the United Fund again fell into Rizzo's bad graces because he disapproved of one of its beneficiaries, a community center that had allegedly sponsored a children's breakfast program in which the Panthers had participated.

In the spring of 1970, thirty-two Philadelphia groups organized COPPAR to combat oppressive practices by the police. COPPAR held its meetings at the Spring Garden Community Center, supported in part by the United Fund. In 1970 the center's director, who had requested a $50,000 contribution, was informed by the fund that Rizzo had called and demanded that the center be denied all financial support because COPPAR was permitted to meet there and the director had become "too involved" with COPPAR. The director was told that he would receive no funding unless he disassociated himself from COPPAR.

COPPAR's co-chairman, Floyd Platton, was employed by the city's water department. He was removed from his job, without being fired, and given no duties for a period of nine months, until a federal court ordered that he be restored to his duties because he had been denied a

statement of reasons for his treatment. Not that the police were not vigilant in searching for reasons: during the period of his idleness Platton
was frequently trailed by CD cars. He also learned that Fencl's file on
him had been turned over to his superior and his phone tapped. COP-
PAR office phones were also tapped and the police-watching project, Operation Alert, organized by COPPAR's co-chairman Mary Rouse, was
infiltrated by a CD informer, while participants in the program were
regularly identified from license plate numbers. Rouse, a former employee of a Philadelphia detective agency, has described police surveillance practices against herself and her organization in a 1970 television
program:

> Well, it's just gone from one thing to the other, from
> stationary surveillance on my house and center to mov-
> ing surveillance of myself and people who visit my
> home, the censor[ing] of my mail, the tapping of my
> telephone and all kinds of threats, you know, when you
> can hear teletypes going in the back of the conversation.

Rizzo tried to make life difficult not only for his organizational foes
but for individual critics as well. Whenever he sensed that a reporter
had become overly critical, he made it a practice to send word back to his
newspaper colleagues that he had better lay off because Rizzo had a file
on him. (He also let it be known that he had friends in the city rooms of
the Philadelphia dailies who kept him posted about hostile doings.)

Lawyers who opposed the police in a professional capacity were regularly harassed. There is no city in the United States where legal advocacy on behalf of minorities and the poor was subjected to such
pressures—surveillance, smears, and abuse, not to speak of attacks by
lower court judges who permitted themselves to become instruments of
Rizzo's program of reprisal.

The OEO-funded CLS was steadily attacked because it undertook the
defense of the rights of victims of police abuses, and was the target of
repeated attempts at infiltration. Its phones were tapped by the Internal
Security Division of the police department, and Rizzo tried, by an appeal
to Washington, to cut off its funds. Similar tactics were used in 1967 to
kill a lawsuit filed in response to the November police attack on high
school demonstrators already discussed. The commissioner first charged
that one of the lawyers was a communist and called Washington to demand that the OEO sponsorship of the lawsuit be withdrawn. A second
lawyer suddenly found himself in tax trouble, and a third was faced with
trumped-up charges of receiving stolen goods.

Rizzo invariably tried to attack his critics as subversive. For example, he let it be known that Spencer Coxe, the energetic director of the Philadelphia ACLU, one of Rizzo's long-time critics, had once been in Communist China.*

In 1969 the Lawyers' Committee for Civil Rights under Law, an American Bar Association committee formed in 1963 at President Kennedy's suggestion (its targeting by the Chicago red squad was discussed on p. 94), learned that the police were taking individuals off the street against their will to participate in line-ups. A young lawyer, Allen Klein, volunteered to work on the lawsuit. In accordance with common practice in cases of this sort, others "similarly situated" (that is, young blacks who had also been shanghaied by the police for this purpose) were invited to participate in the suit if they wished. Rizzo commenced a campaign of pressure against Klein in behind-the-scenes sessions with the Philadelphia bar establishment. In June 1970 he came out into the open and notified the press that he had sent the district attorney's office a lengthy investigative file charging that Klein had violated the canons of professional ethics prohibiting solicitation of professional employment and "stirring up strife and litigation." In August a bar committee rejected the charges, and in September 1970 Federal District Judge Harold Wood banned the practice attacked by the lawsuit.[32]

It is unmistakably clear that during his term as commissioner, Rizzo used the CD file collection as a weapon against police critics and his political enemies. Moreover, the CD record shows that monitoring police critics was a routine CD operational assignment. In one case in 1967 a distributor of leaflets dealing with police abuses was denounced as a "black nationalist" by a police officer. The ACLU wrote to the police commissioner on his behalf, but received no reply. A week later, the complainant, on returning home, found eight members of the CD Squad inside searching his belongings. They had no warrants and explained that they had come in response to a report of a fire, of which there were no signs on the premises. A second incident was described by Attorney Jack J. Levine in an interview with the author:

> During the latter part of April 1971 considerable public attention was drawn to an incident many years ago during which former Police Commissioner Frank Rizzo struck a demonstrator at the State Office Building. Mr. Rizzo was accused by the governor and state attorney general of having violated the law in apprehending one

---

* According to Coxe, the source for this tidbit was his FBI file.

Eugene Dawkins. During the public debate over this incident, a number of concerned citizens held an informal hearing to hear witnesses to the beating describe what they saw of the incident. The meeting was held on May 13, 1971, at the First Unitarian Church at 2125 Chestnut Street. . . .

As the meeting began, I saw a man whom I believed to be a police officer and member of the CD Squad. I approached him, identified myself, and asked him whether he was an officer. He looked at me and very nicely explained that, no, he was not a police officer; yes, he would likewise object if undercover police were present because he, himself, had been mistreated in the past by a police officer. He gave his name as "Taney" or "Teaney" and said he works "in the credit department at Lit Brothers." I apologized to him for my suspicion and together we agreed that undercover police at a meeting of this sort would be unwarranted and a disgrace.

On Tuesday, August 10, 1971, at about 1:00 P.M., I observed the same gentleman sitting in a police vehicle on a plainclothes detail at 15th and Chestnut Streets. I approached him and asked him if he were a police officer. He replied, "Yes." I asked him his name and he replied, "Taney."

Rizzo's ruthlessness in stifling criticism of the department was a clue to a similar modus operandi in the corridors of power. During his term as police commissioner, Rizzo placed important police functionaries in other city departments. He waged a campaign against judges who displeased him, warning them that he would single them out by name and work against their reelection if they did not change what he considered to be an overly permissive attitude toward defendants and the sentencing process. When a city councilman took a public stand against him, he leaked his dossier through a right-wing organization in the Philadelphia area. Rizzo feuded endlessly with the late Richardson Dilworth, a prominent Philadelphian, lawyer, banker, former mayor, and president of the school board, who had earlier (in 1967) clashed with the vengeful commissioner about policing the public schools.

Independence Mall Becomes a Potemkin Village

By the early 1970s the CD's blueprinted role as an understanding mediator gave way altogether to the tactics of bogus raids and invented bomb plots. Not only were the powers of the police used for illegal and unconstitutional purposes, but a network of lower court judges could be counted on to implement the CD's abuses by fixing high bail, refusing to permit effective cross-examination of police witnesses, sanctioning search raids on insufficient or fabricated evidence, and granting repeated stalling adjournments requested by the district attorney's office in order to avoid the trial of charges against individuals for which there was no foundation in the first place. A dramatic demonstration of the transformation of the CD, the permanent substitution of the scowling mask for the smiling one, occurred on October 20, 1972, when President Nixon, at the invitation of Mayor Rizzo, came to Philadelphia to participate in a public bill-signing ceremony, a move intended as a show of the city's support for Nixon's reelection bid. A group of Philadelphia organizations, opponents of the administration's Vietnam and domestic policies, made plans to conduct a protest vigil beginning at 9:00 P.M. on October 19 and continuing the next day in front of Independence Hall, where the president was scheduled to speak.*

At about 7:00 in the morning, Fencl and his superior, Joseph O'Neill, Rizzo's successor as police commissioner, required those demonstrators carrying signs or distributing leaflets to move a block away to a location far removed from the site of the ceremony. Some sixteen demonstrators who carried signs were arrested, and only those who carried no signs or who surrendered them were permitted in the area, despite a warning by an attorney from the district attorney's office to the police that they had no right to bar sign-carrying demonstrators from an area otherwise open to the public.† Fencl and O'Neill offered to release all of those arrested on condition that they refrain from carrying signs. Fifteen sign carriers forming a second group were also arrested and offered releases on the same condition. But both groups refused to accept.

* The following organizations participated in the protest: Philadelphia Resistance, Vietnam Veterans against the War, Philadelphia Labor Committee for McGovern-Shriver, Local 1357, Retail Clerks International Association, Military and Draft Information Centers, Philadelphia Area Indo-China Peace Campaign, Friends Peace Committee, and Philadelphia Area Peace Action Coalition.
† There is no dispute about the fact that the area from which signs were banned had not been quarantined by the Secret Service as a "security" area. Nevertheless, it may have been possible that such a request came from a member of the presidential party, mindful of President Nixon's sensitivity to such picket displays. John W. Dean III told the Senate Watergate Committee that when Nixon one day in the late winter of 1971 looked out of an upstairs White House window and spied a lone picket with a sign in Lafayette Park far across Pennsylvania Avenue, his "displeasure" was so intense that an aide immediately set out looking for "thugs" to remove the offender.

Shortly before 1:00 P.M. Federal Judge Daniel Huyett III, acting on a petition filed by a counsel for some of the demonstrators, issued a restraining order forbidding interference "in any manner whatsoever" by the police with the constitutional rights of the complaining demonstrators and organizations, including "the carrying of signs in any area in the vicinity of Independence Hall where the public is likewise permitted to assemble."*[33]

Thereafter a number of pickets and leaflet distributors tried to use the judge's restraining order to gain entry into the area, but were barred either by uniformed officers or by plainclothesmen wearing buttons with the letter *E*, a coded designation for CD plainclothesmen. All the officers to whom the order was displayed refused to comply with it and continued to insist that official instructions barred the entry of anyone with signs. A number of demonstrators, including one who started to photograph the police actions, were arrested and detained for five hours.[†] It was not until President Nixon's departure at 2:00 P.M. that signs began to appear in the crowd on the mall.

In a subsequent hearing to determine whether the police had defied the court's order, the police contended that surrendering the signs was optional and not mandatory. But this defense collided with the offer of release on condition that the arrestees relinquish their picket signs. Besides, the videotapes made by the police themselves refuted this argument: they showed Fencl himself reaching out to seize a picket sign. While the contempt case was pending before Judge Huyett, the determination of the police to flout the rights of demonstrators even at the risk of contempt of court was made clear by a police attack on October 25 on an orderly group of demonstrators outside the Bellevue-Stratford Hotel where, this time, Mrs. Nixon was being feted at a luncheon ceremony. One of the demonstrators, an attorney, who was addressing the gathering through a PA system about the legal issues presented by the October 20 police action, was rushed and assaulted by a phalanx of plainclothesmen, who ripped the microphone from his hands and fled with it before the eyes of the police functionaries, including Fencl, who refused either to make or order an arrest.

---

* The assistant city solicitor pleaded in vain with the district attorney's office to charge the protesters with "disorderly conduct" to provide a legal basis for the arrests and a defense in a civil action instituted in federal court against Mayor Rizzo and the police for violating the plaintiffs' civil rights.

† The frustrated photographer was kept in custody for an additional hour without being notified of the charges against him or given the opportunity to make a telephone call. He was searched, fingerprinted, photographed, and finally released still without notification of charges.

As the demonstrators were preparing to use a second microphone that had been hastily procured and plugged into the sound system, a flying wedge of five plainsclothesmen forcibly seized the entire unit—microphone, amplifier, and loudspeaker—and again fled into the hotel. One person addressing the gathering was injured and two demonstrators were physically assaulted, the first for carrying a picket sign and the second for coming to his aid when he was attacked by the police. No arrests were ever made, although witnesses identified the plainclothesmen involved in sworn statements.

On June 22, 1973, Judge Huyett ruled in a sweeping decision that the police had acted in willful contempt of his injunction. The court stressed the fact that all of the defendants had been deprived of rights protected by the First Amendment. In addition the court found that Fourth Amendment protections against unreasonable searches and seizures were denied those picketers detained after the issuance of the injunction because there was no "probable cause" for such detention. The court rejected attempts by Fencl and O'Neill to escape liability, pointing out that they directed the exclusion of picketers from the Independence Mall area and "admittedly did nothing to change" the policy after the issuance of the injunction.[34]

Since no legal proof of Rizzo's complicity was presented, he was dropped from the contempt case. Still, it would be naive to assume that O'Neill and Fencl took it on themselves to adopt a policy of preventive detention, an extraordinary departure from legal norms even in Philadelphia. There can hardly be a mystery about what happened: Mayor Rizzo, an ardent supporter of the president, was determined to show him that he could make a public appearance in his city without encountering a single visible (or audible) indication of dissent from his policies. By means of the CD and other police units, Rizzo converted Independence Mall into a Potemkin Village, a tranquil haven of conformity. And the demonstration of his power, in a traditionally Democratic city with a strong peace movement, could hardly escape the notice of the kingmakers whose favor he had courted ever since he was a rookie on a beat. To be sure, a federal court had disapproved. But calculated illegality and defiance of court orders had always seemed a cheap enough price to pay for the time he needed to consolidate his political power.

The Political Imperative: The View from City Hall

A dilemma confronted the power holders who obtained urban office in the late sixties and early seventies through the essentially negative techniques of intelligence-mongering—how to expand a constituency unified by fear, anxiety, and social bigotry into an effective consensus necessary to respond to the stubborn urban problems of the time. Rizzo had ravaged the New Left, antiwar, and black protest movements and politicized the police department in his ascent to the mayoralty. But the politics of fear and confrontation could not divert attention from his inability to cope with the city's proliferating social and economic problems. Having campaigned on a platform against crime in the streets and permissiveness in the schools, Rizzo was helpless when confronted with mounting inner-city crime and an educational system that was in continuing decline. His critics were no longer confined to civil libertarians and fringe activists; theatrics, patronage, and assorted fixes no longer worked to shield him from criticism and investigation by the press. His response to a crisis in the school system revealed his administration's desperation.

In the course of a teachers' strike in the winter of 1973, picketers and demonstrators were placed under continuing surveillance and subjected to police photography. On one occasion in February 1973 about one hundred members of the Citizens' Committee for Public Education, a coalition of concerned citizens, assembled to meet with a councilman and to demonstrate in front of his house. At least ten detectives photographed the group and recorded the license numbers of the cars in which they arrived. The police also harassed individuals protesting their exclusion from city council meetings, required by law to be open to the public.

Rizzo's career dramatically illuminates the simple truth that power diminishes the perception of risk. The reprisal tactics that had served the police commissioner so effectively were even more recklessly deployed against the mayor's opponents. On August 25, 1973, Philadelphia papers revealed that Rizzo had set up a 33-member "plumber"-style police unit with an assignment to investigate two political opponents, Peter J. Camiel, a Democratic city council committee chairman, and George X. Schwartz, city council president. This unit, which included three full staff inspectors, five lieutenants, and some twenty-four detectives and policewomen, conducted its investigations in secret and reported directly to Rizzo and his deputy mayor.[35] After a public outcry Rizzo turned the squad back to the police department under the leadership of a police inspector operating out of separate headquarters.

Other important targets of the special unit's snooping included Governor Milton Shapp, Rizzo's chief political opponent. John R. Bunting, a leading banker, told reporters that after a disagreement with the mayor in the summer of 1973, he was warned that the police were investigating him. In the wake of these charges another claim of surveillance came to light from Mark R. Shedd, former superintendent of schools and a sharp critic of Rizzo's conduct as police commissioner. Shedd charged that after the November 17, 1967, school disturbance described above he was tailed for months by Rizzo's police. "Two plainclothesmen in an unmarked car parked outside the administration building and followed me everywhere I went. At night they parked in front of my house. I used to go outside and say goodnight to them." In mid July 1969 Shedd's home was burglarized and ransacked. Some time after the burglary, Shedd received an anonymous late-night call from a man who said he had overheard two off-duty detectives in a bar discussing how they had burglarized Shedd's home.[36]

When confronted with these allegations, Rizzo admitted that much of the surveillance had, indeed, taken place, but insisted that it was "legal" and that "honest men have nothing to fear from the police." In the welter of charges and countercharges, Rizzo also admitted that he had occasionally, in the past, told "white lies" in order to protect policemen charged, unfairly in his view, with misconduct. He also intimated that he had "spies" in the offices of the *Inquirer* and the *Bulletin*. In fact, he had gained access to the *Inquirer's* exposé of his snoop squad before it was printed and then leaked it to the *Bulletin* in the hope of getting more favorable treatment.[37]

Rizzo hoped for vindication in the arrest record of his special squad, but according to an analysis in the press in mid September, not only were its achievements limited, but the results, as the district attorney's office put it, reflected "routine police work that has nothing to do with corruption and doesn't require a special squad of investigators." In order to refute charges that the squad was staffed by ordinary gumshoes who lacked investigative expertise, Rizzo beefed it up with ten more policemen, a lawyer, and a financial expert. His press release then referred to the squad as a "strike force." But as a commentator put it, "There is a look of desperation in these . . . correctives."[38]

In the meantime a grand jury probing the special squad's activities received evidence uncovered by the Pennsylvania Crime Commission that Inspector Fencl (he was promoted in January 1973) had improperly accepted a gratuity from a Philadelphia insurance company for "special services." This, too, like the special unit, is a familiar abuse by urban police on labor assignments and one expressly prohibited by Philadelphia's charter. In this case the "special services" were suspected by many to include intelligence background data about Resistance picketers protesting the company's investments in South Africa.[39] Early in 1974, after an eighteen-month investigation, the Pennsylvania Crime Commission issued a massively detailed report charging the Philadelphia police with widespread and systematic corruption and accusing Rizzo of actively attempting to block its investigation.[40]

The 1973 special unit exposé was a product of local press initiatives that seriously discredited Rizzo and jeopardized a success formula in which favorable media coverage was the keystone. His unique relationship with the press—both as a news source and as a personal friend of leading reporters—was institutionalized when Rizzo became mayor: he placed a score of media representatives on the payroll, many of them in high posts for which they had neither the requisite training nor expertise. As his closest advisor he chose the veteran *Inquirer* and *Bulletin* reporter Albert Gaudiosi,* who, as already noted, was co-author of the series on Philadelphia's radicals. But despite his courtship of the media, the press soon posed a serious threat to Rizzo's political ambitions—such a contrast to the old days when each successive bomb plot set the stage for a fresh epiphany, radiantly emerging in the morning from the *Inquirer* and in the evening from the *Bulletin*, constantly renewing the gratitude to Rizzo of the faithful for their rescue from destruction.

In March 1973 the *Inquirer* joined other media critics in Rizzo's doghouse with the publication of a crude spoof by a columnist of Rizzo's equally crude bigotry. After fruitless efforts to stop its publication by private appeals and a court injunction, he filed a $6 million libel suit against the *Inquirer* and offending columnists, charging that "ultra liberals have gained control of the press and they're using it to destroy people who do not have the same philosophy as them."[41] On the afternoon of March 29, while the suit was in progress, a mob of 250 members of the Building and Construction Trades Council blockaded the *Inquirer*'s offices for ten hours, barring all access and delaying editions of the paper until federal marshals finally dispersed the crowd. Although several *Inquirer* employees were physically restrained from entering the building by the pickets, the uniformed police refused protection or escort. They threatened the frustrated employees—rather than their attackers—with assault charges if they persisted in trying to enter the building. The *Inquirer*'s telephone calls for relief to the city police commissioner, solicitor, and Rizzo himself were rebuffed or ignored.[42]

---

* Gaudiosi subsequently announced his candidacy in the 1978 mayoralty race.

The Bicentennial Disruption Plot

On May 27, 1976, Mayor Rizzo broke a two-year boycott of the press and granted the *Inquirer* an "exclusive" interview for publication in its Sunday (May 30) edition. The five-column headline story, which dominated the front page, announced that the mayor had requested 15,000 Army troops to keep order in the Philadelphia streets during the national July 4 Bicentennial celebration. The request was prompted, he said, by the discovery of a leftist plot to "come here in thousands from all over the country . . . under the guise of the Bill of Rights to disrupt a celebration that should be so great."[43] By Monday morning Rizzo's planned request, further ventilated by radio and television stations, emerged as a prime news item, both locally and nationally. By a significant coincidence, that Monday was the scheduled date for the release by a citizen's committee of the signature totals in a petition for an election recalling the mayor.[44] (The requisite number of signatures was obtained, but the recall was set aside on appeal on procedural and constitutional grounds; charges were made that the mayor had collected political IOU's from some of the court's judges.) It can hardly be doubted that Rizzo's plot revelations were intended to undercut the recall movement and to restore the "tough cop," city-savior image that had served him so well in the past. The mayor's intelligence sources (both local and federal) identified the principal organizational conspirators as two anti-establishment coalitions planning counter-rallies: Get-the-Rich-off-Our-Backs and the July 4 Coalition. According to the mayor's representative, these umbrella groups were planning violent confrontations, including the capture of Independence Hall by Get-the-Rich-off-Our-Backs. No supporting evidence was adduced,* and the representatives of both groups

---

* The NCLC, a right-wing rival of the Get-the-Rich-off-Our-Backs Coalition, prepared a polemic accusing it of "terrorist" intentions. Ironically, this group was a descendant of the Fraser-Borgmann NCLC. In a quest for acceptance and respectability, the NCLC had launched a "counter terrorist" campaign, initially implemented by collaboration with federal and urban intelligence structures. In Philadelphia, the NCLC became a vociferous defender of the Rizzo administration. At the time of the Bicentennial, it not only fed Rizzo bogus charges of an impending terrorist coup but distributed on the streets a scare brochure, *Who Runs the Smear Campaign against the Philadelphia Police Department and How Is It Financed?* charging, inter alia, that the *Inquirer* was the instrument of "a small group of the nation's wealthiest bankers" in a sinister conspiracy to destroy the Rizzo administration. These same conspirators, it was charged, had funded a pyramid of terrorist groups (such as the ACLU, the Emergency Civil Liberties Committee, and Philadelphians for Equal Justice) bent on a violent takeover of the Bicentennial celebration.

insisted that protest would be wholly peaceful. After an FBI investigation, the Department of Justice rejected the troop request, citing the lack of persuasive evidence of a serious disruptive threat. "The blood is on their hands not mine," Rizzo said in a telecast when the Justice Department turned him down. There remained political mileage in a belated appeal to the governor, whom he hoped to replace. After Governor Shapp rejected Rizzo's initial request for the assignment of National Guard contingents to keep order, the mayor unsuccessfully renewed his request. "We want it on the record," his aide Gaudiosi explained.[45]

Both coalitions conducted their protests in a peaceful and orderly fashion. During the five-day period of the celebration between June 30 and July 5, and including counter-rallies and parades, not a single one of the 30,000 dissidents who participated was arrested. Confrontation and conflict with the police were barely in evidence. But Rizzo's performance cost the city dearly: many organizations and tourists, frightened by Rizzo's message of violence and danger, changed their plans. Seventy-eight bands and 15,000 marchers were frightened away; the tourist figures were sharply below expectations. And this attempt to stifle expressions of dissent in a celebration of two hundred years of freedom on the site of the birth of the Republic was marked by another wrong: a few days later it was revealed that an article attacking Rizzo had been removed from 40,000 copies of *Hustler* magazine by the United News Company, Philadelphia's major news distributor.[46]

The Last Act: 1976–1980

But the pattern of police state practices did not end with the Bicentennial fiasco. Fencl testified in August 1976 that his civil affairs unit* (as it was then called) covered "just about every demonstration . . . any type of group that is protesting anything."[47] The systematic monitoring and harassment of dissidents and protest groups focused heavily on Philadelphia's black minority.

Nationwide publicity centered on the city's police as a consequence of their attack on MOVE, a mostly black back-to-nature cult residing communally in Philadelphia's Powelton Village, an area that had long been a prime target of Fencl's plainclothesmen.[48] MOVE's abusive rhetoric, dis-

---

* In November 1976 the 50-member unit absorbed the 32-member labor squad; already under Fencl's command, the squad had covered the *Inquirer* blockade discussed above ("Fencl Unit Absorbs Police Labor Squad," *Philadelphia Bulletin*, November 7, 1976).

ruption, and threats of violence—not to speak of its health-endangering rejection of rudimentary sanitation regulations—had resulted in complaints by some of its neighbors. From May 1977 to August 1978, Fencl orchestrated a massive offensive against MOVE (at one time a thousand uniformed and plainclothes police were deployed), including a seven-week blockade of a four-block area designed to starve the group out, implemented by eight-foot-high fences, the screening of area residents, their families, and guests, and arrests for such offenses as crossing the street without permission. The siege, which cost the taxpayers more than $2 million, climaxed in a wild shoot-out in which a policeman was killed and twelve police and firemen were injured, as well as six MOVE members and supporters. In manifest reprisal for the death of one of their own, the police brutally assaulted a MOVE leader, Delbert Africa, as he tried to surrender. Because the *Inquirer* printed a series of chilling photographs of the sequence of assaults on the unarmed leader[49] (also shown on network television), the police, in street clothes, picketed its office in still another shutdown attempt.

Despite the earlier judicial condemnation of raid tactics, local police units, sheriff's deputies, and the FBI conducted a series of raids against the Afrikan Peoples Party (APP) on October 20, 1975, October 26, 1976, and February 4, 1977. Although the claimed purpose of each raid was to locate a fugitive, no lawful search warrants were displayed by the search parties, doors were broken, weapons flourished, the residences ransacked, money stolen, the occupants (including children) threatened at gunpoint, and a visitor detained as a warning against associating with his host. The October 20, 1975, raid followed an APP campaign to support unemployed black street vendors threatened with removal under pressure from center-city merchants. The other two raids also appear to have been reprisals for protest activities against police abuses.* A similar motivation explains the harassment of members of the Guardian Civic League, a black policemen's organization. A largely undenied complaint filed in court in October 1978 charged that Guardian members had been followed by plainclothesmen in unmarked cars, subsequently grilled about their involvement in sessions to improve police-community relations, and required to identify those in attendance and report what local leaders said at public meetings.[50]

---

* An investigative report by American Friends Service Committee staff members concluded that "the chronology of harassment of the APP by various police agencies" reflected a pattern of reprisal for APP activism. See also "Chilling FBI Raid on APP House Angers N. Phila. Resident," *Philadelphia Tribune*, March 9, 1976; "African Peoples Party Sues Police," *Philadelphia Sunday Bulletin*, February 27, 1977; "APP Goes to U.S. Court to Halt Raids," *Philadelphia Tribune*, March 1, 1977.

When in 1978 the voters rejected Rizzo's politics of fear along with his racist appeal ("Vote white"), the full costs of police government began to emerge. In virtually every area, the city had gone downhill.[51] A study of Rizzo's claimed law-and-order credits revealed that he had not really reduced the crime rate: his figures had all along been the result of statistical flim-flam and tilted reporting. Moreover, he had not hesitated to use his powers as mayor to instigate taps of the phones of his predecessors and continued to damage the city's justice system by bullying judges and blaming their softness for his failure to control crime.[52] Perhaps most shocking were the disclosures of the pervasiveness of police brutality and the use of deadly force by the police without justification.

In April 1979 charges of extraordinary racist violence by the police were formally aired by the Federal Civil Rights Commission. Witnesses also charged the department with flagrant cover-up maneuvers, systematic suppression of records of police abuse, and withholding of evidence from both prosecutive and legislative investigators.[53] But, to the mayor, it was all an old story: "Militants and anarchists" and "biased, prejudiced, or unfair" newspaper accounts by reporters who "scream 'the First Amendment' " were joined in a conspiracy to traduce dedicated police officers.[54]

The April Civil Rights Commission session heard startling admissions from a banker, John Bunting, and Thatcher Longstreth, head of the Chamber of Commerce, that acquiescence of the business community over the years in police abuses and brutality was simply an updated version of the "Bargain": support or tolerance of police misconduct in exchange for a safe city. As Longstreth put it, "Most businessmen . . . feel that police protection is so good that they are willing to put up with instances which, if they happened in their own family, would be intolerable." More bluntly put, the business community agreed that the police could betray the public interest, engage in corrupt practices, and do what they pleased to minorities and the lower orders generally as long as they left the Philadelphia elite undisturbed.[55]

The record indicates that some traditional liberals and reformers were so influenced by Rizzo's scare tactics that they too sacrificed civic values and reformist goals to Rizzo's planted fears of imminent destruction of the city (a posture reminiscent of nineteenth-century fears of the "dangerous classes").* But a more concerned, activist sector of the citizenry,

* As one biographer put it: "The city . . . had become polarized concerning Rizzo and the police, and much of it by his own design. By eliminating the dangerous middle ground of opinion, Rizzo felt that people would have to choose between law and order on the one hand, and lawlessness and chaos on the other.

daunted by the repressive political climate, resorted faute de mieux to litigation to challenge particular abuses. As a result, a series of court decisions periodically condemned police misconduct in connection with raids, surveillance, file compilation, and related areas, but it turned out that the plaintiffs won all the battles but lost the war. Although some nine of these rulings rebuked recurrent abuses, they had virtually no impact as precedent. For example, Judge Huyett's powerful contempt ruling of June 1973 denouncing interference with public protest did not prevent an initial administrative turndown of permit applications by the two dissident Bicentennial coalitions, forcing petitions for judicial relief.[56]

In the same way, dossiers were distributed to private parties both while litigation challenging such dissemination was pending and after the practice was judicially proscribed.* In the former case, damages were ultimately awarded by the court to demonstrators whose dossiers were obtained by the Insurance Company of North America, and in the latter, Mayor Rizzo himself, in defiance of the court's decision in the Tate case, disseminated the police file of a former police officer who opposed his 1978 bid for a third term.[57]

If you were for Frank Rizzo, you stood up for law and order; if you criticized him, you were a coddler of criminals" (Hamilton, Rizzo, pp. 282–83).

* "City Agrees to Keep Police Files a Secret," Philadelphia Daily News, June 18, 1976. This agreement was based on an appellate court decision in the federal case of Philadelphia Yearly Meeting v. Tate, 519 F 2d 335 (CA3, 1975), affirming 382 F Supp. 549 (E.D. Pa.) 1974 (see p. 224) ruling that it is unlawful for public officials to disclose the contents of political dossiers and that the subjects of such disclosures are entitled to compensation. Litigation challenging surveillance practices was substantially blocked by the Supreme Court decision in the case of Laird v. Tatum, 408 U.S. 1 (1972), holding that the jurisdiction of a federal court could not be invoked where there was no immediate threat to the individual's constitutional rights and any chilling effect was purely subjective. However, the appellate court in the Tate case reversed the lower court's dismissal (on the authority of Laird v. Tatum) of those portions of the complaint charging that the dissemination of information as on the telecast discussed in the text violated the plaintiffs' constitutional rights. "It cannot be doubted that the disclosure on nationwide television that certain persons or organizations are subjects of police intelligence files has a potential for a substantial adverse impact" especially "when joined with the absence of a lawful purpose" so as to make an adequate showing of unconstitutional police action. Problems not only of standing to sue but of jurisdiction as well have plagued litigation challenging police abuse. In March 1973 federal Judge John Fullam, in a detailed 83-page decision reviewing charges of police brutality ordered Philadelphia city officials to submit a comprehensive plan for dealing with citizens' complaints. But the Supreme Court in a 5–3 decision reversed the lower court's decision as an unwarranted intrusion by the federal judiciary into the authority of local officials. Rizzo v. Goode 423 U.S. 362 (1976).

The reason for the ineffectiveness of judicial restraints came to light at the 1979 Civil Rights Commission hearings. Police Commissioner Joseph O'Neill, a Rizzo protégé, insisted that there was nothing particularly disturbing about the retention without discipline of policemen found guilty of misconduct by courts or the continuation of judicially condemned practices. The "courts' particular views," he explained, "were not . . . in and of themselves binding on the department." The disclosures at the hearings reinforced the growing sense of many Philadelphians, including substantial numbers who had succumbed to Rizzo's law-and-order appeal, that the entrenchment of an urban version of a police state had resulted in a frightening and escalating racial polarization as the police resorted to ever more desperate measures to crush efforts to protest racial injustice—much of it originally traceable to Rizzo's forces.

The disclosures also finally led to a long-deferred Department of Justice decision to bring legal action against the city and its police administrators. On August 13, 1979, a judicial weapon of last resort was deployed against police city, a landmark civil lawsuit by the Justice Department's Civil Rights Commission charging the city itself, Mayor Rizzo, and eighteen top city and police officials with condoning systematic police brutality. Alleging for the first time in American history that an entire police system violated the civil and constitutional rights of a city's residents—especially its blacks and Hispanics—the complaint stated that the official cover-up of police brutality "shock[ed] the conscience" and required a court injunction and the cut-off of federal aid until the system was changed.[58] Noting the ineffectiveness of piecemeal judicial remedies, the complaint observed that seventy-five persons were shot by the police each year and civilian complaints totaled more than 1,100 annually. The complaint further alleged that political leaders, minority groups, and police critics were harassed and surveilled by the police department. Without passing on its merits, a federal court judge ruled in October that the attorney general lacked standing to bring the suit, a conclusion subsequently affirmed on appeal.[59] Although Rizzo denounced the suit as politically inspired "hogwash" and yet another unfair attack on the long-suffering police ("Most people out there in this great country respect the police and support them"), it renewed the sense that police curbs were a necessity to restore democratic government, to eliminate institutional lawlessness, and to change the city's image.

Following a meeting early in 1980 with police critics, the new city administration under Mayor William Green announced in July that the police intelligence countersubversive file collection had been destroyed, that the police department would in the future monitor and maintain records on individuals and groups only where there was a "potential for violence," and that photographs and other records would be destroyed following a demonstration or investigation if no violent or criminal activity took place.[60]

But the new administration could not wholly escape the consequences of the police abuses in the Rizzo years when the force had enjoyed carte blanche as a result of the hands-off bargain with the power structure and Rizzo's protective posture. Shortly after Mayor Green took office, a scandal erupted over the habitual resort by police to unjustifiable deadly force, a practice encouraged, according to a newly appointed assistant district attorney dealing with police misconduct, by the sense of the rank and file "that they could do anything they wanted . . . and there wouldn't be any price to pay."[61]

While Philadelphians were still dealing with these disclosures, a second scandal rocked the city: beginning in 1981 a federal investigative team uncovered evidence of police corruption that, over a four-year period, yielded convictions of twenty-nine police officers, including, in addition to patrolmen, a former deputy commissioner,* a chief inspector, a captain, and three lieutenants for offenses such as extortion, racketeering, and bribe-taking involving numbers operations, massage parlors, and illegal gambling. These developments furthered darkened Rizzo's political image, contributing to his last hurrah in May 1983, when he was defeated in a comeback campaign by Wilson Goode, who became the city's first black mayor. But the Rizzo legacy of police corruption continued to haunt the city; in July 1986 a narcotics officer and six former members of his unit were indicted by a federal grand jury for racketeering conspiracy and extortion of at least $400,000 plus quantities of cocaine from drug dealers.[62]

Goode's administration promptly became involved in another legacy of the past—the MOVE vendetta—which was played out in May 1985 when the police dropped a bomb on MOVE's fortified headquarters in an

---

* Disclosures of police corruption in Philadelphia have repeatedly raised the cry *Quis custodiet custodes ipsos?* but never so sharply as in the case of Deputy Commissioner James Martin. Convicted in August 1984 of extorting payoffs, Martin headed the department's Major Investigations Division, which monitored police misconduct ("Philadelphia Police Undergoing Major Shake-Up," *New York Times*, February 23, 1986; "James Martin Is Dead at 54; Ex-Philadelphia Police Aide," ibid., January 28, 1986).

assault launched to serve arrest warrants on four members of the group barricaded with their associates inside their row house. The resulting fire killed 11 individuals, including 5 children, destroyed 61 homes, and left 250 men, women, and children homeless. In March 1986 a commissioner appointed to investigate the tragedy concluded after lengthy hearings that the mayor, the city's managing director, and the police commissioner were variously at fault for planning the attack, approving the use of explosives, and permitting the operation to continue despite its manifest failure.[63] In findings critical of the police, the commission—one of its eleven members dissenting—pointed out the "firing of over 10,000 rounds of ammunition in under 90 minutes at a row house containing children was clearly excessive and unreasonable"; that "the failure of those responsible for the firing to control or stop such an excessive amount of force was unconscionable" (Finding #18); and that police gunfire prevented some occupants "from escaping from the burning house to the rear alley" (Finding #28). The commission unanimously concluded that the deaths of the children "appear to be unjustified homicides which should be investigated by a grand jury" (Finding #29). Despite the fact that the city was governed by a black mayor, Wilson Goode, the commission asserted that racism, deeply rooted in the Philadelphia force, strongly influenced the tactics in the MOVE affair: the use of bombs, the excessive shooting, and allowing the fire to burn in a row house occupied by children. Such practices would not have been authorized, the commission concluded, if the target house had been located in a white neighborhood and its occupants had been white.*

Students of the Philadelphia police force and its autonomous growth under Rizzo also found noteworthy the fact that the police were operationally gung-ho, eager to "get even" for the death of one of their fellows in the 1978 confrontation and to avenge a humiliation at the hands of this violence-prone cult. The extraordinary hostility of the police to the probe was reflected in their obstructive responses to the investigation as seen in the tactics of their representative, Lodge 5 of the

---

* On May 3, 1988, a Philadelphia grand jury cleared everyone involved, including the mayor and other top officials, of criminal liability for the death and destruction resulting from the confrontation; it was, however, critical of their "morally reprehensible behavior" as well as their "incompetence" and "cowardice." However, William H. Brown III, the chairman of the Special Commission, stated, "It seems to me that there was more than sufficient evidence to indicate that there should have been indictments returned by this grand jury." See "Grand Jury Clears Everyone in Fatal Philadelphia Siege," *New York Times*, May 4, 1988.

Fraternal Order of Police, and gave fresh evidence of the rejection of accountability and protection from criticism institutionally fostered by Rizzo.[64] On another level the hatred felt by the police echoes in the first words spoken at the outset of the assault by Police Commissioner Gregore J. Sambor over the bullhorn: "Attention, MOVE! This is America!"

7   The Los Angeles Police Department

Defenders of the
Free Enterprise Faith

*The Los Angeles Red Squad and the
Political Culture in Which It Was Rooted*

The patterns of overkill in the selection of targets, operational abuse, and harassment that emerge from a study of the Chicago, New York, and Philadelphia political intelligence units are also reflected in the Los Angeles experience—but with certain noteworthy differences. In the former three cities the core nativist creed that has historically nourished countersubversion in the American political culture was influenced or modified by special local circumstances. But in Los Angeles, an undiluted nativism enduringly shaped the red squad's agendas and operations and assigned its police chiefs a special superordinate role as the city's autonomous guardians of morality and righteousness.

In the same way, while all urban intelligence units functioned as protectors of propertied interests, this mission was, with the passage of time, masked or curbed in the other three cities (by reform movements, labor unions, libertarian pressures, media hostility, and judicial and statutory restraints). In Los Angeles, however, more than in any other city in the country, the role of the police department and its red squad as clients of business interests in combating dissent and unionism was from the start openly proclaimed and was implemented over the years with only minimal concessions to changes in political climate, accountability requirements, reform movements, recurring corruption scandals, and adverse court decisions.[1] Finally, the political intelligence component of the LAPD is unique because of its unabashed right-wing commitment. To be sure, all of the red squads were guided by highly conservative political values, but in Los Angeles right-wing zealotry reigned supreme. This extremist bias accounts for the unit's operational aggression, persistent racism, failure to deal with right-wing bombings in the sixties, operational collaboration with legislative witch-hunts, and the autonomous power of its Big Men.

The most revealing measure of the Southern Californian nativist political culture was the extraordinary burgeoning of far-right political movements in the fifties and early sixties. These patriotic pipers marched in an assortment of organizations under the banner of anticommunism. (They also opposed big government, the United Nations, integration, the income tax, the Supreme Court, and the fluoridation of drinking water.) Dr. Fred C. Schwarz's Christian Anti-Communist Crusade, the most popular of these groups, attracted 12,000 supporters to a Hollywood Bowl rally in October 1961 and a television audience estimated at four million for a three-hour anticommunist rally. A week-long school in Los Angeles on the same theme netted the crusade $214,000; its income in 1961 was estimated at over $1 million, of which one-third was contributed by Southern Californians. The fringe sector of the right-wing movement included nativist guerrilla groups committed to armed paramilitary-style conflict. Of these forces in Southern California the Minutemen were the most prominent; in the sixties some 2,400 of these ideological warriors were organized into twenty-three guerrilla bands that dominated the extremist sector, and it was in this sector that the successive waves of bombings that plagued the Los Angeles area from the early sixties on erupted.[2]

William H. Parker: Hail to the Chief, Savior of Civilization

When LAPD Chief William H. Parker died on July 16, 1966, at the age of sixty-four, the power structures of the city and state paid him spectacular tribute.[3] Thousands of admirers streamed past his coffin as he lay in state in the city hall rotunda attended by a police honor guard. Following a requiem mass conducted by Cardinal James McIntyre, the funeral procession, led by 300 police motorcycles and 280 squad cars, solemnly proceeded to the cemetery, where six rookies carried the coffin to the grave site.[4]

Parker joined the LAPD in 1927 and for several years served as administrative assistant and drumbeater for Chief James E. Davis and subsequently as a departmental prosecutor of errant policemen. When, after sixteen years as chief, he died in harness, he was not only an internationally recognized authority on police administration but probably the most respected public figure in Southern California and, next to J. Edgar

Hoover, the most celebrated law-enforcement official in the country. His writings and lectures on police themes were widely reprinted for use in police circles, and his speeches—he was a popular after-dinner guest speaker—were widely circulated. In an authoritarian mold made familiar by a succession of Los Angeles chiefs, he was an indefatigable preacher and prophet. But, in contrast to his counterparts, he offered a more grandiose version of the bargain: in exchange for trust in and respect for the police, society would be rescued from destruction. His world was divided into a Manichean polarity between the forces of evil and the defenders of freedom—a conflict in which the demonic hosts were slowly but surely winning. Thus he attributed the fall of Babylon, Egypt, Greece, and Rome, not to invasion by external enemies, but to the fact that "the walls crumbled and the enemy poured through when barbarianism within rotted the morale of supporting timbers."[5] Parker assumed the role of a traffic cop assigned by history to reroute us from the path of Ozymandias. His apocalyptic pronouncements were highly useful in promoting the role of the police—and Parker himself. Because of its immorality and softness, society as a whole, and not the police, was to blame for increasing crime rates.

In his Jeremiads he inveighed against the flabbiness and permissiveness of American society contrasted with the discipline of the communist revolutionaries. The godless, disciplined communists were poised to crush the nation, already corrupted by the weakness of its people. Was it not plain that the communists were linked to the criminal elements in a plot against constituted authority (the police), which would succeed unless we shaped up? His public utterances and writings are filled with the glorification of the role of the "thin blue line"—to use a phrase of his own coinage—in shielding American society from barbarism. How could we tolerate criticism of this bastion of civilization, knowing that loss of public confidence in law enforcement would ease the path to a communist takeover? And how could civil rights leaders permit themselves to become agents or dupes in this blueprint for conquest?[6] In testifying in 1965 before the McCone Commission investigating the Watts riot, he complained that "black leaders seemed to think that if Parker can be destroyed officially, they will have no trouble in imposing their will upon the police of America . . . because nobody else would dare stand up."[7]

Parker's anticommunist strictures were shaped by the Cold War—an updated version of Richard Hofstadter's "paranoid style." The long twilight struggle was beginning, cosmic forces were moving toward Armageddon, could America, undermined by secularism and immorality, still be saved? With so much at stake, every police program had to be viewed in a global perspective. For example, in describing a campaign to deal with the threat of organized gambling, he told an assemblage of police officers: "This plan goes deeper than a means of saving Los Angeles from the stigma of vice. We are protecting the American philosophy of life. It is known that Russia is hoping that we'll destroy ourselves as a nation through avarice, greed and corruption in government. Hence this program has a wider application than in the Los Angeles area alone."[8]

In addition to his homiletic passion, Parker shared many other personality traits with FBI chief J. Edgar Hoover. Like Hoover, he was consumed by an insatiable hunger for publicity and acclaim. He not only sponsored his own television program ("The Thin Blue Line"), but actively collaborated in a series of programs that glorified the LAPD and its leaders. And, again reminiscent of Hoover, he was contentious and intolerant of criticism (given the massive egos of both men, it is hardly surprising that they feuded), demanded blind loyalty, and treated any deviation from his rules of conduct as a stain on his reputation deserving for that reason alone the severest punishment. He undermined the Los Angeles Board of Police Commissioners, the titular managing command of the police, and achieved virtually unchallenged autonomy during his long tenure as chief.[9]

Parker personified the Southern California ultra-rightist sensibility. He was a John Birch Society hero—in the Parker years the society became a powerful departmental force—and his picture was reproduced on the front cover of its official organ, *American Opinion* (September 1967). He was also a participant in the weekly right-wing radio discussion group, the "Manion Forum," presided over by Clarence Manion, a member of the John Birch Society's National Council. On May 30, 1965, in a nationwide 300-station hook-up, Parker unburdened himself to the forum audience; he denounced the courts as coddlers of criminals, deplored their concern for civil liberties,[10] and decried what he saw as a "socialistic trend" threatening American society.* Also revealing the

---

* Parker's anger at the courts for curbing police violations of basic individual rights reflected an occupational hostility that pervaded the police world in the sixties. See Yale Kamisar, "Criminals, Cops, and the Constitution," *Nation*, November 9, 1964. In the case of California, obsession with countersubversion had generated conflicts with the courts beginning in the Hynes era (see pp. 59–61). And subsequently judicial protection of First and Fourth Amendment rights cast the courts in the role of national standard-bearers of the Jeffersonian democratic tradition and thus the symbolic foe of nativism, with its claim to the exclusive stewardship of a higher law. This conflict in our political culture is reflected in

chief's ultra-right politics was his enthusiasm for Dr. Fred Schwarz's Christian Anti-Communist Crusade; he thought that its work was so important that he negotiated with the Schwarz group for a special police tuition rate in order to stimulate attendance.

Giant of the Police Intelligence Community

When Parker joined the force in 1927, he was assigned to work as an undercover agent in radical groups. Throughout his career his passion for intelligence work remained undimmed. The standard police text on police intelligence brackets Parker with J. Edgar Hoover as "giants of the police intelligence community."[11] Political intelligence was highly attractive to Parker because it implemented his conservative politics, nourished his ego, and afforded him a means of discrediting critics. That Parker viewed the department's surveillance and filing activities as an instrument of personal power is made clear by a departmental statement issued in the early fifties not long after he took office: "The Intelligence Division maintains its own filing system and all files therein are the property of the Chief of the Police; not only are official police records not subject to subpoena—these files are not open to perusal by members of the department." It was widely rumored that Parker had "the goods on everybody" and that his secret files on enemies and critics made him politically invulnerable.

It is clear that Parker enjoyed this file fear and did nothing to dispel it. For example, there can be no doubt that he used this personal resource to keep tabs on members of the Board of Police Commissioners.[12] He also used the assumed existence of file documentation to lend credibility to unproved charges that his critics were subversive.

When in 1954 the widely respected constitutional lawyer A. L. Wirin brought a suit challenging the legality of LAPD's wiretapping practices, Parker angrily denounced him "as identified with the defense of Communists in practically every action he has been involved in" and born in Russia for good measure. Similarly a characterization of Parker's political

---

the John Birch Society's sixties battle cry "Impeach Earl Warren" and in the Reagan era in the movement to block Senate approval of Sandra Day O'Connor's nomination to a Supreme Court post unless she promised to disregard in the future the Court's prior rulings on the abortion issue, as well as in a series of right-wing measures to deprive the courts of jurisdiction in areas such as busing, abortion, and prayer in the schools.

views as "extremist" by Thomas L. Pitts, head of the California AFL-CIO, brought the retort that such charges were a tactic used by communists in their never-ending plots against the police.[13]

Parker did not inherit a highly active intelligence operation. Under Republican Mayor Fletcher Bowron's reform administration (1938–50), LAPD intelligence operations shrank considerably. As a result of the exposés of the La Follette Committee and a changed political climate, police involvement in labor matters largely ended. The traditional monitoring of subversion was, at first, recast into more discreet modes as red squad personnel were reassigned to the metropolitan division. Shortly before Parker took over, a new intelligence unit was formed that retained the discredited red squad's antiradical mission and stewardship of its file collection. When Parker ascended to the leadership of LAPD, he revived the old red squad, but without its more flamboyant operational style, using the fifties rationale, already referred to, of linking subversion and organized crime as activities uniquely requiring an intelligence response.[14]

Parker's intelligence unit expanded in response to Cold War stimuli, the postwar spy scare, the need to develop leverage in the mainstream political process, the intensive monitoring of the left-liberal sector of the Hollywood community, demands for operational assistance by the FBI, and requests of both federal and state countersubversive committees for surveillance and file data. In 1975 a Los Angeles writer and film maker, Robert Cohen, discovered from documents released under the Freedom of Information Act that the Los Angeles intelligence unit had, during the Parker era, spied on groups such as the Beverly Hills Democratic Club, Hollywood Democratic Club, Los Angeles Committee for a Sane Nuclear Policy, First Unitarian Church, and ACLU.

When the occasion arose, Parker sacrificed secrecy—a requirement of professionalism repeatedly stressed by him as the sine qua non of intelligence work—to political necessity. In the early 1950s, for example, Mayor Bowron was locked in combat with a diehard business coalition over his plans for a federally financed low-cost housing program. In 1952, at a key point in the conflict, Parker presented the mayor with a dossier on Frank Wilkinson, the Housing Authority's public relations officer. However, Bowron would have none of this attempted smear and told Parker that he was a long-time friend of Wilkinson's family and had great confidence in his loyalty. Furious at Bowron, the vengeful Parker did not hesitate the next year, on the eve of the mayoralty election, to read Wilkinson's dossier at a televised state legislative committee hearing and to reveal the fact that Bowron had rebuffed him. This disclosure created a sensation and contributed to Bowron's overwhelming defeat by

Norris Poulson and the subsequent abandonment of the controversial housing project.*

Wilkinson's home and the office of an organization he headed (the Citizens' Committee to Preserve American Freedoms) were bombed, as were the homes of Unitarian and Lutheran ministers, the offices of the Communist Party and the American Association for the U.N., and the Valley Peace Center (which housed a number of liberal groups)—in some instances more than once. The intelligence unit responded with a mixture of apathy and hostility. None of the presumably right-wing perpetrators were ever identified; on the contrary, the police stance was that the victims somehow brought destruction on themselves in order to get publicity and scapegoat the right. For example, they questioned Wilkinson in an effort to establish that he had bombed his own home and office.[15] This bias in favor of the ultra-right was also reflected in the police response to public meetings. Although vigilant in protecting rightist groups, the police refused to intervene when liberals and dissenters sought protection.[†] For example, the police refused in October 1963 to clear the entrance of a meeting hall besieged by hostile picketers identified with right-wing Cuban exile groups seeking to bar entrance to a meeting sponsored by the Fair Play for Cuba Committee. In contrast, a parade the following week by members of these anti-Castro groups was afforded full police protection.[16]

Parker's Thin Blue Line: Racism and Reaction

Even before Parker ascended to its leadership, the LAPD had acquired a national reputation for its vigorous espousal of right-wing politics. In

---

* In 1961 when Yorty defeated Poulson, Parker was charged with using his files to discredit the Yorty forces ("Yorty Police Charges to Be Pressed," *Los Angeles Times*, June 13, 1961). However, Parker quickly moved to make peace with Yorty, who had become a convert from the left to the anticommunist right.

† This is not to invite approval of surveillance of right-wing groups for purposes unrelated to law enforcement or peace-keeping. My stress on the unremedied hemorrhage of bombings and threats indisputably traceable to the far right seeks to call the reader's attention to the PDID's distorted priorities in sacrificing the claims of law enforcement to professionally unjustifiable but politically more congenial pursuits. It is conceivable—but barely—that this skewed pattern reflected not conscious value preferences but a bureaucratic lag in responding to change that preserved obsolete manpower assignment priorities. But even such a strained justification does not improve the case for PDID. When other police units abandon conventional crime prevention and detection in a particular area of recurrent crime, we reasonably suspect some form of corruption or bribe-taking; but in the case of the PDID, the systematic failure to respond to repeated acts of politically motivated violence did not result in criticism extensive enough to bring about a reordering of the unit's target priorities.

the Parker years members of the force even more openly than in the past promoted their right-wing creed by inter alia distributing extremist literature, sponsoring prominent right-wing speakers (Dr. Fred C. Schwarz was a favorite), and showings at the police academy of the far-out film *Communism on the Map*.[17] The John Birch Society, which in the fifties began wooing a national police constituency, gained a substantial following in the Los Angeles law-enforcement community—an estimated 2,000 members.[18] Such unconcealed political loyalties inevitably influenced policy and decision making in the political intelligence sphere and seriously compromised the impartiality required in maintenance of public order and related areas of actual or potential confrontation.

The spearhead of the Birch operation was the Firemen's and Policemen's Protective League and its research organization (Fi-Po), which published a Birch-style exposé newsletter (*Fi-Po News*), lobbied for countersubversive legislation, promoted far-right rallies and lectures, polemicized against the opinions and writings of moderates in the field of policing, and, for a fee, conducted loyalty checks, based on official file entries, for approved requesters in the business community. Despite the fact that it was supposed to be a purely private group, it enjoyed semiofficial status and the enthusiastic collaboration of many watch commanders. Indeed, the head of the outfit during the Parker years was none other than the ultra-rightist Edward M. Davis, who later succeeded Parker as chief.[19]

Parker's apocalyptic style flamed from the newsletter. In April 1963 *Fi-Po News* announced, "We know the U.S. will be a socialistic nation that will eventually fall under the domination of Russian rule if we continue our 'new frontier' progress. . . . According to Khrushchev's openly published schedule of conquests . . . we have . . . two more years of 'freedom.' " Under the headline "Know Your Candidates—What the News Media Failed to Tell You," a *Fi-Po News* item for June 1970 proclaimed that Wilson Riles, a black educator running for state superintendent of public instruction against a rightist, Max Rafferty, had once been connected with an organization, the Fellowship of Reconciliation, condemned as subversive by none other than J. Edgar Hoover (but a Hoover spokesman denied that he had ever so characterized the organization). In 1975, in the wake of another scandal, Fi-Po disbanded, and its files—copies of official documents—were secretly transferred to the right-wing United Community Churches of America.[20]

In August 1965 the Watts riot exploded—an event of unprecedented destructiveness marked by looting and burning; property damage estimated at $40 million; countless assaults and injuries, 34 deaths and approximately 4,000 arrests. Festering resentment of the LAPD's racism was the key cause.[21] Prior to the riot, Parker, quite blind to the gathering storm, smugly reported that Los Angeles had nothing to fear from racial unrest. After the riot, Parker delivered himself of a litany of complaints; the police were being made scapegoats; they were hounded by a vicious press; he himself was unjustly condemned for discontinuing juvenile crime prevention programs that were clearly, in his eyes, "unprofessional" and, in addition, improperly assigned "sociological" functions to the police. Why had his critics ignored his statement that "G-2," as he called the intelligence unit, had identified communist troublemakers in the ghetto?

Despite Parker's paranoid outbursts, the fact remained that "G-2" had utterly failed to perform its blueprinted intelligence function of alerting the authorities to the impending disturbance.[22] But neither "G-2's" failure nor his own had an impact on Parker's standing in Los Angeles's WASPish middle-class home-owner and business community or altered the Los Angeles establishment's trust in the police as a barrier against disorder. On the contrary, the outbreak renewed in the citizenry a sense of dependence in the face of unforeseen future disruptions by the city's minorities. Unconsciously, Parker gave voice to this continued perception of the protective "thin blue line" role of the police when, after the riot subsided, he smugly compared the positions of the police and ghetto dwellers: "Now we're on the top and they're on the bottom."[23]

Parker's contributions to police management and discipline, admirable though they were in other respects, intensified the inward-facing, tightly knit, hierarchical character of his force and institutionalized the countersubversive stereotypes that had long dominated its intelligence operation. He was succeeded after his death by Thomas J. Reddin, who led the department for two years (February 1967–May 1969) before departing for greener pastures—a $100,000-a-year post as a television commentator.[24] While Reddin tried with mixed success to alter the perception of the force as racist and violence-prone, the department's intelligence coverage in the political area was expanding.

An endless round of speeches, to an assortment of groups, in the ornate rhetoric made familiar by Parker established Reddin as a right-wing standard bearer in tune with the values of the business community. In 1967 the city was shaken by a police riot in which a large number of demonstrators, along with children and invalids, protesting in front of the Century Plaza Hotel, where President Johnson was being feted, were clubbed and brutalized by police equipped with helmets, guns, and nightsticks.[25] According to an investigative report of the Southern California ACLU, the decision to disperse the demonstrators was unjustified in view of the fact that they were not violent or threatening and did not violate the terms of their parade permit.*[26] Protesters against the police actions were subsequently denied a hearing and forcibly ejected from city council chambers.[27] As in the 1965 riot, criticism of the police in no way reduced the police chief's standing.

Edward M. Davis: Sermons from a Bully Pulpit

We now come to the third of the Los Angeles prophets in blue, Edward M. Davis, the police chief who presided over the department from 1969 until he resigned in January 1978 to run (unsuccessfully) for the Republican gubernatorial nomination.[28] Like his predecessors, the first Davis (James E.—no relation) and Parker, Davis was a "culture bearer," a larger-than-life figure who embodied and symbolized the extremely conservative political tradition identified today with President Ronald Reagan. Davis, a native of Southern California, is a product of its lily-white superpatriotic political culture. In the classic Southern California style, he equated social protest—particularly in its activist mode—with a threat to the nation's survival and was quick to link dissent generally with immorality and libertinism.

Again, like Parker, Davis had a colossal ego and an obsession with power, a hunger for publicity and a self-righteousness that rejected all criticism. During his eight years as chief, he poured out a steady stream of blasts and put-downs, such as a proposal that airplane hijackers be summarily hanged right at the airport, denunciations of gun control, and a suggestion that farm workers join the gay rights movement to

---

* The report points out: "Amateurish intelligence work prior to the march helped police misread the size and character of the crowd they would be facing. A private detective, hired by attorneys for the hotel, attended planning sessions conducted by the parade organizers and returned with lurid tales of conspiracies and diabolical plans: to unleash mice, cockroaches, and stink bombs in the hotel, and other such outlandish schemes. The meetings were in fact open to the public and many of the detective's stories were based on suggestions offered by members of the audience. None was ever taken seriously by the planning committee.

"However, such tales seem to have reinforced police beliefs that they were dealing with kooks and subversives. Certainly these impressions were widespread among the rank-and-file officers assigned to control the crowd. . . . Statements submitted to the ACLU are filled with quotations of the police indicating they regarded the crowd as made up of disreputable people: 'Get that damn Jew,' 'A bunch of dirty, Goddamned communists,' 'Animals and commies, that's all they are' " (ACLU, *Day of Protest, Night of Violence: The Century City Peace March* [Los Angeles: Sawyer Press, 1967], pp. 31–32).

form a "United Fruit Party." In a speech to the National Rifle Association in 1975, he described one section of Los Angeles as "a cesspool of pornography, fruit bars, and bottomless bars, thanks to the United States and California Supreme Courts," and explained that if he did not hold the line on the recruitment of minorities, gays, and women as police officers, "I could envision myself on the stage on graduation day [at the police academy] giving a diploma to a 4'1" transvestite moron who would kiss me instead of saluting."

In 1975 he ordered a large contingent of police into action at a rock concert, arresting a total of 511 persons, most on marijuana charges. After the raids, Mayor Tom Bradley said he thought the pot busts posed "a serious question about the priorities in assignment of personnel" by the police. Davis claimed the concert was "a dope festival" and vowed he would "never allow mass wholesale violations of the law in the city of Los Angeles."[29]

When in early 1971 a demonstration against police brutality was scheduled by leaders of the Mexican-American community, he warned them: "If they don't watch out, their young men will be exploited. . . . Now is the time to prevent swimming pool communists and sophisticated Bolsheviks who have worked for this sort of thing around the world, who always avoid arrest, from making victims of Mexican-Americans as prison fodder."[30]

As his term wore on, the flow of reckless announcements quickened; he inveighed increasingly against the softness of the courts, the weakening of the "moral fibre" of society, the "disintegration of the family," and the "desecration of the relationship between men and women." What America needed, he insisted, was more "men with male gonads."

The ACLU's Southern California chapter regularly drew outraged denunciations. When the group obtained an injunction banning his prejudicial comments on a pending case against the police, he replied, "I'm not saying they're Communists, but I've noticed that when the Communist Party takes a deep breath, the ACLU's chest goes out." Mumbling through a handkerchief tied around his mouth, he added, "Bar your doors, buy a police dog, call us when we're available and pray. I am under a gag rule imposed by the American Civil Liberties Union. I'm one of the few men in the country without freedom of speech."[31]

The Public Disorder Intelligence Division (PDID): Updating the Red Squad

In 1970, not long after Davis took over the department, he reconstituted the red squad as the Public Disorder Intelligence Division (PDID) and severed it from the Intelligence Division, where it had been sheltered for more than three decades. The historic style, mission, and target priorities of the LAPD's political intelligence operation continued unchanged. As with so many police functionaries, the adversary that stirred Davis's juices was not the criminal but the subversive—an embodiment of the demonic foe barring the road to the New Jerusalem, the Zion promised by the Lord, a justification for police spying and a means of discrediting criticism of the police. In October 1970, in testimony before the Senate Internal Security Committee, he echoed Parker's thesis that "the government is being overthrown" by militant left-wing groups that encourage attacks on police officers. "We have revolution on the installment plan." Davis explained:

> Public officials are absolutely at the mercy of conspirators who have decided to overthrow this form of government. They're doing it with impunity and immunity at this time, and it's going to get worse.
>
> It is a tragic irony that revolutionaries are running free on the streets and that the people are locked in their homes and even in their public buildings.

Consequently, Davis stated, he was compelled to "divert a good percentage of [his] manpower to intelligence and security efforts."[32]

Lawsuits filed in the early 1970s make it quite clear that the PDID's favored operational mode was indiscriminate spying on legitimate dissent wholly unrelated to law enforcement, revolution, or the preservation of public order. Files in the office of the Los Angeles city attorney established in 1970 that the LAPD had infiltrated the UCLA campus to gather information for use in the compilation of dossiers on organizations and individuals (students and professors) suspected of "conspiratorial activities." Two individuals arrested as students in connection with a campus demonstration on February 20, 1970, Harry Ted Kozak and James McMurray, were identified as undercover PDID agents. Both Kozak and McMurray are recorded in the files as having played provocative roles in the demonstration. Kozak was prominent in UCLA radical circles* and McMurray sat on the steering committee of Students for a Democratic Society (SDS). A third undercover PDID agent, who called himself "Stephen Smith," while not an enrolled student like his two colleagues, was an active participant in campus dissident activities.[33]

---

* He also wrote articles for the campus newspaper, the *Daily Bruin,* in support of the Students for a Democratic Society (SDS). Kozak was mistakenly taken into custody by the police, who were unaware of his cover.

A spokesman for Chief Davis acknowledged the existence of the campus infiltration program.[34] The police practice did not sit well with the faculty's academic senate, which in October 1970 received an investigative report confirming the existence of a police infiltration program and concluding that the evidence established the presence of spies who acted as agents provocateurs. The investigative report was followed by a federal court lawsuit by thirteen students and faculty members. When this suit was dismissed on jurisdictional grounds, a second lawsuit was filed in a state court by Professor Hayden V. White, charging that undercover police agents had infiltrated his classes. A unanimous decision in the *White* case, handed down by the California Supreme Court in 1975, rejected a lower court's ruling upholding the practice: "Given the delicate nature of academic freedom, we visualize a substantial probability that this alleged undercover police surveillance will chill the exercise of First Amendment rights [and] also constitute a violation of the explicit 'right of privacy' recently added to the State Constitution."[*][35]

The LAPD also received input in the form of wiretap tapes from the Los Angeles Community College District, which is responsible for the operation of a chain of community colleges. A lawsuit filed in 1972 revealed that the Los Angeles Technical College had wiretapped and compiled dossiers on political and social activities of both students and faculty members.[†][36] The fruits of this program were shared with the PDID operatives, who also tested the electronic equipment prior to its installation and conducted workshops for the campus police. The practices unearthed by the lawsuit prompted an investigation by a state legislative committee, which revealed LAPD collaboration in an extensive pattern of electronic surveillance at all of the community colleges, covering a range of organizations from women's liberation groups to the Southern Christian Leadership Conference (SCLC).

The *White* case was paralleled by an equally revealing controversy involving the scope of targeting and operational modes of the PDID. In June 1970 a lawsuit (*Cannon v. Davis*) on behalf of three Los Angeles taxpayers against Chief Davis charged that public funds were being improperly used to develop and maintain intelligence files concerning a wide range of church, political, educational, and social welfare groups and individuals associated with them. The alleged organizational subjects

---

[*] The constitutional amendment referred to was approved after the adverse decision of the lower court and shortly before the appellate court's reversal.
[†] Disclosure of the program came from an unusual source, Harold Cole, a campus security officer. The embittered Cole was subsequently harassed and threatened by supervisory campus police personnel.

of surveillance files included the American Baptist Home Mission Society; the United Church of Christ Board of Home Ministries and Board of Missions; the Methodist Church Board of National Missions; the United Presbyterian Church, U.S.A.; the Catholic Committee for Urban Ministries; the Executive Council of the Episcopal Church; the General Board of Christian Concerns of the Methodist Church; the National Catholic Conference for Inter-Racial Justice; the Constitutional Rights Foundation; the American Jewish Committee; the Inter-City Cultural Center; and Operation Breadbasket, sponsored by the Southern Christian Leadership Conference.

The surveillance files on individuals, the complaint alleged, reflected such norms as "engaged in protest," "agitator," "militant," "controversial," "anti-establishment," "racist," "anti-police," "anti-white," "use foul language," "subversive," and "oppose the enforcement of the House Un-American Committee's revised Internal Security Act of 1969." The supporting documents referred to or reproduced in the files include records of church membership; voter registration documents; lists of books used in a public school leadership program at the University of California at Los Angeles; the curriculum of a federally funded educational project; texts of leaflets, pamphlets, and other publications dealing with civic and educational matters; and a statement by a member of the Board of Supervisors of Los Angeles County in support of a complaint against the police.[37]

The complainants' allegations were no paranoid fantasies but were based on dossiers publicly disclosed as part of a broad offensive to discredit the principal Los Angeles components of the federal antipoverty program.

From May 1967 to February 1968, PDID Sergeant Robert G. Thoms had served as a community relations officer (ironically enough, part of Chief Reddin's program to reduce racial unrest), working with many of the groups and individuals he subsequently charged with subversion. In a detailed presentation to the Senate Internal Security Subcommittee in January 1970,[38] Thoms charged that some forty-seven organizations and ninety-five individuals were either themselves subversive or the tools of subversion. Thoms insisted one could not afford to ignore the fact that the innocent-seeming groups were really sinister "umbrella organizations" that deliberately sponsored innocuous civic associations as a calculated cover "to give an air of respectability."

One such deceptive umbrella organization, Thoms charged, was the Inter-Religious Foundation for Community Organization (IFCO), which supported a variety of community organizations, most notably, the Black

Congress of Los Angeles, a coalition of black community groups. The Black Congress, Thoms testified, was "violent and subversive" because of its sponsorship of "anti-establishment" demonstrations. Similarly the federally funded Educational Opportunities Program designed to help support needy students was not as innocent as it seemed: no fewer than 43 student beneficiaries—out of 604 in the program—belonged to "militant organizations." The publication and circulation of Thoms's testimony in March 1970 produced a wave of almost incredulous protests against its inaccuracies and wildly strained inferences.[39]

In the wake of the Thoms scandal, it came to light that the initial release of files was part of an offensive to undermine a cluster of area social agencies. On May 20, 1970, it was disclosed that the city council's president, John S. Gibson, Jr., and council member Arthur Snyder (both quite conservative) had used a series of red squad files stamped "Confidential" to compile a 48-page report charging that certain federally funded antipoverty agencies were "aiding and abetting militant groups" and that police critics as well as political opponents of the two councilmen espoused "revolutionary change."* The Gibson-Snyder document was prepared to brief participants in a Chamber of Commerce Los Angeles "Leadership Trip" to Washington, D.C., for use in persuading government legislators and officials to bar further funding of objectionable projects and to provide establishment support for the earlier Thoms-Davis charges.[40]

The airing of the Gibson-Snyder document set off a second barrage of complaints by those prominently identified with the attacked programs, who pointed out that the councilmen's sponsorship of the report had been used to clothe it with official sanction.[41] But police critics were stirred more deeply by two other circumstances: the facility with which "confidential" documents were obtained and disseminated and, an echo from the past, the readiness of the police chief to place the department's resources at the disposal of the Los Angeles business establishment. It is hardly open to doubt that in both cases Davis knew that the file materials would be made public. It seems equally clear that Davis gave the two councilmen access to the file material used in the report not only to implement his own policies but to gain approval for an upcoming request for a budgetary increase.

A year later, the entire attack, initiated by Thoms and reinforced by the Chamber of Commerce, was exposed as part of a statewide campaign

---

* Councilman Snyder represented East Los Angeles, a heavily Hispanic constituency that was at the time in the process of freeing itself from Anglo domination.

of surveillance and harassment. The report by a federal investigative team in April 1971 charged that the Reagan state administration had used a large part of the federal yearly contribution of $800,000 to the state Office of Economic Opportunity for surveillance-related purposes to discredit antipoverty agencies.*

Aggressive Intelligence: Theme and Variations

As we have seen, the law-enforcement justification for political surveillance has been frequently thwarted by a variety of intelligence-related barriers, from unwillingness to identify an informer to illegal procedures—such as wiretapping—in the collection of evidence. The LAPD's intelligence practices not only blocked bona fide law enforcement but generated a series of lawsuits, of which the *Cannon* and *White* cases were forerunners, charging the unit with illegal practices. In addition to the cases referred to in later sections of this chapter, two legal actions illustrate the role police misconduct played in litigation. Both of them involve a relatively rare phenomenon in urban intelligence work: the assignment of police officers—usually in plainclothes—to surveil an individual target. Such permanent assignments were used to monitor high-priority targets: in the Los Angeles practice, the plainclothes tails typically made themselves known to their targets, slashed the tires on their cars, photographed them over and over again, verbally abused them, threatened them with arrest and jail terms, and detained them on pretexts—especially bogus charges of law-breaking, withdrawn after a few hours.[42] In addition, these surveillants looked the other way when subjects were harassed or assaulted by rightist ideological adversaries.

A dramatic illustration of this aggressive style of surveillance came to light in a case involving Seymour Myerson, a 70-year-old political leftist. Myerson was repeatedly cursed and physically assaulted by his PDID tail, Clifford E. Ruff, while participating in protest activities. In an inci-

---

* One agency, the California Rural Legal Assistance Program (CRLA), was accused by Governor Ronald Reagan of "acting like a bunch of ideological ambulance chasers." The federal investigators referred to in the text were bombarded by anonymous complaints solicited by the Reagan-controlled state OEO in letters to lawyers, judges, community leaders, and others. A subsequent review of the CRLA by a panel of Reagan-appointed judges cleared the agency of all charges of misconduct. See "Federal Report Charges State Spends OEO Funds for Spying," *Los Angeles Times*, April 30, 1971; Jeff Stein, "Officer Ed Meese," *New Republic*, October 7, 1981; and Elizabeth Drew, "A Reporter at Large," *New Yorker*, March 1, 1982 (reprinted in *Congressional Record*, March 15, 1982, pp. S2104–8).

dent in July 1976 Ruff shouted obscenities at him outside his home and drove back and forth across his lawn. Minutes later, Myerson was ordered from his home by four uniformed policemen, who pointed loaded firearms at him, forced him to place his hands behind his head, and searched his house. The police told Myerson that they had received a radio dispatch saying that he was armed with a rifle and was threatening to shoot people on the street and in passing cars. No weapon was found either on Myerson's person or in his house. Ruff, responsible for the message, obviously designed to set up Myerson for armed attack by the police, received a five-day suspension and his victim a letter of apology. Subsequently the department agreed to pay Myerson $27,500 in settlement of a lawsuit charging a variety of police abuses and dirty tricks and seeking damages.[43]

In May 1972 Ron Ridenour, a leftist photographer-reporter, was arrested for "interfering with an officer" while he was photographing the police beating a paraplegic veteran in attendance at an anti-Nixon demonstration. After being booked on a charge of interfering with the police, Ridenour discovered that his film had been exposed and ruined. Despite eyewitness testimony that Ridenour had been no closer than fifteen feet from the scene of the beating, he was sentenced by a judge, himself a former LAPD officer, to a year in jail. In May 1973 an appeals court reversed the conviction.[44]

An aggressive surveillance style also marked the operations of the LAPD's Criminal Conspiracy Section (CCS). According to its organizational blueprint, CCS is responsible for the investigation of criminal conspiracies of all kinds, while a unit called Criminal Investigation and Identification (CII) is supposed to serve its intelligence needs. In fact, CCS-CII concentrated primarily on political offenses—other conspiracies were the responsibility of the division assigned to handling the particular substantive crime involved. The PDID's intelligence functions overlapped the CII's, and both fed material to the CCS. Groups considered militant or violence-prone (typically race-related) were targeted by the CCS and infiltrated by highly aggressive informers, conscious role-players, ready to engage in violence and deception both as cover and provocation.[45]

A key case that emerged from this program involved Donald Freed, a West Coast teacher and writer, and Shirley Sutherland, the then wife of screen actor Donald Sutherland and the activist daughter of a liberal former premier of Saskatchewan.[46] In March 1969 Freed and Sutherland helped organize "Friends of the Black Panthers," a white, middle-class group. Later that year, the group was infiltrated by James Jarrett, who claimed to be a former CIA Green Beret and assassination specialist in the Indo-Chinese war theater. What he did not say was that he had been recruited to help train the LAPD Special Weapons and Tactical Squad (SWAT)[47] and was attached to the CCS.

The Friends had been plagued by harassments, vandalism, assaults, and the rape of a group member—the work of right-wing Cuban exiles—and accepted Jarrett's offer of instruction in self-defense techniques and the first aid despite their suspicion and fear of him. Jarrett's manner, vocabulary, and everyday behavior were extraordinarily spookish, wary, and melodramatic. The enemy was everywhere! His style somehow made everyone else in his company feel that he was absurd or that they, by speaking and acting naturally, were somehow taking foolish risks. His speech was dense with verbal shorthand and code words, the clichés of spy thrillers: a single overheard verbal slip might cause the fall of nations. He had a way of testing a phone and then pronouncing it "secure" and of conducting a conversation as though the walls had ears, familiar mannerisms of certain intelligence types. Freed recalled in an interview: "When he would enter a room, he would check: he would never sit with his back to the door; he would permit no one to take his picture. And if he would enter a drugstore to buy a pack of gum, he would enter as if it were staked out. He was never without his dark glasses; he made one feel as though he wore them to bed." In some ways, paradoxically enough, Jarrett's furtive, James Bondish style became a sort of cover to neutralize suspicion that in fact he was a spy. If his style dismally failed to convince the targets that he held the same values as they did, it nevertheless went far to persuade targets that he was opposed to the same institutions as they were.* Jarrett naturally did not reveal a range of racist and macho views that would have repelled the Friends and have ultimately led to his ostracism.

A few months after Jarrett's infiltration, Freed asked him to furnish some chemical spray such as mace for self-defense purposes and to pick up from Ms. Sutherland a check for $100 to reimburse him. At 4:30 A.M. on October 29, 1969, Jarrett made his appearance at Freed's apartment with a box neatly wrapped in brown paper and demanded payment,

---

* It is hard to say whether Jarrett's style was an acquired occupational response (a pattern of reflexes developed to reduce the risks of his undercover work abroad), a projection of his fantasies about domestic enemies, or simply an act put on to impress his targets. It was probably a blend of all three. In any event, Jarrett's style became more familiar to Americans as a result of the Watergate disclosures. Jarrett belongs in the same gallery of types as G. Gordon Liddy and E. Howard Hunt. See Tad Szulc, "The Spy Compulsion," *New York Times Magazine*, June 3, 1973.

much to the surprise of Freed in view of the prior arrangement for Ms. Sutherland to handle details of the payment. Quite unaware that the newly delivered box did not contain the requested spray but explosives obtained from a Navy arsenal, Freed responded to Jarrett's request for payment by making out a check for $90—hardly a form of payment one would expect in a criminal transaction. Before Jarrett left, he repeatedly but unsuccessfully tried to get Freed to say that the "stuff" was for the Black Panthers and not for the defense of members of the Friends.* Minutes after Jarrett's departure, Freed's home was invaded by a combined raiding party of agents of the LAPD, the FBI, and the Treasury Department. At about 5:30 A.M. Ms. Sutherland, who had put the $100 Jarrett had asked for in her rural delivery–style mailbox for Jarrett to pick up (again another unlikely payoff scenario in a criminal situation), was, along with her screaming children, awakened by a second raiding party of about twenty agents, who left the place a shambles.†

After an arraignment on federal charges of illegal possession of explosives, the defense lawyers hired an experienced West Coast investigator, Michael McCowan (himself a former policeman). McCowan needed help and so looked up another former cop, one Sam Bluth, who was assigned to dig into Jarrett's background. For two months, Bluth also worked as a police infiltrator in the defense camp, collaborating in break-ins at the offices of a defense attorney and McCowan and in the theft of files, tapes of interviews with the defendants, and lists of witnesses. The police not only chauffeured the spy-recruit, but even provided him with burglar's tools. His role as double agent was a perfect cover.

All this came to light because on January 20, 1970, the police turned over the stolen tapes, files, and records to U.S. Attorney Matthew Byrne, who felt obliged to make full disclosure not only to the defendants but to the court.[48] Judge Warren Ferguson ultimately dismissed

---

* The Intelligence Division later admitted that Jarrett was wired with a transmitter that was beamed at police stakeout cars in the area to tape-record the conversation with Freed, but they later claimed that this particular tape, curiously enough, was inaudible because of defective transmission.

† Ms. Sutherland recalled: "Jarrett was running around there singing in a sort of singsong, 'I've got the two biggies, I've got the two biggies.' It was weird. And then someone said, 'She seems very calm,' and Jarrett said, 'Of course, it's her Communist training. Her father's the head of the Communist Party in Canada!' They kept telling Jarrett that he might as well go home, but he insisted on going down to the jail with me. When we finally got there he said, 'I know you'd like to see everyone out of here.' I didn't know what he was talking about and then he said, 'They're all poor people—all the rich criminals are out on the street.' Finally he turned to me with tears in his eyes and asked to talk to me when I got out. I've never seen him again."

the case on technical grounds, noting in reproof of police entrapment tactics that Jarrett himself had committed the very crime for which Freed and Sutherland were later indicted.

There was an even graver problem, which ultimately forced the abandonment of the prosecution: the LAPD had conducted warrantless wiretaps of conversations of the defendants with their lawyers. Under a 1971 Supreme Court decision, such warrantless "national security" telephone interceptions were illegal. Moreover, it was obvious that a warrant would in any event never have been granted for the purpose of recording lawyer-client conversations.

What seems clear is that this case, with its pattern of wiretaps, burglaries, break-ins, thefts, and provocations, reflected an attempt to implement an intelligence program blueprinted to destroy the Panthers by a combined federal–local intelligence assault. This view of the case is confirmed by the ease with which the explosives were obtained from a Navy arsenal and the role of LAPD informers in implementing federally inspired anti-Panther initiatives. *

Another CCS superstar was Louis Tackwood. A streetwise black con man and hustler, Tackwood began his career as a police tipster. In the early sixties he began to inform the police about criminal activities in the ghetto while pursuing his own specialties—armed robbery, car theft, and drug peddling.[49] After the 1965 Watts riot, he moved over to political and racial targets and ultimately became a key asset; his services were compensated with cash ($5,000 to $7,000 over the period of his connection with the CCS) and a free hand to pursue his own criminal career. Credible evidence indicates that he was given exoneration for crimes such as burglary and drug peddling. When Tackwood surfaced in the summer of 1971, his disclosures—sometimes subsequently repudiated or altered—were received with some skepticism. But the core of his allegations has survived challenge and is corroborated by other evidence.

On November 22, 1971, after Tackwood had surfaced, he testified under oath in the trial of the Los Angeles Panther 13, which arose out of a 3 A.M. raid on December 8, 1969, by the LAPD SWAT squad on Panther

---

* The planting of contraband seems to have been only one step in a multifaceted dirty tricks offensive. In addition to the harassments already noted, a number of homes of Friends' leaders were burglarized; indictments were handed down on false charges (such as harboring a fugitive) and promptly dismissed; on one occasion Jarrett tried to press a packet of newspaper clippings on some Friends (students in his first-aid class) who had previously given first aid to a wounded Panther, for the purpose of establishing after the fact that they knew that the wounded man had been involved in a police shoot-out. This was accompanied by a series of harassments of the Panthers by the LAPD discussed below.

headquarters. One of those arrested was Melvin ("Cotton") Smith, the number three man in the Panther hierarchy. At the trial two years later there were two surprises: Smith, who had been deeply involved in the defense strategy, turned up as a prosecution witness. The prosecution claimed that Smith had turned state's evidence to escape prosecution. But Tackwood testified under oath that Smith had not made a last-minute switch, but had been a CCS plant, designated as Tackwood's contact when he infiltrated the Panther group prior to the raid. Probably as a result of Tackwood's testimony, Smith's credibility was shattered, and after eleven days of deliberation, the jury found nine of the defendants guilty only of the minor charge of conspiracy to possess illegal weapons. It returned acquittals or was deadlocked on the remaining charges of conspiracy to commit murder and assault on a police officer. They were never retried.

In 1976 Tackwood testified as a defense witness in the Marin County trial of a number of blacks and Hispanics, prisoners and former prisoners, accused of participating in an escape attempt on August 21, 1971, in the course of which the black author George Jackson, three guards, and two inmate trustees were killed in the prison. Tackwood's testimony implicated the CCS in the planned assassination of Jackson.* Although the prosecutor called the testimony "absurd," he made no attempt to refute it by calling any of the seventeen named participants in the alleged state plot.[50]

Two other Tackwood charges have never been seriously challenged: (1) He was assigned by CCS to infiltrate the campaign staffs of two members of the "Black Caucus" running for the Berkeley City Council, equipped with a listening device to record what was said and to eavesdrop on a number of strategy sessions; (2) the CCS supplied him with funds to transmit to Ron Karenga, the leader of a black nationalist organization that was the rival of the Panthers, for use in funding armed attacks on the latter, a program conceived by the FBI and implemented locally. The Karenga assignment was part of a combined LAPD-FBI operation to foment a violent feud between the two groups. The operation

---

* Tackwood, in a day-long interview with the author in August 1971 and in sessions with reporters, claimed that the subsequent shoot-out in the Marin County courthouse where the escape case was being tried could have been prevented. He was, he insists, sent to Santa Cruz to investigate a Panther "hit squad" trained to invade the courthouse and seize hostages. But, he claims, the plan was abandoned on the morning it was scheduled when it appeared that the courthouse was too well guarded. But no one remembered to tell Jonathan Jackson, George Jackson's 17-year-old brother, who went ahead on his own and was killed in the subsequent shoot-out.

was highly successful and resulted in the killings of two Panther activists—Alprentice Carter and John Huggins—for which several members of Karenga's group were convicted.

The master key to the operations of Jarrett and Tackwood is the already-mentioned program to destroy the Panthers. As a result of a series of brutal raids and other harassment, the Panthers were forced to leave Los Angeles in the late sixties. When they returned in January 1971, the LAPD, through its intelligence resources, renewed its efforts to wipe out the group. This second round, only slightly less vicious than the first, was marked by intensive intimidating physical surveillance—from boats, cars, and helicopters—of Panther meetings and individual leaders; confrontations accompanied by verbal abuse, slashed tires, and threats with revolvers and shotguns; repeated interference with the sale of the party's newspaper and the destruction of literature; pretextual detentions and arrests on charges ranging from kidnapping to defective license plate lights; attempts to frame Panther members on drug charges; warnings to third parties to shun them; unauthorized searches of persons and homes; and refusal to accept charges of abuses by police officers and the arrest of the complainants.* Ironically the surveillance failed to uncover any criminal activity. The repeated detentions rarely resulted in charges, and, even when such charges were made, failed to produce a single conviction for Panther activities.

The More the PDID Changes, the More It Remains the Same

In April 1975 the Los Angeles Police Commission announced the planned destruction of some 2 million secret police intelligence files kept on individuals and organizations over the preceding half-century. The files covered the activities of an estimated 55,000 undisclosed individuals and groups and extended, in the words of the commission's press release, "from the Wobblies of the Twenties to the labor agitators of the Thirties, the interned Nisei of the Forties, the alleged subversives of the Fifties and some antiwar demonstrators of the Sixties." According to a commission estimate, about 2,500 active files survived the purge, completed the next year.[51]

Along with the announced file destruction, new filing guidelines were proposed, the result of stocktaking begun in 1973 at a time of mounting

---

* A number of Panther activists also belonged to a group known as the Coalition against Police Abuse (CAPA), a circumstance that intensified police harassment.

disclosures of intelligence abuses nationally and locally and the emergence of the civil suit for injunctive relief and damages as a weapon against surveillance abuses. The 1975 guidelines were jointly sponsored by the mayor's office, Chief Davis, and the Board of Police Commissioners, and were drafted by Davis. The commission lauded the guidelines as "an important and valuable police innovation for which Chief of Police Edward M. Davis and his staff are to be highly recommended . . . a contribution . . . in the best leadership traditions of the Los Angeles Police Department."[52]

But such hosannahs were hardly justified. To begin with, file destruction thwarted the opportunity for examination by surveillance targets authorized by courts elsewhere and spared Davis the embarrassment of public disclosure of the targeting of prominent citizens and civic organizations, including members of the family of at least one police commissioner. More important, as we shall see, the files were hidden, not destroyed. The guidelines themselves were much ado about very little. They were confined to norms for the retention in files of intelligence data and placed no curbs at all on the PDID's methods of gathering intelligence. Moreover, the PDID's operational freedom was not even limited to Los Angeles; the unit was authorized to monitor potentially disruptive activities anywhere in the country "reasonably expected to affect the city of Los Angeles," as well as the conduct of persons resident in Los Angeles who might commit proscribed acts elsewhere and then return to the city.

There is no reason to doubt the good faith of the commission's assurance that the guidelines were aimed at restructuring the intelligence process to shift the emphasis from the holding of ideas to "the performance or threatened performance of criminally disruptive acts." The commission genuinely hoped to divert the intelligence division's focus on personal and political beliefs based on ideology, race, creed, sexual orientation, and the like to the public disorder area, but it scrupulously avoided limiting the operational freedom of the intelligence division to accord with these objectives. In addition to target selection and operational carte blanche, the guidelines were so loosely worded that they could be construed—as in fact they were—to apply only to the maintenance of files formally entered into an official departmental collection and not desk files, the compilation of raw data used in ongoing investigations.

The commissioners rejected contentions that the victims of surveillance should be told—even privately—that they had been file subjects in the past, on the grounds that such disclosure would destroy the "complete confidentiality" required by the PDID's delicate mission. Similarly the demand for file access in the future was considered unacceptable because, the commissioners cryptically explained, "to state publicly that a person was not or is not the subject of a file could be taken as some form of official approval" and "could only create a legal and administrative quagmire."*

A hearing on April 26, 1975, on the proposed guidelines released a torrent of complaints both against the self-protective motivation for the file destruction and the inadequacy of the guidelines in protecting nonviolent groups from operational surveillance. Moreover, critics protested that the retention of some 2,500 active files in alleged conformity with the new guidelines in itself established the guidelines' inadequacy to protect political expression. Another focus of protest was the PDID's failure to cope with repeated bombings by extremist groups on the right.[53]

These April interim guidelines were revised in December 1975 and made permanent a year later, but they remained a sham and continued (until 1980) to be limited to filing practices alone. As disclosures of indiscriminate targeting and operational abuses mounted between 1976 and 1980, it seemed to many that the commissioners were seeking to convey a misleading impression of cleansing and reform.

The Terrorism Hoax

On December 4, 1975, a second public hearing was held on the interim guidelines, which many observers considered the most telling protest against political surveillance ever held in Los Angeles. A series of seventeen witnesses testified on behalf of such organizations as the Los Angeles County Bar Association, the NAACP, the ACLU, the Citizens' Commission on Police Repression (CCPR), Women's Strike for Peace (WSP), and the Legal Aid Foundation. Chief Davis himself, who was

* The guidelines purported to limit the dissemination of intelligence to other LAPD personnel and law-enforcement agencies in other jurisdictions on a "need to know" basis. But this standard was hazily defined as a requirement that the information be useful in preventing disruption of the public order in cities or areas with a mission comparable to the PDID's. In a sworn deposition in 1971, the coordinator of the Intelligence Division files, Sergeant George Bell, stated that in the late sixties such files were freely released to the press: the practice was to retrieve requested index cards and, after they had been examined, to release the files to which they made reference. Under Davis the practice was continued but was made conditional on the approval of an assistant chief. See "Police Admit Opening Files for Writer on Alioto," Los Angeles Times, March 11, 1971. In the post-guideline years, file access and dissemination were continued, but on a selective basis.

present most of the time, did not raise his voice in defense of the guidelines.[54] But, a few days after the hearing, and in the wake of extensive media coverage of the testimonial objections to the guidelines, Davis issued a press statement insisting that his two intelligence operations (Organized Crime and PDID) "have been worth their weight in gold." And there was a new "enemy" that required scouting even more zealously than in the past: international terrorism, the "growing pace of bombings, kidnappings, hostage extortions, killings and other terrorist activity." This new rationale for doing business at the old stand was flawed by a grave difficulty: the kind of left-oriented terrorism referred to by Davis was, at the time, almost nonexistent in Los Angeles. But Davis had the answer: "the relative freedom from serious harm . . . from terrorist activities" in Los Angeles, the Davis press release insisted, "is largely attributable to the creation of a highly sophisticated, totally lawful and extremely effective public disorder intelligence function within the police department." But what was perhaps most striking about Davis's PDID apologetics was his silence about a form of terrorism quite prevalent in Los Angeles: right-wing bombings. In the spring of 1975, official data revealed that in the previous year Los Angeles continued, as it had in the past, to lead the nation in bombings: a total of 152—almost 3 a week. In the first five months of 1975, no fewer than 18 terrorist-style bombings took place in the Los Angeles area, for which groups such as the American National Socialist Party, the Nazi Liberation Front, the anti-Castro Cuban Action Commandos, the Ku Klux Klan, and the Jewish Defense League were responsible.*[55]

In May 1976, to counter a proposal by Mayor Bradley to reduce by half the 91-member PDID, Davis again pronounced the PDID as the city's savior from the menace of terrorism. The mayor, himself a former police officer, was convinced that the PDID's functions unnecessarily duplicated those of federal, state, and county investigative units, and that top priority should be given to increasing the number of patrol officers in the drive against street crime. But the city council by a large majority voted to restore 30 of the proposed 46 PDID staff reductions. The council was apparently persuaded by the chief's contention that the PDID had

---

* Among the targets were the Committee to Reopen the Rosenberg Case; the Socialist Workers' Party; Unidos Bookstore (operated by the leftish October League); the Long March Bookstore; KCET, a Public Broadcasting Service television station; the National Committee on Repressive Legislation; the Progressive Labor Party; and a Jewish seminary. Only one arrest was made—that of a member of the Jewish Defense League—and this without the involvement of PDID.

cleansed the city of terrorism and specifically by Davis's boast that the Weather Underground had been discouraged from operating in the city "thanks to PDID." Subsequent attempts by journalists to obtain documentation for Davis's defense of the PDID were frustrated.

Davis repeatedly insisted that professionalism prevented him from revealing the PDID's impressive record in thwarting riots and criminal conspiracies, but the results were scanty. As early as 1974, for example, he cited in support of his budgetary request on behalf of the PDID the 1970 case of a plot to assassinate Judge Alfred Getelson, who had issued the city's first school desegregation order. In this case five members of a white racist group were arrested after one of them allegedly offered two undercover officers $1,000 to kill the judge and then plunge a metal stake with a racist note attached to it into his forehead. Four of the defendants were convicted on various charges—but only two served jail sentences, one a year in the county jail and the other five weeks there.

A second frequently cited assassination case was the unsuccessful 1977 plot by three Ku Klux Klan members to murder Irv Rubin,* area head of the Jewish Defense League. Of the three arrests in this case, one defendant Klansman received a jail term concurrently with a life sentence he was already serving on another charge.

In 1980 a press briefing by the intelligence division's assistant chief cited as success stories, in addition to the above two assassination plots, three vaguely described planned killings of police officers allegedly averted by the police; but no corroborative details were offered except that the would-be murderers were thwarted by "additional security precautions."[56] In addition, five occasions were cited in which the PDID had allegedly either forestalled bombing plots or developed information leading to the arrests of extremist (right-wing) bombers. But again, no supporting proof was offered even of arrest records. Indeed, the departmental spokesman conceded that in many cases no arrests were made, a failure ascribed in part to unwillingness to reveal identities of informers in cases with limited prospects of conviction. What is, in any event, abundantly clear is that all of the cited examples of the PDID's effectiveness involved situations that are classically the responsibility of conventional criminal intelligence forces.

Over the entire Davis era only one cited example of a claimed success of PDID infiltration of leftist targets emerges from the record. In Sep-

---

* The PDID documents called him "Jerry Rubin," confusing him with the New Left activist of the sixties.

tember 1976 Davis charged that a violence-prone Mexican-American group, the Brown Berets, had conspired to set fires near a downtown hotel where then Governor Reagan was scheduled to speak and to detonate explosives at another site. The Brown Berets were duly indicted and ultimately tried in 1970 on conspiracy and arson charges. The prosecution's case was built almost entirely on the testimony of an LAPD infiltrator, Lieutenant Fernando Sumaya, who claimed to have intimate knowledge of the alleged conspiracy. The defendants denied the existence of a plot and charged that the arson and other illegal acts were the work of Sumaya alone. The jury was not persuaded by Sumaya's testimony. The case thus became another in a series in which the role of the PDID as a law-enforcement resource was discredited, a consequence concealed by Davis in his congressional testimony citing these arrests as a demonstration of the value of intelligence.

The leader of the indicted Chicanos, Carlos Montes, fled Los Angeles prior to the trial because he feared that he would be killed by a PDID officer, Sergeant José Ceballos, who had repeatedly threatened his life. After deliberating for seven hours, the jury, in November 1979, acquitted Montes of all charges and indicated subsequently that they had chosen to believe Montes's charges that the arrests were the product of a police frame-up.[57]

The PDID Runs into Trouble

Intelligence units typically outrun their missions for a variety of reasons, ranging from the passions of their leaders to a misplaced sense of invulnerability. What is remarkable about the PDID is both the grossness of its operational abuses and the small price it was forced to pay when these abuses came to light. In 1978, after Davis had left in search of higher office* and Daryl F. Gates had become chief, the department was shaken by a series of exposés, including revelations about spying on the city council, the release of extensive lists of investigative targets, and the unmasking of a spy network.

---

* We cannot take leave of Chief Davis without taking note of what can only be called a sea-change in some of his attitudes and values. In 1984, while serving as a state senator, he admitted in an interview that there were probably improprieties in the PDID's operation while he was chief. And in the same year Davis, once a virulent homophobe, took a leading role in a legislative campaign to promote a "gay rights" measure! ("Davis Says Spy Unit May Have Erred under Him," *Los Angeles Times*, March 12, 1984; "Davis Gay-Rights Stand a Resistance to Pressure," ibid., February 23, 1984).

On February 25, 1978, a three-man videotaping crew and a still photographer were deployed to photograph a city council meeting attended by many antinuclear activists concerning a nuclear power plant (Sundesert). When the council became aware of what was happening, it ordered the police cameramen from the chamber and later voted to confiscate the film that they had shot. The council president, who admittedly knew of the crew's presence, explained that the LAPD had requested permission to make a training film for the police academy. Some council members and many hearing participants were outraged, however, and demanded an investigation by the Board of Police Commissioners. The board reported later that day with a different story: the police had "received an intelligence report that there was a violent disruption planned for the hearing."[58] The department explained that it routinely sent photographers to potentially disruptive meetings to obtain evidence for possible use in prosecutions. Chief Gates conceded that it was "an unfortunate mistake" and promised that there would be no future recurrence.

The widely reported Sundesert incident renewed skepticism about the credibility of earlier assurances of PDID operational restraint and of greater respect for personal rights. These doubts increased in the summer of 1978 when a police-reform coalition, the Citizens' Commission on Police Repression, circulated a previously leaked official list of some 200 organizations under PDID surveillance through the year 1975 (after the adoption of the April 1975 guidelines). Of the total listings, only about 20 groups could be considered violence-prone and for that reason legitimate subjects of investigation, including the Ku Klux Klan, Alpha 66, Mexican Mafia, Black Guerrilla Family, American Nazi Party, and National Socialist White People's Party. The names of another 20 groups (headed by the John Birch Society) were crossed through, evidently deleted from the surveillance agenda. The remainder were either Third World groups (Congress of African People, Sunni Muslims, Pan African Union) or, more predominantly, liberal and left-of-center organizations concerned with issues of peace, equality, free speech, and social change in this country, such as the National Committee to Abolish HUAC, Peace Action Council, South Bay Asian Involvement, Asian Americans for Peace, First Unitarian Church of Los Angeles, Gay Community Services Center, Southern California Council for Soviet Jews, Los Angeles Committee to Defend the Bill of Rights, Operation PUSH, Southern Christian Leadership Conference, National Council of Churches, National Organization for Women, Chicana Service Action Center, Socialist Workers' Party, World Peace Council, United Farm Workers union,

Women's Strike for Peace, Welfare Rights Organization, Black Social Workers' Union, Tax Rebellion Group, and Gay Community Alliance. A numbered grading system, from one to six, classified the degree of dangerousness attributed to each organization. For example, Women's Strike for Peace and the World Peace Council were graded number one ("Communist or affiliated or sympathetic with the Communist Party"); the Southern Christian Leadership Conference and the National Council of Churches were rated number two ("Public advocacy of social or political change through violence or law-violation"); in categories three and four (violence-oriented groups), we find the Klan and others listed above; category five ("Participation in or advocacy of any activity intended to create disorder") included the National Organization for Women and the United Farm Workers of America; category six was assigned to, among others, the Black Social Workers' Union and the Pakistan-American Friendship League.

Chief Gates did not deny the authenticity of the list and held off reporters with the disclaimer, "I don't know what police spying is."[59] He also stated that the number of organizations under surveillance had been considerably reduced. But it was not long before this assurance was clouded by a chain of revelations of informer infiltration.

The PDID Scout Corps

Between 1978 and 1981 lawsuits and clues supplied by litigation led to the exposure of a spy network that established that even after the adoption of the revised guidelines in 1976 and even after Chief Gates's asserted target-paring, surveillance of nonviolent civic groups continued.[60] Earlier versions of the PDID had made extensive use of planted informers, especially in labor unions and strike situations. These were drawn both from LAPD ranks and from among private detective agency operatives, who were supervised and assigned by LAPD personnel. Beginning in the thirties the unit was also served by volunteer spies eager to contribute to the conquest of subversion. The late Carey McWilliams charged, for example, that in the thirties at least one member of the board of directors of every liberal-reformist organization in town turned out to be a police spy. Another prominent civic figure (Reuben Borough) recalled that members of the city's elite—including one entire family—joined the spy ranks. In the sixties and thereafter the spy coverage ranged from Hollywood to the Vietnam Veterans against the War (VVAW) and the American Indian Movement (AIM). In addition, the CCS ran a group of its own spies, which included sworn personnel as well as paid infiltrators such as "Cotton" Smith and Tackwood, usually recruited from the ranks of individuals in trouble with the law. A third type of spy operation was jointly sponsored by the LAPD and federal agencies such as the FBI and Alcohol, Tobacco and Firearms units of the Treasury Department.

Davis took the view that there was nothing objectionable about secretly infiltrating any organization—however peaceful its goals or nonviolent its tactics.* When it was revealed that he had planted a policewoman on the staff of an alternative newspaper (*Valley News*), he justified the assignment as a form of cover to facilitate future access to violence-prone targets—the first of a number of deceptions devised to minimize and justify the ecumenical monitoring of Los Angeles dissenters.[61]

The infiltration process in the seventies was typically implemented by sworn personnel. Take the case of Edward Camarillo—a PDID officer. Beginning in 1975, and for a three-year period, Camarillo infiltrated a Hispanic group, the Center for Autonomous Social Action (CASA). In January 1978 after CASA disbanded, Camarillo became active in the CCPR, which had begun exposing a number of LAPD infiltrators. Camarillo's infiltration became particularly embarrassing to the PDID when it was revealed in May 1980 that he had served as a research aide to Councilman Zev Yaroslavsky in the drafting of a proposed "freedom of information" ordinance requiring the release of police intelligence files to their subjects. But a subsequent documentary disclosure (in November 1981) was even more embarrassing: Camarillo had in 1974 and 1975 reported on private meetings between Mayor Bradley and the United Farm Workers of America (UFW) concerning an endorsement of the UFW's boycott of Gallo wines.[62]

Another police informer planted for purposes unrelated to law enforcement was Connie Milazzo, who along with an LAPD colleague, Georgia Odom, infiltrated the Coalition against Police Abuse (CAPA) and ultimately became its secretary. Milazzo also spent fourteen months as an informer inside the avowedly militant left-wing Progressive Labor Party (PLP).[†] Also exposed as police informers were Eddie Solomon,

---

* Davis cited the analogy of scouting in an athletic contest, apparently untroubled by the fact that a scout who secretly infiltrated an opposing team under a false cover would be regarded as a disgrace to his sponsor.
† Milazzo's arrest along with twenty-seven members of the PLP in a clash with the police resulted in her exposure and the dismissal of eight felony charges against PLP members on the grounds that Milazzo had participated in attorney-client conferences—yet another instance of the fatal impact of surveillance on

John Dial,* and Cheryl Bell. Their targets included the National Alliance against Racist and Political Repression (NAARPR; Eddie Solomon was its salaried coordinator); a string of already-mentioned groups, along with Campaign for Democratic Freedoms (CDF); *Vanguard,* a community-based newspaper; the Democratic Socialist Organizing Committee (DSOC); Young Workers' Liberation League; Alliance for Survival (an antinuclear coalition); Committee on Nuclear Information; and Citizens' Research and Investigation Committee (CRIC). In addition, subsequently released intelligence reports established that the LAPD had engaged in spying on the movement for racial integration of the Los Angeles schools.

Even city council meetings were covered. For example, CAPA informer Georgia Odom came to a city council committee meeting in September 1977 and relayed to the police observations of Councilman David Cunningham on police abuses. Cheryl Bell reported on the proceedings of the already-described Sundesert hearings, including a list of supporters and opponents of various issues, along with their comments. (Ironically, although the participants successfully demanded the ouster of the photographers, they were unaware that there was a spy in their midst.) In the course of a prolonged infiltration of a local campus chapter of the Alliance for Survival, Bell became its president. The spy documents also revealed the participation of city council members in the activities of a variety of peaceful, nonviolent groups. In the same way the released documents included accounts of hearings by the Board of Police Com-

---

law enforcement. Misdemeanor charges against others were dismissed when the court was told that the department had in 1975 shredded records of police brutality complaints against the officers involved. See "LAPD Red Squad Losing Punch," *Los Angeles Free Press,* March 22, 1978; "Suspect Cleared—She's Policewoman," *Los Angeles Times,* August 5, 1977; "LAPD's Intelligence Activities Back in Spotlight," *Los Angeles Herald Examiner,* March 6, 1978.

* Trained in karate and electronic communications, Dial infiltrated a variety of organizations that prized him for his practical skills. In the early 1970s he was assigned to protect actress Jane Fonda when she took the stump to denounce the Vietnam War. During this period, Dial was assigned to make contact with a group of targets in Mexico, posing as a student Marxist organizer. So effective was his deception that he was tortured by the Mexican police along with his radical targets until he established his identity. Dial vanished in the summer of 1977 when Milazzo's police-informer role was brought to light and, ironically, was feared by his victims (organized into a rescue mission, Friends of John Dial) to have been done in by the police. In the spring of 1978, a reporter revealed that Dial was not only alive but had married his companion in spying, Connie Milazzo ("Vanished Leftist Activist Believed Alive and Wed," *Los Angeles Times,* March 15, 1978).

missioners at which complaints were aired concerning indiscriminate use of firearms, beatings of blacks, and other abuses.

The PDID's indiscriminate infiltration practices were further exposed in 1981 when the lawsuit, consolidated at the time to include over 120 individual and organizational plaintiffs represented by the ACLU, charged that a trio of informers had infiltrated a number of nonviolent groups and had surfaced in 1979 or early 1980—long after the final guidelines were in effect.[63]

Richard Gibbey, one of the defendants in the 1981 lawsuit, joined the LAPD in 1972 and in 1974 was assigned to infiltrate the Socialist Workers' Party, of which he remained a member at least until 1979.* He was also a founding member of a local chapter of the Alliance for Survival and served as a security aide at an alliance rally in 1979. Another LAPD member exposed in late 1979 was Frank Montelongo, who, over a five-year period of infiltration, was prominently involved in a wide variety of Native American activities, including legal defense committees and sacred prayer meetings called sweat lodges.

Nothing more clearly exposes the pretextual character of the claimed concern only with targets with a propensity for violence than the PDID's concentration on police critics and antispying organizations with no record of violent propensities. In sworn testimony in pretrial discovery proceedings, a PDID spokesman, Lieutenant Charles Kilgo, admitted that it was standard PDID practice to infiltrate any group concerned with police intelligence-gathering. No fewer than five police agents were planted in community groups concerned with police abuses. Thus laid bare in litigation were Camarillo's infiltration of the CCPR and the coverage by an infiltrator, Connie Milazzo, of the predecessor of the CCPR, the Committee for Democratic Freedoms, an antispying group she served as a steering-committee member.

Another reflection of the PDID's paranoid obsession with police critics was its practice of routinely infiltrating or investigating peaceful gatherings of ad hoc groups formed in response to specific acts of police violence. It not only sent two of its agents, Jennifer Drake and Carol Hill, to monitor a public hearing investigating the shooting in April 1979 of a

---

* Gibbey's spy role was confirmed when he responded in uniform to a burglary report early in 1980 by a former leader of the Socialist Workers' Party. In all of the PDID's spy operations, one is struck by the inconsistency between the claims that even the scrutiny of a proposed budget request would endanger the lives of PDID undercover agents and the failure to reduce the risks of exposure to the agents.

black woman, Eulia Love, but admittedly planted a spy in a community group formed to protest the killing.*

The Accountability Duel: Gates versus the City Council

Chief Daryl Gates, like his predecessors, must be identified as a true believer in the Southern California gospel of countersubversion. A protégé of Chief Parker's and prominent in the intelligence field, he served for seven years on Parker's staff and thereafter as Davis's operational chief. In the tradition of Edward Davis and Parker, Gates took a dim view of critics and was quick to assume the mantle of preacher-prophet.[64]

In his dealings with the city council, however, Gates could not muster the clout of a Parker or Davis. Gates's problems with the council were initially sparked by the disclosures of spying on that body and its members—most notably in connection with the Sundesert incident and the Camarillo infiltration. In addition, the emergence of a vigilant police critic, Councilman Zev Yaroslavsky, a hostile press, the vigorous monitoring of the police by the CCPR, and a series of lawsuits all contributed to a changing climate and (for the first time) demanded a public accounting of challenged police practices.

In the spring of 1980 a departmental official, on Gates's instructions, refused to reveal to the council's finance committee, even in executive

---

* The record in the Love case shows that two policemen fired eight bullets killing Love, who had threatened a utility company employee when he attempted to shut off her gas and then flashed a knife at the officer called to the scene. The officers were exonerated of wrongdoing in an inquiry by the department, a conclusion that sparked a series of protests and demands for a police review board. Chief Gates at first denied that the PDID had covered the Love meeting but later reversed himself and explained that one of the organizations represented at the hearing was the subject of a PDID file; he refused to identify the group and conceded that it presented no threat of violence or disruption of the meeting. Gates never explained why the police targeted the Friends of Ron Burkeholder (an unarmed man killed by a police officer in August 1977) and a similar group, the Anthony Brown Defense Committee. The infiltration of the Love protest group is described in "Did LAPD Spy on Protesters?" and "LAPD Spy in Eulia Love Group?" *Los Angeles Herald Examiner*, February 8, 1982; "Probe Planned of Eulia Love Group Spying," ibid., February 10, 1982; "Officer Helped Organize Love March, Suit Says," *Los Angeles Times*, February 9, 1982; "Alleged Spy Was Officer, LAPD Says," ibid., February 10, 1982; "How Eulia Love Case Still Haunts the City of Los Angeles," *Los Angeles Herald Examiner*, February 15, 1982.

session, information in support of a PDID budget request, on the grounds that answers to such routine questions as whether the PDID borrowed manpower from other divisions would endanger the lives of undercover officers. In that event, as Gates subsequently explained, if an undercover officer were killed, "each council member would naturally become suspect." Gates was forced to capitulate when the city attorney issued a formal opinion that the police department was legally required to respond to questions about the financing of undercover activities. The hearings were finally held in executive session, over the protests of the CCPR and the *Los Angeles Times*.*

In his exposition to the city council, Gates professed to see nothing wrong per se with the targeting and infiltration of peaceful groups. If the target had not done anything wrong, why all the fuss? In a vein made familiar by his predecessor, he justified Camarillo's infiltration of a peaceful target (the CCPR) as standard PDID practice—a means of developing a cover to facilitate penetration of (unspecified) more appropriate targets. But this justification was plainly a pretext in view of the fact that Camarillo made detailed reports on the CCPR, its activities, and its personnel, a step hardly necessary if his sole purpose had been to develop a cover. Similarly, the comprehensive scope of Camarillo's reports exposed as fraudulent the alternative claim of Chief Gates that peaceful, nonviolent groups like the CCPR were infiltrated to develop information only on pin-pointed participants in such groups regarded as violence-prone.[65]

The controversy sparked by the council's Camarillo inquiry raged over many months as newly released documents further confirmed that the PDID had substituted for its antiterrorist mission a vacuum cleaner–style spy coverage of peaceful dissidents and their activities. There was not even a hint of an arrest to prevent an act of terrorism.

Pressures on the chief and the commissioners mounted when, on June 4, Mayor Bradley, breaking a long silence, responded to the file release, saying, "I will not tolerate the gathering of intelligence information on individuals or organizations that are not involved in either criminal or terrorist activities." Shortly after the Bradley statement, two former

* The *Times* had gradually become critical of the PDID's practices. Subsequent to the Sundesert hearings, it noted editorially that "there can be no justification for the peaceable conduct of the public's business becoming raw material for police intelligence files" ("The Police Cross the Line," *Los Angeles Times*, March 2, 1978). Two years later it joined the campaign of the CCPR for an ordinance modeled on the federal Freedom of Information Act ("A Check on Political Spying by Police," ibid., April 4, 1980).

PDID spies assigned to its Black Power section gave an anonymous interview to the *Herald Examiner* detailing surveillance in the mid 1970s of such targets as the Christian Leadership Conference–West, the NAACP, black teachers' unions, Jesse Jackson's People United to Save Humanity (PUSH), the Congress of Racial Equality (CORE), and Bishop H. H. Brookins, a highly respected Los Angeles black leader. The two embittered and humiliated black detectives stated that they had never heard of surveillance operations conducted for the protection of the targets—a justification previously invoked by department apologists. Mayor Bradley was outraged at these new disclosures and again announced that he would seek an accounting from Chief Gates.[66]

The Death Throes of the PDID

In April 1980, when criticism of the unit could no longer be contained, a set of interim operational guidelines was issued by the Board of Police Commissioners. While the guidelines made some concessions to its critics, the stated mission of the PDID continued vaguely to prescribe surveillance practices deemed (presumably by the department itself) to be "necessary to protect the people of Los Angeles from unlawful disruption of the public order." Activities subject to surveillance were those with a "potential for disorder," that could or would result in disruption, or that "probably" would pose "crowd control problems"—terms that typically cloak invasions of basic rights. Once again, promises made to the hope were broken to the ear.

A similar ambiguity characterized the guidelines' operational strictures. Although the use of illegal collection methods was barred, no meaningful description of excluded techniques was offered: it was broadly assumed, for example, that infiltration, even of peaceful groups, was authorized. Also questionable was the fact that the guidelines were structured in such a way as to assume the necessity for threshold exploratory overkill, which was then to be correctively screened at higher levels. Thus "preliminary investigations" were authorized of targets that might "be engaged in activities" falling within the PDID's mission. These guidelines, like the earlier ones, gave predominant stress to filing and dissemination standards, to which, the commission insisted, "adherence . . . must be particularly stringent," and continued to skim over line functions of target selection and data collection. The sole operational concession in the new guidelines appeared to be the adoption of a more deceptive operating style to prevent future embarrassing exposure or infiltration—hardly a reassuring innovation.

Evidence of post-guidelines surveillance of nonviolent political dissenters and police critics emerged, as in Chicago, in the form of surreptitious photography. LAPD officers were discovered surreptitiously photographing a march sponsored by the Committee in Solidarity with the People of El Salvador (CISPES). And the countersubversive bias of the unit continued to be reflected in its laxity in monitoring the violence-prone right. In September 1980 a bomb exploded in the local Communist Party headquarters on Wilshire Boulevard. A few days later an attempt was made to plant a bomb in the Socialist Workers' Party headquarters, which was forestalled by the early arrival at the site of two SWP members. On October 1, 1980, the ACLU's Los Angeles office also received a telephone threat: "You goddamned commies better run for your lives!" Just as in the case of the earlier bomb scares, in which right-wing bombings regularly occurred for which Nazi, Klan, and anti-Castro groups publicly claimed credit and in some cases gave bragging interviews, these episodes generated neither arrests nor prosecutions. Instead, as earlier, the actual or intended victims of violence were subjected to harassment by the CCS—questioned about their politics and taunted for refusing to submit to lie-detector tests.[67]

By the end of 1980, the public furor over police abuses had somewhat subsided, despite that year's disclosure of spying on public figures. The PDID emerged as the most active unit of its kind on the police scene. In contrast to the cutbacks of police surveillance in New York, Philadelphia, and Chicago, the Los Angeles operation remained in place. But the calm was interrupted by the disclosure in March 1981, through additional batches of police intelligence documents obtained in pretrial litigation, of the PDID's recorded surveillance of Mayor Bradley himself. And in 1982 scandals finally brought PDID down.

We begin in January with the great Summer Olympics red scare. Concerned about PDID's future and faced with the possibility of budget cuts, Chief Gates, like Davis before him, played the terrorist card. On January 21 he released a pamphlet, assertedly based on intelligence reports, indicating a Soviet plot to send "dangerous criminals" posing as Jewish émigrés to this country with a mission to disrupt the 1984 Summer Olympics in Los Angeles. Cries of outrage came from all quarters: the Jewish community and its Soviet émigré component, the Olympic Committee president, and the president of the Board of Police Commissioners, who rebuked Gates for "crying wolf" to gain approval of budgetary requests. In a press conference, Gates retreated and admitted that the report was no more than "speculation." But, again in accents reminiscent of Davis, he justified the report as a necessary alert, a "worst case scenario" to impress a decent, but naive, citizenry with the need for additional personnel and appropriations in order to expand intelligence-gathering activities.[68]

The Olympics red scare had barely subsided when pretrial discovery in February 1982 revealed the infiltration of the groups protesting the Eulia Love shooting (see pp. 76–77). As in the past, the Police Commission made a rescue attempt. In March it came through with a third set of proposed guidelines, which it anointed with the pronouncement (of highly questionable accuracy) "that no other metropolitan police department in this country has imposed such far-reaching restrictions on its own behavior," which moreover "far exceed existing judicial and statutory requirements." Despite objections that the guidelines were extremely vague with respect both to target selection and operational norms, riddled with loopholes, lacked provision for civilian oversight, and ignored court rulings governing informer infiltration of political organizations, they were unanimously adopted, subject only to possible amendment in public hearings.[69]

The commission's protective stance was not helped by the Myerson case settlement in April (see pp. 260–61) and the filing in June of a lawsuit charging the PDID with campus surveillance of the student body of California State University.*[70] But that was just the beginning. In September the ACLU released forty documents obtained in litigation establishing that the PDID had systematically spied on the Citizens' Committee on Police Repression (CCPR). Although the bare fact of such surveillance had become known when Camarillo was exposed, the newly released documents indicated an operation of much greater scope and penetration than had previously been assumed. These documents detailed information about meetings with a city councilman and a state senator, as well as a variety of CCPR legislative activities; the personal affairs of the CCPR's then director, Linda Valentino; the goals of the CCPR and planned legal action against the LAPD. What was perhaps even more startling about the reports was the fact that they established

---

* This action, the sixth filed against the police and other defendants, was added to those in the already-consolidated lawsuit. Efforts to settle the litigation from time to time were unsuccessful. See, for example, "5 Spying Suits May Be Settled out of Court," *Los Angeles Times*, February 24, 1982; "Police Commission Tries to Settle Spy Suits," *Los Angeles Daily Journal*, February 25, 1982; "Progress Reported in Police Spying Suits," *Los Angeles Times*, March 12, 1982. The consolidated case was popularly known as *CAPA v. Gates*, but occasionally called *CCPR v. Board of Police Commissioners*. The six case numbers involved are LASC C 243 458, LASC C 317 528, LASC C 374 660, LASC C 381 339, LASC C 399 552, and LASC C 413 904.

that Gates had misled the city council, the Police Commission, and the public in 1980 when the Camarillo infiltration had been brought to light. He had asserted then that the CCPR was a peaceful organization and hence of no interest to the PDID,* and that the infiltration was for "cover" purposes only, when in fact the CCPR was intensively surveilled and detailed reports about its activities were transmitted up the PDID's chain of command.[71]

The commission responded by announcing a probe into whether Gates had lied to them in the CCPR matter.[†] Measurably greater pressure was exerted by the ACLU lawsuit. Gates admitted under oath in pretrial testimony that when he succeeded Davis in April 1978, he had reviewed and authorized the continuation of all undercover surveillance operations then pending. When confronted with the fact that briefing reports on noncriminal intelligence targets were found in police records despite the guidelines' prohibition against data compilation on individuals' political beliefs and peaceful activities, he answered that since the data reported by informers were not recorded in the index-card format termed a "file" by the police, the prohibition did not apply.[72]

The deposition also made clear what had been previously fudged: it was Gates alone who was responsible for the selection of new targets for surveillance after he took office. There was an outraged response to his claim that Linda Valentino, the former director of CCPR and the chief plaintiff in the lawsuits, might have been engaged in criminal activities, echoing a contention advanced earlier by a lawyer for the city that Valentino and her group might have been involved in a "criminal conspiracy" to "illegally" expose undercover police officers.[73]

The winds of controversy continued to howl around Gates and the PDID with the publication on October 11, 1982, of summaries of newly

---

* On March 23, 1980, Gates denied to the Police Commission that PDID had surveilled CCPR: "I wish everyone understood that we have absolutely no interest in peaceful groups. If we have an interest we can obtain all the information we want to obtain from the media. I keep asking the question why they believe we are interested in them. I just have difficulty with that question."

† This was a second investigation of the chief's behavior in 1982. In May an investigation was ordered by the Police Commission into alleged insulting comments by Gates directed at ethnic and racial minorities; the commission rebuked him both for his words and his response to criticism over what he had said. Treading in the footsteps of "Crazy Ed," Gates had stirred protest over his characterization of Hispanic officers as "lazy," remarks after the Eulia Love shooting, his characterization of a blonde newscaster as an "Aryan broad," and a suggestion that blacks might be more susceptible than "normal people" to fatalities when police use a "choke hold" on suspects ("Police Chief on Defensive," *New York Times,* May 7, 1982).

released documents detailing the fruits of surveillance of another group critical of police practices active in the 1970s, the Coalition against Police Abuse (CAPA).[74] In his deposition Gates had offered no plausible explanation of why, despite his insistence on PDID's law-enforcement mission, no fewer than four agents had been planted in CAPA. Moreover, the documents were prepared, as were the CCPR dossiers already discussed, after the Police Commission had issued its final guidelines in 1976 instructing the police to avoid interference with constitutional rights.

Apart from the questionable practice laid bare in the targeting of these two organizations, it became apparent that deception of the Police Commission was itself a PDID project. This new potential scandal was particularly challenging to the Police Commission: had not Gates repeatedly insisted that after the undercover agents had written down everything they saw and heard, any material irrelevant to a criminal investigation was sifted out and locked away until it could be destroyed? It accordingly expanded its month-old investigation and ordered Gates to explain whether or not he had systematically violated the procedures established to control the filing and dissemination of political intelligence data. These disclosures cast serious doubt on the city's ability to mount a successful defense against the pending lawsuits and led a city councilman to urge a quick settlement.[75]

The commission also called on Gates to investigate and explain a seeming embarrassment of a different sort. A leftist group, the Revolutionary Communist Party (RCP), appealed in December 1982 for the appointment of a prosecutor to deal with an assortment of police abuses in connection with a case brought against eight RCP members for allegedly assaulting police officers at a May Day 1980 demonstration. In cross-examination, a PDID spy admitted that during his seventeen months' undercover infiltration, he had never heard anyone in the RCP propose the commission of a crime or an act of violence and never saw any weapons. Moreover his testimony revealed that he had played a leading role in the May Day demonstration, which resulted in a bloody clash, with many injured and twenty-eight arrested, and that it was he who had shouted slogans through a bullhorn to encourage the demonstrators.[76]

Early in November 1982 winds began to blow from another quarter, bringing new embarrassment to the Police Commission. The press disclosed that after the commission had in 1975–76 ordered the massive file destruction (referred to on p. 266), the associate superintendent of the Los Angeles Unified School District had been approached by "sergeant-level" LAPD personnel and offered 300 files on school employees.[77]

The school official also disclosed that a PDID detective, Jay Paul, a research analyst and photographer with a twelve-year service record, had expressed concern about files in his possession containing information about the school desegregation drive, along with briefing reports on the issue prepared for the office of the chief of police. Paul, it was soon revealed, had removed the files to preserve them from destruction. Armed with search warrants, investigators uncovered more files in his mobile home and other locations—an estimated ninety cartons of files were seized. Dossiers were discovered on two current police commissioners and a former commissioner, who subsequently became a U.S. court of appeals judge. There followed in January 1983 an order by the Police Commission deactivating the PDID within forty-five days.[78]

As the file probe continued, ten more boxes of files—in addition to the ninety previously surrendered—were turned over by Paul, including dossiers on California State Supreme Court Judge Jerry Pacht tracing in detail almost four decades of his public life for the stated purpose of exploring his possible bias against police intelligence-gathering practices. Also uncovered in this same batch of documents was a "connections" report written in 1982 seeking to establish the subversive character of the two major police-reform groups—CAPA and CCPR, the plaintiffs in the police lawsuit—and the Coalition for Economic Survival, an advocate of low-rent housing and related policies. These documents attempted to discredit the three groups by linking them to communism through strained inferences and guilt by association and had been drafted by Detective Paul on assignment by a PDID captain.[79]

It soon became apparent that file fetishism, an occupational disease of countersubversive intelligence zealots (see pp. 70–71) had afflicted the entire PDID. The effort to portray Paul as a maverick acting on his own was completely shattered when Paul named almost a dozen fellow detectives who had participated in the file coup and numerous others, including lieutenants and captains, who had sanctioned it. Further, he charged that the removal of the files to circumvent the destruction order was an organized project: boxes were officially requisitioned for the purpose of stashing the documents; various officers were assigned to complete portions of the removal project; the division's command staff allowed Paul to work at home, provided him with supplies—including materials to set up a photographic lab at home—and reimbursed him for expenses such as telephone calls.

These charges and admissions were confirmed by a scathing attack by City Attorney Ira Reiner on the PDID. Urging an immediate cut-off of funds for the unit, Reiner charged that, despite contrary claims, the 1982 guidelines were purely cosmetic, and that PDID officers had fed surveillance data into a computer for the use of others and tapped into a computerized system maintained by private sources. These charges were supported by the discovery in the cartons surrendered to the investigators by Paul of intelligence data from a cluster of federal and state agencies involved in the countersubversive trade. Gates remained (externally) unfazed by Reiner's charges: "I'll bet there are several terrorists clapping their hands in glee over the panic that has set in . . . [who] are not going to go away by having the City Council withhold funds from PDID."[80]

Hardly able to dismiss the evidence of its misconduct, Gates finally confessed failure to give proper direction to the PDID, but stubbornly insisted that his critics were intentionally misleading the public and concealing their indifference to the threat of terrorist activity. But the rain continued to fall on the PDID during the spring and summer of 1983, with disclosures that top brass were involved in the scheme to evade the file-destruction order and that Reiner himself had been an intelligence target.[81]

These embarrassments made way for the passage of a freedom-of-information ordinance—considerably watered down in response to police objections—providing public access to police files. This was followed by a court-ordered release of documents stashed away by Jay Paul. These in turn produced further embarrassments, including the record of a decision to evade the 1976 destruction order by labeling files as "notes" or "briefing" papers. This batch of documents also revealed more dossiers on Police Commission members, judges, lawyers, politicians, and critics of the PDID. Three reports written by Paul in 1977 and 1978 on Burt Pines, then city attorney, based on "confidential sources" in his office, suggest that Pines and his staff were politically biased against the police.[82]

The lawsuit was unaffected by the dissolution of the PDID and its replacement in July 1983 by the "Anti-Terrorist Division." Indeed, the lawsuit, combined with the grand jury proceedings and a departmental investigation of Detective Paul, brought to light new facts about the PDID operation that confirmed many previously unsupported charges and rumors.* Of these, the most important was Paul's deep involvement

---

* The in-house hearing revealed that a number of PDID members, including supervisory echelons, either authorized or participated in private storage of intelligence files. Los Angeles Herald Examiner: "Commander Wants Second Officer to Face PDID Charges," February 7, 1984; "Two Retired PDID Captains Blamed for Not Keeping Jay Paul under Control," February 8, 1984; "Second

in the Western Goals Foundation, a privately funded ultra-right operation headed by the late Congressman Larry McDonald, who was also the
national leader of the John Birch Society. In bits and pieces it was
learned that Paul had fed LAPD intelligence data into a computer network maintained by Western Goals, with a terminal located in his wife's
law office in Long Beach, using $100,000 worth of equipment purchased
by Western Goals, who also paid Ms. Paul $30,000 a year for the use of
her office. This arrangement was approved by the PDID brass on the
condition that police be given access to Western Goals' data bank in return. The computer base that Paul had begun building for Western
Goals was also fed by tapping into the computer of the RAND Corporation, a conservative, Santa Monica–based think tank.[83]

Depositions of detectives and supervisors taken in connection with
the ACLU lawsuits produced a continuing stream of disclosures. A suspended detective in the Organized Crime Intelligence Division testified
that his unit had collected information on "at least a half dozen public
officials," including Mayor Bradley; that he was twice instructed by his
superiors to ferret out information on the sex lives of two "public officials"; that information had been gathered on John van de Kamp, local
district attorney, when he entered the race for state attorney general.
The testimony also revealed that information on public officials was
channeled to a two-man team who provided Gates with weekly briefings—a practice, the witness said, to enable Gates to influence certain
political figures and dating back to the days of Chief Parker.[84]

PDID detective Kenneth M. Rice testified that Paul's Western Goals
connection was not unique: he himself and his partners exchanged data
with Research West, an operation founded by FBI agents, which sold

Officer Charged in PDID Case," February 10, 1984; "Officer Says There Were
No Rules on Storing Files at Home," February 23, 1984; "Official Testifies
LAPD Permitted Officers to Trade in Spy Data," February 25, 1984; "Gates
Agrees to Turn over Subpoenaed Police Documents," March 10, 1984; and
"Paul Tells Board He Stored PDID Data Ordered Destroyed," March 29, 1984.
Los Angeles Times: "2nd Police Officer May Be Charged in Spying Inquiry,"
February 8, 1984; "Spy Charges Filed on 2nd L.A. Officer," February 10, 1984;
"Paul's Ex-Boss Says He OKd Data Exchange," February 25, 1984; "PDID Chief
OKd Storing Files in Car, Ex-Officer Testifies," March 7, 1984; "Former Police
Spy Unit Chief Disputes Officers' Testimony," March 20, 1984; "Paul Contra-
dicts Testimony of Ex-Chief of Police Spy Unit," March 29, 1984; "Paul Con-
cedes Passing Data to Editor for Private Group," March 30, 1984; and "Gates to
Release 'Sanitized' Reports in Police Spy Case," March 10, 1984. "Ex-Supervisor
in Spy Unit Suspended, Ordered to Face Police Board Hearings," Los Angeles
Daily Journal, February 10, 1984. Subsequently, the California attorney general
concluded that no laws were broken by Paul's file-stashing.

background information to corporations and made loyalty checks on their employees. In addition, a former PDID sergeant testified at a departmental disciplinary hearing on the suspended Detective Paul that he was paid by a local bank for consulting work and that he shared intelligence information with other private organizations, including the Exxon Corporation.[85]

Depositions in the fall of 1983 included an admission by a former PDID lieutenant that he had hidden material (deceptively labeled "investigator's notes") from the police commissioners when they conducted audits. These charges were subsequently confirmed in a deposition in October 1983 by Detective Joel Berk, who stated that prior to a 1982 Police Commission audit, on the orders of his superior, Lieutenant Elmer Schiller, nine PDID officers hid documents containing an assortment of information gathered and retained despite the guidelines and the destruction order barring the retention of data recording lawful activities. This material was reportedly hidden by officers in their car trunks and returned to the files after the audit was completed. What caused some eyebrow-raising among the now jaded police-reform constituency was the fact that the same Schiller who had ordered this caper was assigned to lead the new Anti-Terrorist Division's undercover program.*[86]

The documents obtained in the ACLU lawsuits fueled still another scandal in the seemingly never-ending chain. The files revealed the extent of the police vendetta against Councilman Yaroslavsky, the LAPD's gadfly critic, including the fact that a PDID officer had been assigned to investigate Yaroslavsky. Moreover, despite its claim to prevent terrorist activity, the PDID had learned of a right-wing death threat against the councilman, but neglected to inform him of the danger.[87]

The combined impact of the consolidated lawsuit (by the fall of 1983 depositions had been taken from almost 100 witnesses, whose testimony

---

* Skepticism about the mission of the Anti-Terrorist Division began to emerge in August 1982, when one of its representatives appeared before Senator Jeremiah Denton's Subcommittee on Security and Terrorism to denounce the 1982 guidelines along with the Freedom of Information ordinance, lawsuits challenging intelligence activities, and the proliferation of revolutionary groups, which "pose a dire threat to public peace," and the nationwide assault on intelligence agencies as "threats to the nation's ability to cope with the efforts of the enemy within who are committed to its destruction." His documentation consisted mainly of a highly selective mixture of genuine terrorist threats then present, the recycling of acts of violence by radicals in the 1960s, and a hyperbolic characterization of nonviolent groups (such as the National Lawyers' Guild) as terrorists. Apparently referring to the ACLU lawsuits in Los Angeles, he was particularly bitter about the fact that the nation was being left defenseless by the reliance of suspect groups on First Amendment protection.

filled over 200,000 pages), the grand jury probe into possible violations of the California statute criminalizing the unauthorized transfer of government files, and the prominent press airing of the disclosures eroded public confidence in the entire intelligence operation and, beyond that, in the LAPD and its leadership. This concern led to a decision in October 1983 for a joint investigation by the city council and the Police Commission, an undertaking (predictably) denounced by Gates as "petty politics" aimed at "destroying" him.[88] In February 1984, after months of deliberation and on the eve of the scheduled trial, the city council voted to approve an out-of-court settlement to be divided equally between the 144 plaintiffs and their attorneys (discussed in detail on pp. 355–56 below).[89]

A Final Reckoning

On paper it would appear that the November 1983 testimony by an educational superintendent of the attempt to evade the 1976 file-destruction order and the subsequent Jay Paul disclosures constituted the *fons et origo* of the offensive against the police. But the diversion of files to private groups for a political purpose was an old story in Los Angeles. One need only recall the use of LAPD files by Fi-Po—not only to document its newsletter but for loyalty checks on behalf of employers; the preparation of a brief for the Chamber of Commerce in May 1970 based on red squad files; and the practice of giving press favorites access to the files. Nor can we, in the light of the history of the red squad, attribute its downfall primarily to the extraordinary scope of its targeting of lawful groups or of a councilman. Similarly, Gates's effort to exploit a bogus terrorism threat to rescue himself from adverse criticism cannot be cited as the coup de grace; Ed Davis had played even more transparently manipulative variations on this same theme.

We must look elsewhere for an answer to the question, How was such a unit—which over the years had led the pack of urban red-hunters both in the scope of its targeting and in operational daring, consistently mocked the oversight responsibilities of the Board of Police Commissioners, and successfully invented justifications for questionable operations—so quickly wiped out? At root the answer must be that the PDID—and for that matter the entire LAPD—had become imprisoned in the assumptions and stereotypes of the California countersubversive tradition in a changing urban climate. Ironically, the perception spread that the hunter had become more dangerously ideological than his prey. The events of 1982 thus released a compression of disapproval built up over the years: the mounting disturbance in libertarian circles not only over political repression but over police racism and brutality as well; the concern of the business establishment over the LAPD's image with the 1984 Summer Olympics looming ahead; a complete media turnabout; and changing demographics that challenged the traditional nativism long entrenched in the LAPD. As is frequently the case with change movements, personal factors heightened the perception that police practices had to be overhauled. Gates's attempts to deal with the stream of scandals and embarrassments—beginning with the great Olympics terrorist–Soviet émigré fiasco*—confirmed that he was cast in the same mold as the three Big Men who preceded him: James Davis and Gates's two revered mentors, William H. Parker and Ed Davis—arrogant, moralizing, intolerant of critics, and hostile to dissent generally. Like his predecessors, Gates personified the California countersubversive tradition and inherited the legacy of extremism that has long flourished in Los Angeles's political culture.

For all of his scare-mongering and bitter put-downs—so reminiscent of Davis's and Parker's responses to critics—Gates was unable to reverse the sense in broad social and political circles of the city that the PDID resembled a corps of soldiers wandering in the enemy's backlands years after the war had been lost. And even the Board of Police Commissioners was belatedly forced to recognize that it had served over the years not as the blueprinted guardian of the LAPD against political influence and corruption but as a cover, accomplice, and dupe in a rogue operation.

---

* Gates's Olympics-terrorism warnings were crowned by a Hollywood-style hoax. On Monday, August 14, 1984, shortly before the closing ceremonies of the Summer Olympic games, a police officer, Jimmy W. Pearson, seized a large explosive device from a bus at the Los Angeles airport carrying the Turkish Olympic team's baggage, seemingly rendered it inoperative while it was still ticking, and dashed to an isolated area, where he tossed it away. As Chief Gates hailed the officer's feat ("a helluva courageous act"), thousands of travelers were evacuated from three of the airport's terminals, flights were rerouted, and a massive investigation begun. Hours later, Pearson admitted placing the bomb—which contained explosive powder but no detonating fuse—in order to win acclaim for his bravery and earn him a transfer. Instead, he was arrested on criminal charges. See *Los Angeles Times*: "Bomb Disarmed at Airport, Turkish Team Threatened," August 14, 1984; "Admits Hoax, Wanted to Be Noticed by Superiors," August 14, 1984; "Planted Bomb to Get Transfer, Officer Quoted," August 17, 1984.

8 Political Surveillance in Second-Tier Cities

Detroit, Baltimore, Birmingham, New Haven, and Washington, D.C.

Police surveillance operations in Detroit reflect a pattern that, with marginal variations, is repeated in cities of similar size such as Buffalo and Cleveland. All of them were initially run by bureaucratic specialists who made little effort to conceal their surveillance activities either from their targets or the public. The surveillance units of such cities were nurtured and publicized over a twenty-year period by congressional antisubversive committees and by the local press.

Prior to the sixties, political surveillance operations were conducted largely in public and enjoyed a greater degree of autonomy than other police operations. The early sixties saw the beginning of a new modus operandi: a more muted style, a professional image, more sophisticated cover resources, and channels for the exchange of information with similar operations in other cities. In addition, they were assimilated into command structures with blanket jurisdiction over the emerging, modish specialty of "intelligence" and bracketed with vice, narcotics, and organized crime squads. This bureaucratic reshuffling was accompanied by a reduction in the visibility of both command and line forces, a transformation that reflected the influence of covert surveillance procedures, the availability of new technological resources, and the fear of arousing public hostility through the disclosure of objectionable practices in both the selection of targets and surveillance techniques. This last concern also forced an increasing reliance of law enforcement as a cover or justification for ever-expanding surveillance systems.

During both stages in the history of political surveillance police squads, these units were viewed with an ever-increasing hostility by their targets (including labor unions and their leaders) and by libertarian and allied forces. In turn, this hostility was perceived by the police as a form of deviance and in itself became a justification for surveillance and

290

increasingly punitive response to dissent of all kinds. As this mutual antagonism escalated, the police—already suspicious of conduct challenging the status quo—became more politicized through patrolmen's associations and alliance with right-wing supporters. The dominant issues of the sixties—black unrest and antiwar protest, especially by New Left standard bearers—accelerated this polarity. These two movements all but replaced the old (communist) left as target priorities. In the case of antiwar activities, adversarial response by local red squads was repeated in cities all over the country and monitored as well by the FBI. But the ghetto-police confrontations were more isolated, confined as they were to cities with concentrations of black residents.

A number of cities, of which Detroit is a prime example, reflected in their police structures and target priorities a similar urban pathology ("the urban syndrome"): a decaying black ghetto, widespread poverty, a city administration left fiscally impotent by the flight of the white middle class to the suburbs and ravaged by the corruption of politicians who retained power by exploiting the tension between black and white racial enclaves (thus further polarizing the city), the emergence of potentially violent black and white groups, and the development among white policemen of a siege mentality.

Both before and after the ghetto riots of the late sixties, self-help and violence inevitably came to be regarded in both camps—police and ghetto—as vital means of survival. "Law and order" became a coded battle cry as the police were transformed into an army defending white power and the status quo. In this confrontation, the urban intelligence unit played a key role. Blacks—their organizations and activities—became prime targets for ongoing surveillance regardless of their political views, not unlike the foreign-born of an earlier day. In the same way, when the peace movement slackened in the late sixties, the police continued their former surveillance practices against white targets. Despite the fact that red squad activities frequently implicated the protected freedoms, the police were left free of statutory or other official restraints (beyond budget limitations) in their surveillance practices. Given these circumstances, it was inviting for a demagogic and ambitious local official to use his power to strike in dramatic ways at the radical or ghetto enemy and to play the role of savior.

The Detroit Red Squad: The Pacesetter for the Second-Tier Cities

The Detroit Red Squad underwent enormous growth in the sixties in response to New Left and black protest activities, particularly by the

Black Panther Party. Testimony by representatives of the city and state red squads before the House Internal Security Committee, the Senate Internal Security Subcommittee, and the McClellan Committee[1] makes it apparent that the Detroit area had become the theater of a form of guerrilla warfare in which adversarial confrontations between the hunted and the hunters had become commonplace: both sides—activist protesters and the police—viewed this mutual and ever-intensifying hostility as part of a war for survival. What is clear from the pattern of these clashes is that, despite the justifiable rationale for police intervention in some situations to prevent disorder and crime, the police response was indiscriminate, harshly retaliatory, and vindictive: to their targets, the police came to symbolize the substantive evils they were protesting. *

Nothing more dramatically demonstrates the emptiness of the prediction-prevention justification for intelligence activities in Detroit than the total lack of useful advance and on-site information made available to the military forces called in to quell the 1967 riots, in which forty-three were killed, hundreds wounded, and 7,200 arrested, not to speak of many millions of dollars of property damaged. Prior to the 1967 outbreak, the Detroit police had recognized the need to monitor the mounting civil rights demonstrations and for that purpose had formed a demonstration detail within the Special Investigation Bureau (SIB) that functionally overlapped the responsibilities of an established subversive unit in the Criminal Investigation Bureau—a situation that drew professional criticism.[2] Each of these units ran its own informers, kept separate files, and maintained contact with other intelligence agencies. The demonstration detail gained notoriety in 1965 in the aftermath of the slaying in Alabama (discussed below) of Violet Liuzzo, a Detroit resident, because in a press conference called by the Ku Klux Klan a spokesman recited data about Liuzzo's personal life and problems drawn from SIB files.[3]

In the decade beginning in the mid sixties, target priorities and operations shifted and expanded markedly. Activities of the New Left and black protest movements became major concentrations, overshadowing the old (communist) left and labor activists. File collections—individual

---

* This conflict was sharply reflected in the attacks on the Black Panther Party from the late sixties to the seventies. See, for example, "Police Draw Blank in Panther Raid," *Detroit Free Press*, June 6, 1969; "Panthers Target of Crackdown," ibid., June 12, 1969; "Panthers Victims of Hoax Call," ibid., December 12, 1969; "15 Black Militants Surrender after a 9-Hour Confrontation with Detroit Police," *New York Times*, October 26, 1970; "The Panthers and the Red Squad" and "Police Spying in Michigan," *Newsletter* of the Citizens' Committee to End Political Surveillance, February/March 1977.

and organizational, "subjects" and events—grew enormously, as did data exchange. The old liaison networks were revitalized with new ties (to Army intelligence) and much closer ones to the FBI on the federal level and close operational collaboration with state and area police generally, as well as with college units such as the Wayne State University campus security police.

In addition to traditional physical surveillance of organizations, individuals, and events, photography became routine.[4] In late 1967 a large group of police officers (from forty to sixty) were recruited for intensive training in the use of photographic equipment. Photographic surveillance was conducted in unmarked police vehicles and on foot. Not only demonstrations and rallies, but organizations' officers and supporters were also photographed and sometimes videotaped. A typical practice was to park an unmarked car outside the office of a target group—such as the BPP or the East Side Improvement Association—and photograph entering and departing visitors, even following particular targets whenever considered necessary. The enormous photographic harvest was entered into swollen scrapbooks (side by side with newspaper-clipping scrapbooks) and selectively fed to congressional investigating committees.

A number of aspects of the Detroit surveillance program, rarely found elsewhere, warrant notice. Police officers, notably blacks in sympathy with the civil rights movement, were systematically photographed and otherwise surveilled. In the same way, a sizable contingent, typically from the Detroit Police Officers' Association, appeared at some gatherings as "private" citizen-observers.[*5] As in Chicago, their efforts at concealment—through, for example, grubby apparel—were betrayed by their age, grooming, and clustering together. Finally, and most important, there was the close operational collaboration of the city and state units. Planted informers and sworn personnel conducted both open and covert surveillance in partnership, a unique team play epitomizing shared concern for curbing dissent. The conservative state government played an aggressive role in this enterprise.

Activists who were surveilled were convinced that their phones were being tapped, but hard evidence is lacking to support this contention. What is uncontroverted is the disclosure that a retired police department inspector, formerly in charge of departmental wiretapping ("police science laboratory"), became chief of security at Michigan Bell, the super-

---

* There are rare examples of greater involvement, such as distributing literature as a surveillance cover.

visor of its wiretap operations and responsible for red squad liaison. It is clear that wiretapping targets included the already-mentioned maverick police officers.[6]

In July 1974 a modest grass-roots consumer group, the Michigan Association for Consumer Protection, filed suit against the Michigan State Police (MSP), charging that it had been illegally investigated and surveilled by the MSP at the instigation of a state legislator who opposed a consumer protection bill it sponsored. Within a year, the suit had become a class action suit, with fourteen named plaintiffs, and the list of defendants had been expanded to include the Police Commission of the city of Detroit, Detroit's police chief, and its mayor, Coleman Young. The state police promptly admitted the illegality of the surveillance.[7] By the summer of 1975, the plaintiffs and their attorneys had amassed evidence that the city police had, from the 1930s to the 1970s, gathered and often disseminated intelligence concerning the political activities of between 60,000 and 110,000 individuals and organizations,* and that 38,000 subjects had been targeted by the state police.

The scope of the Detroit Police Department's intelligence-gathering is reflected in the range of plaintiffs, which included an attorney with activist clients, a professor, a labor leader, a radical political activist, a consumer protection advocate, a nonprofit alternative newspaper, and an attorney for pro-Arab groups. Later, UAW officials and other individuals prominent in public life joined the suit. As the lawsuit progressed, it catalyzed long-dormant opposition in the Detroit community to police surveillance and related operations that served as surveillance covers.

---

* "Police to Release Espionage Files," *Detroit Free Press,* December 19, 1980; "Inside the Red Squad Files," ibid., December 21, 1980; "Michigan to Release Its Files about Political Surveillance," *New York Times,* December 27, 1980. A more accurate quantification is difficult to arrive at, principally because of duplications and overlapping coverage of the various file collections. For example, in the late sixties, two separate police details collected information about the same political targets. According to an account by the investigative reporter Claudia Capos, "Forbidden Files," *Detroit Free Press,* December 6, 1981, an audit commissioned by the police, disclosed that, "The files contain the names of more than 1.4 million individuals . . . and 1450 organizations . . . [which] appear on 135,000 index cards that fill five cabinets." Although based on a police audit, these figures do not help us quantify the number of file subjects since individual and organizational files are littered with names not all the subjects of separate files. The enormous number of names of individuals and organizations is, however, not without relevance: it confirms the fact that the dominant purpose of the surveillance operation in Detroit, as elsewhere, was proscriptive identification. See *Benkert et al. v. Michigan State Police et al.,* No. 74–023–934–AZ (Wayne Cty. Cir Ct. Mich.), deposition of Jesse Coulter, August 6, 1975, pp. 79–80.

The pressures of the lawsuit were reflected in the harassment of the original plaintiff, Walter J. Benkert, who charged that he had been continually intimidated, his house broken into, the files of the Michigan Association for Consumer Protection ransacked, his documents stolen, his phone tapped, his movements continuously surveilled by helicopters manned by pilots equipped with binoculars, and that efforts had been made by unidentified individuals to run him off the road.[8]

The litigation established that the unit had operated over the years totally without restraining standards of target selection or operations. One unit chief testified that investigations were conducted against "any organization or individual that would tend to appear a potential police problem," including "super super liberals" or any targets that "by action, statements or ideology present an actual or implied threat to city, state or national government, their representatives or citizenry."[9] Another claimed the unit's mission to be the investigation of "militant activity" or, for targets falling short of a militant rating, "subversive activity."[10] A third averred that the unit's operations were directed at "groups . . . trying to foment discord."[11]

Depositions of these witnesses and others established the existence of an extensive network of paid informers—compensated for each item submitted, or on salaries as high as $1,000 a month—as well as unpaid civilian volunteers or sworn personnel and cadets, usually assigned, but sometimes serving as "interested citizens."[12] Other collection modes were likewise extraordinarily thorough and included garbage searches and the pilfering of targets' documents and literature.[13] The information collected by the squad concerning individuals or organizations was stored in master files, which bulged with inter-office memoranda, third-party interviews (utilities, employers, landlords), newspaper clippings, documents and literature "lifted" by informers, and a variety of public records. Filed information included a subject's address, spouse, vital statistics, criminal history (if any), and a photograph when available. In addition, such personal information as "localities frequented," friends, personal characteristics, and traits were recorded. Thus, one lawyer's Intelligence Exchange (IE) card commented that he "worked without fee for Sirhan Sirhan"; a reporter's card documented the fact that he "wears tight pants"; and another card read, mysteriously, "This subject is very bad. Has an Eastern accent." The IE card of another subject recorded the fact that he attended a rally at which one woman speaker had been "recently divorced." The core entries dealt with political activities—meetings and demonstrations at which a subject had been observed, or to which his car's license plate number had been traced; positions of leadership within a subject organization; speeches; publications; out-of-town trips; and so forth. These data were coded to master files dealing with organizational activities. Mere attendance at a rally, meeting, forum, or demonstration was frequently sufficient to trigger the data collection process. The record also reflected an active data dissemination and exchange system involving the state police, local and more remote red squads, the FBI, the Secret Service, and Army intelligence.[14]

The scope of the targeting ranged from antiwar and student groups to consumer, environmental, feminist, and gay groups. The targets included organizations such as the American Friends Service Committee, the Detroit Coalition to End the War Now, the American Civil Liberties Union, Wayne County Legal Services Organization, and Concerned Parents for Peace. (During the recession of 1974–75, the protest activities of the unemployed became a surveillance focus.) Individual targets were equally ecumenical, covering city officials and employees, Congressman John Conyers, and an assortment of professionals and journalists. The file of an attorney, Abdeen Jabara, was over fifty pages long and listed all the gatherings he had attended over several years and the names of more than one hundred of those present at rallies where he had spoken, along with the license plate numbers and home addresses of some of them. The file of Professor James B. Jacobs records his home address (by courtesy of the Detroit Edison Company), the fact that his name had been found on a list belonging to a political activist, his attendance at a rally, and his visit to a home where music and dancing were observed. Stuart Dowty—a student movement activist of the late sixties who worked on an antiwar education project with David Stockman (later the Reagan administration's budget director), the subject of a state red squad file*—was so closely surveilled that the entries in his file record

* The state unit's files, which date from 1950, were as wide-ranging as the city's and reflected the surveillance of such subjects as state and city legislators and employees, UAW officials, and activists of all kinds—civil rights workers, feminists, gay rights advocates, environmentalists, and busing and antibusing advocates. Prominent dissidents whose names were missing from the list of file subjects complained that the list had been "sanitized." Police officials denied the charge, but admitted that the files had been "updated" and purged. The state unit was also embarrassed by disclosures of improper dissemination. In one case, file information was admittedly transmitted to the Panox Corporation, a conservative Michigan-based newspaper chain, for use in making background checks on employees and job applicants. See "Inside the Red Squad Files," December 21, 1980; "Hiring Linked to Red Squad," December 13, 1981; "Rep. Stockman Named in Files Kept by Police," December 29, 1980; "State 'Red Squad' Watched Thousands," January 9, 1979; and "State Police Subversive File Used by Newspaper Chain," March 1, 1977, all from the *Detroit Free Press*, and

the fact that his wife (also a file subject) picked him up after work, and that they went to a grocery store and then home. More serious was the evidence in his file establishing that after a stint at the Chrysler Dodge truck plant, he was not rehired (although the company was rehiring at the time) because he was suspected of being a radical. Other evidence established that Chrysler was actively involved in blacklisting politically suspect employees.

For years, Chrysler provided the Detroit unit and the FBI with information from its voluminous files concerning the political activities of workers and allowed the Detroit Red Squad to place informers and undercover agents inside various plants. In return, the police provided Chrysler with membership lists of allegedly subversive organizations and in some cases recommended the firing of activist employees. Thus, an SIB file contains the following entry about a Chrysler employee: "Industry has been cautioned on occasion re: one of these people who have obtained employment within their company. But they have failed to get rid of the subject until he has involved himself so heavily in the union that it is impossible to do so without large labor problems."[15]

In 1976, in a landmark decision and order, Judge James Montante invalidated as unconstitutional the legislation invoked to justify surveillance on the state level and ordered both the state and Detroit police to halt the surveillance practices complained of and work out a method of notifying the victims of surveillance that their records were on file and available for return.[16] In 1980 the state police finally agreed to begin a process of notification and return of files to the victims.[17] However, arrangements to develop a parallel procedure on the local level were stymied. Mayor Young simply ordered the political unit abolished and its files transferred to the custody of the Board of Police Commissioners,[18] an edict that did not, however, deal with the substance of the surveillance issue either in the past or future. And when the city council began the consideration of an ordinance sharply curbing political surveillance, Mayor Young expressed his opposition on the grounds that such a measure would impinge on his executive power, exercised in this case by his appointed Board of Police Commissioners.[19] A highly restrictive council measure was nevertheless passed, which included provisions for civil remedies and damages, but it was subsequently vetoed by the mayor on questionable grounds.[20] Many found the mayor's balky response ironic in view of the fact that Young himself had been victimized by the red

---

"Police Computer Spied on 'Subversives' " (Michigan State University) *State News*, January 24, 1977.

hunt of the fifties and had been subpoenaed as an unfriendly witness before the House Un-American Activities Committee.[21] As a concession to his critics, however, Young promoted the issuance of a brief police order in 1982 prohibiting investigations into "beliefs, opinions, attitudes, statements, associations and activities" of persons or organizations except when they were "reasonably suspected of violation of the law."[22]

A number of circumstances in addition to Judge Montante's decision brought the city's countersubversive operations to an end: shifting demographics, a change in political climate reflected in the election of a progressive mayor, a press turnabout, and the red squad's loss of its "friends"—the auto makers, congressional committees, UAW, and state and federal structures. The dissemination of files on thousands of subjects not remotely identifiable as a threat to any legitimate interest provoked bewilderment, anger, and laughter—and a sort of pride. Howard Simon, executive director of the Michigan Civil Liberties Union, put it this way: "It really is a mark of distinction, a badge of commitment. Several people have called me and said, 'Thank God I got my red squad notice!' Others can't understand why they didn't get one."[23]

Baltimore's Red Squad: The Operational Arm of Police Commissioner Donald Pomerleau

For some fifteen years (1966–82) Police Commissioner Donald Pomerleau dominated police activities in Baltimore as a "Big Man" easily matching his counterparts of earlier times. During this period, Pomerleau presided over and directed a huge countersubversive operation, which he also used to enhance his prestige and intimidate his critics.

Baltimore's red squad—formally known as the intelligence section of the Inspectional Services Division (ISD)—was launched on July 1, 1966, coinciding with the date of Pomerleau's appointment as commissioner. In addition to an organized crime unit, the intelligence section sheltered an antisubversive squad responsible for "gathering information regarding the activities of subversive, extremist and militant groups."[24] The ISD was blueprinted as "the operational arm of the Police Commissioner,"[25] the only branch of the police department required to report directly to the commissioner. Pomerleau's annual report for 1968 tells us: "The primary purpose of the Intelligence Section is to serve as the eyes and ears of the Police Commissioner."[26] According to its charter, "The primary mission of the Intelligence Section . . . in the active surveillance of individuals or groups outside the normal criminal behavior, has always been to attempt to spot potential areas of violence."[27]

The ISD's operational scope was extremely broad and typically unrelated to violence prevention. Without guidelines or restraints of any kind, ISD agents under Pomerleau's direction targeted some 125 groups, ranging from the American Friends Service Committee, American Civil Liberties Union, Black United Front (a broad-based, interracial civic group), tenants' organizations, and "Operation Breadbasket" (a project of the Southern Christian Leadership Conference) through collectives and communes of the counterculture to the Black Panther Party, Young Communists, and community associations in various parts of the city (concerned with such matters as road improvement and the elimination of rodents). In addition, all area colleges and universities were surveilled and campus groups infiltrated.[28] The ISD employed familiar surveillance instruments such as wiretapping, photography, and informers, as well as a network of private and governmental sources, including the Chesapeake and Potomac Telephone Company, credit bureaus, and federal agencies. This network fed the ISD material upon informal, verbal requests, which concealed their purpose.

In covering meetings of target groups, ISD personnel were instructed to identify leaders and activists and report the name of every person in attendance, including representatives of the press and electronic media. So ubiquitous was the ISD in its coverage that one former ISD agent cautioned members of his family never to stop at any rally or picket line even out of curiosity because someone might submit their names to the police. This, he feared, could result in them being considered a "potential threat."[29]

Reports compiled by ISD operatives were processed through an elaborate system of index cards, complete with dates and places of meetings and even head counts. These cards were supplemented by "background reports" (including highly personal data), "activity folders," and dossiers detailing a subject's earnings, close associates, debts, and creditors. According to one veteran ISD officer, "The more information you could gather, this, in the eyes of your superiors, made you a better officer."[30]

The ISD's surveillance modes included not only passive identification of targets but more aggressive practices such as discharge pressures, stakeouts, 24-hour spying on organizations, and follow-up interviews with individuals. For example, after a speaker remarked to a law students' group that, "At other schools when demands weren't met, there have been boycotts and sit-ins," he was visited by two ISD agents, who demanded an explanation of his remarks.[31] Such intimidating practices were sometimes followed up by destructive raids, provocation, and pretext arrests.

Two aspects of the ISD operation are noteworthy. First was the unit's ties with the federal surveillance community—a relationship undoubtedly cemented by Baltimore's geographical closeness to the nation's capital. No fewer than five ISD members had been trained in intelligence-related matters at the Military Intelligence School at Fort Holabird, Maryland. ISD directors in the sixties and seventies were former FBI agents. In its campaign to destroy the city's Black Panther group, the ISD deployed informers already recruited by the FBI.

The second, and perhaps more striking, facet of the ISD operation that claims our attention is the manner in which the unit was used to advance the interests, silence the critics, and massage the formidable ego of Police Commissioner Pomerleau. The commissioner deployed the ISD to fish in the waters of mainstream politics for useful material to use as leverage against potential critics and adversaries. The political campaigns of candidates for federal, state, and local office were watched and in some cases infiltrated.[32] The ISD also regularly monitored meetings of government agencies in Baltimore such as the city council, the school board, the liquor board, and utility-rate-increase and expressway hearings. In some cases, ISD detectives and infiltrators covering such gatherings were equipped with concealed recording devices.

Pomerleau did not hesitate to make it known to those who incurred his disfavor that he "had everything on everybody"[33] and made a practice of scouring ISD files in advance of meeting an individual not familiar to him. Pomerleau's passion to silence his critics was reflected in the assignment of ISD personnel to review local and regional newspapers systematically for articles mentioning the commissioner or the department. Critical journalists were harassed through "dirty tricks." In addition, radio and television broadcasts were selectively screened for comments or criticism of the commissioner or the department.[34]

Of all the five police units discussed in this chapter, none placed so heavy a reliance on informers as Baltimore's ISD. A corps, estimated at about one hundred, of police department members, cadets, recruits (not infrequently "hooked" by means such as threats of drug arrests or probation violation charges), volunteers, and FBI cast-offs flooded target groups and individuals. Pomerleau's deployment of informers to feed his insatiable hunger for information sometimes led to weird results. Thus he planted ISD agents in the highly respected Black United Front (BUF), which included the city's elite and was dedicated to promoting racial peace. Even more strange was his spying on groups cooperating with the police Community Relations Division (CRD). This project, launched in the pre-Pomerleau days, won national acclaim for its professionalism.

Police attached to the CRD openly participated in meetings of neighborhood groups and contributed to their discussions and planning. But this did not prevent Pomerleau from planting ISD agents in these groups—and, in the process, compromising the entire program.[35]

Pomerleau's grandiosity and fury were most graphically reflected in his legendary dirty war against the BPP, conducted pursuant to a program targeting the Panthers initiated by the then U.S. attorney general, John Mitchell. Thus in the fall of 1969 the police installed a movie camera in a building across the street from Panther headquarters. The record abounds with examples of the repressive conduct of the red squad agents and their informers. In 1969 a Panther rally for which a permit had been obtained was being held in a city park when suddenly there appeared on the scene ten buses loaded with 400 policemen to "maintain order." Fortunately, the invaders were persuaded to leave the scene and position themselves where they would not be visible. On another occasion, on February 25, 1969, six Panthers were arrested for allegedly interfering with police during the arrest of a seventh "Panther," who was later found by the press to be working for the police department. At the trial a year and a half later, the state prosecutor, Hilary Kaplan (later appointed to the Maryland supreme court bench), admitted that he had no evidence to incriminate the defendants and dropped all charges with prejudice although the allegations had been sworn to by no less than eight police officers.

The most disturbing confrontation in this crusade took place on May 1, 1970, when the police staged massive raids on Panther hangouts, homes, and offices. (Approximately 150 heavily armed policemen wearing bulletproof vests participated.) Four party members were arrested on weapons charges; six were arrested for murder and eleven more sought. Police Commissioner Pomerleau claimed that the arrests were linked to the discovery of the body of one Eugene Anderson, a twenty-year-old Baltimore resident, said to be a Panther, tortured and murdered by other Panthers because he was suspected of being a police informer.[36]

At about the same time, a young white lawyer, Arthur Turco, and seventeen Panthers were charged with Anderson's murder. The case ultimately collapsed, a disaster traceable to the jury's distrust of the state's witnesses. One of the latter, Mahoney Kebe, was supplied by the FBI to the red squad and more specifically to a Colonel (then Major) DuBois, who was appointed to head the red squad at the height of the campaign against the BPP. At Turco's trial the judge, on his own motion, ordered Kebe, the star witness, removed from the stand for his perjurious testimony, which was ordered stricken. Another, Samuel Walters (Agent 94), was an undercover operative for the Baltimore red squad. He was first assigned to infiltrate the peace movement and then told, in February 1969, to monitor Turco. He first broke cover to testify at Turco's trial and claimed that Turco was a leader of the Panthers, an inherently implausible mantle to be draped around the shoulders of a young white lawyer who had only recently come to Baltimore. When Walters's reports were submitted in court, they made no mention of Turco. Confronted with this fact, he testified, "My superiors told me to implicate Turco." (Kebe, Walters, and a third informer, it developed, were paid fifty dollars a week each and given free room and food for two years prior to their testimony.)[37]

The indictment against Turco and his alleged accomplices was accompanied by an attempt by Pomerleau to seek an injunction against the distribution of the Black Panther newspaper in the city, which Pomerleau justified on the grounds that two police officers had been shot to death in west Baltimore and that Panther literature was left at the scene. He successfully persuaded the state attorney general to seek an injunction, which was granted without a hearing. This extremely broad injunction banned the distribution of any literature by the Panthers that in any way criticized or disparaged the Baltimore Police Department. Ultimately, despite Pomerleau's ardent pursuit of the matter, the injunction was severely narrowed by a federal court to ban only the publication of material that might result in imminent danger to the police.[38]

Pomerleau also made the counterculture, and in particular antiwar activists, priority targets. Although infiltrators dressed in properly deceptive "movement" garb, worked hard to gain acceptance, and contributed financially to the proper causes, their capacity to deceive was limited. The efforts developed by their victims to expose ISD agents yielded substantial returns. However, the informer saturation was not without its impact: suspicion reduced morale and led to unfounded accusations.[39]

One agent, Glenn Ehasz, became an unpaid news photographer for an underground newspaper, *Harry*. A departmental spokesman, responding to protests over this form of compromising press freedom, explained, "We were not interested in *Harry* [but wanted] to solidify [Ehasz's] cover in the community."[40]

In response to a stream of press disclosures of widespread surveillance practices and abuse of power by Pomerleau's unit, the Maryland Senate Committee on Constitutional and Public Law conducted a series of preliminary public hearings in January 1975 to determine whether an investigation was warranted.

On February 18, the scheduled date of Pomerleau's appearance before the committee, the panel received a letter stating his refusal to appear on the grounds that "the Senate is being used as an instrument to disrupt the last bastion of order in Baltimore." The letter further charged that the entire investigation was not only illegal but "immoral," amounting to "a daily rehashing of past activity solely based on the statements of those who would like to change our system of government other than by the lawful process of the law."[41]

Subsequently, after a train of obstructive maneuvers condemned by the committee, including the destruction of relevant ISD files on the eve of the investigation, the commissioner relented, and on October 18, 1975, he explained, among other things, to the committee what action he had taken when he received information about the son of a community leader:

> I called that individual's mother and said, you know, I think it would be wise if you came into the office and bring your son with you and we had a discussion and that individual, when I read to him what I had in two different source documents, got on his knees and said, please don't do that to me and the mother assured me that she would make some proper input.[42]

As this testimony suggests, Pomerleau saw himself as the savior of the city, the embodiment of righteousness. He viewed his office as a pulpit, and from it he denounced such evils as parental permissiveness, judicial laxity, and lack of patriotism. His homiletic passions were the projection of an authoritarian personality, a mesh of character traits that he, along with Frank Rizzo, shared with J. Edgar Hoover, a revered mentor.[43]

Another authoritarian trait manifest in Pomerleau's style is what T. W. Adorno and his associates refer to as an "intolerance of ambiguity." Pomerleau viewed the world through Manichean lenses: the good Americans (under his leadership) doing endless battle with evil subversives. For example, in February 1971 the commissioner lashed out against participants in a broad-based antiwar demonstration, denouncing them, in a hastily called press conference, as part of "a revolutionary movement which is Communist-oriented." He told the assembled newsmen that in view of the violence of the demonstration—eleven policemen were injured and many windows were smashed in the downtown area—he had ordered his men in the future "to move directly to the baton" in dealing with unruly demonstrators; that some of "these miserable creatures" had "only recently returned from Cuba," and that in the future policemen would "stop and frisk" demonstrators to search for concealed missiles. A professor at the University of Maryland, Paul Lauter, along with other organizers of the march, blamed the police for provoking the violence. Lauter, who was himself arrested, protested: "It's odd that the violence in the area where I was was provoked and started by the police on horseback coming into the crowd."[44]

The state senate committee's report rebuked the ISD for its monitoring of nonviolent groups and rejected the now-familiar justifications: the need to pinpoint particular individuals suspected of criminal activities ("closing for the criminal closing" in Pomerleau's ornate usage), to maintain an agent's cover, and to prepare for outbreaks of violence. How, the committee wondered, could such justifications apply to the ISD agent's report of the debate between George Russell and his opponent, Clarence Mitchell III, in a mayoralty race, which included such details as whether Commissioner Pomerleau was mentioned and whether future meetings were scheduled?[45]

The committee also noted that the assessment of the material collected by the ISD was as flawed as its target selection and operational practices. For example, Pomerleau undertook, on the basis of gossip and hearsay, to assess the politics of certain applicants for public employment. As the committee pointed out:

> Information was, after all, obtained from informants and covert operatives, as well as sworn personnel, and was oftentimes of a hearsay nature. Intelligence-gatherers had license, oftentimes poetic, to make subjective judgments in reports concerning such things as an individual's character, beliefs, political leanings, motivations, personal habits, associates, and ambitions.[46]

The panel's modest recommendations focused in part on the fact that the Baltimore ISD—along with the state police and four county departments (also engaged in political surveillance, frequently in partnership with the ISD)[47]—lacked adequate guidelines. The absence of guidelines coupled with the ISD's control by a commissioner with delusions of grandeur made serious abuse of power all but inevitable. What further intensified the dangers posed by an ISD run wild, the panel concluded, was the total lack of departmental accountability. The Baltimore Police Department had, for over a century, operated under the supervision and control of the state government, which was ill equipped to meet its responsibilities in this area. The committee recommended a transfer to city administration and control and the appointment of a commissioner by the mayor rather than by the governor.

The committee's report, completed in December 1975 and released in January of the next year, confirmed in substantial part the complaints of ISD victims. But even before it appeared, Pomerleau's supporters rallied to his defense. Both Baltimore's Mayor William Schaefer and Governor Marvin Mandel praised the commissioner without calling on him to defend himself against the panel's well-documented charges. The business community, led by the Advertising Club of Baltimore, insisted that he deserved the city's Man of the Year Award and pointed to the need for protection promised by Pomerleau against a recurrence of the devastation caused by the 1968 riots.[48] When the committee's recommendation of local selection of a police commissioner was implemented in 1978, Pomerleau was appointed to a six-year term.*

The state senate report was followed in 1978 by the enactment of a law, based on federal models, limiting the scope of the collection of information by government agencies and granting individuals, subject only to narrow limitations, access to file data. These measures finally closed the door to Pomerleau's manic spy operations. In 1982, before his term had expired, Pomerleau resigned.

Birmingham: Bull Connor's Race War

On April 9, 1960, the *New York Times* published a front-page article on Birmingham, Alabama, by Harrison E. Salisbury, a Pulitzer prize–winning correspondent back from twenty years of reporting on the Soviet Union under Stalin and Khrushchev. Birmingham, wrote Salisbury, is a city of "fear, hatred and terror":

> No New Yorker can readily measure the climate of Birmingham today. Whites and blacks still walk the same streets. But the streets, the water supply and the sewer system are about the only public facilities they share. . . .
>
> Every channel of communication, every medium of mutual interest, every reasoned approach, every inch of middle ground has been fragmented by the emotional dynamite of racism, reinforced by the whip, the razor, the gun, the bomb, the torch, the club, the knife, the mob, the police, and many branches of the state's apparatus.[49]

---

* According to one observer, there was a noticeable lack of opposition to the commissioner's continuing in office from the very people who would ordinarily have been delighted to see him go, inviting the suspicion that the possession of secret files by the commissioner played some role in this matter.

Birmingham was polarized by all of the major struggles of the civil rights movement: the Freedom Rides, school desegregation, lunch-counter protests, sit-ins, bombings and the failure to curb them, Black Panther Party activities, union organization by blacks, conflicts over police brutality, and interference with rights to public protest. For ten years the political and social climate of Birmingham—Salisbury's "emotional dynamite"—was profoundly influenced by the energy and conflicting activism of such prominent figures as Rev. Martin Luther King, Jr., Rev. Fred Shuttlesworth, Ralph Abernathy, and Hosea Williams aligned against Governor George Wallace, Police Commissioner Eugene ("Bull") Connor, States' Rights Party leaders Dr. Edward Fields and J. B. Stoner, and Imperial Wizard Robert Shelton of the Ku Klux Klan.

Under Connor's leadership, the Birmingham police became a bulwark of southern resistance to the call for civil rights and racial justice. Photographs flashed around the globe: Birmingham policemen directing waterhoses at black demonstrators, Birmingham police releasing dogs to attack marchers accused of "parading without a permit," Birmingham police officers "subduing" a lone woman demonstrator and committing other acts of violence against demonstrators. "We're not going to have white folks and nigras segregatin' together in this man's town,"[50] Connor announced to the world. In his view, it was the responsibility of the police to enforce traditional southern race relations. As he stated in 1958: "We don't give a damn about the law. Down here we make our own law."[51]

Forced to retire as police commissioner in 1953 after he was caught in flagrante delicto with his secretary in a hotel room, Connor was reelected in 1957 in the wake of increased racial tension brought on by the 1954 Supreme Court decision in *Brown v. Board of Education* condemning racial segregation in the schools.[52] During his years as commissioner, both in his earlier stint in the fifties as well as his later term in the sixties, bombings of black homes in previously white fringe areas repeatedly took place without serious police efforts to investigate and arrest the suspected Klan perpetrators.* (In the only case in which the bombers were caught and convicted, an all-white jury freed them, subject only to probation.)[53]

Connor made his "own law" in other ways: police justifications for assaults on blacks were accepted without question; peaceful marches and demonstrations were brutally disrupted; city police were ordered to ar-

---

* These were preceded by unsolved bombings of synagogues also attributed to the Klan.

rest and detain civil rights activists on invented charges. Connor's vendetta against Rev. Fred Shuttlesworth, the city's black civil rights leader, became legendary. In 1958 he charged that Shuttlesworth was responsible for bombing his own home two years earlier and announced that he intended to force him to submit to a lie-detector test. Predictably, he accused Shuttlesworth of being a communist tool charged with disrupting the city's peaceful race relations. In October of the same year he ordered the arrest without charges of three black ministers from Montgomery who had come to discuss the bus boycott with Shuttlesworth. Connor held them incommunicado for several hours and subjected them to a lengthy interrogation. Shortly after the ministers' arrest and jailing, he ordered his men to arrest and fingerprint a white staff member of the New York–based Fellowship of Reconciliation, who had come to Birmingham to counsel Shuttlesworth and the Alabama Christian Movement for Human Rights on peaceful methods to resist segregation, and to confiscate his personal effects and papers. Connor condemned this visit as proof of a larger strategy in support of a communist plot.[54]

In the early days of the civil rights movement, Connor's police collaborated with white racist organizations in defense of the racial status quo. Such cooperation, however, was nothing new for the Birmingham police. As early as 1930, a member of the Alabama Knights of the Ku Klux Klan, John G. Murphy, testified before the House Special Committee to Investigate Communist Activities in the United States (the Fish Committee) that the Klan had cooperated with the Birmingham police (and the U.S. Department of Justice) in anticommunist intelligence investigations. According to Murphy, the Klan trailed communists to party meetings, checked license plates at the doors, and then "immediately got in touch with Chief Kelley, who sent several men there, arrested Johnson, M. Bunkin . . . and possibly one other."[55]

Under Connor, cooperation between city officials and the Ku Klux Klan could no longer be as open as formerly. Though it was common knowledge that some police officers were Klan members and that many of them, along with their superiors, sympathized with Klan objectives, by 1961 public dealings with the Klan were out of the question. Even the House Committee on Un-American Activities listed the KKK as a "subversive" organization "committed to force and violence in order to deny others their rights under the Constitution of the United States."[56] New liaison modes had to be devised.

Assigned to the job of maintaining covert contact with the Klan was one of the most committed members of the Birmingham police, Detective Sergeant Tom Cook, a specialist in "racial matters," prominently perched in the Gallery of the Obsessed, and commander of the Birmingham police intelligence unit (or "subversive squad," as the FBI called it).

On April 13, 1961, Detective "Red" Self, on assignment by Sergeant Cook, approached a member of the Eastview Klavern of the Klan. Self told the Klansman that Cook wanted to arrange several meetings to discuss matters "of interest" to the Klan. The Klansman agreed to meet with Cook, and a time and place were set for April 17. At that meeting, Cook furnished the Klansman with names of various "inter-racial organizations," the locations of civil rights meetings, and the membership lists of these groups for publication by the Klan. At the same meeting, Cook warned the Klansman that the Klan's plans to "make trouble" during a speech by poet John Ciardi should be canceled. An undercover FBI informant, Cook told the Klansman, had infiltrated the Eastview Klavern and had reported KKK plans back to the FBI. The meeting at which Ciardi was to speak "would definitely be covered" by the FBI. Cook offered the Klansman help in a task of mutual interest to both: determining the identity of the FBI informer.[57]

What Cook did not know was that the Klansman with whom he was meeting was, in fact, the FBI informer in question: Gary Thomas Rowe, known to his friends as Tommy and to his FBI contact agents as BH 248 PCI (RAC),* had joined the Klan approximately a year before and had reported his experiences faithfully back to the FBI. What Cook also didn't know was that even as he spoke to Rowe, he was being watched from across the room by two FBI agents. Cook felt sure that Rowe was trustworthy. Even after being told by Imperial Wizard Robert Shelton that Rowe was "100%," Cook had called Special Agent C. B. Stanbery of the FBI to make sure that Rowe was not "one of your boys."[58] Stanbery, of course, denied knowing Rowe. Cook was convinced and continued feeding information to Rowe, who in turn passed it on to both the leadership of the Klan and the FBI Birmingham office.

On April 20, Cook and Rowe met again. Cook provided the KKK, through Rowe, with three internal police documents concerning Martin Luther King, Jr., and the Birmingham Council on Human Relations, a local civil rights group. According to one FBI memo, Cook told Rowe to pass the documents on to Klan leaders to "determine whether the material therein could be printed on the Klan press and distributed to Klan members"[59]—a "disinformation"-style tactic made familiar by the FBI's COINTELPRO operation. The document on Martin Luther King, Jr.,

---

* BH stands for Birmingham, PCI for potential criminal informant, and RAC for racial.

written by Cook and directed to the attention of Police Commissioner Connor, began:

> On January 1, 1958, the power hungry Negro leader, Martin Luther King, Jr., led a pilgrimage for public schools on Emancipation Day. . . . This school integration propaganda gesture is another in a long series of racial agitation activities led by King and, as usual, was reported in the *Worker* with full approval of the Communist Party official organ.[60]

When Rowe met to return the documents to Cook on April 24, Cook told him

> that any information he had in his files would be made available to the Alabama Knights, Knights of the Ku Klux Klan, Incorporated. Informant [Rowe] stated at that time Cook opened two file drawers in his office and told informant to help himself to any material he thought he would need for the Klan.[61]

The FBI's suspicion that Cook was acting under Connor's supervision was confirmed when the sergeant suggested to Rowe that a meeting be arranged of higher-ups. Rowe arranged several meetings attended by Hubert Page, a Birmingham Klan leader; Imperial Wizard Robert Shelton; Bull Connor; Cook; and occasionally Rowe. The primary topic of discussion at these sessions, held in late April and early May, was the impending arrival on May 14 of two busloads of Freedom Riders sponsored by the Congress of Racial Equality (CORE). The Freedom Riders were making their way south from Washington, D.C., to New Orleans on integrated buses, testing southern compliance with laws regarding the desegregation of interstate transportation facilities. The Klan leadership and the police leadership agreed that a response was necessary to convey to the world the southern answer to the call for integration.

On May 11 the members of Eastview Klavern #3 met to discuss the reception planned for the arrival of the buses in Birmingham. Sixty Klansmen were to meet the buses at the terminal. Hubert Page announced that Sergeant Cook was to leave for Anniston and Atlanta to verify the arrival time of the buses in Birmingham. According to Page, Connor promised that fifteen to twenty minutes would elapse before police officers arrived on the scene. During those fifteen to twenty minutes, the Klan could use its own discretion in teaching the Freedom Riders a lesson. If blacks entered the restroom in the depot, Connor said that the Klan should beat them, "make them look like a bulldog got hold of them," then remove the victims' clothing and leave them nude in the restroom. Anyone leaving the restroom nude would be arrested, Connor promised, and sent to the penitentiary. Furthermore, Connor himself would see to it that the Klansmen, if arrested, would be let off with light sentences.[62] The general attitude of the police toward the Freedom Riders was summed up by Cook in a conversation with Rowe a few days before the Freedom Riders arrived in Birmingham: "I don't give a damn if you beat them, bomb them, murder or kill them. I don't give a shit. I don't want them in Alabama when you're through with them."[63] The Klan's response to the police suggestions was nothing short of enthusiastic; as Shelton stated, "We'll give them one hell of a welcome they'll never forget."[64]

Gary Thomas Rowe and Tom Cook were assigned as liaison agents between the police force and the Klan. On May 14, when the Freedom Riders arrived in Birmingham, Rowe was in constant contact with Cook from a telephone booth near the Greyhound bus terminal. When Cook was informed that one of the Freedom Ride buses had been attacked outside of Anniston and was now destined for the Birmingham Trailways depot, Cook immediately notified Rowe who dashed over to the Klansmen at the Greyhound terminal and sent them on to Trailways.

When the bus arrived at the Trailways station, the Klansmen were ready. "I could see a mob lined up on the sidewalk only a few feet from the loading platform," recalled James Peck, a Freedom Rider wounded in Birmingham. "Most of them were young—in their twenties. Some were carrying ill-concealed iron bars. A few were older men. All had hate showing on their faces." As Peck and another Freedom Rider entered the white waiting room and approached the lunch counter, they were grabbed and pushed into an alleyway out of sight of onlookers in the waiting room. "Six of them started swinging at me with fists and pipes. . . . Within seconds I was unconscious on the ground."[65]

The assault continued for approximately fifteen minutes. By the time the police arrived, most of the Klansmen were gone. Rowe, who was still fighting, remembers that a police officer ran over to him and shouted, "Goddammit, goddammit, get out of there. Get 'em out of here. Your fifteen minutes are up and we're sending the crew."[66]

The public reaction to what was viewed as police inefficiency was immediate and severe. Nevertheless, no one suspected a conspiracy between the police and the KKK. Bull Connor was taken at his word when he responded: "It happened on a Sunday, Mother's Day, when we try to let off as many policemen as possible so they can spend the day at home with their families. We got the police to the bus station as quick as we possibly could."[67]

Gary Thomas Rowe remained in the Ku Klux Klan until 1965, when he surfaced in connection with the investigation of the Montgomery murder of civil rights worker Violet Liuzzo. The issue of police collaboration in the Trailways bus station incident was forgotten until 1975, when Rowe testified before Senator Frank Church's Senate Select Committee on Intelligence. The main issue before the Church Committee and the principal complaint of a lawsuit against the government focused on the fact that despite the fact that Rowe had notified the FBI of the impending violence weeks before the Mother's Day incident, the FBI took no effective action to avert the catastrophe. FBI officials justified their inaction on the grounds that the agency was charged not with law enforcement, but only with intelligence-collection functions. The proper FBI action, officials insisted, was to notify the appropriate local law-enforcement units of Klan plans and then step out of the picture. This the FBI did, but since the local law-enforcement agency was part of the conspiracy, the information served no purpose.*

There is no indication that the Ku Klux Klan ended its partnership with the Birmingham police before 1963, when Connor lost his job as police commissioner. Connor's legacy was a blatantly racist police force notorious for its aggressiveness in repelling protest and related abuses, as well as for its failure to curb a series of bombings, beginning in the fifties, directed at blacks and associated with a campaign of intimidation by white hate groups.[68] This jihad accelerated in 1963, when no fewer than five bombings directed at blacks shook Birmingham and terrorized its residents. The most destructive of the explosions occurred on September 15, 1963, when the 16th Street Baptist Church was dynamited, causing the deaths of four young black women. (Although many were convinced of their identities, the perpetrators of the first three bombings

---

* Government records disclosed, in the course of a lawsuit filed in 1978 by two Freedom Riders (Walter and Frances Bergman), that the FBI supplied information to the Birmingham Police Department and its Intelligence Unit on the Freedom Riders' planned activities on the date of their arrival, knowing that many members of the department belonged to the Klan and that the bureau's police contact, Tom Cook, was a Klan agent ("FBI Tracked Freedom Riders for Klan-Infested Alabama Police," *Detroit Free Press*, August 20, 1978; "FBI Knew Policeman Was Leak for Klan Freedom Riders," *Washington Post*, August 19, 1978). The supportive role of the FBI in the Klan attack is described in the court's opinion in *Peck v. United States*, 78 Civ. 983 (S.D.N.Y. 1983).

were never caught; the investigation of the fourth was bungled for more than a decade and finally resulted in the conviction of Robert E. Chambliss, a Klan leader.)[69]

The overwhelming evidence of white racist violence did not alter the bias and bigotry of the police. Instead, they preferred to view civil rights and white hate groups as equally deviant and, under the leadership of Lieutenant M. H. House and Detective Marcus Jones, subjected both to "intelligence" treatment. This bogus even-handedness was rooted in a surveillance program launched by Connor in the late fifties, in which mass meetings of the Alabama Christian Movement for Human Rights (ACMHR) were monitored by uniformed police and smaller organizational meetings by plainclothesmen.

During the sixties, police surveillance operations were increasingly intensified and directed at the ACMHR under Rev. Fred Shuttlesworth and Rev. Edward Gardner and at Martin Luther King, Jr., Hosea Williams, Ralph Abernathy, and the Southern Christian Leadership Conference (SCLC). Also targeted was the racist, anti-Semitic National States' Rights Party (NSRP) led by Dr. Edward Fields, J. B. Stoner, Jerry Dutton, Matt Murphy (a lawyer for the hate groups), and their associates. The police also monitored the Klan, the American Nazi Party, and the Student Nonviolent Coordinating Committee (SNCC), but concentrated on the ACMHR, SCLC, and NSRP. *Every* ACMHR and NSRP meeting held in Birmingham was attended by police intelligence officers for at least a decade. Civil rights meetings, typically held in churches, were regularly surveilled by teams of two white detectives—occasionally as many as four attended—equipped with a tape recorder; they made no effort to conceal their presence.

From the records now preserved in archives at the Birmingham Public Library—a treasure trove of documents accidentally discovered—we can measure the extent of police involvement in the civil rights movement. For example, a statistical sampling of reports on the ACMHR from 1963 to 1967 reveals that from May 8 to December 20, 1963, detectives covered fifty-two meetings (held in twelve churches) and produced seventy-five reports, of which twenty-three duplicated other reports on the same meetings. Comparable figures for the period from January 5 to December 29, 1965, show coverage of forty-three meetings yielding forty-four reports; in the period from January 3 to December 25, 1966, no fewer than eighty-two meetings were monitored and reported on; while in the 44-week period from January 3 to November 10, 1967, twenty-eight meetings were covered. These reports were filled out with explanatory and background material such as informers' reports, profiles of leading civil rights activists, photographs, and summaries of articles dealing with race problems in various publications.

Coverage extended not only to the ACMHR but also to such groups as the Birmingham Council on Civil Rights, the Birmingham Ministerial Alliance, and the SCLC. Nothing was too trivial to transmit. The racist mission of the surveillance is clearly demonstrated by the prominence given in the reports to "race mixing": the reports on all civil rights meetings invariably include racial tallies. Similarly, whites who were socially involved with blacks became ipso facto the subject of reports.*

A related concern that repeatedly erupts from the reports is a gossipy focus on sexual matters, fed by a fundamentalist version of Christian morality rooted in southern nativism and common in the Klan world. Thus, the reports gave great emphasis to rumors of interracial sex relations and of adultery and sexual kinkiness in white circles. Though the police never seem to have used this information for blackmail or disruptive purposes, the apparent assumption in the reports was that such material might provide useful police leverage in the future.

Innuendoes about sex-related activities crowd the reports. White women are often given descriptions such as "slender brunette," "sexy," "attractive," "good figure," "blonde hair." A memo on a reputed unnatural ménage à trois in the right-wing hierarchy[70] is followed by a report containing this item: "It is talked that Martin Luther King and Lena Horne have a real big affair going. Also, that King's wife, who has several children, is raising hell and threatening a divorce."[71] A 1968 report by a detective notes that one SDS woman's dress "was about four or five inches above her knees and she was the usual type that follows these student movements."[72] On one occasion we learn: "They seemed to be just having one big party, lying around on the floor naked, making love and drinking."[73] A police report notes that during a plane trip the lawyer for the NSRP, consistently characterized as sex-obsessed, did not

---

* For example, on April 28, 1964, an intelligence officer reported (the names of the subjects are deleted here): "We have information that [X] and his wife, who are white, of 1006 32 Street South, have been entertaining Negro company recently. I went next door to this address. . . . On the Sunday previous the neighbors, including the fellow named London, had attempted to take pictures of the Negroes and get the tag numbers. . . .

"On Sunday I contacted [Y] and told him that there were rumors in the neighborhood that [X] was entertaining Negroes and it was also rumored that he still worked for him. [Y] denied this stating that [X] had not worked for him since last summer. He was very upset and said he would go on television and radio and make a public statement that [X] did not work for him anymore."

read the book in his hand, "but watched the stewardess the whole time."[74]

The reports typically focus on the leadership of the target group and the quarrels dividing it—an emphasis perhaps rooted in the hope of gaining an informer recruit. For example, a report in January 1965 details a rumored conflict between Fred Shuttlesworth and Martin Luther King, Jr.: "Shuttlesworth claims that he has assembled the Alabama Christian Movement for Human Rights in Birmingham to put King on the road to fame and the Nobel Prize, and if there had not been a Birmingham, Alabama, there would have been no Nobel Prize for King."[75]

The surveillance of groups in meetings was supplemented by other forms of surveillance. The police regularly engaged in tailing subjects, following cars, watching houses and windows, talking to neighbors and friends of subjects, and photographing individuals and crowds. They listed the license plates and car owners of all those attending a dinner honoring a Presbyterian minister who was moving to a northern church.

For the full week of October 7 to October 14, 1963, the police conducted "surveillance and stakeouts" at the home of Rev. A. D. King (brother of Martin Luther King, Jr.) and at the headquarters of the National States' Rights Party. On October 14, detectives followed the car of a woman "dating" A. D. King, but "lost her at Center Street."[76] Rev. Fred Shuttlesworth was a high-priority surveillance target. For example, a memo tells that "our source of information called Shuttlesworth this morning" and then relates the details of the conversation.[77]

Birmingham police surveillance of civil rights leaders became so oppressive that they often found it preferable to try to live with the process and in this way to blunt its edge. When Ralph Abernathy arrived in Birmingham in June 1969, for example, he made several calls from the airport. One was to Detective Marcus Jones, Birmingham's top police intelligence operative, to inform Jones of his day's itinerary.[78] Surveillance at ACMHR meetings was taken for granted; as Rev. Edward Gardner made clear to the congregation at the weekly ACMHR meeting (at which Detective Jones was present): "We are watched over by God and City Hall. No matter what else is going on on Monday night, we have two detectives with us. Two inside and four outside. They are watching over us. When we holler, they better jump."[79]

At both ACMHR and NSRP meetings, the detectives and/or informers paid particular attention to attacks on the police or on the city government. Detective Marcus Jones, who preferred to write about himself in the third person, was generally the butt of the attacks on the Birmingham police force, and Jones seemed to enjoy repeating these attacks in his reports. At the ACMHR meeting of April 28, 1969, Jones reported: "There was much discussion of Detective Jones. . . . It was decided they would send the Chief a telegram and make demands about Detective Jones."[80]

At NSRP meetings, attacks were generally leveled at the city government under Mayor Albert Boutwell (1963–67). The police reported these attacks in detail and their files on the NSRP are filled with typical statements by the NSRP leader Edward Fields concerning the city government and the police department: "The Birmingham police department is controlled by Jews," "Eight, six, four, two, Albert Boutwell is a Jew," and so on.

Over time the intelligence unit became, in a sense, the guardian of the establishment. Planned demonstrations, internal disputes, and complaints against the city and police were known by the intelligence officers before the ACMHR or NSRP chose to announce them. As one ACMHR supporter complained in 1969, the ACMHR could not "pull a single surprise of which the Police Department [is] not aware."[81] On occasion, police surveillance in defense of the city government overlapped into the political sphere. When Richmond Flowers opened his campaign for mayor with the blessing of the local civil rights organizations in March 1966, the police were there counting the numbers of blacks present and transcribing his speech.[82] At a subsequent Flowers rally, federal civil rights functionaries attached to the Community Relations Service are reported by the detectives to have "been very outspoken against detectives being in the meeting."[83]

The grudging acceptance by ACMHR officials of police attendance at meetings* was occasionally revoked. While open police attendance at public meetings could be tolerated, leaders of the civil rights movement resented police use of informers or infiltrators attending meetings covertly.

On April 25, 1969, Detective Jones overstepped his bounds in the eyes of the civil rights leaders. In his own words:

> On Friday night, April 25, 1969, Detective Jones picked
> up Donald Kidd at his home near the airport. He went in
> the house and Donald's mother helped Detective Jones
> and Donald arrange a wireless mike under his arm and

* A detective's report of February 3, 1964, records an announcement at a mass meeting in a church that "everyone in the building was supposed to have Membership Cards but the Law."

under his shirt. Detective Jones gave Donald some mint drops and money to put in the collection plate. Detective Jones put Donald out at 8th Avenue and 15th Street. As Donald walked up the street Detective Jones saw a Negro man come out of the bushes. . . . this Negro man and one more came to where he was sitting and asked him if Detective Jones had brought him to the meeting, which he denied. . . . They searched him and found the wireless mike, which brought on lots of screams and lots of loud and hard talk. Hosea Williams took charge of the boy and after much questioning the boy told them part of the truth. . . . They carried the mike and placed it on the pulpit and then Hosea Williams preached Detective Jones a one-half hour sermon.[84]

The ACMHR was outraged. Its meetings were temporarily closed to the police. ACMHR leaders and workers also suspected that their headquarters and a church at which many ACMHR meetings were held were bugged.[85]

Detectives learned a great deal from inside sources about the internal workings and plans of both the civil rights groups and the hate network. In both worlds, committed individuals provided information—sometimes because of differences with the leadership, power rivalries, or simply the feeling that they had nothing to hide. In the case of black sources, one must conclude that in some cases Jones exploited their trust and innocence. The hunted unwittingly joined the hunters. One can also conclude that among black leaders, traumatized by fears of further bombings, Jones's reassurances of a protective mission were accepted without challenge—especially when the bid for "cooperation" was baited with morsels of information about what the rightists were up to. And some were pragmatically motivated: the Klan would not dare bomb a church while two whites were in attendance.* Whatever the motivation may have been, the reports establish that, in addition to conventional informers, Jones had "cooperative" sources—"informants" rather than "informers" (with its overtones of betrayal)†—in

---

* Like many such concerns, the fear of bombing became a matter for jest. At a meeting in August 1967, Lucinda Robey, an ACMHR vice president, told the audience "how lucky they were" to have the detectives present, saying, "At least if a bomb was put in the church, the detectives would go up with it." At an earlier meeting (June 28, 1967), she announced a scheduled committee meeting in her home and, again in jest, invited the police to attend, complaining that "the police used to come and flash their lights around."
† The betrayal of trust, the record shows, was by the police.

both camps who supplied material that could not have been obtained in any other way.

A compelling example is an unsigned, undated report, obviously from an insider, describing a meeting in the spring of 1968, prior to the Poor People's March, of Ralph Abernathy and Hosea Williams, leaders of the march, along with four of their followers and President Johnson. We are told what the petitioners wore, what was said (the "talk got off on a sour note" because the delegation was twenty minutes late), the rejected demand for a full cabinet meeting, what happened when the meeting ended, what the news media were told ("that they had never been treated as bad as the President of the United States just treated them"), an unsuccessful attempt to meet with the secretary of agriculture, and so on. The police source clearly appears to have been someone in Abernathy's delegation who furnished the information about the conference; the same source followed up the account of the conference with a description of meetings of the Birmingham Ministerial Alliance and the Southern Christian Leadership Conference that discussed the White House session.

Reliance was also placed on traditional planted informers. A campus network developed by Detective Jones and his superior, Lieutenant House, is described in a series of reports in 1963 dealing with the campus activity at Birmingham Southern College, then all-white, with a reputation for liberalism. In September of that year, "Detective M. A. Jones," in the language of a report, "contacted a young lady who is a senior at Birmingham Southern College" who informed him of the appearance on the campus of a former white student, expelled for his interracial activism, in the company of black youths. She was instructed to make further contact ("if she was not scared") and to report back. A few days later Jones met with his regular campus informer ("S") along with his recruit. "Carried both girls to dinner. They compared notes. Were pretty much informed on the same people." However, the recruit subsequently reported back that in view of the fact that the college president, Howard Phillips, had warned the students on pain of expulsion not to join an outlaw group such as SNCC, "she was scared to go to any more meetings unless there was some way" to get protection. No problem: on October 17, 1963, Jones met with President Phillips and gave him the names of students attempting to organize a "Student Non-Violent Unit" on campus and named faculty members who "might" be involved. Phillips, Jones reported,

> said he appreciated the Birmingham Police Department working with him and wanted our continued help.

> Talked to him [Phillips] about using a source of informa-
> tion from his campus and if he could take care of the
> party if she joined SNIC [SNCC] and went to the meet-
> ings. He said that he would take care of her . . . Presi-
> dent Phillips told Detective Jones he had informed these
> people to stay off his campus and that he would prose-
> cute any of them with the help of the police
> department.[86]

Subsequently, Jones talked to a college administrator and "gave him a report on information from informer on Southern campus. They have agreed to take care of this girl." What Jones did not mention, of course, was the fact that Phillips's cautionary speech threatening expulsion was made at the instigation of Jones himself.

The NSRP and its rivals were also ready targets of informers. The white hate sector was riddled with dissension, resulting in a bounteous supply of mavericks and factional elements. The prime informer source in monitoring the right was "J," who provided a stream of information both in reports and by telephone, including such felicities as the fact that two rightist leaders "have got new suits and clothes." In the spring of 1964, however, "J" was thrown out of the NSRP as an informer.

By the close of the sixties, it became evident that the existing modes of surveillance had to be supplemented by more covert tactics. This need became especially demanding as the focus of surveillance shifted from groups to the individual leaders. In this area, the ideal form of surveil-lance was eavesdropping, either through wiretaps or through bugging.

The record reveals that when Martin Luther King, Jr., was arrested in Birmingham in 1963, his telephone call to his wife, Coretta, was tapped. Also noteworthy is an unsigned 1967 police document dealing with a visit to the city that year of Vice President Hubert Humphrey, which stated that "just before the Vice-President left Birmingham, he took off privately to make several phone calls. We know that one of them was to Reverend [Edward] Gardner." This was followed by a summary of what the vice president said to Gardner.[87] In a number of instances, it is clear from the verbatim reproduction of conversations that some form of elec-tronic eavesdropping was the source of a report. In one instance a pri-vate conversation between Fred Shuttlesworth, then in Cincinnati, and Martin Luther King, Jr., in Atlanta is reported in considerable detail.[88]

The cutback on more overt modes of surveillance and the need to individuate coverage also resulted in the increased use of informants and casual "sources" within the groups surveilled.[89] For the same reason, the record reveals, the police resorted to letter opening.[90] Another useful source of information was the press. A "Memorandum" of December 4,

1963, by Detective Jones states that he and a *Birmingham News* reporter attempted to photograph two white girls attending the funeral of the four black girls killed in the bombing of the 16th Street Baptist Church. A *News* lawyer subsequently confirmed that the reporter had "cooperated" with city police, the sheriff's office, and the FBI while covering the civil rights movement. (Both mainstream newspapers in town, it should be noted, were largely unresponsive to the police abuses and the victims' complaints and confined their reaction to bewailing the tarnishing of the city's image.)[91] Similarly, police surveillance was fed from other sources: in the spring of 1963, when the demonstrators and the police were locked in bitter conflict, a call from Eastern Airlines at 2:00 A.M. reported that "a group of 10 Jewish rabbis and 35 black males had just unloaded from their New York flight."* Other sources were the Birmingham National Bank, the sheriff's department, and the FBI.[92]

All of the channels for collecting data—from the surveillance of meetings to third-party interviews—focused primarily, as the sixties progressed, on the train of outdoor expressions of protest: rallies, demonstrations, marches, vigils, and "indignation meetings" protesting police misconduct. Ultimately the prime justification for the vast surveillance program was, through advance knowledge, to intervene in, thwart, or dampen the seemingly unending demonstrations. When these tactics failed, water hoses, police dogs, indiscriminate arrests, and photography were used to intimidate the marchers.[93] The outdoor protest mode was viewed as threatening to the city's image, a perception that intensified the punitive police response, which, in turn, further damaged the city's image and, more important, brought sympathy and support both to the demonstrators as individuals and to their causes. By the late seventies, the gradual triumph of integration and the consequent power shifts in city government brought reform to the police department, including the phasing out of the intelligence unit.

New Haven: A Tangled Tale of Tapping

Throughout the sixties, the city of New Haven, under Mayor Richard C. Lee, enjoyed a national reputation for enlightened administration. It

* The rabbis' trip to Birmingham was frustrated by a delegation of local rabbis who met the travelers at the airport and successfully persuaded them to turn back on the grounds that their visit would simply aggravate the situation. This fear that protest would only add fuel to the flames was pervasive among the city's white moderates and resulted in widespread self-censorship. Such fear of an accelerated conflict was shared by a group of conservative blacks who similarly opposed protest against the racial status quo.

was regarded as a preeminent "Model City" in developing urban renewal plans and policies and indeed, received more urban-renewal funds per capita than any other city in the country. As mayor from 1953 to 1969, Lee was touted as a reformers' reformer. The mayor's police chief from 1968 to 1970 was James Ahern; it was during this period that an illegal wiretap operation targeting activities protected by the First Amendment came to full flower. As M. Mitchell Morse, the chief counsel to the New Haven Board of Police Commissioners, put it, "The number of people whose conversations have been intercepted is absolutely mind boggling."

The institutionalization of wiretapping as a form of intelligence-gathering in much larger cities than New Haven, with its relatively small population (about 126,000), was frequently impeded by problems of acquiring equipment and lack of technical know-how and operational expertise. But these difficulties in New Haven were overcome by James Ahern's brother Stephen, an ambitious young officer whose rise from the ranks of the New Haven Police Department was phenomenal. Although phones had been tapped by the New Haven police to a limited extent as early as 1943,[94] the story of wiretapping in that city really began in 1957 after Ahern learned the technology of telephone surveillance from Richard K. Sulman, a sophomore engineering student at Yale.[95] In the years 1966 to 1971 the operation was greatly expanded to include political targets and became the subject in 1977 of an exposé by investigative journalist Andrew Houlding published in the *New Haven Journal Courier*.

"Members of the New Haven Police Department tapped the telephones of more than one hundred New Haven residents in a major, secret and illegal wiretapping operation conducted between 1966 and May 1971, according to sources with personal knowledge of the intelligence-gathering operation." Thus began a series of articles by Houlding on the front page of the *Journal Courier* on the morning of January 24, 1977. Additional front-page reports followed on four consecutive days.[96] It was an exposé that, if true, placed New Haven in a leading position among American cities engaged in warrantless—hence illegal— wiretapping.* Houlding's articles charged that:

---

* Actually, warrantless wiretapping had been illegal both on federal and state levels for decades. But in 1968, climaxing a series of Supreme Court decisions striking down warrantless wiretapping and other forms of electronic eavesdropping as violative of the Fourth Amendment's ban on unreasonable searches and seizures, Congress enacted Title III of the Omnibus Crime Control and Safe Streets Act banning wiretapping and bugging by federal authorities except in

—Warrantless phone taps were installed and monitored by New Haven police on a fairly consistent basis starting in 1966. Lines tapped initially were those of suspected criminals—primarily gamblers—but during the "times of trouble" in the late sixties and early seventies, the focus shifted to political radicals, or those the police identified as radical. Conversations with attorneys were regularly monitored.

—At least one mayor during that period was reported to have known of the tapping, and two chiefs of police sanctioned the operations.

—The Southern New England Telephone Company, headquartered in New Haven, was implicated.

—Summaries of the taps, distributed to the police intelligence division, misleadingly identified the source of this information as "confidential informant." Often it was used to prepare search and arrest warrants—clearly illegal—which eventually contributed to convictions.

—Wiretapping provided the police with information about the people tapped as well as those with whom they conversed, their activities, personal lives, and whereabouts, emboldening some officers to resort to phone threats, obscene calls, harassment, and damage to their property.

—The wiretapping operation was well known to personnel both of the FBI and the Connecticut State Police Division of Intelligence. FBI agents were involved in various phases of the operation. A former director of the state police Intelligence Division frequently spent time in the wiretap room listening to tapped conversations.

---

certain carefully circumscribed areas. Moreover, permissible activity could not be undertaken without the explicit authority of a federal court, unless it involved a foreign security matter. This interdiction applied to state and local officers as well. Title III stated specifically that any state activity in this area would be permissible only if preceded by a state legislative grant of such authority. However, this authority could not be less restrictive than the standards established by the federal government. The Congress, in adopting this legislation, was determined not only to punish unjustifiable interception, disclosure, or use of wire communications; it sought to ban the manufacture, distribution, possession, or advertising of intercepting equipment. Thus the act provided criminal sanctions for possession or use of the machines: five years in jail, a $10,000 fine, or both. In addition, civil suits were authorized: if an individual proved his phone was tapped, he could collect $100 for each day tapped, or $1,000, whichever was greater, plus punitive damages and legal fees from the tap operator. As will be seen, this civil remedy played an important part in the New Haven story. Given this federal legislative authorization, and as a consequence of the New Haven wiretapping described here, Connecticut in 1971 enacted sections 54–41a through 54–42s of the general statutes, which are more restrictive than Title III. *Only* state police and prosecutors are permitted to initiate wiretaps. Local police are wholly barred from such practices.

Although journalists in other cities contributed to the airing of police misconduct, they typically developed and followed up disclosures already brought to light through other channels (in some cases as the result of litigation). But Houlding on his own dug up the basic elements of the New Haven wiretapping affair. Prior to the 1977 disclosures, Houlding had developed a reputation as an investigative reporter, attracting an assortment of whistle-blowers, mavericks, defectors, and guilt-ridden retirees willing to feed him information about matters that would otherwise never have become publicly known, and who trusted him to protect their identities.

The core facts reported by Houlding were corroborated under oath by the testimony of police officers in an investigative hearing, in courtroom documents, and in administrative proceedings. Prosecution was rendered moot, since the five-year statute of limitations had run out by the time the wiretapping program came to light. However, a civil suit against the city of New Haven and various police officers was begun in 1977.

The Board of Police Commissioners began an investigation a month after Houlding's exposé. From the middle of February through June of 1977, Special Counsel Mitchell Morse and his co-counsel conducted extensive investigations involving interviews with more than sixty-five individuals (some more than once), the taking of sworn statements, an audit and analysis of tapes related to the wiretapping, including scrutiny by fingerprint experts, a thorough review of pertinent police department documents, and use of a polygraph expert. Following this investigative activity, the board convened public hearings at which testimony was given about the wiretapping. According to the interim report of the board, the hearings "disclosed irrefuted [*sic*] evidence of a long-standing massive illegal wiretap operation conducted by the New Haven Police Department, during which many thousands of private telephone calls were monitored."[97]

Almost all witnesses who testified were members of the police force and had been involved in the wiretap operation. Corroborative testimony was presented that Stephen Ahern fathered the New Haven wiretapping operation from his apartment, beginning in the late fifties, with a machine that he himself had purchased. At that time, this activity, initially directed at gamblers, went on to include prostitutes and drug dealers, and then, in the late sixties, political activists and an assortment of students, professionals, and intellectuals. From 1964 on, Ahern had succeeded in acquiring more equipment (apparently with public funds illegally used for this purpose) and institutionalizing the tapping operation over the years by installing recorders in various locations at police headquarters.

The wiretap operation at police headquarters was at first conducted in a sergeant's closet, but was ultimately moved to a room specifically prepared with acoustical tile and closed to members of the force who were not privy to its operation. Logs were kept of phone calls tapped, detailing information considered essential for intelligence purposes. Inspector Nicholas Pastore testified that at the time in the late 1960s when Chief James Ahern won national acclaim as a "new breed" of liberal cop, he had, on more than one occasion, ordered the bugging of meetings of the police board through a wireless transmitter placed under the table in the police commissioners' conference room.*[98] Moreover, testimony revealed that the cell block phone in the police department used by individuals incarcerated there to contact their lawyers or arrange for bail was tapped.

Sergeant Walter P. Connor, assigned to monitoring the wiretapping equipment from April 1968 to the summer of 1969, testified that Chief James Ahern, who had visited the wiretap room after its removal from police headquarters to the fourth floor of an office building in downtown New Haven in 1969, told him that if a stranger came to the door, "throw the fucking machines out the window."

Although the criminal and civil sanctions of the Omnibus Crime Control Act of 1968 put teeth into its strictures against wiretapping, the New Haven police wiretappers were obviously not deterred. Some were quite unaware of the statutory ban; others perceived no danger in view of the collaboration by FBI agents in the wiretap operation.[99] Bureau agents had provided expertise in the installation of the equipment and supplied the tapes required for recording; three agents of the FBI had visited the wiretap room on numerous occasions, obtained information from the tap machines, and had access to a special phone number in the wiretap room they could call for information without needing to visit the premises. All doubts about the role of the FBI in wiretapping targets in the New Haven area were resolved when documents were released

---

* Former Chief James Ahern broke a six-month silence, hotly denied Pastore's testimony, and attacked the credibility of the lie-detector test passed by Pastore ("Ahern Says Pastore Lied, Questions Polygraph Value," *New Haven Register,* June 20, 1977). Ironically, Ahern had in 1974 attempted to introduce the results of a polygraph test on his behalf in an incident involving his conviction for disorderly conduct following an altercation outside a restaurant in Westport, Conn.

under the Freedom of Information Act establishing an eighteen-month pattern of FBI wiretapping,[100] which overlapped the longer span of the police operation.

The January 1977 newspaper exposé referred to the FBI role and led to a U.S. Department of Justice announcement that an inquiry had resulted in exoneration of FBI personnel. Michael A. Shaheen, Jr., head of the Department of Justice's Office of Professional Responsibility, responding to the Connecticut Civil Liberties Union's request for a federal investigation, first pointed out that the statute of limitations barred a criminal investigation. Further, the department "did conduct an administrative inquiry . . . into the allegation that FBI agents were aware that the New Haven Police Department was engaged in illegal wiretapping."[101] The agents denied any involvement and Justice intended to end the matter there. The police commissioner's counsel, with masterly understatement, said that he had "reason to believe" that the Justice Department's conclusion "may not be accurate."[102] But despite an announced reexamination of the charges, the department took no action.

The FBI's crusade against the Black Panther Party (BPP) in the late sixties is an oft-told tale: it included informer infiltration, physical surveillance, wiretapping, provocation, and, most important, an assortment of dirty tricks.[103] New Haven was a primary area of FBI surveillance because of the BPP's effectiveness and growth there, successes to which white liberal and radical students made substantial contributions. If the BPP enjoyed strong, supportive ties with the "gown," its relationship with the town was largely negative. Local residents, especially ethnic hard hats and small merchants whose perception of the academic community was already resentful, were enraged by the militance of student protesters and even more by their black ghetto counterparts.

In this context of fear and hostility, it is clear that not only the Panthers and their student allies, but all the city's white-collar, liberal sectors were welcome police targets, and that an operational alliance with the FBI was inevitable. At one point, the city's fear flashed into a panic. The fuel for this transformation was the murder of Alex Rackley, a BPP member, and the turmoil that ensued in the wake of the trial of the Panther suspects. At its threshold the Rackley affair provided confirmation for a phenomenon pervasive in the sixties: the failure of prevention-oriented surveillance (especially wiretapping) to achieve its claimed purpose.

A police tap had been placed on the phone of an apartment on Orchard Street in New Haven in 1969, where BPP members were holding Rackley, a New York member of the group accused of being a police agent. There he was apparently subjected to interrogation and torture by party members.[104] According to ex-Chief James F. Ahern's book, *Police in Trouble*,[105] "information" alerted the police that Rackley was being held in the Orchard Street apartment. Police occupants in several unmarked cars kept the apartment under surveillance. However, there was not enough information available, Ahern claims, to make an arrest. When he was alerted that there had been a sudden burst of agitated activity at the apartment, he dispatched more unmarked cars to the location. Before they could arrive, the Panther members had emerged, and, knowing they were being observed, writes Ahern, dispersed in four vehicles and left in different directions. "The radio was crowded with noise as our men sorted the cars out. Three were followed. In the confusion, the fourth slipped away." Unfortunately, it was the car that "slipped away" that held Rackley and those who were shortly thereafter to kill him in a rural area thirty miles north of New Haven.

Ahern made no reference in his book to the wiretap his men had placed on that apartment. An FBI memorandum, subsequently released under the Freedom of Information Act, shows that the bureau received information from the police taps on Panther headquarters during the time of Rackley's murder. What may never be known is whether, as some allege, both the FBI and New Haven police deliberately refrained from any attempt to stop the murder so that they might move to break a group considered highly threatening during the charged days of the late sixties. The police moved quickly, following discovery of the body the next day, and ultimately thirteen people were arrested. (Fatefully, Bobby Seale, national chairman of the Panther Party, had visited the apartment during the period in which Rackley was held there and was later charged with conspiracy to commit murder. In *Police in Trouble*, Ahern recalls being astonished that the state's attorney asked for Seale's indictment despite the apparent paucity of evidence.)

Thus began the unfolding of the drama of New Haven May Day, 1970. Some of the Panthers had been placed on trial for the murder of Rackley. As a result, a nationwide appeal went out to Panther friends to assemble on the New Haven Green across the street from the courthouse to demonstrate on their behalf. The combination of events—the alleged mistreatment of those on trial; May Day, historically the occasion for left protest, plus President Nixon's announcement of the bombings in Cambodia—gave promise of dire happenings. Yale President Kingman Brewster questioned whether the Panthers could get a fair trial. Vice President Spiro Agnew excoriated Brewster. Thousands of national guardsmen were dispatched to the New Haven area, and the New

Haven police force was buttressed by several hundred Connecticut state police. A few incidents occurred (the most serious of which was a bombing at the Yale Ingalls Skating Rink; Chief Ahern conjectures that the perpetrators could have been either pro- or anti-Panther),[106] but the weekend passed and the city survived.

In *Police in Trouble*, Ahern deplores the panicky response on both federal and state levels to the planned demonstration. He particularly criticizes the overreaction of the federal government, insisting that he had carefully reviewed the scene and judged the nature of the threats so accurately that he succeeded in preventing any undue violence without provocation. What was not known at the time, however, was that his brother Stephen Ahern and his men were constantly listening to phone conversations about the plans of the May Day organizers. These made it clear that these organizers would make every effort to stage a nonviolent demonstration. It is safe to conclude, therefore, that the determination by the Panther organizers to keep the rally nonviolent, plus the restraint of the New Haven police (who were privy to this knowledge) in avoiding provocation, resulted in the entirely peaceful gathering on the New Haven Green over the May Day weekend of 1970.

Indeed, the surprisingly peaceful character of the demonstration catapulted James Ahern to a position of national prominence—a consequence reminiscent of the Arthur Woods experience in New York City in 1914 (see pp. 30–31). Appointed to the Presidential Commission on Campus Unrest, as well as to the Democratic Party's National Policy Council, he was hosted as a celebrity, appeared on a television program along with Yale President Kingman Brewster, and even lectured to the local ACLU branch on the evils of wiretapping.

Of those convicted for the Rackley murder, Lonnie McLucas received a twelve- to fifteen-year sentence on conspiracy charges. He had served four years and three months of this sentence when he was released on bail after the filing of a series of appeals by his lawyers, Theodore and Michael Koskoff, of Bridgeport, Connecticut, directed at overturning his original conviction. All others convicted had been released by this time.

The Koskoffs had exhausted all avenues of appeal on behalf of their client—that is, until evidence about illegal wiretapping by the New Haven police pointed to interception of conversations between the Koskoffs and McLucas. Subsequently, the state supreme court released McLucas on bail again, pending a hearing on whether the police wiretapping had tainted his trial.[107]

There was no evidence that State's Attorney Arnold Markle knew of the wiretapping. Clearly, however, enough solid evidence had been presented that policemen with whom he had regular contact were wiretapping Panther phones and securing information that had to be passed on to Markle. Whatever the precise reason, Markle's assistant went before the Connecticut sentence review board in February 1978, did a complete about-face, and recommended that "justice will be served if McLucas' sentence is reduced to time served."[108]

The wiretapping of the Panthers did not end with the 1970 Panther trial, but continued under Police Chief Biagio DiLieto, appointed in 1971 to succeed the retiring James Ahern. The force reportedly was unhappy with his elevation. A period of unease set in, particularly for Stephen Ahern, who remained as chief inspector. In a sense, the "outs" were "in," and those formerly "in" were beset by fears that their illegal wiretapping activities would be brought to light.

The wiretap operation initially ceased when DiLieto became chief, though nothing was done or said about past transgressions. However, when a Panther demonstration was planned in early 1971, focused on the separate trials of the Panther leader Bobby Seale and Ericka Huggins, Ahern and his followers appealed to Chief DiLieto to tap the Panthers. Although DiLieto acquiesced for a period, Deputy Vincent DeRosa later testified that, following Chief DiLieto's decision to permit renewal of the tapping, DiLieto sought advice about a purported threat from Stephen Ahern to disclose the new chief's involvement in this illegal business and ultimately responded to urgings that he dispose of the equipment.[109]

Sergeant Francis R. DeGrand testified that DiLieto asked him secretly to destroy three wiretapping machines. DeGrand and an associate, in the dark of night, carried the machines from the chief's office out to the trunk of a rented car and took them to the basement of DeGrand's home, where he rendered them inoperable with a hammer.[110]

In view of these disclosures, many residents demanded that Mayor Frank Logue dismiss DiLieto. Logue's reluctance was attributed to political caution. New Haven is a strongly ethnic city; two major groups in competition for political power were the Irish and Italians. Mayor Logue, Irish, had, as a reform candidate, replaced an Italian mayor in 1975 and, more important, ousted the Italian Democratic Party boss. Undaunted, the Italian politicos were intent on regaining power; their mayoral choice appeared more and more to be Biagio DiLieto.

The charges against DiLieto were not easy to refute, though he attempted to do so—in the press and in self-serving *ex parte* statements,*

---

* DiLieto had made statements to the investigators and appeared before the commission prepared to testify, but reneged when he was denied an opportunity

but not under oath and subject to cross-examination at the board's public hearing. DiLieto ultimately resigned his position a few months later, in June 1977, in an effort to shield himself from board sanctions, and shortly thereafter began an active campaign for the Democratic nomination for mayor (the only viable one in New Haven), challenging incumbent Logue.[111]

By this time, DiLieto had become a hero among his supporters and followers. Had not Benny (his nickname) DiLieto successfully protected us from those dangerous radicals, and black radicals at that? DiLieto assumed the role of a savior preventing the city's destruction by these bestial elements. And how could one be critical of the tapping of gamblers, pimps, and so on? Besides, if those overheard were innocent of wrongdoing, why should they complain? As DiLieto pursued his campaign, his stance on wiretapping shifted from disavowal until he was claiming—jaw thrust forward in pugnacious political challenge—that if the community were similarly threatened in the future, he would wiretap again.[112]

DiLieto lost a primary challenge to Mayor Logue in September 1977 by only 243 votes out of a total of 22,000. Though defeated, he was now the knight *sans peur et sans reproche*, intransigent, refusing even to support Logue, his party's nominee in the election. He had nowhere to go but up, and he knew it. Two years later, in November 1979, he was elected overwhelmingly as New Haven's mayor, having decisively defeated Frank Logue in that September's primary. Indeed, his involvement in the wiretap mess may have eased his path to the mayor's office.

An interim report by the police commissioners issued in January 1978 confirmed massive misconduct by police personnel and identified several of the culprits. (Those still members of the force ultimately received official reprimands.) The report made a series of recommendations designed to prevent a recurrence of the practices under investigation.*

---

to read a prepared statement. The reasonableness of this request, frequently granted in investigative hearings, seemed to some to confirm DiLieto's charge that the panel was biased.
* The board recommended that the department (1) revamp training programs to stress better knowledge of laws relating to police work, including wiretap laws; (2) establish guidelines for cooperation with other law enforcement agencies; (3) implement a study by the board of all the ramifications of police intelligence-gathering activity, with the goal of spelling out procedures; (4) reexamine the structure and operation of the Internal Affairs Division, which had been charged with investigating improper police conduct and had obviously failed in its responsibility; (5) revise rules and procedures to ensure that (a) officers did not

The board investigation was one of the few instances in which an official urban body undertook a public probe of massive misconduct by a police department. But it was criticized on a number of grounds, such as its failure to probe dirty tricks connected with the tapping. "Tail teams" had been set up to use information about the comings and goings of the tap targets. These teams went beyond the scope of surveillance duties and threatened and harassed political activists. Several tap victims charged that they had received threatening phone calls and, in some cases, been pelted with a variety of obscene epithets. An activist house-wife claimed that sugar had been dumped in the gas tank of her car and its tires slashed at locations where, in all likelihood, the culprit(s) had to have monitored her movements. (*Journal Courier* reporter Houlding re-called the following incident reported to him by a police officer: the lat-ter was tapping a phone when he heard a loud noise, which brought an abrupt halt to the conversation; the explanation became clear to him later that evening when fellow officers returned to the police station and gleefully recounted that they had fired a shotgun blast into the living-room window of the wiretapped subject's home.)

Those familiar with the inquiry also claimed that the board deliber-ately curtailed the scope of its inquiry in other ways. For example, In-spector Nicholas Pastore, according to these sources, was prepared to testify at much greater length at the hearings and offered to do so if the commission wanted to ask more questions. This was not done, assertedly because, first, Mayor Logue was interested primarily in damaging DiLi-eto's reputation, and, secondly, the commission members were concerned that the exposure of too much malfeasance could be too costly—in ac-tual dollars—for the city of New Haven.

The board was also faulted for its lackadaisical response to the resis-tance to subpoenas of key figures (DiLieto, the Aherns, and FBI agents). Here, too, it would appear that the board's failure to compel testimony of recalcitrant witnesses was based on the fear of providing support and documentation for a damage suit that might drain the city's treasury.

An extraordinary civil suit seeking damages in a federal court under the 1968 statute referred to above soon picked up some of the slack in the board's investigation.[113] While civil actions for damages for police

---

blindly obey unclear orders from above, (b) a report of corruption or unlawful conduct was obligatory, (c) statements about malfeasance were made under oath, and (d) a procedure was established to permit reports to an ombudsman or to the board about alleged unlawful order; and, finally, (6) involve the board itself more fully in operational and policy matters.

misconduct were hardly unique in the seventies, this lawsuit stands out: the core of the complaint was not garden-variety surveillance, but wiretapping, a practice condemned by federal statute as well as by the Constitution. Further, it charged not merely passive eavesdropping but dirty tricks facilitated by the eavesdropping. But perhaps most important was its enormous scope: from an initial roster of 52 plaintiffs who claimed (and were ultimately awarded) damages, the suit ballooned to over 1,200 plaintiffs, and this figure refers only to those who joined the suit, not the total number of individuals victimized by the illegal taps (estimated at more than 3,600). The number of telephone calls monitored was estimated to have been at least 10,000.

Police wiretapping of political subjects in the sixties and seventies was typically directed at the office or headquarters of an organization, rarely at individuals. Such eavesdropping yielded information about the group, its members, activities, and plans, which was commonly used to support or supplement the work of police infiltrators or informers. In New Haven, organizational targets with offices and telephones were quite rare. As a result, the tapping of individuals became institutionalized.

The defendants in the New Haven suit included the Ahern brothers, Mayor DiLieto, ex-Mayor Lee, four FBI agents, several police officers, the city of New Haven, and the Southern New England Telephone Company. The principal attorney for the plaintiffs was John Williams, a feisty criminal lawyer in New Haven with a record of successfully redressing police abuse on behalf of victims.*

Williams's civil action was plagued by conflicts and contradictions involving both the FBI and the city of New Haven. For example, the New Haven corporation counsel filed papers in court on behalf of the police officers charged with illegal wiretapping, denying that they had wiretapped anyone—despite public admissions under oath by some of these same officers. Thus the Police Commission, an agent of the city, collected the incriminating evidence while the corporation counsel, another agent of the city, fought to prevent its disclosure in the civil lawsuit. Understandably, the Logue administration's stance was primarily moti-

---

* At the time the suit was commenced in May 1977, Williams had devoted a third of his practice to litigation against police misconduct and brought well over a hundred cases. Roughly a third of these had been successful, well above the 10 percent national average. A board attorney stated in an interview that more than one police officer confided to him that all that held them back from more harassment of New Haven citizens was the knowledge of John Williams's presence and the fact that he would be likely to sue them. Recognition of Williams's efforts grew: he has taught the techniques of litigation against police officers at the Yale Law School as well as in seminars in Connecticut and for practicing attorneys.

vated by a desire to minimize the potentially staggering money damages that could be assessed against the city on behalf of the aggrieved parties.

There were two major issues to be resolved following the filing of the civil lawsuit: (1) how to make known to potential plaintiffs that their phones and/or conversations had been illegally and secretly tapped, and (2) how to obtain the evidence in the form of wiretap records held by the Board of Police Commissioners. As noted above, the city of New Haven fought yielding any of this information, arguing that the privacy of those individuals should be protected.

Federal Judge Jon Newman ruled in July 1978 that the named plaintiffs should receive these records, but denied Attorney Williams's request to notify others who were unaware that they had been tapped. The resolution of the problem of publicizing the names of potential plaintiffs from police records of overheard conversations resulted in a conflict between the defenders of the right of privacy and those who insisted that disclosure should prevail. The Civil Liberties Union adopted the view that this information, while permitting victims to learn that their rights had been violated and thus to sue if desired, would invade privacy and should therefore not be divulged. The city of New Haven also took this position, not on privacy grounds, but in order to limit its potential liability. Attorney Williams argued that ethical considerations, state laws, and court decisions tilted the balance in favor of disclosure. The commissioners, who were opposed to public disclosure, fought a ruling releasing the disputed data by the Connecticut Freedom of Information Commission. The dilemma was ultimately resolved by notifying those listed on police index cards, who could then obtain the relevant file documents, including logs of wiretapped conversations.[114]

In April 1981, two days before the state legislature's Judiciary Committee was scheduled to deal with a bill banning political surveillance by law-enforcement officers, the press identified several prominent citizens overheard on the police taps, including Joseph Lieberman, formerly majority leader of the state senate, elected in 1988 to the U.S. Senate; State Treasurer Henry Parker and his wife; a New Haven police commissioner; an assistant state's attorney; and the distinguished Yale professors Vincent Scully and R. W. B. Lewis. In spite of these disclosures, the Judiciary Committee refused to submit the surveillance measure for a vote by the full committee.

The May 13, 1981, issue of the *New Haven Advocate*, then edited by Andrew Houlding, was devoted almost entirely to the New Haven scandal ("THE WIRETAPPED CITY" the caption ran). The lead story listed, from "confidential sources," more than three hundred individuals directly identified with tapped phones and, in a separate story, so that it would not be possible to identify those referred to, aired items taken from index cards compiled by the tappers. The reproduced data nowhere provided a hint or clue that the subjects tapped for political purposes—as opposed to narcotics and gambling—were involved in activity threatening to any interest even remotely related to police concerns. The items reproduced included the following:

"Subject is a liberal Prof. at Yale and lives with —————   . . . "

"————— is separated from his wife. . . . Mrs. ————— is slightly disturbed mentally. Has a daughter and son named ————— and —————.
————— is a religious nut. Mr. ————— left Mrs. after 25 years of marriage and this has affected her mentally. Is lonely and insom."

"Does photo. work. Is involved in every subversive group in the city. Was head marshall for the May Day Rally."

"————— (daughter of above subj.) stayed at 520 Chapel St. on 3-28-29, 70."

"Girlfriend of ————— . Had relations with her on 4-5-70 at approx. 12:00 P.M. Has a jealous husband whom she fears. Also has a couple of children."

"Indication is that ————— has relations with this female on occasion. More than likely pays for it."

"Member of the Associated Press. Has been known to contact ————— . Also took a comment statement from him on 9-27-70, on the the report of the Presidents commission on Campus unrest. See phone index and first name index."

"BBP Attorney. Presently defending against A—————."

"This subject is friendly with ————— . (NHPD)* Worked to organize the Yale strike in support of Bobby Seale and other BPP."

"Subj. is an Attny and is assoc with BPP and ————— group. Is the New Haven Attny. for Bobby Seale. Office is at 865 Chapel St. Tele: 777–5752."

"————— is a folk guitarist. Participates in many left wing and radical affairs such as the Huey Newton Rally on the Green. Is scheduled to make an appearance at Hillhouse on 10-15 for the Teach-In. See first name index."

---

* A file reference, not to the New Haven Police Department but to the New Haven Panther Defense Committee. Among other file entry abbreviations, "W" by a name stands for "white," "C" for "colored." The "PH" after some names evidently indicates that the spelling of the name is a phonetic rendering and not necessarily accurate. The frequent use of abbreviations is sometimes practiced by intelligence units to limit access to files.

"Acquaintance of ———— . Subj. is Chaplain at Dwight College Yale. Offered ———— to appear at a board meeting to solicit funds for N.H.P.D. The Board has contributed funds to Seale Defense Fund."

In support of a motion for "class action" certification permitting similarly situated individuals to join the suit as plaintiffs, Attorney Williams, in January 1983, filed a list of some three thousand individuals victimized by the wiretap operations. In addition to the prominent figures already mentioned, the list included nine lawyers, several physicians, journalists, clergymen, and Yale faculty members. Among those listed as potential plaintiffs were Rev. William Sloane Coffin, a Yale University chaplain during the 1960s and 1970s; the former Black Panther leaders Huey Newton and Eldridge Cleaver; the defense lawyer William Kunstler; Dr. Benjamin Spock; and activists Tom Hayden and John Froines. The list also included the Associated Press, the *Hartford Courant*, the Bridgeport radio station WNAB, and the Yale radio station WYBC.

In 1983 the suit was granted "class action" certification and the total number of aggrieved individuals who joined the suit ballooned to 1,238 out of a total of 3,000 identified victims. The city agreed to settle the claims of the plaintiffs for a total of $1.75 million.[115] Individual plaintiffs were awarded damages ranging from $1,000 to $6,000. In 1983 the Southern New England Telephone Company settled with a payment of $150,000, while at the same time denying any wrongdoing.

The fact that the final settlement included the withdrawal of charges against then Mayor DiLieto produced its share of irony and, in some circles, bitterness. Attorney John Williams had, in a 1983 speech, quoted DiLieto's vow to a federal judge, "I will never settle this case. I don't care how much it costs taxpayers." Pasquale Carrieri, a retired police sergeant, complained: "I think it's very unfair that we came out bearing responsibility for what occurred and he [DiLieto] came out bearing no responsibility." The lawyer for the Aherns was outraged that his clients were excluded from the settlement while DiLieto was dropped as a defendant altogether.* But the city's corporation counsel responded that the Aherns "were the chief architects and organizers of the wiretaps . . . and the only officials of the city of New Haven who refused to testify in the 1977 Commission hearings."[116] (The latter claim seems questionable in view of DiLieto's stonewalling.)

The most striking commentary on the New Haven police story—and one that raised eyebrows among those involved—was not the 1984 court

---

* The Aherns settled in 1984 for $35,000.

settlement, but the observation back in 1971 of a born-again James Ahern at a Princeton University conference on the FBI. In describing his city's intelligence operations, its former police chief recalled:

> We collected very little political data; we were not interested in it. Local police departments don't have the sophistication to gather political information and they wouldn't know what to do with it if they got it. If they pass it on, it's generally useless. Anybody who would listen to their ideas about who's politically dangerous would have to be crazier than they are most of the time.[117]

Throughout the furor generated by the 1977 exposé and investigation, the university authorities—an important component of the city's establishment—remained silent, despite the disclosure of extensive wiretapping of faculty members and student activists over a three-year period. During the earlier mayoralty term of Richard Lee, the university's voice was heard in public discussions of civic issues, especially those dealing with curbs on protest. But by the late seventies it shunned such involvement—perhaps a reflection of an altered climate.

Although the Yale campus police were "sworn personnel" attached to the New Haven force, they apparently played a minor role in the wiretapping affair. (A campus police officer did introduce Stephen Ahern to the Yale student Richard Sulman, his first source in his wiretapping career.) However, the campus component worked closely with the FBI, especially in the selection of campus surveillance targets and recruitment of potential informers. But in other city and town sites of colleges and universities, the campus police, typically autonomous, worked closely with local and state police units.

The District of Columbia: Keeping Demonstrators at Bay

The surveillance that flourished in the District of Columbia from the late sixties to the mid seventies was rooted in police responsibility for keeping order at the torrent of rallies and demonstrations that flooded the capital. Local demonstrations and outdoor meetings of residents were usually monitored by the police, uniformed or plainclothes, from the periphery of the assemblage. When the decision was made for muscle-flexing, a police van marked "Identification Division," mounted with a mugging camera, was driven close by. A three-man crew then photographed individual and group targets while the speaker addressed the audience.

By the end of the sixties, the city had become the nation's outstanding theater of protest—increasingly focusing on the Vietnam War.[118] In the face of this challenging surge, the police moved from the use of surveillance to prevent violence and disorder to aggressive surveillance and disruption as ends in themselves, quite unrelated to any peacekeeping function. Moreover, by the early seventies, the maintenance of order had ceased to be the primary police mission. In a familiar progression, the prime responsibility claimed by the police became the security of the nation itself against subversive plotters. Thus whereas in 1968 the total departmental budget for "subversive intelligence" was $2,100, by 1972 expenditure in this respect had increased more than thirty-three times to $70,500.[119]

It would be hard to find a police surveillance operation with a comparably vague and extensive range of coverage of political targets. As the record of a 1976 lawsuit (*Hobson et al. v. Wilson et al.*)* reveals in testimony by former Police Inspector Thomas J. Herlihy, responsible head of the Intelligence Division, the surveillance program was conducted without guidelines of any kind; the range of targets was extraordinary. As Herlihy further testified, all dissident activities involving public issues were considered a proper subject of police interest: "I just can't say what we weren't interested in."[120] Another functionary, Captain George R. Suter, head of the security information unit from May 1968 to December 1970, insisted that any organization opposed to the Vietnam War was "subversive" and a threat to the government.[121] These elastic standards resulted in targeting for surveillance of peaceful organizations with a commitment to nonviolence and no record of past violence. The organizations surveilled by the police and the FBI included a wide range of groups, such as the Washington Area Peace Action Committee (WAPAC), New Mobe, Vietnam Moratorium Committee (VMC), Emergency Committee on the Transportation Crisis (ECTC), Black United Front, and People's Coalition for Peace and Justice (PCPJ). In justifying its program of infiltrating such groups not remotely suspected of violence, the defendants in the *Hobson* case resorted to now-familiar justifications: first, that involvement in nonviolent activities provided a "cover" for informers to sniff out violence-prone trouble-

---

* The *Hobson* lawsuit was brought by eight individuals, all active in antiwar and other issues during the late sixties and early seventies. In addition, two organizations, the Washington Peace Center (a group affiliated with the Society of Friends) and the Women's Strike for Peace (another peace organization), were also plaintiffs. The defendants in the *Hobson* case included both District of Columbia and FBI officials considered responsible for the activities challenged. The *Hobson* trial record is a key source: in 1974 the Intelligence Division of the Metropolitan Police Department shredded all of its political surveillance files.

makers and, second, that the surveillance was intended as protection for the demonstrators.

The Metropolitan Police Department (MPD), through its Intelligence Division, conducted surveillance operations against dissidents in close partnership with the FBI—both its Washington Field Office and its national headquarters' desks. Unquestionably the deployment of informers was the form of surveillance most favored both by the police and the FBI. Indeed, on occasion, informers were jointly sponsored by both agencies. The Intelligence Division, which is our primary concern here, instructed its informers to seek positions of leadership and control and—as will be seen—from these positions of trust, aggressively to try to sabotage the aims of their targets, such as plans and preparations for orderly demonstrations.

The use of sworn personnel as informers and for related duties was routine. Members of the police department were enrolled, at the city's expense, at the American University, Howard University, George Washington University, and Federal City College. These officers were assigned to identify campus leaders, attend meetings and rallies, collect information, and file reports with the director of the Intelligence Division. [122]

Among other targets, police agents were dispatched to surveil the Institute for Policy Studies (a left-wing think tank), a rock concert, a supermarket picket line, and speeches by public officials. While his wife spied on Tina Hobson, the wife of activist Councilman Julius Hobson, James Binsted, an admitted undercover agent with the MPD, trailed such leftist leaders as Rennie Davis, Tom Hayden, Jane Fonda, and Abbie Hoffman around Washington. A second agent stole a target's mail, while a third rifled IPS garbage cans for clues to subversive activities and a fourth, a Mexican-American posing as an Apache, infiltrated the American Indian Movement. [123]

An undercover officer, Harold Bynum, was assigned to infiltrate ECTC, an antifreeway group led by *Hobson* plaintiffs Reginald Booker and Sammie A. Abbott. Bynum became Booker's constant companion and would drive him to speaking engagements, including events out of town,* even though other MPD informers were assigned to monitor the same gatherings. [124]

---

* On one occasion when Booker was scheduled to speak against urban freeways as a guest of a local citizen's group in Toledo, Ohio, he was closely questioned about his visit by the local police. Bynum had preceded Booker to Toledo—a bit of zealotry quite inconsistent with the claim that the surveillance was conducted solely for the purpose of planning for demonstrations within the city.

At an ECTC demonstration planned by Abbott and Booker, an especially vociferous "demonstrator" urged the crowd of over a thousand to disregard instructions given by Abbott, whom he called a "coward and sell-out artist," and to march instead to an off-limits area where police were waiting to tear gas them. Abbott later learned the "demonstrator" was Jan Francis, an agent of the Metropolitan Police.[125] Another D.C. agent was Detective Tom Okeson who, among others, infiltrated the Washington Peace Council (WPC)* and copied private addresses from its file cards for his superiors.[126]

Both passive and disruptive surveillance modes were facilitated by the fact that almost all of the peace targets (VMC, New Mobe, and PCPJ) operated from offices in the same building, 1029 Vermont Avenue. These offices were riddled with informers of all kinds—MPD, FBI, and CIA. On the eve of a major demonstration, the MPD informers were instructed to "smash all [the Vermont Avenue office] duplicating equipment . . . to go ahead and bash it up," with the result that the machine, shared by several peace groups, became inoperable.[127]

At about the same time, an Intelligence Division supervisor instructed one of his informers at 1029 Vermont Avenue, Charles Marcum, to break into a peace group's office at night and take a metal strongbox in which the police hoped to find documents indicating the source of funding for the peace movement. The contents of the box, some stock certificates, were photographed and then turned over to the FBI.[128] This was standard operating procedure: informers were permitted or encouraged by their control agents to steal private membership lists, mailing lists, mail, "everything we could get our hands on . . . and turn it over to the office," provided they could do so "without being caught."[129]

Several paid MPD informers achieved considerable prominence. The most spectacular of them was Earl Robert Merritt, who fled to Washington in 1968 after writing several bad checks in his West Virginia hometown, and subsequently was recruited as an informer by Intelligence Division Sergeant Christopher Scrapper.[130] Desperate for spy hands to cover an upcoming series of rallies scheduled for a period from April 24

---

* The WPC was charged with the training of marshals for major demonstrations and worked closely with the New Mobe, PCPJ, and WAPAC. The fact that it was responsible for training individuals to keep order did not spare it either from surveillance or from a burglary in July 1973, which focused on mailing lists and spurned items of monetary value. This disruptive attack on the WPC is explained by the importance of its role in providing housing information for out-of-town demonstrators.

to May 5 (May Day) organized by the New Left and a range of peace groups, Scrapper offered Merritt fifty dollars a week plus expenses to provide confirmation about May Day, its sponsors and supporters. After accepting the offer, Merritt was informed by Scrapper that the May Day rally was part of a communist plot that would be exposed by obtaining floor plans of the offices at 1029 Vermont Avenue; the names and telephone numbers of the occupants; the dates, times, and locations of all meetings; and copies of the publications of sponsoring organizations. Scrapper further instructed Merritt to do whatever he "felt was necessary even if it meant bending the law to do so." Merritt was not given a gun, but told he should hide a large hatpin in his sleeve or jacket collar. If attacked, he could then puncture his attacker's chest or throat with the pin.

On April 23, the day before the first of the May Day demonstrations, Merritt cut the wires of the sound system—his first act of sabotage. He was further assigned to give out false information in the streets—wrong directions to rally sites, the wrong place or time for an action—in short, to confuse the action in the streets. His control also directed him to infiltrate the "Pig Patrol" (a group that attempted to identify, shadow, and photograph undercover agents operating in the area).

Merritt collected information relating to planned demonstrations at the Democratic and Republican conventions in Miami, and since he was homosexual he was also assigned to spy on the gay community and cultivate radicals believed to be homosexuals. In June 1972, shortly after the Watergate break-in, MPD officers tried to induce Merritt to "get close" to the lawyer for the Watergate burglars, a rumored homosexual "associated with Communist causes" and to develop a sexual relationship with him.

After Merritt surfaced in the fall of 1972, he gave extraordinarily detailed accounts of his four-year career as a spy based on files he had kept. According to Merritt, the range of surveilled targets included the American Civil Liberties Union, the D.C. Statehood Party, Common Cause, the Gay Activists Alliance, *Off Our Backs* (a monthly feminist magazine), the Catholic Peace Fellowship, the American Friends Service Committee, the Tenants' Rights Workshop, and the Middle East Resource and Information Project. In addition to the disruptive activities already mentioned, Merritt admitted involvement in delivering mail stolen from the Institute for Policy Studies to the MPD and the FBI; being trained by a D.C. policeman to forge a draft card (in violation of federal statutes); and breaking into the Community Bookshop at the behest of the police to steal petitions.

Another highly prized MPD informer was Ann Kolego-Markovich ("Crazy Annie"), who was recruited in 1969 while she was a student at George Washington University.[131] During her three years undercover— she surfaced in the fall of 1973—she entrenched herself, despite her seeming flightiness,* in peace groups such as the PCPJ, the Anti-War Union, an anti-Nixon campaign, and the Miami Convention Coalition. Throughout this entire period she worked and lived with antiwar activists. She rendered a particularly valuable service in reporting on the plans of antiwar activists developed during meetings at an apartment rented by Kolego-Markovich for $200 a month and paid for by the police. The apartment was also bugged.

Annie showed up at the 1972 Republican Convention in Miami where, by a revealing coincidence, the Intelligence Division's Sergeant Christopher Scrapper—Annie's control for three years—was posted "on leave" to the Dade County, Florida, police to help in handling demonstrators. In the thick of the D.C. contingent, she was arrested several times on flimsy charges (such as "loitering")—a circumstance resulting from Scrapper's need to debrief her and at the same time improve her cover. When the convention protesters returned home, they found that the apartment and office of a prominent activist had been burglarized and ransacked. The sole loot was political material.

After she surfaced, her betrayed friends realized that there was a method in Kolego-Markovich's seeming madness. She had committed violence and urged others to do so, not out of craziness, but to provoke violence by others. In this spirit also, she disrupted an otherwise peaceful demonstration at the Capitol in 1971 by taunting police and hurling tear-gas canisters at them.

George Washington University also provided a second spy, Jody Gorran, a student with a flair for commercial enterprise. When Gorran appeared on the campus, he had acquired a franchise for the sale of tear-gas canisters for use in controlling demonstrators. Warned by the Secret Service against selling his product to student dissidents, he approached the FBI to prove his antiradical qualifications and became a bureau spy in the Students for a Democratic Society. Not only would such a relationship prove his qualifications, but he would receive fifteen dollars a report into the bargain. Gorran came through until a cutback in agents led to his transfer to the MPD, which put him on a $60 weekly retainer. In May 1969, fed up with the contrast between the creepy assumptions

---

* According to a high-ranking MPD official, "Her cover was to act a little goofy" ("FBI Acted to Disrupt Left," *Washington Post*, March 29, 1975).

of his MPD control and the placid reality, Gorran shed his cloak and dagger, publicly admitting (no, regretting) his spy role.*

By virtue of its mission to gather information about "persons, groups and organizations whose activities might be detrimental to the proper functioning" of the federal government and the ancillary responsibility to maintain "intelligence liaison with other governmental agencies and organizations," the MPD's Intelligence Division developed close ties not only with the FBI, but with the Army, Secret Service, Treasury Department, Justice Department, and CIA.[132] These linkages did not apply merely to information exchange, but included a shared use of informers and duplication of informer operations. Thus, CIA informers infiltrated such MPD targets as the WSP, WPC, SNCC, CORE, and Mobe. But the CIA's most important contribution to the surveillance program was in the area of electronic eavesdropping.

In 1964, the then police chief, Robert V. Murray, asserted in a police department general order: "Since assuming office on December 1, 1951, my policy has been NOT to permit the use of wiretapping or 'bugging' equipment by members of the Force."[133] However, on March 29, 1971, a general order from Police Chief Jerry V. Wilson entitled "Intercepting Oral Communications" rescinded Chief Murray's 1964 order on wiretapping and bugging. Under the new rules, electronic surveillance was permitted when in accordance with the law and when approved by an upper-level police official.[134] By mid 1973 an electronic surveillance unit had been established to maintain and recommend purchase of "contact microphones, head sets, surveillance kits, pen registers, pre-amplifiers, radio frequency recorders, recorder starters, touchstone decoders, transmitters and radio scanners."[135]

---

* When the House Internal Security Committee subpoenaed Gorran to testify before it on July 22, 1969, it was apparently unaware of Gorran's defection. However, the panel might have realized they had a turncoat on their hands from his testimony, which rejected most of its accusatory scenarios and defended the SDS against violence charges. But this oversight led to a third-act climax. During a recess called by the committee to permit the showing of a film, Gorran spilled what was left of the beans to reporters: his sponsors had used him for their own ends (a complaint that had also embittered Merritt); had considered him "expendable" by instructing him to surveil an American Nazi Party (ANP) meeting without protection; and were plainly ignorant of the peaceful nature of the student movement. All in all, he told them, he didn't think the police belonged on campuses. He explained that he had come in from the cold because of "revulsion" over what he was doing to people with whom he had come to sympathize. See House Internal Security Committee (HISC) Hearings, 1969: *Investigation of Students for a Democratic Society*, pt. 3–A, pp. 688–709, and "Student Describes Career as FBI Spy," *Washington Post*, July 23, 1969.

The availability of informers enabled the MPD to engage in "consensual" eavesdropping: the monitoring of a phone by consent of one of the parties, which was not illegal providing the informer who gave consent was present. But, under the statute applicable at the time, if the informer was not present, as was frequently the case, the monitoring technically became illegal. In these operations, the CIA contributed expertise and equipment. Another CIA specialty was an ingenious bugging device that could be installed in lamps.[136] Among the other services provided to the MPD by the CIA were instructions in lock-picking, photography, and surveillance; the use of CIA cars, drivers, and radios as well as a safe house and photographic facilities. In exchange, the department performed security checks for the CIA, provided cover for CIA agents, and assisted in the training of apprentice agents. The CIA, in turn, showered MPD personnel with all kinds of gifts and gratuities, including dinners honoring retiring MPD inspectors.*[137]

The MPD also served as an operational arm of the White House in dealing with threatened disruption in connection with the 1971 May Day antiwar demonstrations. So it was that Police Chief Wilson, in responding to the charges of police misconduct before, during, and just after the demonstrations, stated enigmatically, "If you want to find fault with [police behavior], you can blame the President." This statement was clarified by the disclosure in 1972 that Chief Wilson had attended eight meetings with high Nixon administration officials, including Attorney General John Mitchell, White House aide John Ehrlichman, Richard Kleindienst, Robert Mardian, and William Rehnquist (later appointed to the Supreme Court) to plan a tough response to the 1971 demonstrations.†[138]

---

* Army intelligence also contributed its mite, $150,000 to aid in the MPD's intelligence collection effort ("Army Aided D.C. Police Spy Efforts," *Washington Post*, March 8, 1975).
† In a 1971 speech to the 78th Annual Convention of the International Association of Chiefs of Police, "Common Sense in Dealing with Demonstrations" (*Police Yearbook*, 1972, pp. 15, 23), D.C. Police Chief Jerry V. Wilson told his audience that "the president instructed me explicitly that violations of the law were to be dealt with fairly—but firmly." However, in a subsequent lawsuit, described in the text, juries as well as trial and appellate courts upheld claims that plaintiffs were arrested, imprisoned, and prosecuted without probable cause in violation of the Fourth Amendment and that the arrests and prosecutions were conducted in a manner violative of their rights under the Fifth and Sixth Amendments (*Dellums v. Powell*, 566 F. 2d 167, cert. denied 438 U.S. 916 [1977]; *Dellums v. Powell*, 568 F. 2d 216 [1977]; *Sullivan v. Murphy*, 478 F. 2d 938, cert. denied 414 U.S. 880 [1973]).

The implementation of the blueprint for handling the May Day rallies resulted in serious misconduct by both the MPD and the Capitol police force. During the entire period of May Day demonstrations from April 24 to May 5, some 14,500 people were arrested on a variety of dubious charges. Demonstrators were indiscriminately clubbed and beaten and arrested without probable cause. More than 1,000 of them were rounded up in mass arrests on May 3, 4, and 5 successively, bypassing legal arrest procedures, and stuffed into tiny cells for as long as seventy-two hours. Most of the cases were dropped before reaching court.[139]

After approximately 3,000 cases had gone through the courts with only about 10 convictions, an appellate court halted prosecution of all demonstrators—an estimated 4,000—if there was no adequate evidence to link an individual with the charge against him or her. Shortly thereafter, an additional 2,400 cases were dropped. A trial judge then complained that the Washington police and prosecutors had chosen "order at the expense of citizens' rights" in their handling of the May Day protesters.

On June 16, seventeen cases in an ever-dwindling docket were dismissed by a court because the prosecutors claimed they were not ready for trial. The government's woes continued to mount: the next month, charges were dismissed in fifty-six more cases, accompanied by a judicial rebuke of governmental misconduct. In addition, earlier proceedings against over one hundred veterans who had demonstrated on April 21, 1971, freed all of them.[140]

The largest groups of demonstrators were those arrested on May 5 on the steps of the Capitol listening to speeches by political figures. One of the speakers, Congressman Ronald V. Dellums, became the leading plaintiff in a class action lawsuit brought by the ACLU, which, after protracted litigation, resulted in a court award of over $2.5 million in damages to the people arrested on May 5 on the House steps.* Congress subsequently appropriated more than $600,000 in additional monies to settle other May Day litigation involving arrests on May 3 and 4, 1971.

In 1976 a classified report by the U.S. attorney's office detailed cooperation by the FBI and the MPD's Intelligence Division in monitoring antiwar activists and organizations from 1969 to 1971. The report charged that, among other surveillance abuses, D.C. police intelligence officers had, on at least two occasions, burglarized private apartments. Although the evidence included testimony by intruding police, the MPD denied the break-in charges.

---

* Two of Dellums's aides were arrested, and the congressman himself was hit with a nightstick and pushed down the steps by the police.

The 1974 shredding of the files did not destroy evidence establishing that the Intelligence Division had maintained files on city council members Julius Hobson and Marion Barry (later mayor) and council head Sterling Tucker, as well as on congressional delegate Walter Fauntroy and other public figures. Hobson promptly became a plaintiff in a lawsuit (see pp. 335–37) that, on December 23, 1981, resulted in awards of $711,000 to the plaintiffs to be paid by the fourteen federal and District of Columbia defendants.[141]

On June 8, 1984, the court of appeals for the District of Columbia issued an opinion and order in the *Hobson* case, reversing, on statute of limitations grounds, trial judgments in favor of three of the plaintiffs against the FBI defendants, and, on grounds of insufficiency of the evidence, trial judgments against the individual MPD defendants and the District of Columbia; affirming the findings of liability against certain of the FBI defendants, however, including an award of punitive damages against an FBI agent; and remanding the case for a reconsideration by the trial court on other issues.[142] The court—a three-judge panel dominated by two highly conservative appointees of the Reagan administration—viewed the record of MPD misconduct as simply a good-faith effort to develop a police program to gather information for preventative purposes despite the fact that no credible evidence was introduced that the surveillance, both passive and aggressive, contributed to the peaceful character of the demonstrations. The court wholly ignored the fact that the demonstrations were, by and large, quite peaceful because the sponsoring groups had not only secured permits but had cooperated with the local police agencies in matters such as sites, times, places, and logistics.

Similarly, the court concluded that the Intelligence Division's exchange of information with other agencies, such as the FBI, was sanctioned by other presidential task forces. This construction of the evidence would also appear to ignore the motive that unifies and explains the entire record—namely, the drive to forestall expressions of protest through intimidation and disruption. Equally questionable is the court's treatment of the conceded misconduct as the discrete acts of mavericks violative of the legitimate policies of the MPD, a conclusion that seems strained in view of the repeated indications that the acts complained of resulted from instructions by higher-ups.

Prompted by a determination of the city council to bring an end to the abuses of the past,* a more cautious police leadership, the creation of

---

* City fathers are typically reluctant to challenge the police, and the District of Columbia was no exception: a city government, largely black and uncertain of its

a climate favorable to whistle-blowing, the fear of further damage suits, and disclosures that council members had been surveilled and dossiered, the door was sealed against future repressive surveillance practices by the adoption in 1976 of strict guidelines confining intelligence operations to areas not invasive of the protected freedoms.[143] This process of repudiating an embarrassing past was hastened by the Watergate disclosures and the perception that the administration's role in masterminding the lawless response to the May Day demonstrations was a projection of the same siege mentality that had motivated the Watergate break-in. Finally, as in so many other cities and towns where the curtain on police surveillance finally came down by the mid seventies, costly litigation and the fear of future damage suits were effective spurs.

---

course, was confronted by a well-entrenched white police hierarchy determined to resist a shake-up of any kind. See, for example, "Shun D.C. Council Spy Quiz, Police Union Advises 5," *Washington Post*, July 24, 1975. But, as elsewhere, the untouchability mystique was pierced by disclosures of corruption and misconduct, buttressed by the charges of a House committee. "D.C. Police Named in $1.1 Million Damage Suit," *Washington Post*, November 30, 1971; "Probe of Police Sought," ibid., January 13, 1972; "D.C. Police, Drugs, under Jury Probes," ibid., February 3, 1972; "Judge Criticizes U.S. Prosecutor in Police Case," ibid., October 27, 1972; "Lieutenant Tells of Taking Bribes of $150 a Month," ibid., August 31, 1972.

Epilogue

The Haymarket Legacy: The End or a Flickering New Beginning?

The urban political intelligence operations detailed here typify, with variations in priorities, the target selection, surveillance (overt and covert, passive and aggressive), threat assessment, and filing and dissemination practices that flowered during the sixties in urban police departments throughout the nation. But, beginning in the early seventies, a backlash against police spying made itself felt. This critical social mood was fed by hoarded disapproval of police excesses in the sixties, a delayed "morning after" sense—reminiscent of past patterns of recurrent repression and repentance—that our democratic commitment had been compromised and violated. Fueling this backlash was the fact that by the early seventies the activism of the previous decade had cooled, leaving the defenders of the police without a "menace" to exploit. Moreover, ordinary citizens became more receptive to charges of police repression as the result of Senate investigations of Watergate and inquiry into federal intelligence abuses by the Church Committee. This mood of social repentance was also shaped by the media, which not only supported criticism of the police, but participated in exposing previously secret practices. So pervasive was this climate that in some areas—Chicago (the Cook County Grand Jury), Baltimore, New Haven, Los Angeles, and the District of Columbia, to name the most prominent—official bodies undertook investigations of politically repressive police actions.

Urban forces seeking an airing of past misconduct and measures to prevent a recurrence in the future were sometimes frustrated: while they knew that abuses had occurred, they were unable to provide details of a sort that might yield corrective measures. This lack was filled in a

345

variety of ways, ranging from leaks to the press, the surfacing of under-cover agents and informers in criminal prosecutions, testimony of police officers before congressional countersubversive committees, pretrial disclosures, and documents released under freedom of information statutes and ordinances. From these and other sources* a syndrome of six abuses by police in the sixties emerged: (1) indiscriminate targeting of a wide range of peaceful dissenting groups and individuals; (2) spying on such targets by questionable tactics, ranging from physical surveillance, photography, and letter-opening to informer infiltration and wiretapping; (3) aggressive intelligence measures such as incitement to violence, provocation, and disruption and harassment of peaceful groups; burglaries, raids, and dissemination of information (calculated to do injury to the target) to third parties (such as landlords and employers); and stealing, copying, and destruction of documents and correspondence; (4) maintenance and dissemination of files and dossiers; (5) failure to justify the intelligence activities of the previous decade by persuasive evidence on either crime-prevention or peacekeeping grounds; and (6) resort to ideological rationales ("national" or "internal" security) similarly perceived as implausible or invented.

The retreat from political intelligence operations took various paths. In some cities and towns the operation was simply ended without formal action. In larger cities restrictive guidelines were adopted to avoid more drastic, embarrassing, and expensive measures. But such administrative remedies were properly viewed with skepticism: nothing prevented the revival of the former objectionable practices and, in any event, they were subject only to departmental interpretation. The Seattle city fathers enacted an ordinance broadly banning practices violative of the protected freedoms and scrupulously monitoring borderline areas.

But the most favored form of remedy against the police and local authorities in the seventies was litigation—under a variety of federal (the Civil Rights Act of 1871, the First Amendment, and the Freedom of Information and Privacy Acts) and state provisions (privacy, free speech,

---

* Information sometimes came to potential plaintiffs quite serendipitously. For example, in the course of a federal court trial early in 1984 in which black officers charged the Columbus, Ohio, Police Department with discriminatory practices, testimony was given by a police officer that in the early seventies, with the knowledge of his superiors, he had placed hidden microphones in the offices of the NAACP and two other civil rights groups. A second officer testified that, on assignment, she had monitored several NAACP meetings in 1979 and 1980 and had written reports for her superiors. On December 3, 1984, the NAACP filed a lawsuit seeking $2 million in compensatory damages and $10 million in punitive damages.

and freedom of information statutes). These actions—at least thirty in number—were brought by individuals, or a larger cluster of complainants, or on a broad-scale basis on behalf of all persons within a victimized class. Of the red squads discussed in these pages, seven were involved in federal or state lawsuits seeking judicial relief* and, in some cases (Los Angeles, New Haven, Chicago, District of Columbia), civil damages. Some lawsuits were settled after lengthy pretrial depositions. These widely publicized proceedings generated public concern in other cities with respect to surveillance, resulting in pressures, including lawsuits, for an accounting and reform.

The forerunners of the mainstream seventies litigation were a series of cases in the early part of the decade attacking—with mixed results—such police practices as photography, surveillance, and the maintenance of files. One such case was *Holmes v. Church*, in which surveillance practices, including the tracing of telephone calls, by the New Rochelle, New York, Police Department directed against a number of civic leaders and a draft counseling agency were disclosed in a congressional hearing (see pp. 75–76). (A detailed file on the prominent black actor, writer, and director Ossie Davis was subsequently publicized.) These practices were judicially banned in November 1971 by a federal court after the plaintiffs' files were turned over to them.[1] A parallel state court case emerged in 1970–71 in a Los Angeles suburb, Hermosa Beach, based primarily on the discovery of a confidential memo, "Ecology Action Committee—Intelligence Report," submitted by a police chief's administrative assistant with the notation "Active files are being maintained as you directed." A lawsuit by the individuals named followed and was ultimately settled by the adoption of guidelines designed to protect peaceful political activity of all kinds from police encroachment.[2] In both these cases surveillance and the responsive legal action were extensions of passionate political conflicts between conservatives and their liberal adversaries.

In 1972 the Supreme Court decided the case of *Laird v. Tatum*. In a 5–4 ruling, the court held that the plaintiffs had not adequately demonstrated a personal stake in the outcome of the litigation and that "allegations of subjective 'chill' are not an adequate substitute for a claim of specific present objective harm or a threat of specific future harm." Thereafter, the effectiveness of lawsuits in obtaining judicial relief against political surveillance by police required a showing that the acts complained of were directed against the plaintiff and were "proscrip-

* Chicago, Philadelphia, New York, Los Angeles, Detroit, New Haven, and the District of Columbia.

tive," that is, conducted (in the absence of concrete proof of personal damage) for politically punitive, rather than law-enforcement, purposes or through intrusive methods conflicting with constitutional rights. In order to meet this standard, litigants were typically forced to rely on secret internal file and dossier collections. The data assembled for status-enhancement reasons and to ensure institutional continuity (see pp. 70–71) became, paradoxically, the greatest threat to such continuity. Thus, police departments under siege in the seventies sought to conceal, purge, or destroy their once-cherished intelligence files in order to avoid damaging litigation.* A prominent example is the file destruction in Memphis, Tennessee.

In 1976 the Memphis Police Department and the mayor's office received a request from a local resident to be allowed to inspect his intelligence files. In response, Mayor Wyeth Chandler ordered the police to burn all the files of the Domestic Intelligence Unit (DIU, as the local red squad was called) and to abolish the unit altogether.[3] In compliance with the mayor's order, 180 boxes of files were reportedly destroyed on September 10, 1976, at the very time the ACLU was in court to obtain a restraining order to preserve the files in support of a lawsuit brought under the federal civil rights statute and the First Amendment.[4] But the destruction backfired: first, the allegations of improper surveillance were sustained by pretrial depositions of police officers in the fall and winter of 1976–77; second, embarrassing documents were unearthed in the basement of a building formerly used by the red squad that had escaped the mayor's destruction order; and, third, the act of destruction itself generated an inference of wrongdoing, not to speak of adverse publicity, which provided a justification for a restrictive settlement decree used as a model in other litigation and legislative efforts. But before examining the Memphis decree, we should glance at the pretrial record in the lawsuit.

Overlapping the mission of the Criminal Intelligence Squad, the DIU was assigned jurisdiction over strikes, demonstrations, and rallies and was authorized to maintain files on potentially disruptive political activities, organizations, and individuals. A memo directed the intelligence

---

* A variation on the resistance by police to file disclosures was the effort of the Mississippi state authorities to bar access to the files of its Sovereignty Commission, created in 1960 by the legislature to defend segregation, and dismantled seventeen years later. As with other file collections, the resistance was based on the fear of the disclosure of damaging information that might generate litigation. Again, paralleling developments elsewhere, an effort was made to negotiate a settlement in order to avoid disclosure ("Dispute in South over Secret Files," *New York Times*, November 25, 1984).

unit to focus on "local subversion, disorders, civil rights activist activities, and union and Negro coalition activities."[5]

A wide range of personal, as well as political, information was collected and recorded. Police Captain Patrick Ryan, chief of the intelligence unit, explained: "You tried to gather as much information as you possibly could about whatever particular investigation you were involved in . . . to put it all together, and see what you came out with."[6] In addition, the DIU's operation was openly racist on every level. For example, in contrast to conventional categories of intelligence files, the DIU files were divided into two specially coded categories, "White" and "Black."[7] In order to justify their surveillance of such moderate groups as the NAACP and the SCLC, DIU officials were forced to invent a potential for criminal behavior on the part of these groups. To this end, the DIU's Lieutenant Ely Arkin referred to the NAACP as "a fairly militant group" in one Intelligence Division memo.[8]

In addition to individual dossiers and data on political organizations, the DIU files also included a number of intelligence "threat assessments." For example, one document retrieved after the destruction of the files was entitled "Summary of the Plans of the Black Extremists in the United States of America." Another, more specific memo listed "Militant Black Power Advocates in Memphis." In addition to these memos, the DIU prepared a monthly intelligence report concerning political trends and activities both in the Memphis area and nationwide.

Among the groups targeted by the DIU were the Communist Party, the All-African People's Republic Party, PUSH, the ACLU, a number of "motorcycle gangs," the SCLC, the Black Panther Party, the Invaders (a militant black group), the Memphis Sanitation Workers' Union, and the National Committee against Repressive Legislation. The DIU planted informers (paid and unpaid) in most target groups, and some were penetrated by police undercover agents.[9] The DIU also used bank records, FBI information, still photographs, films, credit checks, phone company checks, and other sources in the course of investigations. In addition, the DIU developed liaison relationships with the FBI, the Secret Service, the Treasury Department, the Immigration and Naturalization Service, and the IRS.

The pretrial discovery proceedings simply reinforced the inference from the file destruction that the unit had engaged, not as a casual or optional matter, but continuously and systematically, in practices designed to curb dissent and protest. Under these circumstances, the defendants agreed in September 1978 to an injunction against the collection of political intelligence, broadly defined to cover activities protected by the

First Amendment.* More specifically, the defendants (both mayor and police officials) undertook *not* to:

—maintain a unit for surveilling legitimate political activity;

—infiltrate legitimate political groups;

—harass political groups by disseminating derogatory information or other disruptive tactics;

—photograph or otherwise identify those attending gatherings protected by the First Amendment.

In addition, the defendants agreed to procedures for authorization, review, and minimization of intrusion in lawful investigations of criminal conduct involving the exercise of First Amendment rights. Finally, the city was ordered to make the terms of the agreement known to its officials and police officers through publication, public posting, and other means. The court retained jurisdiction to ensure that violations of the decree would be promptly dealt with. As in the case of other settlement agreements, it was probably more far-reaching than a postlitigation judicial decree in favor of the plaintiffs.[10]

The Memphis settlement decree spurred a movement in Seattle to curb intelligence abuses by its intelligence unit.[11] This countersubversive operation, an update of a surveillance program that had originated in the post–World War I era (see p. 37), was extremely active in the thirties.[†] It received a new lease on life in 1956 as the Subversive Activities Unit and later merged with a criminal intelligence squad that was little more than a cover for its predominantly political priorities.[12] Over the years, disclosures of broad targeting and questionable tactics created a favorable

---

* The decree defines *political intelligence* as "the gathering, indexing, filing, maintenance, storage or dissemination of information, or any other investigative activity, relating to any persons, beliefs, associations or other exercise of First Amendment rights" (*Kendrick v. Chandler*, No. 76–449 [W.D. Tenn.]).

† A 1936 Seattle news item states: "Swinging clubs and blackjacks, 100 vigilantes raided the first classroom session of the Seattle Social Science school, badly beat students, teachers, and visitors, and drove them into the street. Police made no attempt to interfere with the attackers, but arrested five allegedly 'radical' teachers and students. One student was traced to a hospital, where he was receiving treatment for a head injury, and hauled off to jail" (quoted in the *Progressive*, June–July 1984, p. 33). In January 1970 the Seattle Police Department made national headlines as a result of the ambush murder of an unarmed black veteran, Larry Ward, in which the police, acting on a tip from an FBI informer, staked out and killed the victim (Donner, *The Aims and Methods of America's Political Intelligence System* [New York: Knopf, 1980], p. 231; "Seattle Divided by Controversy over Slaying of Black by Police," *New York Times*, May 31, 1970).

climate for remedial efforts. Thus, in 1974 the Seattle police chief informed the city council that he had purged all political intelligence files dealing with some 730 subjects—yet another example of file destruction as survival tactic—a disclosure that startled and angered many civic-minded residents.

To combat these disclosed abuses and to prevent their recurrence, the local chapters of three organizations—the American Friends Service Committee (AFSC), the ACLU, and the National Lawyers' Guild—in September 1976 formed the Coalition on Government Spying (COGS), which launched a resourceful and ultimately successful campaign to ban police surveillance practices. Public pressure generated by the coalition campaign led to the release of police documents on the functions of its intelligence unit, which concealed more than they revealed about the unit's operations. [13]

In June 1977 thirty-six individuals and six organizations under the COGS umbrella filed a complaint for inspection of their intelligence files based on a Washington state statute providing for "full access to public records so as to assure continuing public confidence . . . in government processes." After continued stonewalling by the police and city authorities in response to demands for file access, the police authorities admitted in pretrial discovery proceedings that some 170 individuals and organizations—including the three plaintiff groups and fifteen individual plaintiffs—were the subjects of current files. [14] But, relying on a statutory exception to the disclosure requirements that file access can be denied if "non-disclosure is essential to effective law enforcement," the police continued to resist disclosure efforts.

The defendants were unable to provide proof requested by the court for nondisclosure on law-enforcement grounds. Here, as in Memphis, the defendants' submissions did little more than embarrass them. The reluctantly surrendered files virtually wiped out the resistance in the police hierarchy to the plaintiffs' charges. The files submitted to the coalition elaborated a wide range of intelligence activities and confirmed the complainants' charges of spying tactics wholly unrelated to law enforcement. [15] One report dealing with a civic leader, the head of a local Chicano service organization, states, "On 12-13-75 it was reported that Roberto Maestas was still trying to get some bombs made by an unknown U.W. [University of Washington] student and has the promise of AFSC [American Friends Service Committee] to pay for the costs involved." Although the files on both the AFSC—described as a "national pacifist organization" on an index card—and Maestas recorded this information, no action was taken by the police to verify it. [16]

The files were dense with misinformation, irrelevance, inaccuracies, and trivia. For example, a special file ("A Profile of Miscellaneous Indicators") contains a copy of a letter written to the editor of the *Seattle Times* discussing President Carter's policies on the B-1 bomber. A 78-page file on the National Lawyers' Guild reveals an extraordinary range of surveillance tactics: photographs, physical surveillance, informers, and the use of computers—largely premised on the view that lawyers for suspected radicals needed watching. In addition to leaflets and other documents distributed to the public, the file also records personal information on guild members.[17]

As the flames of the lawsuit mounted around the intelligence unit, its chief, Lieutenant V. L. Bartley, shipped off certain intelligence files to the zone commander of the LEIU in Santa Clara, California (see p. 81n) with a letter complaining that the coalition's lawsuit sought "to force us to disclose our files" and further stating, "It would not surprise me if the mayor seized our files at any time." This move produced a vigorous response: the plaintiffs in the lawsuit moved to hold Bartley in contempt, he was removed from his post, and the presiding judge ordered the documents returned.[18]

These two developments—the denial of access to the files and the effort to remove them from further scrutiny—advanced the coalition's drive for the passage of a city ordinance. In the course of its campaign, the coalition published a basic resource document with respect to the surveillance issue, "Principles for Effective Legislation," which was endorsed by more than fifty groups, from the League of Women Voters to the King County Bar Association. This initiative was also supported by Mayor Charles Royer, a newsman who had himself been the subject of red squad investigation and who had made a campaign promise to curb police intelligence-gathering activities unrelated to law enforcement. The city council held hearings on the proposed ordinance in the summer and fall of 1978 in which evidence was presented by the coalition.

A landmark ordinance was finally passed in 1979, effective as of January 1, 1980. This measure banned political surveillance per se and provided inter alia that no person "become the subject of the collection of information on account of a lawful exercise of a constitutional right or civil liberty" and no information be collected or used for political purposes. Furthermore, police may not collect "restrictive information" (defined to include the political or religious beliefs or activities of an organization or individual) except in connection with criminal investigations or the protection of visiting dignitaries. In addition, the police are barred from collecting political information on associates of suspects or, more broadly, those holding similar political views.[19]

Rigorous authorization requirements by higher officers are mandated in "mixed" investigations, that is, those in which a law-enforcement inquiry overlaps the area of free expression and association. The deployment of infiltrators and informers likewise requires specific authorization in writing by the police chief, including a statement that such investigation will avoid "unreasonable infringement upon . . . rights, liberties and freedoms."[20]

Perhaps the most noteworthy provisions of the ordinance are those mandating the appointment by the mayor and the city council of a civilian auditor to audit the police files at unscheduled times, not less than 180 days apart. The auditor is required to report to the mayor as to whether the ordinance has been obeyed by the police. In addition, the police chief is also required to submit an annual statistical report to the mayor. But most important is an unprecedented provision that the city government may be held civilly liable for damages resulting from the willful violation of the ordinance.[21]

In April 1981, sixteen months after the effective date of the Seattle ordinance, a settlement agreement in the Chicago litigation echoed the major provisions of the Seattle measure. The Chicago settlement agreement, signed by the parties on April 24, 1981, and subsequently approved by a federal judge, came six years after the grand jury report condemning the department's police state practices.[22] Under this agreement the police are permanently barred from gathering any information concerning political activities, whether from public or private sources, in the absence of prior evidence of criminal intent. Moreover, such data collection cannot exceed its legitimate crime-suppression purpose, must be authorized by the police superintendent or an aide, and is limited to the least intrusive investigative techniques. Where advocacy of unlawful violence is the investigative justification, it must be in a context that creates a credible threat. The deployment of informers and infiltrators is authorized only for crime-suppression purposes and is affirmatively banned for information-gathering in the First Amendment area. Additional provisions limit the compilation and dissemination, including by leaks to the press, of dossiers on groups and individuals unless related to criminal conduct. All information dealing with First Amendment–related activities collected in the course of a legitimate criminal investigation must be purged from police files as soon as the purpose of the investigation is achieved. Finally, all of these restraints are implemented by review and auditing requirements.[23]

But rejoicing over this settlement proved to be premature. The settlement had included an agreement vesting the court with continuing jurisdiction, and in April 1982, shortly after the order was signed by Judge

Susan Getzendanner enjoining the conduct set forth in the agreement, the Chicago police violated the order by filming an anti–nuclear arms race demonstration. In a sharply worded opinion, the judge gave the police a month to conform to all the requirements of the settlement order—although it was then more than a year old, it had never been implemented—and warned that future violations would result in an order compensating the victims of such practices and assessing the city court costs and attorneys' fees. (By mid 1983, the city's court-ordered disbursements for plaintiffs' attorney fees exceeded $2 million.)[24]

Still the ghost of Captain Schaack continued to roam the police department's corridors. In December 1982, only a few months after the court's contempt finding of July 15, an accounting firm hired by the police board to audit compliance with the injunction urged some ninety-two changes in police investigative procedures as necessary to avoid future contempt citations. For example, the auditors found that covert photographs of public events were taken without prescribed authorization or approval, protected "First Amendment activities" had not even been defined as guidance for investigators, and permission to conduct investigations in this area was either not sought or not documented as required by court order. In other cases, key police units assumed that they were not covered by the injunction or that the prescribed safeguards could be ignored. What is at least as striking as what the auditors called "major exposures to potential future judgment order violations" was the audit's almost total silence about the specific conduct discovered to be violative of the injunction. It was then revealed that the firm had been directed to deal primarily with future implementation of the consent agreement and told to downplay cases of noncompliance at the time of the audit.[25]

But the Chicago story was not yet ended. In June 1984 a federal court jury awarded $60,000 in damages to a Chicago Puerto Rican community group, the Spanish Action Committee of Chicago, for aggressive surveillance in violation of the constitutional rights (see pp. 140–41) of the organization and its members.* There remained to be litigated in the Chicago case the damage claims of twenty-five plaintiffs based on surveillance alone of peaceful political expression. In July 1984 U.S. District Court Judge Getzendanner approved a settlement providing for payment in damages by the city of Chicago of $335,000 to eight organizations, in-

---

* The city attorney sought to justify the police disruptive program as a prevention measure, but the jury accepted the contention of plaintiff's counsel, Richard Gutman, that arrests were the proper responses to illegal conduct and that there was no evidence of wrongdoing by the plaintiff and its members.

cluding the ACLU, AFSC, Community Renewal Society, and Medical Committee for Human Rights, and seventeen individuals (among them Jesse Jackson, a congressman, two city aldermen, and a cluster of activists, journalists, and civic leaders).[26] This was followed by a second settlement agreement dated October 21 and approved November 14, 1985, allotting twenty plaintiffs a total of $306,250 in damages.[27]

On December 30, 1985, Judge Getzendanner handed down a final decision in the eleven-year-old *Alliance to End Repression v. City of Chicago* case in favor of the remaining plaintiffs.[28] The court's ruling, not appealed by the defendants, was unprecedented in scope. A series of prior cases had held, on the authority of *Laird v. Tatum*, that infiltration of an organization and the maintenance of files on surveillance targets are not per se justiciable in the absence of actual disruption or harassment. But the judge found in the *Alliance* case that the mere existence of a subversive file on an individual plaintiff (Lucy Montgomery) was sufficiently damaging and violative of her rights under the First Amendment to create grounds for legal complaint, without further evidence that the file was ever used proscriptively or even that Montgomery knew of its existence. Further, Montgomery's standing to sue was bolstered because her file included extensive information about her private life. The court thus distinguished the Supreme Court's decision in the *Laird* case by confining its scope to the gathering of publicly available information.* In the case of the organizational plaintiffs, the court found justiciability on two separate grounds: (1) public dissemination of derogatory charges, and (2) spying by infiltrators on private meetings. (The opinion further suggests that police infiltration is justiciable when the informer is directed to maintain a duplicitously friendly relationship with the target.)

Finally, in contrast to the rulings in other cases, the court approved a specific standard, an objective level of evidence, "a reasonable suspicion of criminal conduct," for investigating First Amendment–related activities—a standard, the court ruled, not met by the record in the *Alliance* case.

In Los Angeles a settlement agreement between the plaintiffs in the consolidated lawsuit was signed and approved in February 1984[29] providing, in addition to the $1,800,000 settlement (see p. 288), that investi-

---

* The court went further in narrowing the *Laird* case: "It seems there should be some point [at which], in tenaciously tracking and piecing together the details of a person's life from multifarious sources, the resulting probe becomes so intrusive as to amount to an invasion of privacy even if individual pieces of the probe are public sources. Such an intrusion has happened here."

gations of individuals and organizations by the Anti-Terrorist Division that had replaced the PDID must be based on "a reasonable and articulated suspicion" that the target is "planning, threatening, attempting or performing a significant disruption of the public order." In addition, "undercover investigations" by officers "who assume a fictitious identity" to obtain information are banned unless there is a "good faith reason" to believe that the target is committing or seeking to commit "significant disruptions of the public order." Moreover, a precondition for such investigations is authorization by two members of the Police Commission. The agreement further mandates periodic audits by a second pair of police commissioners, as well as an annual report to the city council, a written record of the decisions authorizing undercover investigations, and public disclosure of the number of such authorized investigations. Although the agreement does not distinguish as clearly as it might between "political" and "criminal" investigations, it does bar run-of-the-mill political investigations, which were for so long the PDID's stock in trade. Here, too, as in Memphis and Chicago, the court retained jurisdiction for the purpose of reviewing unilateral changes in or violations of the new standards, and it was further agreed that the court was empowered to enjoin conduct or operations found objectionable, that is, violative of the settlement agreement.

In May 1971 the plaintiffs in the New York City lawsuit, the *Handschu* case, filed charges in federal court on behalf of those formally named and all others similarly aggrieved (as in Chicago, a class action lawsuit) charging the New York red squad—the Special Services Division, as it was then called—with a range of abuses for the purpose of impairing or suppressing the exercise of First Amendment rights, including the planting of informers (civilians as well as police officers), the provocation and incitement of criminal acts, intimidating surveillance and confrontation, and wiretapping. Lack of adequate funding and support slowed the pace of the litigation, so that it was not until December 1980 that a settlement stipulation was signed by the plaintiffs' and defendants' attorneys.[30]

Many of the members of the class whose rights were assertedly violated by the defendants became critical of the settlement on a variety of grounds, ranging from overly restrictive file access, narrow definition of the scope of activity protected from surveillance, and a waiver of civil damages claims that was extremely broad in scope to the role and composition of the entity ("the Authority") charged with oversight of the settlement agreement and guidelines: two police officers and a mayoral appointee.[31]

Finally, on March 11, 1985—some fourteen years after the filing of the complaint—federal judge Charles Haight approved the settlement package, rejecting the claim that it lacked important substantive provisions protecting constitutional rights and limiting police powers set forth in its counterparts in other cities and in the Seattle ordinance. Despite the subsequent affirmance of Judge Haight's decision, many continued to doubt whether the settlement would serve as an effective barrier to renewed political surveillance in the future,[32] doubts that, it will be seen (see pp. 365–66), were well-founded.

The wide-ranging scope of political surveillance and file dissemination in the not-too-distant past came to light in December 1984, when it was disclosed that for about a decade, beginning in the mid sixties, 159 agencies, including 100 municipal police departments, had engaged in exchanging political intelligence file data with the Chicago police.* These "transmittal files" record the same target priorities, operational procedures, threat assessment, filing, and dissemination practices as those described in these pages.[33]

The Chicago transmittal files also illuminate the path to a revival of political intelligence-gathering practices, not through the embattled red squads, but rather through county and state units—a survival tactic not uncommon in the intelligence community when particular units or operations fall into disfavor. According to the transmittal files, sixteen county sheriffs' offices were involved in intelligence data exchange with the Chicago police. In the sixties a few aggressive county sheriffs or law-enforcement officers, such as Michael D'Amico of Erie County (Buffalo, New York) and Lawrence Kihnel of Jefferson Parish (New Orleans), became dominant partners with local units in intelligence operations or launched such programs on their own.

---

* In addition to ten of the thirteen agencies already discussed here, some of the police departments that received from or sent to the Chicago Police Department's Intelligence Division information about lawful political activities of particular subjects were Huntsville, Ala.; Phoenix, Tempe, and Tucson, Ariz.; Anaheim, Bakersfield, Delano, McFarland, Newark, Oakland, Orange, San Francisco, San Jose, Santa Ana, and Torrance, Calif.; Aspen and Denver, Colo.; Miami Beach, Miami, Orlando, Tallahassee, and Tampa, Fla.; Honolulu, Hawaii; Carbondale, Crystal Lake, Decatur, Evanston, Galesburg, Grayville, Highland Park, Peoria, Rockford, and Skokie, Ill.; Anderson, East Chicago, and Gary, Ind.; Cedar Rapids and Des Moines, Iowa; Columbia and Kansas City, Kans.; Louisville, Ky.; New Orleans, La.; Houlton, Maine; Boston, Fitchburg, and Medford, Mass.; Ann Arbor, Flint, and Saginaw, Mich.; St. Louis, Mo.; Omaha, Nebr.; Reno, Nev.; Atlantic City and Camden, N.J.; Beacon and Yonkers, N.Y.; Akron, Canton, Columbus, Dayton, Steubenville, and Toledo, Ohio; Eugene and Portland, Oreg.; Pittsburgh, Pa.; Providence, R.I.; Knoxville and Memphis, Tenn.; Dallas, Fort Worth, and Houston, Tex.; Salt Lake City, Utah; and Milwaukee, Wis.

In December 1983 Floridians learned that an Orange County, Florida, sheriff's investigator, using an assumed identity, spent seven months undercover in the Central Florida Nuclear Freeze Campaign on an infiltration assignment. The sheriff's office claimed that the freeze campaign posed a danger to the county's security because several of its members had been previously arrested in Tampa for civil disobedience.[34] In Orange County, California, Sheriff Bradley Gates has been sued for an assortment of surveillance practices including wiretapping, bugging, and harassment of three political opponents and critics—a judge, a private investigator, and a college professor—who claim they were targeted in order to silence them.[35]

Data exchanges are also recorded between the Chicago Police Department and twenty-six state law-enforcement agencies.* The record further demonstrates that state units in California, Connecticut, Maryland, Michigan, New Jersey, New York, and Ohio, among others, staked out their own countersubversive turf and continued their surveillance activities in the late sixties and thereafter when urban operations were attacked or suspended.

In 1980 the New Hampshire State Police, working with a private pronuclear group headed by the extremist Lyndon LaRouche, infiltrated the Clamshell Alliance, a coalition of nuclear power opponents. When a number of demonstrators were arrested for criminal trespass, one of them turned out to be a state police undercover agent.[36] During 1983 and 1984 evidence emerged of surveillance and infiltration of a group demonstrating against the death penalty by the Georgia Bureau of Investigation (GBI) under a newly enacted Georgia statute, the Anti-Terrorism Task Force Act. The demonstration was also videotaped by an agent, who disguised himself by wearing a green ribbon, which was used for identification by opponents of the death penalty. In addition, identifying data were collected by uniformed troopers. The GBI also targeted a number of claimed "terrorist" groups for surveillance with no record of violent activities.[37] The cloak-and-dagger obsession of the GBI's director, J. R. Hamrick, led in 1986 to the targeting of the Campaign for a Prosperous Georgia, a consumer group with an antinuclear agenda, despite the fact that a GBI investigator had cleared the group of charges of

---

* A variety of other state cadres also operated in secret collusion with local red squad units. This was especially true in the South. State agencies in Alabama, Louisiana (Joint Legislative Committee on Un-American Activities), and Mississippi (Sovereignty Commission) supplied red squads with funds and operational manpower in a joint crusade against black activism. In these efforts, white citizens' councils also played a collaborative role.

illegal activities. But Hamrick was unpersuaded: he feared that the "international situation," particularly the "conflict between the United States and Libya" created "the potential for a terrorist attack."

In October 1983 it was disclosed that, under an Arizona statute passed in 1975 to investigate drug trafficking, the Arizona Criminal Intelligence Systems Agency had deployed infiltrators in two towns where copper miners were on strike; these mingled with the strikers and attended union meetings, tactics claimed to be justified by a "potential threat of violence." Subsequently it was discovered that the same agency had infiltrated the ranks of anti–cruise missile demonstrators at an Air Force base as part of an investigation into "radical terrorist groups."[38]

In areas where national defense facilities are targets of protests and demonstrations, state police units are increasingly deployed both on their own and in collaboration with other agencies. In Connecticut political surveillance for purposes unrelated to law enforcement has routinely been conducted by the Connecticut State Police in the New London area, the site of a Navy laboratory, a submarine base, and a General Dynamics submarine yard. Moreover, in the recent past, state police officers have routinely photographed demonstrators at other sites, assertedly for "future intelligence purposes"; documents establish that in 1982 undercover troopers infiltrated a student gathering at Wesleyan University, where students were planning an anti-Klan rally. Documents also record surveillance of other demonstrations where certain participants were labeled "pacifists" and "Marxists." In 1984 it was revealed that included in the Connecticut State Police collection of 24,000 "raw intelligence reports" was a file on a respected former state supreme court justice, initiated by an anonymous telephone call.[39]

Nothing demonstrates the persistence of the latter-day surveillance drive as the disclosure that despite the dismantling of the Michigan State Police (MSP) intelligence unit in 1976 (see p. 297), state troopers, operating under the cover of another branch of the MSP, infiltrated peace groups protesting the construction of nuclear weapons at a plant in a Detroit suburb.[40]

The revival of political surveillance may also be spurred by the private sector. Surveillance and file maintenance of alleged or suspected subversives has for a long time been a priority of ultra-right groups in this country, working on their own or, more commonly, with police agencies. In the sixties, and even earlier, a substantial majority of the police forces in large American cities—including New York, Philadelphia, Chicago, Detroit, Cleveland, Buffalo, and Birmingham—had close operational or file-sharing ties with right-wing groups. In some cases, local and state forces aided paramilitary groups such as the Minutemen in frustrating federal arrests and even in operational initiatives.[41]

The look-the-other-way encouragement of Klan violence, typically communicated to police headquarters in the planning stage by an informer (as in Birmingham), subsequently emerged in striking detail in a civil trial initiated in March 1985 by a communist group, five of whose members were killed on November 3, 1979, by Klansmen and Nazis. The story begins with Klansman Edward Woodrow Dawson, who in the fall of 1979 became a paid informant for the Greensboro, North Carolina, Police Department. Having worked in that capacity for the FBI from 1969 to 1976, Dawson began attending meetings of the Communist Workers' Party (CWP) in Greensboro and gathering literature and other "intelligence" on that group. It soon became clear that Dawson and his Greensboro Police Department (GPD) control agents, Detective Jerry "Rooster" Cooper and Lieutenant Robert Talbott, were focusing on a communist-sponsored anti-Klan march and conference to be held in Greensboro on November 3, 1979.

In the course of attending Klan meetings and functions during this period, Dawson reported to Cooper that the Klan had met in Lincolnton on October 20 and that eighty-five Klansmen had expressed their intent to counter-demonstrate on November 3; that they had inquired about bringing guns with them to Greensboro; that they planned to "disrupt" the march (at least by assaulting the demonstrators with rotten eggs); that Grand Dragon Virgil Griffin was soliciting the attendance of Klan leaders from other states; and that there was at least a "rumor" that some members of the Klan living in the Winston-Salem area had obtained a machine gun and possibly other weapons, and that they planned to come to Greensboro on November 3 and "shoot up the place."

On the morning of November 3, 1979, the Klan and Nazis began gathering at the home of Brent Fletcher, a Klan activist (now deceased). Dawson called Cooper sometime before 9:00 A.M. to report that several Klansmen were in town, including Grand Dragon Virgil Griffin, and that he had seen at least three weapons in their possession. Dawson had driven over the parade route hours earlier with these out-of-town Klansmen. After obtaining a copy of the parade permit (which included a map of the march route) the day before at Detective Cooper's behest, Dawson then went to Fletcher's house, where he observed at least three handguns and nine long guns. He called Cooper again and relayed this information. In the meantime, Cooper had driven by the Fletcher house, seen the Confederate flag flying, taken down the license plate numbers of the cars parked there, and returned to police headquarters for a 10:00 A.M.

briefing of the leaders of the tactical units assigned to cover the march. Cooper told the officers present at this meeting that the Klan was assembling at Fletcher's home and that some of them were armed.

For reasons that are hardly inscrutable, the threat of a violent confrontation was ignored both by Cooper and by the leaders of the tactical units, for following this meeting, Cooper headed back to the Fletcher house and the tactical squad leaders declared a lunch break. Cooper encountered the Klan caravan stopped on a highway ramp and for the next twenty minutes or more reported its progress toward the starting point of the march—Morningside Homes, a predominantly black housing project. While Cooper reported from behind the caravan ("shots fired" and then "heavy gunfire"), most of the tactical squads' police officers were still at lunch.

There were at least two officers, however, who were not at lunch as the caravan proceeded on its deadly course to Morningside. Officer April Wise, along with another officer, had been dispatched to an address approximately a block and a half from the starting point of the parade to answer a domestic "disturbance" call. Though they had not been assigned to cover that specific zone on that particular day, they responded to the call because the area was mysteriously without its normally assigned patrol cars or officers at the time. They arrived at Morningside at 10:34 A.M. About ten minutes later, they received what Officer Wise later recalled as a most unusual inquiry from the police communications center asking how long they expected to be on the call and advising them to "clear the area as soon as possible." At 10:57 A.M. they did so. The Klan caravan, led by Eddie Dawson and trailed by Detective Cooper, was on its way to Morningside. Twenty minutes later, five demonstrators lay dead or dying on the streets, assassinated in broad daylight by avowed members of the Ku Klux Klan and American Nazi Party, without a uniformed police officer in sight.

In June 1985, six years after the event, in contrast to earlier acquittals in state and federal criminal trials of those accused of the murder of CWP members, a civil jury awarded $409,000 in damages to some of the victims and survivors. In addition to two Klan members and three Nazi sympathizers, the jury held liable two Greensboro police officers and informer Dawson.

It was hardly a ringing victory. The award was confined to liability for the death of only one of the slain demonstrators, and the jury failed to find, as the complaint alleged, that the defendants had violated the plaintiffs' civil rights or engaged in a conspiracy. Still, the jury made it clear that the police cannot in the name of neutrality abandon their responsibility for protecting free speech and assembly against violence in the streets.[42]

A more common form of collaboration with extremist groups is file-sharing. As we have seen, the besieged Los Angeles PDID, through Detective Jay Paul, used the computerized files of the extremist right-wing organization Western Goals to evade threats of disclosure and destruction of PDID files. During the sixties, the LEIU, wearing the mask of a nongovernmental entity, became a channel for concealing as well as disseminating political intelligence files. To be sure, the LEIU's later (1979) guidelines on the face of it barred a political-intelligence orientation, but it would be foolhardy to assume that the guidelines will not once again be stretched or ignored.

Moreover, the politicization of the LEIU stirs similar concerns about the potential transformation of other "private" police entities purportedly dealing with criminal intelligence, but formally excluding political spying. One example is the Regional Organized Crime Information Center (ROCIC). Headquartered in Memphis, Tennessee, the ROCIC was one of seven multistate regional intelligence projects funded by grants from the LEAA. The predecessor of the ROCIC, known as "Metropol," was formed in 1967 and was a private organization composed of local and state law-enforcement officers in the southeastern United States as a clearinghouse and mechanism for the formal exchange of information on crime among law-enforcement authorities. Access to the files and records of the ROCIC was limited to "members," who were carefully screened and had to conform to unspecified security regulations established by the ROCIC. Additionally, the ROCIC provided "field agents" to local law-enforcement agencies in need of surveillance expertise, informers, electronic monitoring, and other covert operational resources. The ROCIC also supplied funding for raids and "sting" operations.[43]

The Chicago transmittal files provide new evidence of liaison arrangements, operational collaboration, and file dissemination linkages with right-wing groups.[44] One document discloses that the Chicago police requested data on subversives from the Minutemen, headed by Robert B. dePugh, after the latter had offered access to its files on "75,000 individuals that either belonged to the Communist Party or various subversive front groups." On March 14, 1968, the New York red squad's Chief Deputy Inspector William Knapp inquired of his Chicago intelligence peers what information was available regarding Edgar C. Bundy, head of the Church League of America, a far-right group with a huge countersubversive file collection and publisher of News & Views, a newsletter dealing with the never-ending threat of subversion.* According to Knapp, a "confidential background investigation" was being conducted, presumably to check out Bundy's credentials in connection with a file-sharing offer. Chicago's reply could hardly have been more enthusiastic: *News & Views* had been regularly sent to the red squad and "has been very helpful in the past," as had the Church League's file collections. In November of the same year, apparently as part of a Church League outreach project, the Philadelphia police sent the Chicago unit an inquiry concerning an individual representing the Church League who offered his services "in the investigation of subversive and militant organizations"—a partnership that the league had assertedly forged with other municipal police departments. Again the reply reported: "This Division has on many occasions used the files of the Church League of America when conducting background investigations on persons affiliated with [*sic*] subversive activities. This organization has been completely cooperative with us in the past."

The prospects for a renewal of countersubversive extremism with an attendant police involvement are shadowy but hardly fanciful. The American political scene has historically been a fertile breeding ground for countersubversive vigilantism, punitive self-help, and scapegoating during periods of social tension and political polarization like the present. The symptoms of the renewal of such practices are visible in the burgeoning of fifties-style rightist neo-Nazi and paramilitary networks, in the train of bombings of abortion facilities by anti-abortion forces, and in the new Alabama-based private mercenary (Soldiers of Fortune) movement to supply arms and manpower to the Nicaraguan contras, Angolan guerrillas, and other forces considered friends of the West.[45]

The leaders—lay and clerical—of our nativist constituencies and their allies stand ready to fill the gaps created by the dismantling of the federal countersubversive committees and cutbacks in FBI political intelligence-gathering activities. Nor is renewed cooperation between these private groups, free as they are from government restraint—not the least of their freedoms is immunity from file-disclosure requirements

---

* CLA brochures boast that its file collection contains not only newspaper clippings and similar data but also reports by infiltrators who spied on liberal and leftist groups. According to Bundy, the CLA library included seven million index cards listing every person, organization, movement, and publication that has been tied to dissenting movements. Bundy has claimed that the collection is "the most reliable, comprehensive and complete second only to those of the FBI" ("Who Shall Lead the Righteous?" *Chicago Sun-Times* [suburban ed.], November 16, 1984).

imposed by freedom of information measures—and nonfederal police forces precluded. (Only the settlement agreements in Chicago and Memphis forbid such collaboration.)

Finally, it should be remembered that private surveillance is not confined to spying by right-wing extremists on their political enemies. Beginning in the late seventies, public utilities, through in-house and hired operatives, have continuously monitored organizations, movements, and demonstrations protesting the use of nuclear power as an energy source.[46] These operations have frequently been launched in tandem with forces in the public sector such as urban police, sheriffs' deputies, and state troopers. Nor, in assessing a political-surveillance threat, can we ignore the rapidly growing body of security personnel serving private industry and now reportedly outnumbering the nation's urban police forces. These cadres, too, may well become a countersubversive resource acting both independently and in collaboration with police units.

If history, both recent and more remote, is a guide, the triggering mechanism for a renewal of repression by the police may well be the response to protest and unrest generated by such developments as an economic downturn, racial disturbances, growth in the area of nuclear power and weaponry, and military intervention abroad. To be sure, existing barriers to a full-scale renewal of surveillance cannot be ignored: fear of damage actions; judicial restraints; control of police target selection, missions, and tactics by reconstituted city councils (as in Chicago and Los Angeles); and an anti–urban surveillance political climate and constituency. Thus, prompt and effective protests have ensued in the wake of discovery of police surveillance of demonstrations in opposition to the administration's foreign policies.[47] However, all that may be needed to stir a traditional countersubversive response in a society programmed for fear and quick to forget the costly and repressive follies of the past ("social amnesia" in Russell Jacoby's phrase) is the mythification of the extent and gravity of the threat. We may once again emerge from a cyclical repentence ritual to entrust to the police the very powers now denied them.

Given the grip of countersubversion on our political culture, the reluctance of civilian authorities to interfere with or restrain police policies and practices for fear of damaging consequences in both the law-enforcement and peacekeeping realms, and the Haymarket legacy that makes the defense of the status quo a prime police mission, the achievements of the movement to depoliticize police investigations and to safeguard invasions of constitutional rights have been extraordinary. Efforts

in courtrooms and legislative chambers to prevent a recurrence of politically motivated investigations, and for accountability as to the past,
have created models for, as well as a climate favorable to, further ad-
vances in dealing with police abuses in urban America. And perhaps the
most effective therapy has been the pocketbook sanction, civil damage
actions—like the SACC lawsuit—against cities, their police departments,
and individual malefactors.

But the danger of a revival of past abuses cannot be ignored—not
even in the cities with police departments already subject to external
restraints, not to speak of those in which remedies have been confined to
internal administrative guidelines or those that, untouched by litigation,
have retained unfettered political surveillance resources. (As we have
seen in the case of Chicago, no new threat or menace was necessary to
cause police disregard of a clearly worded judicial ban.) Moreover, the
Haymarket legacy triumphed in all of the cities discussed here despite
the institutionalization of nondepartmental civilian controls, a long-
standing goal of reformers, intended to curb the evils of the past. Indeed, it would be difficult to find in the entire history of red squad
operations significant evidence of intervention by civilian overseers. (In
New Haven, it will be recalled, the review panel entered the picture after
public disclosure of extensive illegal surveillance operations.)

In assessing the likelihood of a recurrence of traditional, run-of-the-
mill political surveillance in urban America, we are not confined to the
record of politically motivated surveillance in the sixties and seventies.
In the summer of 1987 New York City was confronted by the specter of
racially motivated police surveillance thought to have been banished by
the consent decree in the *Handschu* case (see pp. 356–57) in which a
federal court placed limits on surveillance. Moreover, the police misled
the Handschu Authority set up to ensure compliance with agreed upon
guidelines. In effect, the police department rewrote the meaning of the
consent decree. Investigative reports disclose that the police Intelligence
Division taped and reported on comments on a radio talk show by black
community leaders and engaged in related practices, including the surveillance of black activists and undercover monitoring of meetings such
as press conferences. In the face of legal charges of contempt of court,
these activities were curbed by the police commissioner. Subsequently, in
November 1987, the authority ruled that most of the targets' allegations
were well founded. A month later the police retreated from earlier denials and admitted undercover surveillance of a civil rights group in violation of the *Handschu* decree, an operation especially questionable
given that the initial spur to the surveillance was criticism by the targets

of police conduct in race-related situations. The court subsequently (in July 1989) upheld the contention that the police had broken the *Handschu* pact.[48]

During the same period, in what a civil liberties advocate calls "a case dripping with irony," fifteen political action and advocacy groups sued the city of Philadelphia and federal officials for violating the constitutional rights of their members and supporters to free speech and association in celebration of the bicentennial of the Constitution. One of the target groups, the nonviolent Pledge of Resistance, was infiltrated by an undercover policeman; associates of all the plaintiff groups charged that the police had encircled and barricaded three hundred of their number to bar their entry into Independence Mall, the site of the festivities, and that individuals were denied the right to wear protest buttons dealing with political issues (such as military intervention in Central America and apartheid) or to carry any signs or banners, however peaceful their import. One of those barred was told that the celebration was only for "Reagan people" and those without protest messages of any kind. A court decision in July 1987 postponed the judge's decision on the spying, stating that it was a "close Constitutional question," and ruled that protesters were to be allowed access to the Mall—too late to correct the abuses complained of. Mayor Wilson Goode dealt with the court's ruling on the infiltration by transferring the authority to approve proposed infiltration of groups engaged in political expression and protest from the police to the city's managing director and two high-level functionaries, thus for the first time in Philadelphia placing responsibility for informer misconduct in civilian hands.[49]

Beyond these revealing developments, the sheer number and diversity of cities with red squads stir doubts about the likelihood of depoliticizing red squad operations across the board nationally. It will be recalled that in the seventies the LEIU alone had some 230 member agencies. The CIA instructional and liaison program during the same period likewise involved at least 44 local and county units.*

---

* To be sure, not all LEIU members were urban units or engaged in political intelligence. The original LEIU membership requirements were that the agency seeking admission must be a police or sheriff's office with an intelligence unit of at least one officer working full time on intelligence matters (Nino John LoSchiavo, "Law Enforcement Intelligence Unit," *Police Chief*, February 1975). The CIA may perhaps have furnished training or equipment to more than the 44 mentioned above. According to one released document, 83 units were briefed on "trace-metal detection techniques" (Philip Melanson, "The C.I.A.'s Secret Ties to the Local Police," *Nation*, March 26, 1983).

Restoration of the Haymarket legacy requires a "subversive" reference group—communists (or "Marxist-Leninists," the trendy substitute) have long been the official choice faute de mieux, but "terrorism" is becoming the current favorite—posing a new/old threat of subversion, violence, betrayal, and overthrow, historically so effective in politicizing police functions. If the past is a guide, "terrorist" may well be converted into an all-purpose taint or stigma against an expandable body of targets—potential terrorists, fronts, suspects, supporters, and sympathizers. Not only are terrorists suitably fear-engendering as a negative reference group, but already they are being broadly invoked to justify repression of peaceful dissenters.* Equally noteworthy is the cooperation between the FBI and the local police in the Joint Terrorist Task Force in monitoring the political scene for terrorist subjects, a linkage that has already emerged in a number of cities with a distinctive modus operandi. According to one account, in 1983 the Naval Investigative Service infiltrated an anti–nuclear weapons group planning a demonstration at the Naval Weapons Station in Concord, California. The informer-infiltrator was apparently a police agent attached to the local force. The infiltrator's report was then transmitted to the FBI's Domestic Terrorism Unit.[50]

A campaign to develop and exploit a market generated by the fear of domestic terrorism[51] has already been launched by private groups. In Idaho, Michigan, Ohio, Connecticut, Arizona, and other states "seminars," primarily for law-enforcement personnel, have been conducted by Dan-Cor Ltd., a firm headed by James Davis, a former California police functionary with ties to state law-enforcement circles organized under Governor Reagan. The presentations are typically sponsored by local officers (police chiefs, sheriffs, state police officials), and the participants' fees are paid for with public funds. The agendas of the workshops typically have very little to do with terrorism—understandable enough given that domestic terrorist incidents have become quite rare. (By 1985 the number of such incidents had "declined," according to FBI chief William Webster, "for the fourth consecutive year to only seven.")[52] Instead, the conference agendas include such subjects as "Anti-Nuke Organizational Structure," "The New Peace Movement," "Communist Front Groups," "Sanctuary and Underground Railroad Activity," "Update: Central American Support Groups, Intelligence Tips for Demonstration Control, the Structure of Dissident Groups, Use of Special

---

* For example, in 1985 the mayor of Providence, R.I., established a Terrorist Extremist Suppression Team (TEST) to "keep tabs" on "extremists"—that is, left-wing political groups and peace activists.

Operations Personnel," and "Developing an Associative Matrix" (for identifying members and leaders of groups).

A similar operation, "Anti-Terrorism '86," a "symposium featuring state of the art tactics, strategies and operational techniques" was sponsored by the Law Enforcement Communication Network in conjunction with the California Peace Officers' Association. The literature of the operation listed an impressive array of sponsors, including public figures, headed by then Vice President George Bush. This group appealed to the fears of corporate executives of threats to persons and property by a new breed of subversives.

The disclosures in the eighties of a series of Soviet espionage connections have stirred demands for closer joint federal-local counterintelligence operations.[53] The development by local agencies of a loose partnership with the CIA in the counterintelligence sphere cannot be discounted when we recall that, in the sixties, the CIA, despite a ban on internal security functions, coopted many local police units, and that it is today expressly authorized to engage in domestic intelligence operations. Nor can we discount the prospect of an aggressive FBI partnership with local police on the counterintelligence front. The bureau has already established a program, "Development of Counter-intelligence Awareness" (DECA), to help some 14,000 defense contractors combat the threat of infiltration by foreign agents.

There are already glimmerings of a potential FBI partnership with local law-enforcement units in the monitoring and harassment of critics of U.S. Central American policies. The grounds offered by the FBI for its sprawling pursuit, beginning in 1981, of a wide range of individuals and organizations, as disclosed in documents dealing with its targeting of the Committee in Solidarity with the People of El Salvador (CISPES), are counterintelligence and counterterrorism. In the CISPES case and other instances, red squad file items were channeled to FBI agents via a private right-wing surveillance network in which the *Information Digest* published by John Rees, a veteran informer for the FBI and local police, and Western Goals played principal roles. As a source on the Senate Select Committee on Intelligence stated: "There is a concern [among members] that there has been a return to the red squads and the use of local resources in an improper way." Senator William Cohen, a committee member, noted that the committee planned to probe whether there were not "too few constraints on the [FBI's] investigative activities in the field." Not only resort to a new breed of targets but the emergence of more protective operational modes may invite renewal of political surveillance. The risk of renewing such surveillance may well officially be perceived as reduced by stricter secrecy than in the past, while deniability may be preserved through greater deception and reliance on private-sector proxies (as in the Iran-Contra affair), as well as by newer, less traceable surveillance technology, which also (through computers) has made the maintenance and dissemination of files easier to conceal.[54]

Notes

Notes to the Introduction

1. "History of Police Intelligence Operations, 1880–1975 (Final Draft)" (report prepared by Legal Development Division, Technical Research Services Division, International Association of Chiefs of Police, Gaithersburg, Md., 1976), p. 3, hereafter cited as IACP "History."

2. See, for example, Albert J. Reiss, *Police and the Public* (New Haven: Yale University Press, 1971), pp. 147, 155; Robert W. Balch, "The Police Personality: Fact or Fiction," *Journal of Criminal Law and Criminology* 63, no. 1 (Spring 1972): 106–19; Robert Reiner, *The Blue-Coated Worker: A Sociological Study of Police Unionism* (New York: Cambridge University Press, 1978), p. 137; Jerome Skolnick, *The Politics of Protest* (New York: Ballantine Books, 1969), p. 252, hereafter cited as Skolnick; David H. Bayley and Harold Mendelsohn, *Minorities and the Police* (New York: Free Press, 1969), pp. 4, 15, 28, 33; Rodney Stark, *Police Riots* (Belmont, Calif.: Focus Books, 1972), p. 10.

Notes to Chapter 1

1. The domestic exploitation of fears engendered by the Paris Commune of 1871 in order to justify repression was a commonplace in subsequent years. See, for example, George L. Cherry, "American Metropolitan Press Reaction to the Paris Commune of 1871," *Mid-America* 32, no. 1 (January 1950); Samuel Bernstein, "American Labor and the Paris Commune," *Science and Society* 15, no. 2 (Spring 1951): 144–62. Kenneth Stampp describes the invocation of the Commune by ex-slaveholders to promote resistance to radical Republican reconstruction and the warning that universal male suffrage would usher in a version of the Commune (*The Era of Reconstruction: America after the Civil War, 1865–1877* [New York: Vintage Books, 1965], p. 205, hereafter cited as Stampp).

2. Goldwin Smith, "The Labour War in the United States," *Contemporary Review* 30 (September 1877), quoted in Robert V. Bruce, *1877: Year of Violence* (Indianapolis: Bobbs-Merrill, 1959), p. 26, hereafter cited as Bruce, *1877*.

3. Quoted by Richard Drinnon, *Rebel in Paradise: A Biography of Emma Goldman* (Boston: Beacon Press, 1970), p. 226, hereafter cited as Drinnon.

4. The history of the Pinkerton Agency is well presented in Frank Morn, *"The Eye That Never Sleeps": A History of the Pinkerton National Detective Agency* (Bloomington: Indiana University Press, 1982). See also James D. Horan, *The Pinkertons: The Detective Dynasty That Made History* (New York: Crown Publishers, 1967); James D. Horan and Howard Swiggett, *The Pinkerton Story* (New York: Putnam's, 1951); Thomas A. Repetto, *The Blue Parade* (New York: Free Press, 1978), pp. 258–63.

5. On the Molly Maguires, see Wayne G. Broehl, *The Molly Maguires* (Cambridge, Mass.: Harvard University Press, 1964); Arthur H. Lewis, *Lament for the Molly Maguires* (New York: Harcourt, Brace & World, 1964).

6. The discussion of the Great Upheaval is based on the following sources: Philip S. Foner, *The Great Labor Uprising of 1877* (New York: Monad Press, 1977); Bruce, *1877*, passim; Jeremy Brecher, *Strike!* (1972; repr., Boston: South End Press, 1977), pp. 1–25; Richard Schneirov, "Chicago's Great Upheaval of 1877," *Chicago History* 9, no. 1 (Spring 1980); Herbert C. Gutman, "Trouble on the Railroads in 1873–1874: Prelude to the 1877 Crisis," *Labor History* 2, no. 2 (Spring 1961): 215–35.

7. Gerald Astor, *The New York Cops: An Informal History* (New York: Scribner's, 1971), p. 199; Augustine E. Costello, *Our Police Protectors: A History of the New York Police*, repr. from 3d ed. (Montclair, N.J.: Patterson Smith, 1972), p. 475. The most notorious disturbance in New York City is discussed by Herbert C. Gutman, "The Tompkins Square Riot in New York City on January 13, 1874: A Re-Examination of Its Cause and Aftermath," *Labor History* 5, no. 1 (Winter 1965).

8. The sources for the discussion of the response by Chicago authorities to the Great Upheaval in that city include, in addition to the citations above, Bessie Pierce, *History of Chicago* (New York: Knopf, 1957), 2: 248ff.; John J. Flinn and John E. Wilkie, *History of the Chicago Police* (Chicago, 1887; reprint, New York: Arno Press, 1971), pp. 153ff., hereafter cited as Flinn and Wilkie; Carolyn Ashbaugh, *Lucy Parsons: American Revolutionary* (Chicago: Charles H. Kerr, 1976), pp. 21–27, hereafter cited as Ashbaugh; William J. Adelman, *Pilsen and the West Side* (Chicago: Illinois History Society, n.d.), pp. 9–19; Edgar Bernhard, Ira Latimer, and Harvey O'Connor, eds., *Pursuit of Freedom: A History*

of Civil Liberties in Illinois, 1787–1942 (Chicago: Chicago Civil Liberties Committee, 1942), pp. 172–73, hereafter cited as *Pursuit of Freedom.*

9. The backlash also resulted in the passage of conspiracy laws to curb worker unrest. The Chicago Citizens' Association also promoted the purchase of a new police weapon—the rapid fire Gatling gun, capable of firing as many as 1,000 shots a minute (Ashbaugh, p. 25).

10. The principal sources of the discussion in the text of the Haymarket tragedy are Paul Avrich, *The Haymarket Tragedy* (Princeton: Princeton University Press, 1984), hereafter cited as Avrich; Henry David, *The History of the Haymarket Affair* (New York: Farrar & Rinehart, 1936), hereafter cited as David; Ashbaugh; Dyer D. Lum, *A Concise History of the Great Trial of the Chicago Anarchists in 1886* (1887; repr., New York: Arno Press, 1969), hereafter cited as Lum; two publications of the Illinois History Society by William J. Adelman: *Haymarket Revisited* (Chicago, 1976) and *Pilsen and the West Side*; and contemporary press accounts.

11. The eight were Albert Parson, August Spies, Samuel Fielden, Michael Schwab, George Engel, Adolph Fischer, Louis Lingg, and Oscar Neebe. Of the eight, Parsons and Fischer had left the meeting before it was over, Neebe and Engel were at home at the time, and Lingg was not at the scene of the meeting.

12. Herbert Asbury, *Gem of the Prairie: An Informal History of the Chicago Underworld* (New York: Knopf, 1940), pp. 93–94.

13. Bureau of the Census, *Statistics of the Population* (Washington, D.C.: GPO, 1883), 19: 508.

14. Flinn and Wilkie, p. 232. For further accounts of Bonfield's violent proclivities, see Ashbaugh, pp. 60–61; Henry Barnard, *Eagle Forgotten: The Life of John Henry Altgeld* (Indianapolis: Bobbs-Merrill, 1938), p. 79, hereafter cited as Barnard; Avrich, pp. 97–98; Waldo R. Browne, *Altgeld of Illinois: A Record of His Life and Work* (New York: B. W. Huebsch, 1924), pp. 110–11. In his address to the jury, defendant August Spies charged that Bonfield was responsible for the bombing since it was an act of revenge for the brutality of his detail against the McCormick pickets—a view subsequently expressed by Governor Altgeld in his pardon statement.

15. John P. Altgeld, *Reasons for Pardoning Fielden, Neebe and Schwab* (1893; repr., Chicago: Charles H. Kerr for the Illinois History Society, 1986), hereafter cited as Altgeld, *Reasons;* Barnard, pp. 103–4.

16. David, p. 221; Ray Ginger, *Eugene Debs: A Biography* (New York: Collier Books, 1962), pp. 47–49, hereafter cited as Ginger; Lum, p. 80; Herman Kogan, "William Perkins Black: Haymarket Lawyer," *Chicago History* 5, no. 3 (Summer 1976); Harvey Wish, "Governor Altgeld Pardons the Anarchists," *Journal of the Illinois State Historical Society* 31 (December 1938): 83–84. Seven of the ultimate defendants

were arrested by May 14; the eighth, Albert Parsons, turned himself in on June 21, the opening day of the trial.

17. David, p. 538.

18. Quoted in Barnard, pp. 189, 210; Ginger, pp. 78–79, 84.

19. The original publisher of Schaack's *Anarchy and Anarchists* was a Chicago firm, F. J. Schulte & Co., associated with publishers in New York, Philadelphia, St. Louis, and Pittsburgh.

20. David, pp. 486–87.

21. On the post-Haymarket climate, see Lewis P. Wheelock, "Urban Protestant Reactions to the Chicago Haymarket Affair" (Ph.D. diss., University of Iowa, 1956), passim; Robert J. Goldstein, "The Anarchist Scare of 1908," *American Studies* 15 (1974): 40–44; Richard Sennett, "Middle-Class Families and Urban Violence," in *Nineteenth-Century Cities: Essays in the New Urban History*, ed. Stephen Thernstrom and Richard Sennett (New Haven: Yale University Press, 1969), pp. 386–88.

22. Drinnon, pp. 226–27.

23. Finley Peter Dunne, *Mr. Dooley Remembers: The Informal Memoirs of Finley Peter Dunne* (Boston: Little, Brown, 1963), p. 62.

24. Byrnes also acquired a yacht and a country estate on the Shrewsbury River in New Jersey. "It's All News to Mr. Byrnes," *New York Times*, July 25, 1893; "Superintendent's Yacht Won," ibid., August 7, 1894; "Byrnes and His Money," ibid., December 3, 1894.

25. "Wrecked Valhalla Hall," *New York Times*, August 18, 1893; "Anarchists Were to Blame," ibid., August 20, 1893.

26. "Anarchy's Dingy Stronghold," *New York Times*, August 22, 1893; "Anarchists Kept in Check," ibid., August 20, 1893.

27. "He Rules through Fear," *New York Times*, December 10, 1893.

28. *New York Times:* "Chief Byrnes Retired," May 28, 1895; "Mr. Byrnes Goes to Europe," October 23, 1895; "Byrnes Starts a Bureau," December 23, 1895.

29. Philip Taft and Philip Ross conclude that the United States has had "the bloodiest and most violent labor history of any industrial nation in the world," but that worker hostility and violence flowed primarily from employer resistance to organizing efforts ("American Labor Violence: Its Cause, Character and Outcome," in *Violence in America*, ed. Hugh Davis Graham and Ted Robert Gurr [New York: Bantam Books, 1969], pp. 281, 380–81). See also Philip Taft, "Violence in American Labor Disputes," *Annals of the American Academy of Social and Political Science* (March 1966): 127–40; Val Lorwin, "Reflections on the History of the French and American Labor Movements," *Journal of Economic History* 17 (March 1957): 25–44. A thoughtful statement of the views on labor violence of Progressive Era liberals is presented in T. S. Adams, "Violence in Labor Disputes," *Proceedings of the American Economic Association*, December 1905, hereafter cited as Adams,

"Violence." See also "The Violence of American Trade Unions," *Living Age*, 7th ser., 10 (February 1913); and Anthony Oberschall, "Group Violence: Some Hypotheses and Empirical Uniformities," *Law and Society Review* 3, no. 4 (August 1970): 61–92. A Marxist view on employer violence is summarized in Bruce Johnson, "Taking Care of Labor: The Police in American Politics," *Theory and Society* 3, no. 1 (Spring 1976).

30. C. P. Connolly, "Protest by Dynamite," *Collier's*, January 13, 1912.

31. That the fear of imminent class conflict survived in the industrial era is suggested by a 1912 novel, *Philip Dru—Administrator: A Story of Tomorrow* (New York: B. W. Huebsch, 1912), written by Colonel Edward House (future advisor to President Wilson). It warned that "the seething radical elements of the political cask—today under pressure of rising prices for the poor and greater privilege for the rich—[might] literally burst into one great conflict, the second Civil War."

32. See, for example, Adams, "Violence."

33. Altgeld, *Reasons*.

34. Robert Hunter, *Labor in Politics* (Chicago: Socialist Party, 1915), pp. 281–82.

35. Commission on Industrial Relations (1912), *Final Report and Testimony* (Washington, D.C.: GPO, 1916), 1: 56, hereafter cited as C.I.R. *Final Report*.

36. Ben Blumenberg, "Making Open Air Meetings Successful," *Socialist World* 2, no. 12 (June 1922); Charles Leinenweber, "Socialists in the Streets: The New York City Socialist Party in Working Class Neighborhoods, 1908–1918," *Science and Society* 41 (Summer 1977): 152–71.

37. John Berger, "The Nature of Mass Demonstrations," *New Society*, May 1968.

38. *Mother Earth*, May 1911.

39. Edward A. Ross, "Freedom of Communication and the Struggle for Right; Presidential Address," in American Sociological Association, *Papers and Proceedings of the Annual Meeting* 9 (1914): 4–5.

40. C.I.R. *Final Report*, 3: 2563.

41. Documented in the testimony devoted to the strikes in these cities in C.I.R. *Final Report*, chs. on Lowell, Passaic, Akron.

42. *New York Times*: "To Drive Anarchists Out of New York," September 11, 1901; "Hiss the Red Flag," July 5, 1905; "Social Democratic Speakers Arrested," August 16, 1905; "Again Stop Meeting of Social Democrats," August 17, 1905; "Ban on Meeting Taken Off," August 18, 1905; "Socialists Have Only Hisses for Hearst," October 16, 1905.

43. "Nightsticks, Fists and Blackjacks Used by Police on Striking Cloakmakers," (New York) *Call*, August 15, 1908.

44. "Bomb Explosion in St. Patrick's," *New York Times*, October 14, 1914.

45. *New York Times*, 1915: "Woods Sees Swann on Bomb Inquiry," March 6; "Too Many Lawyers Halt Bomb Hearing," March 7; "I.W.W. Prisoner a Sleuth," March 16; "30 Anarchists Fail to Shake Polignani," March 31; "No Danger in Bomb, New Defense Plea," April 1; "In Cell for Threat at the Bomb Trial," April 2; "Detective Lit Bomb, Abarno Tells Court," April 3; "Convict Bomb Men in Cathedral Plot," April 13; (New York) *Call*, 1915: "Letters Show Church Bomb Spy Tried to Incite 40 Boys," March 8; "Detective Tells of Buying Part of Material in Cathedral Bomb," March 31; "Frame Up Forced on Abarno Is His Charge," April 3. See also Emma Goldman, "The Barnum & Bailey Staging of the 'Anarchist Plot,' " *Mother Earth*, April 1915.

46. "Police in Two Years Tapped 350 Phones," *New York Times*, May 17, 1916.

47. "Open Campaign on Anarchists," *San Francisco Chronicle*, March 3, 1908; "Assistant Chief Schuetter Examining Prisoners Taken in Round-up of Anarchists," *Chicago Examiner*, March 4, 1908; "Police Have Proof of Well-Laid Plot," *Milwaukee Sentinel*, March 4, 1908; Drinnon, pp. 122–23.

48. Coverage nearly every day in the *Chicago Daily Times*, February 10–21, and the *New York Times*, February 11–19, 1916.

49. "Make Mills, 85, Ex-Lieutenant of Police, Dies," *Chicago Tribune*, September 25, 1956; "Make Mills Rites Set; Former Police Officer," *Chicago Sun-Times*, September 25, 1956.

50. *Fourth Annual Message of Samuel Ashbridge, Mayor of the City of Philadelphia . . . for the Year Ending December 31, 1902* (Philadelphia: City of Philadelphia, 1903), introduction, p. xii. See also pp. 8, 37. These annual reports are cited hereafter as Philadelphia, *Mayor's Annual Report* [date].

51. Philadelphia, *Mayor's Annual Report*, 1908, introduction, p. xiv. See also pp. 6–12.

52. Emma Goldman, *Living My Life: An Autobiography* (1931; 1 vol. ed., Garden City, N.Y.: Garden City Publishing, 1934), pp. 456–59.

53. The discussion of the political setting of the LAPD and the historic role of its red squad is based on Carey McWilliams, *Southern California Country* (New York: Duell, Sloan & Pearce, 1946), pp. 272–82, hereafter cited as McWilliams; Robert Gottlieb and Irene Wolt, *Thinking Big: The Story of the Los Angeles Times, Its Publishers and Their Influence on Southern California* (New York: Putnam's, 1977), pp. 45–47, hereafter cited as Gottlieb and Wolt; David Halberstam, *The Powers That Be* (New York: Knopf, 1979), pp. 94–101, hereafter cited as Halberstam; and Joseph Gerald Woods, "The Progressives and the Police: Urban Reform and the Professionalization of the Los Angeles Police" (thesis, Urban Policy Research Institute, 1973), pp. 15–43, hereafter cited as Woods.

54. C.I.R. *Final Report*, p. 5860; *Los Angeles Times* editorial, June 11, 1911.

55. IACP "History," p. 8.

56. Joan M. Jensen, *The Price of Vigilance* (Chicago: Rand McNally, 1968), pp. 173, 223, hereafter cited as Jensen.

57. Jensen, pp. 245–70; IACP "History," pp. 10–11.

58. The impact of these attacks can be traced in newspaper coverage in the *New York Times*, for example.

June 3, 1919: [Nott story]	MIDNIGHT BOMBS FOR OFFICIALS IN 8 CITIES BOMBERS DIE AT ATTORNEY GENERAL'S HOUSE TWO VICTIMS AT JUDGE NOTT'S HOUSE HERE BOMBS IN BOSTON, CLEVELAND, PITTSBURGH
[Round-up story]	Attacks in 6 Other Cities House of Boston Justice Who Sentenced Reds Is Shattered Bomb to Pittsburgh Judge Cleveland Mayor's House Damaged—Attempt on Philadelphia Church Paterson Scene of Attack House of a Legislator in the Bay State Is Badly Wrecked
June 4, 1919: [Pittsburgh story]	PITTSBURGH BOMBER'S NAME IS GIVEN TO POLICE NATIONWIDE SEARCH RESULTS IN 67 ARRESTS RIOTERS KILLED, TOLDO ASKS FOR TROOPS
[Philadelphia story]	See Philadelphia as a Plot Center That City Is Searched to Find Washington Bombing Antecedents Police Round Up I.W.W.s Reputable Residents of Italian District Aid in Disclosing Anarchist Reports
[Cleveland story]	Arrest 45 Suspects in Cleveland Raids Police Find Red Banner and Pictures of Bolshevist Leaders in "Automobile School"
[Round-up story]	See Reign of Terror as Aim of Plotters Head of Legislative Committee Puts Number in This City at Hundred of Thousands
June 5, 1919:	Philadelphia Finds Trail of Red Who Died in Washington Explosion; Flynn Begins Nationwide Search Question Radicals Here Police to Investigate Activities of 20,000 on Their Lists

Seek for Bomb Clues
Detectives Visit Russian People's House and Question Supporters of Soviets
Police Aid Other Cities
Detectives Go to Philadelphia, Paterson, and Pittsburgh to Hunt for Conspirators
Pittsburgh Thinks Plot Began Here
Police Believe Bolshevist Conspiracy Is Back of the Bomb Explosions
Irishmen Made Bombs?
House of I.W.W. Secretary Is Minutely Searched by the Authorities
Dragnet for Reds All Over Country
Associates Will Be Rounded Up—Twelve Radicals Now under Surveillance There

[Cleveland story]   Cleveland Proposes to Deport All Reds
Thirty Suspects Arrested Give No Clue to the Bombing of Mayor Davis's Home

[Boston story]   Boston Finds Bomb Source
Branch Red Group Had Dynamite Stolen from Contractor

June 6, 1919:   Irish I.W.W. Chief Held in Pittsburgh
[New York story]   Federal and Local Detectives Plan for United Efforts to Reach the Conspirators

[Philadelphia story]   European Reds May Have Set Bombs

June 7, 1919:   Center Hunt for Bomb Gang in New York
[New York story]   Co-operation to an Unexampled Degree of the Nation's Police Agencies
Bomb Squad Reinforced
Police Make a Census of All Anarchists Here on Night of the Explosions

[Detroit story]   2 Held in Detroit as Bomb Suspects; Both Have I.W.W. Cards.

See also Stanley Coben, *A. Mitchell Palmer: Politician* (New York: Columbia University Press, 1963), pp. 205–8.

59. See, for example, testimony from the chiefs of police from Bessemer, Pa., and Baltimore, Md., in *Proceedings of the 26th Convention of the International Chiefs of Police* (1919), pp. 18ff. and 103ff.

60. The general source for this account is Dennis Earl Hoffman, "An Exploratory Analysis of the Response of Urban Police to Labor Radicalism" (Ph.D. diss., Portland State University, 1979).

61. The account of the 1919 strike is based principally on these sources: Interchurch World Movement of North America, Commission of Inquiry, *Report on the Steel Strike of 1919* (New York: Harcourt, Brace & Howe, 1920), hereafter cited as IWM *Report;* U.S. Senate, *Report Investigating Strike in Steel Industry,* 66th Cong., 1st sess., 1921 (S. Rept. 289, vol. 1); David Brody, *Labor in Crisis: The Steel Strike of 1919* (Philadelphia: Lippincott, 1965); and William Z. Foster, *The Great Steel Strike and Its Lessons* (New York: B. W. Huebsch, 1920).

62. Interchurch World Movement of North America, Commission of Inquiry, *Public Opinion and the Steel Strike* (New York: Harcourt, Brace, 1921), p. 177, hereafter cited as IWM *Public Opinion.*

63. IWM *Report,* pp. 32–38, 220–32.

64. IWM *Public Opinion,* pp. 174–77.

65. IWM *Report,* pp. 27–31.

66. See, for example, Robert K. Murray, "Communism and the Great Steel Strike of 1919," *Mississippi Valley Historical Review* 38, no. 7 (December 1951), hereafter cited as Murray.

67. Julian F. Jaffe, *Crusade against Radicalism: New York during the Red Scare, 1914–1924* (Port Washington, N.Y.: Kennikat Press, 1972), pp. 80–82, hereafter cited as Jaffe.

68. New York State, Lusk Committee, *Revolutionary Radicalism* (Albany, N.Y., 1920), pp. 21–23.

69. Jaffe, pp. 132–33.

70. For example, in reviewing the squad's first year of operation, Mayor Thomas B. Smith boasted: "All meetings of [radicals] were carefully investigated and details of uniformed and plainclothes men were present in each occasion when the slightest intimation was given that radicalism might prevail. Complete cooperation with the U.S. Department of Justice was effected in subduing all traitors to the Government" (*Mayor's Annual Report,* 1919, p. 9).

71. *Mayor's Annual Report,* 1921, pp. 23–24.

72. Gladys L. Palmer, *Union Tactics and Economic Change* (Philadelphia: University of Pennsylvania Press, 1932), p. 19.

73. "Rough House Methods for Garment Makers," *Philadelphia Daily News Record,* March 21, 1921.

74. American Civil Liberties Union, *Annual Report,* 1928, pp. 31–32. The American Civil Liberties Union is cited hereafter as ACLU.

75. Murray, p. 215. On orders of Mayor James Cozzens, the Detroit police were not operationally involved in the Palmer Raids in January 1920, when some 800 Detroit residents were arrested and treated with

lawlessness and cruelty. See also James B. Jacobs, "The Conduct of Local Police Intelligence" (Ph.D. diss., Princeton University, 1977), hereafter cited as Jacobs.

76. Norman Hapgood, ed., *Professional Patriots* (New York: A. & C. Boni, 1927), p. 4. See also Better American Federation, *Newsletter*, June–September 1920; McWilliams, pp. 291–93.

77. Los Angeles Police Department, *Daily Bulletin*, November 15, November 22, and November 24, 1919.

78. John W. Caughey, *Their Majesties the Mob* (Chicago: University of Chicago Press, 1960), p. 9 and passim. See also Clinton J. Taft, *Fifteen Years on Freedom's Front* (Los Angeles: ACLU, Southern California Branch, 1939), hereafter cited as Taft.

Notes to Chapter 2

1. On the vital role of outdoor and indoor meetings in left politics and the harassment of such gatherings by the police, see "Party Notes," *Proletarian*, May 1922–October 1927; Rose Karsner, "Building the I.L.D.," *Labor Defender*, March and June 1926; "The New York Sacco and Vanzetti Meeting," ibid., March and August 1927; "Ten Millions Continue Their Demand," ibid., August 1927; A. Jakira, "Organizing Mass Meetings," ibid., January 1930. Sites large enough for mass meetings were available in large cities such as New York (Union Square) and Chicago (Bughouse Square). Public as well as private meeting halls abounded in virtually all American cities and towns; in some cities, the new surge of radicalism led to the reopening of disused or abandoned meeting places.

2. The Fish Committee hearings (House Special Committee to Investigate Communist Activities in the United States) are in six multivolume parts. The committee's report (71st Cong., 3d sess., H. Rept. 2290) is in part 6. Hereafter cited as Fish Committee Hearings.

3. Illustrative examples may be found in testimony from Fish Committee Hearings: St. Louis (pt. 1, vol. 4, p. 322); New York (pt. 3, vol. l, p. 191; pt. 3, vol. 4, pp. 211–13); Seattle (pt. 3, vol. 4, p. 1); Boston (pt. 3, vol. 5, pp. 1–9, 21, 60–65); Flint, Mich. (pt. 4, vol. 1, pp. 1–16); Detroit (pt. 4, vol. 1, pp. 1–17, 110–14, 174–93, 282–90); the South (pt. 6, vol. 1, pp. 1–304).

4. ACLU, *Annual Report*, 1934, pp. 53–56.

5. Ibid., pp. 72–76; IACP "History," pp. 38–39.

6. Frank Donner, *The Age of Surveillance: The Aims and Methods of America's Political Intelligence System* (New York: Knopf, 1980), pp. 52–79, hereafter cited as Donner, *Age*.

7. IACP "History," p. 42.

8. Donner, *Age*, pp. 240–49; id., "Electronic Surveillance: The National Security Game," *Civil Liberties Review* 2, no. 4 (Summer 1975), hereafter cited as Donner, "Electronic Surveillance"; Victor Navasky and Nathan Lewin, "Electronic Surveillance," in *Investigating the FBI*, ed. Pat Watters and Steven Gillers (New York: Doubleday, 1973), pp. 297–337. The Watters and Gillers collection is hereafter cited as Watters and Gillers, *Investigating the FBI*.

9. Among the cities with such ordinances were: McKeesport, Erie, and York, Pa.; Jacksonville and Miami, Fla.; New Rochelle, N.Y.; Cambridge, Mass.; and Los Angeles (IACP "History," p. 50).

10. IACP "History," p. 57.

11. See, for example, Donald F. Crosby, "The Politics of Religion," in *The Specter: Original Essays on the Cold War and the Origins of McCarthyism*, ed. Robert Griffith and Athan Theoharis (New York: New Viewpoints, 1974), pp. 18–38.

12. Fish Committee Hearings, pt. 2, vol. 1, pp. 177ff., in Executive Session.

13. Lowell J. Limpus, *Honest Cop: Lewis J. Valentine* (New York: Dutton, 1939), p. 128, hereafter cited as Limpus.

14. "Boring into Business, Schools and City Bureaus, Whalen Warns, Asks Curb," *New York Times*, March 9, 1930, quoted in *Police Lawlessness against Communists in New York* (New York: ACLU, April 1930).

15. Ernest J. Hopkins, *Our Lawless Police* (New York: Viking Press, 1931), pp. 52–53, hereafter cited as Hopkins.

16. Charles Garrett, *The La Guardia Years: Machine and Reform Politics in New York City* (New Brunswick, N.J.: Rutgers University Press, 1961), pp. 254, 280; August Heckscher, *When La Guardia Was Mayor* (New York: Norton, 1978), pp. 56, 64, 122–29. La Guardia's hands-off policy in strikes and demonstrations infuriated his first police commissioner, General John F. O'Ryan, who resigned after nine months. He was succeeded by Lewis J. Valentine, who for decades gave the department outstanding leadership, sharply reducing graft and corruption as well as police intervention in political protest activities. See Limpus, pp. 235–37, 254–55; Lewis J. Valentine, *Nightstick: The Autobiography of Lewis J. Valentine* (New York: Dial Press, 1947), passim.

17. Anthony Bouza, "The Operations of a Police Intelligence Unit" (M.A. thesis, John Jay College of Criminal Justice, City University of New York, 1968), p. 19. Bouza was a member of BOSS for eight years (1957–65) and considered an expert on urban political intelligence. He became chief of the Minneapolis Police Department; his wife was arrested for trespass in a peace demonstration in 1983 ("130 Arms Demonstrators Arrested in Minneapolis," *New York Times*, April 19, 1983).

18. Fish Committee Hearings, pt. 4, vol. 2.

19. *Pursuit of Freedom*, pp. 155–60; ACLU, *Annual Report*, 1931–32, p. 22; ACLU *Annual Report*, 1934, p. 42.

20. House Special Committee on Un-American Activities Hearings, *Executive Session*, vol. 4, pp. 1512–53 (1938). Hereafter cited as Dies Committee Hearings. Established in 1938 and succeeded in 1945 by a standing House Committee on Un-American Activities (HUAC), the Dies Committee was the second Un-American Activities Committee. Its predecessor of the same name—the McCormack-Dickstein Committee—investigated Nazi as well as Communist activity in 1934–35.

21. See Howard B. Myers, "The Policing of Labor Disputes: A Case Study" (Ph.D. diss., University of Chicago, 1928).

22. Studs Terkel, *Hard Times: An Oral History of the Great Depression* (New York: Avon Books, 1971), p. 182.

23. See William H. Burk, "The Memorial Day 'Massacre' of 1937 and Its Significance in the Unionization of the Republic Steel Corporation" (M.A. thesis, Graduate College of the University of Illinois, 1975).

24. Frank J. Heimoski, remarks to the annual meeting of the Law Enforcement Intelligence Unit (LEIU), 1963. See American Friends Service Committee, *The Police Threat to Political Liberty* (Philadelphia: AFSC, 1979), p. 88 and n. 28, hereafter cited as *Police Threat*.

25. ACLU *Annual Report*, 1932–33, p. 49.

26. Philadelphia, *Mayor's Annual Report*, 1929, p. 21: a total of 335 radical meetings surveilled; 1930, p. 22: 352 radical meetings surveilled; 1932, p. 28: 2,112 open-air meetings and 87 indoor meetings surveilled; 1934, p. 37: 2,187 outdoor and 25 indoor; 1936, p. 26: 585 outdoor, 14 indoor, in addition 167 strikes "handled with extreme caution"; 1937, p. 58: 376 outdoor, 31 indoor.

27. "Phila. Raids Bare Reds' Foothold in Key Industries," *Philadelphia Public Ledger*, April 13, 1940; "Raids on Reds' Office Here Ruled Illegal by Court," *Philadelphia Inquirer*, May 4, 1940.

28. The discussion of the Detroit red squad has drawn extensively on "The Conduct of Local Police Intelligence" by James B. Jacobs (cited in ch. 1, n. 75), dealing with the political intelligence operations of the Detroit police.

29. Fish Committee Hearings, pt. 4, vol. 1, pp. 174–93.

30. Ibid., p. 105.

31. Ibid., pp. 1–15, 111–13.

32. Murray B. Levin, *Political Hysteria in America: The Democratic Capacity for Repression* (New York: Basic Books, 1971), p. 66.

33. Sidney Fine, *Frank Murphy: The Detroit Years* (Ann Arbor: University of Michigan Press, 1975), pp. 389–90, hereafter cited as Fine.

34. Fine, pp. 410–41.

35. For a measure of this disillusionment, see two articles by Mauritz A. Hallgren in the *Nation*: "Detroit's Liberal Mayor," May 13, 1931, and "Grave Danger in Detroit," August 3, 1932.

36. See Lorraine Majka, "Organizational Linkages, Networks and Social Change in Detroit" (Ph.D. diss., Wayne State University, 1981), hereafter cited as Majka.

37. See Jacobs, pp. 113, 115; Majka, pp. 103–8; Kenneth T. Jackson, *The Ku Klux Klan in the City* (New York: Oxford University Press, 1967), pp. 127–43.

38. Quoted in Majka, p. 127.

39. 1938 hearings in Washington and Detroit focusing on Detroit, detailed in pt. 4, vols. 1–2.

40. ACLU, *Civil Liberties in American Cities: Survey Based on 332 American Cities of over 10,000 Population* (1939).

41. Robert S. Mowitz, "State and Local Attack on Subversion," in *The States and Subversion*, ed. Walter Gellhorn (Ithaca, N.Y.: Cornell University Press, 1952).

42. Hynes's career is traced in H. Bloom, "The Passing of 'Red' Hynes," *Nation*, August 2, 1952; La Follette Committee Hearings, pp. 19062–387, 23507–664, and issues in the thirties of the Southern California Branch of the ACLU's weekly newsletter, *Open Forum*. Some examples: *1931*: "Hynes Turns on Labor Paper," January 10; "Freedom of Press Violated by Judge in Citizen Case," January 31; "The Blood of the Martyrs" and "Police Wreck Cooperative," February 28; "Police Prevent Speaking at Anti-War Demonstrations," August 8; "There's No Police Brutality but Go to the Courts," October 24; "Pasadena Scores Red Raiders" and "F.S.U. Meeting in Pasadena Prevented by Red Squads," November 7; "Score Free Speech in Pasadena; L.A. as Usual!" November 14; "Our Lawless Police," November 24; *1932*: "Making for Revolution," January 9; "L.A. Red Squad Stages Raid at Beach, Arresting Two Hundred," January 23; "Police Brutality and Lawlessness Rampant," January 30; "Hynes Investigates Himself," March 19; "Prejudice vs. Justice" and "Captain Hynes' Brave Red Squad Bans Paris Commune Concert," March 26; "Official Banditry in Los Angeles," April 16; "Foster Seized at Plaza on C.S. Charge, Later Released," July 9; "Hynes Pays for Destruction of Films at Demonstration," August 6; "Police Reign of Terror in L.A.," October 8; "Investigation of Red Squad Demand of Methodist Pastors," October 22; "Thousands Demonstrate for Mooney," November 19; "Peace or War—Which Hynes?" December 3; "How Vicious Is the L.A. Red Squad?" December 10; "B.A.F. [Better America Federation] Blocks Way to Progress," December 31; *1933*: "Bigger and Better Police in L.A.," January 21; "Demands That Chief Steckel Investigate Gallagher Attack," March 4 (involved a brutal physical assault by Hynes on a civil liberties attorney); "Damages Suits Filed in L.A." and "Appellate Court Scores Red Squad Lawlessness," March 25; "Injunction Halts Red Squad," April 8; "The Los Angeles Terror," April 29; "More C.L.U. Civil Suits Filed," July 1; *1934*: "What about It, Mayor Shaw?" May 12; "L.A. Red Squad Branded as

Most Brutal in U.S.; Abolition Urged," July 7; "Capt. Hynes Pays," November 17; "Red Squad Practice of Arresting Reds on Suspicion of C.S. Stopped," November 24; *1935*: "Red Squad Head Excoriated," October 5; *1937*: "California Police Officers Flout the Bill of Rights," September 25; "L.A. Red Squad Head to Be Quizzed," November 13; "Captain Hynes Pays," November 20. In the late thirties, Hynes became involved in a variety of activities spreading the word of the gruesome red menace, including a period of service for the Los Angeles business establishment. His most notable contribution was the huge 1937 *Report* to the California Peace Officers' Association, "The Communist Situation in California," drafted by Hynes, who headed the association's Subcommittee on Subversive Activities. The report is not only noteworthy because it projects Hynes's scary style and rhetoric but is graced with illustrations, "Subversive Exhibit Panels of Banners and Placards" seized in raids by the Hynes crew.

43. Fish Committee Hearings, October 9, 1930, pt. 5, vol. 4, pp. 54ff.

44. Taft, pp. 30–33, 38–40; American League against War and Fascism, *California's Brown Book* (pamphlet, 1934), pp. 12–14; *Open Forum*, February 3, 1934, "A. L. Wirin Attacked by Vigilantes"; ibid., May 12, 1934, "Valley Vigilantes on Rampage Again"; La Follette Committee Hearings, pp. 23640–8.

45. See, for example, Hopkins, pp. 38–39, 54–55; Marna Leigh, "Class Warfare in California," *Labor Defender*, August 1930.

46. La Follette Committee Hearings, part 64, exhibit 10213, "Statement of William F. Hynes, Commanding Officer of Intelligence Bureau, Outlining Scope and Function of Bureau," pp. 23509–10.

47. "Cossack War Tactics Menace Peaceful Citizens' Assemblage" and "The Iron Heel Descends," *Open Forum*, November 7, 1931.

48. "Making For Revolution," *Open Forum*, January 9, 1932.

49. ACLU *Annual Report*, 1934, pp. 34–35, appendix, items 65, 67.

50. "Mayor Porter, Chief Steckel Deny Protests, Accuse Citizens of 'Red' Tendencies for Asking Free Speech" (Los Angeles) *Record*, October 10, 1931 (Hynes); Woods, pp. 291–93 (Thorpe).

51. Woods, pp. 240, 250, 323–29.

52. Captain Kynette's gamey proclivities are documented in the L.A. Police Commission's *Minutes* of April 21, 1926, to December 21, 1929. Although a trial board found him guilty of extortion and recommended dismissal, the Police Commission overrode the recommendation. Shortly thereafter he was promoted to sergeant and transferred to the intelligence unit. L.A. Police Commission *Minutes*, October 25, November 15, 29, December 13, 20, 1927.

53. Bruce Henstall, "When the Lid Blew off Los Angeles," *Westways*, November 1977. See also Woods, pp. 357–61. Press coverage in

the *Los Angeles Daily News* and the *Los Angeles Examiner* between mid January and March 1938 is quite complete.

54. Carey McWilliams, "Mr. Tenney's Horrible Awakening," *Nation*, July 23, 1949.

55. The contents of the Burns files are discussed in "Schrade Defends Senate Files on State Subversive Activities," *Los Angeles Times*, March 14, 1971; "Senate Red Files List Legislators," *San Francisco Chronicle*, March 15, 1971; "Abolish Un-American Activities Panel" and "One Flack for the Snoop File," *Los Angeles Times*, March 15, 1971; "Un-American Group Spies on Legislators, Mills Says," ibid., March 21, 1971; "Move Begun to Reverse Senate Loyalty Group," ibid., April 3, 1971.

56. James E. Mills, "Locking up the Tenney Files," *Nation*, July 5, 1971.

Notes to Chapter 3

1. Federal Bureau of Investigation, *FBI Annual Report, Fiscal Year 1965* (Washington, D.C.: GPO, 1965), p. 23, hereafter cited as *FBI Annual Report* [year].

2. Ibid., "Counterintelligence Activities," pp. 21–29.

3. Frank Donner, "Theory and Practice of Political Intelligence," *New York Review of Books*, April 22, 1971, hereafter cited as Donner, "Theory."

4. Court decisions and a changed political climate had sharply restrained such "crowd control" police tactics as physical violence, harassment, and arbitrary arrests. Except in right-wing political circles—see, for example, Raymond M. Momboisse, *Blueprint of Revolution: The Rebel, the Party, the Techniques of Revolt* (Springfield, Ill.: Charles C. Thomas, 1970)—the crowd phobias of the past, the "riff-raff" theories, lost credibility. Compare Gustave Le Bon's *The Crowd: A Study of the Popular Mind* (London: T. F. Unwin, 1910) with Elias Canetti, *Crowds and Power* (New York: Viking Press, 1962), pp. 16–21. Although some police intelligence experts and consultants cited the urban riots as proof of their charges that the West had become the target of a vast "guerrilla warfare" operation, such claims failed to attract support (S. J. Makielski, *Beleaguered Minorities: Cultural Politics in America* [San Francisco: W. H. Freeman, 1973]).

5. See Donner, "Theory."

6. Ibid.

7. Garry Wills, *The Second Civil War: Arming for Armageddon* (New York: New American Library, 1968); "Police Go Space Age in Big Cities and Small, to Dismay of Critics," *Wall Street Journal*, August 9, 1971; Lee Webb, "Repression—A New 'Growth Industry,' " in *Policing*

America, ed. Anthony Platt and Lynn Cooper (Englewood Cliffs, N.J.: Prentice-Hall, 1974), pp. 77–79, hereafter cited as Platt and Cooper, *Policing America;* Vince Pinto, "Weapons for the Home Front," in Platt and Cooper, *Policing America,* pp. 80–89. On the role of the Law Enforcement Assistance Administration (LEAA—established in 1968) in furthering the technological resources of the urban police units, see *LEAA Activities, July 1, 1969, to June 30, 1970* (Washington, D.C.: GPO, 1970); *Grants and Contracts, Fiscal Year 1970* (Washington, D.C.: GPO, 1970); Joseph C. Goulden, "The Cops Hit the Jackpot," *Nation,* November 23, 1970.

8. Frank Donner, "Political Intelligence: Cameras, Informers and Files," in *Privacy in a Free Society: Final Report, Annual Chief Justice Warren Conference on Advocacy in the United States, June 7–8, 1974* (Cambridge, Mass.: Roscoe Pound–American Trial Lawyers Foundation, 1974), p. 69, hereafter cited as Donner, "Political Intelligence."

9. Ibid.

10. Ibid.

11. Donner, "Electronic Surveillance"; Victor Navasky and Nathan Lewin, "Electronic Surveillance," in Watters and Gillets, *Investigating the FBI,* pp. 297–337.

12. "How Riots Are Stirred Up: Interview with Senator McClellan," *U.S. News and World Report,* May 1, 1968, reprinted in the *Congressional Record,* May 8, 1968, vol. 114, p. 12346. Senate Permanent Subcommittee on Investigations of the Senate Subcommittee on Government Operations Hearings, passim. These hearings are in 25 parts, covering 1967–69, and are hereafter cited as McClellan Committee Hearings.

13. See police testimony, McClellan Committee Hearings, pt. 1, p. 157 (Houston); pt. 2, pp. 664–79 (Nashville); pt. 6, pp. 1419–51 (Detroit); pt. 8, pp. 1649–761 (Newark); pt. 14, pp. 2861–70 (Wilmington, Del.); pt. 18, pp. 3675–76 (New Orleans); pt. 19, pp. 3826–63 (Oakland); pp. 3865–912 (San Francisco); pp. 3912–48, 4097–116 (Los Angeles); pp. 4117–52 (St. Louis); pt. 20, pp. 4210–311 (New York City); pp. 4320–46 (Denver); pp. 4394–404 (Jersey City, N.J.); pp. 4460–98 (Chicago); pt. 22, pp. 4860–84 (Greensboro, N.C.); pt. 24, pp. 5550–56 (Puerto Rico).

14. House Committee on Internal Security Hearings regarding Newark, N.J., pt. 4 (1968), hereafter cited as HISC Hearings [year].

15. Ibid., pt. 4, p. 1958. Kinney also played a prominent role in the McClellan Committee Hearings (see pt. 8, pp. 1649–761).

16. See HISC Hearings: *Subversive Involvement in the Disruption of the Democratic National Convention* (1968); *Students for a Democratic Society* (1969), pt. 1A–7B; *Subversive Involvement in the Origin, Leadership, and Activities of the New Mobilization Committee to End the*

War in Vietnam (1970), pts. I–III; *National Peace Action Coalition (NPAC) and People's Coalition for Peace and Justice (PCJP)* (1971), pts. I–IV; *Subversive Influences Affecting the Military Forces of the U.S.* (1972), pts. I–II.

17. Senate Subcommittee to Investigate the Administration of the Internal Security Act Hearings, *Gaps in Internal Security Laws* (1967), in 12 parts, hereafter cited as SISS Hearings [year].

18. LEIU, *15th Annual Conference, May, 1970*.

19. SISS Hearings, 1970: *Extent of Subversion in New Left*, pt. 6, pp. 889–90.

20. SISS Hearings, 1975: *Nationwide Drive against Law Enforcement Intelligence Operations*, p. 9.

21. *Report of the National Advisory Commission on Civil Disorders* (New York: Bantam Books, 1968), p. 487. This is the Kerner Commission.

22. Bruce J. Terris, "The Role of the Police"; Jerome H. Skolnick, "Police and the Urban Ghetto"; Peter Henig and Randy Furst, "Cops: Same Role, New Tactics"; all in *The Ambivalent Force: Perspective on the Police*, ed. Arthur Niedenhoffer and Abraham S. Blumberg (Waltham, Mass.: Ginn, 1970), pp. 44–45, 230–34, and 318–21 respectively. See, too, the President's Commission on Law Enforcement and Administration of Justice, *Task Force Report: The Police* (Washington, D.C.: GPO, 1967), pp. 144–207. The leading theorist on the police response to riots and "urban guerrilla warfare" is Major Rex Applegate, whose book *Riot Control: Materiel and Techniques* (Harrisburg, Pa.: Stackpole Books, 1969) advocates close liaison with groups sponsoring demonstrations, not only for logistic purposes, but in order to facilitate the compilation of photographs, histories, and records of professional demonstrators and agitators (pp. 44, 58). Similar recommendations are embodied in such authoritative manuals as *Prevention and Control of Collective Violence* (Washington, D.C.: Department of Justice, June 1973), a five-volume set of guidelines for local police developed by W. Thomas Callahan and Richard L. Knoblauch of Operations Research, Inc., Silver Spring, Md., under LEAA Grant NI-71-097-G, issued in the Criminal Justice Research series from the National Institute of Law Enforcement and Criminal Justice.

23. "Riot Plot Seen by Jersey P.B.A.," *New York Times*, May 17, 1968.

24. Sectors of the New Left were "into drugs," but such traffic and use were not widespread and did not extend to hard drugs. For examples of far-fetched attempts to subversify all drug use and traffic, hard and soft, see the following SISS Hearings: *World Drug Traffic and Its Impact on U.S. Security* (1972–73), pts. 1–7; *Hashish Smuggling and Passport Fraud* (1973); *Marihuana-Hashish Epidemic and Its Impact on*

United States Security (1973–75), pts. 1–2; and the SISS Report, *Marihuana and the Question of Personnel Security* (1975). The terrorist-scare campaign to revive countersubversive programs is discussed in the following articles by the author in the *Nation:* "Terrorist as Scapegoat," May 20, 1978; "Rounding up the Usual Suspects," August 7–14, 1982; letter exchange, pt. 2, October 2, 1982. See also Donner, *Age,* pp. xi–xiii, 409–10, 455–60 and Victor Navasky, "Security and Terrorism," *Nation,* February 14, 1981.

25. The LEIU is not a public agency, and its records are not published but distributed in typescript or mimeographed copies to police agencies. The literature dealing with the LEIU, which is the source of this section, has proliferated in recent years as a result of lawsuits against urban police agencies, legal actions under state public disclosure laws, leaks, the hearings and reports of state investigating committees in California and Michigan, and the investigations of journalists. It embraces 250 pages of documents in the files of the Seattle Police Department; a release in the course of litigation against the Chicago red squad of face cards disseminated by the LEIU dealing with noncriminal subjects; a series of documents from FBI files released to the author dealing with the LEIU and its internal affairs and annual meetings; pleadings and other papers in a lawsuit brought by the Northern California ACLU and other plaintiffs against state authorities under the California Public Records Act; proceedings of regional conferences of the LEIU; Charles Marson, "The LEIU: A Fact Sheet," *First Principles,* February 1977; Linda Valentino, "The LEIU: Part of the Political Intelligence Network," *First Principles,* January 1979; Linda Valentino and Greg Goldin, "The L.E.I.U.—McCarthyism by Computer," *Nation,* August 25–September 1, 1979; Rory O'Connor, "Antinuke Movement Spooked?" *Rolling Stone,* June 1, 1978; George O'Toole, *The Private Sector: Private Spies, Rent-a-Cops, and the Police-Industrial Complex* (New York: Norton, 1978), pp. 127ff.; Senate Committee on the Judiciary, Subcommittee on Constitutional Rights, Hearings, 1974: *Criminal Justice Data Banks* (2 vols.); "Campaign for Political Rights" [news release], September 22, 1978; Joe Morrissey, "America's Police Network," *FOCUS,* February 1977; American Friends Service Committee, "Program on Government Surveillance and Citizen Rights," Briefing Paper for Conference on LEIU, March 9, 1978; *The Police Threat to Political Liberty* (Philadelphia: American Friends Service Committee, 1979), hereafter cited as AFSC, *Police Threat.* In addition, valuable data may be found in: California Department of Justice, Consolidated Data Center, Hearings, October 18, 1976: *IOCI—Automated System Functional Design;* Grant Award from LEAA to California Department of Justice, grant no. 77SS-99-6005, January 6, 1977; "Police Intelligence Cooperative Drops Houston Department over Illegal Wiretap Charge," *New York Times,* May 18, 1975; "Police Intelligence

Files Disclosed," *Palo Alto Times*, May 14, 1975; "Police Build a 'Private' U.S.-Financed Data Exchange System," *Washington Star-News*, May 14, 1975; "Ex-Police Agent Tells of Spying on Citizens," *Washington Post*, May 15, 1975; David Power, "Police in the United States Could Be Spying on you!" *Seattle Times*, August 21, 1977; Rich Riggs and Bill Parks, "How Crime Data Bank Works," *Hayward* [Calif.] *Daily Review*, May 17, 1975; "States Defend Intelligence Role," *New York Times*, November 6, 1976; "Wiretap Dispute Widens in Texas," ibid., July 10, 1975.

26. Michigan, House of Representatives, Civil Rights Committee, Subcommittee on Privacy, *Report on the Law Enforcement Intelligence Unit*, October 11, 1978, pp. 4–5.

27. Memorandum, Station Agent in Charge (SAC), San Francisco, to FBI Director J. Edgar Hoover, November 7, 1962.

28. LEIU Eastern Zone Regional Conference, *Report of the Host Committee*, November 2, 1963. See also *Police Threat*, pp. 81ff.

29. Address by Lt. Frank J. Heimoski, Eastern Zone Regional Conference, November 1, 1963. See also *Police Threat*, pp. 81ff.

30. Memorandum, SAC, Las Vegas, to FBI Director Hoover, May 3, 1965.

31. McClellan Committee Hearings, pt. 2, pp. 661–64.

32. LEIU Central and Eastern Zone Conference, Bar Harbor, Fla., "Program," October 2–5, 1968.

33. Fourteenth Annual LEIU Conference, Palm Springs, Calif., "Agenda," April 16–18, 1969.

34. Campaign for Political Rights news release, September 22, 1978. See also "Ex-Cop Spied on Non-Criminals," *San Francisco Chronicle*, May 18, 1975; "How Crime Data Bank Works," *Hayward* [Calif.] *Daily Review*, May 17, 1975.

35. "Ex-Police Agent Tells of Spying on Citizens," *Washington Post*, May 15, 1975.

36. Michael Klare, "City Surveillance," in *Police on the Homefront* (Philadelphia: National Action Research on the Military-Industrial Complex [1971]), p. 98.

37. LEAA, *Second Annual Report* (Washington, D.C.: GPO, 1968), pp. 63–64, 19–100.

38. The discussion of the CIA's involvement with local police personnel is based on 189 "sanitized" documents (327 pages) released to the author by the CIA. See also Philip Melanson, "The C.I.A.'s Secret Ties to the Local Police," *Nation*, March 26, 1983, hereafter cited as Melanson, and the following news stories: "Cuban Exiles Recall Domestic Spying and Picketing for C.I.A.," *New York Times*, January 4, 1975; "Records Show C.I.A. Trained Washington Area Police," ibid., January 12, 1976; "C.I.A. Got Credentials of Police to Use in Local Operations,"

ibid., February 10, 1976; "Charge C.I.A. Aided Red Squad," *Chicago Tribune,* April 24, 1978; "C.I.A. Data: Spy Chief Here Fired on Choice of Targets," *Chicago Sun-Times,* April 24, 1978.

39. Melanson, passim.

Notes to Chapter 4

1. "Police Spying Heaviest Ever," *Chicago Daily News,* June 21, 1969.

2. CPD, General Order no. 71–11, May 31, 1971; "Improper Police Intelligence Activities: A Report by the Extended March 1975 Cook County Grand Jury," November 10, 1975 (hereafter cited as "Cook County Grand Jury Report"); CPD, General Order no. 73–5, April 1, 1973.

3. CPD, Intelligence Division, Special Order no. 74–3, issued April 1, 1974, by Division Commander Thomas M. Hanley. This document was turned over to the plaintiffs in response to interrogatories in the lawsuit (discussed below) by the Alliance to End Repression (AER). One target of this program was the Chicago chapter of the National Lawyers' Guild. See also "Anti-Social Groups Still a Police Target" and "Spy Unit Got Directive in 1974," *Chicago Daily News,* December 9, 1975.

4. Citizens ALERT press release, October 26, 1976, and attached file documents; "Cop Spy Files on 105,000 Destroyed: Daley Lawyers," *Chicago Sun-Times,* October 27, 1976; "Cops Admit Destroying Spy Records," *Chicago Tribune,* October 27, 1976; "The Files That Police Destroyed," *Chicago Tribune,* October 29, 1976; "Reveal Police Files on Political Beliefs," *Chicago Daily News,* October 29, 1976. In addition to the admitted destruction of files, it was charged that a fake fire was set in a room at Chicago police headquarters where intelligence files were stored to create a pretext for withholding files ordered to be surrendered to the AER plaintiffs four days later ("Destroyed Spy File on 105,000: Cops," *Chicago Daily News,* October 16, 1976; "Claim Fake Fire in File Cover-up," ibid., March 26, 1975; "Rochford Burns Secret Files," *Chicago Sun-Times,* January 12, 1975).

5. "Cook County Grand Jury Report."

6. For a useful summary of red squad files released in the course of litigation, see the two-part report by David Moberg, "The Truth about Police Spying in Chicago," *Chicago Reader,* February 18, 25, 1977. The targeting of churches and ministers is reported in a press release and attached documents by the United Methodist church, February 9, 1977; "Police Keeping Watch on Cleric," *Chicago Tribune,* July 20, 1975; "Care and Feeding of Watchdogs," *Chicago Sun-Times,* July 26, 1975; "Casual Remark Got Pastor in Chicago Subversive File," *Rockford* [Ill.] *Morning Star and Register Republic,* November 11, 1975; "United

Methodist Leaders Demand Rochford Spy Apology," *Chicago Sun-Times,* February 10, 1977; "Police Spying and Its Toll on the Methodists," *Chicago Sun-Times,* February 12, 1977; "Police Spying on Priests Revealed," *National Catholic Reporter,* September 16, 1977. Examples of campus spying are presented in "Police Spied on Loop College Class Activities," *Chicago Tribune,* August 23, 1977; "Cops Spied on Class at College, Files Show," *Chicago Sun-Times,* August 23, 1977; "Circle Campus Spying by 'Red Squad' Revealed," *Chicago Tribune,* June 21, 1978, and of the surveillance of civic groups (in this case Business and Professional People for the Public Interest) in "Spy Report's Wording Hints Literary Theft," *Chicago Daily News,* March 25, 1975. A list of an assortment of seventy-seven targets was released by the Chicago Police Department in January 1981.

7. The CRS files are described in a four-part *Chicago Tribune* investigative report, "Chicago Police Used for Political Spying," June 19–22, 1977. This series is noteworthy not only because of its detailed disclosures but as a turning point in the *Tribune's* long acquiescence in and collaboration with red squad operations.

8. See "Spy Targets Bare Files, Assail Cops" and "List of 16 Citizens Revealing Dossiers," *Chicago Sun-Times,* January 6, 1977; "Files Show 24 Spy Targets of Police Were Law-Abiding," *Chicago Tribune,* January 6, 1977; "Spy Humor Turns Dark," *Chicago Daily News,* January 6, 1977; "Leading Chicagoans Assail Police Spying on Political Actions, Seek to End Practice," *Los Angeles Times,* January 6, 1977; "Hundreds of Daley Foes in Police Files," *Chicago Daily News,* March 21, 1975; "Dossiers on Carey, Newhouse," ibid., March 21, 1975; "Police Intelligence Files Pinpointed Foes of Daley," *Chicago Sun-Times,* March 22, 1975; "Singer, Other Daley Foes Listed," *Chicago Daily News,* March 26, 1975; "Percy Raps Spying on Black Legislators," *Chicago Defender,* May 12, 1977; "Percy Raps Tactics of Police 'Red Squad,'" *Chicago Daily News,* July 1, 1969; "Chicago: The DIA," *Newsweek,* April 7, 1975; "Row Cuts Rochford Trip Short," *Chicago Tribune,* March 22, 1975.

9. Mike Royko, "Dan Came Out as Mr. Clean," *Chicago Daily News,* April 11, 1975.

10. "Opposed to Police Infiltration—Daley," *Chicago Daily News,* March 21, 1975; "Daley Defends Police Spying, Denies Ordering It," *Chicago Sun-Times,* March 26, 1975; "Court Is Told Daley Involved in Cop Spying," *Chicago Sun-Times,* August 12, 1975; "Won't Let Daley Off in Spying—Judge," *Chicago Daily News,* September 10, 1975; "Judge Rules Daley Must Face Spy Quiz," ibid., March 8, 1976; "Rules Daley Must Reply or Face Jail," ibid., March 25, 1976; "Firm on Daley Reply," *Chicago Sun-Times,* March 27, 1976; "Police Spy Deadline Extended," *Chicago Tribune,* March 26, 1976; "Daley Told to Answer in

Spy Case," *Chicago Sun-Times*, April 13, 1976; "Daley Is Questioned on Police Spying on Community Groups," *Chicago Tribune*, May 2, 1976; "Daley Oath: Didn't Know about Spies," *Chicago Daily News*, August 26, 1976; "Daley Aides Given Files—Rochford," ibid., March 26, 1975; Mike Royko, "Daley's Stand on Police Spies," ibid., March 27, 1975.

11. "Cop Spying Protects Public, Daley Says," *Chicago Daily News*, March 26, 1975; "Police Top Brass Got Spying Briefs Weekly Court Told," *Chicago Sun-Times*, March 25, 1976.

12. Released file; see also "Police Spying on Priests Revealed," *National Catholic Reporter*, September 16, 1977; "Daley's Office Given Spying Data on Priest," *Chicago Daily News*, March 25, 1977; "Hint Daley Put Spies on Catholic Leader," *Chicago Tribune*, May 25, 1977.

13. The Clarke connection was first revealed by two *Chicago Sun-Times* reporters: "How Judge Supervised Spying on Dissidents," May 13, 1973. For follow-up news stories see "Chicago Courts, Staffed by Daley Men, under Attack," *New York Times*, May 20, 1973; "Daley Aide Indicted on Tax Charge," *Chicago Daily News*, June 26, 1973; "Clarke, Ex-Daley Spy, Pleads Not Guilty to Spy Charge," *Chicago Sun-Times*, July 10, 1973; "Ask Judge Power to Respond on Spy Supervisor Reports," ibid., May 15, 1973; "Judge's Spy Produced Fake Panther Witnesses," ibid., May 16, 1973; "A Mini-Watergate in Chicago?" ibid., May 18, 1973; "Hint Power Defied Court's Edict," ibid., May 23, 1973; "Ask Inquiry Unit: Probe Power," ibid., June 1, 1973; "Bugging of Cells by Daley Spy Told," ibid., June 20, 1973. Shortly after the Clarke disclosures, Judge Power withdrew from the controversial Black Panther raid case, but refused to comment on the charges that he was Clarke's control ("Power Drops out of Panther Case," ibid., May 17, 1973).

14. In September 1968, Clarke prepared a secret report to the Chicago Department of Investigation that revealed many of the surveillance and sabotage operations described in the text that he performed as Mayor Daley's personal spy. The report was released in August 1978.

15. "Daley Aide Indicted on Tax Charge," *Chicago Daily News*, June 26, 1973; "Grand Jury Indicts Daley Spy," *Chicago Sun-Times*, June 27, 1973; "U.S. Attorney Eyes Clarke Role in Panther Probe," ibid., July 19, 1973; "John Clarke Pleads Guilty to Filing False Tax Returns," ibid., December 4, 1973; "Thompson Rips Daley in Blackmail Case," *Chicago Daily News*, December 7, 1973; "Reveal Clarke's Attempt to Blackmail Thompson," *Chicago Sun-Times*, December 7, 1973.

16. The AAPL began a suit in 1970 charging racial discrimination, which was subsequently merged with a similar action begun by the Civil Division of the Department of Justice. Early in 1975 a federal court ordered the Chicago Police Department to turn over its relevant files to the plaintiffs. For press accounts describing these files and the background of the lawsuit, see "Arrest Afro Police Leader; Charge 'Frame,' " *Chicago*

Daily Defender, September 16, 1969; "Black Police Leader Charges Harassment in His Arrest," *Chicago Tribune*, September 16, 1969; "Aldermen Hit Cop Abuse of Robinson," *Chicago Daily Defender*, September 18, 1969; "Black Police Leader Suspended," *Chicago Daily News*, February 17, 1970; "Files on Afro League Going to U.S. Judge," *Chicago Sun-Times*, February 14, 1975; "Call Afro Cop Files 'Scrapbook,' " ibid., February 15, 1975; "Yield Police Afro Files 'Now,' U.S. Judge Orders City," ibid., February 19, 1975; "Ratings Suffered, Says Dissident Cop," *Chicago Daily News*, March 11, 1975; "Robinson Testifies Cops Warned Him of Firing," *Chicago Sun-Times*, March 12, 1975; "Renault Robinson Tells Harassments by Police Bosses," *Chicago Tribune*, March 13, 1975.

17. "The Quiet Quest of Alliance to End Repression," *Chicago Tribune*, April 13, 1975.

18. In addition to the voluminous file of documents made public about the surveillance of the AER, the most useful press stories are "Two Infiltrated Civic Group," *Chicago Daily News*, June 6, 1975; "Police Memos List Reasons for Spying on Citizen Group," ibid., November 4, 1976; "Spied on for Seeking Rights," *Chicago Defender*, November 8, 1976; and "Foe of Police Spying Finds Data Complimentary," *Chicago Sun-Times*, November 5, 1976.

19. On the very day that Chicago Mayor Bilandic and Police Superintendent James M. Rochford announced measures to curb and monitor police intelligence gathering, their lawyers were urging the Supreme Court to overturn decisions by the lower courts rejecting a claimed right to spy on the legal preparations of the AER's team of lawyers. "Community-Action Unit Wins Spy Ban," *Chicago Sun-Times*, November 11, 1976; "Ruling Will Help Spy-Case Plaintiffs," *Chicago Daily News*, October 4, 1977; "Police Spy Ban Here Let Stand," *Chicago Sun-Times*, October 4, 1977; "High Court Refuses to Let Police Use Spy Evidence," *Chicago Tribune*, October 4, 1977; "A Lesson for Cop Spies," *Chicago Sun-Times*, November 12, 1976; "The Trouble with Spying," *Chicago Tribune*, November 16, 1976; "Alliance Lawyer Attacks City Plan to Appeal Spying Ban," *Chicago Sun-Times*, December 15, 1976; "Injunction Barring Cop Spying Upheld," ibid., March 3, 1977; "Appeals Court Upholds Ban on Police Spying," *Chicago Tribune*, March 3, 1977; "Tell City's Defense of Police Spies," *Chicago Sun-Times*, June 3, 1977.

20. "Repression to End Alliance?" *Chicago Sun-Times*, September 20, 1977; "Rights Group: Cops Out to 'Destroy' Us," *Chicago Defender*, September 19, 1977; "Cop Spies Told: Disable Rights Group," *Chicago Tribune*, September 19, 1977; "Smear by Police 'Red Squad' Charged," *Chicago Sun-Times*, September 19, 1977.

21. "City Hid Cop Spy Documents, Plaintiffs Charge," *Chicago Tribune*, September 13, 1977.

22. Deposition of John Hill in *Alliance to End Repression et al. vs. James Rochford et al.,* No. 74 C 3268 (N.D. Ill. November 10, 1975), pp. 60, 64–65.

23. SISS Hearings, 1975: *The Nationwide Drive against Law Enforcement Intelligence Operations,* pt. 2, pp. 41–201. See also "Chicago Police 'Handicapped' by Subversives, Says Senator," *Chicago Daily News,* July 11, 1975; "Money to Fight Crime Goes to Communist-Front Organizations Seeking to Destroy Law Enforcement," Conservative Party press release, November 1976.

24. "Activists Stymie Undercover Work: Chicago Cops," *Chicago Tribune,* January 13, 1976; "Senate Panel Bares 'Red-Front' Charges by Police," *Chicago Sun-Times,* January 13, 1976; "Civic Groups, Media Harassed Us: Police," *Chicago Daily News,* January 13, 1976; "Of Repression and Repressors," *Chicago Sun-Times,* January 14, 1976; "Rochford's Rubbish File," *Chicago Daily News,* January 14, 1976.

25. HISC Hearings, September 1978: testimony of Superintendent James O'Grady.

26. "Bare Police Spying on 5 Civic Groups," *Chicago Daily News,* March 20, 1975; "Sought Data for Traffic, Says Spiotto," ibid., March 20, 1975; "Citizen Groups Blast Use of Police 'Spies,' " *Chicago Tribune,* March 21, 1975; "Police Tell Infiltrating, Spying on 5 Civic Groups," *Chicago Sun-Times,* March 21, 1975; "3 Portraits: These 'Activists' Were Spies," ibid., March 22, 1975; "City Brushes Off Spy-Cop Subpoena," ibid., March 22, 1975; "CAP Spy Left in Cold on Reasons for Police Assignment," *Chicago Daily News,* March 25, 1975.

27. Court's memorandum opinion and order, March 26, 1976; "Judge Tells Cops to Name Informers Used as Cops," *Chicago Daily News,* March 29, 1976; "Cops Must Open Spy Files," ibid., March 30, 1976; "Rule Court 'Not Cop Spy Tool,' " ibid., April 1, 1976.

28. "Cook County Grand Jury Report," p. 5.

29. The literature on the convention, as well as on earlier confrontations involving the Chicago police, is enormous. A useful summary of the repressive proclivities of the Chicago unit during the sixties is presented by Skolnick, pp. 243, 246–48, 265, 274–75. See also National Commission on the Causes and Prevention of Violence, *Rights in Conflict* (Washington, D.C.: GPO, 1968), hereafter cited as Walker Report; "Verdict on Chicago," *New York Times,* December 3, 1968. Mayor Daley's defense of the Chicago police, blaming provocation by revolutionaries for the outbreaks, along with supporting material, is reprinted in over sixty-seven columns of the *Congressional Record,* September 4, 1968, pp. 8257–70.

30. Sparling Commission, *Dissent and Disorder: A Report to the Citizens of Chicago on the April 27 Peace Parade* (August 1968), p. 21, hereafter cited as Sparling Commission, 1968.

31. Sparling Commission, 1968, p. 40.

32. Discussed in Sparling Commission, *Dissent in a Free Society: A Report to the Citizens of Chicago on the City's Handling of Public Dissent in the Streets and Parks* (August 1969), p. 17, hereafter cited as Sparling Commission, 1969.

33. The account in the text of the 1966–67 wave of infiltrators in Chicago is based on a variety of sources: leaks by employees of the city of Chicago; the files of the Chicago branch of the American Civil Liberties Union and of the Alliance to End Repression Task Force on Surveillance; court records (especially pretrial depositions); the research and writings of Chicagoan Sidney Lens, including an unpublished paper, "Chicago's Mini-CIA"; press stories (especially in the *Chicago Daily News*, the Lerner Booster Newspapers, the *Chicago Journalism Review*, *Second City*, and *FRED* (the latter two sources are "alternative" papers); interviews by the author with lawyers and police officers (who at their request cannot be named), as well as with individuals who have had firsthand experience with infiltration and surveillance of several groups, including the Chicago Peace Council (CPC), Latin American Defense Organization (LADO), Communist Party (CP), West Side Organization (WSO), Students for a Democratic Society (SDS), National Conference on New Politics (NCNP), Politics for Peace, Young Socialist Alliance (YSA), Center for Radical Research (CRR), Medical Committee for Human Rights (MCHR), Fellowship of Reconciliation (FoR), Chicago Area Draft Resistance (CADRE), and the Free School Conducted at the University of Chicago. For a useful summary, see "The Secret Police in Chicago," *Chicago Journalism Review* 1, no. 5 (February 1969), hereafter cited as "Secret Police."

34. Frankin was a star defense witness in an action brought by John Rossen for a court order requiring the city to issue him a license for operating a movie theater, three times denied him because of his leftist affiliations. The quotation in the text is from the court record: *Illinois, ex rel., vs. Cine Lajoy Corp.*, No. 67 L 16971 (Cook County Cir. Ct.), pp. 4–5, 10–11, 12, 17–18, 28, 30, 34–35. See also "Cop Tells of Infiltrating Leftists," *Chicago Tribune*, January 3, 1968; "Key Pacifist Unmasked as Chicago Police Spy," *Chicago Daily News*, December 5, 1967.

35. Karl Meyer and ACLU attorneys David Long and Kermit Coleman, interviews with the author. See also "Peace Group Tells Police Infiltrators: We Can Use You," *Chicago Sun-Times*, December 2, 1967; "Police Peace-Group Role Hit," ibid., December 8, 1967; "ACLU Moves to Halt Police Spying Tactics," *Chicago Daily News*, December 6, 1967; "Peace Unit Unmasks 2 More Police Spies," ibid., December 7, 1967.

36. The discussion in the text of the spy operations of Valkenburg and his partner, Michael Randy, is based primarily on depositions given by them on May 9 and May 21, 1979, respectively, in a consolidated

pretrial discovery proceeding in three federal court lawsuits brought by the AER, the American Civil Liberties Union, and the Chicago Lawyers' Committee for Civil Rights under Law. This detailed, sworn testimony is perhaps the most revealing ever adduced from nondefecting, adversarial informer-witnesses. The extraordinarily candid recitals of both witnesses followed a long period of resistance after their self-incrimination pleas were rejected in March 1978 by Judge Alfred Y. Kirkland on the grounds that they had been granted immunity in the course of the Cook County Grand Jury investigation. A month later they were held in contempt for continuing to refuse to answer questions. In May the two were ordered to pay escalating fines of twenty dollars a day until they answered questions put by plaintiffs' lawyers. In February 1979 Judge Kirkland signed an order committing them to jail for their continuing recalcitrance. One of them (Valkenburg) was jailed briefly, but his partner (Randy), who had unsuccessfully appealed the contempt verdict, submitted to questioning to avoid being jailed. The following news stories discuss the Valkenburg-Randy infiltration and its background: "2 Chicago Peaceniks Unmasked as Cops," *New York Post*, December 7, 1967; "Former Police Spy Reveals 2 Break-ins in '67," *Chicago Sun-Times*, May 2, 1979; "Cops Told to Shun 5th, Talk in Spying Case," *Chicago Tribune*, March 29, 1978; "Reply Ordered from 'Red Squad' Cops," *Chicago Sun-Times*, March 29, 1978; "2 Former Cops Are Held in Contempt in Spy Case," *Chicago Sun-Times*, April 19, 1978; "Mum on Red Squad, Two Ruled in Contempt," *Chicago Tribune*, April 19, 1978; "2 Silent Red Squad Cops Face Daily Fine for Their Silence," *Chicago Sun-Times*, May 31, 1978; "Fine 'Red Squad' up to $20 a Day," *Chicago Defender*, June 1, 1978; "Ex-Red Squad Cops Ordered to Jail," *Chicago Tribune*, February 7, 1979; "2 in 'Red Squad' Ordered to Jail," *Chicago Sun-Times*, February 7, 1979; "Ex-Red Squad Member Stays Mum, Goes to Jail," *Chicago Tribune*, February 8, 1979; " 'Red Squad' Ex-Member Surrenders to Marshal," *Chicago Sun-Times*, February 8, 1979; "Two 'Red Squad' Members Jailed," *Chicago Tribune*, February 7, 1979.

37. Files of the Chicago branch of the ACLU; "Peace Group Tells Police Infiltrators: We Can Use You," *Chicago Sun-Times*, December 9, 1967.

38. Randy claimed, as a cover, that his livelihood was derived from retrieving golf balls by diving into a pond at a suburban golf course, an exotic free-lance pursuit that would be difficult to verify. Randy deposition (see n. 36 above), pp. 22–23.

39. Karl Meyer, Chicago Peace Council, interview with author.

40. Files released by the Chicago Police Department.

41. "War Critics Liken Chicago to Prague," *New York Times*, August 25, 1969. Police preparations for the convention are detailed in the department's released files; Sparling Commission, 1968 and 1969; Walker

Report, pp. 78–81; "The Battle of Chicago: What Really Happened," *Chicago American*, September 9, 1968; "Strategy of Confrontation: Official White Paper," *Chicago Daily News*, September 8, 1968 (the last mentioned reports are special inserts of twelve and eight pages respectively). A three-part hearing dated October 1, 3, and 4, 1968, on *Subversive Involvement in Disruption of the Democratic National Convention* by the House Un-American Activities Committee, hereafter cited as HUAC Hearings [date], also covers (in pt. 1) convention-related intelligence activities.

42. "Police Spying Heaviest Ever," *Chicago Daily News*, June 21, 1969.

43. "Cop Who Infiltrated Hippies Kept Many away from City," *Chicago Tribune*, September 7, 1968.

44. Information about Bock's activities as a spy in the peace movement is derived from interviews by the author with Sholem Leibovitz, Stewart Meacham, and Sidney Lens, peace activists who had close contact with Bock. Printed sources are the HISC Hearings, April 7, 1970: *Subversive Involvement in the Origin, Leadership, and Activities of New Mobilization Committee to End the War in Vietnam*, p. 3855, and the record in the "Chicago 8" (then 7) conspiracy case, *United States v. David T. Dellinger et al.*, Docket 69 CR 180 (N.D. Ill.) (Chicago: Commerce Clearing House, 1970), 15–16: 6464–7258, hereafter cited as *U.S. v. Dellinger*. See also "Second Confrontation in Chicago," *New York Times Magazine*, March 29, 1970, and the following *New York Times* stories: "Police Agent Says 2 Chicago Defendants Plotted Firebombings," November 14, 1969; "Trial of Chicago 7 Goes into Overtime," November 15, 1969; "Witness Denies Seeing Chicago 7 Commit Violence," November 19, 1969; " 'Chicago 7' Judge Denies Motion for Mistrial by Lawyer Who Charges Bias," November 20, 1969.

45. The principal source of the account of William Frapolly's spy career is an interview by the author with an SDS activist who knew Frapolly well. Additional sources are an interview by the author with one of his college instructors and the record in the conspiracy case, *U.S. v. Dellinger*. See also Jason Epstein, *The Chicago Conspiracy Trial* (New York: Random House, 1970), pp. 239–43, hereafter cited as Epstein.

46. Pierson testified before the House Internal Security Committee (see HISC Hearings, pt. 1, pp. 2931–38). Sources for the discussion in the text are a series of interviews by the author with Jerry Rubin and his associates Stewart Albert and Judy Clavir; Rubin's book *Do It: Scenarios of the Revolution* (New York: Simon & Schuster, 1970), pp. 181–85; McClellan Committee Hearings, *Riots, Looting and Burning*, pt. 20, p. 204; Epstein, pp. 200–203. Pierson also published an article, "Behind the Yippies' Plan to Wreck the Democratic Convention" (*Official Detective*, December 1969), but subsequently disavowed it.

47. "Cop Becomes 'Longhair' to Clip Yippies' Plans," Chicago Tribune," August 31, 1968. See also James H. Wechsler, "Preview," New York Post, September 25, 1968.

48. Court's memorandum opinion and order, March 5, 1976, 75 F.R.D. 430 (N.D.Ill. 1976); "Cops Must Open Spy Files," Chicago Daily News, March 30, 1976; "Judge Acts to Disclose Some Data," ibid., March 30, 1976; "Judge Tells Cops to Name Informers Used as Spies," ibid., March 27, 1976.

49. "Housewife Infiltrated Civic Group," Chicago Daily News, June 6, 1971; "Civilians Still Supply Data," ibid., June 10, 1975; and see the discussion at pp. 92–93.

50. "Secret Police." See also "225 Students Stage Sit-In in U.C. Offices," Chicago Tribune, January 31, 1969.

51. In its September 1960 issue, the John Birch Society's official organ, American Opinion, featured an article by David Gumaer, "The ACLU—Lawyers Playing the Red Game," which condemns the ACLU as a communist front. An account of Gumaer's career is presented in Donner, Age, p. 430.

52. "Spy Reports Short on Credibility," "Ex-Spy Speaks Out," "Chicago Police Spies Pried in Suburbs," Evanston [Ill.] Review, August 3, 1978.

53. Sheli Lulkin's spy role was demonstrated by her repeated failure to list herself in her reports of meetings she was known to have attended and by a derogatory reference to Joyce Stover, another infiltrator, with whom, it was widely known, she was feuding. Lulkin's career as an informer is documented in a series of reports made to her controls (she had a number of them, including Irwin Bock) as well as in her answers to plaintiffs' interrogatories in the AER lawsuit. (Lulkin was represented by legal counsel paid for by the city despite the fact that she was not an employee and was paid only her expenses while serving as a spy.) In the response to interrogatories, she listed the following organizations as surveillance subjects: Al Fatah; Alliance to End Repression; Bail Bond Task Force; Cairo Task Force; Police Brutality Task Force; American Indian Movement; American Nazi Party; AMEX (American Exiles in Canada); Angela Davis Defense Committee; Black Panther Party (and support groups); Chicago Area Draft Resistors (CADRE); Chicago Area Group on Latin America (CAGLA); Chicago Committee to Save Lives in Chile; Chicago Peace Council; Citizens' Committee to Investigate Police Disorder; Clergy and Laity Concerned (CALC); Communist Party, U.S.A.; Committee on Defense against Terrorist Attacks (DATA); Harrisburg Defense Committee; Impeach Nixon Committee; Intercommunal Survival Committee; International Socialist League; International Women's Day Coalition; Iranian Student Association; Labor Today; Legion of

Justice; May Day Tribe; Miami Conventions Coalition; Modern Book Store; National Committee for Universal, Unconditional Amnesty; National Committee to Save Lives in Chile; National Committee for Trade Union Action and Democracy; National Committee on Latin America (NACLA); National Peace Action Coalition; National Tenants' Organization; National Welfare Rights Organization (NWRO); New American Movement; New Mobe (New Mobilization Committee to End the War in Vietnam); New University Conference; New World Resource Center; October League; Organization of Arab Students; Palestine Liberation Organization; Peace and Freedom Party; People's Bicentennial Commission; People's Coalition for Peace and Justice; People's Peace Treaty; Progressive Labor Party; Revolutionary Brigade; Revolutionary Communist Party–U.S.A.; Revolutionary Student Brigade; Revolutionary Union; Revolutionary Youth Movement I & II; Rising Up Angry; SCLC Black Labor Leaders Conference; Socialist Workers' Party; Sons and Daughters of Liberty; Sojourner Truth Organization; Soviet-American Friendship Society; Sparticist [*sic*] League; Stockholm Peace Committee; Stop ABM Movement; Student Mobilization Committee; Students for a Democratic Society; Teacher Action Committee; Teachers' Committee for Peace in Vietnam; The Guild; The Other Cheek; Teachers for a Free Chicago; Teachers for a Radical Change in Education; U.S.-China Friendship Association; Venceremos Brigade; Veterans for Peace in Vietnam (Vets for Peace); Vietnam Veterans against the War (VVAW-WSO); War Resistors' League; Weathermen; Winter Soldier Organization (VVAW-WSO); Women for Peace; Women's International League for Peace and Freedom; Women Strike for Peace; Workers' World Party; World Federation of Democratic Youth; World Federation of Trade Unions; World Peace Council; Yippies (Youth International Party); Young Socialist Alliance; Young Workers' Liberation League; Youth against War and Fascism; Zippie.

The following press accounts summarize the Lulkin informer file and her sworn response to interrogatories: "2 Named as Police Informants in Cop Spying Unit," *Chicago Tribune*, November 18, 1976; "Teachers' Union Aide a Cop Spy," *Chicago Daily News*, November 18, 1976; "2 with *Chicago Tribune*, Peace Council Accused of Spying for Cops," *Chicago Sun-Times*, November 19, 1976; "Who's Spying Now?" *Chicago Reader*, December 3, 1976; "Spy Suspect Quits Teacher Union Posts," *Chicago Sun-Times*, December 5, 1976; "Charge Union Bigwig Is Informer," *Guardian*, December 8, 1976; "Teacher Admits Cop Spy Role," *Chicago Daily News*, December 29, 1976; "Lulkin Admits to Being FBI Stool Pigeon," *Guardian*, January 19, 1977; "Chicago Union Official Admits Red Squad Ties," *Militant*, January 28, 1977; "Two-Piece Spy Suit," *Chicago*, January 1978.

54. "Citizen Unit Target of '68 Spying," *Chicago Sun-Times*, December 23, 1977; "Police Infiltrated Panel Critical of Cops, Data Show," *Chicago Daily News*, December 23, 1977.

55. "German-Iranian Terror Link Feared in U.S." and "Six Honored in Struggle against Tyranny," *Chicago News-World*, July 30, 1978.

56. The discussion in this and the sections that follow is based in part on transcripts of a series of taped interviews conducted by members of a National Educational Television (NET) crew in connection with a television program "Surveillance: Who's Watching?" aired by WNET /Channel 13 on January 31, 1972, and discussed below. The transcripts record interviews with, among others, Renault Robinson, head of the Afro-American Patrolmen's League; Richard Rubensteen, associate professor of political science at Roosevelt University; David Anderson, a Lerner Booster Newspapers reporter; Courtenay Esposito, Susan Jordan, and other members of the People's Law Office; two black members of the red squad; Abe Schrager, the proprietor of a camera store; Mort Schaffner, a radical activist; Gil and Robbyelee Terry, publishers of *Second City*, an alternative newspaper; and U.S. Attorney Thomas Foran.

57. In addition to the sources cited in n. 56 above, the account in the text is based on court records; police files including Patrick Dailey's reports; and an interview by the author with Chris Mason, one of the defendants in the bomb-plot trial. Details of the trial are reported in "Loop Firebombing Plot Told by Police," *Chicago Tribune*, September 27, 1968.

58. "Policeman Cited, Posed as Hippie," *Chicago Daily News*, November 15, 1969.

59. The description in the text of Dailey's overt operations is based on interviews by the author with a number of activists. See also Detroit, federal grand jury testimony of Martha Real, July 9, 1970; affidavit of Martha Real, August 25, 1973; "Out of the Blue I: Recycling the Red Squad," *Chicago Reader*, February 27, 1978; " 'Hope Neighbors and I See a Lot of Each Other' New Community Relations Cop Says," Lerner Booster Newspapers, December 10–11, 1977.

60. "Police Spying Heaviest Ever," *Chicago Daily News*, June 21, 1969; Tom Wicker, "In the Nation: Brief Encounter at the Coliseum," *New York Times*, June 22, 1969.

61. Newsmen were not wholly thwarted: delegates sold them information about the proceedings. And, of course, the SDS conference was heavily infiltrated by informers.

62. "SDS Convention Bars Press; Police Keep Watch," *Chicago Sun-Times*, June 19, 1969: "A reporter knocked on the door of the room from which the cameras were aimed and a man opened the door a crack. 'Sorry,' he said, 'we can't tell you who we are.' Three other men could be seen behind him before he closed the door."

63. "Freedom for Dissenters" (letter to the editor by James L. Fulton), *New York Times*, July 4, 1969.

64. "Task Force Goes into Evanston," *Chicago Daily News*, October 11, 1969; "Undercover Policeman Attacker Being Hunted," ibid., October 14, 1969.

65. "50 from SDS Touch All Bases in Protest as Policemen Yawn," *Chicago Tribune*, September 11, 1970. The heavily surveilled SDS rally and march were staged by the anti-Weatherman Progressive Labor (PL) faction of the SDS and was entirely peaceful. The Chicago police, however, made no distinction among the SDS factions and turned out en masse because all the SDS units were considered violence-prone revolutionaries.

66. "Panthers Charge Police Harassing 8," *Chicago Daily News*, July 9, 1970.

67. Attorneys Jeffrey Haas and G. Flint Taylor, interviews with the author; "Panther Lawyers Charge Police Surveillance Here," *Chicago Daily News*, June 5, 1975; affidavit of Charles Bradley, a U.S. postman who delivered mail to the People's Law Office, stating that he was offered a job with the police department in exchange for mail data.

68. A by-product of this arrangement was free access by newspaper publishers to police intelligence files to check the political backgrounds of reporters. Both *Chicago Today* and the *Chicago Tribune* enjoyed this privilege.

69. The role of newsmen as surveillance operatives is covered in a spirited story by Ron Dorfman, "Watching the Watchers," *Chicago Journalism Review* 4, no. 4 (January 1971), hereafter cited as Dorfman. See also J. Anthony Lukas, *The Barnyard Epithet and Other Obscenities* (New York: Harper & Row, 1970), pp. 62–63; "Prosecution Witness Aids Chicago 8," *Chicago Daily News*, October 17, 1969; "Two of 'Chicago Eight' Are Denied Paris Trip to Discuss P.O.W.s," *New York Times*, October 25, 1969.

70. Here are some samples of "inside dope" stories Ronald Koziol shared with his *Tribune* readers, typically assuring them in the lead that the story was based on "documents obtained yesterday" or "confidential files": "Black Panther Records Show Misuse of Funds," September 19, 1969; "City High Schools Targets of SDS in Strategy for Havoc," October 6, 1969; "Get Police—Theme That Led Rioters," October 13, 1969; "37 Chicago Area Cane Cutters Return from Cuba Next Week," April 24, 1970; "Probe Source of Cane Cutters Bus Fare Back from Canada," April 28, 1970; "Radicals Making Plans to Disrupt Washington," August 11, 1970; "Yippie Is Linked to Escapers," November 9, 1970. See also *Chicago Tribune*, August 30 and 31, 1968; January 31, 1969; May 15, 1969.

71. "Youth Tells of Police Bid to Turn Spy," *Chicago Daily News*, January 13, 1970; "Policeman Censured for Posing as *Sun-Times* Reporter," *Chicago Sun-Times*, March 13, 1971; "Cop Posing as Reporter Censured," *Chicago Daily News*, March 13, 1971; Joel Havemann, " . . . and More Spies," *Chicago Journalism Review* 3, no. 7 (April 1971): 13. Havemann's account of the incident concludes: "Reporters have a hard enough time getting information from groups such as militant black students, who are naturally suspicious of the establishment press. If these groups begin to suspect that every reporter they talk to may be a policeman, our job will become impossible."

72. Columns by Robert Wiedrich in the *Chicago Tribune*, September 3 and 4, 1966.

73. Dorfman.

74. The account that follows is based on interviews by the author with Marc Weiss and two members of his camera crew (Joel Sucher and Howard Blatt). The 2½-hour-long NET film was aired on January 31, 1972. See also Ron Powers, "Hey Mac, Want Some Secret Info?" *Chicago Sun-Times*, January 31, 1972; "Ex-Army Spy is GOP Sleuth Here," *Chicago Daily News*, February 3, 1972.

75. *Marc Weiss, Joel Sucher and Howard Blatt v. Sgt. Edward Wodnicki, et al.*, No. 73–C–2512 (N.D. Ill.).

76. "Cook County Grand Jury Report," p. 20.

77. Ibid.; "Lawyer Data Winds Up in Police Files," *Chicago Daily News*, April 9, 1975.

78. "CIA Spying in Chicago," an index-digest of documents describing a broad pattern of CIA activities directed against Chicago area dissidents and the ramified linkages of the CIA and the Chicago intelligence detail, was released to the plaintiffs in the AER lawsuit and made public on May 9, 1978. See also "CIA Helped Cops Here on Files: Helms," *Chicago Daily News*, June 13, 1975; "Charge CIA Aided Red Squad," *Chicago Tribune*, April 24, 1978; "CIA Data: Spy Chief Here Fired on Choice of Targets," *Chicago Sun-Times*, April 24, 1978; "CIA, Chicago Police Links Are Detailed," *Washington Post*, April 24, 1978; "Blacks Targets of CIA," *Chicago Defender*, May 10, 1978; "CIA Got Police Data on Chicagoans," *Chicago Tribune*, May 10, 1978; "Bare Cops, CIA Anti-War Spy Link," *Chicago Sun-Times*, May 10, 1978; "The CIA's Chicago Front Man," *Chicago Reader*, February 2, 1979; John Kelly, "CIA in America," *Counterspy*, Spring 1980. It has also been charged (but not convincingly proved) that the CIA used the Legion of Justice as one of its Chicago assets (Mike Royko, "Ex-Terrorist Tells CIA Ties," *Chicago Daily News*, January 21, 1975).

79. Dennis Chudoba and Robbyelee Terry, "The Legion of Justice: An Informational Report" (MS, 1975) provides a documented account of the activities of the Legion of Justice. See also "Legion of Assholes,"

Second City, July 1970, and "Surveillance in Chicago," ibid., April 1975. File material and testimony about the Legion of Justice produced in the Cook County Grand Jury hearings and in the course of litigation, as well as follow-up investigative journalism, are summarized in the following press stories (from 1975 except where indicated):

Chicago Daily News: Mike Royko, "Ex-Terrorist Tells CIA Ties," January 21; Mike Royko, "Telow Tells of Aiding Cops," March 25; "Report Cops Aided 4 Right Wing Raids," April 8; "Seizures of Tapes, Files Told," April 8; "Bare Army Role in Terror Here," April 12; "Russ Ballet One Target of Rightists," May 1; "Police Spies Tied to 2 Gas Bombings," May 1; "Link Cops to Spying in 'Chicago 7' Trial," May 5; "Charge Aid in Break-In at Church," May 5; "Witness Links Cops to Terror Activities," July 22; "Working with Legion of Justice," July 22; "Terrorists' Ties to Cop Spies Told," July 23; "Spy Figure Told: Talk or Else . . . ," July 24; "Cop Spying Witness Admits Lies," July 28; "Links Cops to Source of Tear Gas," July 29; "Second Witness Ties Terror Group to Military Spy Unit," August 1; "Cops 'Encouraged' Terrorist Rampage by Right Wingers," November 10; "3 Cops 'Admit by Silence' They Plotted Spying," February 7, 1977;

Chicago Tribune: "Robbery and Other Charges Dropped against Informer in Police Spy Probe," June 15; "Testimony of Police Spy Figure Stricken," August 13;

Chicago Sun-Times: "Harasser of Anti-War Groups Tells of Police Assistance," July 23; "Hear Cop Planned to Run Rightist Unit," July 30; "Right Winger Believes Army Spies Engineered Passport," August 1.

See also "Chronology—Partial List of Recent Right Wing Terrorists' Activities," *Second City*, April 1979; *Z in Chicago*, a Report of the Independent Voters of Illinois; Report by the Cook County Grand Jury and transcript of testimony before the grand jury by Orville Herbert Brettman, July 23, 1975, pp. 2–56, summarized in "Centerville President Planned Illegal Spying, Burglaries," "Brettman, Legion of Justice: Terror on the Right," and "Orville Brettman: Spy, Burglar, Cop, Politician," *Daily Courier News*, January 6, 1979.

80. "Socialist Office Here Was Looted," *Chicago Daily News*, March 24, 1975; "Treason Must Be Punished," Lerner Booster Newspapers, August 9, 1970.

81. SISS Hearings, 1970: *Extent of Subversion in the New Left*, pt. 7, pp. 1051–66. The testimony is discussed in "SISS Mischief," *Christian Century*, March 24, 1971.

82. AER press release and attached file documents, October 8, 1980; "Suit against Police Discloses '75 ITT Spying," *Washington Post*, October 9, 1980; "Papers Linked to Suit in Chicago Suggest Political Spying by I.T.T.," *New York Times*, October 10, 1980.

83. "Keep Files Intact Judge Tells Police," *Chicago Daily News*, March 21, 1975.

84. "Hint 2nd Jury Quiz on Spying by Cops," *Chicago Daily News*, October 18, 1975; "Reveal Cop Unit Sought to Fix Charges against a Police Spy," *Chicago Daily News*, October 16, 1975.

85. "City Hall, Police 'Frustrated' Probe," *Chicago Daily News*, November 10, 1975; "Carey Failed to Prove Case—Rochford," *Chicago Daily News*, November 10, 1975.

86. The use of charges of subversion as a response to protest and unrest is an old story in Chicago. In the course of the 1965 civil rights demonstrations, the mayor stirred widespread protest by his charges that the civil rights activities were prompted by communists. See, for example, "Daley Gives Talk Despite a Threat," *New York Times*, July 2, 1965. In 1978 Daley's successor, Mayor Bilandic, issued a self-serving and superficial committee report clearing the police of charges of wrongful spying from August 1977 on ("Spy Probe Here Clears Police but Calls for New Safeguards," *Chicago Sun-Times*, August 30, 1978). Chicago police officials appeared before at least five congressional hearings between the sixties and 1982 to justify their department's practices. In addition, the Chicago Police Department undertook a program of reform in 1974 that, according to Chicago civic groups, it subsequently ignored.

87. "House Crushes Bill to Reduce Police Spying," *Chicago Daily News*, May 21, 1975; "Police-Spying Curb Rejected by Senate Unit," *Chicago Tribune*, June 19, 1977.

Notes to Chapter 5

1. Senate Judiciary Committee, Subcommittee on Constitutional Rights, Hearings, 1971: *Federal Data Banks, Computers and the Bill of Rights*, pt. 1, pp. 292–93.

2. Interview by the author with a BOSS agent; "City Has Its Own Police to Keep Dossiers on Dissidents," *New York Times*, August 8, 1969; Bouza, quoted in "Thesis Provides Clues on Undercover Police," *New York Times*, March 8, 1971; Nat Hentoff, "BOSS—Persons of Special Interest," *Village Voice*, January 14, 1971.

3. "City Has Its Own Police to Keep Dossiers on Dissidents," *New York Times*, August 8, 1969.

4. John Henry Faulk, *Fear on Trial* (New York: Simon & Schuster, 1964), p. 326.

5. Interviews by the author with bar applicants. The practice was apparently abandoned as part of a departmental reform effort in 1971. "Police Scrutiny of Radicals Rises," *New York Times*, January 19, 1972; "Use of Police Red Squad Data," ibid., September 14, 1976; "Panthers and the Police: The Local Scene," *New York Post*, December 29, 1969;

"Blacks at Parley Allege Harassing," *New York Times*, July 19, 1971. According to an exhibit submitted by a police official in the *Handschu* case, file data were transmitted to no fewer than seven federal agencies, seven state agencies, and a variety of urban units, including Yonkers, Los Angeles, Cleveland, Philadelphia, Miami, and Kansas City.

6. *New York Times*: "Detective Draws Jail for Bribery," April 30, 1971; "Inquiry on Police Corruption Queries Captain Accused of Abetting Bribery," November 12, 1970; "Police Pensioner Arraigned Again," July 3, 1970; "Detective in Disputed Retirement Is Arrested Here," June 25, 1970; "Detective Goes on Trial in Sale of Data Despite Plea of Illness," November 14, 1970.

7. Bouza, pp. 13, 15.

8. Ibid., p. 174.

9. Ibid., p. 8.

10. Ibid., p. 14.

11. Ray Schultz, "Meet Captain Finnegan Who Solved the Great Pig Caper," *New York Free Press*, December 19–25, 1968.

12. John Finnegan was also spotted at rallies in Fort Dix, N.J., and New Haven, Conn. (Nat Hentoff, "John Lindsay, Mayor of Prague?" *Village Voice*, June 3, 1971, and interviews by the author with activists).

13. Kenneth G. Gross, "Bad Show for Reporters," *Nation*, November 18, 1968.

14. "Boring into Business, Schools and City Bureaus, Whalen Warns, Asks Curb," *New York Times*, March 9, 1930.

15. Reported in front-page coverage in the *New York Times*, May 4, 1968.

16. See Nat Hentoff, "Now Playing: The Rule of Law," *Village Voice*, December 18, 1969; interview by the author with Jonah Raskin. The use of excessive force in monitoring protest activities by both the red squad plainclothesmen and uniformed policemen was routine in the late sixties. See, for example, the following *New York Times* accounts of police abuses at an anti-Nixon demonstration, an area within the red squad's responsibility: "Rights Group Scores Police Handling of Protest," December 31, 1969; "2 Arrested at Anti-Nixon Protest Say They Were Beaten by Police," December 14, 1969; "7 Policemen Hurt as 3,000 Protest Nixon's Visit," December 10, 1969. See also "Conduct of Police at Rally Scored," April 29, 1968; "Police Review Unit Gets Accusations against 2 Officers," April 30, 1968.

17. The account in the text is based on interviews by the author with Howard Blatt, Stephen Fischler, and Joel Sucher. The latter two were also targets of the Chicago security unit (see pp. 141–43). The police harassment of the film makers is described in Nat Hentoff, "John Lindsay: Mayor of Prague?" *Village Voice*, June 3, 1971.

18. "Scenes," *Village Voice*, September 5, 1968.

19. Undenied allegations in plaintiffs' *Memorandum in Support of Motion to Suppress Eavesdropping Warrants,* Sup. Ct., New York County, 1848 / 69, pp. 18–33; applications for wiretap warrants by Eugene Gold, district attorney of Kings County and supporting affidavits of Angelo Galante and Richard Hodgson in the Supreme Court of the State of New York (November 1968–March 1969); trial record in Panther 13 case, *People v. Lumumba Shakur, et al.,* pp. 4375–4691; "Police Admit Panther Lied and Was a Mental Patient," *New York Times,* May 22, 1970; "Police Informer Asserts He Was Aiding Panthers," ibid., June 2, 1970; "Police Informer Called Double Agent," *New York Post,* May 26, 1970.

20. "Police Contact SJU Rep for NSA Data," *Downtowner,* February 24, 1967; *Collegiate Press Service,* March 8, 1967.

21. HUAC Hearings, 1959: *Investigation of Communist Activities, New York Area,* pts. 3 and 4, pp. 820–989, 1668–70.

22. SISS Hearings, 1953: *Communist Underground Printing Facilities and Illegal Propaganda,* pp. 261–87; SISS Hearings, 1957: *Scope of Soviet Activity,* pt. 79, pp. 4571–76.

23. "New Chief Named for Policewomen," *New York Times,* November 23, 1963.

24. Frank Ferrara's brief career at Columbia University is described in "Long-Haired Infiltrator Aids Police in Campus Hall Action," *New York Times,* May 23, 1968. See also Nat Hentoff, "Columbia's Gift to the Mayor," *Village Voice,* December 18, 1969. On the infiltration of the Columbia University campus, see James Ridgway, "Columbia's Real Estate Ventures," *New Republic,* May 18, 1968. Weiner's spy activities are described in interviews by the author with one of the defendants (Richard Palmer). Details of the affair are given in "Bomb Plotters Here Sentenced," *New York Times,* May 8, 1971, and "6 Are Identified as Weathermen in an Attempt to Bomb Bank Here," *New York Times,* December 5, 1970.

25. The discussion that follows in the text is based on the court records in the four cases. The media sources cited reflect the testimony and exhibits in these cases.

26. Media accounts of this case may be found in Claudia Dreifus, "BOSS Is Watching," *Nation,* January 25, 1971; "Say Woods Urged Shrine Blast," *New York Post,* January 4, 1965; "Hero Cop Went to Jail to Break the Bomb Case," ibid., February 19, 1965; "Detective Admits Rights Activities," *New York Times,* May 21, 1965; Sandra S. Adicks, "Bonnie and Clyde in Blackface," *Realist,* August 1967; "Arrogance on the Left," *Manhattan Tribune,* April 19, 1969; "Statue of Liberty Plot," *New York Post,* May 25, 1965; "Statue of Liberty Plot Called Detective's Idea," *New York Times,* June 3, 1965; Murray Kempton, "A Policeman's Plot," *New York Post,* August 14, 1965, hereafter cited as Kempton.

27. In addition to the court record, the following sources are illuminating: "Witness Links Ferguson to Assassination Talk," *New York Times,* June 6, 1968; "Gun Seizure Cited in Ferguson Trial," ibid., June 13, 1968; "Jury Deliberate on Ferguson Case," ibid., June 15, 1968; "2 Black Militants Ordered to Prison in Death Case," *New York Post,* July 9, 1968; "Ferguson and Harris Sentenced to 3½ to 7 Years in Murder Plot," *New York Times,* October 4, 1968.

28. In addition to the court record, see also stories in the *New York Times:* "Black Group Plan Mobilization of Aid for Harlem Five on Trial as Plotters," May 2, 1971; "Harlem Five Say They Are Victims of a Police Plot," May 12, 1971; "Lawyer in Harlem Five Case Sees Vindication," May 15, 1971.

29. *New York Times,* May 17, 1968.

30. This case involving three Panther defendants is the subject of an illuminating book by a lawyer, Paul Chevigny, *Cops and Rebels: A Study of Provocation* (New York, Curtis Books, 1972). In addition, see "Trial Opens Here for 3 Panthers," *New York Times,* April 3, 1970; "3 Ex-Panthers Acquitted of Conspiracy to Murder," ibid., September 27, 1970; "Police, FBI Infiltrators Stir Trouble for Panthers," *Civil Liberties,* December 1970; "Cop Spy: Hero or Svengali?" *New York Post,* April 30, 1970; Paul Chevigny, "Red Squad: The Verdict Is Entrapment," *Village Voice,* February 11, 1971.

31. "Black City Policemen Say Inside Corruption Stalls Fight on Drugs," *New York Times,* June 12, 1971. The Guardians charged that narcotics enforcement was slighted in favor of political surveillance and infiltration by black detectives.

32. The trial record, interviews by the author with defendants and their attorneys, and the following books and articles document the discussion in the text of the Panther trial: Kempton; Stephen Chaberski, "Inside the New York Panther Trial," *Civil Liberties Review* 1, no. 1 (Fall 1973); Robert Cover, "A Year of Harassment," *Nation,* February 2, 1970; Edwin Kennebeck, "Not Guilty of What?" ibid., October 4, 1971.

33. Aspects of Ralph White's career and testimony are described (in addition to the sources cited in n. 32 above) in the following stories from the *New York Times* (all from 1971): "Detective Joined Panthers in 1968," February 2; "Agent Got High with Panthers," February 3; "Panther Lawyer Tried to Show Detective as a Woman Chaser," February 4; "Agent Says Panthers Made Him Teach about Guns," February 5; "Panther Defense Presses Witness," February 12; "Detective Tells of Panther Role," February 17; "Detective Kept 'Cover' Job's Pay," February 24; "Agent Is Queried at Panther Trial," March 2; "Panthers: How Some Say 'Kill,' " March 3; "Accounts Differ at Panther Trial," April 8.

34. Another BOSS infiltrator who engaged in intimacies with his victim was Carlos Ashbrook; like Ralph White, he asserted that such ca-

vorting was a reluctant concession to the need for cover (*New York Post:* "A Panther Spy's Anecdotes," March 5, 1971; "Another Fake Panther on Grill," March 25, 1971).

35. Supplementing the books and magazine articles dealing with Gene Roberts cited in n. 32 above are the following newspaper stories from 1970: "Panther Jurors Hear Cop," *New York Post*, November 10; "Under Cover Agent Tells of Panther Drills and Plots," *New York Times*, November 11; "Police Agent Is Back on Panther Stand," *New York Post*, November 12; "Witness Tells of a Panther Bombing List," *New York Times*, November 13; "Detectives Tell How They Recorded Conversations of Panthers," ibid., November 17; "Hid Mike Panther Cop Says," *New York Post*, November 16; "Agent Says He Transmitted Meetings of Panthers," *New York Times*, November 20; "Undercover Agent Recalls How Role Was Almost Discovered by Black Panthers," ibid., December 2; "Policeman Tell [*sic*] Panther Trial of His Attempt to Save Malcolm X," ibid., December 3; "Police Agent in Panther Case a Boyhood Friend of Defendant," ibid., December 3; "Undercover Agent in Panthers 'Feared' the Police," ibid., December 4; "Detective Defends Role He Played as a Panther," ibid., December 9; "Panther Defense Pressing Detective," ibid., December 10; "No-Flap Panther Witness," *New York Post*, December 16; "Detective Heard on Panther Trial," *New York Times*, December 16; "Black Panther Defense Finishes Cross-Examining of Infiltrator," ibid., December 23.

36. "13 Panthers Here Found Not Guilty on All 12 Counts," *New York Times*, May 14, 1971.

37. *People v. Collier*, 85 Misc. 2d 529, 376 N.Y.S. 2d 554 (N.Y. County Ct. 1973); "Justice Quashes 2-Year-Old Indictment Decrying Secret Infiltration by Police," *New York Times*, July 29, 1975; Edwin Kennebeck, "Looking for Trouble: A Spy Story," *Nation*, November 15, 1975.

38. Franklin Siegel, "Red Squad Bills Force Inquiry into Police Surveillance," *Guild Notes*, January 1976.

39. According to the New York Police Department's responses to interrogatories in the *Handschu* case, between 1974 and 1977, 10,385 index cards were added to BOSS's files; 213 groups were surveilled and 14 infiltrated. In the ten-year period 1968–77, approximately 4,462 demonstrations were surveilled. See *Handschu v. Special Services Division*, No. 71–2203 (S.D.N.Y.), filed May 18, 1971, *Handschu v. Special Services Division*, 349 F. Supp. 766 (S.D.N.Y., 1972), and the Settlement Agreement, *Handschu v. Special Services Division*, No. 71–2203, signed by attorneys, December 30, 1980, but not by the judge.

40. The account in the text of the conflict between the New York Police Department and the Lindsay administration is based primarily on interviews by the author with Aryeh Neier and Ira Glaser, both former

directors of the New York Civil Liberties Union who subsequently became directors of the national organization.

41. *New York Times*, 1968: "New Police Group Is Incorporated," August 9; "New Group Fights Suspension of Patrolmen in Beating Case," September 3; "New Police Group Maintains Stand," September 14; "Many Police in City Leaning to the Right," September 6; "One Law for All," September 7. See also "A Close Inspection of LEG from Three Points of View," *New York Post*, September 6, 1968.

42. *New York Times:* "Off Duty Police Here Join in Beating Black Panthers," September 5, 1968; "Mayor and Leary Warn Policemen in Panther Melee," September 6, 1968; "Case Dismissed in Panther Attack," April 28, 1970. This affray finally brought a credible condemnation from the mayor and police commissioner. The PBA itself also condemned the LEG as a blot on the department because of its "unlawful, antisocial or violent acts." By this time, the Cassese "get tough" directive was allowed to languish when it became apparent that it had been issued to circumvent the LEG movement's threat to the PBA leadership ("P.B.A. Condemns New Police Group," *New York Times*, September 13, 1968). But this tactical retreat in no way curbed the police revolt.

43. *New York Times*, 1970: "2 Protest Groups Meet on Wall Street," May 13; "Police Assailed by Mayor on Laxity at Police Rally," May 14; "Police Enjoined on War Protest," May 29; "Court Nullifies Order to Police," May 30.

44. "Police Weapons Buildup in Cities Intensifies Fear of Summer Clashes," *Wall Street Journal*, March 11, 1968; "The Fear Campaign" and "The Police Need Help," *Time*, October 4, 1968; "Administration Shapes Stop Gap Plans to Avert Racial Violence in 1968," *Wall Street Journal*, April 6, 1967.

45. "A State Hearing Set on Actions by City's Police," *New York Times*, May 16, 1985.

Notes to Chapter 6

1. The chapter epigraph is quoted in Joseph R. Daughen and Peter Binzen, *The Cop Who Would Be King: Frank Rizzo* (Boston: Little, Brown, 1977), p. 8, hereafter cited as Daughen and Binzen. In addition to the sources specifically cited, this chapter is based on the following sources: materials supplied by a research group at the University of Pennsylvania Law School; newspaper and magazine reports; documents from the files of a number of Philadelphia organizations concerned with police abuses, civil rights, and civil liberties; interviews by the author with representatives of organizations that may have been targets of surveillance, with lawyers specializing in civil rights and civil liberties

matters, and with a Philadelphia councilman, David Cohen; and supplementary research by Robert Koulish.

2. Jim Riggio, "The Year of the Bull," *Philadelphia Magazine*, March 1973, hereafter cited as Riggio; Lenora E. Berson, " 'The Toughest Cop in America' Campaigns for Mayor of Philadelphia," *New York Times Magazine*, May 16, 1971, hereafter cited as Berson, "Toughest Cop"; Mike Mallowe, "Watch Out! Here Comes Frank the Tank," *Philadelphia Magazine*, October 1975, hereafter cited as Mallowe.

3. Accounts of the early Rizzo include Greg Walter, "Rizzo," *Philadelphia Magazine*, June 1967; Bernard McCormick, "God Bless Frank Rizzo . . . or God Save Us?" ibid., August 1969; Fred J. Hamilton, *Rizzo* (New York: Viking Press, 1963), pp. 83ff., hereafter cited as Hamilton; Berson, "Toughest Cop"; Riggio; Mallowe; Daughen and Binzen, pp. 59–91.

4. "Police 'Spies' Watch School Conference on Racial Problems," *Philadelphia Inquirer*, December 12, 1967.

5. The best account of Rizzo's relationship with the press appears in Hamilton, ch. 6. See also Joe McGinnis, "He'll Always Be Car One" [*MORE*], December 1971, and Berson, "Toughest Cop."

6. "How to Handle Demonstrations," *Time*, December 9, 1966.

7. SISS Hearings, June 24, 1966: *Gap in Internal Security Laws*, pt. 2, pp. 25–29.

8. *United States v. Eqbal Ahmad et al.*, Crim. No. 14950 (E.D. Pa. February 22, 1972), pp. 109–10; testimony in text quoted from pp. 98–102.

9. "Ex SNCC Aide Pleads Guilty in Dynamite Case," *Philadelphia Bulletin*, October 17, 1968.

10. Between August 13 and 23, 1966, Rizzo gave the press no fewer than twenty-five statements elaborating on the claim that the raid had rescued the city from disaster.

11. "Dynamite Charge against 2 Dismissed," *Philadelphia Inquirer*, May 10, 1968; "Classic Frame-Up: SNCC Unit Dies," *National Guardian*, May 27, 1967.

12. "4 Racists Accused of Cyanide Plot to Kill Hundreds Here," *Philadelphia Bulletin*, September 27, 1967. For an account of the hearing at which prohibitively high bail ($10,000) was set, see " 'Black Guard' Assailed in Court by DA," ibid., August 9, 1967.

13. *Philadelphia Inquirer*, 1967: "Guerilla War Planned, RAM Informer Says," October 16; "Pride at Stake in RAM Hearing," December 16.

14. "Bail Cut Is Refused Activist," *Philadelphia Inquirer*, November 13, 1968; "DA Drops Case in RAM Hearing," *Philadelphia Bulletin*, May 10, 1969.

15. The SDS "bomb plot" account in the text is based on interviews by the author; files of the Philadelphia ACLU and the American Friends Service Committee; lawyers for the defendants in court cases; and the Philadelphia ACLU's publication, *Civil Liberties Record,* April 1969.

16. Quoted in *Bomb Plot Conspiracy,* a pamphlet published by the Fraser-Borgmann Defense Committee (n.d.).

17. The description of the raids on the Panthers in the text is documented by the following sources in addition to those specifically cited: interviews by the author with Panther leaders and their lawyers; the files of the American Friends Service Committee and the Philadelphia ACLU; Bernard McCormick, "The War of the Cops," *New York Times Magazine,* October 8, 1970; a feature article by a team of investigative reporters, "Controversy Still Rages over Raids on Panthers," *Philadelphia Bulletin,* September 30, 1970; and another by an *Inquirer* staffer, "A Week of Violence: The Facts and the Meaning," *Philadelphia Inquirer,* September 6, 1970.

18. "Bugs in the Office," *Philadelphia Free Press,* September 1969.

19. "7 Seized in North Philadelphia Raid," *Philadelphia Bulletin,* March 11, 1970; "N. Philadelphia Fortress Raided; 7 Arrested, Arms Seized," *Philadelphia Inquirer,* March 12, 1970. An ACLU press release of March 13, 1970, protested as "irresponsible and malicious" the attempt to link the Panthers with criminal activity.

20. Quoted in Berson, "Toughest Cop." In an interview Rizzo stated: "We let idiots like this survive under our form of government. Maybe we'll have to change it." "Writer Protests Police Action in Raids on 3 Black Panthers," *Philadelphia Bulletin,* September 3, 1970.

21. Rizzo insisted even after the disclosure of police excesses that it was "clearly evident . . . that the police acted with remarkable restraint" ("Report of Panther Weapons Led to Raids," *Philadelphia Inquirer,* September 4, 1970).

22. "Panther Conference Opens after Court Victories," *New York Times,* September 6, 1970.

23. That Rizzo hated the *Free Press* and especially Biggin because of his stand on police issues is made clear by the testimony of Philadelphia Police Inspector Robert Wolfinger in SISS Hearings, October 8, 1970: *Assaults on Law Enforcement Officers,* pt. 3, p. 213.

24. The account of the harassments of the *Free Press* in the text is based on undisputed allegation of a legal complaint, discussed on p. 221, and a series of interviews by the author with Biggin. The police case against Biggin and the *Free Press* is reflected in two *Philadelphia Bulletin* articles from July 28, 1970: "Head of Rebel Paper Is Central Figure in New Left Here" and "100 Here Called Hardcore Revolutionaries." See also a series of stories by Albert Gaudiosi from the *Philadelphia*

Bulletin of July 29, 1970: "Petite New Leftist Studied for a Year in England"; "Free Press No. 2 Man Assails Bicentennial"; "City Social Worker David Cross Doubles as Free Press Staffer"; "Dougherty High Dropout Is Free Press Editor."

25. "Police Keep Close Tabs on Leftist Groups Here," *Philadelphia Bulletin*, April 12, 1970.

26. "Visitor Reports Talk of Bombs in Powelton," *Philadelphia Bulletin*, July 30, 1970.

27. *Philadelphia Bulletin*, 1970: "Powelton Man Denies Charges about Bombs," July 30; "Series on Radicals Evokes Praise, Denials, Concern," August 2.

28. "Rizzo Charges Plot against Police," *Philadelphia Bulletin*, September 1, 1970.

29. *Free Press et al. v. Frank L. Rizzo et al.*, Civil Action No. 70–3175 (E.D. Pa.), stipulation and consent decree.

30. *Avirgan et al. v. Frank L. Rizzo*, Civil Action No. 70–477 (E.D. Pa.), stipulation of counsel. Three months prior to this stipulation, on April 6, 1971, a number of peace groups filed a complaint in the same court challenging the file-keeping and dissemination practices telecast in the "First Tuesday" program discussed above. The Federal Court of Appeals later upheld significant portions of the complaint (*Philadelphia Yearly Meeting et al. v. Tate*, 519 F 2d 1335, 1338 [3d Cir. 1975]).

31. Joe McGinnis, "The Techniques of Frank Rizzo," *Philadelphia Inquirer*, August 18, 1967. McGinnis's criticism of Rizzo stirred the wrath of Walter Annenberg, then the *Inquirer's* owner. Following confrontation with Annenberg, McGinnis left the newspaper.

32. "Bar to Probe Rizzo Charge of Solicitation," *Philadelphia Bulletin*, June 24, 1970; "Lawyers Stand Firm on Public Service Issue," ibid., August 6, 1970; "Police Enjoined on Forced Line-Up," *New York Times*, September 10, 1970.

33. "Anticipating the Bicentennial," *Nation*, July 30, 1973.

34. Judge Huyett's 28-page contempt decision is reported in *Farber et al. v. Rizzo et al.*, 363 F. Supp. 386 (E.D. Pa. 1973). Excerpts from the decision including the portions quoted in the text were reprinted in "Law Officers Continued to Display Contempt of Court," *Philadelphia Inquirer*, June 27, 1973. A memorandum and order approving the damage claim settlement were issued on April 26, 1974.

35. "Rizzo Puts a Police Squad on Trail of Schwartz, Camiel," *Philadelphia Inquirer*, August 25, 1973; "33-Man Police Unit Acts as Rizzo's Espionage Arm," *Philadelphia Bulletin*, August 26, 1973; "O'Neill on Special Police Squad," ibid., August 25, 1973.

36. "Shedd Claims He Was Tailed by Rizzo's Police," *Philadelphia Bulletin*, August 8, 1973; "4 Rizzo Foes Aren't Surprised by Police Tactics," *Daily News*, August 9, 1973.

37. "Nothing Wrong with Surveillance," *Daily News*, August 9, 1973.

38. "Mayor Will Add '8 or 10' to His Special Squad," *Philadelphia Inquirer*, August 9, 1973; "Special Squad Has Done Nothing," ibid., September 12, 1973.

39. "Jury Probes Fencl in Gratuity Case," *Philadelphia Inquirer*, August 21, 1973.

40. Pennsylvania Crime Commission, *Police Corruption and the Quality of Law Enforcement in Philadelphia* (March 1974). This 1,400-page report concluded that police corruption in Philadelphia is "ongoing, widespread, systematic and occurring at all levels of the police department." See "Police in Philadelphia Called Corrupt; Panel Says Rizzo Tried to Bar Inquiry," *New York Times*, March 11, 1974; "Charges against Rizzo Police Force May Prove to Damage Him Politically," ibid., April 17, 1974. Not only did Rizzo attempt to block the investigation, but the police sought to enjoin distribution of the report itself ("Police Inquiry Set for Philadelphia," *New York Times*, March 12, 1974), which treats the Fencl charges at pp. 290–92.

41. The mayor characterized the article as "garbage," "filth," and "treason" ("Rizzo Takes the Stand and Accuses the *Inquirer*," *Philadelphia Inquirer*, March 19, 1976; "Rizzo Drops Request for Injunction against *Inquirer*," ibid., March 20, 1976; Tony Green, "Bicentennial Brawl in Philadelphia" [*MORE*], May/June 1976).

42. "*Inquirer* Blocked by Protesters," *Philadelphia Inquirer*, March 20, 1976; "*Inquirer* Protests Picketing," ibid., March 21, 1976; "The Thug Rule," ibid., March 21, 1976; "FBI Urged to Probe Picketing That Blocked *Phila. Inquirer*," *Philadelphia Bulletin*, April 5, 1976.

43. "Rizzo Asks 15,000 Troops to Protect City on July 4," *Philadelphia Inquirer*, May 30, 1976.

44. The recall drive was greatly spurred by the *Inquirer* shutdown controversy in March. "Mayor Rizzo Gets Black Eye out of Ruckus at *Inquirer*," *Philadelphia Sunday Bulletin*, March 28, 1976; "Where Was the Law and Order Mayor?" (letter to the editor), *Philadelphia Bulletin*, March 30, 1976; "Drive on to Recall Rizzo," ibid., March 31, 1976; "The Rule of Law Has Been Threatened" (letter to the editor), *Philadelphia Inquirer*, March 25, 1976; "The Siege at the Inquirer," *Philadelphia Bulletin Forum*, March 20, 1976; "Business Faction Asks Rizzo to Pledge Faith in Constitution," *Philadelphia Bulletin*, March 31, 1976; "Philadelphia's Embattled Mayor Rizzo, Facing Recall Petition, Nevertheless Is 'Unconcerned,'" *Wall Street Journal*, July 29, 1976; "Philadelphia Action Report," *Common Sense*, May 1–15, 1976; and "Rizzo Solidifies Power in Philadelphia," *New York Times*, May 25, 1976. In May, aware of the burden of a hostile press in the recall campaign, Rizzo held out the olive branch to the Philadelphia press corps. "Rizzo Offers Truce to

Press, Aide Says," *Philadelphia Bulletin*, May 12, 1976; "Text of Mayor Rizzo's Interview," *Philadelphia Inquirer*, May 30, 1976; and "3 Mugwumps Mugging the People's Will," *Daily News*, June 18, 1976.

45. "FBI Probing Phila's Need for Troops," *Philadelphia Bulletin*, May 30, 1976; "FBI, City to Discuss Troop Bid," *Philadelphia Inquirer*, June 11, 1976; "Meeting Set in Washington to Review Troop Plea," *Philadelphia Bulletin*, June 12, 1976; "The Troops Aren't Needed Here on July 4th," *Philadelphia Inquirer*, June 20, 1976; "City Told: No Street War, No Troops," *Philadelphia Bulletin*, June 21, 1976; "U.S. Refuses Troops for City, ibid., June 22, 1976; "Shapp Won't Send Pa. Guard," ibid., June 22, 1976; "Rizzo Renews Bid for Troops on July 4 in Letter to Shapp," ibid., June 23, 1976.

46. "Mag Article Critical of Rizzo Is Censored," *Daily News*, July 6, 1976; "*Bulletin* Prints, *Inquirer* Rejects Magazine Ad about Rizzo Article," *Philadelphia Bulletin*, July 8, 1976.

47. Deposition, *Dyketactics et al. v. Fencl*, Civil Action No. 75–3641 (E.D. Pa.), p. 9.

48. The account that follows is based on an interview by the author with a Philadelphia police officer; Jim Quinn, "The Heart of Darkness," *Philadelphia Magazine*, May 1978; "Judge Balks Philadelphia Effort to Isolate Revolutionary Group," *New York Times*, March 3, 1978; "Prime MOVEr 'John Africa' No Mystery," *Philadelphia Inquirer*, July 14, 1977; "He's Trusted by the City and MOVE," ibid., March 3, 1978; "Police Are Winning a War of Attrition," *Daily News*, July 14, 1977. For the background of the controversy, see "MOVE Members Speak Out—Loudly," *Philadelphia Inquirer*, April 21, 1975; " 'MOVE' the Seed of Fascism," *Drummer*, April 2, 1974.

49. *Philadelphia Inquirer*, August 9, 1978. Africa was first struck, then grabbed by the hair and dragged to the sidewalk, where an officer kicked his head and stomped him.

50. "Black Cops Tell O'Neill: Quit Spying," *Philadelphia Journal*, October 7, 1978; "Black Policeman Files Complaint against Police Commissioner O'Neill," *Philadelphia Tribune*, October 7, 1978.

51. A biting review of Rizzo's mayoral reign was aired in a 75-minute television presentation, "Rizzo," January 21, 1979. See also, John J. O'Connor's *New York Times* television column of that day; Christopher Davis, "Integrity in Philadelphia," *New York Times*, July 23, 1978; and Michael J. McManus [syndicated column], "In Philadelphia, Ding, Dong the Witch Is Dead," *Norwalk* [Conn.] *Hour*, November 25, 1978.

52. Gene Gilmore, "One Year with Frank Rizzo," *Nation*, December 25, 1972; "Violence and Terror by Street Gangs Arouse Public Outrage in Philadelphia," *New York Times*, May 24, 1973; "Roundhouse Punches," *Newsweek*, July 4, 1977; "Rizzo Call for 'Openness' Must Apply to Police Too," *Philadelphia Inquirer*, December 22, 1977; James

Steele and Ron Bartlett, "Justice in Philadelphia," *New Republic,* May 26, 1973 (a summary by two *Inquirer* reporters of a seven-month investigation of Philadelphia's court system).

53. "U.S. Panel Hears Criticism of Phila. Police," *Philadelphia Inquirer,* April 17, 1979; "Police Image Hurts Phila., Rights Unit Told," *Philadelphia Bulletin,* April 17, 1979.

54. *New York Times:* "Mayor Rizzo in Familiar Form, Defends Police in Brutality Hearings," April 18, 1979; "Philadelphia Police Law to Themselves," April 22, 1979.

55. "Illegal Police Abuse: The Course Is Command," *Philadelphia Inquirer,* April 19, 1979.

56. "Dissidents Win Right to Rally; Tent City Denied," *Philadelphia Inquirer,* June 16, 1976.

57. "Rizzo Cheered, Jeered at Meeting in Northeast," *Philadelphia Bulletin,* October 26, 1978; *Philadelphia Resistance v. Insurance Co. of North America* (E.D. Pa.), filed 1973, settled 1974.

58. Complaint in *United States v. City of Philadelphia et al.,* Civil Action No. 79–2937 (E.D. Pa.); "U.S. Files Its Civil Rights Suit Charging Philadelphia Police with Brutality," *New York Times,* August 14, 1979; "Rizzo Calls Suit on Police Abuse a Political Move," ibid., August 14, 1979; "Justice Accuses Philadelphia of Police Abuses," *Washington Post,* August 14, 1979.

59. Order by Judge J. William Ditter, October 30, 1979, dismissing complaint in the case cited in n. 58 above in all but minor respects; "Suit Dismissed," *Daily News,* November 1, 1979; "Philadelphia Police Upheld on U.S. Suit," *New York Times,* October 31, 1979; "Judge Dismisses Last Part of Police Brutality Suit," ibid., December 14, 1979; "Verdict in Cop Suit 'Triumph'—Rizzo," *Daily News,* October 31, 1979; "Would-Be Successors Join Rizzo in Criticizing Police Abuse Suit," *Washington Post,* August 15, 1979; "Philadelphia Police—'Toughest in the World,'" ibid., August 14, 1979. Philadelphia's city solicitor pronounced the city's police "the best in the United States," accused the *Washington Post* of "lies, half-truths and deceptions" in the article last cited, and threatened a lawsuit unless a retraction was made ("Police Officials Threaten Suit," *Washington Post,* August 16, 1979). Judge Ditter's dismissal action was upheld on December 29, 1979.

60. "Philadelphia Police Destroy Intelligence Files," *Organizing Notes,* July/August 1980.

61. Quoted in ABC News Closeup, "The Shattered Badge," television broadcast, December 27, 1980 (script, p. 18).

62. See, for example, *New York Times* stories: "Sometimes Bad Apples Come by the Bushel," September 2, 1984; "Official Who Restored Respect to Philadelphia Police Resigns," May 28, 1988; "Philadelphia Officer Indicted," July 20, 1988.

63. Philadelphia, *Findings, Conclusions and Recommendations of the*

Philadelphia Special Investigation Commission, March 1, 1986. A recent treatment of the MOVE case is Margot Henry, "*Attention, MOVE! This Is America!*" (Chicago: Banner Press, 1987).

64. See, for example, "Philadelphians' Careers at Stake as Hearings Approach on Police Bombings," *New York Times*, October 7, 1985.

Notes to Chapter 7

1. The discussion of the political setting of the Los Angeles Police Department (referred to throughout as the LAPD) and the historic role of its red squad is based on McWilliams, pp. 272–82; Gottlieb and Wolt, pp. 45–47; Halberstam, pp. 94–101; and Woods, pp. 15–47.

2. "Rightist Revival Thrives in So. Cal.," *Open Forum*, November 1961; William Wingfield, "California's New Vigilantes," *Progressive*, February 1968; William Turner, *Power on the Right* (Berkeley: Ramparts Press, 1971), hereafter cited as Turner; Richard Popkin, "The Strange Tale of the Secret Army Organization (USA)," *Ramparts*, October 1973.

3. An extensive literature describes William H. Parker's career. The most useful sources are "Chief Parker" (five-part series), *Los Angeles Mirror-News*, June 17–21, 1957; Ed Cray, "The Police and Civil Rights," *Frontier*, May 1962; Wesley Marx, "The Cop as Crusader," *Los Angeles*, August 1962 (hereafter cited as Marx, "Cop as Crusader"); Bill Davidson, "The Mafia Can't Crack Los Angeles," *Saturday Evening Post*, July 30, 1965; Paul Jacobs, "The Los Angeles Police: A Critique," *Atlantic Monthly*, March 1969. Parker's early speeches and articles are collected in *Parker on Police*, ed. O. W. Wilson (Springfield, Ill.: Charles C. Thomas, 1957, hereafter cited as *Parker on Police*). His later output includes "Introduction to Showing of Filmstrip, 'Communism on the Map,' " July 17, 1961; "Internal Threat to American Freedom," November 3, 1962; "Guarantor of Freedom," April 1, 1963; and "Final Address," July 15, 1966. His early efforts on behalf of Chief James E. Davis are sampled in his article as a police lieutenant, "L.A. Police Center Rooted in Davis' Dream," *Police Journal*, May 1938, and his pioneering exploitation of television as a publicity channel for the LAPD is usefully charted in "The LAPD? What Channel Is It On?" in "The LAPD: How Good Is It?" (special report), *Los Angeles Times*, December 18, 1977.

4. See, among numerous other articles, "Thousands Mourn at Funeral Rites for Chief Parker," *Los Angeles Times*, July 21, 1966.

5. Quoted from *Parker on Politics* in "Chief Parker Story," *Los Angeles Mirror-News*, June 21, 1957, hereafter cited as "Chief Parker Story."

6. See, for example, "Chief Parker Defends Force—Hits Critics," *Los Angeles Herald Examiner*, June 25, 1964.

7. Quoted in Robert M. Fogelson, *Violence as Protest: A Study of Riots and Ghettos* (Garden City, N.Y.: Doubleday, 1971), p. 252, hereafter cited as Fogelson.

8. Quoted in Jack Webb, *The Badge* (Englewood Cliffs, N.J.: Prentice-Hall, 1958), p. 253.

9. "Politics and the Police Department" (special report), *Los Angeles Times*, December 18, 1977.

10. Parker also had police trainees attend showings of "Operation Abolition," a propaganda film issued by the House Committee on Un-American Activities defending the conduct of the police in the committee's 1960 San Francisco hearings. See Turner, p. 79.

11. Donald O. Schultz and Loren Norton, *Police Operational Intelligence* (Springfield, Ill.: Charles C. Thomas, 1968), dedication and p. vii; Marx, "Cop as Crusader."

12. "Chief Parker Story"; Southern California ACLU files.

13. Wirin is discussed in "Chief Parker Story." Pitts is denounced in "Extremism Now Laid to Police, Parker Charges," *Los Angeles Times*, November 21, 1964. See also "CDC Accuses Police of Attacking Civil Rights," ibid., April 13, 1964.

14. *Parker on Police*, passim.

15. The pursuit of Wilkinson is extremely detailed in file documents of the Southern California ACLU. See also Stephen H. Fritchman, "The New 'Know Nothings,' " sermon of the month, delivered February 11, 1962 (First Unitarian Church of Los Angeles) and February 25, 1962 (Berkeley); "Valley Peace Center Will Not Move Out," *Los Angeles Times*, January 3, 1964; Kay Hardman, "Terrorism, Apathy and the American Community," *Liberal*, April 1964.

16. Southern California ACLU files.

17. Robert Conot, *Rivers of Blood, Years of Darkness: The Unforgettable Classic Account of the Watts Riot* (New York: Bantam Books, 1967), pp. 172–73, hereafter cited as Conot; Turner, pp. 105, 265.

18. Turner, p. 264.

19. Fogelson, p. 156.

20. "Riles Red Link Claim Unfounded, Group Says," *Los Angeles Times*, October 16, 1970; Donner, *Age*, p. 439 and n.

21. Conot, pp. 91–103, 160–61; Paul Jacobs, "The Los Angeles Police," *Atlantic Monthly*, March 1969; Fogelson, pp. 68–69, 200–204.

22. This failure was documented by the McCone Commission. See Conot, pp. 415–30.

23. Quoted in Conot, pp. 348–49.

24. Reddin subsequently (in 1975) unsuccessfully ran for mayor on a law-and-order platform. Useful accounts of Reddin's leadership style are Robert Conot, "The Superchief," *Los Angeles Times West*, June 9, 1968; Linda M. Mathews, "Chief Reddin—New Style at the Top," *Atlantic*

Monthly, March 1969, pp. 84ff.; "Special Report," *Los Angeles Times,* December 18, 1977; and "Police: The Thin Blue Line," *Time,* July 19, 1968, reprinted in *Congressional Record,* p. E1720, August 1, 1968.

25. *Los Angeles Times,* 1967: "The Anti-War March—What Did Happen?" and "Anti-War Protest Nearly Drove President out of Los Angeles," July 2; "Girl Undercover Agent Says She Heard Plot" and "Unruh and Burns Hit Antiwar Demonstrators for L.A. Action," June 30; "City Agencies Move to Probe Clash of Marchers and Police," June 28; "Police Win Council Vote of Confidence," June 30; "Safety of President Dictated Course of Action, Reddin Says," June 27.

26. In addition to the ACLU report referred to in the text and the *Los Angeles Times* coverage cited in n. 25 above, see Turner, p. 104, and these additional stories in the *Los Angeles Times,* July 2, 1967: "Anti War Acts Predicted by Underground Paper" and "Incidents Set Pattern for Impending Violence."

27. "Protestors Ejected from City Hall in Row over Police Action," *Los Angeles Times,* June 27, 1967.

28. In addition to the specific source references, this section relies on the following articles: William J. Drummond, "There Is More to Chief Davis Than Meets the Ear," *New West,* August 15, 1971; William Turner, "LA's Top Cop and His Plan to Straighten up the Statehouse," *San Francisco Bay Guardian,* December 29, 1971 (hereafter cited as Turner, "LA's Top Cop"); Barry Farrell, "The Power Politics of Ed Davis: A Cop Who Would Be King," *New West,* December 19, 1971; Jane Gassner Patrick, "Discipline in the LAPD: May the Force Be with You," *New West,* November 21, 1977; "LAPD's 'Crazy Ed' Davis Shoots for Calif. Governor in 1978," *Black Panther,* January 7, 1978; "Lore and Legend of Ed Davis" (special report), *Los Angeles Times,* December 18, 1977. See also Woods, pp. 505–6; "Retiring Los Angeles Police Chief, in Governor Race, Stresses Morals," *New York Times,* January 14, 1978; "In Cops' Eyes, Gay Community Is a Threat" (special report), *Los Angeles Times,* December 18, 1977.

29. "The Meanest Police Chief," *Militant,* May 1975.

30. "Reds Seek to Use Latin Youths as 'Prison Fodder,' Davis Says," *Los Angeles Times,* January 15, 1971.

31. Turner, "LA's Top Cop."

32. SISS Hearings, 1970: *Assaults on Law Enforcement Officers,* pt. 4, p. 327. See also SISS Hearings, 1969: *Extent of Subversion in the New Left,* pt. 2, p. 144.

33. "Report of UCLA Faculty Committee on Academic Freedom" (October 12, 1976); records in the cases of *Bagley v. City of Los Angeles Police Department* and *White v. Davis,* 13 C. 3d 757; 120 Cal. Rep. 94, 33 P. 2d 222 (1975); UCLA sections in the *Report of the President's Commission on Campus Unrest* (June 19, 1970). See also "Undercover

Police" and "Undercover Agents Identified on Campus" (UCLA) *Daily Bruin*, June 3, 1970; "13 UCLA Students, Faculty File Suit over Police 'Spies,' " *Los Angeles Times*, January 22, 1971.

34. "Widespread 'Snooping' Denied," *Los Angeles Times*, March 26, 1975.

35. *White v. Davis* (cited n. 33 above).

36. Record in *Martin et al. v. Los Angeles Community College District, et al.*, C 25402 (L.A. Sup.). See also the following news stories from 1972: "Students Spied On," *Los Angeles Free Press*, March 10; "Ruling Due on Local College Wiretapping," *Los Angeles Herald Examiner*, March 21; "Colleges Charged with Wiretapping in Class Action," *Metropolitan News*, March 21; "L.A. Colleges District Hit by Illegal Wiretapping Suit," *Valley News and Green Sheet*, March 21; "Surveillance Charged to Campus Police," *News Press*, March 21; "Suit Claims Police at Junior Colleges Spied on Activists," *Los Angeles Times*, March 21; "Junior College Trustee Asks Wiretap Probe," *Los Angeles Times*, March 22; "Colleges Trustee Demands Probe of 'Bugging,' " *Chronicle*, March 22; "Trustees Declare 'Bugging' against Policy of Board," *Valley Star*, March 23; "L.A. College Trustees Agree to Probe Bugging Charges," *Los Angeles Times*, March 23; " 'Bug' Suit Upsets College Trustees," *Los Angeles Daily Journal*, March 23; "Trustees Ask Probe on Illegal Wiretap Charges," *Valley News and Green Sheet*, March 23; "Three Community Colleges File Suit on Eavesdropping," *Californian*, March 23; "Suit to End Wiretapping Filed by WCLP [Western Center on Law and Poverty]," *Herald Dispatch*, March 23; "Superior Court Suit Asks for End to Junior College Surveillance," *Brooklyn-Belvedere* [Calif.] *Comet*, March 23; "Three Community Colleges File Suit on Eavesdropping," *East L.A. Tribune*, March 23; "AFT Charges District with 'Spying,' " *Los Angeles Collegian*, March 24; "Lawsuit Challenges School Wiretapping," *Los Angeles Free Press*, March 24–30; "Recording of L.A. City College Phone Calls Stirs Controversy," *Los Angeles Times*, March 28; "Suit Challenges Wiretapping of Students and Faculty," *Los Angeles Free Press*, March 30; "Suit Hits Wiretapping Filed Here," *Herald Dispatch*, March 30; "Surveillance Is Bane of Freedom," *Valley Star*, April 6; "Surveillance on Campus," *Los Angeles Times*, April 6; "Officer in Colleges Wiretap Suit Takes Fifth Amendment," *Los Angeles Times*, April 28; "Meetings 'Bugged' Twice, Dean at L.A. Trade Tech Testifies," ibid., May 3; "Spying on Students and Teachers Continues at Local Colleges," *Los Angeles Free Press*, May 4; "4 in Bugging Case Silent," *Los Angeles Times*, May 5; "Witness Balks at Testifying in Wiretap Case," ibid., June 6; "Judge Rules Suit Can Be Filed for Wiretapping at College," *Los Angeles Free Press*, September 1.

37. See uncontroverted allegations in the case of *J. Alfred Cannon, Philip L. Carter, and Opal C. Jones v. Edward M. Davis*, No. 978116

(Cal. Super. Ct.) and No. 41761 (Ct. App. 2d App. Dist.), and "Suit Seeks to Bar Police Keeping Files on 'Militants,' " *Los Angeles Times*, June 2, 1970.

38. SISS Hearings, 1970: *Extent of Subversion in the New Left*, pt. 1, pp. 1–44.

39. But one group mentioned by Thoms, the Congress of Mexican Unity, was promptly denied funding, and another, the Black Congress, was abandoned by former contributors frightened away by Thoms's testimony (*Los Angeles Times:* "Groups Deny Link to Violence, Subversion," March 25, 1970; "Implications Denied on Fund for Militants," April 24, 1970).

40. The document's cover reads: "THIS MATERIAL IS SUPPLIED BY THE PRESIDENT OF THE LOS ANGELES CITY COUNCIL TO THE MEMBERS OF THE LOS ANGELES AREA CHAMBER OF COMMERCE LEADERSHIP TRIP TO WASHINGTON, D.C. AND TO MEMBERS OF THE LOS ANGELES FIVE COUNTY DELEGATION IN CONGRESS FOR INFORMATION AND USE AS DEEMED APPROPRIATE BY THE RECIPIENTS, April, 1970."

41. "Report That Militants Get Poverty Funds Hit," *Los Angeles Times*, May 5, 1970.

42. The most revealing descriptions of the LAPD's aggressive intelligence modes are set forth in trial records in two 1970 state court cases stemming from a "shoot-out" between the LAPD and members of the Black Panther Party: *People v. Bryan*, LASC A-253348, and a companion case, *People v. Taylor*, LASC A-227425. See also the uncontroverted allegations in two 1970 federal court cases involving police responses to protest activities by Hispanics: *Ramirez et al. v. Ceballos et al.*, No. 70–2746–FW, and *Sanchez v. Los Angeles Police Department et al.*, No. 69202-HP. These lawsuits were brought on behalf of the victims of police misconduct by the Western Center on Law and Poverty (WCLP), whose files are a rich source of documentation in this area. Also highly useful is a memorandum dated May 17, 1978, to then Police Chief Darryl Gates by William Vaughn, Robert Vanderet, and Peter Leone on "The Department's Relations with the Black Panther Party" setting forth in careful detail (57 pages) the misconduct pattern summarized in the text.

43. The vendetta against Seymour Myerson was probably honed by his involvement in causes centering on police misconduct. The text briefly summarizes Myerson's voluminous personal files, the record of an interview with the author in July 1981, and undenied allegations supporting his legal action. For a press treatment, see "Taking a Peek at LAPD Intelligence Activities," *Los Angeles Herald Examiner*, August 13, 1978. The settlement agreement is described in "LAPD Agrees to Pay Damages," *Los Angeles Times*, and "City Settlement with ACLU in Police Spying Case Told," *Los Angeles Daily Journal*, both April 15, 1982.

See too "Good Judgment Missing in Action," *Los Angeles Times*, April 19, 1982. Meyerson's account of his harassment by the police appears in Bud and Ruth Schultz, eds., *It Did Happen Here: Recollections of Political Repression in America* (Berkeley: University of California Press, 1989), pp. 303–17.

44. "Ridenour's Own Story," *Review of Southern California Journalism*, December 1972; Ridenour Defense Committee, "Frame by Frame" (n.d.); "Judiciary Overkill," *Long Beach* [Calif.] *Press-Telegram*, October 6, 1972; and record on appeal in *People v. Ronald Ridenour*, No. 309, 423 (Los Angeles Mun. Ct.).

45. The style, priorities, and structure of the CCS, and in particular its active collaboration with the FBI, are described in the *Bryan* case record, cited in n. 42 above. A more general treatment appears in Louis E. Tackwood, in collaboration with the Citizens' Research and Investigation Committee, *The Glass House Tapes* (New York: Avon Books, 1973), passim, hereafter cited as *Glass House Tapes*. The claim has persisted in left circles that the CCS was complicit in the wave of terrorism against the left that engulfed Los Angeles in the mid seventies. See, for example, "LAPD Spies on You," *Los Angeles Free Press*, July 4, 1975.

46. The account in the text is based primarily on the extensive files made available to the author by Donald Freed, including radio interviews, reports by private investigators, checks, photographs, correspondence, reminiscences by the principals, disseminations by Justice for All (a defense organization), and Freed's MS, "The C.I.A. Comes Home" (1970). Informative press treatment may be found in "Sorry about That Jack Webb," *Scanlan's Monthly*, May 7, 1970; Nat Hentoff, "Civics Lessons for July 4," *Village Voice*, June 25, 1970; D. J. R. Bruckner, "Free Society Could Be Big Loser in War between Police and Panthers," *Los Angeles Times*, October 30, 1970; and David Wesley, "Freed Sutherland Case—Knock at Midnight," *Rights* 17, no. 7 (June 1970).

47. SWAT was a guerrilla-style police operation formed in the aftermath of the Watts riot. It won notoriety as a result of its unjustifiable use of deadly force in the May 1974 ambush and shoot-out with the Symbionese Liberation Army (SLA). See Larry Remer, " 'SWAT': The Police Berets," *Nation*, May 24, 1975; "The SWAT Squads," *Time*, June 23, 1975; and Center for Research on Criminal Justice, *The Iron Fist and the Velvet Glove* (Berkeley: CRCJ, 1975), pp. 48–52.

48. Memorandum of Fact, *United States v. Donald Freed, Shirley Jean Sutherland*, No. 4846-(WF)-CD (C.D. Cal. n.d.).

49. Inspired in part by revelations of Daniel Ellsberg, an antiwar activist who rejected his past as a hawkish intellectual, Tackwood laid bare his career as a police agent in *Glass House Tapes* and in an interview with the author on August 29, 1971. The most useful newspaper stories are "Web of Intrigue Tightens on Police Informer," *Los Angeles Times*,

October 17, 1971; "Informer Says Police Prompt Radical Acts," *New York Times*, October 25, 1971; "Los Angeles Police Agent Reveals Frameup of Left," *Guardian*, November 10, 1971; "Tackwood," *Seattle Sound News*, November 24, 1971; "Own Man or Pawn," *Los Angeles News Advocate*, February 4–10, 1972.

50. "3 Cleared, 3 Guilty in San Quentin Case," *New York Times*, August 13, 1976.

51. "The Public Disorder Unit of the Los Angeles Police Department" (statement of the Los Angeles Board of Police Commissioners, April 10, 1975); "Police Purge Nearly 2 Million Dossiers," *Los Angeles Times*, April 11, 1975; "Coast Police Unit Purges Its Files," *New York Times*, April 12, 1975.

52. "Public Disorder Unit of the Los Angeles Police Department."

53. See "Testimony by Ramona Ripston, Executive Director, American Civil Liberties Union of Southern California" (released document, April 26, 1975); "LAPD Spies on You," *Los Angeles Free Press*, July 4, 1975.

54. "Intelligence Unit Rules Elude Police Panelists," *Los Angeles Times*, December 28, 1975.

55. Political Rights Defense Fund, "Chronology of Recent Terrorist Attacks in Los Angeles" (released document, n.d.); "Quick Action Saves Lives in Bombing," *Los Angeles Times*, February 5, 1975; "Small Pipe Bomb Explodes at KCET; Another Found," *Los Angeles Times*, February 24, 1975; "County Ranks No. 2 in Bombings," *San Jose News*, March 28, 1975; "Iraqi Airways Office in Hollywood Bombed," *Los Angeles Times*, April 7, 1975; "Second Bombing Unidos Bookstore," ibid., April 16, 1975; "Three Bombings Alert ACLU to Active Terrorist Force," *Open Forum*, March 1975; "Local Nazis Admit to Rosenberg, Socialist Bombings," *Los Angeles Free Press*, March 21, 1975; "Nazis Claim Credit For Two Bombings," *Santa Monica Evening Outlook*, February 27, 1975; "A 12-inch Pipe Bomb Exploded," *Los Angeles Times*, May 5, 1975; "Anti-Castro Group Claims SM Explosion," *Santa Monica Evening Outlook*, May 5, 1975; National Socialist Liberation Front, *The Future Belongs to the Few of Us Still Willing to Get Our Hands Dirty— Political Terror It's the Only Thing They Understand* (leaflet, n.d.); National Socialist White People's Party, *Uptight about School . . . or Just about the Niggers??* (leaflet, n.d.); "Nazis Choose Pasadena for Race-Hate Campaign," *Pasadena Guardian*, May 2, 1975; "Right-Wing Terrorists Strike Again in L.A.," *Militant*, May 2, 1975; "New Rightist Bombing Hits L.A. Socialists," *Militant*, May 16, 1975; "Cops Are Political Soldiers" and "I'll Never Reach My 30th Birthday" (interviews with a leader of the provisional wing of the National Socialist Liberation Front), *Los Angeles Free Press*, August 22–28, 1975; "Demand L.A. Cops Halt Terror Bombings," *Militant*, June 20, 1975. The bombings of

offices of leftist groups continued into the eighties: "La Casa Nicaragua Attacked by Rightists Linked to Somoza," *Militant*, July 30, 1982.

56. "Police Side of Spying Story," *Los Angeles Herald Examiner*, June 9, 1980.

57. The trials and tribulations of Carlos Montes and his associates are chronicled in documents publicized by the Montes Defense Committee.

58. The intelligence report was never produced. "Noncalendared Item re Filming in City Council Chambers" (minutes, Los Angeles Police Commission meeting, February 28, 1978); "Police Taking A-Plant Critics' Photos Ousted," *Los Angeles Times*, March 1, 1978; "The Police Cross the Line," ibid., March 2, 1978; Southern California Alliance for Survival, press release (n.d.); American Friends Service Committee, "Statement to the Members of the Los Angeles Police Department Board of Commissioners," March 14, 1978; Los Angeles Board of Police Commissioners, "Report" to American Civil Liberties Union and American Friends Service Committee, March 6, 1978; "Police Filming Protested by Civil Liberties Groups," *Los Angeles Times*, March 15, 1978; "Report Promised on Police Filming at City Council," ibid., April 5, 1978; Los Angeles Board of Police Commissioners, "Final Report," May 30, 1978; "LAPD Accused of Political Spying" (report of lawsuit filed by the ACLU arising out of the Sundesert incident), *Los Angeles Times*, June 9, 1978. The angry response to the city council spying resulted in the formation of the Citizens' Commission on Police Repression (CCPR).

59. The list is reproduced in "Police Spying on L.A. Activist Groups Scored," *Los Angeles Times*, July 19, 1978. See also "A Problem for Gates," *Los Angeles Herald Examiner*, July 21, 1978; " 'Police Spying' on Local Groups Charged," *Altadena* [Calif.] *Chronicle*, July 20, 1978; "Hard to Love That Guy Who's a Spy," *Los Angeles Times*, July 27, 1978. Corroboration of the scope of the spying had already surfaced in the airing of the Cohen files in 1976 ("Police Spied on Democrats in '60's," *Los Angeles Times*, April 12, 1976).

60. The discussion of the PDID's infiltration network is based on pleadings, released documents, and pretrial discovery testimony aired in lawsuits filed on June 7, 1978, in the Superior Court of California case of *Coalition against Police Abuse (CAPA) et al. v. Gates et al.*, and on March 25, 1980, in the case of *Citizens' Commission on Police Repression (CCOPR) et al. v. Police Commission et al.* These lawsuits along with four others subsequently filed were consolidated into a single action with eighty-eight individuals and twenty-one organizational plaintiffs, in which the ACLU served as counsel (Los Angeles Super. Ct. C 243 458, C 317 528, C 374 660, C 381 339, C 399 552, C 413 904). A number of the original complaints joined the Los Angeles Police Commission as defendants because it had assertedly failed to redress the abuses com-

plained of, which included targeting of peaceful organizations, attempt by infiltrators to incite such groups to engage in criminal acts, pretext arrests, "dirty tricks," and the surveillance of political and religious leaders. Many of these activities were detailed in media accounts such as "LAPD Accused of Political Spying," *Los Angeles Times*, June 9, 1978; "LAPD Accused of Spying on Anti-Spying Citizen's Group," *Los Angeles Herald Examiner*, March 25, 1979; "Citizens' Coalition Suit Charges Political Infiltration by Police, Asks Court Ban," *Los Angeles Times*, March 26, 1980; "Police Commission to Probe LAPD 'Spying,' " *Los Angeles Herald Examiner*, March 26, 1980; "The Investigators," ABC News Closeup, broadcast April 29, 1980; Jeff Gottlieb, "My Tennis Partner Was an Agent," *In These Times*, October 19–25, 1977.

61. Interview by *Valley News* editor and staffers with former LAPD chief Ed Davis, March 17, 1978.

62. "Spy Exposed," *Rap Sheet* (CCPR), April 1980; CCPR release of discovery documents (n.d.); "L.A. Police Scouting of Private Bradley Meeting Revealed," *Los Angeles Times*, November 18, 1981.

63. Allegations of complaint, *Santa Monica–Venice Alliance for Survival et al. v. Police Commission of the City of Los Angeles et al.*, No. 0723460 (Los Angeles Super. Ct.), described and investigatively confirmed in "Southland Indian Groups Infiltrated by Police Spy," *Los Angeles Times*, November 21, 1980; "Behind the Latest Suit against LAPD Spying on Civilians," *Los Angeles Herald Examiner*, July 16, 1981; "New Suit Charges LAPD Spying on Peaceful Groups," *Los Angeles Times*, July 16, 1981; "ACLU Lawsuit Charges LAPD with Spying," *Los Angeles Herald Examiner*, July 15, 1981; "Statement by the Citizens' Commission on Police Repression on the Lawsuit against Los Angeles Police Department Spying," July 15, 1981; Michael Balter, "Will the Real Anti-Nuke Activists Please Stand Up?" (Pacifica News Service, n.d.).

64. "Gates Appointed as L.A. Police Chief; Commission Calls for New Direction," "Gates' Rise to the Top Began Early in Career," and "Gates Will Be the Image of Parker, Officers Say," *Los Angeles Times*, March 25, 1978; "Gates Issues Broad Attack on Crime and Drugs," ibid., September 11, 1980. Because Gates was Parker's protégé and in addition promoted the LEIU, he was an FBI bête noire: "FBI Kept an Eye on Gates," *Los Angeles Times*, October 13, 1978. For his LEIU connection, see Captain Darryl Gates, "The Law Enforcement Intelligence Unit," *California Peace Officer*, January/February 1965.

65. "Police Spy's Ploy to 'Impress' Violent Group Disclosed," *Los Angeles Times*, July 26, 1980; "Yaroslavsky: Police Officer–Spy Sought Cover as a Leftist," *Los Angeles Herald Examiner*, July 25, 1980; "Council Panel Sees No Abuse by Police Spy," *Los Angeles Times*, July 24, 1980; "Behind Closed Doors, Gates Discusses Spying," *Los Angeles*

Herald Examiner, July 24, 1980. The background of the accountability controversy and its ultimate resolution are detailed in the following news reports from 1980: "Dogging the Watchdogs," *Los Angeles Herald Examiner*, May 8; "Major Police Official Defies Council Panel," *Los Angeles Times*, May 9; "Council Panel Denied Answers by LAPD," *Los Angeles Herald Examiner*, May 9; "Yaroslavsky Asks Gates to Reveal Data," *Los Angeles Times*, May 12; "Dear Burt: An Open Letter to Our City Attorney," *Los Angeles Herald Examiner*, May 12; "Gates Answers Yaroslavsky: No," ibid., May 13; "Gates Affirms Stand on Releasing Intelligence Data," *Los Angeles Times*, May 13; "LAPD's Obligation," ibid., May 13; "On Gates' Rebuff of Yaroslavsky," *Los Angeles Herald Examiner*, May 14; "Cunningham Raps Gates on Refusal to Give Data," *Los Angeles Times*, May 14; "Gates Will Be at Council Meeting," ibid., May 15; "Gates, Yaroslavsky Hold 'Closed Summit,' " *Los Angeles Herald Examiner*, May 15; "PDID Funding Given OK by 4 on Council," *Los Angeles Times*, May 16; "Burt Pines Does the Right Thing," *Los Angeles Herald Examiner*, May 16; "Gates Gives in, Tells Council about Spying," ibid., May 16; "Farrell Protests Secret Meeting," *Los Angeles Times*, May 20; "Council to Get Data on Police 'Spy' Unit," ibid., May 27; "Ruling Sought on Open Police Hearing," ibid., May 31; "Council Opens Closed Sessions—to Its Members," ibid., June 18; "Closed Police Spy Hearings Restricted," ibid., July 1; "Court Order Keeps Spy Hearing in Open," *Los Angeles Herald Examiner*, July 1; "Gates Asks Judge to Lift Ban on Closed Meetings," *Los Angeles Times*, July 18; "Judge Rules Gates Can Talk in Private Council Spy Session," *Los Angeles Herald Examiner*, July 19.

66. "Bradley Takes on the Police," *Los Angeles Herald Examiner*, June 5, 1980; "Two LAPD Spies Tell Their Story," ibid., June 16, 1980; "Los Angeles Police Find Image of Efficiency Fades," *New York Times*, June 16, 1980; "Bradley Will Ask Gates to Report on Spy Charges," *Los Angeles Herald Examiner*, June 18, 1980.

67. "Where's PDID? Right Launches Attack on Left . . . Again," *Rap Sheet*, October 1980.

68. "Gates Rebuked for Comments on Olympic Plot," *Los Angeles Times*, January 25, 1982; "Police Aide on Coast Says Spies May Pose as Jewish Emigres," *New York Times*, January 23, 1982; "Police on Coast Detail 'Russian Mafia' Cases," ibid., January 28, 1982; "Jewish Leaders Meet Police on Reports of Russian Mafia," ibid., January 30, 1982; "Gates Calls Police Report of Soviet Plot on Olympics Speculation," *Los Angeles Times*, January 23, 1982; Greg Golden, "The Olympics Game," *Nation*, March 6, 1982.

69. Los Angeles Board of Police Commissioners, "Press Release," "Submission of Proposed Guidelines," and "Standards and Procedures for the Collection of Intelligence Information by the Los Angeles Police

Department, Public Disorder Intelligence Division," all February 24, 1982. Also, CCPR, "Brief Summary of Major Objections to Police Commission's Proposed New Guidelines for PDID," February 24, 1982; "Guidelines 'Far Exceed' Requirements," *Los Angeles Herald Examiner,* February 24, 1982; "Guidance for the New Guidelines," ibid., March 1, 1982; "Guidelines on Intelligence Activities by Police Adopted," *Los Angeles Times,* March 3, 1982; "Police Commission Gives Unanimous Approval to Controversial Spying Rules," *Los Angeles Herald Examiner,* March 3, 1982; "New Guidelines on Police Spying Rapped," *Los Angeles Times,* May 19, 1982; "LAPD's New Spying Guidelines Protested," ibid.; "Police Panel Told New Guidelines Are Too Vague," ibid., May 20, 1982; Los Angeles Board of Police Commissioners, "Audit Report, Public Disorder Intelligence Division," November 17, 1981.

70. "LAPD Infiltrated California Campus," *Organizing Notes,* June/July 1982; "Student Group Sues over Police Spying," *Los Angeles Daily Journal,* June 11, 1982.

71. Los Angeles Board of Police Commissioners, "In the Matter of Presentation by Citizens' Committee on Police Repression," March 25, 1980, p. 20; "Police Spying Data Channeled to Top Brass," *Los Angeles Times,* October 11, 1982.

72. *Los Angeles Times:* "Gates' Role in Undercover Work Told," January 5, 1983, and "Gates' Stand on Keeping Data Assailed," March 11, 1984.

73. *CAPA v. Gates et al.,* 243–458 (L.A. County Ct.), Gates deposition, vol. 1, December 30, 1982, pp. 60–61; "Gates' Role in Undercover Work Told," *Los Angeles Times,* January 5, 1983.

74. "Police Spying Data Was Channeled to Top Brass," *Los Angeles Times,* October 11, 1982.

75. *Los Angeles Times:* "Spying Probe Expanded by Police Board," October 13, 1982; "Police Spying Unit Hid Data, Officer Reveals," September 23, 1983; "Police Spy Unit Hid Work as Part of Policy, Councilman Told," September 29, 1983; "L.A. Seen Losing in Police Spying Suits," October 12, 1983. Also "Police Spying Suits Called 'Indefensible,' " *Los Angeles Daily Journal,* October 12, 1983.

76. Other embarrassing details emerged as well. With the approval of his superior, the infiltrator had engaged regularly in sex with a woman member of the group, and he had witnessed (apparently without intervening) the murder of an RCP leader during a rally at a housing project. In still another complication, a police lieutenant had tampered with the PDID files on the case (*Los Angeles Times:* "Use of Special Prosecutor in Spy Case Urged," December 12, 1982; "New Probe Ordered on Spying by LAPD," December 15, 1982).

77. *Los Angeles Times:* "LAPD Offered Files to Schools, Official Says," November 8, 1982; "Classification of Police File Reports Asked,"

December 9, 1982; "Police Intelligence Probe Intensified," January 5, 1983; "Grand Jury Probe of Police Asked," December 15, 1982; "New Probe Ordered on Spying by LAPD," December 15, 1982.

78. *Los Angeles Times*, 1983: "Officer Admits to Storing Police Files at Home," January 7; "Hidden Police 'Spy' Files Seized," January 8; "Police Board to Scrap Spy Unit," January 12; "Disorderly Conduct" (editorial), January 14; and "Commission to Abolish Police Intelligence Unit," January 19. Also "Los Angeles Police Subject of Inquiry," *New York Times*, January 17, 1983; "Bye-Bye, PDID" (editorial), *Los Angeles Herald Examiner*, January 20, 1983.

79. On the Pacht probe, see "Police Kept File on Him, Official Says," *Los Angeles Times*, January 11, 1983; "Los Angeles Police Unit Is Being Dismantled," *New York Times*, February 28, 1983; "File on Judge Found in Police Spy Documents," *Los Angeles Times*, January 17, 1983. On targeting of judges, see "Judge Finds His Name in LAPD Intelligence Files," *Los Angeles Times*, February 1, 1983; "Police Commission Delays Decision on Releasing Files to Judge, Officials," *Los Angeles Daily Journal*, February 9, 1984; "Police Spying Case—Is Anybody Safe?"*Los Angeles Times*, February 6, 1984; "Judge Was Transferred after Probe by PDID," ibid., March 6, 1984.

80. "Police 'Zealots' Spying on Own Reiner Charges," *Los Angeles Times*, January 18, 1983; "Reiner Defense of LAPD Questioned after Spy Criticism," *Los Angeles Herald Examiner*, January 19, 1983; "Reiner Defends PDID Blast," *Los Angeles Times*, January 20, 1983.

81. "City to Study Ending Police Spy Defense," *Los Angeles Times*, January 22, 1983.

82. "Proposed Ordinance to Open Police Files Wins Heavy Support," *Los Angeles Times*, February 15, 1983; "Tempers Flaring over L.A.'s Information Act," *Los Angeles Herald Examiner*, May 24, 1983; "Council Passes Watered-down File Law," *Los Angeles Times*, July 7, 1983; "Information Act Officially Passes, 9–5," *Los Angeles Herald Examiner*, July 14, 1983; "LAPD's Files Violated Rights, ACLU Charges," *Los Angeles Times*, July 21, 1983. Only a short time after the Freedom of Information ordinance was enacted, the LAPD's newly organized Anti-Terrorist Division turned down all but one of 122 requests for intelligence files, without stating grounds for the denials. These rejections fueled charges that the ordinance was being shafted and that the Anti-Terrorist Division was simply the old PDID with a new name.

83. *Los Angeles Times*: "Detective in Spying Case Linked to Birch Leader," May 24, 1983; "LAPD Must Turn over Spy Files," March 25, 1983; "L.A. to Pay for Defense in Police Spying Scandal," August 20, 1983; "New Police Anti-Terrorist Unit Being Formed," January 27, 1983. Detective Jay Paul's connections with Western Goals and Congressman McDonald and in the LAPD are described in two detailed fea-

ture stories: "L.A. Police Spy Probe Leads to Prominent Right-Wing Lawmaker," *Los Angeles Times*, June 5, 1983, and "Death of Rep. McDonald Disrupts Anti-Red Group," *Washington Post*, December 9, 1983. See also "Western Goals Striving to Keep Tabs on the Left," *Guardian*, September 28, 1983; "Red Faces for L.A.'s Red Squad," *Newsweek*, January 24, 1983; "Police Files on Leftists Funneled to Birchite Group," *Guardian*, June 15, 1983.

84. *CAPA v. Gates et al.*, depositions of Michael J. Rothmiller, vol. 1, August 12, 1983; Mayor Bradley (pp. 74–75), public officials (pp. 39–41), team reporting to Gates (pp. 68, 69), van de Kamp (pp. 78, 79) and Thomas Scheidecker, vol. 2, October 19, 1983, p. 74; "ACLU Wins Look at New Cache of PDID Data," *Los Angeles Herald Examiner*, September 13, 1983; "Judge Limits ACLU Access to LAPD Data," *Los Angeles Times*, September 25, 1983; "LAPD Spying Inquiry Aims at Lieutenant," ibid. July 27, 1983.

85. *CAPA v. Gates et al.*, deposition of Kenneth Rice, vol. 1, August 2, 1983, pp. 57, 59. *Los Angeles Times:* "PDID Detective Distrusted by Peers, Testimony Shows," August 25, 1983; "LAPD Approval of Role in Study of Subversives Shown," August 12, 1983; "Bank Paid Spy Unit Officer, Hearing Told," March 27, 1984.

86. *CAPA v. Gates et al.*, deposition of Thomas Scheidecker, vol. 1, September 20, 1983, p. 57; deposition of Joel Berk, October 12, 1983, p. 101. *Los Angeles Times:* "Police Spying Unit Hid Data, Officer Reveals," September 23, 1983; "Police Spy Unit Hid Work as Part of Policy, Councilman Told," September 29, 1983; "Anti-Terrorism Officer Tied to Hiding Data," October 18, 1983.

87. *Los Angeles Times:* "Yaroslavsky Learns of '76 Death Threat," September 8, 1983; "Police Order for File on Yaroslavsky Cited," October 28, 1983.

88. "Council, Police Commission Plan Joint Spy Investigation," *Los Angeles Times*, October 27, 1983.

89. "Police Spy Case Accord Voted; L.A. City Council Approves $1.8-Million Settlement," *Los Angeles Times*, February 4, 1984; "L.A. Approves Police Spy Case Settlement; Council Hopes $1.8-Million Award Will Keep Dispute out of Court," ibid., February 4, 1984; "City OKs Settlement of Police Spying Suit," ibid., February 22, 1984; "Council Approval of Award Settles Police Spying Litigation," *Los Angeles Herald Examiner*, February 22, 1984; "1.8 Million to End Police Spying Suit," *Los Angeles Daily Journal*, February 22, 1984; "Decree Leaves L.A. with Toughest Police-Spy Rules," *Los Angeles Times*, February 23, 1964; "The Case Is Closed," *Los Angeles Herald Examiner*, February 23, 1984; "Los Angeles Settles Police Spying Case," *New York Times*, February 23, 1984; "ACLU Attorneys: L.A. Settlement May Be Just the Start" (Los Angeles) *Daily News*, February 23, 1984; "Police

Spying Suit," *Los Angeles Daily Journal*, February 27, 1984; "Agreement on Spying Lawsuit between Union, Police Reached" (California State) *University News*, March 1, 1984; Frank del Olmo, "Improper Police Spying Causes a Chill That Lasts," *Los Angeles Times*, March 1, 1984; Dave Lindorff, "Police Spies in the City of the Angels; Return of the Red Squads," *Nation*, May 5, 1984. The ACLU announced that $100,000 from the lawyers' share of the award would be used to establish an ACLU Police Practices Litigation Fund. This fund would be used to hire a lawyer to monitor compliance with the settlement and to explore other police-spying suits, possibly against the county sheriff's department and the FBI.

Notes to Chapter 8

1. HISC Hearings, 1969: *Investigation of Students for a Democratic Society*, pt. 6B; 1970: *Black Panther Party*, pt. 3. SISS Hearings, 1970: *Assaults on Law Enforcement Officers*, pt. 3; 1970: *Extent of Subversion in the New Left*, pt. 9; McClellan Committee Hearings, 1968: pts. 5, 6, and 7. The discussion of the Detroit red squad draws extensively on "The Conduct of Local Political Intelligence" (1977), a Princeton University doctoral dissertation by James B. Jacobs, dealing with the political intelligence operations of the Detroit police, hereafter cited as Jacobs.

2. L. Loukopolis, "The Detroit Police Department: A Research Report" (MS, May 1970), pp. 69–70.

3. Jacobs, p. 297.

4. The patterns of surveillance targeting and operations from the mid sixties to the mid seventies are documented with photographs and interviews in a detailed investigative report, "Political Surveillance," submitted by S. E. Bordwell to the Michigan Civil Liberties Union in March 1971, hereafter cited as Bordwell Report; in a series of depositions subsequently recorded in the case of *Benkert et al. v. Michigan State Police et al.*, 74–023–934 A2 and 76–610–100 C2 (Wayne County Cir. Ct., 1974), hereafter cited as Benkert lawsuit; in SISS Hearings, 1970: *Extent of Subversion in New Left*, pt. 9, pp. 1225–78; and in Marc Stickgold, "Yesterday's Paranoia Is Today's Reality: Documentation of Police Surveillance of First Amendment Activity" (University of Detroit) *Journal of Urban Law* 55, no. 4 (Summer 1978): 877–929.

5. Bordwell Report, pp. 2–58, appendices 1–16.

6. Bordwell Report, appendices 1–11.

7. Bordwell Report, p. 8, appendix 11.

8. Benkert lawsuit (filed July 28, 1974); "Consumer Group Sues State Police," *Detroit News*, July 27, 1974; "Michigan Police Admit to Illegal Probe of Group," *Detroit Free Press*, August 24, 1974.

9. Benkert lawsuit, deposition of Jesse Coulter, August 1, 1975, pp. 21–22, 77.

10. Benkert lawsuit, deposition of Harold Mertz, August 5, 1975, pp. 19, 114.

11. Benkert lawsuit, deposition of John Ware, November 19, 1975, p. 33.

12. Benkert lawsuit, depositions of Allen Crouter, pp. 56–57, 131–32; William McCoy, pp. 30, 38–43, 109, 146; Harold Mertz, pp. 9, 49.

13. Benkert lawsuit, deposition of Harold Mertz, p. 30.

14. "Comments and Index to Detroit Police Department Documents Released by Plaintiffs in Benkert v. State Police on Thursday, July 31, 1975," passim; "Officials Disputed on Spying," Detroit Free Press, August 1, 1975.

15. Detroit Police Department, Special Investigation Bureau, file entry (n.d.). See also "Chrysler–FBI–Detroit Police Joint Spying Exposed," Michigan Free Press, March 8, 1976; Benkert lawsuit, depositions of John Ware, November 19, 1975, pp. 47–49, 53–61, 68–70; Robert J. Van Raaphorst, November 10, 1975, pp. 21, 24–38, 52, 78.

16. Order granting partial summary judgment, Benkert lawsuit, June 9, 1976. The court invalidated three statutes: the Subversive Activities, Communist Control, and Criminal Syndicalism acts. The Benkert suit was paralleled by a second, separate action, which also resulted in the invalidation of the legislation authorizing the state red squad. This suit was subsequently consolidated with the Benkert lawsuit for the purposes of devising a formula for distribution of the files. See "Michigan to Release Its Files about Political Surveillance," New York Times, December 27, 1980, and Jim Jacobs and Richard Soble, "A Blow against the Red Squads," Nation, February 14, 1981.

17. Order on method of notification and content of files, Benkert lawsuit, December 22, 1980.

18. "Political Files Kept by Detroit Police," Detroit Free Press, July 31, 1975; " 'Red Squad' Files Transferred," ibid., December 21, 1980; "Red Files Will Go to Civilians," Detroit News, February 12, 1981.

19. Proposed article 52, amendment to chapter 2, code of the city of Detroit, passed December 3, 1981; "Council OK's Limit on Police Spying," Detroit Free Press, December 4, 1981.

20. Veto statement of Mayor Coleman Young, December 11, 1981.

21. HUAC Hearings, 1952: Communism in the Detroit Area, pt. 1, pp. 2878–93.

22. Detroit Department of Police, special order, January 7, 1982.

23. "Inside the Red Squad Files," Detroit Free Press, December 21, 1980.

24. Baltimore Police Department, Annual Report, 1968 (June 30, 1969), p. 13, hereafter cited as BPD Annual Report, 1968.

25. Maryland General Assembly, Senate Investigating Committee Established Pursuant to Senate Resolutions 1 and 151 of the Maryland General Assembly, *Report to the Senate of Maryland* (December 31, 1975), p. 23, hereafter cited as Maryland Senate *Report*. The report is discussed in detail on pp. 302–5.

26. BPD *Annual Report, 1968,* p. 13.

27. Maryland Senate *Report,* p. 24.

28. Ibid., pp. 27–28.

29. Ibid., p. 28n.

30. Ibid., p. 29.

31. Letter dated January 19, 1971, to John Roemer III, director of the Maryland Civil Liberties Union.

32. Maryland Senate *Report,* pp. 17, 27.

33. Police Commissioner Pomerleau boasted of the thick ISD file on David Glenn, then Baltimore's director of human relations, with whom he had clashed. He subsequently let it be known that Glenn was a dangerous fellow, citing his attendance at meetings of extremists—a claim that was totally false. Maryland Senate *Report,* pp. 17, 33; telephone interview by the author with David Glenn, October 1984, and Glenn's recorded memoir.

34. Maryland Senate *Report,* pp. 19, 31, 143–48.

35. Interview by the author with a former CRD member, March 1972.

36. Maryland Civil Liberties Union, "Black Panthers: A Chronology of Panther Raids Harassment" (April 25, 1970).

37. The account in the text is based on court records and interviews by the author. See also Donner, "Hoover's Legacy," *Nation,* June 1, 1974, and the following newspaper articles from 1971: "State's Attorney Blasts Panther Indictments," *Baltimore Afro-American,* May 25; "Ex-Prosecutor Testifies Panther Witnesses Aided," *Baltimore News American,* June 18; "Police Admit Paying Witnesses in Panther Slaying Case," *Washington Post,* June 18; "Turco Trial: 'Agent 94' Testifies," ibid., June 19; "Kebe Faces New Quiz in Turco Trial," *Baltimore News American,* June 22; "Key State Witness's Testimony Stricken in Turco Trial," ibid., June 23; "Turco Case: Kebe Withdrawn, Testimony Stricken from Record," *Baltimore Afro-American,* June 26.

38. Private (office) memoir by William Zinman, October 1984.

39. The discussion of infiltration of collectives and peace groups is based primarily on interviews by the author with targets and suspected infiltrators, arranged in 1972 by John Roemer III, director, Maryland Civil Liberties Union.

40. "Agent Bridged 2 Worlds," *Baltimore Sun,* October 11, 1971.

41. "Pomerleau Refuses to Testify," *Washington Post,* February 19, 1973.

42. Maryland Senate *Report*, p. 34.

43. Donner, *Age*, pp. 120–23; T. W. Adorno, Else Frenkl-Brunswik, Daniel J. Levinson, and R. Nevitt Sanford, *The Authoritarian Personality* (New York: Harper & Row, 1950), pp. 239ff.

44. "City Police Take Tough Riot Stand," *Baltimore Sun*, February 12, 1971; Interviews by the author with demonstrators, March 1972.

45. Maryland Senate *Report*, pp. 27, 36–37, 149.

46. Ibid., pp. 32–33, 40–41.

47. Garry Wills, *Nixon Agonistes: The Crisis of the Self-made Man* (1970; reprint, New York: New American Library, 1971), pp. 260–61, 266–67; "ACLU Requests Probe of Police," *Annapolis Evening Capital*, April 29, 1971; "Glenn Burnie Activists Eyed by Authorities," *Baltimore Sun*, December 28, 1971; "Police Watch Possible Subversives," *Baltimore Evening Sun*, December 28, 1970; "Statement of Allen Lenchek," Prince George's County Council Meeting, May 21, 1973; "Students Fear Political Activity," *Diamondback* (University of Maryland student newspaper), April 29, 1971; "Police Served as Informant Here," ibid., May 18, 1971.

48. "Mr. Pomerleau's Protectors," *Baltimore Sun*, January 19, 1976.

49. "Fear and Hatred Grip Birmingham," *New York Times*, April 9, 1960. The article subsequently generated an unsuccessful libel suit; the plaintiffs, all Birmingham officials, were led by Eugene Connor. Charles Morgan, Jr., *A Time to Speak* (New York: Harper & Row, 1964), pp. 68–72, hereafter cited as Morgan.

50. Morgan, p. 249.

51. Alan F. Westin and Barry Mahoney, *The Trial of Martin Luther King* (New York: Crowell, 1974), p. 18; Robert G. Corley, "The Quest for Racial Harmony: Race Relations in Birmingham, Alabama, 1947–1963" (Ph.D. diss., University of Virginia, 1979), p. 163, hereafter cited as Corley.

52. Corley, pp. 83–85, 159–61.

53. Corley, p. 147.

54. Corley, pp. 163ff.

55. Fish Committee Hearings, 1930: vol. 1, pt. 6, p. 193.

56. Ibid.

57. Federal Bureau of Investigation, memorandum, April 29, 1961, "To: Director, FBI, From: SAC [Special Agent in Charge], Birmingham, Subject: 'Infiltration of Law Enforcement Agencies by Klan-Type Organizations,' Racial Matters." These memoranda are cited hereafter as FBI memo.

58. FBI memo, April 24, 1961, "To: Director, FBI, From: SAC, Birmingham."

59. Birmingham Police Department, inter-office communication, April 24, 1961, "To: Commissioner Eugene Connor, From: Tom Cook,

re: Martin Luther King, Jr. and Communism" (appended to FBI memo, April 24, 1961).

60. FBI memo, April 26, 1961, "To: Director, FBI, From: SAC, Birmingham."

61. Ibid.

62. Deposition of Gary Thomas Rowe, *Peck v. United States*, No. 76 Civ. 983 (S.D.N.Y.) (n.p.).

63. Ibid.

64. James Peck, *Freedom Ride* (New York: Grove Press, 1962), pp. 98–99.

65. Ibid.

66. Senate Select Committee to Study Governmental Operations with Respect to Intelligence Activities, Hearings: *Federal Bureau of Investigation*, December 2, 1975, testimony of Gary Thomas Rowe, vol. 6, p. 118.

67. Ibid.

68. Much of this discussion is based on the collection of records generated by the Birmingham Police Department from 1940 to 1982, which include the Eugene Connor Papers (1959–63), Albert Boutwell Papers (1963–67), W. C. Hamilton Papers (1963–67), and George Seibels Papers (1967–75). Documents from these collections dealing with police matters include reports of detectives that are variously called "Notes," "Report," "Memorandum," "Inter-Office Memorandum," or lack a designation altogether. They are cited here as "Police Intelligence Reports," followed by a date whenever it is given.

69. George McMillan, "The Birmingham Bombers," *Saturday Evening Post*, June 6, 1964; Howell Raines, "The Birmingham Bombing," *New York Times Magazine*, July 24, 1983. The Raines article reveals that the case against Chambliss "was built on information from a small secret network of women with Klan ties [and] . . . that much of that information originated with Chambliss's wife."

70. Police Intelligence Report, November 6, 1963.

71. Police Intelligence Report, November 22, 1963.

72. Police Intelligence Report, August 26, 1966.

73. Miscellaneous Police Notes, January to May 1967.

74. Police Intelligence Report, September 21, 1963.

75. Police Intelligence Report, January 15, 1965.

76. Police Intelligence Report, October 4, 1963.

77. Police Intelligence Report, October 9, 1963.

78. Police Intelligence Report, June 19, 1969.

79. Police Intelligence Report, June 28, 1965.

80. Police Intelligence Report, April 28, 1969.

81. Police Intelligence Report, April 29, 1969.

82. Police Intelligence Report, March 31, 1966.

83. Police Intelligence Report, April 1, 1966.

84. Police Intelligence Report, April 25, 1969.

85. Police Intelligence Reports, April 28 and 29, 1969.

86. Police Intelligence Report, October 17, 1963.

87. "Police Surveillance in Birmingham Once Extended to a Vice-President," *New York Times*, June 21, 1978; Police Intelligence Report, January 15, 1965.

88. Police Intelligence Report, February 1967.

89. Police Intelligence Reports, April 18, October 6, and September 29, 1972.

90. "There is a white girl, age 17 . . . We have a copy of a letter that she has written to the communists . . . [She] is a threat to any other girls around her" (Police Intelligence Report, November 21, 1966). A photocopy of the letter is attached to the report.

91. Corley, pp. 167–69; Police Intelligence Report, December 4, 1963, recounting how Detective Jones and a reporter for the *Birmingham News* attempted to photograph white mourners attending the funeral of the victim of the 16th Street church bombing.

92. "Police Surveillance in Birmingham Once Extended to a Vice-President," *New York Times*, June 21, 1978.

93. A report dated February 27, 1967, describes a march sponsored by the Alabama Christian Movement for Human Rights, the route, leaders, and behavior of the marchers ("orderly"), and concludes, "Detectives B. J. Cooper and W. D. Nelson took pictures. Cooper used a 35MM camera . . . Nelson used the special detail polaroid camera." A second report dated March 7, 1967, and exemplary of the coverage of other marches that month, is similarly detailed and concludes, "Detective Vernon T. Hart and I [the reporter] photographed the march concentrating on the people we did not know and the leaders of the march."

94. Statement of retired Police Chief Francis V. McManus, "Police Wiretap Machines Found," *New Haven Journal Courier*, January 27, 1977. This statement was subsequently alternately denied and readmitted.

95. Testimony of Richard Sulman at public hearings of the New Haven Board of Police Commissioners, June 1977, "Report of Proceedings," pp. 68ff.

96. *New Haven Journal Courier*, 1977: "City Police Used Illegal Phone Tap," "Lee, Ahern, DiLieto Deny Tap Ties," January 24; "Taps Become Tips," January 25; "Pro-Panther Rally Spurred Taps," January 26; "Police Tap Machines Discovered," January 27; "FBI, State Police Knew," January 28.

97. New Haven Board of Police Commissioners, "Interim Report," p. 7; "Aherns Visited Tap Operation Police Officers Reveal in Probe," *New Haven Register*, June 8, 1977.

98. "Police Surveillance Put on Judge," *New Haven Register*, June 5, 1977; "Pastore: Warned DiLieto, Says Ahern Bugged Board," *New Haven Journal Courier*, June 27, 1977; "Ahern, Ex-New Haven Police Chief, Linked by Witnesses to Wiretapping," *New York Times*, June 31, 1977.

99. "F.B.I. Documents Confirm Federal Wiretaps in City," *New Haven Register*, July 12, 1977; "F.B.I. Memo Says Agency Kept Data on Panther Phones," *New York Times*, March 1, 1978.

100. " 'Whitewash' Alleged in Inquiry on New Haven FBI," *New York Times*, May 1, 1977; "F.B.I. Documents Confirm Federal Wiretaps in City," *New Haven Register*, July 12, 1977.

101. "Justice Department Asks F.B.I. to Renew New Haven Taps Inquiry," *New York Times*, July 6, 1977.

102. " 'Whitewash' Alleged in Inquiry on New Haven FBI," *New York Times*, May 1, 1977.

103. See Donner, *Age*, pp. 324, 336, 340.

104. "City Police Had Wiretap during Rackley Torture," *New Haven Journal Courier*, November 2, 1977.

105. James F. Ahern, *Police in Trouble* (New York: Hawthorn Books, 1972), pp. 31ff.

106. Ibid., pp. 64–65.

107. "Wiretaps Putting McLucas on Bail," *New Haven Journal Courier*, October 21, 1977; "Court Review in Murder Case May Shed Light on Wiretaps," ibid., November 2, 1977; "Much Rides on McLucas Trial," *Hartford Courant*, October 26, 1977; "Tap Tainted McLucas Conviction," ibid., October 19, 1977.

108. "Markle Supports McLucas in Bid to Cut Sentence," *New Haven Journal Courier*, March 1, 1978; "Review Board Frees McLucas," ibid., April 10, 1978; "Sentence Ends for Ex-Panther," *New Haven Register*, April 10, 1978.

109. "Police Official Says Chief Was Told Wiretap Illegal," *New Haven Register*, June 29, 1977. *New Haven Journal Courier*: "Tap File Burned on Police Orders," July 1, 1977; "Lie Tests Taken by Police," April 21, 1977; "Testimony on Taps Contradicts Chief," June 2, 1977; "Chief Questioned about Tap Letter," June 7, 1977.

110. "DeGrand Tells of DiLieto Order," *New Haven Journal Courier*, June 23, 1977; "Probe Told DiLieto Said to Dump 3 Tape Machines," *New Haven Register*, June 4, 1977.

111. "DiLieto Retires as Chief to Enter Mayoral Derby," *New Haven Register*, June 14, 1977.

112. "Boosters Set Tone of Debate," *New Haven Journal Courier*, August 3, 1977.

113. *Abramovitz et al. v. James Ahern et al.*, Civil Action No. 77–207 (D. Conn.), filed May 12, 1977; "$1.3 Million Sought in Wiretap

Suits," *Hartford Courant*, May 13, 1977; "Taps Aimed at Leftist Groups, Suit Claims," *New Haven Register*, May 13, 1977; "52 Suing for $1 Million In Illegal City Wiretapping," ibid., May 12, 1977; "Ahern Property in Trust," *New Haven Journal Courier*, May 13, 1977; "52 to File Wiretap Lawsuits," *Hartford Courant*, May 12, 1977; "Federal Suit Filed by 52 Persons Charging New Haven Wiretapping," *New York Times*, May 13, 1977; "Aherns Say Tap Victims Broke Law," *New Haven Register*, August 17, 1977; "Tap-Suit Plaintiffs Engaged in Crimes, Aherns Charge," *New Haven Journal Courier*, August 17, 1977.

114. "Wiretap Plaintiffs to Get Records," *Hartford Courant*, July 6, 1978.

115. "Wiretap Case Nears an End," *New York Times*, May 13, 1983; "Board Seeks 'Taps' Settlement," *New Haven Journal Courier*, June 21, 1983; "Board Lets 'Taps' Case Veto Stick," ibid., July 1, 1983; "Board Seeks an End to Wiretap Case," *New York Times*, July 10, 1983; "Deal Reached in Wiretap Case," *New Haven Journal Courier*, April 20, 1984; "$1.75 Million Agreement Reached in Wiretap Case," *Norwalk* [Conn.] *Hour*, April 20, 1984; "City Ponders New Wiretap Settlement," *New Haven Register*, April 29, 1984; "Illegal Wiretapping Suit Costs City $1.75 Million," *Norwalk* [Conn.] *Hour*, June 27, 1984.

116. "7 Years of Wiretap Woes Ending for DiLieto," "Police Sank Suit, Lawyers Say," *New Haven Register*, July 8, 1984.

117. Watters and Gillers, *Investigating the FBI*, p. 134.

118. "Law Enforcement Men to Outnumber Protesters at March of Poor in Capital," *New York Times*, March 4, 1968; Jerry W. Wilson, "Common Sense in Dealing with Demonstrations," *Police Yearbook*, September 1971 (according to Wilson, then the District of Columbia police chief, in the calendar year 1970, police handled 361 demonstrations). See also "Police Have Handled 289 Demonstrations in Past Year," *Washington Post*, April 24, 1971.

119. District of Columbia, "Police Intelligence Activities Report," March 7, 1975, Attachment "K."

120. Record in *Hobson et al. v. Wilson et al.*, 556 F Supp. (D.D.C.) 1982, R. 268 at 97, hereafter cited as Hobson Record.

121. Hobson Record, R. 268 at 865–66.

122. "Campus Turmoil Aftermath," *Washington Post*, July 17, 1970.

123. Hobson Record, R. 263 at 126–27. *Washington Post:* "D.C. Police Officer Led Double Life as an Apache Indian," February 3, 1973; "Police Surveillance: Two First-Hand Views" (letters by Tina Hobson and James D. Binsted), March 11, 1976.

124. Hobson Record, R. 263 at 121–22, R. 264 at 349, R. 272 at 68–69.

125. Hobson Record, R. 264 at 334–35, 336–37, R. 263 at 123–25.

126. Hobson Record, Pl. Exh. 91 at 9–10, R. 263 at 218–19.

127. Hobson Record, Pl. Exh. 90.

128. Hobson Record, Pl. Exh. 88 at 34, Pl. Exh. 91 at 10.

129. Hobson Record, Pl. Exh. 5 at 4, Pl. Exh. 88 at 34, Pl. Exh. 91 at 10.

130. The discussion of Merritt's career as an informer is based on the following sources: "FBI Informer Confesses, an Exclusive Interview," *Daily Rag,* October 5–12, 1973; "Revelations of a Gay Informant," *Advocate,* pt. 1, February 23, pt. 2, March 9, 1977; Tim Butz and John B. Hayes, *WIN Magazine,* "Biography of an Informant: The Recruitment Trap," pt. 1, March 14, "Biography of an Informant: Dirty Tricks and Other Games," pt. 2, March 21, "Biography of an Informant: In from the Cold," pt. 3, March 28, 1974; "Police Unit Bemoans Use of Informers," *Daily Rag,* October 12–19, 1973; "Informers Spied on D.C. Activists," *Washington Star,* October 7, 1973; "Informers for Police Exposed," *Washington Post,* October 7, 1973; "Police Disrupt Left, Police Officer Cites Tactics on Activists," ibid., March 20, 1975; "Informant's Data Most Irrelevant," ibid., March 28, 1971; "Informant Says Police Urged Theft," ibid., March 14, 1975.

131. The activities of Ann Kolego-Markovich as an informer are described in "Citizens Finger Prize Police Informer," *Daily Rag,* September 25–October 5, 1973; "Albert Ferguson Discusses Police Intelligence Activities," *Washington Post,* March 20, 1975; and "Police Chief Releases Report on Past Surveillance," ibid., March 13, 1975.

132. "Organization, Functions, and Staffing of the Intelligence Division," District of Columbia, Metropolitan Police Department general order no. 7-G-4 (A), ser. 1966, December 24, 1969.

133. Metropolitan Police Department general order no. 5, 1964.

134. Metropolitan Police Department general order no. 12, March 29, 1971.

135. Metropolitan Police Department general order no. 5, ser. 603, June 7, 1973.

136. *Washington Post:* "Police Chief Releases Report on Past Surveillance," March 13, 1975; "Justice Department Probes D.C. Police and FBI Surveillance," October 12, 1975.

137. Rockefeller Commission, *Report to the President by the Commission on Central Intelligence Agency Activities in the United States* (Washington, D.C.: GPO, 1975), ch. 17, pp. 151–52, 236–39, appendix 7.

138. "Administration Says It Planned for Mayday," *Washington Post,* February 21, 1972. On May 10, 1971, Attorney General Mitchell lauded the tactics of the "valiant Washington policemen" as exemplary ("Mitchell Asserts Tactics Exemplary," *Washington Post,* May 11, 1971; see also "Nixon Backs D.C. Police on Mayday," ibid., June 21, 1971, and "Mitchell Reiterates His Praise of Wilson," ibid., June 17, 1971). On

August 14, 1972, then Attorney General Richard Kleindienst stated that not only did he approve of the Mayday police actions, but insisted that under similar circumstances, "I would do substantially that again" ("Miami Beach Arrests Backed by Kleindienst," Washington Post, August 15, 1972).

139. Washington Post, 1971: "7,000 Arrested in Demonstration," "Justify Arrests Judge Orders Police," May 4; "1200 Protesters Arrested," May 6; "The Demonstration, the Law and the City" (editorial), May 6; "Judge Halleck Says Demonstrators Pressured over Pleas," May 11; "15 Sue over Arrests during City Disorder," May 14; "Protest Arrests Held Not Justified," May 12.

140. Washington Post, 1971: "Court Halts Prosecution of Most Mayday Cases," May 27; "Prosecution Drops 2500 Mayday Cases," May 28; "2400 Free of Mayday Charges," May 31; "Mayday Weakens Court, Police Ties," May 30; "17 Capital Arrest Cases Dismissed by D.C. Judge," June 17; "Judge Clears 56, Hits Mayday Partisanship," July 10. See also "The Incredible Conduct of the Mayday Prosecutors" (editorial), ibid., June 2, 1971.

141. "Council Member, 7 Others Sue Police, FBI for Spying on Them," Washington Post, July 17, 1976; "Way Cleared for Trial of Aides in '71 Protest," ibid., December 14, 1976; "Jury Weighs a $1.8 Million Damage Claim by 7 Activists in Capital," New York Times, December 18, 1981; "Ex-Activists Win $711,000 in Red Squads Case," ibid., December 24, 1981; "Jury Awards $711,937.50 to Demonstrators," Washington Post, December 24, 1981.

142. Julius Hobson et al. v. Jerry Wilson et al., 737 F. 2d 1 (Ct. App. D.C., 1984); "City Held Responsible for Police Misconduct," Washington Post, July 27, 1981; news release, American Civil Liberties Union, National Capital Area, May 4, 1981; "Payments in 'May Day' Suits Near," Washington Star, April 22, 1981.

143. "DC Police Admit Keeping Files on Political Figures," Washington Post, February 13, 1975; "Council Asks Specific Data on D.C. Surveillance Files," "Police Unit to Make Intelligence Rules," ibid., February 19, 1975; "Cullinane Puts Emphasis on Criminal Intelligence" (covering a report by Police Chief Maurice Cullinane), Washington Star, March 30, 1975; "Bill Would Limit D.C. Police Files," Washington Post, April 23, 1975; "Intelligence Work and the District Police" (editorial), ibid., March 14, 1975; "Intelligence Gathering Curbs Clamped on District Police," Washington Star, July 2, 1976; "Controlling Police Surveillance" (editorial), Washington Post, July 23, 1976.

Notes to the Epilogue

1. Holmes v. Church, 70 Civ. 5691 (S.D.N.Y.), judgment, June 10, 1971; SISS Hearings, 1969: Extent of Subversion in Campus Disorders,

pp. 191–289. See also coverage in the *New Rochelle* [N.Y.] *Evening Star:* "Testimony of N.R. Detective Revealed," January 28, 1970; "Police Surveillance Issue Taken to City by Citizens" and "Commissioner Carey Explains Circumstances of Testimony," February 20, 1970; "Police Testimony 'Misused' " and "Ottinger Charges 'New McCarthyism,' " February 28, 1970; "Full Text: City Manager's report to Mayor, City Council," March 16, 1970; "Carey Rips into Fuerst on P.D.," November 15, 1972; "Police File Shows Ossie Davis Was Surveillance Target in 1960's," January 27, 1985; and coverage in the *New York Times:* "Police 'Spy' at Meeting Rouses Ire," February 26, 1970; " 'Spying' Defended in New Rochelle," March 18, 1970; "Police Head Is Out in New Rochelle," April 25, 1970; "Westchester Group Sues to Bar Police Surveillance of Lawful Persons," June 23, 1971.

2. *Libby and Valdes v. Berlin*, complaint for injunction (Cal. Super. Ct.), February 2, 1970; Hermosa Beach, Calif., Police Department, "General Statement of Principles: Function of the Local Police Department concerning Intelligence Information," October 26, 1972; "Ecology Action Committee," intelligence report by Wallace Moore, administrative assistant to Chief William Berlin, March 31, 1970. See also coverage in the *South Bay* (Calif.) *Daily Breeze*, "Police Shift Quiets Hermosa 'File' Rumors," December 15, 1970; "Hermosa Skirts Dossier Issue," January 6, 1971; "Hermosa Silence Due for Attacks," January 5, 1971; " 'Dossier' Denied by Chief Berlin," January 7, 1971; "Berlin Denies Dossier Charge," January 8, 1971; "Hermosa Police Chief Sued" and "Council Backs Police," February 3, 1971; "Key Witness Mum in Dossier Case," May 30, 1971; "Hermosa Denies 'Dossier Case' Fee," August 18, 1971; "Police Guidelines Accepted by Council," October 25, 1972; and coverage in other area newspapers: "New Evidence of Surveillance Focuses Police Issue," *Beach People's Easy Reader*, January 23–February 6, 1971; "Dossier Case Seems Headed for High Court," *Los Angeles Times*, June 27, 1971; "Plaintiffs Drop Suit over 'Dossier Case' Fee," ibid., October 24, 1971; "Former Hermosa Beach Policeman Admits 'Deal' with Councilman Ben Valentine," *Hermosa Beach* [Calif.] *Review*, August 19, 1971; "Guidelines OK'd on 'Police Spying' " *Los Angeles Times*, October 27, 1972.

3. "Order Too Late: Police Burn Intelligence Files" and "ACLU Wants Explanation of Burning of Police Files," *Memphis Press-Scimitar*, September 11, 1976; "Mayor Dissolves Police Unit, Has Files Burned," *Memphis Commercial Appeal*, September 12, 1976; "Memphis Mayor Disbands Intelligence Unit of Police," *New York Times*, September 12, 1976; "Another Police Fire," *Memphis Commercial Appeal*, September 13, 1976; "Former War Protestor Says Name Can't Be Used in Suit," *Memphis Press-Scimitar*, September 14, 1976; "ACLU Files Suit over Police Files," *Memphis Commercial Appeal*, September 19, 1976.

4. An enlightening analysis of the Memphis litigation appears in Paul Chevigny, "Politics and Law in the Control of Local Surveillance," *Cornell Law Quarterly* 70, no. 3 (April 1984), hereafter cited as Chevigny, "Politics and Law."

5. *Kendrick v. Chandler*, No. 76–449 (W.D. Tenn.), deposition of Lieutenant Ely Arkin, p. 403.

6. Ibid., deposition of Captain Patrick Ryan, November 17, 1976, p. 128.

7. Ibid., deposition of Lieutenant Ely Arkin, December 14, 1976, p. 561.

8. Ibid., p. 600.

9. Ibid., pp. 110, 176, 191, 261–63, 418, 430–50, 594, 597, 622, 631, 633, 644, 648; deposition of Captain Patrick Ryan, pp. 145, 178, 214, 232, 317, 328–31. See also "ACLU Says Newswoman Named in Controversial Police Reports," *Memphis Press-Scimitar*, September 14, 1978; "Police Kept Tabs on Memphis PUSH Chapter, Data Indicates," *Memphis Commercial Appeal*, September 15, 1978.

10. *Kendrick v. Chandler* (cited in n. 5 above), order, judgment, and decree. This document is reproduced with commentary in "Domestic Intelligence Opinion—a Court Order against a Red Squad," *First Principles* 3, no. 2 (October 1978). See also Chevigny, "Politics and Law," pp. 751–54; "Memphis Police Facing Controls on Surveillance" and "Police Information to Be Made Public," *Memphis Press-Scimitar*, September 13, 1978; "ACLU Opens Doors on Police Intelligence Gathering," *Memphis Commercial Appeal*, September 14, 1978.

11. A useful account of the attempts to curb police spying in Seattle is Kathleen Taylor, "Seattle," in American Friends Service Committee, *The Police Threat to Political Liberty* (Philadelphia: AFSC Program on Government Surveillance and Citizens' Rights, 1979), pp. 25–35. This volume, hereafter cited as AFSC, *Police Threat*, records the AFSC program's investigative findings in four additional cities: Los Angeles, Philadelphia, Baltimore, and Jackson, Miss. See also Kathleen Taylor, "The New Seattle Ordinance to Control Police Spying: How It Was Put Together," *First Principles* 4, no. 2 (October 1979).

12. The modern history of the Seattle intelligence unit is traced in an undated confidential manual compiled by Major E. R. Connery, Inspectional Services Division. According to this document, the formation of the subversive activities unit was inspired by the newly launched LEIU.

13. "Citizens' Rights Must Be Protected" (editorial), *Seattle Post-Intelligencer*, December 2, 1975; AFSC, *Police Threat*, p. 26; Coalition on Government Spying, "Report to the Mayor and the Seattle City Council on Seattle Police Intelligence Activities, August 23, 1978," hereafter cited as "Seattle Report"; "Get Moving on Intelligence Curbs" (editorial), *Seattle Post-Intelligencer*, January 30, 1978.

14. "Citizens, Groups, Watched by Police," *Seattle Times,* November 30, 1977.

15. "Police Spy Critics Lash 'Abuses,' " *Seattle Post-Intelligencer,* August 16, 1978; "Police Files Denounced as 'Useless, Damaging,' " *Seattle Times,* August 15, 1978; "Keeping Tabs on the Rads," *Weekly* (a Washington State area journal), September 5, 1978; "Police Spied on International District Group," *International Examiner,* July 1978.

16. "Seattle Report," p. 304; AFSC, *Police Threat,* pp. 26–27.

17. "Seattle Report," p. 11; AFSC, *Police Threat,* pp. 28–29; Roxanne Park, "Police Spying in Seattle," *Inquiry,* June 12, 1978; "Long-Secret Police Spy File Revealed," *Seattle Post-Intelligencer,* April 10, 1978.

18. Coalition on Government Spying, press statement, May 25, 1978; "Police Intelligence Chief Suspended for Releasing Files," *Seattle Times,* May 26, 1978; "Police Spy Unit Chief Removed," *Seattle Post-Intelligencer,* May 26, 1978; "Contempt Motion Filed against Seattle Police," ibid., May 27, 1978; "Police Face Contempt Hearing for Moving Files," *Seattle Times,* May 28, 1978; "Decision to Transfer Intelligence Files Was a Joint One, Says Captain," ibid., June 1, 1978; "Judge to Ban Transfer of Disputed Police Files," ibid., June 5, 1978; Coalition on Government Spying, memorandum to Seattle media, June 6, 1978; "No Ruling on Police Records," *Seattle Post-Intelligencer,* June 6, 1978; "Police Misled Council, Says Anti-Spying Group," *Seattle Times,* June 7, 1978; "Officer Won't Be Held in Contempt for Shifting Files," ibid., June 7, 1978; "The Bartley Affair—What Happened to the Intelligence Files?" and "Spy Files: Did Bartley Act Alone?" *Seattle Sun,* June 7, 1978; "Hidden Police Files May Be Returned," *Seattle Post-Intelligencer,* June 8, 1978; "Police Files on Way Back, Judge Is Told," ibid., June 10, 1978; "Cops Discussed Spy Files," *Seattle Sun,* June 14, 1978; "Police Finish Probe of File Transfer," *Seattle Post-Intelligencer,* June 23, 1978.

19. See Seattle municipal code, ch. 14.12 (1980).

20. Ibid., ch. 14.12 150 (C), 160.

21. Ibid., ch. 14.12 330 (A), ch. 14.12 350–60.

22. *Alliance to End Repression v. City of Chicago,* 561 F. Supp. 537 (N.D. Ill. 1982), agreed order, judgment, and decree.

23. Ibid., "City Agrees to Spying Ban," *Chicago Sun-Times,* April 28, 1981; "Chicago Agrees to Bar Political Spying by Police," *Los Angeles Times,* April 29, 1981; Matthew J. Piers, "The Struggle against Abuse," *Rights,* (October–November 1981); Nat Hentoff, "Chicago Shows Us Yokels How to Leash a Red Squad," *Village Voice,* June 24–30, 1981.

24. Memorandum opinion and order, No. 75 C3295 (N.D. Ill., July 12, 1982). See also "Police Violated Order on Spying, Suit Claims," *Chicago Tribune,* April 12, 1982; "Police Accused of Violating No-Spy

Pact," *Chicago Law Bulletin*, April 12, 1982; "Cops Photographed Nuke Crowd: Lawyer," *Chicago Sun-Times*, "Suit Charges Police Spying," ibid., April 13, 1982; May 14, 1982; "Judge Hits Cops for Violating Spy Ban," ibid., July 12, 1982; "Police Guilty of Spying on Protest Rally," *Chicago Tribune*, July 15, 1982; "City to Pay Record High Legal Fees," *Chicago Sun-Times*, January 23, 1983.

25. "Police Spying Violations Bared," *Chicago Sun-Times*, January 28, 1983.

26. "City to Pay $335,000 for Illegal Spying," *Chicago Tribune*, July 25, 1984.

27. "Police 'Spy' Payoff," *Chicago Sun-Times*, October 22, 1985; "20 in Chicago Settle Police Spying Case," *New York Times*, November 15, 1985; "$306,250 Settlement in Red Squad Suit," *Chicago Tribune*, November 15, 1985; Alliance to End Repression, "City of Chicago to Pay $306,250 to Chicago Red Squad Victims" (press release), March 21, 1985.

28. *AER v. Chicago* (cited n. 22 above), memorandum opinion and order, No. 14 C. 3268.

29. *Coalition against Police Abuses v. Board of Police Commissioners*, No. 243–458 (Los Angeles County Ct., February 22, 1984), stipulated consent decree and judgment, and attached appendix, "Standards and Procedures for the Anti-Terrorist Division (ATD)," January 31, 1984. See also "City OKs Settlement of Police Spying Unit," *Los Angeles Times*, February 22, 1984; "Council Approval of Award Settles Police Spying Litigation," *Los Angeles Herald-Examiner*, February 22, 1984; "City Agrees to Pay $1.8 Million to End Police Spying Suit," *Los Angeles Daily Journal*, February 22, 1984; "Decree Leaves L.A. with Toughest Police-Spy Rules," *Los Angeles Times*, February 23, 1984; "5 Years Later, Decree Ends PDID Case" and "The Case Is Closed" (editorial), *Los Angeles Herald-Examiner*, February 23, 1984; "Los Angeles Settles Police Spying Case," *New York Times*, February 23, 1984; "ACLU Attorneys: L.A. Settlement May Be Just the Start," *Los Angeles Daily Journal*, February 23, 1984; "Police Spying Suit," ibid., February 27, 1984; "Agreement on Spying Lawsuit between Union, Police Reached," (California State) *University News*, March 1, 1984; "Improper Police Spying Causes a Chill That Lasts," *Los Angeles Times*, March 1, 1984; Dave Lindorff, "Police Spies in the City of the Angels," *Nation*, May 5, 1984.

30. *Handschu v. Special Services Division*, No. 71–2203 (S.D.N.Y.), settlement agreement, signed by attorneys December 30, 1980, but not by the judge.

31. See Nat Hentoff in the *Village Voice*, 1981: "NYPD Red Squad's Biggest Scam—Going Legit," June 3–9; "Afeni Shakur v. New York Civil Liberties Union," June 10–16; "How We All Got Screwed in the

N.Y. Red Squad Case," June 17–23; and "Chicago Shows Us Yokels How to Leash a Red Squad," June 24–30. See also Aryeh Neier, "A Time to Settle," *Village Voice*, July 1–7, 1981; Larry Tell, "Liberals See Red over Red Squad Pact," *National Law Journal*, July 6, 1981; and "The Red Squad Settlements Controversy," *Nation*, July 11, 1981.

32. *Handschu v. Special Services Division*, memorandum opinion and order, 605 F.S. at p. 1384, affirmed, U.S.C.A. 2 (April 9, 1986).

33. "City Police Shared Spy Secrets Nationwide," *Chicago Tribune*, December 5, 1984; "Nationwide Police Spying in 60's Documented," *New York Times*, December 6, 1984; "Police Spying Unit Network Disclosed," (Lake County, Ill.) *News Sun*, December 6, 1984; "Highland Park Rabbi a 'Red Squad' Target," ibid., December 6, 1984; "Knoxville Police Linked to 'Red Squad' Spying," *Knoxville News-Sentinel*, December 6, 1984; "Huntsville Police Linked to Spying Unit in '60s, '70s," *Huntsville* [Ala.] *Times*, December 6, 1984; "1960s Intelligence Request Defended by S.L. Officer," *Salt Lake City Tribune*, December 6, 1984; "California Agencies Got Spy Dossiers on Non-Criminal Groups from Chicago Police," *Los Angeles Times*, December 6, 1984; "Bay Police Shared Data on Dissidents with Chicago in '60s," *San Francisco Chronicle*, December 7, 1984; "Seattle-Chicago Connection in Surveillance Shown," *Seattle Times*, December 7, 1984; "Bay State Police Requested Information on Activists," *Boston Sunday Globe*, December 9, 1984; "Police Checked School Applicant's Activities," *Dallas Times Herald*, December 14, 1984; "Keeping Tabs—Texas Police Often Used Chicago Dossiers" and "After '60s, Dallas Reined in Intelligence Probes," *Dallas Times Herald*, December 16, 1984; "Chicago Spy Squad Linked to RI Police," *Quad-City Times*, December 21, 1984; "Fitchburg Police Requested Information from 'Red Squad,' " *Fitchburg-Leaminster* [Mass.] *Sentinel*, December 27, 1984; "Chicago 'Red Squad' Shared Files on Activists, New Evidence Shows," *Washington Post*, December 29, 1984; "Files Show Local Police Probed 60s Activists," *Rockford* [Ill.] *Register Star*, January 10, 1985.

34. ACLU files; coverage in *Orlando* [Fla.] *Sentinel*, 1983: "MBI Agent Infiltrates Nuke Group," December 17; "Lamar Okayed Spying on Nuke Freeze Group," December 20; "Sheriff's Snooper out of Line," December 20; "Lawyer Warned Freeze Group," December 21; "Agent Finds Freeze Group Not Violent," December 22; "Sheriff Right to Monitor Nuclear Freeze Group Because of the Pershing 2" (editorial), December 23; "ACLU Offers Legal Aid to Nuke Group," December 30.

35. "Judge Youngblood, 2 Others Probed in Alleged Bribery Plot," *Los Angeles Times*, April 16, 1983; "Youngblood Accuses Gates of Recruiting Bounty Hunters to Frame Him," *Orange County* [Calif.] *Register*, May 26, 1983; "Magistrate to Review Material Sought in Suit against Sheriff," ibid., November 28, 1984; "Court Seeks Sheriff's Files

on Opponents," *Los Angeles Times*, November 28, 1984; "Group Suing Sheriff Can Have Lumber Records, Court Rules," *Orange County Register*, December 4, 1984; "Sheriff's File on Judge, Private Investigator, Is Big, Could Get Bigger," *Los Angeles Times*, December 12, 1984; "Court Discloses Civil Rights Probe of OC Sheriff's Office," *Orange County Register*, December 18, 1984; " 'Sting' Claim Is Made in Youngblood Hearing," ibid., February 13, 1985; "Youngblood's Ex-Wife Says Sheriff's Unit Gave Her Drugs to 'Set Up' Judge," ibid., April 10, 1985; "Judge Will Ask Probe of Sheriff Unit," *Los Angeles Times*, April 10, 1985; "Santa Ana Private Investigator Files Suit against Anaheim, OC Officials," *Orange County Register*, April 30, 1985; "Youngblood Warns Colleagues on 1986 Sheriff, Judicial Races," *Los Angeles Daily Journal*, August 2, 1985; "Youngblood to Run against Sheriff Gates," *Los Angeles Times*, August 16, 1985; "Youngblood Decides to Leave Bench Early to Run for Sheriff," *Orange County Register*, October 22, 1985; "Court Says Youngblood Can View Gates' Files," *Los Angeles Times*, December 24, 1985; "Youngblood's Investigator Cleared of Misdemeanor Charges," *Orange County Register*, December 28, 1985; "Judge Won't Release Imprisoned OC Financier," ibid., December 28, 1985; "Detective, a Foe of Gates, Cleared of Misdemeanors," *Los Angeles Times*, December 28, 1985; "Youngblood's Lawsuit against Gates Delayed," ibid., January 17, 1986; "Judge Refuses to Order Turnover of Documents in Youngblood Case," *Santa Ana* [Calif.] *Register*, January 22, 1986; "Suit against Gates Partly Dismissed," *Orange County Register*, March 7, 1986.

36. Donner, *Age*, ch. 12, "Countersubversive Intelligence in the Private Sector," p. 433 and p. 520 n. 28.; Steve Burkholder, "Red Squads on the Prowl," *Progressive*, October 1988.

37. Text of speech by Phil Peters to Atlanta Metropolitan Crime Commission, May 17, 1983.

38. "State Agents Photographed Protests" and "Nuclear Protesters Get Sympathy in Court, Community Work to Do," *Tucson Daily Citizen*, December 29, 1983; "Crime Agency Tried to Infiltrate Missile Protestors," "A Tinge of 1984," and "DPS, Sheriff Say They Didn't Invite Agency to Spy on Demonstrators," (Arizona) *Daily Star*, December 30, 1983; "D-M Campers Photographed, Agency Says," ibid., December 31, 1983; "The Spies among Us: When Will They Ever Learn?" (editorial), ibid., January 4, 1984; "Mawhinney Says Agency Doing Its Job in Probe of Peace March," *Tucson Daily Citizen*, January 4, 1984.

39. "Big Brother Is Watching—State Police Secretly Spy and Collect Information on Activists" and "State Police Spying Indefensible," (Connecticut) *Fairpress*, December 19, 1984; "What It Means When Police Spy," ibid., December 26, 1984; "ACLU Director Says Police May Have Broken Law," *Waterbury* [Conn.] *Republican*, December 27, 1984; Opening Statement of Lester Forst before Judiciary Committee, Decem-

ber 28, 1984; and coverage in the *Hartford Courant:* "Excerpts from Grand Jury Testimony in Torrington Probe," December 28, 1984; "Prosecutor's Retirement Fuels Police-McGuigan Dispute," January 1, 1985; "Governor Steps into Feud between Police, McGuigan," January 3; "McGuigan Names Buckley to Probe Possible Wiretap Leaks," January 5; "Turf Wars: How Gossip Ignited Forst-McGuigan Feud," January 13; "A Vicious Smear That Won't Go Away" (editorial), January 20.

40. George Corsetti, "Patterson Throws the Book," (Detroit) *Metro Times,* April 4–10, 1984.

41. Donner, *Age,* ch. 12, "Countersubversive Intelligence in the Private Sector," pp. 414–15; O'Toole, *Private Sector,* passim; Barbara Durr, "The Challenge to Privacy and Constitutional Rights from Private Corporate Security," *Council on Economic Priorities* 5 (1980).

42. The account of the Greensboro trial is based on the trial record in the case. See also Greensboro Civil Rights Front, press release (n.d.); "Federal Jury Finds 8 Liable in Communist's Death," *Winston-Salem Journal,* June 8, 1985; "Plaintiffs Consider Verdict of Klan-Nazi Trial a 'Victory,' " *Greensboro News & Record,* June 11, 1985. For a more comprehensive exploration of the Greensboro civil action and the confrontation that gave rise to it, see Paul Bermanzohn, "The Greensboro Massacre: Police-Vigilante Nexus," in Bud Schultz and Ruth Schultz, *It Did Happen Here: Recollections of Political Repression in America* (Berkeley: University of California Press, 1989), pp. 335–46, and the following stories and articles: "Ex-Officer Says Dispatcher Told Her to Leave before CWP Members Shot," *Greensboro News & Record,* November 28, 1984; " 'Greensboro Massacre' Retrial Set to Start Today in North Carolina," *Los Angeles Daily Journal,* March 11, 1985; "Klan-Nazi Shooting Cops' Fault, Suit Says," *Chicago Tribune,* March 7, 1985; "3d Trial in Fatal Klan Clash with Leftists Starting Today," *New York Times,* March 11, 1985; "Another Trial Begins in Greensboro Deaths," *USA Today,* March 11, 1985; "Greensboro: Explosive Case Comes to Trial—Again," (Pine Ridge County, N.C.) *Journal,* March 11, 1985; "Judge Wants Black Jurors in Klan Trial," *USA Today,* March 12, 1985; "Civil Trial Opens on Greensboro Clash," *Washington Post,* March 16, 1985; "Countersuits Anger Black Leaders," *Greensboro News & Record,* March 17, 1985; Jack D. Novik, "Greensboro Triggers," *New York Times,* March 23, 1985; "1979 Shootings Haunt N.C. City," *USA Today,* March 21, 1985; "Lawsuit on Deaths of Communists Goes to Trial in North Carolina," *New York Times,* March 26, 1985; Isaiah Singletary and Lewis Cohen, "Five Years Later, the Widows Get Their Day in Court," *Guardian,* March 27, 1985; "N.C. Suit against Klan-Gov't Goes to Court," *Militant,* March 29, 1985; Guy Seay, ed., "The Greensboro Massacre," *Carillon: The Chronicle Magazine* 1, no. 10 (March 27, 1985): 1–8; "Klan Trial a Sharp Contrast with 2 Earlier Ones," *New*

York Times, March 31, 1985; "Nov. 3 Gunfire Widow Says Anti-Klan Crowd Lashed Out at Police," Greensboro News & Record, April 12, 1985; "Killings at Anti-Klan Rally Still Haunt Greensboro, N.C.," Boston Sunday Globe, April 7, 1985; "Attorney Says Trial Reveals Conspiracy," Carolina Peacemaker, April 13, 1985; "Witness Says He Suggested Klan Attend Rally," Greensboro News & Record, April 13, 1985; "Dawson Says His Testimony in '80 Concerned Police," ibid., April 14, 1985; "Police Were Told about the Rally, Informant Says," Winston-Salem Journal, April 14, 1985; "Officer Relates Alert to Klan Plan," Greensboro News & Record, April 15, 1985; "Informer Testifies Police Knew about Klan Intent," New York Times, April 15, 1985; "Police Movements Told at Klan Trial," ibid., April 22, 1985; "Police Give Conflicting Testimony on Details of '79 Carolina March," ibid., April 29, 1985; "Agent Tells of '79 Threats by Klan and Nazis," ibid., May 12, 1985; "Aide Recalls Advice to Police before 1979 Anti-Klan Rally," ibid., May 27, 1985; "8 Found Liable in Slaying at Anti-Klan Rally in 1979," ibid., June 8, 1985; William K. Tabb and Martha Nathan, "Civil Rights, the Klan & Reagan Justice: The View from N.C.," Nation, August 21–28, 1982; and David J. Garrow, "Klan and State in North Carolina; the Greensboro Boys," ibid., August 6–13, 1983.

43. FBI file documents released March 27, 1984; House Committee on Government Operations, Subcommittee on Government Information and Individual Rights, Investigation of Multi-State Regional Intelligence Projects, statements of William J. Anderson, General Accounting Office, and James M. Howard, chief civil deputy prosecutor, Pima County, Arizona, May 27, 1981, and Rex P. Armistead, director, Regional Organized Crime Information Center, May 28, 1981; U.S. Comptroller General, "The Multi-State Regional Intelligence Projects—Who Will Oversee These Federally Funded Networks?" December 31, 1980; "Under Cover: Super-Secret Police Intelligence Network Operates in Memphis amid Controversy," Memphis Press-Scimitar, May 21, 1980; "Ex-Housewife Says She Worked Undercover to Halt Drug Flow," Nashville Tennessean, July 8, 1981; "Private Law Agency Has Spa Connections," Hot Springs [Ark.] Sentinel Record, March 25, 1981.

44. Correspondence in Chicago transmittal files: November 21, 1967 (Minutemen); March 14, 1968 (Church League of America); November 27, 1968 (Church League of America); February 14, 1969 (John Rees). There is an abundance of accounts concerning the partnership in the sixties between the police and the right. See, for example, Max Gunther, "The New Political Police," True Magazine, June 1970; "Birch Policemen Tell Their Beliefs, Fears," New York Herald Tribune, April 3, 1966; "Cops Tip Off Minutemen," Liberation News Service, October 14, 1968; "Police Chief's Club Called Klan Front," New York Times, February 24, 1966; "Hentel: State Trooper Spied for Minutemen," World Journal Tri-

bune, November 4, 1966; "Minutemen Leader Seen as 'Kook, Genius, Joker' " and "U.N. Newsman Target of Minutemen," *World Journal Tribune*, November 6, 1966; "Minutemen Accused of Having Informer among State Police," *New York Times*, November 6, 1966; "Minutemen Case Is Dropped Here," *New York Times*, October 19, 1971.

45. "Special U.S. Links to Mercenaries," *Covert Action Information Bulletin* 6, no. 2 (Fall 1984); Jon Lee Anderson and Lucia Annuziata, "A Fragile Unity Is Born," *Nation*, March 9, 1985. For examples of other recently launched extremist groups and movements, see "Violence against Mercenaries on the Increase," *Congressional Record*, February 19, 1981, p. H525; "Links of Anti-Semitic Band Provoke 6-State Parley," *New York Times*, December 27, 1984; "Computer Network Links Rightist Groups and Offers 'Enemy' List," ibid., February 15, 1985; "20 Held in 7 States in Sweep of Nazis Arming for 'War' on U.S.," ibid., March 3, 1985; James Ridgeway, "Reagan's Slow Defeat in Nicaragua," *Village Voice*, March 12, 1985; and "In Alabama's Woods, Frank Camper Trains Men to Repel Invaders," *Wall Street Journal*, August 19, 1985.

46. Symposium on "Civil Liberties Implications of Nuclear Power Development," *Review of Law and Social Change* 10, no. 2 (1980–81); Jay Peterzell, *Nuclear Power and Political Surveillance* (Washington, D.C.: Center for National Security Studies, 1981); Donna Warnock, "Nuclear Power vs. Political Rights," (Campaign for Political Rights) *Organizing Guide*, April 1979; "Nuclear Power Critics and the Intelligence Community," *First Principles* 3, no. 5 (April 1979); "Assault on Nuclear Opponents Intensifies," *Organizing Notes*, March/April 1981; "Papers Show Kerr-McGee Used Spying in Waste Fight," *Chicago Sun-Times*, January 10, 1985. In the early seventies, John Rees, referred to above, infiltrated a Georgia antinuclear group under clerical cover ("Reverend John Seeley") on behalf of the security department of the Georgia Power Company (Donner, *Age*, pp. 448–49).

47. See, for example, "City to Investigate Police Spy Caper," *Chico* [Calif.] *News & Review*, May 17, 1984; "Police Resist Controls on Political Investigations," ibid., December 13, 1984; "Police Arrest 14 Protestors in Burlington," *Burlington* [Vt.] *Free Press*, May 8, 1985; "Protest and Police: Under the Covers," *Vanguard Press*, May 12–19, 1985; "Law & Order—What Hath Chief Bill Burke Wrought?" ibid., September 8–15, 1985.

48. "City Cops Tuning in Black Radio," *Newsday*, June 28, 1987; Earl Caldwell, "The Ghost of J. Edgar Hoover Rises Here," (New York) *Daily News*, June 29, 1987; "Police Unit Spies on Blacks; 'Black Desk' Watches Leaders," *New York Newsday*, July 1, 1987; Earl Caldwell, "Police Hark Back to Some Bad Old Days," (New York) *Daily News*, July 1, 1987; "Cop Spying; Ward Says 'I've Done Nothing Wrong'; Denies

Surveillance of Black Community; Giuliani to Discuss Civil Rights Questions," "Ward, Koch Call on WLIB," "Court Puts Cop Files on Hold," "Not Sorry for Tailing Station," *New York Newsday*, July 3, 1987; "Police Are Caught Eavesdropping," *New York Times*, July 5, 1987; "Top Cops Briefed on N.Y. Eight," "A TNT Plan to Spring Two," (New York) *Daily News*, July 5, 1987; "Bright Lights & Big City Spies," ibid., July 6, 1987; "Parks Crew 'Routinely' Films Events," *New York Newsday*, July 31, 1987; "Four Plan to Sue on Monitoring by Police Dept.," *New York Times*, October 1, 1987; Dave Lindorff, "Filing Grievances: Red Tape at 'Red Squad' Headquarters," *Village Voice*, October 6, 1987; "Panel: Cops' 'Black Watch' Was Legit," *New York Newsday*, October 9, 1987; "Panel Rejects Civilian Claims of 'Black Desk,' " *New York Times*, October 10, 1987; "Cops Surveillance Guidelines Tested," *New York Newsday*, October 11, 1987; "Snoop Rules: Careful How You Use Them," ibid., October 12, 1987; "Black Radio, Blue File: Judge Unseals WLIB Notes," ibid., October 26, 1987; "Police Focused on Taped Views of Noted Blacks," *New York Times*, October 27, 1987; "Lawyers: Cops Lied about Radio Summaries," *New York Newsday*, November 20, 1987; "Police Admit Surveillance Violated Pact," *New York Times*, December 19, 1987; "Group Asks Police to Explain Surveillance," ibid., December 20, 1987; and "Suit by Four Blacks Charges Illegal Surveillance by Police," ibid., June 10, 1988. See also "Memorandum in Support of Motion for Sanctions" and "Notice of Motion—Sanctions," filed by the plaintiffs in *Handschu v. Special Services Division* charging violation of the *Handschu* settlement, and "Intelligence Pact Broken by Police, Judge Rules," *New York Times*, July 22, 1989.

49. *Pledge of Resistance et al. v. We the People 200, Inc. et al.*, Civil Action No. 87–3975, memorandum and order (E.D.Pa.); "Is the Constitution Getting Too Much Police Protection?" *Philadelphia Inquirer*, June 30, 1987; "15 Political Groups Sue Officials of Bicentennial," *New York Times*, June 30, 1987; "Civilian Review of Surveillance Okd," ibid., July 16, 1987; "Reagan People Only," *Progressive*, September 1987; "Managing Director Must OK Police Spying," *Philadelphia Daily News*, September 16, 1987; and "The 'Non-violent but Hardly Docile' Pledge Celebrates the Constitution," *Pledge of Resistance Newsletter*, Fall 1987, p. 2.

50. *ACLU State Lobbyist*, May 1984.

51. "Training Bulletin," issued for the Northwest Terrorism Conference, sponsored by the Idaho Department of Law Enforcement, April 29, 30, and May 1, 1985; Bruce Schapiro, "Teaching Cops about Terrorism," *Nation*, October 12, 1985; "Police Get Lesson on Fighting Terrorism," *Hartford Courant*, February 19, 1985; Frank Donner, "The Terrorist as Scapegoat," *Nation*, May 20, 1985; "Anti-Terrorism '86" (advertisement), *Wall Street Journal*, March 14, 1986.

52. House Judiciary Committee, Subcommittee on Civil and Constitutional Rights, *FBI Authorization Request for Fiscal Year 1987*, open session, March 14, 1986, opening statement of William H. Webster, director, FBI.

53. See, for example, Francis J. McNamara, *United States Counterintelligence Today* (Washington, D.C.: Nathan Hale Institute, 1985).

54. See Gary Marx, "I'll Be Watching You—Reflections on the New Surveillance," *Dissent* 32 (Winter 1985): 26–34.

Select Bibliography

Materials for the study of official and unofficial political repression in America are scattered and often fugitive. The list even of published materials is immense. This bibliography lists only major works cited in the text and notes. It excludes personal communications, transcripts of interviews and broadcasts, materials contained in files released during judicial proceedings or disclosures obtained through requests under the Freedom of Information Act (FOIA), newspaper stories, and local, state, or federal government documents, unless the story or document reports significant research. Items cited but not listed are in the personal possession of the author, who has arranged for their eventual deposit in the Yale University Law School Library.

Adams, T. S. "Violence in Labor Disputes." In *Proceedings of the American Economic Association*, December 1905. Cited as Adams, "Violence."

Adelman, William J. *Haymarket Revisited: A Tour Guide of Labor History Sites and Ethnic Neighborhoods Connected with the Haymarket Affair.* Chicago: Illinois Labor History Society, 1976.

————. *Pilsen and the West Side: A Tour Guide to Ethnic Neighborhoods, Architecture, Restaurants, Wall Murals, and Labor History with Special Emphasis on Events Connected with the Great Upheaval of 1877.* Chicago: Illinois Labor History Society [1977].

Adorno, T. W., Else Frenkl-Brunswik, Daniel J. Levinson, and R. Nevitt Sanford. *The Authoritarian Personality.* New York: Harper & Row, 1950.

Ahern, James F. *Police in Trouble.* New York: Hawthorn Books, 1972.

Altgeld, John P. *Reasons for Pardoning Fielden, Neebe and Schwab.* 1893. Rev. ed., Chicago: Charles H. Kerr for the Illinois History Society, 1986. Cited as Altgeld, *Reasons.*

American Civil Liberties Union. *Annual Reports*. 1928, 1931–32, 1932–33, 1934.

——— . *Civil Liberties in American Cities: Survey Based on 332 American Cities of over 10,000 Population*. New York: ACLU, 1939.

——— . Southern California Branch. *Day of Protest, Night of Violence: The Century City Peace March*. Los Angeles: Sawyer Press, 1967.

——— . *Police Lawlessness against Communists in New York: The Facts, and Remedies to Check Future Violence and Force a Changed Police Policy*. New York: ACLU, 1930.

American Friends Service Committee. *The Police Threat to Political Liberty*. Philadelphia: American Friends Service Committee, 1979. Cited as AFSC, *Police Threat*.

——— . "Program on Government Surveillance and Citizen Rights." Briefing Paper for Conference on the LEIU, March 9, 1978.

American League against War and Fascism. *California's Brown Book*. Los Angeles: American League against War and Fascism, 1934.

Anderson, Jon Lee, and Lucia Annuziata. "A Fragile Unity Is Born." *Nation*, March 9, 1985.

Applegate, Rex. *Riot Control: Materiel and Techniques*. Harrisburg, Pa.: Stackpole Books, 1969.

Asbury, Herbert. *Gem of the Prairie: An Informal History of the Chicago Underworld*. New York: Knopf, 1940.

Ashbaugh, Carolyn. *Lucy Parsons: American Revolutionary*. Chicago: Charles H. Kerr, 1976. Cited as Ashbaugh.

"Assault on Nuclear Opponents Intensifies." *Organizing Notes*, March/April 1981.

Astor, Gerald. *The New York Cops: An Informal History*. New York: Scribner's, 1971.

Avrich, Paul. *The Haymarket Tragedy*. Princeton: Princeton University Press, 1984. Cited as Avrich.

Balch, Robert W. "The Police Personality: Fact or Fiction." (Northwestern University Law School) *Journal of Criminal Law and Criminology* 63, no. 1 (1972): 106–19.

Baltimore Police Department. *Annual Report, 1968* (June 30, 1969). Cited as BPD *Annual Report, 1968*.

Barnard, Henry. *Eagle Forgotten: The Life of John Henry Altgeld*. Indianapolis: Bobbs-Merrill, 1938. Cited as Barnard.

Bayley, David H., and Harold Mendelsohn. *Minorities and the Police*. New York: Free Press, 1969.

Berger, John. "The Nature of Mass Demonstrations." *New Society*, May 1968.

Bernhard, Edgar, Ira Latimer, and Harvey O'Connor, eds. *Pursuit of Freedom: A History of Civil Liberties in Illinois, 1787–1942*. Chicago: Chicago Civil Liberties Committee, 1942. Cited as *Pursuit of Freedom.*

Bernstein, Samuel. "American Labor and the Paris Commune." *Science and Society* 15, no. 2 (Spring 1951): 144–62.

Berson, Lenora E. " 'The Toughest Cop in America' Campaigns for Mayor of Philadelphia." *New York Times Magazine.* May 16, 1971. Cited as Berson, "Toughest Cop."

Blumenberg, Ben. "Making Open Air Meetings Successful." *Socialist World* 2, no. 12 (June 1922).

Bordwell, S. E. "Political Surveillance: Report Submitted to the Michigan CLU." MS. March 1971. Cited as Bordwell Report.

Bouza, Anthony. "The Operations of a Police Intelligence Unit." M.A. thesis. John Jay College of Criminal Justice, City University of New York, 1968. Cited as Bouza.

BPD *Annual Report, 1968.* See Baltimore Police Department.

Brace, Charles Loring. *The Dangerous Classes of New York and Twenty Years' Work among Them.* New York: Wynkoop & Hallenbeck, 1872.

Brecher, Jeremy. *Strike!* San Francisco: Straight Arrow Books, 1972. Repr. with a new introduction. Boston: South End Press, 1977.

Brody, David. *Labor in Crisis: The Steel Strike of 1919.* Philadelphia: Lippincott, 1965.

Broehl, Wayne G. *The Molly Maguires.* Cambridge, Mass.: Harvard University Press, 1964.

Browne, Waldo R. *Altgeld of Illinois: A Record of His Life and Work.* New York: B. W. Huebsch, 1924.

Bruce, Robert V. *1877: Year of Violence.* Indianapolis: Bobbs-Merrill, 1959. Cited as Bruce, *1877.*

Burk, William H. "The Memorial Day 'Massacre' of 1937 and Its Significance in the Unionization of the Republic Steel Corporation." M.A. thesis. Graduate College of the University of Illinois, 1975.

California Department of Justice, Consolidated Data Center. *IOCI—Automated System Functional Design.* Hearings, October 18, 1976.

Canetti, Elias. *Crowds and Power.* Trans. Carol Stewart. New York: Viking Press, 1962.

Caughey, John W. *Their Majesties the Mob.* Chicago: University of Chicago Press, 1960.

Center for Research on Criminal Justice. *The Iron Fist and the Velvet Glove.* Berkeley: Center for Research on Criminal Justice, 1975.

Chaberski, Stephen. "Inside the New York Panther Trial." *Civil Liberties Review* 1, no. 1 (Fall 1973).

Cherry, George L. "American Metropolitan Press Reaction to the Paris Commune of 1871." *Mid-America* 32, no. 1 (January 1950).

Chevigny, Paul. *Cops and Rebels: A Study of Provocation.* New York, Curtis Books, 1972.

———. "Politics and Law in the Control of Local Surveillance." *Cornell Law Quarterly* 70, no. 3 (April 1984). Cited as Chevigny, "Politics and Law."

———. "Red Squad: The Verdict Is Entrapment." *Village Voice*, February 11, 1971.

Chudoba, Dennis, and Robbyelee Terry. "The Legion of Justice: An Informational Report." MS. 1975.

C.I.R. *Final Report.* See U.S. Commission on Industrial Relations (1912).

"Civil Liberties Implications of Nuclear Power Development." Symposium. *Review of Law and Social Change* 10, no. 2 (1980–81).

Coalition on Government Spying. "Report to the Mayor and the Seattle City Council on Seattle Police Intelligence Activities, August 23, 1978." Cited as Seattle "Report."

Coben, Stanley. *A. Mitchell Palmer: Politician.* New York: Columbia University Press, 1963.

Conot, Robert. *Rivers of Blood, Years of Darkness: The Unforgettable Classic Account of the Watts Riot.* 1967. New York: Morrow, 1968. Cited as Conot.

Cook County, Illinois. "Improper Police Intelligence Activities: A Report by the Extended March 1975 Cook County Grand Jury." November 10, 1975. Cited as "Cook County Grand Jury Report."

Corley, Robert G. "The Quest for Racial Harmony: Race Relations in Birmingham, Alabama, 1947–1963." Ph.D. diss., University of Virginia, 1979. Cited as Corley.

Costello, Augustine E. *Our Police Protectors: A History of the New York Police.* 1885. Reprinted from the 3d ed. Montclair, N.J.: Patterson Smith, 1972.

Cover, Robert. "A Year of Harassment." *Nation*, February 2, 1970.

Crime Commission. See U.S. President's Commission on Law Enforcement and Administration of Justice.

Crosby, Donald F. "The Politics of Religion." In *The Specter: Original Essays on the Cold War and the Origins of McCarthyism,* ed. Robert Griffith and Athan Theoharis, pp. 18–38. New York: New Viewpoints, 1974.

Daughen, Joseph R., and Peter Binzen. *The Cop Who Would Be King: Frank Rizzo.* Boston: Little, Brown, 1977. Cited as Daughen and Binzen.

Daunt, William J. O. *Eighty-Five Years of Irish History, 1800–1885.* London: Ward & Downey, 1886.

David, Henry. *The History of the Haymarket Affair.* New York: Farrar & Rinehart, 1936. Cited as David.

Davidson, Bill. "The Mafia Can't Crack Los Angeles." *Saturday Evening Post*, July 30, 1965.

Davis, David Brion. *The Fear of Conspiracy: Images of Un-American*

Subversion from the Revolution to the Present. Ithaca, N.Y.: Cornell University Press, 1971.

Dies Committee. See U.S. Congress. House. Special Committee on Un-American Activities.

"Domestic Intelligence Opinion—A Court Order against a Red Squad." *First Principles* 3, no. 2 (October 1978).

Donnelly, Ignatius. *Caesar's Column: A Story of the Twentieth Century.* 1890. Reprint. Cambridge, Mass.: Harvard University Press, Belknap Press, 1960.

Donner, Frank. *The Age of Surveillance: The Aims and Methods of America's Political Intelligence System.* New York: Knopf, 1980. Cited as Donner, *Age.*

———. "Electronic Surveillance: The National Security Game." *Civil Liberties Review* 2, no. 4 (Summer 1975). Cited as Donner, "Electronic Surveillance".

———. "Hoover's Legacy." *Nation,* June 1, 1974.

———. "Political Intelligence: Cameras, Informers and Files." In *Privacy in a Free Society: Final Report, Annual Chief Justice Warren Conference on Advocacy in the United States, June 7–8, 1974.* Cambridge, Mass.: Roscoe-Pound–American Trial Lawyers' Foundation, 1974. Cited as Donner, "Political Intelligence."

———. "Rounding Up the Usual Suspects." *Nation,* August 7–14, 1982; and letter exchange, pt. 2, ibid., October 2, 1982.

———. "The Terrorist as Scapegoat." *Nation,* May 20, 1978.

———. "Theory and Practice of Political Intelligence." *New York Review of Books,* April 22, 1971. Cited as Donner, "Theory."

Dorfman, Ron. "Watching the Watchers." *Chicago Journalism Review* 4, no. 4 (January 1971). Cited as Dorfman.

Dreifuss, Claudia. "BOSS Is Watching." *Nation,* January 25, 1971.

Drinnon, Richard. *Rebel in Paradise: A Biography of Emma Goldman.* Boston: Beacon Press, 1970. Cited as Drinnon.

Dunne, Finley Peter. *Mr. Dooley Remembers: The Informal Memoirs of Finley Peter Dunne.* Boston: Little, Brown, 1963.

Durr, Barbara. "The Challenge to Privacy and Constitutional Rights from Private Corporate Security." *Council on Economic Priorities* 5 (1980).

Edelman, Murray. "Myths, Metaphors and Political Conformity." *Journal for the Study of Interpersonal Processes,* August 1967.

Epstein, Jason. *The Chicago Conspiracy Trial: An Essay on Law, Liberty and the Constitution.* New York: Random House, 1970. Cited as Epstein.

Faulk, John Henry. *Fear on Trial.* New York: Simon & Schuster, 1964.

Fine, Sidney. *Frank Murphy: The Detroit Years.* Ann Arbor: University of Michigan Press, 1975. Cited as Fine.

Fish Committee. See U.S. Congress. House. Special Committee to Investigate Communist Activities in the United States.

Flinn, John J., and John E. Wilkie. *History of the Chicago Police.* 1887. Reprint. New York: Arno Press, 1971. Cited as Flinn and Wilkie.

Fogelson, Robert M. *Violence as Protest: A Study of Riots and Ghettos.* Garden City, N.Y.: Doubleday, 1971. Cited as Fogelson.

Foner, Philip S. *The Great Labor Uprising of 1877.* New York: Monad Press, 1977.

Foster, William Z. *The Great Steel Strike and Its Lessons.* New York: B. W. Huebsch, 1920.

Freed, Donald. "The C.I.A. Comes Home." MS. 1970.

Garrett, Charles. *The La Guardia Years: Machine and Reform Politics in New York City.* New Brunswick, N.J.: Rutgers University Press, 1961.

Gates, Darryl. "The Law Enforcement Intelligence Unit." *California Peace Officer,* January/February 1965.

Gilmore, Gene. "One Year with Frank Rizzo." *Nation,* December 25, 1972.

Ginger, Ray. *Eugene Debs: A Biography.* New York: Collier Books, 1962. Cited as Ginger.

Glass House Tapes. See Tackwood, Louis E.

Golden, Greg. "The Olympics Game." *Nation,* March 6, 1982.

Goldman, Emma. *Living My Life: An Autobiography.* 1931. 1 vol. ed. Garden City, N.Y.: Garden City Publishing, 1934.

Goldstein, Robert J. "The Anarchist Scare of 1908." *American Studies* 15 (1974): 40–44.

Gottlieb, Robert, and Irene Wolt. *Thinking Big: The Story of the* Los Angeles Times, *Its Publishers and Their Influence on Southern California.* New York: Putnam's, 1977. Cited as Gottlieb and Wolt.

Goulden, Joseph C. "The Cops Hit the Jackpot." *Nation,* November 23, 1970.

Gross, Kenneth G. "Bad Show For Reporters." *Nation,* November 18, 1968.

Gutman, Herbert C. "The Tompkins Square Riot in New York City on January 13, 1874: A Re-Examination of Its Cause and Aftermath." *Labor History* 5, no. 1 (Winter 1965).

——— . "Trouble on the Railroads in 1873–1874: Prelude to the 1877 Crisis." *Labor History* 2, no. 2 (Spring 1961): 215–35.

——— . *Work, Culture and Society in Industrializing America.* New York: Vintage Books, 1977.

Halberstam, David. *The Powers That Be.* New York: Knopf, 1979. Cited as Halberstam.

Hallgren, Mauritz A. "Detroit's Liberal Mayor." *Nation,* May 13, 1931.

——— . "Grave Danger in Detroit." *Nation,* August 3, 1932.

Halliday, Samuel B. *Lost and Found; or, Life among the Poor.* New York: Blakeman & Mason, 1859.

Hamilton, Fred J. *Rizzo.* New York: Viking Press, 1973. Cited as Hamilton.

Hapgood, Norman, ed. *Professional Patriots.* New York: A. & C. Boni, 1927.

Hardman, Kay. "Terrorism, Apathy and the American Community." *Liberal*, April 1964.

Havemann, Joel. ". . . and More Spies." *Chicago Journalism Review* 3, no. 7 (April 1971).

Hecksher, August. *When La Guardia Was Mayor.* New York: Norton, 1978.

Henry, Margot. *"Attention, MOVE! This Is America!"* Chicago: Banner Press, 1987.

Hentoff, Nat. "Afeni Shakur v. New York Civil Liberties Union." *Village Voice*, June 10–16, 1981.

———. "Chicago Shows Us Yokels How to Leash a Red Squad." *Village Voice*, June 24–30, 1981.

———. "Civics Lessons for July 4." *Village Voice*, June 25, 1970.

———. "Columbia's Gift to the Mayor." *Village Voice*, December 18, 1969.

———. "How We All Got Screwed in the N.Y. Red Squad Case." *Village Voice*, June 17–23, 1981.

———. "John Lindsay: Mayor of Prague?" *Village Voice*, June 3, 1971.

———. "A Lengthening List." *Village Voice*, January 20, 1972.

———. "Now Playing: The Rule of Law." *Village Voice*, December 18, 1969.

———. "NYPD Red Squad's Biggest Scam—Going Legit." *Village Voice*, June 3–9, 1981.

Higham, John. *Strangers in the Land: Patterns of American Nativism, 1850–1925.* 1955. Reprint. New York: Atheneum, 1963.

HISC. See U.S. Congress. House. Committee on Internal Security.

"History of Police Intelligence Operations, 1880–1975 (Final Draft)." Report prepared by Legal Development Division, Technical Research Services Division, International Association of Chiefs of Police, Gaithersburg, Md., 1976. Cited as IACP "History."

Hoffman, Dennis Earl. "An Exploratory Analysis of the Response of Urban Police to Labor Radicalism." Ph.D. diss., Portland State University, 1979.

Hofstadter, Richard. *The Paranoid Style in American Politics, and Other Essays.* New York: Knopf, 1965.

Hofstadter, Richard, and Michael Wallace, eds. *American Violence: A Documentary History.* New York: Knopf, 1970.

Hopkins, Ernest J. *Our Lawless Police.* New York: Viking Press, 1931. Cited as Hopkins.

Horan, James D. *The Pinkertons: The Detective Dynasty That Made History.* New York: Crown Publishers, 1967.

Horan, James D., and Howard Swiggett. *The Pinkerton Story.* New York: Putnam's, 1951.

House, Edward. *Philip Dru—Administrator: A Story of Tomorrow.* New York: B. W. Huebsch, 1912.

HUAC. See U.S. Congress. House. Committee on Un-American Activities.

IACP "History." See "History of Police Intelligence Operations, 1880–1975 (Final Draft)."

Idaho. Department of Law Enforcement. "Training Bulletin." Issued for the Northwest Terrorism Conference, sponsored by the Idaho Department of Law Enforcement, April 29, 30, and May 1, 1985.

Interchurch World Movement of North America. Commission of Inquiry. *Public Opinion and the Steel Strike.* New York: Harcourt, Brace, 1921. Cited as IWM *Public Opinion.*

———. *Report on the Steel Strike of 1919.* 1920. Reprint. New York: Da Capo Press, 1971. Cited as IWM *Report.*

International Chiefs of Police. *Proceedings of the 26th Convention of the International Chiefs of Police.* 1919.

IWM *Public Opinion.* See Interchurch World Movement of North America. Commission of Inquiry.

IWM *Report.* See Interchurch World Movement of North America. Commission of Inquiry.

Jackson, Kenneth T. *The Ku Klux Klan in the City.* New York: Oxford University Press, 1967.

Jacobs, James B. "The Conduct of Local Police Intelligence." Ph.D. diss., Princeton University, 1977. Cited as Jacobs.

Jacobs, Jim, and Richard Soble. "A Blow against the Red Squads." *Nation,* February 14, 1981.

Jaffe, Julian F. *Crusade against Radicalism: New York during the Red Scare, 1914–1924.* Port Washington, N.Y.: Kennikat Press, 1972. Cited as Jaffe.

Jensen, Joan M. *The Price of Vigilance.* Chicago: Rand McNally, 1968. Cited as Jensen.

Johnson, Bruce. "Taking Care of Labor: The Police in American Politics." *Theory and Society* 3, no. 1 (Spring 1976).

Kamisar, Yale. "Criminals, Cops, and the Constitution." *Nation,* November 9, 1964.

Kelly, John. "CIA in America." *Counterspy: Covert Action Information Bulletin,* Spring 1980.

Kempton, Murray. "A Policeman's Plot." *New York Post,* August 14, 1965. Cited as Kempton.

Kennebeck, Edwin. "Looking for Trouble: A Spy Story." *Nation*, November 15, 1975.

———. "Not Guilty of What?" *Nation*, October 4, 1971.

Klare, Michael. "City Surveillance." In *Police on the Homefront*. Philadelphia: National Action Research on the Military-Industrial Complex [1971].

Kogan, Herman. "William Perkins Black: Haymarket Lawyer." *Chicago History* 5, no. 3 (Summer 1976).

La Follette Committee. See U.S. Congress. Senate. Committee on Education and Labor. Special Subcommittee.

Le Bon, Gustave. *The Crowd: A Study of the Popular Mind*. New York: Macmillan, 1896.

Leinenweber, Charles. "Socialists in the Streets: The New York City Socialist Party in Working Class Neighborhoods, 1908–1918." *Science and Society* 41 (Summer 1977): 152–71.

Levin, Murray B. *Political Hysteria in America: The Democratic Capacity for Repression*. New York: Basic Books, 1971.

Lewis, Arthur H. *Lament for the Molly Maguires*. New York: Harcourt, Brace & World, 1964.

Liberal Unionist Association. *The Speaker's Handbook on the Irish Question*. London: Cassell, 1889.

Limpus, Lowell J. *Honest Cop: Lewis J. Valentine*. New York: Dutton, 1939. Cited as Limpus.

Lindorff, Dave. "Police Spies in the City of the Angels." *Nation*, May 5, 1984.

Lorwin, Val. "Reflections on the History of the French and American Labor Movements." *Journal of Economic History* 17 (March 1957): 25–44.

Los Angeles Board of Police Commissioners. "Final Report." May 30, 1978.

———. "In the Matter of Presentation by Citizens' Committee on Police Repression." March 25, 1980.

———. "The Public Disorder Intelligence Function of the Los Angeles Police Department." Statement of the Los Angeles Board of Police Commissioners, April 10, 1975.

———. "Report." Report to American Civil Liberties Union and American Friends Service Committee, March 6, 1978.

Los Angeles Police Department. "Standards and Procedures for the Collection of Intelligence Information by the Los Angeles Police Department, Public Disorder Intelligence Division." February 24, 1982.

Los Angeles Mirror-News. "Chief Parker Story." June 21, 1957. Cited as "Chief Parker Story."

Los Angeles Times. "Politics and the Police Department." Special report. December 18, 1977.

LoSchiavo, Nino John. "Law Enforcement Intelligence Unit." *Police Chief*, February 1975.

Loukopolis, L. "The Detroit Police Department: A Research Report." MS. May 1970.

Lowenthal, Leo, and Norbert Guterman. *Prophets of Deceit: A Study of the Techniques of the American Agitator.* New York: Harper, 1949. 2d ed. Palo Alto, Calif.: Pacific Books, 1970.

Lukas, J. Anthony. *The Barnyard Epithet and Other Obscenities.* New York: Harper & Row, 1970.

Lum, Dyer D. *A Concise History of the Great Trial of the Chicago Anarchists in 1886.* 1887. Reprint. New York: Arno Press, 1969. Cited as Lum.

Lusk Committee. See New York.

Lynd, Helen. *England in the Eighteen-Eighties: Toward a Social Basis for Freedom.* New York: Oxford University Press, 1945.

McClellan Committee. See U.S. Congress. Senate. Committee on Government Operations. Permanent Subcommittee on Investigations.

McCormick, Bernard. "God Bless Frank Rizzo . . . or God Save Us?" *Philadelphia Magazine*, August 1969.

———. "The War of the Cops." *New York Times Magazine*, October 8, 1970.

McGinnis, Joe. "He'll Always Be Car One." *[MORE]*, December 1971.

———. "The Techniques of Frank Rizzo." *Philadelphia Inquirer*, August 18, 1967.

McManus, Michael J. [syndicated column]. "In Philadelphia, Ding, Dong the Witch Is Dead." *Norwalk* [Conn.] *Hour*, November 25, 1978.

McMillan, George. "The Birmingham Bombers." *Saturday Evening Post*, June 6, 1964.

McNamara, Francis J. *United States Counterintelligence Today.* Washington, D.C.: Nathan Hale Institute, 1985.

McWilliams, Carey. "Mr. Tenney's Horrible Awakening." *Nation*, July 23, 1949.

———. *Southern California Country: An Island on the Land.* New York: Duell, Sloan & Pearce, 1946. Cited as McWilliams.

Majka, Lorraine. "Organizational Linkages, Networks and Social Change in Detroit." Ph.D. diss., Wayne State University, 1981. Cited as Majka.

Makielski, S. J. *Beleaguered Minorities: Cultural Politics in America.* San Francisco: W. H. Freeman, 1973.

Mallowe, Mike. "Watch Out! Here Comes Frank the Tank." *Philadelphia Magazine*, October 1975. Cited as Mallowe.

Marson, Charles. "The LEIU: A Fact Sheet." *First Principles*, February 1977.

Marx, Gary. "I'll Be Watching You—Reflections on the New Surveillance." *Dissent* 32 (Winter 1985): 26–34.

Marx, Wesley. "The Cop as Crusader." *Los Angeles*, August 1962. Cited as Marx, "The Cop as Crusader."

Maryland General Assembly. Senate Investigating Committee Established Pursuant to Senate Resolutions 1 and 151 of the Maryland General Assembly. *Report to the Senate of Maryland*, December 31, 1975. Cited as Maryland Senate *Report*.

Maryland Civil Liberties Union. "Black Panthers: A Chronology of Panther Raids Harassment." April 25, 1970.

Melanson, Philip. "The C.I.A.'s Secret Ties to the Local Police." *Nation*, March 26, 1983. Cited as Melanson.

Michigan House of Representatives. Civil Rights Committee. Subcommittee on Privacy. *Report on the Law Enforcement Intelligence Unit.* October 11, 1978.

Miller, Wilbur P. *Cops and Bobbies.* Chicago: University of Chicago Press, 1977.

Mills, James E. "Locking Up the Tenney Files." *Nation*, July 5, 1971.

Moberg, David. "The Truth about Police Spying in Chicago." *Chicago Reader*, February 18, 25, 1977.

Momboisse, Raymond M. *Blueprint of Revolution: The Rebel, the Party, the Techniques of Revolt.* Springfield, Ill.: Charles C. Thomas, 1970.

Morgan, Charles, Jr. *A Time to Speak.* New York: Harper & Row, 1964. Cited as Morgan.

Morn, Frank. *"The Eye That Never Sleeps": A History of the Pinkerton National Detective Agency.* Bloomington: Indiana University Press, 1982.

Morris, William O'Connor. *Ireland, 1798–1898.* London: A. D. Innes, 1898.

Morrissey, Joe. "America's Police Network." *FOCUS*, February 1977.

Mowitz, Robert S. "State and Local Attack on Subversion." In *The States and Subversion*, ed. Walter Gellhorn. Ithaca, N.Y.: Cornell University Press, 1952.

Murray, Robert K. "Communism and the Great Steel Strike of 1919." *Mississippi Valley Historical Review* 38, no. 7 (December 1951). Cited as Murray.

Myers, Howard B. "The Policing of Labor Disputes: A Case Study." Ph.D. diss., University of Chicago, 1928.

Myerson, Seymour. "The Lawlessness of the LAPD Red Squad." In *It Did Happen Here: Recollections of Political Repression in America*, ed. Bud Schultz and Ruth Schultz, pp. 303–17. Berkeley: University of California Press, 1989.

The Nation. "The Red Squad Settlements Controversy." July 11, 1981.

Navasky, Victor. "Security and Terrorism." *Nation*, February 14, 1981.

Neier, Aryeh. "A Time to Settle." *Village Voice,* July 1–7, 1981.

New York. Lusk Committee. Report. *Revolutionary Radicalism.* Albany, N.Y., 1920.

Niedenhoffer, Arthur, and Abraham S. Blumberg, eds. *The Ambivalent Force: Perspective on the Police.* Waltham, Mass.: Ginn, 1970.

"Nuclear Power Critics and the Intelligence Community." *First Principles* 3, no. 5 (April 1979).

Oberschall, Anthony. "Group Violence: Some Hypotheses and Empirical Uniformities." *Law and Society Review* 3, no. 4 (August 1970): 61–92.

O'Connor, Rory. "Antinuke Movement Spooked?" *Rolling Stone,* June 1, 1978.

O'Connor, T. P. *The Parnell Movement: Being the History of the Irish Question from the Death of O'Connell to the Present Time.* New York: Cassell, 1891.

O'Toole, George. *The Private Sector: Private Spies, Rent-a-Cops, and the Police-Industrial Complex.* New York: Norton, 1978.

Palmer, Gladys L. *Union Tactics and Economic Change.* Philadelphia: University of Pennsylvania Press, 1932.

Park, Roxanne. "Police Spying in Seattle." *Inquiry,* June 12, 1978.

Parker, William H. *Parker on Police,* ed. O. W. Wilson. Springfield, Ill.: Charles C. Thomas, 1957. Cited as *Parker on Police.*

Peck, James. *Freedom Ride.* New York: Grove Press, 1962.

Pennsylvania Crime Commission. "Police Corruption and the Quality of Law Enforcement in Philadelphia." March 1974.

Peterzell, Jay. *Nuclear Power and Political Surveillance.* Washington, D.C.: Center for National Security Studies, 1981.

Pierce, Bessie. *History of Chicago.* 2 vols. New York: Knopf, 1957.

Philadelphia. *Mayor's Annual Report.* 1902, 1908, 1919, 1921, and 1929.

——— . Special Investigation Commission. *Findings, Conclusions and Recommendations of the Philadelphia Special Investigation Commission.* March 1, 1986.

Philadelphia Bulletin. "Controversy Still Rages over Raids on Panthers." September 30, 1970.

Philadelphia Inquirer. "A Week of Violence: The Facts and the Meaning." September 6, 1970.

Platt, Anthony, and Lynn Cooper, eds. *Policing America.* Englewood Cliffs, N.J.: Prentice Hall, 1974. Cited as Platt and Cooper, *Policing America.*

Popkin, Richard. "The Strange Tale of the Secret Army Organization (USA)." *Ramparts,* October 1973.

Quinn, Jim. "The Heart of Darkness." *Philadelphia Magazine,* May 1978.

Raines, Howell. "The Birmingham Bombing." *New York Times Magazine,* July 24, 1983.

Reiner, Robert. *The Blue-Coated Worker: A Sociological Study of Police Unionism.* New York: Cambridge University Press, 1978.

Reiss, Albert J. *Police and the Public.* New Haven: Yale University Press, 1971.

Remer, Larry. " 'SWAT': The Police Berets." *Nation*, May 24, 1975.

Repetto, Thomas A. *The Blue Parade.* New York: Free Press, 1978.

Ridgway, James. "Columbia's Real Estate Ventures." *New Republic*, May 18, 1968.

———. "Reagan's Slow Defeat in Nicaragua." *Village Voice*, March 12, 1985.

Riggio, Jim. "The Year of the Bull." *Philadelphia Magazine*, March 1973. Cited as Riggio.

Rockefeller Commission. See U.S. National Commission on Central Intelligence Agency Activities in the United States.

Rubin, Jerry. *Do It: Scenarios of the Revolution.* New York: Simon & Schuster, 1970.

Rudé, George. *The Crowd in History: A Study of Popular Disturbances in France and England, 1730–1848.* New York: John Wiley & Sons, 1964. Rev. ed. London: Lawrence & Wishart, 1981.

Schaack, Michael J. *Anarchy and Anarchists.* Chicago: F. J. Schulte, 1889.

Schapiro, Bruce. "Teaching Cops about Terrorism." *Nation*, October 12, 1985.

Schneirov, Richard. "Chicago's Great Upheaval of 1877." *Chicago History* 9, no. 1 (Spring 1980).

Schultz, Bud, and Ruth Schultz, eds. *It Did Happen Here: Recollections of Political Repression in America.* Berkeley: University of California Press, 1989.

Schultz, Donald O., and Loren Norton. *Police Operational Intelligence.* Springfield, Ill.: Charles C. Thomas, 1968.

"Seattle Report." See Coalition on Government Spying.

"The Secret Police in Chicago." *Chicago Journalism Review* 1, no. 5 (February 1969). Cited as "Secret Police."

Sennett, Richard. "Middle-Class Families and Urban Violence." In *Nineteenth-Century Cities: Essays in the New Urban History*, ed. Stephen Thernstrom and Richard Sennett, pp. 386–88. New Haven: Yale University Press, 1969.

Siegel, Franklin. "Red Squad Bills Force Inquiry into Police Surveillance." *Guild Notes*, January 1976.

Siringo, C. A. *Two Evil-Isms, Pinkertonism and Anarchism.* Chicago: C. A. Siringo, 1915.

SISS. See U.S. Congress. Senate. Subcommittee to Investigate the Administration of the Internal Security Act and Other Internal Security Laws.

Skolnick, Jerome. *The Politics of Protest: A Report.* New York: Ballantine Books, 1969. Cited as Skolnick.

Sparling Commission. *Dissent and Disorder: A Report to the Citizens of Chicago on the April 27 Peace Parade.* Chicago: April 27th Investigation Commission, August 1968. Cited as Sparling Commission, 1968.

————. *Dissent in a Free Society: A Report to the Citizens of Chicago on the City's Handling of Public Dissent in the Streets and Parks.* Chicago: Citizens' Commission to Study the Disorders of Convention Week, August 1969. Cited as Sparling Commission, 1969.

Stampp, Kenneth M. *The Era of Reconstruction: America after the Civil War, 1865–1877.* New York: Vintage Books, 1965. Cited as Stampp.

Stark, Rodney. *Police Riots.* Belmont, Calif.: Focus Books, 1972.

Stickgold, Marc. "Yesterday's Paranoia Is Today's Reality: Documentation of Police Surveillance of First Amendment Activity." (University of Detroit) *Journal of Urban Law* 55, no. 4 (Summer 1978): 877–929.

Szulc, Tad. "The Spy Compulsion." *New York Times Magazine,* June 3, 1973.

Tackwood, Louis E., in collaboration with the Citizens' Research and Investigation Committee. *The Glass House Tapes.* New York: Avon Books, 1973. Cited as *Glass House Tapes.*

Taft, Clinton J. *Fifteen Years on Freedom's Front.* Los Angeles: ACLU, Southern California Branch, 1939. Cited as Taft.

Taft, Philip. "Violence in American Labor Disputes." *Annals of the American Academy of Social and Political Science,* March 1966, pp. 127–40.

Taft, Philip, and Philip Ross. "American Labor Violence: Its Cause, Character and Outcome." In *Violence in America,* ed. Hugh Davis Graham and Ted Robert Gurr. New York: Bantam Books, 1969.

Taylor, Kathleen. "The New Seattle Ordinance to Control Police Spying: How It Was Put Together." *First Principles* 4, no. 2 (October 1979).

Tell, Larry. "Liberals See Red over Red Squad Pact." *National Law Journal,* July 6, 1981.

Terkel, Studs. *Hard Times: An Oral History of the Great Depression.* New York: Avon Books, 1971.

Thompson, E. P. "The Moral Economy of the Crowd in the Eighteenth Century." *Past and Present,* February 1971.

Tilly, Charles. "Repertoires of Contention in America and Britain, 1750–1830." In *The Dynamics of Social Movements,* ed. Mayer N. Zald and John D. McCarthy. Cambridge, Mass.: Winthrop, 1979.

————. *The Vendée.* Cambridge, Mass.: Harvard University Press, 1964.

Turner, William. "LA's Top Cop and His Plan to Straighten Up the Statehouse." *San Francisco Bay Guardian,* December 29, 1971. Cited as Turner, "LA's Top Cop."

————— . *Power on the Right*. Berkeley: Ramparts Press, 1971. Cited as Turner.

U.S. Bureau of the Census. 10th Census. *Statistics of the Population*. Washington, D.C.: GPO, 1883.

U.S. Commission on Industrial Relations. 1912. *Final Report and Testimony*. Washington, D.C.: GPO, 1916. Cited as C.I.R. *Final Report*.

U.S. Comptroller General. "The Multi-State Regional Intelligence Projects—Who Will Oversee These Federally Funded Networks?" December 31, 1980.

U.S. Congress. House. Committee on Government Operations. Subcommittee on Government Information and Individual Rights. Hearings, *Investigation of Multi-State Regional Intelligence Projects* (1981).

————— . Committee on Internal Security [HISC]. Hearings, especially *America's Maoists* (1971), *Black Panther Party* (1970), *Investigation of Students for a Democratic Society* (1969), *New Mobilization Committee to End the War in Vietnam* (1970), and *Subversive Influences on Riots, Looting and Burning* (1968). Cited as HISC Hearings [year].

————— . Committee on the Judiciary. Subcommittee on Civil and Constitutional Rights. Hearings, especially the annual budget hearings, *FBI Authorization Requests*, and *FBI Undercover Operations* (1982).

————— . Committee on Un-American Activities [HUAC]. Hearings, especially *Communism in the Detroit Area* (1952), *Investigation of Communist Activities, New York Area* (1959), *Investigation of Students for a Democratic Society* (1969), *National Peace Action Coalition (NPAC) and People's Coalition for Peace and Justice (PCPJ)* (1971), *Subversive Influences Affecting the Military Forces of the U.S.* (1972), *Subversive Involvement in the Disruption of the Democratic National Convention* (1968), and *Subversive Involvement in the Origin, Leadership, and Activities of the New Mobilization Committee to End the War in Vietnam* (1970).

————— . Special Committee on Un-American Activities [Dies Committee]. Hearings, 1938–40.

————— . Special Committee to Investigate Communist Activities in the United States [Fish Committee]. Hearings, 1930.

————— . Subcommittee on Courts, Civil Liberties, and the Administration of Justice. Hearings, especially *Wiretapping and Electronic Surveillance* (1974).

U.S. Congress. Senate. *The Anti–Viet Nam Agitation and the Teach-In Movement: The Problem of Communist Infiltration and Exploitation; A Staff Study*. 89th Cong., 1st sess. (1965), S. Doc. 72.

————— . *Report Investigating Strike in Steel Industry*. 66th Cong., 1st sess. (1921), S. Rept. 289, vol. 1.

————— . Committee on Education and Labor. Special Subcommittee [La Follette Committee]. Hearings, *Violations of Free Speech and*

Rights of Labor (1936–40). 74 parts. Cited as La Follette Committee Hearings.

———. Committee on Government Operations. Permanent Subcommittee on Investigations [McClellan Committee]. Hearings, 1967–69.

———. Committee on the Judiciary. Subcommittee on Constitutional Rights. Hearings, especially *Criminal Justice Data Banks* (1974) and *Federal Data Banks, Computers and the Bill of Rights* (1971).

———. Select Committee to Study Governmental Operations with Respect to Intelligence Activities. Hearings, especially *Covert Action* (1975) and *Federal Bureau of Investigations* (1975) (pts. 6 and 7 of *Intelligence Activities, S.R. 21*).

———. Subcommittee on Security and Terrorism. Hearings, especially the annual budget hearings, *FBI Oversight and Budget Authorization* (title varies after 1986).

———. Subcommittee to Investigate the Administration of the Internal Security Act and Other Internal Security Laws [SISS]. Hearings, especially *Assaults on Law Enforcement Officers* (1970), *Extent of Subversion in Campus Disorders* (1969), *Extent of Subversion in the New Left* (1970), *Gaps in Internal Security Laws* (1966–67), *Hashish Smuggling and Passport Fraud* (1973), *Marihuana and the Question of Personnel Security* (1975), *Marihuana-Hashish Epidemic and Its Impact on United States Security* (1973–75), *The Nationwide Drive against Law Enforcement Intelligence Operations* (1975), *Terroristic Activity* (1974–76, especially *Terroristic Bombings and Law Enforcement Intelligence*, pt. 7, 1975), and *World Drug Traffic and Its Impact on U.S. Security* (1972–73).

U.S. Federal Bureau of Investigation. *FBI Annual Report, Fiscal Year.* Washington, D.C.: GPO. Cited as *FBI Annual Report* [year].

U. S. Law Enforcement Assistance Administration (LEAA). *LEAA Activities, July 1, 1969, to June 30, 1970.* Washington, D.C.: GPO, 1970.

———. *LEAA Annual Report of the Law Enforcement Assistance Administration, Fiscal Year.* Washington, D.C.: GPO. Cited as *LEAA Annual Report* [year].

———. *Grants and Contracts, Fiscal Year 1970.* Washington, D.C.: GPO, 1970.

———. Law Enforcement Intelligence Unit. "Confidential Manual." Compiled by E. R. Connery for the Inspectional Services Division. N.d.

U.S. National Advisory Commission on Civil Disorders [Kerner Commission]. *Report of the National Advisory Commission on Civil Disorders.* New York: Bantam Books, 1968.

U.S. National Commission on the Causes and Prevention of Violence [Walker Commission]. *Rights in Conflict.* Washington, D.C.: GPO, 1968. Cited as Walker Report.

U.S. National Commission on Central Intelligence Agency Activities in the United States [Rockefeller Commission]. *Report to the President by the Commission on Central Intelligence Agency Activities in the United States.* Washington, D.C.: GPO, 1975.

U.S. President's Commission on Campus Unrest. *The Report of the President's Commission on Campus Unrest.* Washington, D.C.: GPO, 1970.

U.S. President's Commission on Law Enforcement and Administration of Justice [Crime Commission]. *The Challenge of Crime in a Free Society: A Report.* Washington, D.C.: GPO, 1967. Commonly known as the Crime Commission Report.

————. *The Police: Task Force Report.* Washington, D.C.: GPO, 1967.

Valentine, Lewis J. *Nightstick: The Autobiography of Lewis J. Valentine.* New York: Dial Press, 1947.

Valentino, Linda. "The LEIU: Part of the Political Intelligence Network." *First Principles,* January 1979.

Valentino, Linda, and Greg Goldin. "The L.E.I.U.—McCarthyism by Computer." *Nation,* August 25–September 1, 1979.

Walker Commission. See U.S. National Commission on the Causes and Prevention of Violence.

Walter, Greg. "Rizzo." *Philadelphia Magazine,* June 1967.

Warnock, Donna. "Nuclear Power vs. Political Rights." (Campaign for Political Rights) *Organizing Guide,* April 1979.

Washington, D.C., Metropolitan Police Department. "Organization, Functions, and Staffing of the Intelligence Division." General Order No. 7-G-4 (A), Series 1966. December 24, 1969.

Watters, Pat, and Steven Gillers, eds. *Investigating the FBI.* New York: Doubleday, 1973. Cited as Watters and Gillers, *Investigating the FBI.*

Webb, Jack. *The Badge.* Englewood Cliffs, N.J.: Prentice-Hall, 1958.

Weighley, Russell E., ed. *Philadelphia: A 300-Year History.* New York: Norton, 1982.

Westin, Alan F., and Barry Mahoney. *The Trial of Martin Luther King.* New York: Thomas Y. Crowell, 1974.

Wheelock, Lewis P. "Urban Protestant Reactions to the Chicago Haymarket Affair." Ph.D. diss., University of Iowa, 1956.

Wiebe, Robert. *The Search for Order, 1877–1920.* New York: Hill & Wang, 1967.

Wills, Garry. *Nixon Agonistes: The Crisis of the Self-Made Man.* Boston: Houghton Mifflin, 1970. Reprint. New York: New American Library, 1971.

————. *The Second Civil War: Arming for Armageddon.* New York: New American Library, 1968.

Wilson, Jerry W. "Common Sense in Dealing with Demonstrations." *Police Yearbook,* September 1971.

Wingfield, William. "California's New Vigilantes." Progressive, February 1968.

Wish, Harvey. "Governor Altgeld Pardons the Anarchists." Journal of the Illinois State Historical Society 31 (December 1938): 83–84.

Woods, Joseph Gerald. "The Progressives and the Police: Urban Reform and the Professionalization of the Los Angeles Police." Thesis, Urban Policy Research Institute, 1973. Cited as Woods.

Woodward, C. Vann. Tom Watson, Agrarian Rebel. London: Oxford University Press, 1955.

Z in Chicago. Report of the Independent Voters of Illinois. N.d.

Index

469

Compositor: BookMasters, Inc.
Text: 10/13 Aldus
Display: Aldus
Printer: Edwards Brothers, Inc.
Binder: Edwards Brothers, Inc.